THE NEW AMERICAN COMMENTARY

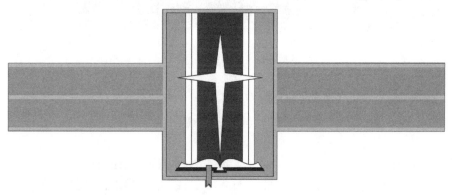

An Exegetical and Theological
Exposition of Holy Scripture

THE NEW
AMERICAN
COMMENTARY

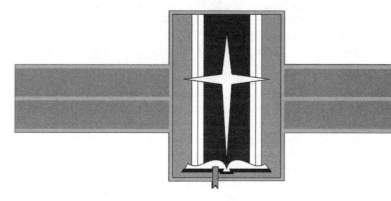

Volume
25B

JOHN 12–21

Gerald L. Borchert

PUBLISHING GROUP

Nashville, Tennessee

© 2002 • B&H Publishing Group
All rights reserved
ISBN: 978-0-8054-0143-1
Dewey Decimal Classification: 226.5
Subject Heading: Bible. N.T. John
Library of Congress Catalog Number: 96–26847
Printed in the United States of America
17 16 15 14 13   12 11 10 9 8 7 6

Cataloging-in-Publication Data

Borchert, Gerald L.
   John 12–21 / Gerald L. Borchert.
    p. cm. — (The new American commentary ; vol. 25B)
   Includes bibliographical references and indexes.
   ISBN 0-8054-0143-1 (hardcover)
    1. Bible. N.T. John XII–XXI—Commentaries. I. Title. II. Series:
New American commentary ; v. 25B
   BS2615.3.B58 2002
   226.5' 077—dc20

Dedicated to

The Church of the Future
and to

Elissa Ann,

Timothy William,

Seth Joseph,

and

Jessica Lynn

Editors' Preface

God's Word does not change. God's world, however, changes in every generation. These changes, in addition to new findings by scholars and a new variety of challenges to the gospel message, call for the church in each generation to interpret and apply God's Word for God's people. Thus, THE NEW AMERICAN COMMENTARY is introduced to bridge the twentieth and twenty-first centuries. This new series has been designed primarily to enable pastors, teachers, and students to read the Bible with clarity and proclaim it with power.

In one sense THE NEW AMERICAN COMMENTARY is not new, for it represents the continuation of a heritage rich in biblical and theological exposition. The title of this forty-volume set points to the continuity of this series with an important commentary project published at the end of the nineteenth century called AN AMERICAN COMMENTARY, edited by Alvah Hovey. The older series included, among other significant contributions, the outstanding volume on Matthew by John A. Broadus, from whom the publisher of the new series, Broadman Press, partly derives its name. The former series was authored and edited by scholars committed to the infallibility of Scripture, making it a solid foundation for the present project. In line with this heritage, all NAC authors affirm the divine inspiration, inerrancy, complete truthfulness, and full authority of the Bible. The perspective of the NAC is unapologetically confessional and rooted in the evangelical tradition.

Since a commentary is a fundamental tool for the expositor or teacher who seeks to interpret and apply Scripture in the church or classroom, the NAC focuses on communicating the theological structure and content of each biblical book. The writers seek to illuminate both the historical meaning and contemporary significance of Holy Scripture.

In its attempt to make a unique contribution to the Christian community, the NAC focuses on two concerns. First, the commentary emphasizes how each section of a book fits together so that the reader becomes aware of the theological unity of each book and of Scripture as a whole. The writers, however, remain aware of the Bible's inherently rich variety. Second, the NAC is produced with the conviction that the Bible primarily belongs to the church. We believe that scholarship and the academy provide an indispensable foundation for biblical understanding and the service of Christ, but the editors and authors of this series have attempted to communicate the findings of their research in a manner that will build up the whole body of Christ. Thus, the commentary concentrates on theological exegesis while providing practical, applicable exposition.

THE NEW AMERICAN COMMENTARY's theological focus enables

the reader to see the parts as well as the whole of Scripture. The biblical books vary in content, context, literary type, and style. In addition to this rich variety, the editors and authors recognize that the doctrinal emphasis and use of the biblical books differs in various places, contexts, and cultures among God's people. These factors, as well as other concerns, have led the editors to give freedom to the writers to wrestle with the issues raised by the scholarly community surrounding each book and to determine the appropriate shape and length of the introductory materials. Moreover, each writer has developed the structure of the commentary in a way best suited for expounding the basic structure and the meaning of the biblical books for our day. Generally, discussions relating to contemporary scholarship and technical points of grammar and syntax appear in the footnotes and not in the text of the commentary. This format allows pastors and interested laypersons, scholars and teachers, and serious college and seminary students to profit from the commentary at various levels. This approach has been employed because we believe that all Christians have the privilege and responsibility to read and seek to understand the Bible for themselves.

Consistent with the desire to produce a readable, up-to-date commentary, the editors selected the *New International Version* as the standard translation for the commentary series. The selection was made primarily because of the NIV's faithfulness to the original languages and its beautiful and readable style. The authors, however, have been given the liberty to differ at places from the NIV as they develop their own translations from the Greek and Hebrew texts.

The NAC reflects the vision and leadership of those who provide oversight for Broadman Press, who in 1987 called for a new commentary series that would evidence a commitment to the inerrancy of Scripture and a faithfulness to the classic Christian tradition. While the commentary adopts an "American" name, it should be noted some writers represent countries outside the United States, giving the commentary an international perspective. The diverse group of writers includes scholars, teachers, and administrators from almost twenty different colleges and seminaries, as well as pastors, missionaries, and a layperson.

The editors and writers hope that THE NEW AMERICAN COMMENTARY will be helpful and instructive for pastors and teachers, scholars and students, for men and women in the churches who study and teach God's Word in various settings. We trust that for editors, authors, and readers alike, the commentary will be used to build up the church, encourage obedience, and bring renewal to God's people. Above all, we pray that the NAC will bring glory and honor to our Lord who has graciously redeemed us and faithfully revealed himself to us in his Holy Word.

SOLI DEO GLORIA
The Editors

Author Preface

It seems most appropriate that after concluding the commentary of John 1–11 on Palm Sunday of 1996 I should be writing the Preface of this second volume in the Palm Sunday glow five years later, having just returned from the lands of the Bible for about the thirty-third time.

Even though I am now immersed in the somewhat tedious task of reviewing all the doctoral theses of students at Northern Baptist Seminary as the director of doctoral work, the writing of this second volume of the commentary has been one of the most spiritually renewing experiences of my entire life. Following the last days of Jesus' life on earth with the Johannine evangelist has been, for me, an extended experience of incomparable blessing which I pray I may have communicated to readers in the pages of this work. And now from our home in Wheaton, Illinois, many years after I was born on Palm Sunday in Edmonton, Alberta, Canada, I can echo with the saints of the church: "Thank, you, God, for giving us this marvelous 'Spiritual' Gospel."

But prefaces are places where authors are able to thank specific people as well. And so my sincerest gratitude is expressed to my associate, Barbara Wixon, who has transferred my pencil scribblings to the computer keyboard and thus allowed me the freedom to revise my thoughts a number of times. She has been not only an incredible assistance in this typing marathon but also a gift of God in the doctoral office.

To Ben Bergfalk, my student assistant, I also express my heartfelt thanks for his faithful chasing down of incomplete bibliographical citations and thus freeing me from this task. And to the staff of the Grow Library at Northern Baptist Theological Seminary, with its highly computerized technology, I also express my sincere thanks.

Finally, to Doris Ann, my dear wife and colleague in seminary teaching who has endured for many years my very late nights and early mornings, I express my overwhelming love and gratitude. Moreover, since I have dedicated the first volume of this commentary to her, our family (all of whom as I have noted in the first volume are graduates of seminary), and to my former students (from whom I have learned much), it is perhaps fitting to dedicate this work to the church of the future and to our grandchildren: Elissa, Will, Seth, and Jessica, all of whom have brought great joy and blessing to us. It is our earnest prayer that they, like their parents (our children), will come to acknowledge Jesus as "the Lamb of God who takes away the sin of the world" and accept him as the Lord of their lives.

Moreover, I pray that every reader of this commentary may ponder afresh and come to know more fully the great significance not only of Palm Sunday but also the strategic meaning of the self-giving Passion and powerful Resurrection of the "Word" who became flesh for us, our Lord and Savior Jesus Christ!

—Gerald L. Borchert
Wheaton, Illinois
Palm Sunday 2001

Abbreviations

Bible Books

Gen	Isa	Luke
Exod	Jer	John
Lev	Lam	Acts
Num	Ezek	Rom
Deut	Dan	1, 2 Cor
Josh	Hos	Gal
Judg	Joel	Eph
Ruth	Amos	Phil
1, 2 Sam	Obad	Col
1, 2 Kgs	Jonah	1, 2 Thess
1, 2 Chr	Mic	1, 2 Tim
Ezra	Nah	Titus
Neh	Hab	Phlm
Esth	Zeph	Heb
Job	Hag	Jas
Ps (pl. Pss)	Zech	1, 2 Pet
Prov	Mal	1, 2, 3 John
Eccl	Matt	Jude
Song	Mark	Rev

Apocrypha

Add Esth	*The Additions to the Book of Esther*
Bar	*Baruch*
Bel	*Bel and the Dragon*
1,2 Esdr	*1, 2 Esdras*
4 Ezra	*4 Ezra*
Jdt	*Judith*
Ep Jer	*Epistle of Jeremiah*
1,2,3,4 Mac	*1, 2, 3, 4 Maccabees*
Pr Azar	*Prayer of Azariah and the Song of the Three Jews*
Pr Man	*Prayer of Manasseh*
Sir	*Sirach, Ecclesiasticus*
Sus	*Susanna*
Tob	*Tobit*
Wis	*The Wisdom of Solomon*

Commonly Used Sources for New Testament Volumes

AB	Anchor Bible
ACNT	Augsburg Commentary on the New Testament
AGJU	Arbeiten zur Geschichte des antiken Judentums und des Urchristentums
AJBI	Annual of the Japanese Biblical Institute
AJT	*American Journal of Theology*
AJTh	*Asia Journal of Theology*
ANF	Ante-Nicene Fathers
ANQ	*Andover Newton Quarterly*
ATANT	Abhandlungen zur Theologie des Alten and Neuen Testaments
ATR	*Anglican Theological Review*
ATRSup	*Anglican Theological Review Supplemental Series*
AusBR	*Australian Biblical Review*
AUSS	*Andrews University Seminary Studies*
BAGD	W. Bauer, F. W. Arndt, F. W. Gingrich, and F. Danker, *Greek-English Lexicon of the New Testament*
BARev	*Biblical Archaeology Review*
BBR	*Bulletin for Biblical Research*
BDF	F. Blass, A. Debrunner, R. W. Funk, *A Greek Grammar of the New Testament*
BETL	Bibliotheca ephemeridum theologicarum lovaniensium
BETS	*Bulletin of the Evangelical Theological Society*
Bib	*Biblica*
BJRL	*Bulletin of the John Rylands Library*
BK	*Bibel und Kirche*
BLit	*Bibel und Liturgie*
BR	*Biblical Research*
BSac	*Bibliotheca Sacra*
BT	*The Bible Translator*
BTB	*Biblical Theology Bulletin*
BVC	*Bible et vie chrétienne*
BZ	*Biblische Zeitschrift*
BZNW	Beihefte zur *ZAW*
CBC	Cambridge Bible Commentary
CBQ	*Catholic Biblical Quarterly*
CCWJCW	Cambridge Commentaries on Writings of the Jewish and Christian World
CJT	*Canadian Journal of Theology*

CNTC	Calvin's New Testament Commentaries
CO	W. Baur, E. Cuntiz, and E. Reuss, *Ioannis Calvini opera quae supereunt omnia,* ed.
Conybeare	W. J. Conybeare and J. S. Howson, *The Life and Epistles of St. Paul*
CQR	*Church Quarterly Review*
CSR	*Christian Scholars' Review*
CTM	*Concordia Theologial Monthly*
CTQ	*Concordia Theological Quarterly*
CTR	*Criswell Theological Review*
Did.	*Didache*
DJD	Discoveries in the Judaean Desert
DNTT	*Dictionary of New Testament Theology*
DownRev	*Downside Review*
DSB	Daily Study Bible
EBC	Expositor's Bible Commentary
EDNT	*Exegetical Dictionary of the New Testament*
EGT	*The Expositor's Greek Testament*
EGNT	*Exegetical Greek New Testament*
EKKNT	Evangelisch-katholischer Kommentar zum Neuen Testament
ETC	English Translation and Commentary
ETL	*Ephemerides theologicae lovanienses*
ETR	*Etudes théologiques et religieuses*
ETS	Evangelical Theological Society
EvT	*Evangelische Theologie*
EvQ	*Evangelical Quarterly*
Exp	*Expositor*
ExpTim	*Expository Times*
FNT	*Filologia Neotestamentaria*
FRLANT	Forschungen zur Religion und Literatur des Alten und Neuen Testaments
GAGNT	M. Zerwick and M. Grosvenor, *A Grammatical Analysis of the Greek New Testament*
GNBC	Good News Bible Commentary
GSC	Griechischen christlichen Schriftsteller
GTJ	*Grace Theological Journal*
HBD	*Holman Bible Dictionary*
HDB	J. Hastings, *Dictionary of the Bible*
Her	Hermeneia
HNT	Handbuch zum Neuen Testament

HNTC	Harper's New Testament Commentaries
HeyJ	*Heythrop Journal*
HTKNT	Herders theologischer Kommentar zum Neuen Testament
HTR	*Harvard Theological Review*
HUCA	*Hebrew Union College Annual*
IB	*The Interpreter's Bible*
IBS	*Irish Biblical Studies*
ICC	International Critical Commentary
IDB	*Interpreter's Dictionary of the Bible*
IDBSup	Supplementary Volume to *IDB*
Int	*Interpretation*
INT	Interpretation: A Bible Commentary for Preaching and Teaching
ISBE	*International Standard Bible Encyclopedia*
JAAR	*Journal of the American Academy of Religion*
JANES	*Journal of Ancient Near Eastern Studies*
JAOS	*Journal of the American Oriental Society*
JBL	*Journal of Biblical Literature*
JES	*Journal of Ecumenical Studies*
JETS	*Journal of the Evangelical Theological Society*
JJS	*Journal of Jewish Studies*
JR	*Journal of Religion*
JRE	*Journal of Religious Ethics*
JRH	*Journal of Religious History*
JRS	*Journal of Roman Studies*
JSNT	*Journal for the Study of the New Testament*
JSOT	*Journal for the Study of the Old Testament*
JSS	*Journal of Semitic Studies*
JTS	*Journal of Theological Studies*
JTT	*Journal of Translation and Textlinguistics*
LB	*Linguistica Biblica*
LEC	Library of Early Christianity
LouvSt	*Louvain Studies*
LS	Liddel and Scott, *Greek-English Lexicon*
LTJ	*Lutheran Theological Journal*
LTP	*Laval théologique et philosophique*
LTQ	*Lexington Theological Quarterly*
LW	Luther's Works
LXX	Septuagint
MCNT	Meyer's Commentary on the New Testament
MDB	*Mercer Dictionary of the Bible*

MM	J. H. Moulton and G. Milligan, *The Vocabulary of the Greek Testament*
MNTC	Moffatt New Testament Commentary
MQR	*Mennonite Quarterly Review*
MT	Masoretic Text
NAB	New American Bible
NAC	New American Commentary
NASB	New American Standard Bible
NBD	*New Bible Dictionary*
NCB	New Century Bible
NCBC	New Century Bible Commentary
NEB	New English Bible
Neot	*Neotestamentica*
NICNT	New International Commentary on the New Testament
NIDNTT	*New International Dictionary of New Testament Theology*
NIGTC	New International Greek Testament Commentary
NIV	New International Version
NorTT	*Norsk Teologisk Tidsskrift*
NovT	*Novum Testamentum*
NovTSup	Novum Testamentum, Supplements
NPNF	Nicene and Post-Nicene Fathers
NRSV	New Revised Standard Version
NRT	*La nouvelle revue théologique*
NTD	Das Neue Testament Deutsch
NTI	D. Guthrie, *New Testament Introduction*
NTM	*The New Testament Message*
NTS	*New Testament Studies*
PC	Proclamation Commentaries
PEQ	*Palestine Exploration Quarterly*
PRS	*Perspectives in Religious Studies*
PSB	*Princeton Seminary Bulletin*
RB	*Revue biblique*
RelSRev	*Religious Studies Review*
ResQ	*Restoration Quarterly*
RevExp	*Review and Expositor*
RevQ	*Revue de Qumran*
RevThom	*Revue thomiste*
RHPR	*Revue d'histoire et de philosophie religieuses*
RSPT	*Revue des sciences philosophiques et théologiques*
RSR	*Recherches de science religieuse*

RSV	Revised Standard Version
RTP	*Revue de théologie et de philosophie*
RTR	*Reformed Theological Review*
SAB	*Sitzungsbericht der Preussischen Akademie der Wissenschaft zu Berlin*
SBJT	*Southern Baptist Journal of Theology*
SBLDS	SBL Dissertation Series
SBLMS	SBL Monograph Series
SBLSP	SBL Seminar Papers
SE	*Studia Evangelica*
SEAÛ	*Svensk exegetisk aΩrsbok*
SEAJT	*Southeast Asia Journal of Theology*
Sem	*Semitica*
SJT	*Scottish Journal of Theology*
SNTSMS	Society for New Testament Studies Monograph Series
SNTU	*Studien zum Neuen Testament und seiner Umwelt*
SPCK	Society for the Promotion of Christian Knowledge
ST	*Studia theologica*
Str-B	H. Strack and P. Billerbeck, *Kommentar zum Neuen Testament*
StudBib	Studia Biblica
SWJT	*Southwestern Journal of Theology*
TB	*Tyndale Bulletin*
TBC	Torch Bible Commentaries
TBT	*The Bible Today*
TCGNT	B. M. Metzger, *A Textual Commentary on the Greek New Testament*
TDNT	G. Kittel and G. Friedrich, eds., *Theological Dictionary of the New Testament*
TEV	Today's English Version
Theol	*Theology*
ThT	*Theology Today*
TLZ	*Theologische Literaturzeitung*
TNTC	Tyndale New Testament Commentaries
TRE	*Theologische Realenzyklopädie*
TrinJ	*Trinity Journal*
TRu	*Theologische Rundschau*
TS	*Theological Studies*
TSK	*Theologische Studien und Kritiken*
TTZ	*Trierer theologische Zeitschrift*
TU	Texte und Untersuchungen

TynBul	*Tyndale Bulletin*
TZ	*Theologische Zeitschrift*
UBS	United Bible Societies
UBSGNT	*United Bible Societies' Greek New Testament*
USQR	*Union Seminary Quarterly Review*
VD	*Verbum Domini*
VE	*Vox Evangelica*
WBC	Word Biblical Commentary
WEC	Wycliffe Exegetical Commentary
WP	*Word Pictures in the New Testament,* A. T. Robertson
WTJ	*Westminster Theological Journal*
WUNT	Wissenschaftliche Untersuchungen zum Neuen Testament
ZDPV	*Zeitschrift des deutschen Palästina-Vereins*
ZNW	*Zeitschrift für die neutestamentliche Wissenschaft*
ZRGG	*Zeitschrift für Religions- und Geistesgeschichte*
ZST	*Zeitschrift für systematische Theologie*
ZTK	*Zeitschrift für Theologie und Kirche*

Contents

Introduction 21
   V. The Centerpiece of the Gospel: Preparation of the Passover Lamb
      for Glorification (12:1–50) 29
   VI. The Farewell Cycle (13:1–17:26). 71
   VII. The Death of the King (18:1–19:42) 213
   VIII. The Resurrection Stories (20:1–21:25) 287

Excursus 11: The Son of Man and the Son of God 49
Excursus 12: A Note on Glorification 55
Excursus 13: Satan and the Prince of the World 58
Excursus 14: Foot Washings and Sacramental Interpretations 83
Excursus 15: Peter and the Beloved Disciple 92
Excursus 16: John's Gospel on the Trinity 117
Excursus 17: The "World" in John and Gnosticism 153
Excursus 18: Nonabandonment in John and the Cry of Dereliction . . . 181
Excursus 19: The Structure of John 17 185
Excursus 20: The Political and Judicial Situation in Israel during
               the Time of Jesus 224
Excursus 21: The Roman Scourging of Jesus and His Condition. 246
Excursus 22: The Site of Golgotha 262
Excursus 23: The Crucifixion of Jesus 263
Excursus 24: On Allegorical Interpretations 267
Excursus 25: On the Reality of Jesus Christ's Death 276
Excursus 26: Archaeology and the Tomb of Jesus 283
Excursus 27: The Resurrection Perspective and the Purpose of
               the Gospel 287
Excursus 28: The Twelve. 311
Excursus 29: Jerusalem and Galilee 323
Excursus 30: The Sons of Zebedee, the Beloved Disciple, and
               Oblique References in John 324
Excursus 31: John 21:1–14 and Luke 5:1–11: A Form and
               Redactional Note 331
Excursus 32: The Community "We" and Their Confession 342
Excursus 33: Questions of Eternity—Where Is the Place? What Is
               It Like? How Do We Get There? 360
Excursus 34: Characterization in Literature 369

Appendix 1: A Summary of Johannine Theology 345
Appendix 2: Characterization in the Gospel of John 369
Selected Bibliography 381
Selected Subject Index. 385
Person Index. 387
Selected Scripture Index 393

John 12–21

--------- THE STRUCTURE AND MESSAGE OF THE ---------
SECOND HALF OF THE GOSPEL

For the sake of those who do not immediately have in hand the first vol-ume of this two-volume commentary, it is appropriate to include a restate-ment of the structural map of the first half of the Gospel. That "triptik"[1] carried the reader from the magnificent Prologue to the climactic decision of the high priest to sacrifice Jesus as an expedient victim in order to "save" the nation (John 11:50). But John understood that the high priest's declara-tion of expediency, coming in the context of the readiness for Passover, was the divine signal (12:51) that the Lamb of God (cf. 1:29,35), who was being prepared for a divinely appointed hour (2:4; etc.), would, in fact, die very shortly as the Savior of the world (cf. 4:42).

Because the reader should begin the second half of the journey[2] with a clear understanding of the purpose for which the Gospel was written, it is well to be reminded that John wrote this book.

In order that you might believe that Jesus is the Christ, the Son of God, and that believing you might have life in [or by virtue of] his name![3]
(John 20:31, author translation)

Then the first half of the map with John follows:

Trip Map 1

The first segment of the journey is a most profound Prologue that introduces the reader to the incarnation of the preexistent "Word" of God, who became human in order to communicate the purposes of God to humanity (1:1–18). The next segment highlights the forerunner, the one whom God chose to intro-duce his messenger/agent to the world (1:19–28). This introduction is accom-plished by three Cameos of Witness in which the various aspects of the messenger's role are briefly suggested. The focus of this segment is set upon the agent's task as the Passover Lamb of God (1:29–51).

---

[1] "Triptik" is the registered name for the AAA sectional map books.
[2] See my comments in G. Borchert, *John 1–11* (Nashville: Broadman & Holman, 1996), 95.
[3] Ibid.

The evangelist then turns to present the first (2:1–4:54) of three cycles that will carry the messenger to his goal of serving as the Passover Lamb who "takes away the sin of the world" (1:29). This first cycle I have designated as the Cana Cycle because it begins and ends at Cana and leads to the clarification of the meaning of authentic believing in Jesus. This cycle is composed of five segments involving two signs that form an inclusio[4] on the manner in which Jesus works and human believing operates. Thus our road map leads us from the disciples who believed because of a sign at Cana (2:1–12) to the proleptic Passover sign of Jesus cleansing the temple (2:13–22), with a crucial insight on the nature of believing (2:23–25).

Our map next directs us to Nicodemus, who was unable to understand the nature of spiritual rebirth through the lifting up of Jesus as a sign. The discussion then expands into the implications for believing in terms of both salvation and judgment. By way of contrast, however, trust was pointedly exemplified in John the Baptizer (3:1–36). Then our trip compass points to the fascinating story of the Samaritan woman at the well with the intriguing implications of the Savior's coming for ethical living, genuine worship, theological perception, and clarity in mission (4:1–42). This cycle finally concludes with another Cana story involving the official who modeled believing in the word of Jesus before he saw the sign (4:43–54).

The next cycle, which I call the Festival Cycle (5:1–11:57), takes us on a journey through the experiences of Jewish festivals and the reality of opposition and hostility to Jesus. This cycle begins where the Jewish experience of reflection and worship ought to have been primary: namely, with the Sabbath and its proper understanding. Thereafter the cycle involves the second major inclusio in the Gospel, one that runs from Passover to Passover (6:4; 11:55). More particularly, the cycle begins with a sign concerning the paralytic and Jesus' healing on the Sabbath, an act that immediately engendered hostility from the Jews and led to a declaration of Jesus' rights as God's agent (5:1–47).

Next the reader is led to an exodus context at Passover time and is shown within the framework of two signs (a miraculous feeding and power over the sea) that Jesus' listeners should not have been seeking to eat more than manna, indeed to digest the bread of life. In this context one is reminded of the murmuring in the desert and that true discipleship involves decision making (6:1–71). In the next segment of the Johannine journey we are led through a three-chapter (7–9) reflection on the significance of Tabernacles in terms of the meaning of the water ceremony in which Jesus is the living Water and an emphasis on Jesus as the Light of the world (cf. the pillar of fire) who makes it possible to travel as a freed slave in the midst of darkness. Throughout this section the hostility against Jesus continues to develop, and the segment ends with a vivid illustration or sign of the blind man who is given light and new life

---

[4] An inclusio is a kind of literary envelope in which the first and last elements of a discussion are closely related and thus enclose the argument in a unified presentation.

through Jesus. But as a follower of Jesus he must pay for his new freedom from bondage by exclusion from the synagogue (9:34).

In chap. 10, the next segment, we traverse the territory of messianism and the Festival of Dedication or Hanukkah, the time when Jewish messianic expectations introduced in the popular Festival of Tabernacles were viewed as anticipating their realization in calling to remembrance the Jewish freedom that had earlier been achieved for a brief period through Judas Maccabeus. In this chapter there is also explained the true nature of God's shepherd or messiah, but Jewish hostility reaches such a level that the Jews were willing to stone Jesus, the Messiah, on the spot (10:31). The cycle then turns to its conclusion at Passover time when Jesus performs his ultimate sign of the first half of the Gospel, the raising of Lazarus (11:43), the prefiguring of the resurrection of Jesus at the conclusion of the Gospel. This event was regarded by the Jewish establishment to be such a significant act that they were forced to decide the ultimate question of either accepting Jesus or disposing of him. And so the Passover plot was hatched at the highest level of Jewish political authority. But strangely, in the high priest's official decree that one should die for the nation, John saw the ironic voice of God indicating that the event of Jesus' death would bring about the ingathering of the people of God (11:49–52).[5]

When we pick up the journey in this present volume, we begin with chap. 12 and the second stage introduction to the Gospel, where the evangelist points the way for us to follow.

Trip Map 2

The first segment of this second part of our journey begins with a rather ominous ring as the evangelist sounded the warning that it was almost Passover time. To make his point clear, he opened this introductory segment with an anointing of Jesus for his burial (12:7). Although the villain Judas would have sought to squelch the act, Jesus refused to entertain his complaint.

The next segment of our literary journey might initially give the reader the impression that this section is not about death but about the elevation of King Jesus as he rode into Jerusalem on a donkey amid shouts of praise from the waiting crowd. But at the same time as the crowd was shouting their hosannas, the disciples were confused by these happenings, the Pharisees were perplexed at what to do with Jesus, and the Greeks just wanted to see him. The evangelist, however, made it quite apparent that Jesus was not misled by these events. Instead, he declared that the hour of his glorification had arrived (12:23). Moreover, even though the prospect of suffering was troubling to him (12:27), Jesus understood that it was the Father's way of sealing the defeat of the evil prince of the world (12:31). This second introduction then concludes with reflections on the rejection of King Jesus in light of human nature.

---

[5] Borchert, *John 1–11,* 95–97.

Our road map takes us next through the third and most complex of the Johannine cycles—The Farewell Cycle, which is presented in the form of a bull's-eye. The first half of the outer ring involves a very vivid act on the part of Jesus in modeling discipleship for his followers by washing their feet at the strategic supper (13:5) and then by identifying that the overarching characteristic of his followers should be "love" (13:34–35). But following the model route of discipleship was not acceptable to the villainous Judas and he departed into the dark night of treachery (13:30).

The first part of the next ring of the bull's-eye leads us to the anxiety of the disciples as they were threatened by the thought of Jesus' departure to the Father, even though it was to be for their benefit (14:2–3). But they wanted to follow him and begged for a route map.

Instead, the reader is led to the section of our journey that takes us into the next ring of the bull's-eye and to the first two of the Paraclete sayings, wherein Jesus promised the disciples that the Holy Spirit would be with them forever (14:16).

After this introduction to the coming of the spiritual companion, the next segment of our journey leads to the core of the bull's-eye, wherein we learn from the *Mashal*[6] of the vine and the branches that abiding in Jesus is the only way to authentic discipleship (15:4–5). Moreover, our sectional map reveals what it means to love and be a friend of Jesus (15:12–17), and we are informed that the context of our journey will be rough because we travel in hostile territory (15:18–25).

From the core we are then directed to move outward again and arrive at the second group of three Holy Spirit sayings. In this segment, which focuses on the fact that the world hates and persecutes the followers of Jesus (15:20), we learn that the presence of our new companion (Paraclete) will be absolutely essential to guard (15:26–16:1), defend (16:7–11), and guide (16:13–14) us as disciples in our hostile context. From that ring we are led back to the next segment, which once again brings us to the setting of the early disciples' anxieties and fears and to the place where the comforting words of Jesus are once again heard (16:20,23,33).

Finally, this Farewell Cycle is concluded in a return to the outside ring of the bull's-eye and to another exemplary act that models a different aspect of discipleship from that of chap. 13. It finishes in chap. 17 with a seven-part exemplary prayer in which Jesus models for his followers the way of dependence upon the Father for true discipleship, safekeeping, unity, and hope. In this prayer the reader is taken into the sanctuary of the divine perspective and,

---

[6] For a discussion on the nature of a *Mashal*, an extended parabolic form (see ibid., 329). There are two such *Mashals* or *Mashalim* in the Gospel of John: the first on the Shepherd in chap. 10 and the second on the Vine and the Branches in chap. 15.

therefore, should be readied to journey with Jesus into the painful setting of the next major section of the Gospel.

In these two next chapters (18 and 19), which I have entitled the Death of the King, the reader is taken into a dark garden where Judas and his arresting band came with torches and weapons (18:3) to seize Jesus. But they discovered the power of the mysterious King who was actually in control (18:6). It was this awesome Jesus who refused Peter's puny help (18:11) and allowed himself to be captured, yet insisted on first taking care of his followers (18:8–9). Our map directs us next to a series of scenes at the courts of Annas and Caiaphas, where everyone including Peter pales in character before the serene Jesus (18:23).

From Caiaphas we follow the path of Jesus, who was sent to Pilate, the vacillating representative of the Roman emperor. Although Pilate acted as though he was in control, it becomes quite evident in the repeated shifting scenes from inside to outside the Praetorium that he had little control of the situation and that only King Jesus evidenced true nobility, even in being condemned (18:34,37; 19:11; etc.). This Jesus was then scourged, mocked, and crucified as the Lamb of God. Although the Jewish leaders gained their wish to rid themselves of Jesus by this horrible act, they could not prevent Jesus from being crucified as the "King of the Jews" (19:21–22)! Indeed, the charge was announced trilingually so that all who passed the cross could read it (19:20). Then, strange as it may seem, the crucifers of Jesus did not determine the exact time of his death because Jesus died at his determined time when his work was finished (19:30), on the day when the Passover lambs were slaughtered (19:14). To the surprise of the crucifers, they did not need to break his bones to hasten his death. He was only stuck with a spear, and thus he died an unblemished, perfect lamb (19:36–37). Finally, the King was buried in a new grave and entombed with enough spices to bury a monarch (19:39–41).

In most cases, journeys such as this one usually end at a sealed tomb that enshrines a hero's body. But our journey does not end in the usual way because a sealed tomb is not our continuing memorial to a dead Jesus. Instead, early on Easter morning the tomb was found to be completely open and empty (20:1–2). The one who had briefly occupied that tomb was no longer there—no longer dead. He was alive! The grave clothes were there in an unusual manner, and although Peter missed the point, those grave clothes brought forth a believing response from that other disciple that the church has linked with John (20:8). Moreover, the weeping Mary was changed into a witness when she simply heard her name spoken by the risen Jesus (20:16,18). Then this Jesus confronted the disciples in their anxiety behind locked doors. There he blessed them with the Spirit and commissioned them for their task as his representatives of salvation. But Thomas missed the blessing, so this realistically skeptical disciple needed to be retrieved. And then Thomas made the most incredible confession—that Jesus was God!—when he was confronted by the reality of the risen Lord (20:28). These testimonies are a wonderful conclusion to our literary journey and surely are more than sufficient for enabling us to confess with the powerful concluding purpose statement of the Gospel (20:30–31) that Jesus is the Christ, the Son of God!

But the Gospel does not end with chap. 20. It contains an important Epilogue that beckons the reader to a slightly longer journey. The trek leads to a miraculous catch of fish and a threefold restoring challenge to Peter. It is always good to review where you left the trail so that you do not make the same mistakes again (21:1–17). Also, it is important to be clear on where discipleship leads: be it to martyrdom with Peter or to old age with the beloved disciple. These important additions our cartographer believed were absolutely essential to prevent misunderstandings concerning Peter and the beloved disciple. Indeed, this extension of the journey is important because it reminds us to maintain our focus on Jesus and not on the disciples.

Finally, our directional map book is completed, but not without the stamp of the authenticating community (21:24) and with a brief binding statement that wraps up our plan book for delivery (21:25). In conclusion, the delivery of this route book is intended for all who would come later and desire to follow in the footsteps of this amazing map-making evangelist who charted the way to find life (20:31) brilliantly for succeeding generations of readers.

I would add: May God bless you, the reader, as you study and make your journey through this inspiring Gospel.

OUTLINE OF JOHN 12–21

V. The Centerpiece of the Gospel: The Preparation of the Passover Lamb for Glorification (12:1–50)
1. The Anointing for Death (12:1–8)
2. A Threefold Transition (12:9–11)
3. The Entry into Jerusalem for Passover and the Various Reactions (12:12–22)
4. The Turning Point and the Perspective of Jesus (12:23–26)
5. The Agony of Jesus and Its Implications (12:27–36)
6. The Centerpiece Summations (12:37–50)

VI. The Farewell Cycle (13:1–17:26)
1. The Foot Washing as Preparation for Passover and Authentic Discipleship (13:1–38)
2. The Great Issue of Loneliness and Anxiety for the Community— Part I (14:1–14)

3. The Role of the Spirit: The Divine Resource for the Community—Part I (14:15–31)
4. The *Mashal* of the Vine and the Bull's-Eye of the Farewell Cycle (15:1–25)
5. The Role of the Spirit—Part II (15:26–16:15)
6. Anxiety and Loneliness—Part II: The Great Reversal (16:16–33)
7. The Magisterial Prayer as the Final Preparation for Passover (17:1–26)

VII. The Death of the King (18:1–19:42)
1. The Garden Arrest of the King (18:1–12)
2. The Jewish Hearings and Peter's Denials (18:13–27)
3. The Roman "Trial" of the King (18:28–19:16)
4. The Crucifixion of the King (19:17–27)
5. The Death of the Lamb/King (19:28–37)
6. The Burial of the King (19:38–42)
7. Concluding Reference in the Death Story (19:42)

VIII. The Resurrection Stories (20:1–21:25)
1. The Resurrection and the First Conclusion to the Gospel (20:1–31)
2. The Epilogue (21:1–25)

V. THE CENTERPIECE OF THE GOSPEL: PREPARATION OF THE
   PASSOVER LAMB FOR GLORIFICATION (12:1–50)
   1. The Anointing for Death (12:1–8)
   2. A Threefold Transition (12:9–11)
   3. The Entry into Jerusalem for Passover and the Various Reactions
      (12:12–22
      (1) The Reaction of the Crowd (12:12–15)
      (2) The Reaction of the Disciples (12:16)
      (3) The Reaction of the Pharisees (12:17–19)
      (4) The Reaction of the Greeks (12:20–22)
   Excursus 11: The Son of Man and the Son of God
   4. The Turning Point and the Perspective of Jesus (12:23–26)
   5. The Agony of Jesus and Its Implications (12:27–36)
   Excursus 12: A Note on Glorification
   Excursus 13: Satan and the Prince of the World
   6. The Centerpiece Summations (12:37–50)
      (1) Wrestling with the Failure to Believe: The Issue of
          Determinism (12:37–43)
      (2) Summarizing the Gospel Message (12:44–50)

— V. THE CENTERPIECE OF THE GOSPEL: PREPARATION — OF THE PASSOVER LAMB FOR GLORIFICATION (12:1–50)

Apart from the Prologue, there is scarcely a more encompassing chapter
than chap. 12, for it serves a unique role in linking the two major sections
of this Gospel together, as will be explained below. Chapter 11 brought the
public ministry to a climax with the strategic raising of Lazarus and the crucial *ex cathedra* statement of the high priest concerning the necessary death
of Jesus. Chapter 12, with the anointing of Jesus and the entry into Jerusalem, prepares the reader for the final cycle—the Farewell Cycle directed to
the disciples of Jesus—and for the Death and Resurrection stories. Thus the
chapter serves as an Introduction to the second major section of the Gospel.
It sets a serious tone with the anointing scene but also offers a foretaste of
the fact that the dying one is also the King of Israel, as is proclaimed by the
crowd at the entry into Jerusalem (12:13).

Many scholars agree in dividing the Gospel into two major sections, yet many also consider chaps. 1–12 as the first section, with chap. 12 being its conclusion. This first segment of John is then variously designated with sectional titles such as Jesus' revelation (of glory) to the world as per Bultmann and Schnackenburg, or the book of Signs as per Brown, or the public ministry in the manner of Beasley-Murray. On the other hand, not only do I regard chaps. 2–11 to contain two well-defined and purposeful cycles, but I consider chap. 12 to be a singularly significant part of John that stands as a strategic unit at the center of the Gospel and serves as a major focal text for understanding the work.[1]

The chapter not only brings to a head the discussion in the previous two cycles and encapsulates the assertion in the Prologue concerning the nonreception of the incarnate Son by his own people, but it also serves as a window into the forthcoming sections of the Gospel; for it signals the arrival of the strategic hour (12:23) as an unmistakable announcement of the imminent coming of the self-sacrificial death of God's Son.

As such this chapter is a magnificent saddle text that touches both that which has gone before and that which is still to come. For those familiar with mountain climbing, the designation of this chapter as a saddle seems to be most appropriate. Saddles unite peaks of mountains and allow climbers the opportunity to move from one mountain to the next. Moreover, these saddles are actually part of both mountains they unite. Similarly, this chapter functions as a linking saddle that contains significant themes from what has been discussed and what is yet to be treated.

This chapter is also important because the writer singles out and identifies persons and groups crucial to understanding the story of Jesus. The sensitive reader, therefore, should be able to position the various parties into categories by how they relate to Jesus. In arriving at these categories, however, it is imperative to recognize how virtually all of the groups or persons are presented as one-dimensional or flat literary characters.[2] The effect of such a presentation is to heighten the portrayal of Jesus, who as a result plays the roles of the magnificent King, the self-giving Son, and the sacrificial Lamb. His call is to die for the world so that he might bring all people to himself.

But the chapter does not end without raising the existential question of believing, which is strategic to the very purpose for which the book was written (cf. 20:30–31). The chapter is thus a masterpiece of literary con-

---

[1] For the usual pattern of structuring this Gospel see D. Deeks, "The Structure of the Fourth Gospel," *NTS* 15 (1968), particularly at 124–26.

[2] For a discussion of the nature of characterization see R. A. Culpepper, *Anatomy of the Fourth Gospel* (Philadelphia: Fortress, 1983), 115–48. See also the concluding section of this commentary, "Characterization in the Gospel of John."

struction, for it involves the complex weaving together of many strands in
the portrayal of God's answer to the world in the Son, Jesus the Christ.

The chapter breaks naturally into a minimum of five subsections: (1)
the anointing scene (12:1–8); (2) a skillful transition (12:9–11); (3) the
entry into Jerusalem at Passover and the various reactions to Jesus (12:12–
21); (4) the crucial turning point and the perspective of Jesus (12:23–26);
(5) Jesus' agonizing acceptance of his coming death (12:27–36); and (6) a
twofold theological summation involving the perturbing failure to believe
by the Jews and a strategic epitomizing of the Gospel's message (12:37–
50).

1. The Anointing for Death (12:1–8)

[1]**Six days before the Passover, Jesus arrived at Bethany, where Lazarus lived,
whom Jesus had raised from the dead. [2]Here a dinner was given in Jesus' honor.
Martha served, while Lazarus was among those reclining at the table with him.
[3]Then Mary took about a pint of pure nard, an expensive perfume; she poured it
on Jesus' feet and wiped his feet with her hair. And the house was filled with the
fragrance of the perfume.**

[4]**But one of his disciples, Judas Iscariot, who was later to betray him, objected,
[5]"Why wasn't this perfume sold and the money given to the poor? It was worth a
year's wages." [6]He did not say this because he cared about the poor but because
he was a thief; as keeper of the money bag, he used to help himself to what was
put into it.**

[7]**"Leave her alone," Jesus replied. "[It was intended] that she should save this
perfume for the day of my burial. [8]You will always have the poor among you, but
you will not always have me."**

The fact that the story of the anointing appears in all four Gospels confirms its significance to the overall presentation of the good news. Given the
general independence of John from the stories in the Synoptics, this fact is
certainly worthy of note, especially since up to this point about all that is
parallel in John with the three other Gospels has been the story of the feeding of the five thousand. Perhaps one could add the temple cleansing (if one
allows for it to be placed at a different point from the Synoptics) and the
story of John the Baptist (if one allows for a different role of the Baptizer in
this book).[3]

---

[3] In addition to the above mentioned pericopes, the story of Jesus walking on the water, though
having a different focus from John 6:15–21, does appear in two of the Synoptic Gospels (Matt
14:22–32 and Mark 6:45–52). On this general topic see "John and the Synoptics" in the Introduction to vol. 1, pp. 37–41.

On the other hand, one who pursues a life of Christ harmony like the one initiated by Tatian in his *Diatessaron* in the second century[4] may find it a little disconcerting to discover that so little of John can be directly coordinated with the other Gospels. Indeed, it may be even more surprising for a reader to find that when one looks at a text like the anointing, where coordination would be possible, even here some variance between John and the Synoptics is evident and that in presentation the Synoptics are not totally coordinated with each other.[5]

Specifically, Mark and Matthew report an anointing of Jesus' head whereas Luke and John speak of the anointing of his feet (Matt 26:7; Mark 14:3; Luke 7:38; John 12:3). Moreover, whereas Bethany (likely to be in Judea) is mentioned in connection with the anointing in Matthew, Mark, and John, the setting in Luke, although not mentioned, would appear to be in Galilee since that was where Jesus was reportedly doing his early ministry at the time (cf. Luke 7:11 for Nain and 8:1,22 villages and the sea of Galilee). Furthermore, the particular site of the reception is said in Matthew and Mark to be the house of Simon the leper while in Luke it is the home of a Pharisee named Simon (Luke 7:40).

In John we are told that Jesus was in "Bethany where Lazarus lived" and that at the dinner Martha was serving, and Lazarus was at the table. So we might suppose that the dinner was in the home of Martha, Mary, and Lazarus, but this is not stated (John 12:1–2).[6] Furthermore, in John the event is placed chronologically six days before Passover (12:1), whereas in Matthew (26:2) and Mark (14:1) it is recounted following a meeting of the Jewish leaders two days before Passover.[7] The Lukan dating is hard to coordinate with either of these dates.

---

[4] See J. H. Hill, *The Earliest Life of Christ Ever Compiled from the Four Gospels Being the Diatessaron of Tatian* (Edinburgh: T & T Clark, 1894) and A. S. Marmarji, *Diatessaron De Tatien* (Beymouth: Imprimerie Catholique, 1935). Rather than writing harmonies today, such as that of A. T. Robertson, the tendency is to provide parallel Gospel texts and remind readers that the contexts are different in the various Gospels. See K. Aland, ed., *Synopsis of the Four Gospels*, Eng. 3d ed. (Stuttgart: United Bible Societies, 1979), 276–79 for the anointing scenes.

[5] For discussions on the comparison of John and the Synoptics see also R. Schnackenburg, *The Gospel According to St. John*, vol. 2 (New York: Crossroad, 1987), 370–71, who posits a development theory of tradition and R. Brown, *The Gospel According to John i–xii*, AB (Garden City: Doubleday, 1966), 449–54, who has a helpful comparison of the various accounts.

[6] C. L. Blomberg suggests that the dinner was at Simon's, "with Lazarus and his family as the invited guests and servers" (*Jesus and the Gospels* [Nashville: Broadman & Holman, 1997], 313). H. Ridderbos agrees from 12:2b that "we do not get the impression that the meal took place in the house of Lazarus and his sisters itself" (*The Gospel of John: A Theological commentary* [Grand Rapids: Eerdmans, 1997], 414).

[7] Blomberg writes that Matthew and Mark "relocate this passage topically, because of the symbolism of preparing Jesus for his burial, sandwiching the narrative between a reference to the later plot of the Jewish leaders to arrest Jesus ... and Judas' arrangement to betray him" (ibid.).

In addition, the woman who anointed Jesus is described by Luke (7:37) as a sinner and contrasted with the self-righteous Pharisee who organized the meal; but there is no such description in Matthew and Mark, and the woman remains virtually unidentified beyond the deed she did. John, on the other hand, identifies her as "Mary" (12:3), whom we assume to be the Mary of John 11, the sister of Lazarus and Martha. It is the particular Lukan designation of the woman as a sinner, however, that in the past has led to speculations that Mary of Bethany must have been a sinful woman and usually that she should be identified with Mary Magdalene, out of whom Jesus cast seven demons (Luke 8:2). But such speculation is merely a later construct of a Tatian-type mentality, and it is important to remember that even Luke, who categorizes Mary Magdalene in such a way, does not identify her with the sister of Lazarus and Martha (Luke 10:39–42).[8]

Given all of these variations, many have concluded that there must have been two anointings of Jesus, one early and one late. A. T. Robertson, for example, lists Luke 7:36–50 without parallel and explains that "this anointing in Galilee must be distinct from the anointing in Bethany, near Jerusalem, more than a year later."[9] The only problem is that just as in the case of the Temple cleansing, there is only one anointing in each Gospel. R. Stein's explanation is that since Luke, for example, chose to include the anointing in Galilee, he left out the anointing in Bethany to avoid having two very similar anointing accounts. He concludes that "it is quite possible that these accounts go back to two separate incidents in Jesus' life," but "as they were told and retold during the oral period, a certain standardization of terminology might have taken place between the stories."[10] I agree that such an explanation is surely possible, although we must be very tentative when formulating a reconstruction of a historical event that is nowhere described as such in any one historical/biblical text.[11] In dealing both honestly and reverently with our texts it is of supreme importance to let each Gospel communicate its own particular inspired message in its given context.

With this perspective in mind, attention is turned to John's strategically

---

[8] In his article on "Mary" E. H. Palmer warns against such synthesizing of identifications (rev. ed. *ISBE* 3.268). Cf. also the interesting comments of D. and F. Stagg in *Women in the World of Jesus* (Philadelphia: Westminster, 1978), 117–21 and 238–39.

[9] A. T. Robertson, *A Harmony of the Gospels* (N.Y.: Harper San Francisco, 1922), 60. See also A. Legault, "An Application of the Form-Critique Method to the Anointings in Galilee and Bethany," *CBQ* 16 (1954): 131–41; A. Feuillet, "Les deux onctions fait sur Jésus, et Marie-Magdeleine," *Revue Thomiste* 75 (1975): 357–94. G. Beasley-Murray (*John*, WBC [Waco: Word, 1987], 206) and Brown (*John*, 1.450–52) also favor a dual tradition.

[10] R. H. Stein, *Luke,* NAC (Nashville: Broadman & Holman, 1992), 235.

[11] C. H. Dodd, on the other hand, attempts to explain how the different texts emerge from one story. His explanations are fascinating, if not totally convincing (*Historical Tradition in the Fourth Gospel* [Cambridge: University Press, 1963], 171–73).

placed story of the anointing and the particular focus that story serves for this evangelist. I will also offer some brief comments on how I think this story relates to the other Gospels.

12:1–2 The scene opens with the reminder that the ominous Passover time was near at hand. Indeed, it was according to John just six days (12:1) before the fateful event. Piecing together the elements of the story, one would speculate that it was Saturday evening after sunset. The Sabbath had apparently passed because Martha, the sister known in Luke 10:40–41 for her engagement in kitchen duties, was hard at work in serving the meal. It is important to note here that the Johannine picture of Martha is quite consistent with the Lukan portrayal of her. So also is the picture of Mary, who is interested more in the relationship to Jesus than with pots and pans.

The notation of six days rather than two days as in Matthew (26:2) and Mark (14:1) reflects the Johannine desire to focus the reader's attention on the fact that the stories in this chapter form a unit around the key idea of the death of Jesus with the anointing serving as a symbolic introduction to the Death Story. The entry into Jerusalem and the triumphant praise of the crowd are, therefore, not in John to be seen as the focal points of this chapter. Thus, the chapter does not begin with them. The focus of the Johannine chapter is on the coming of the hour and the imminent death of the Son of God.

Accordingly, the anointing scene was placed first in this centerpiece of the Gospel. Such placement contrasts with Matthew and Mark, where the use of the anointing seems to be different and therefore follows the entry scene (cf. Matt 21:1–11; Mark 11:1–11 for the earlier entry scenes in those Gospels).

The fact that 12:9 mentions Lazarus's living in Bethany and recounts his raising from the dead so soon after John 11 indicates that these stories were probably told frequently by early Christians prior to being written down and shaped by the Gospel writer into an organizational whole.[12] At the time of writing the Gospel, the stories under inspiration were brought together in a connected narrative. This pattern of narrative setting is particularly observable at 11:2, where the unrelated anointing is mentioned in the context of the resuscitation of Lazarus *prior* to its being reported in John 12.

In the present Gospel story, while no one is directly identified in the account as the host of the dinner in which Martha was serving *(diēkonei)*, Jesus is said to have come to Bethany "where Lazarus was" (the NIV "where Lazarus lived" is certainly the sense); but the fact that Lazarus was among those at the table does not necessarily mean he was the host. It could have been an unmentioned third party. Some scholars, like Sanders, specu-

---

[12] For a brief introduction to Gospel studies see Blomberg, *Jesus and the Gospels*, 77–111.

late that the host may have been a person named Simon to coordinate with the Synoptics and even suggest that such a Simon could be *related* to Lazarus to make the coordination easier.[13]

12:3 During the meal Mary brought to that place a "pound" (*litran*, cf. 19:39, apparently similar to the Roman *libra*, equivalent nearly to our twelve ounces or 327.45 grams)[14] of ointment or perfume (*myron*, either "myrrh" or a generic word for "perfume"). Such ointment is here designated more specifically as being very expensive (*polytimou*, virtually synonymous with the Markan *polyteles*, 14:3, similar to the Matthean *barytimou*, 26:7) and composed of genuine (*pistikēs*, cf. also Mark 14:3) nard. This nard was a special oil probably extracted from the root (and "spike") of the Indian nard plant.[15] While John does not mention the container, there is no reason to doubt the Synoptic description of the perfume or ointment being preserved in a valuable alabaster flask or jar (Matt 26:7; Mark 14:3; Luke 7:37). Such a flask normally had a long thin neck which would be broken (cf. Mark 14:3) in use, and the contents could then be poured out.

The Johannine story has Mary pouring the ointment or perfume over the feet of Jesus and wiping his feet with her hair. As indicated in the John the Baptist story (see my comments at John 1:27), touching the feet of someone was regarded by Jews as a very degrading experience and was normally reserved for slaves and others to whom little "honor" was due. The fact that Mary was willing to do this act at a meal in the presence of others communicates volumes about her elevated regard for Jesus. It might also be argued by some that it indicates a lack of self-worth on her part. But such a theory would seem to fit the Lukan story of the sinful woman more than Mary of Bethany because in Luke the woman was seemingly unburdening herself; she not only anointed the feet of Jesus but also tenderly kissed his feet and dampened them with her tears (cf. Luke 7:38,44–48). In the Johannine story, however, there is no such indication of sinfulness, remorse, or kissing and sobbing over his feet. The story is focused on a proclamation of his death and burial (John 12:7). In this sense the point of the story is not unlike the Markan and Matthean stories, where the anointing serves as an act of Gospel proclamation, but in those Gospels the woman anointed the head of Jesus (cf. Matt 26:13; Mark 14:9).

12:4–7 The reaction to the anointing by Mary is focused here as in

---

[13] J. N. Sanders argues that the Simon of the Synoptics was the father of Lazarus and his two sisters ("Those Whom Jesus Loved," *NTS* 1 [1954]: 29–41).

[14] See BAGD, 475.

[15] For a discussion of nard or spikenard see R. H. Harrison, *Healing Herbs of the Bible* (Leiden: Brill, 1966), 48–49. See also J. E. Bruns, "A Note on Jn 12:3," *CBQ* 28 (1966): 219–22 and R. Koebert, "Nardos Pistike-Kostnarde," *Bib* 29 (1948): 279–81.

Matthew (26:8–9) and Mark (14:4–5) on economic evaluation of the situation. The Lukan story, however, does not concentrate on economics. Instead, the Pharisees charged Jesus with lacking sufficient insight as a prophet to recognize that a sinful woman had touched *(haptesthai)* him. The focus of the Lukan story is, therefore, very different. Yet, unlike John, Matthew and Mark charged the disciples with condemning the woman for her wastefulness. The disciples there thought that the poor could have been the beneficiaries of such a large economic sum. In view of such a charge, Jesus rebuked them because of their misunderstanding of the good or beautiful *(kalon)* thing she had done. Typical of the Markan message, the disciples there had once again misunderstood the events in the life of Jesus. So Jesus had to enlighten them to the effect that the act was an important preparatory symbol of his forthcoming burial (cf. Mark 4:8; Matt 26:12).

The story in John, however, makes a slightly different point. It certainly picks up the burial symbolism (12:7), but it refocuses the picture from the misunderstanding of the disciples to Judas, who was not merely mistaken. In this story John makes it plain that Judas was not an unfortunate, misguided person. He was inherently an evil thief who had no concern for the poor (12:6). Thus John would never agree with some modern portrayals of Judas as a tragic hero who merely misunderstood Jesus. For John, Judas was a devil-man *(diabolos; 6:70)*, a receiver of Satan (13:27), and the son of doom or destruction (17:12). For John, he was the unforgivable betrayer *(ho paradidous)* who stood with the enemies of Jesus (18:5; cf. *paradidonai; 12:5)*. For a discussion of Iscariot, see my comments at 6:71.

According to our Gospel, the role of Judas in the band of Jesus' disciples would be likened to that of the treasurer, indeed a fraudulent treasurer who made the community money box *(glōssokomon,* NIV "money bag") his personal estate. The value of the pure nard, therefore, did not escape his greedy interest. His estimate of its worth was three hundred denarii (12:5; Mark even suggests "more than" three hundred at 14:5), which was the equivalent of a laborer's annual wages (calculated at six days a week less festival days). Such an amount was very significant. Indeed, it could have served as an economic security blanket or, as I have suggested below, as a woman's dowry. Judas's suggestion that the money should have been given to the poor is regarded by the evangelist as a mere hoax or fraud in the mouth of the deceptive thief.

In responding to Judas, Jesus did not engage in any explanation or indicate a correcting spirit, such as he expressed to the disciples, especially in Matthew (26:10–13) and to some extent also in Mark (14:6–9). Judas was not like the other disciples. In those Gospels, Jesus attempted to inform the disciples about the good or beautiful nature of the deed performed by the woman. Here in John, Judas is given the curt reply, "Leave her alone," somewhat like Mark 14:6 but with none of the softening that follows. Instead, what comes next are the somewhat confusing words "in order that she might keep it for the day of my burial."

This Johannine shorthand here concerning "keep" (NIV "save") has led to much debate on the part of scholars. Obviously, it can hardly mean that the perfume or ointment had not all been used and/or that she would keep it (or the remainder of it) until the actual burial date. What then can it mean? Some have suggested that although Mary did not realize what she had done, Jesus understood the implications. Others have posited that "keep" means "keep in mind."[16] Hoskyns and Davey argue that Mary "consciously recognized" what she had done and anticipated the burial.[17] Carson thinks that it is not the anointing itself that is in focus but the burial of Jesus.[18] Daube argues from his rabbinic background that her act was cultically in anticipation of his death.[19]

To what does "keep" refer—to the act, or the nard, or a play on both? Why would a woman "keep" such an expensive item? It must have been very important to her. Could it have been part of a possible dowry? If that was the case, then the gift of the ointment or perfume would be for a woman of marriageable expectation almost the equivalent of an ultimate gift to Jesus. That Matthew (26:13) and Mark (14:9) saw in this gift a significant commitment, worthy of a "Gospel" notation in relation to Jesus' death, is very suggestive indeed. The woman's gift then could be regarded as an incredible expression of attachment to Jesus. Moreover, positioned where it is in John at the point of the coming of the hour (12:23) and the declaration of Jesus' readiness for death (12:27–33), the story of the anointing becomes nothing less than an important signal for the forthcoming glorification of Jesus. Without doubt then the gift of the woman was a tremendous memorial, wonderfully preservable in the light of the forthcoming death of Jesus. It was a marvelous symbol of burial that would answer the ultimate question of life itself; just as Jesus said, seed that dies bears much fruit (12:24). It was an anointing fit for a king who came to save the world (cf. also elaborate spicing at John 19:39–41).[20]

From both the sociological and theological perspectives the response of

---

[16] Cf. C. Barrett, *The Gospel According to St. John* (London: S.P.C.K., 1956), 345. Note also the discussions in B. Newman and E. Nida, *A Translator's Handbook of the Gospel of John* (New York: UBS, 1980), 391–92 and Brown, *John*, 1.449.

[17] See E. Hoskyns, *The Fourth Gospel* (London: Faber & Faber, 1956), 416.

[18] See D. Carson, *The Gospel According to John* (Grand Rapids: Eerdmans, 1991), 429–30.

[19] D. Daube, "The Anointing at Bethany," in *The New Testament and Rabbinic Judaism* (London: Athlone Press, 1956), 312–24.

[20] The reader of John should not miss the fact that the word *litra* (pound) is used in only two places in the entire NT, namely at John 12:3 and at 19:39, both related to the burial of Jesus.

Jesus then is very appropriate here. Since Mary's gift was of such an economic significance, sociologically Mary had depleted her potential of gaining a husband. That move is not to be understood as merely some nice act of honoring the Lord but as a tremendous demonstration of commitment to him. As a result, Jesus graciously accepted the act of dedication that many might consider both strange and wasteful. Thus, Jesus in John gives this act a theological significance far beyond the mere act itself. John recognized the great significance of this act and used this event as a hermeneutical key to introduce in this segment of his book the death of King Jesus.

12:8 Although a few manuscripts omit parts of this verse, there is no compelling reason to omit the words of the text here.[21] It is almost identical to the statement in Matthew (26:11). In interpreting this statement concerning the continuing presence of the poor, it is not to be seen as an excuse for not helping them. But the imminent departure of Jesus ("you will not always have me") supplies the rationale for why the special act of anointing here is fully acceptable in the overall mission of Jesus and the Johannine view of the good news. In censuring Judas (12:7), Jesus was not advocating neglect of the poor (12:8). He was highlighting the importance of the arrival of one of the most significant events in the history of the world—his departure/death.

2. A Threefold Transition (12:9–11)

⁹Meanwhile a large crowd of Jews found out that Jesus was there and came, not only because of him but also to see Lazarus, whom he had raised from the dead. ¹⁰So the chief priests made plans to kill Lazarus as well, ¹¹for on account of him many of the Jews were going over to Jesus and putting their faith in him.

12:9–11 These three verses in this centerpiece section serve as another linkage or minor saddle text between two significant stories, just as occurred earlier at 2:12. These three verses, however, are more complex because the evangelist addressed three pertinent ideas in them. First, in v. 9 he draws the reader's attention away from the anointing scene to the gathering of a crowd that had come to see Jesus (an incredible miracle worker) as well as Lazarus (the recipient of a startling resuscitation). After the healing of Lazarus, Jesus had withdrawn with his disciples from the Jerusalem area to a place called Ephraim (see 11:54). But now the word was out that the healer and the healed both could be found together in the vicinity of Jerusalem. That combination was certain to attract a crowd. John notes the gather-

---

[21] For a discussion of the text of John 12:8 see B. Metzger, *A Textual Commentary on the Greek New Testament* (London: United Bible Societies, 1971), 236–37. See also Newman and Nida, *Translator's Handbook*, 392.

ing of the crowd (12:9; see my comments at 12:12). The crowd of "Jews" here does not imply that they were enemies.

Second, this gathering, in the second place, brought the presence of Jesus and Lazarus to the attention of the enemies of Jesus, who had already plotted his death (11:49–53). The presence of Lazarus as a living witness to the power of Jesus meant that the plot now had to be expanded to include the resuscitated Lazarus (12:10). This verse is an important reminder that an evil thought or deed does not usually remain an isolated event, and those involved in such evil matters are generally forced further into evil in order to "clean up the loose ends."

Third, this "loose end" about the Lazarus raising was having its effect because the narrator tells us that "many" Jews were "departing" from the fold of the authorities and "believing" in Jesus (12:11). The combination of the words "departing" and "believing" could well have also been viewed by the evangelist as a proleptic portrayal of what would happen in the conflict between the early Christians and the synagogue. The preaching and ministry of the early believers led to the departure (exclusion) of Jewish believers/converts from their cradle of Judaism into the fold of the Christian church.

With these three setting statements in mind the evangelist moves from the framing story of the anointing to the story of the Rubicon-like entry into Jerusalem.

3. The Entry into Jerusalem for Passover and the Various Reactions (12:12–22)

Although many people have traditionally designated this crowded, palm-branch experience as the "triumphal entry," such a name hardly fits the significance of this event in John. In the strange intersection of events in my life, I was born on Palm Sunday, then in my youth I was confined to an isolation hospital bed memorizing most of the Gospel of John (see my Preface) until I was released for Palm Sunday. And later when I was teaching John in Jerusalem, I watched a shouting match and a fight take place between Christian priests of different traditions in the Church of the Holy Sepulcher on Palm Sunday! The combination of these events in my life has sensitized me to this "Palm Sunday" story in John.

Although the event is recorded in all four Gospels (Matt 21:1–11; Mark 11:1–11; Luke 19:29–44; as well as here in John), the focus of the stories is not the same in all of them. After pondering the story over the years, I find it completely impossible to designate John's version of the story by the title of the "triumphal entry." That title may apply to Luke's account, where Jesus told the Pharisees that if his followers were to be silenced "the stones" would "cry out" (Luke 19:40a, probably citing Hab 2:11). But John's story is different. It is strategically framed beforehand by the anointing of Jesus for burial (12:7) and afterwards both by the recognition that the hour of his glorification had arrived and by the likening of his time to the death of seeds (12:23–24). Jesus here was not confused about the significance of this event or by the shouting of the crowd. He knew that the meaning of his entry into Jerusalem was an entry into his death.[22]

One of the best ways to read John's story is to give attention to the various people he tells us were at the event. Reflecting on the different reactions can be very enlightening for the reader.

(1) The Reaction of the Crowd (12:12–15)

[12]**The next day the great crowd that had come for the Feast heard that Jesus was on his way to Jerusalem. [13]They took palm branches and went out to meet him, shouting,**

"Hosanna!"

"Blessed is he who comes in the name of the Lord!"

"Blessed is the King of Israel!"

[14]**Jesus found a young donkey and sat upon it, as it is written,**

[15]**"Do not be afraid, O Daughter of Zion;**
  see, your king is coming,
  seated on a donkey's colt."

12:12   The story opens with a typical Johannine introductory phrase "the next day" (cf.1:29,35,43; 6:22). This expression is basically equivalent to the Johannine use of *meta tauta* ("after this," cf. 3:22; 5:1; 6:1; 7:1, etc.) and the frequent *nyn* ("now," cf. 3:25; 4:1,46; 5:19; 6:52,60; 7:25,40,45; 8:12,21; 9:24; 11:17,32,38,45,47 and especially in this chapter 12:1,3,9,20,34). The use of *palin* ("again," cf. 8:12,21; 10:19,31) can also be viewed similarly. If the anointing took place on the evening after Sabbath concluded, this event could be understood to have occurred on Sunday (that would suppose the next day were to be viewed by Roman time designations as the next morning and not by Jewish calculations as starting after sundown of the following day).

Although the term "crowd" occurs in many of the Synoptic stories of Jesus, in John it clusters in chaps. 5–7. The crowd then gives way to the critics of Jesus at 7:49 during the height of the controversy to reappear first at 11:42, then in 12:9, and again here. The presence of the crowd in John, however, is short-lived, and after 12:34 the term disappears from this Gos-

---

[22] For another view see E. Freed, "The Entry into Jerusalem in the Gospel of John," *JBL* 80 (1961): 329–38.

pel. But here the crowd is particularly singled out as being "great" (*polys,* 12:9,12). The festival times in Jerusalem attracted great crowds. Although Josephus, in seeking to impress Hellenistic readers, surely exaggerates in positing that the crowd at one of the Passover feasts prior to the fall of the Temple would have been in excess of an incredible two and a half million people, we can at least conclude that the gatherings must have been very large.[23] Jeremias estimates that over a hundred thousand people, counting the Jerusalemites, could have easily participated in the Passover.[24]

12:13–15 The story of the entry itself is told with a minimal number of words. When the Old Testament references are extracted, what one learns is that the crowd met Jesus with palm branches and acclaimed him. Then Jesus found a young donkey and sat on it. That is the basic story line.

In commenting on the text, Dodd counters the critics who say that palm branches did not grow in Jerusalem because of the weather by reminding readers that pilgrims at feasts (especially at Tabernacles) carried such palm branches from areas nearby.[25] The valley east of Jerusalem (around Jericho) has always been fruitful with various palms. Those who have lived there realize that Jerusalem can get quite cold and that palms might have at times difficulty growing there. But we must not assume that we know what it was like two thousand years ago. The problem is not simply one of weather. It is a problem of the history and geography of Jerusalem involving its many wars, its battered landscape, and the cutting of trees over the centuries. Nevertheless, the text does not demand that the palms grew *in* Jerusalem. It simply says that they "took" (*elabon,* a very general verb) palm branches (*ta baia tōn phoinikōn,* a rather redundant statement like "palm branches of palms," cf. *T. Naphthali* 5:4). Where they obtained them is not stated.

Palm and other branches were traditionally carried to make temporary shelters as part of the Festival of Tabernacles (Lev 23:40; cf. also Neh 8:15). Because of the connection of palms with Tabernacles, T. W. Manson argued that this entrance probably took place at the Feast of Tabernacles.[26] That suggestion, however, is unnecessary because palms were also used as fronds or symbols of welcome for Jewish heros returning from battle or at

---

[23] Josephus, *Wars,* 6.9.3, 422–25.

[24] See J. Jeremias, *Jerusalem in the Time of Jesus* (London: SCM Press, 1969). See also the details in *Zeitschrift des Deutschen Palästina–Vereins* 66 (1943), 24–31.

[25] See Dodd, *Historical Tradition,* 155–56. Contrast W. R. Farmer, "The Palm Branches in John 12:13," *JTS* 3 (1952): 62–66. Cf. the note in Y. Yadin, "More on the Letters of Bar Kochba," *BA* 24 (1961): 34–50, who refers to an instruction for an officer to bring palms from En Gedi to Jerusalem during the Bar Kochba revolt. Palms became a symbol of Israel's messianic hopes and were represented on their coins in the periods of rebellion against Rome. They were also represented on the Roman victory coins. Cf. H. Hart, "Judea and Rome: The Official Commentary," *JTS* 3 (1952): 172–98.

[26] See T. W. Manson, "The Cleansing of the Temple," *BJRL* 33 (1950–51): 272–98.

unusual periods of rejoicing (cf. the ceremony at the welcome of the victor Simon in *1 Macc* 13:51 and at the initiation of Hanukkah with his brother Judas Maccabeus in *2 Macc* 10:7; cf. also *2 Macc* 14:4).

The crowd here obviously came out to meet a hero (12:13), "shouting" their hosannas and pronouncing a blessing on the "one who comes" in the name of the Lord—namely, "the King of Israel!"[27] This statement is a composite acclamation drawn particularly from Ps 118:25–26 and Zech 9:9, where Zion/Jerusalem is called upon to rejoice at the coming of their king. The expression "he who comes" *(ho erchomenos)* is a familiar designation for the expectation of the coming Messiah and the initiation of the messianic age (cf. Ps 118:26 and John 1:9).[28]

The reference to the king of Israel (12:15) should remind the reader that in chap. 1 (in the third Cameo of Witness) Nathanael had already identified Jesus as the "King of Israel" (1:49). But it should also call to mind the fact that Jesus had withdrawn from the people when they attempted to force him into becoming king (6:15). The designation of "king" for Jesus, as will become evident in the further unfolding of the Gospel, was clearly an appropriate title for him, but his kingship was not what people had expected (18:33–37). Not only was he not a political ruler, but he was surprisingly *a king who would die on the cross* (19:19). The crowd might well acclaim him king, but they did not understand what that meant for him.

The crowd attached themselves to the idea of triumph in Zech 9:9.[29] But when Jesus chose a young donkey for his entrance rather than a chariot and horses or a camel (the animals used by Roman and Eastern conquerors), he undoubtedly understood that there was another perspective in that text of Zechariah, a perspective that would not be warmly welcomed by the crowd. That perspective was *humility*.

Moreover, hidden in the boisterous crowd's call of "Hosanna" was an ironic twist of immense proportions. When the crowd shouted Hosanna (from the Aramaic, pronounced *hōša'na,* or Hb. *hōši'āhnâ*), which is a cry for "salvation now," they were begging for something far beyond anything they anticipated. Undoubtedly in the background of their cry of Hosanna here was the great chant of Ps 118 (particularly 118:25), a psalm that was

---

[27] Freed ("The Entry into Jerusalem," 329–38) thinks that the way John uses the OT texts here argues for a dependence on the Synoptics, but I find his discussion to be unconvincing in terms of his comparisons. A better argument here seems to be for Johannine independence in the use of the OT texts. Contrast D. Smith's solution in "John 12:12ff and the Question of John's Use of the Synoptics," *JBL* 82 (1963): 58–64.

[28] See my comments regarding "the coming one" at John 1:9 and the note there. Ps 118:26 was interpreted messianically in connection with the Jewish Festivals.

[29] See F. Bruce, "The Book of Zechariah and the Passion Narrative," *BJRL* 43 (1961): 347. Cf. A. Hanson, *The New Testament Interpretation of Scripture* (London: S.P.C.K., 1980), 167–70.

used in connection with the Festivals of Tabernacles, Dedication, and Passover (note that these are the same three feasts the evangelist chose to highlight in what I have called the Festival Cycle of this Gospel).[30]

The connection between waving branches and the Hosanna of Ps 118:25
should not be missed here. In the Feast of Tabernacles, for instance, the
male participants (both men and boys) waved the *lûlāb* when the Temple
singers reached the crescendo of "Hosanna."[31] The use of the psalm in connection with Passover is also well identified in the tractate on Passover in
the *Mishnah*.[32] But what is most intriguing is the irony in the call of the
crowd for salvation. It was in this entrance to Jerusalem that Jesus said that
his hour had come (12:23). Indeed, it would be on the cross that Jesus
would fulfill the confessional prediction of the Samaritans when they called
him the "Savior of the World!" (4:42). But the crowd's idea of salvation and
their idea of a messianic savior was not what John knew this entrance was
about. If they had only understood the messianic implications of an earlier
verse in that psalm (Ps 118:22), maybe they would have come to realize
that the rejected stone would "become the head of the corner" (cf. the use in
Matt 21:42; Mark 12:10; Luke 20:17; Acts 4:11; 1 Pet 2:4,7; cf. also Eph
2:20). But they did not.

In arriving at a fuller understanding of this story, one further matter
should be addressed. That matter involves the issue of the subtle change
that the evangelist has made in his use of the Zechariah text. Instead of saying, "Rejoice greatly, O Daughter of Zion!" (Zech 9:9), John states, "Do not
be afraid, O Daughter of Zion (John 12:15). It is instructive to notice at this
point that while the text from Zechariah is quoted in Matthew (21:5), the
part quoted above is not used there. The idea of rejoicing, however, is found
in the Lukan story (19:37). But nowhere in these Synoptic stories is there
an encouragement against fear as expressed here in John (cf. John 6:20).
Newman and Nida note the variation between John and Zechariah here and
conclude: "There is no obvious reason why John would have deliberately
changed the wording; the best explanation seems to be that he was quoting
loosely from memory."[33]

I must demur from such logic. Almost nothing in John happens by

---

[30] With the passing of time and the movement of Israel from the countryside to the cities, the
festival interests of Israel changed. In Lev 23 the focus is on *Passover, Weeks* (the early harvest festival), Pentecost, Trumpets, and *Atonement-Tabernacles*. The importance of Weeks diminished,
and in its place arose the new Maccabean festival of Dedication. Pentecost and Trumpets were
minor festivals in the calendar. The italics above indicate the early primary festivals.

[31] The *lûlāb* is a festive bundle of green branches usually composed of palm, myrtle, and wil-
low limbs.

[32] See *M. Pesah* 5.7; 9.3; 10.7.

[33] See Newman and Nida, *Translator's Handbook*, 398.

chance or loose memory. The book is too reasoned an argument to permit such a haphazard perspective. Instead, I believe the answer to the question of why John made this shift is most likely related to the way he has framed the whole event. Although the crowd did not understand the implications of their cry for salvation (Hosanna), John knew Jesus did. He knew that the road to salvation would be a traumatic experience, just as Jerusalem had to learn that there was comfort and hope in the midst of the exile when the Lord God, their shepherd, promised to come to Zion and encouraged them not to fear (Isa 40:1–11). But that was hardly the message the excited crowd wanted to hear. They were in for a shock.

(2) The Reaction of the Disciples (12:16)

[16]At first his disciples did not understand all this. Only after Jesus was glorified did they realize that these things had been written about him and that they had done these things to him.

12:16 The perspective of the disciples at this point can at best be described as foggy or confused. Just as throughout the Synoptic Gospels the disciples seemed unable to "understand" (cf. Mark 6:52; 8:21), the Johannine evangelist indicates here that they were confused ("did not know," *ouk egnōsan,* 12:16). They could be epitomized later in Thomas and Philip, who just could not conceive of where Jesus was going or who the Father was, even though Jesus had sought to teach them (cf. 14:5–11).

Barrett finds this verse to reflect an unreliable tradition and considers it to be "self-contradictory." He wonders why the crowd understood the messianic significance of the entry of Jesus on a donkey and the disciples did not.[34] But the point is that the crowd missed the real point of the entry, and the disciples were confused about the significance of all the events. It did not fit together for them.

But the situation of the disciples was not hopeless, and their fogginess was not a permanent state. At this point the evangelist, as a knowing narrator, provides us with a window into the future reality that helps us understand the transformation that occurred in the disciples. Just as the narrator informed us earlier that the resurrection of Jesus provided the basis for understanding Jesus' statement concerning destroying the sanctuary and in three days he would raise it (cf. 2:19–21), so here he makes clear that the glorification of Jesus would enable the disciples to recall the event in its proper perspective. But at this point they still could not integrate the Old Testament texts, their view of Jesus as the Messiah, and Jesus' life and

---

[34] See Barrett *St. John*, 349. R. Bultmann considers the entire story to be a legend that was developed from some other source such as Mark (*The Gospel of John* [Philadelphia: Westminster, 1971], 418 n. 3).

teachings (cf. the fascinating story of the way to Emmaus when Jesus did so for two of his followers in Luke 24:25–27). That post crucifixion-resurrection perspective, however, would come later.

(3) The Reaction of the Pharisees (12:17–19)

[17]Now the crowd that was with him when he called Lazarus from the tomb and raised him from the dead continued to spread the word. [18]Many people, because they had heard that he had given this miraculous sign, went out to meet him. [19]So the Pharisees said to one another, "See, this is getting us nowhere. Look how the whole world has gone after him!"

12:17–18 Before John turns to identify the reaction of the Pharisees in another brief but very forceful verse (12:19), he reminds the reader of the setting for their reaction by referring to two important contexts. In the first place, he draws attention once again to the climactic sign of the raising of Lazarus and the fact that the people in the crowd that had been at that event were continuing to bear witness of Lazarus having being brought back from the tomb or literally from among the dead ones (*ek nekrōn;* 12:17; cf. 12:9). So startling was that event for everyone that the authorities had moved immediately to hatch their Passover Plot (11:47–50). As they suspected, that situation (11:48) did not improve with the passing of time but in fact got worse.

In the second verse (12:18) John rehearses the fact that the large Jerusalem crowd (a different crowd) had gathered (cf. 12:9,12) in response ("they heard," *ēkousan*) to the witness of the Lazarus crowd. Their interest had been peaked in this sign of the miracle worker and his recipient, who had his life restored (12:9). As a result, if there was going to be a gala reception, they wanted to join the event and went out to meet him. Although the crowd hardly understood John's sense of "sign," here the crowd's acclaim of Jesus raised the concern of the Pharisee power brokers.

12:19 The Pharisees, as representatives of the *religious establishment*,[35] were completely frustrated by this "charismatic" leader who seemed to have sparked a messianic-like revival of passion among the people. As in every age, establishment people are highly threatened by charismatic types, even though as M. Weber has noted such people may have at

---

[35] Carson tries to envisage how the Pharisees' interest in seeking "to endure the occupation" would contrast with the accommodating approach of the Sadducees (*John*, 435). While this information is undoubtedly correct, for John the Sadducees are never mentioned, and the Sanhedrin's decision (11:53) has to be recognized in John as a joint effort. The Pharisees together with the high priesthood represent the Jewish establishment in this Gospel, and *no* philosophical, theological, or sociological distinctions are made between them, except that the high priestly family is portrayed as the administrative heads of the establishment.

one time gained power in a charismatic movement themselves.[36] In their protectionism the "priestly type"/establishment people often estimate that any differences resulting from charismatics (in the social sense) is catastrophic. The situation was not very different in Jesus' day. The establishment had reckoned that the so-called Jesus crowd would ruin everything (the Romans would thus have to take care of restoring order forcibly; cf. 12:48). Their doom-prediction of his growing popular power seemed to be right on target. Indeed, they could only see their political helplessness ("you profit nothing," *ouk ōpheleite;* the NIV reads "this is getting us nowhere") in the face of Jesus' popularity. Thus, in exasperation they cried out, "The [whole][37] world has gone after him!"

The idea of world *(kosmos)* in John is not, as some Christians might have come to think, a negative term (cf. John 3:16–19). Neither is it basically a geographical or territorial designation, but rather a reference to the population of the world. Thus Jesus is the light of the people of the world (1:9; 8:12), and his coming into the world (1:10) was to take away the sin of the people of the world (1:29). But because of hard hearts and rejection, the coming of Jesus also meant the judgment of the world (9:39).

In the present text the reactive cry of the Pharisees was, of course, an exaggeration. Yet for those in the establishment, it probably seemed that their control was collapsing. But for John their statement must have seemed ironic. Jesus had not come to be a political leader, although his entrance into Jerusalem here marked a strategic step in becoming "the Savior of the World" (cf. 4:42).

(4) The Reaction of the Greeks (12:20–22)

20Now there were some Greeks among those who went up to worship at the Feast. 21They came to Philip, who was from Bethsaida in Galilee, with a request. "Sir," they said, "we would like to see Jesus." 22Philip went to tell Andrew; Andrew and Philip in turn told Jesus.

12:20–22 In most commentaries and texts of John a new section is initiated at v. 20. I would not completely demur from this idea because what follows in the argument is clearly connected to these verses. But in a sense

---

[36] For *charisma* see M. Weber's classic study *Economy and Society: An Outline of Interpretive Sociology,* 2 vols. (Berkeley: University of California Press, 1978) as well as *On Charisma and Institution Building,* Selected Papers (Chicago: University of Chicago Press, 1968). Cf. B. Wilson, *The Noble Savages: The Primitive Origins of Charisma and Its Contemporary Survival* (Berkeley: University of California Press, 1975) and P. Berger, "Charisma and Religious Innovation," *American Sociological Review* 28 (1963): 940–60.

[37] The Western family of manuscripts including D, L, Q, *Theta,* and a number of minuscules and versions insert "whole" *(holos)* at this point. Although the evidence is far from convincing for including it in our texts, the possibility of it being there should be noted.

these verses also are related to the previous part of the story because they introduce another group to the picture of those who somehow are reacting to Jesus. The reaction of this group, however, is not tied as tightly to the entry scene as the three previous groups. Instead, these persons are introduced by the general statement "there were some Greeks" *(ēsan de Hellēnes),* and their presence in the story seems to be associated with the festival worship of Passover (12:20).

Although it could possibly be argued that these Greeks were Greek-speaking Jews because they were in Jerusalem for worship, such a view seems unlikely because that group usually would be designated by the term *Hellēnistai* and probably would be identified with the Diaspora (cf. 7:35). One could ask, then, why such a group of Greeks was there. The answer given in the text is that they had "come up" (a typical Jewish way of referring to Jerusalem) to worship at the Passover Feast (12:1,20).

Obviously these Greeks should not be identified as pagan worshipers of the pantheon or of the Eastern cults. They probably would best be identified either as proselytes or God-fearers (those who had not yet committed themselves fully to circumcision and the Jewish rites). The former were numbered among the Jews as converts and permitted into the inner Court of Israel. The latter were still regarded as Gentiles and were permitted only in the Court of the Gentiles, but not allowed beyond the stone wall that threatened death to the unworthy (or to those who encouraged them) if they crossed the boundary (cf. the false charge against Paul in Acts 21:28).

Although Newman and Nida identify the Greeks here as proselytes[38] and Beasley-Murray and Carson would seem to argue in the opposite direction (positing that this event may have hypothetically followed upon a cleansing of the Temple in the Court of the Gentiles as in Mark 11:15–17),[39] it is impossible to tell to which group they belong.

Moreover, it is impossible to determine where these Greeks were from. Passover was a time when adherents and devotees came "up to" Jerusalem from all parts of their world just as they did at Pentecost when Luke

---

[38] See Newman and Nida, *Translator's Handbook,* 403.

[39] See Beasley-Murray, *John,* 211 and Carson, *John,* 436. It must be remembered that while the Synoptics place the cleansing of the Temple close to the time of the entry into Jerusalem, such is not the case in John. From the context of the story here, I lean in favor of these people being "God-fearers," but what troubles me about the methodology proposed here is that it is a construction based on a harmonization that in no way is even remotely suggested by either John or Mark. In R. Fortna's detailed source and redaction analysis it is interesting that, contrary to the scheme suggested by Carson above, he places the restoring (cleansing) of the Temple in Section 10, the conspiracy I designate as the Passover Plot in Section 11, the anointing in Section 12, and the entry in Section 13 (cf. R. Fortna, *The Fourth Gospel and Its Predecessor* [Philadelphia: Fortress, 1988], 120–48). The reality is that reconstructions or harmonizations all have a subjective element that involves certain presuppositions concerning the ordering of the events.

recorded that the empowerment of the Holy Spirit was experienced (cf. the many nationalities listed in Acts 2:5–11). The fact that the Greeks here approached Philip, who was from Bethsaida, for help might suggest that they could have been from the region of the Decapolis, which was near Philip's home. But more likely it was because he had an obvious Greek name and probably spoke Greek.

One cannot help but speculate that the point of these three verses seems to be that nontraditional/non-Jewish persons had become intrigued by this powerful-heroic Jesus and they wanted to become involved with him ("to see" *[idein]* Jesus here means to meet him).[40] In general, displays of power are usually captivating to people on the outside and grab their attention. Sometimes those who are part of the in-group are not quite sure what to do with outsiders and whether they belong. The people in the out-group may also wonder whether the people in the in-group will let them in. So those of the out-group will often seek some opening or means that may help them in. Thus the Greeks, who probably were outsiders here, approached Philip, not Jesus, with the hope of gaining some way to the inside (12:21). Philip, who had earlier brought Nathanael (1:44), a like-minded type, then may possibly have needed some reinforcement in the case of these outsiders. Accordingly, he turned to Andrew (the helper, 12:22; cf. 6:8) who had earlier also shown himself to be a liaison person when he brought Peter to Jesus (1:41). Together they served as intermediaries for the Greeks (12:22).

The coming of the Greeks in a sense was a confirmation of the Pharisees' concern that the world was going after Jesus (12:19). But for John their appearance here hardly was to be interpreted in terms of the Pharisaic view of Jesus. Instead, it is to be associated with a strategic turning point in the ministry of Jesus.

4. The Turning Point and the Perspective of Jesus (12:23–26)

[23]Jesus replied, "The hour has come for the Son of Man to be glorified. [24]I tell you the truth, unless a kernel of wheat falls to the ground and dies, it remains only a single seed. But if it dies, it produces many seeds. [25]The man who loves his life will lose it, while the man who hates his life in this world will keep it for eternal life. [26]Whoever serves me must follow me; and where I am, my servant also will be. My Father will honor the one who serves me.

12:23 This verse opens with the note that (lit.) "Jesus answered them." Whether the "them" means the intermediaries, the Greeks, or both is unclear. What is clear, however, is that this verse marks a turning point in

---

[40] For an interesting commentary on this text see W. Moore, "Sir, We Wish to See Jesus—Was This an Occasion of Temptation?" *SJT* 20 (1967): 75–93.

the Gospel for Jesus. His words "The hour has come for the Son of Man to be glorified" are like an arrival at Waterloo or a crossing of the Rubicon. While the glorification event about which he spoke had not yet occurred (cf. 16:4), for Jesus the alarm clock had definitely sounded. Prior to this verse the evangelist had consistently pointed forward to the hour (cf. 2:4; 4:21,23) and had noted that his enemies were not yet able to complete their death wish for him because it was not yet his hour (7:30; 8:20). Now, however, the dirgelike drumbeat leading to Jesus' death had begun to play. The last act had now started; the hour had arrived (12:23; 13:1; 17:1).

Did the evangelist see the coming of the Greeks as the flashing signal to Jesus that the turning point had arrived? It would seem to be so, yet the entire chapter up to this point has been a kind of signal or flashing light announcing a turning point. The coming of the Greeks certainly can be viewed as a strategic and proleptic sign of their future coming. But not much is made of their coming in the text, and they fade immediately from special attention, unless one would argue that they were specifically the point of the small parable of the seed (12:24). But that statement is more general.

Instead of attention being directed at the Greeks, the focus now falls on Jesus. It is his turn to react, to provide perspective. His view of the events is not triumph in the usual sense. It is victory beyond death—God's great reversal! It is the hour for the Son of Man to be glorified.

Excursus 11: The Son of Man and the Son of God

From the very first chapter of John in the Nathanael story there has been an interweaving of the titles "Son of God" and "Son of Man" (1:49,51). Nathanael chose to refer to Jesus as King of Israel and Son of God while Jesus in that story chose the designation as Son of Man. But that choice surely did not mean the evangelist failed to conceive of Jesus as the Son of God. Quite to the contrary, his frequent references to the relationship of the Son and the Father (cf. 1:18; 3:16–18,35–36; 5:19–26; 8:35–36; 14:13) and the use of the title Son of God (cf. 1:34; 3:18; 5:25; 10:36; 11:4,27; 17:1; 19:7) clearly argue against that notion. Indeed, the purpose statement of the Gospel precisely is constructed to evoke from readers a confession that "Jesus is the Christ, the Son of God" (20:31). Nothing less is expected from the believing community, unless it is a confession that Jesus is God (cf. 1:1; 20:28–29).

Then why did Jesus adopt the designation Son of Man, which in the Synoptics appears to be Jesus' favorite self-designation? The answer to this question has received a great deal of scholarly attention.[41] Briefly summarized, it may be said

---

[41] See also the discussion of M. Hengel, who finds the idea of Son of God to be in the earliest traditions (*The Son of God* [Philadelphia: Fortress, 1976]). Contrast S. Schultz, *Untersuchungen zur Menschensohn-Christologie im Johannesevangelium* (Göttingen: Vandenhoeck & Ruprecht, 1957), 109–39 and *Jesus und der Menschensohn*, Feschrift A. Vögtte, ed. R. Pesch und R. Schnackenburg (Freiburg: Herder & Herder, 1975). See also E. Schweizer, "Discipleship and Belief in 'Jesus as Lord' from Jesus to the Hellenistic Church," *NTS* 2 (1955): 94–95. Cf. Schnackenburg, "Der Menschensohn in Johnnanes-evangelium," *NTS* (1964): 123–37.

that the designation Son of Man probably still was sufficiently vague and non-political so that Jesus could fill it with his particular meaning. Yet in all fairness one must remember that it is difficult to reconstruct fully the thought context of the time of Jesus (namely Second Temple, first-century Judaism). Besides the opinionated views of Josephus, the Dead Sea Covenanters, the intertestamental books, and the rabbinic writings from a later time, our conclusion to the effect that the Son of Man designation for a God-Man or a messianic-like figure was rarely used and must, in fact, remain a theory based primarily on the few references available in Dan 7:13 (where the Son of Man is seen with the Ancient of Days) as well as a few similar references in places like the *Book of Enoch*.[42]

We can, however, assert that the use of the phrase Son of Man in the Gospels is certainly more significant than a general designation for a human being, as evidenced in God's address to the prophet as son of man in Ezekiel (cf. Ezek 2:1; 3:1; 4:1, etc. and the well-known texts in 34:1; 36:16; 37:3; 38:1). The generic use of son of man, such as "sons of man" in Mark 3:28, is not present in John. The word combination "Son of Man" is used in this Gospel only of Jesus. The Son of Man in John is clearly regarded as a unique figure. He was none other than the divine one who had descended from heaven and who thereafter ascended as well (3:13; 6:62). Moreover, as the Son of Man he was a dying, lifted-up one (3:14; 8:28; 12:34) who in 12:34 is equated with the Christ figure and whose death-resurrection was viewed as glorification (cf. 12:23; 13:31). Accordingly, John stated that it was to this divine dying and ascended Jesus that the Father had committed authority for judgment because *(hoti)* "he is the Son of Man" (5:27)! The idea of God's representative, a kind of *shaliach* ("sent one"), who could act for him is clearly in focus here.[43]

It was, therefore, quite natural for the evangelist to speak in the same context about the Son of Man and Son of God (cf. 3:13–18; 5:25–27). For John the two designations have been clearly merged in one person. While some might be tempted to see in these two designations the two sides of the incarnation, it probably is better to envision that both designations would be viewed by John as representative of the incarnation with the Son of Man possessing divine qualities and the Son of God having become a human. They are thus like two sides of the same coin.

12:24   The little parable in this verse, as Dodd has reminded us, is rem-

---

[42] In the Similitudes or Parables of *1 Enoch* the picture of the Son of Man of Daniel 7 is expanded. He is not only linked to the ancient of days but also is the righteous one, the elect one, the one who stands before the head of days, the one who raises kings and serves the Lord of the Spirits, who is the light to the Gentiles, the one chosen before the creation of the world, etc. (*1 Enoch* 46:1–4; 48:1–6; etc.).

[43] Although the Heb. *Shaliach* does not fully encapsulate what is meant by Jesus as God's representative or agent, it approaches some of the aspects of Jesus as a sent agent. For a discussion of these issues see J. Ashton, *Understanding the Fourth Gospel* (Oxford: Clarendon Press, 1991), 310–14; J. A. Bühner, *Der Gesandte und sein Weg im Vierte Evangelium: Die kultur-und religionsgeschichtliche Grundlagen der Johanneischen Sendungschristologie sowie ihre traditionsgeschichtliche Entwichlung* (Tübingen: Mohr-Siebeck, 1977).

iniscent of the agricultural parables of Jesus in the Synoptic Gospels.[44] Jesus knew and understood the mind-set of the common people who labored with their hands, and he chose his illustrations to fit their experiences. They worked with seeds, and so Jesus spoke about seeds and harvest (cf. Mark 4:1–30; John 4:35–38). They understood that the new harvest was the result of dying seeds. Thus, in another double *amēn* ("truly") saying here he directed their attention to the important fact that the phenomenon of seeds and harvest illustrated a reality far beyond the experience of farming and gardening.[45] It was aptly related to the death of Jesus and the reality of their lives. Moreover, the statement that if the seed does not die but "remains alone" or by itself as unplanted, such a condition implies the tragic notion that the harvest would be frustrated. The implication for Jesus was obvious: he had no choice but to accept his coming glorification (death-resurrection) even though it would be traumatic.

12:25–26 The parable in v. 24 is followed by a maxim-like saying concerning loving and hating life. For people of the world, even today the idea of "hating life" seems to be too much to swallow. But one must remember the Semitic love for absolute contrasts in argument.[46] Similar types of argument can be found in Mark 8:35 and Luke 9:24 concerning saving and losing one's life and in Matt 10:39 concerning finding and losing life.[47]

These texts remind us that Jesus' life and teaching were seen by his disciples as paradoxical. Only by understanding Jesus' death and resurrection together can one make sense out of what seems to be the senseless waste of life. For many like Ghandi, however, the death of Jesus remained a senseless waste. Self-sacrifice for a cause can certainly be understood by the world as viable. But a suffering and dying Son of God is hardly viewed as acceptable to popular, power-oriented people of the world. But that is exactly what the Good News is all about.

---

[44] See Dodd, *Historical Tradition*, 366–69.

[45] The idea that the concept of seed dying here is related to parallels in the fertility worship of some ancient religions and particularly of Demeter and Persephone in the Greek religion of Eleusis, as sometimes thought, is remote at best. For a helpful comment see C. Dodd, *The Interpretation of the Fourth Gospel* (Cambridge: University Press, 1958), 372–73.

[46] For examples of Semitic absolutistic contrasts concerning love and hate see Jacob's love for Rachel and hate for Leah (Gen 29:30–31) as well as Malachi's thesis of the Lord loving Jacob and hating Esau (Mal 1:2; cf. Rom 9:13). By contrast, in the Genesis story the Lord speaks of the struggle between the two unborn boys of Rebekah and the service of the younger by the elder (Gen 25:23). But it is Esau who hates Jacob because of the stolen blessing and not God who hates Esau (Gen 27:41). Malachi and Paul, however, in light of history have interpreted the meaning of the servitude prediction and the blessing of Jacob in terms of the Semitic absolute contrast of love and hate. Cf. also the absolute contrast of loving the neighbor and hating the enemy in Matt 5:43.

[47] Cf. C. Dodd, "Some Johannine 'Herrenworte' with Parallels in the Synoptic Gospels," *NTS* 2 (1955): 78–80.

Such a perspective is not to be restricted to Jesus because these two verses are focused not so much on Jesus as on the believers. The model of the self-giving and dying Jesus is to be "followed" by those who would be his servants. It is significant, indeed, that Jesus chose to identify his disciples in this text where he spells out his perspective by the designation of "servant" *(diakonos)*.

This term has since been applied to an officer (deacon) in almost every branch of the Christian church, but one wonders if the idea of self-giving servitude is what is usually foremost in the minds of those who use the term *deacon* today. In this respect it is very instructive to remember the powerful words of Jesus to his disciples from Mark 10:42–45, namely, that authority in the church is not be exercised in the way of the world, but an officer is to be a "slave of all" *(pantōn doulos,* 10:44).

It is the faithful "servant" whom Jesus here says will be honored by the Father (12:26). In an ancient society where shame and honor were extremely significant,[48] the promise of honor for one who accepts a role that has all the markings of little honor is another of the great paradoxes in the message of Jesus. To love God in the Semitic absolute sense is to love God with the whole of one's being (heart, soul, and mind; Deut 6:4; cf. Luke 10:27, heart, soul, strength, and mind). To love God so much means that God has become primary and human existence has become secondary. That was the model set by the self-giving Jesus, and that is the model Jesus calls Christians to follow.

But following Jesus must not be narrowly conceived as merely living in this life. Following Jesus for the disciple may involve the ultimate cost of discipleship, namely the death of the disciple. Yet the disciple is promised the ultimate honor or reward of being "where I am" *(hopou eimi egō)*. This statement is packed with Johannine meaning. Not only does one note the presence of the familiar words *egō eimi* (though in reverse order) but the answer to the questions of "whence" and "whither" or "where" (cf. 8:14) that haunted Jesus' critics are given a new focus. While the critics did not know "where" he was going (8:14), it is precisely "there" (12:26) that his servants "will be" also. This expectation of being with Jesus, which is further discussed in chap. 14, is the promised hope of the faithful "follower" of Jesus.

---

[48] For insights on the issue of shame and honor and social influences see B. Malina, *The New Testament World: Insights from Cultural Anthropology* (Louisville: Westminster/John Knox, 1993) and *The Gospel of John in Sociolinguistic Perspective* (Berkeley: Center for Hermeneutical Studies, 1985). The popular work of Malina and R. Rohrbaugh is at times too brief to be helpful (*Social Science Commentary on the Gospel of John* [Minneapolis: Fortress, 1998]).

5. The Agony of Jesus and Its Implications (12:27–36)

[27]"Now my heart is troubled, and what shall I say? 'Father, save me from this hour'? No, it was for this very reason I came to this hour. [28]Father, glorify your name!"

Then a voice came from heaven, "I have glorified it, and will glorify it again." [29]The crowd that was there and heard it said it had thundered; others said an angel had spoken to him.

[30]Jesus said, "This voice was for your benefit, not mine. [31]Now is the time for judgment on this world; now the prince of this world will be driven out. [32]But I, when I am lifted up from the earth, will draw all men to myself." [33]He said this to show the kind of death he was going to die.

[34]The crowd spoke up, "We have heard from the Law that the Christ will remain forever, so how can you say, 'The Son of Man must be lifted up'? Who is this 'Son of Man'?"

[35]Then Jesus told them, "You are going to have the light just a little while longer. Walk while you have the light, before darkness overtakes you. The man who walks in the dark does not know where he is going. [36]Put your trust in the light while you have it, so that you may become sons of light." When he had finished speaking, Jesus left and hid himself from them.

E. Käsemann, writing primarily on John 17, argued that Johannine Christology was basically docetic and that Jesus in this Gospel is never really confronted by the actuality of suffering in this world.[49] Although there is no question that the resurrection is clearly an underlying presupposition in this Gospel and that the agony *(agōnia)* scene of Gethsemane, where Jesus suffered and his sweat became like clots *(thromboi)* of blood as in Luke 22:44, does not appear in John. But it seems completely unnecessary to conclude that the Johannine Jesus is unaware of trauma. Clearly his agony here is hardly a docetic appearance or, contra Bultmann, an edited Gnostic revelation-discourse.[50]

12:27 This section opens with a powerful emotional statement from Jesus, "Now is my soul *[psychē]* in turmoil *[tetaraktai* or "troubled"]."[51] Jesus had just announced the arrival of his hour (12:23) and defined the hour as his death (12:24). Unless Jesus was an emotionless, docetic, disappearing phantom, the situation could not help but pulsate with a sense of trauma. As W. Thüsing has argued, the verb *tarassein* and its cognates are

---

[49] See E. Käsemann, *The Testament of Jesus* (Philadelphia: Fortress, 1968). See also C. Nicholson's attempt to enhance the theory of Käsemann in *Death as Departure: The Johannine Descent-Ascent Scheme* (Chico, Cal.: Scholars Press, 1983).

[50] See Bultmann, *John*, 420–22.

[51] For the relationship of this statement to the emotion expressed in the Psalms see J. Buetler, "Psalm 42/43 in Johannesevangelium," *NTS* 25 (1978): 33–57.

filled with a deep sense that shock or trauma has come upon a person.[52] And what should one expect? Jesus was not a passionless person in John.

As M. M. Thompson has argued, Jesus is not merely portrayed in John as the powerful Son of God but also in his humanity.[53] To sense his kinship with humanity one needs to reflect on his need for a drink at the well (4:7), his weeping in the Lazarus story (11:35), his zealous attack in the Temple (2:17), his distress with the disciples' failure to understand who he was and the necessity of his departure (14:1–11), his care for his mother at the cross (19:26), and his deep distress over Judas (13:21). Besides being God's own Son, Jesus was also truly human. And what comes next is a confirmation of the genuineness of his feelings of turmoil at this time.

Prayer can be a window into the inner self. That is no less true for Jesus than for us. Although A. Schweitzer's early work showed that it is impossible to psychoanalyze Jesus from a story *about* Jesus,[54] one can nevertheless study what the evangelist considered was Jesus' state of mind at this point. As is the case with anyone who is faced with trauma, Jesus in v. 27 apparently has questions. Part of the nature of trauma is that it forces the psyche to ask questions. Although Jesus' questions may be different from those we may ask in the midst of trauma, it is reassuring to know that the mere presence of questions at such times is not unwarranted. The issue is not the presence of questions but what one does with the questions.

Jesus' question, "What shall I say?" comes to everyone in one form or another in the midst of trauma. It is the question of resetting, redefining, or reasserting one's bearings as the result of trauma. It does not mean that one changes one's direction; it means that one must look intensely at one's direction. One can expect and plan for trauma, but the actual coming of trauma forces one to face the existential questions of one's being. The Gospel of John does not have a temptation story as in the Synoptics (cf. Matt 4:1–11; Mark 1:12–13; Luke 4:1–13), but it does have a reference to Jesus' agony, an agony that confronts him with his question of meaning. Do not overlook the fact that the "prince of the world" is mentioned at 12:31. The devil is a genuine reality in the Gospel of John.

---

[52] See W. Thüsing, *Die Erhöhung und Verherrlichung Jesu in Johannesevangelium* NT Abh 21 (Münster: Aschendorff, 1960), 78–89.

[53] For a discussion of the statements related to the human nature of Jesus in John see M. Thompson, *The Humanity of Jesus in the Fourth Gospel* (Philadelphia: Fortress, 1988).

[54] See A. Schweitzer's study, *The Psychiatric Study of Jesus* (Boston: Beacon Press, 1948), which basically revealed in retrospect that one could not do an analysis of Jesus' psyche from Gospel stories written about Jesus by others.

The next statement beginning with *Pater* ("Father")[55] signals that Jesus' wrestling with trauma took place in context of prayer (for other Johannine prayers see 11:41–42 and the seven petitions of chap. 17). Beasley-Murray is right when he criticizes the UBS Greek Text and most of the translations for making the petition "Father save me from this hour" into a question.[56] Jesus was in the midst of a serious wrestling match as he was in the Synoptics when he prayed in Gethsemane for the removal of the cup of his death (cf. Matt 26:39; Mark 14:36; Luke 22:42). When Jesus was faced with the horrible nature of his forthcoming death, it was a traumatic experience, and he took his plea for escape ("save me") to the only one who was worthy of considering it—God, his Father. But just as in the Gethsemane stories, he answered his own petition. Here he replied with a firm *alla* (strongly negating his own request) and adding the reassertion of his mission in answer to the toll of his fateful hour (*hōra,* 12:27).

12:28 Having thus reaffirmed his course and his commitment to his mission, Jesus once again addressed the Father *(pater)* and made his petition, "Glorify your name!" As Schnackenburg has observed, this brief petition is reminiscent of the first petition in the Lord's/Our Father Prayer "hallowed be your name" (Matt 6:9; Luke 11:2).[57] The idea of "hallowing," or treating as holy the name of God in the Lord's Prayer, is Jesus' way of giving a positive approach to the "third word" of the Decalogue, where Israel is sternly warned against the misuse of God's name (Exod 20:7).[58] In the present text Jesus' petition has a definite Johannine ring, given the use of the verb "glorify."

Excursus 12: A Note on Glorification

There is no question that the Gospel speaks of the glorification of the Son (cf. 1:14; 16:14; 17:4) and also indicates that Jesus would be glorified in and through the disciples (17:10). But in John the glorification of the Son is said to be derived from the glory of the Father (5:40–44; 8:54; 17:5). Moreover, the glorification of the Son is consistently directed to the glorification of the Father (7:18; 8:50; 11:4; 13:31; 14:13; 17:1). Because the glorification of the Son has

---

[55] For a discussion of "Father" see J. Jeremias under the rubric of "Abba" in *The Prayers of Jesus,* 6 SBT (Naperville: Allenson, 1967), 29–54 and E. Lohmeyer, *"Our Father": An Introduction to the Lord's Prayer* (New York: Harper & Row, 1965), 32–51.

[56] Cf. Beasley-Murray, *John,* 212. To make the petition into a question empties the prayer of reality and makes the agony of Jesus into a sham. Carson joins this view as well (*John,* 440). Contrast Brown, *John,* 1.465 and Schnackenburg, *St. John,* 2.385. Barrett thinks it makes "little difference" (*St. John,* 354). So also Newman and Nida, *Translator's Handbook,* 409.

[57] Schnackenburg, *St. John,* 2.387.

[58] For a discussion concerning the relationship of this idea to the Lord's Prayer see R. A. Guelich, *The Sermon on the Mount* (Waco: Word, 1982), 289.

been focused on the glorification of the Father, it has therein removed any sense of selfishness or self-centered ambition from the picture of Jesus.[59]

The Son was consciously said to have chosen the way of obedience—the way that led through the traumatic death on the cross. Thus John identified the way of the cross with the way of glorification. Accordingly, prior to that event he directed the reader's attention forward to that event not only through reference to the coming hour (e.g., 2:4; 7:30; 12:27) but also by reference here to Jesus' glorification. That glorification would, of course, also open the horizon to the post-resurrection period of the era of the Spirit (7:39) and the Son's enthronement in glory alongside the Father, a position which he had "before the world came to be" (17:6). Yet in spite of the victory aspect of glorification, the reader must not submerge the death perspective into the idea of glorification for John. Indeed, the linkage between death and glorification is vividly presented in the Epilogue when the prediction of the death of Peter is described as the way he "would glorify *[doxasei]* God" (21:19).

12:28 (Cont.) In answer to the prayer of Jesus, the evangelist tells us that a voice sounded from heaven. Here is the only place where the heavenly voice is specifically used.[60] In the Synoptics the voice is mentioned in connection with the baptism of Jesus and the transfiguration. In the baptism story in both Mark (1:11) and Luke (3:22) the voice serves as a confirmation to Jesus that he is pleasing to God. In the Matthean text (Matt 3:17) the confirmation of Jesus seems to be used as a kind of announcement concerning who he is. In the transfiguration stories the voice from the cloud seems to serve less as a confirmation to Jesus and more as announcement to the disciples, much like the Matthean baptismal voice. But in the transfiguration stories the voice is directed to correct the misguided Peter and his colleagues concerning the true nature of Jesus (Matt 17:4–6; Mark 9:5–7; Luke 9:33–35). While that voice is not used primarily for confirmation, the experience of the transfiguration seems to be focused on Jesus' preparation for the cross. Indeed, Luke (9:30–31) states pointedly that Moses and Elijah spoke to Jesus about his forthcoming *exodos* ("departure") in Jerusalem. The idea of departure/exodus is a poignant word for any Jew who at Pass-

---

[59] In *The Trinity in the Gospel of John* [Grand Rapids: Baker, 1986], R. Gruenler sought to offset a hierarchical view of the Trinity by emphasizing a community sense of the Trinity in terms of what he called "disposability" or availability as servants of each member of the Trinity for the other. Some corrective to most ideas of the Trinity was necessary, but he probably carried the idea too far in that in speaking to the twentieth century, he probably has slipped into the peril of modernizing the Gospel.

[60] Some have thought that a response might be implied in 11:41–42 because of Jesus' thanking God for having heard his prayer and because of the statement concerning the people who stood by being challenged to believe. But the only voice mentioned in the text is that of Jesus (11:43). For a discussion of this voice see C. Evans, "The Voice from Heaven: A Note on John 12:28," *CBQ* 43 (1981): 405–8.

over time is annually called to remember the deliverance from Egypt and the sojourn in the wilderness. In John there is no direct account of either the baptism or transfiguration of Jesus. The use of the voice that confirmed the work of Jesus thus has been reserved for this centerpiece chapter in the Gospel.

The words of the voice, "I have glorified it, and will glorify it again," are intriguing. The use of the aorist/past tense can hardly refer here to Jesus' preexistent glory but must refer to his life and work as a whole on earth up to the hour. The future when linked with "again" seems to be a reference to his forthcoming death-resurrection experience and his return to the presence of the Father (cf. 17:1–5).[61]

12:29–30 The experience was obviously bewildering to the crowd because they were unsure of what the sound was. Some thought it was thunder; and others, that Jesus had been addressed by an angel. Although it would be inappropriate to categorize the former group with the modern designation of rationalists, these people apparently sought for an explanation based on natural phenomena. But natural phenomena in that day were often linked to nonhuman powers and forces beyond the rational. The other group apparently recognized the event as strange/mysterious and sought another explanation. In the intertestamental period, God was regarded as remote and the word of the Lord was viewed as rare.[62] At that time the people of Israel developed all sorts of theories concerning angels as intermediary beings, both good and bad. Moreover, they developed hierarchies of angels, and their archangels often resembled some of the gods of the Greek pantheon.[63] They were not always sure how they would act, but they often were thought to act on behalf of God.

Neither of the theories advanced by the people here concerning the sound was correct, so Jesus indicated that the voice was for their sakes. At this point Brown asks a difficult question to the effect that if the people were confused about the sound, how could it be for their benefit?[64] Although silence obviously does not speak, one must either presume that the text is confused or assume that there is more to the story than is

---

[61] But Thüsing thinks that the aorist tense includes the hour of Jesus' death and the future tense refers to the resurrection and the exaltation (*Verherrlichung*, 193–97).

[62] The apocalyptic writers of the intertestamental period often related thunder, the sound of many waters, flashes of lightening and the like to the reactions of the divine. Cf. the Johannine version in Rev 4:5; 6:12–14; 11:13, 19; 12:15; 16:18; 19:6). For comparable phenomenological descriptions see the *Similtudes of Enoch*, the *Apoc. Bar.* and *Sib. Or.* 5.343–45.

[63] For the seven archangels see *1 Enoch* 20. Cf. *Sib. Or.* 2.215. See also *Str-B* III, 806. Compared to the intertestamental books, the NT is reserved in its discussion of angels. Moreover, the angelic figures are not given fatelike controlling powers, but as Heb 1:14 argues they are to be viewed as servants of the believers.

[64] See Brown, *John*, 1.477.

reported, namely that some clarity emerged in the situation from the fact that Jesus indicates it was a voice. Such a voice could only be related to the God of heaven.

12:31–33 The clarifying task of Jesus continued as he turned from the topic of the voice of God to the subject of judgment *(krisis),* both negative and positive. The lifting up of the Son of Man is pictured as the way Jesus would die (12:33)[65] and as a divinely oriented dividing line. On the one hand, it meant the "throwing out" or the unseating of the world's prince *(archōn)* or evil authority. On the other hand, it meant the attracting of people to Jesus.

Excursus 13: Satan and the Prince of the World

The leader of evil that is judged here should undoubtedly be understood as none other than Satan, who is described in many ways in the New Testament.[66] For example, he is said to be the ruler (prince) of the kingdom (authority) of the air (Eph 2:2); the god of this age (2 Cor 4:4); the dragon, the ancient serpent, the Devil, the deceiver, and the accuser (Rev 12:7; 20:2); and he is likened to a roaring and devouring lion (1 Pet 5:8). In the Gospel of John he is designated as the prince *(archōn)* of this world (12:31; 14:30; 16:11), the devil *(diabolos,* 8:44; 13:2; cf. Judas in 6:70), the evil one (17:15), and a murderer (8:44). The only use of the name *Satan* in John, however, is at 13:27 in connection with Judas.

The equation of the prince of the world with Satan cannot be found in the Old Testament. In rabbinic times the Hebrew *sâr ha ʿōlām* ("Eternal Prince of the world") is a designation used for God. The Greek term *kosmokratōr* (world ruler) is used only once in the plural in the New Testament (Eph 6:12), and in that text it seems to carry a sense of evil, spiritual powers. Among the Greeks the term was used primarily in astrological texts. The rabbis *transliterated* the word and used it as reference to the Angel of Death.[67] But even the rabbis did not seem to make the equation with Satan. As a result some scholars like Barrett think John has lost "touch with Hebrew and Jewish thought."[68]

But one must not overlook the "prince of spirits" in *Jubilees* (10:8; 11:5ff., etc.; cf. *CD* 20:2) and the "prince of evil," the one who "rules this world" in other texts (cf. *Asc. Isa.* 2:4, etc.).[69] And the texts of Qumran remind us vividly of the contrast between the angel of darkness and the prince of lights (cf. *1 QS* 3.20–22).[70] The Jewish milieu of Jesus and the Gospel of John was not the setting of

---

[65] Note the similar expression to 12:33 at 21:19. Cf. B. Cassian, "John 21," *NTS* 3 (1956): 135–36.

[66] For an excellent treatment on Satan and evil see S. H. T. Page, *Powers of Evil: A Biblical Study of Satan and Demons* (Grand Rapids: Baker, 1995).

[67] See Michaelis's article in *TDNT* 3.913–14.

[68] See Barrett, *St. John,* 355.

[69] Cf. Schnackenburg, *St. John,* 2.527.

[70] For other references see Brown, *John,* 1.468.

the latter rabbis.[71] It was the setting of uneasy conquered Judaism looking for a Messianic ray of hope from heaven and fully prepared to recognize the oppressive power in the world. In this passage of John the evil prince of the world is clearly condemned.

12:31–33 (Cont.)   While judgment ultimately is to be viewed as eschatological, John sees the cross (12:33) as the proleptic dividing point in the history of the world. Thus he can confidently announce that now *(nyn)* is the evil ruler dethroned (12:31) and that whoever refuses to believe in Jesus is already *(ēdē)* condemned (3:18). This "now" of John does not mean, as Bultmann has argued, that "no future … can bring anything new" or that "all apocalyptic pictures of the future are empty dreams."[72] It means that in the "lifting up" of Jesus the decisive event in the history of faith can be identified. Moreover, it means that everyone has been and will be judged in light of that event.

It certainly does not mean that the casting out of the evil prince has ended evil in the world. It means that although he may have engineered the crucifixion, he had no power over Jesus (14:30) but rather that he had been judged by Jesus. The Paraclete would make that fact evident (16:11) to the believers. Also it did not mean that evil would never again gain a foothold in the lives of believers. If such were possible, Jesus would not have needed to pray for their protection from the evil one (17:15). Evil is real, but the message of John is that in the dying (12:33) or the lifting up (12:32) of Jesus evil has been decisively condemned.

The other side of the coin is that it means in the victory the lifted up Jesus has great drawing power. As Carson has correctly observed, "but" *(kago,* "and I") in the NIV at 12:31 is inappropriate[73] because the "lifting up" is *not* an adversative set against the "casting out" of 12:31 because they are part of the same event. In addition, the "lifting up" of Jesus, as indicated earlier, must be understood in the full scope of the Christian confessions involving his death on the cross and his resurrection-exaltation, as presented in texts like the Philippian hymn (Phil 2:8–9), the introduction of Hebrews (Heb 1:3), the Colossian proclamation (Col 1:18), the creedal statement of 1 Timothy (1 Tim 3:16), the traditional affirmation of 1 Corinthians (1 Cor 15:3–5), and the dramatic descriptions in Revelation (e.g., Rev 1:5; 5:6; 19:12–13,16). John sees both aspects intimately bound together in the glorification of Jesus (John 12:23–24, 27–28).

---

[71] For an important discussion by A. Segal of the intersection of Jewish and Christian ideas on this issue, see his "Rules of the World: Attitudes about Mediator Figures and the Importance of Sociology for Self-Definition," *Jewish and Christian Self-Definition*, vol. 2 (London/Philadelphia: SCM/Fortress, 1981), 245–68 and 403–13.

[72] See Bultmann, *John*, 431.

[73] See Carson, *John*, 443.

This "lifting up" of Jesus is the means for drawing all people to himself. Although some manuscripts (including 𝔓⁶⁶) have the neuter plural (*panta,* "all things"), the UBS Greek committee correctly indicated that such a reading is highly unlikely.[74] Although Paul recognized that all creation will ultimately be set free from its bondage to decay (Rom 8:21), John here is concerned with the drawing of all people (*pantas,* the masculine inclusive case is used) to Jesus. We must resist any notion here of interpreting Jesus as "dragging" people irresistibly to himself.[75] The parallel text in 3:14–15 reminds us that the "lifting up" of Jesus provides eternal life to "everyone who believes."

Another caution is also appropriate at this point because the "all" here is not to be interpreted as advocating universalism anymore than "everyone" in 3:15 does. The context of this passage must be remembered. The context has been reactions to Jesus that concluded with the coming of the Greeks (12:20). The way in which Jesus interpreted the event was not that of a heroic Jewish conqueror but of the dying "Lamb of God, who takes away the sins of the world" (1:29). That early strategic Johannine text must always be kept in focus. Here it provides the basis for understanding "all." The meaning of "all," like "the world" in 1:29, is to be seen in contrast to Jewish limitations much in the same way as Jesus said at 10:16 that he had other sheep to bring. This Gospel does not advocate narrow Jewish nationalism. Neither does this Gospel advocate broad universalism, but its scope and appeal are clearly universal. The lifted up arms of Jesus are extended to everyone indiscriminately. He came to be the "Savior of the World" (4:42). But the coming of Jesus is an invitation to all, not a commitment to accept all who reject him.

12:34 The response of the crowd was to contradict Jesus. They combined his statements concerning the Son of Man being glorified and his idea of being lifted up, then they criticized him by referring to the law. Although one might argue with the strict logic of their argument, even the evangelist would have to admit that they heard him and got the point that he was speaking of a dying Messiah. The way they countered the point was by reference to the law.[76] Interpretation of God's purpose is where the major divi-

---

[74] See Metzger, *Textual Commentary,* 238.

[75] See Newman and Nida, *Translator's Handbook,* 412. The verb ἑλκύω is used six times in the NT, five of them in John. Paul and Silas are "dragged" into the marketplace (Acts 16:19), Peter "drew" his sword (John 18:10), the disciples were unable to "haul" in the net (John 21:6), but Peter "dragged" it ashore (John 21:11). In John 6:44 the Father "draws" to Jesus the one who otherwise could not come, and Jesus assures him of resurrection. The point, however, is divine enablement, not divine force.

[76] For a discussion of the idea of law here see S. Pancaro, *The Law in the Fourth Gospel* (Leiden: Brill, 1975), 332–39.

sion occurs between Christians and Jews.

The question is, What does the law say? Assuming that law here probably should be understood generically as the Old Testament, which included the Torah, there may not be any specific text that clearly states the Son of Man or the Messiah would "remain" forever. God of course is eternal. But the Jewish assumption here was a theological construction that, as van Unnik posited, was probably derived from texts such as Ps 89:35–37 (2 Sam 7:13), to the effect that the seed or line of David would continue or be established forever, or Isa 9:6–7, where the promised child's kingdom and the reign of peace would see no end, or Dan 7:13–14, where a Son of Man is said to establish a kingdom that would not be destroyed (cf. Ezek 37:24–25; *Ps. Sol.* 17:4).[77] The people of Israel did anticipate a conquering, triumphant messiah, and they had difficulty conceiving of a temporary messiahship such as presented in *4 Ezra* 7:28–29.[78] Indeed, one of the arguments leveled at Christians in the next century was the one presented by Trypho the Jew in his dialogue with Justin, wherein he cited Dan 7:13–14 that the Son of Man would establish an eternal kingdom.[79] It was impossible for that Jew to integrate the crucifixion of Jesus with an eternal kingdom. But that is precisely the message of John.

12:35–36a The Jews had finished their response in 12:34 with a question, "Who is this Son of Man?" The answer to that question had been Jesus' message throughout his ministry, but they had rejected it (cf. 1:11). This was not the time for another debate. So instead of answering the question of the Jews, Jesus issued a stern warning. Light was with them just a little longer. The issue was whether they would recognize the gravity of the situation or be swallowed up in the darkness.

Light and darkness here are not new themes in John, for they were introduced in the Prologue. Darkness cannot conquer the light (1:5), but it can overcome people. Like Nicodemus (3:2), these Jews were living in the darkness of night. Jesus had proclaimed himself to be the Light of the World and had called people not to walk in darkness (8:12). But unlike the blind man who gained his sight (9:30), they were in imminent danger of becoming just as blind as the unaccepting Pharisees who criticized the former blind man (9:39–41).

Yet the concluding word to the people was not a statement of judgment. Rather it was an invitation to believe and become sons of the light (12:36a). The contrast between sons of light and sons of darkness indicates familiar

---

[77] See W. C. van Unnik, "The Quotation from the OT in John 12:32," *NovT* 3 (1959): 174–79. Cf. also S. Smalley, "The Johannine Son of Man Sayings," *NTS* 15 (1968–1969): 297–300 and B. Chilton, "John xii 34 and Targum Isaiah iii 13," *NTS* 22 (1980): 176–78.

[78] See also *Str-B* 2.552 and 3.823–26.

[79] See Justin, *Dialogue*, 32.1.

self-designations of the Qumran convenanters and their enemies (cf. 1 QS and 1 QM).[80] Similarly, the expressions "sons of light" and "sons of day" are used by Paul in 1 Thessalonians (5:5), and he reminds his readers that believers are not "of the night or the darkness" (cf. also Eph 5:8). The statement here in John is a pointed reminder that the invitational warning is also applicable to disciples, for Jesus had earlier provided a pointed sermonette to his close followers when they were fearful of returning with Jesus to Judea and to the "sleeping Lazarus." Walking in the light and day can guard against stumbling. But the situation is quite different at night (11:9–10). In this text Jesus warned that the darkness was near. It would be signaled again in 13:30 with the tragic departure of Judas.

12:36b   After having said these words, Jesus left and hid himself from the public. According to the Gospel they would not see him again until the Passover events were moving to their conclusion and the Lamb of God was being readied for the slaughter.

6. The Centerpiece Summations (12:37–50)

As the Gospel turns toward its final and decisive movements, the evangelist supplied two brief refrains of reflection. Thus, before he set in motion the third cycle, which is focused on Jesus' concern for his close disciples and prior to his consideration of the death and resurrection stories, he paused in this complex centerpiece and presented two focal summations that should cause readers to ponder how they would have reacted to Jesus if they would have witnessed his words and works.

The questions that underline these summations for readers are: What about you, do you believe? And, if you believe, what does that imply? The careful reader should recognize immediately that these questions in fact parallel the concern in the purpose statement of the Gospel (20:30–31). The symphonic nature of this Gospel has always captivated me as a reader and forced me as a believer to ponder my life in light of God's incredible gift to us as human beings.

(1) Wrestling with the Failure to Believe: The Issue of Determinism (12:37–43)

37Even after Jesus had done all these miraculous signs in their presence, they still would not believe in him. 38This was to fulfill the word of Isaiah the prophet:

"Lord, who has believed our message
and to whom has the arm of the Lord been revealed?"

---

[80] See R. Brown, "The Qumran Scrolls and the Johannine Gospel and Epistles," *CBQ* 17 (1955): 403–19 and 559–74.

³⁹**For this reason they could not believe, because, as Isaiah says elsewhere:**
⁴⁰**"He has blinded their eyes**
   and deadened their hearts,
so they can neither see with their eyes,
   nor understand with their hearts,
   nor turn—and I would heal them."
⁴¹**Isaiah said this because he saw Jesus' glory and spoke about him.**
⁴²**Yet at the same time many even among the leaders believed in him. But because of the Pharisees they would not confess their faith for fear they would be put out of the synagogue;** ⁴³**for they loved praise from men more than praise from God.**

12:37 The rejection of Jesus by the Jews must have been for John (like Paul, cf. Rom 9–11) one of the most difficult realities to understand. Was there not enough proof? What more could be done? The seven signs in the previous cycles should have been more than enough for anyone. And the words of Jesus when linked with signs should have supplied plenty of explanation. The evangelist's conclusion here could be none other than that the problem was not with Jesus. Then what was the reason for the Jewish failure to believe?

12:38–40 If the answer was not in the ministry of Jesus, then perhaps it could be found in the words of the Old Testament. The prophet Isaiah supplied the evangelist with both his question (12:38; cf. Isa 53:1; cf. its use also in Rom 10:16, where Paul modifies the impact by saying not all have listened receptively) and his thesis statement (12:40; cf. Isa 6:10–11;[81] cf. also Acts 28:27 and Matt 13:14, where it serves as an explanation for Jesus' use of parables). The use of these Isaiah verses in several places in the New Testament reminds us that although the early Christians did not carry around the scrolls of all the Old Testament as we carry printed Bibles, they had summary diaries of pertinent texts about the Messiah, sin, and the saving purposes of God which they quoted frequently and to which they referred in their preaching and writing.[82]

Building a kind of proof text from verses in Isaiah 6 and 53 after the manner of Paul's earlier and larger construct in Rom 3:10–18, the Johan-

---

[81] See Brown, *John*, 1.486, who provides a helpful summary of the use of this Isaiah text in the NT in a comparison of the Heb. Massoretic text and the LXX. In the MT he indicates that the statement in Isa 6:11 begins with the situation announcement in an imperative form, "Make the heart of the people ...," whereas in the LXX the text begins with a situation assertion, "The heart of the people ..." Moreover, in the MT the text ends with a general statement, "Convert and be healed," whereas in the LXX it ends with "I shall heal them." The LXX is followed fairly closely in Matt 13:14 and Acts 28:27. But John provides a shorter version in the situation statement and attributes of the blinding God ("He has blinded ...") while ending like the LXX.

[82] For a discussion of summary diaries of OT texts used for preaching, writing, and witnessing see E. Ellis, "Quotations in the NT," *ISBE*, 4.18–25.

nine evangelist formulated his rationale concerning the problem of Jewish unbelief. It was not a simple answer. But like other difficult questions that perplex the mind, the answer for John lay hidden in the mysterious nature of God.[83] For example, Jesus never really supplied the answer to the disciples' perplexing question of theodicy as it applied to the blind man (9:2), but he dealt with the blind man's problem. Pondering the answer here may not be satisfying to the human-oriented mind-set because it seems on the surface to blame God. After all the *hina* at 12:38, usually translated by the vague "to" or "to fulfill" in many English translations, certainly seems to carry the purposive or telic sense of "in order that," despite attempts to argue result or some other solution that would seek to avoid blaming God for the problem.[84]

The implications of the telic sense have generally been avoided by contemporary writers unless they espouse a Calvinistic point of view.[85] But one does not have to espouse such a view to treat fairly a text and recognize it to be telic, as evident in Brown, Beasley-Murray, and others. But in evaluating the telic sense here, I would call readers to think about the presuppositions of the biblical writers in the Old and New Testaments if they are seeking to understand texts like this one as well as others such as Romans 9–11, the Isaiah texts, and the issue of the hardening of Pharaoh's heart, including the apparent conflicting passages of Exod 4:21 (where God is said to have hardened Pharaoh's heart) and 8:15,32 (where Pharaoh is said to have hardened his heart).

Remember the options that were constantly before ancient Israel in the presence of its dualistic neighbors. They could opt for the dualistic heritage out of which they came when Abraham was called from Mesopotamia, a heritage that would permit them as humans the opportunity to choose who to blame or praise and in effect make human choice the measure of reality. Or they could opt for the new way of Abraham, which affirmed only one God (remember also the *Shema Israel*, recited daily by every pious Jew, which states that "the Lord is one!" [Deut 6:8]).

But the latter choice left insoluble questions, questions of who is to blame for disasters and trouble. The only answer in the Old Testament was to turn the question back to God and leave it there. Yet in the case of individuals who have had a significant role in their own pathetic destinies, that answer did not seem to be sufficient because like Adam and Eve (a) they

---

[83] For a controversial view of the issues related to God and the problem of evil see E. F. Tupper, *A Scandalous Providence* (Macon, Ga.: Mercer, 1995), in which he argues for limits on God's activity.

[84] See, for example, J. Painter, "Eschatological Faith in the Gospel of John," *Reconciliation and Hope* (Exeter: Paternoster, 1974), esp. at pp. 46–47.

[85] Cf. the extended discussion of Carson, *John*, 448–50.

had the privilege of choice, (b) were in some sense like God and not mere robots, and (c) chose the way of rebellion or unbelief by moving outside the parameters prescribed by God (cf. Gen 3:1–19). So blame somehow had to be shared. The sharing of both blame and blessing then is part of the uneasy tension concerning human choice that remains at the foundation of the Bible.

But the human mind does not like to accept the tension. It seeks for order, certainty, and clarity where there is mystery. It may raise the status of the tempter, Satan, to the same level as God and like the Gnostics solve the problem by returning to an ontological dualism. Or it may make God so pervasive in human affairs that it accepts what Beasley-Murray labels "naked predestinarianism, even irresistible reprobation."[86] As in other places in the Bible where wrestling with mystery takes place, the Isaiah texts here cited are used to explain the fact that the Jews did not believe because they "could not believe" (12:39). Yet great care must be taken not to blame God for this unbelief in such a way as to excuse these humans for their failure to believe.

Human responsibility for sin and unbelief is never excused in the Bible. That God is clearly said in Isaiah and here in John to have had a hand in human affairs and actions in terms of blinding eyes and petrifying (*epōrōsen,* the NIV uses "deadening") hearts in order that *(hina)* Israel would not come to healing (John 12:40; Isa 6:10) is indisputable. But that original pronouncement was also said in the context of Israel's consistent disobedience. The action of God therefore did not excuse Israel. The same is obviously true in the Gospel with respect to Jesus and his hearers. As my former professors Gerhard von Rad and Otto Piper used to say repeatedly, one has to learn how to keep the various dimensions of the Bible always in focus.[87] I would add that none of us does so consistently, yet it is especially important here not to lose sight of the tension that is inherent throughout this chapter and in the very nature of believing itself. Thus John, having said that they did not believe (12:37), can turn around after having used his proof text about God and then immediately thereafter announce that many believed (12:42), even though it may have been inadequate and secretive believing. It was nevertheless a human response or action, and for that response or action the human is responsible.

12:41   In concluding his citation from Isaiah, the evangelist draws the fascinating and somewhat perplexing observation to the effect that the prophet made this statement because Isaiah saw his glory and spoke about

---

[86] See Beasley-Murray, *John,* 216.

[87] See, e.g., G. von Rad's statements in *The Message of the Prophets* (New York: Harper & Row, 1965), 126. Cf. also Beasley-Murray, *John,* 216.

him. Coming immediately after the question in Isa 6:10–11, it is not impossible that the prophet had in mind the earlier part of that text (Isa 6:1–4), where there is described Isaiah's vision in the Temple of God and the long royal robe. Although the response of the seraph included praise to God for his glory, the passage does not speak precisely of a vision of God's glory. But the Aramaic Targum on this text reads "the glory of the shekinah of the Lord." If the Isaiah text were so interpreted by rabbis at that time, it is not impossible that John saw there a reference to Jesus in a manner somewhat similar to the way he viewed the statement about Abraham seeing his day (cf. John 8:56).

12:42–43 This section closes with the fact that not only the people but many of their rulers or leaders *(archontōn)* believed in him (12:42; quite in contrast to 12:37; cf. the contrast also in 1:11 and 12). "Leaders" here probably implies that they were members of the Sanhedrin or Jewish Council (cf. Nicodemus an *archōn* at 3:1 who met with the leaders in 7:45–52).

But these "believers" were unwilling to confess openly *(homologoun)* their commitments because of pressure from the Pharisees and the potential of excommunication from the synagogues similar to that experienced by the blind man (cf. the fear of the parents in 9:22 and the exclusion of the blind man in 9:34). The church has always had people who remain borderline believers, unwilling to confess openly their attachment to Jesus because of all sorts of pressure. For many today, especially in Muslim countries, the pressure is not merely a matter of membership, prestige, or economics like these secret believers but of life itself, a situation the early Christians soon encountered. The cost of discipleship is often high, and some, like the leaders in this story, remain borderline believers because of fear of exclusion (12:42) or loss of popularity (12:43).

Contemporary readers of the Gospel should not fail to reflect on the implications of this text for themselves. Believing in Jesus is often very costly.

(2) Summarizing the Gospel Message (12:44–50)

[44]Then Jesus cried out, "When a man believes in me, he does not believe in me only, but in the one who sent me. [45]When he looks at me, he sees the one who sent me. [46]I have come into the world as a light, so that no one who believes in me should stay in darkness.

[47]"As for the person who hears my words but does not keep them, I do not judge him. For I did not come to judge the world, but to save it. [48]There is a judge for the one who rejects me and does not accept my words; that very word which I spoke will condemn him at the last day. [49]For I did not speak of my own accord, but the Father who sent me commanded me what to say and how to say it. [50]I know that his command leads to eternal life. So whatever I say is just what the Father has told me to say."

In a few short sentences that follow, the evangelist has unpacked for his readers the meaning of his repeated message in the coming of Jesus, and he directs attention forward. It is thus an overview of his message or a statement in a nutshell.[88] Readers who are familiar with the stories and the reflections up to this point should immediately identify the themes and the core ideas from the chapters they have just read. This summary, accordingly, provides a magnificent launching pad for what is to come next. Clarity in the gospel message is undoubtedly the purpose of this closing section of the centerpiece of the Gospel, which is the reader's preparation for the forthcoming Passover of the Lamb.

12:44a This section opens with the words "Jesus cried out," which sound much like a public proclamation. But at 12:36b it had already been announced that Jesus had finished addressing them and "hid himself." This apparent inconsistency (like the one at 14:31 where Jesus said, "Rise, let us depart hence" and then continued to speak for three more chapters) has led to several suggested revisions in the order of the text, such as that of Bernard, who places this section before Jesus' departure and hiding.[89] Brown merely considers it to be an "unattached discourse" that has been added, and Bultmann completely reworks it in his structuring of John.[90]

12:44b–45 The summary proper begins with a twofold statement not only concerning *believing* and *seeing* Jesus but also believing the one who *sent* him. All three italicized ideas are major themes in this Gospel. This twofold statement furthermore prepares the reader for a third expanded version on *receiving* in the next chapter, which includes an important reference to the ones whom Jesus sent (13:20). This statement occurs in the introductory chapter of the Farewell Cycle, the cycle that focuses on discipleship.

The statement here also highlights the relationship of the Father and the Son in terms of several important themes. It presupposes representative unity that was introduced in the opening verse of the Prologue in terms of the Word and God (1:1) and was stated most emphatically in the conflict setting of the Festival Cycle just before the Jews attempted to stone Jesus (10:30).[91] Moreover, the idea that Jesus had been *sent on mission* to repre-

---

[88] Dodd calls it a "*resumé* of salient points from the discourses" and likens it to Mark's Kerygma of Jesus (*Interpreting the Fourth Gospel*, 382). Brown labels it as an unattached discourse employed as "a summary proclamation" (*John*, 1.489). Carson rejects Dodd's designation, but I believe he has been too hasty in this evaluation (*John*, 451). It may not involve the whole Gospel in the sense of the whole message of the NT, but it is a summary of John's basic teaching to this point.

[89] See J. Bernard, *A Critical and Exegetical Commentary on the Gospel According to St. John*, ICC (Edinburgh: T & T Clark, 1928), 445–48.

[90] For Brown's comments see n. 78 above. For Bultmann see his reworking of the text in *John*, 342.

[91] See Excursus 12 on glorification and particularly n. 56 on Gruenler and the Trinity in John.

sent God and to "make him known" is a theme that is introduced in the concluding verse of the Prologue (1:8). The verbs for "sent" (*apostellein* and *pempein*) form a continual refrain in the Gospel (e.g., 3:17,34; 4:34; 5:23, 24,30,36–38; 6:29,38–39,44,57; etc.). Behind this type of statement stands a concept of Jesus as an agent of God in the carrying out of God's purposes on earth.[92]

The important themes of seeing and believing are clearly interrelated in this Gospel and are basic to understanding what accepting Jesus is all about. The presence of believing in this Gospel is so fundamental that John builds his purpose statement around its necessity (20:31). The idea of seeing is nuanced in a number of ways. It is used as the means for focusing on the signs of Jesus (2:23), serves as a bridge to believing (9:35–38), and acts as a symbol and powerful contrast to blindness and its consequent judgment (9:39–41). As one reaches the conclusion of the Gospel, one is reminded again by the risen Jesus that mere physical sight is not the intention of this presentation (20:29; cf. 2:23–25).

The form of this twofold statement reminds one of Hebrew synonymous poetry, and the construction is not unlike Jesus' negative statement in Matt 10:40 and its positive counterpart in Luke 10:16 (cf. John 13:20; Mark 9:37).

12:46 The summation next moves to a related idea concerning light. The theme of light coming into the world was introduced in the Prologue (1:4–5,9), and the vivid contrast between light and darkness enunciated in the Prologue was forcefully reenunciated in the conflict setting of Tabernacles. There light was presented as the answer to darkness and blindness (8:12; 9:1–5), and light/day was said to be the means for avoiding stumbling (*proskoptein*, 11:9–10; cf. the similar idea of "falling away," of "being paralyzed," *skandalilzein*, in 16:1). The element that seems to have been added to light here is the idea of abiding or remaining, which was introduced by the disciples at the very beginning of their relationship with Jesus (1:32). Although remaining or abiding is used here in connection with the theme of darkness as the opposite to the way of discipleship, it is generally employed as a positive reference to discipleship (e.g., 8:31). Indeed, it becomes the key word for discipleship in the *Mashal* of the Vine, which I have called the bull's-eye of the Farewell Cycle (15:1–11).

12:47–48 These verses have a definite negative ring to them and serve as a warning to the reader. Throughout the Festival Cycle especially, the Jews heard the words of Jesus and debated with him. Hearing him, therefore, was not enough. What was necessary was "keeping" his words. Even his close disciples

---

[92] For an excellent dissertation on the subject of Jesus as God's agent in John see J. R. Venema, "An Apologetic Role for Agency in John Five," Ph.D. diss, Golden Gate Baptist Theological Seminary, 1995.

(the Twelve) were at first in a fog (12:16; cf. 4:27–33) about the implications of his words. Although they did not leave him in Galilee like others who had followed him (cf. 6:66–67), they nevertheless were resistant to his movement, if it meant the potential of danger (11:8–16). And since they had difficulty understanding him and his departure (14:5–10), it is no wonder that someone like Peter, who refused to leave him earlier (6:68), denied him in the Death Story (18:27). If obeying his message was difficult for the close disciples, what about others? Indeed, what about us today?

The coming of Jesus into the world, however, was not intended primarily for judgment but, as clearly stated here and in 3:17, for the salvation of the world's people. Moreover, his coming was not a blessing restricted to Jews only. He was, as the Samaritans discovered, the Savior of the World (4:42). But even though Jesus came to save the world, rejecting him (namely, the failure to believe and receive him and his words) could imply nothing other than judgment.

It is possible to agree with Brown that 12:48 contains a sense of both realized and futuristic eschatology.[93] If a person who rejects Jesus already is judged by his words, then I would argue that, in agreement with the evangelist's statement at 3:18, such a person is already condemned and the wrath of God remains or stays upon him (3:36). On the other hand, John states that there is a sense in which judgment will be finalized on "the last day." As one might expect, Bultmann cannot envisage a futuristic eschatology and therefore assigns the "last day" statement here to an "ecclesiastical editor" in the same manner as he dismissed the futuristic statements of John concerning the resurrection to life and to judgment (5:29).[94] But future reward and punishment, though not at center stage here as in the book of Revelation, are nonetheless fundamental realities for the evangelist. This world and the present are not the only realities of existence, and the reader is forthrightly warned here not to forget the future.

12:49–50   As the evangelist reaches the conclusion to this centerpiece of the Gospel, he returns to a theme that has been for him a crux in his presentation. The message of Jesus did not originate with him. Like a *shaliach,* "sent one," "messenger," or "agent," he was the unique Son of God who was sent by God to provide the world with eternal life (3:16; cf. the purpose statement at 20:31). He did not speak or act on his own (5:19). Like a faithful representative, he acted in conformity to the will of the one who sent him (5:30; 7:16–17).

His words therefore were not to be interpreted as mere human words. Accordingly, John uses at this point the designation "commandment,"

---

[93] Cf. Brown, *John,* 1.491.

[94] See Bultmann, *John,* 345, n.6.

which has not been previously applied to Jesus' teaching. But it will be hereafter as he links love and commandment together in the Farewell Cycle (13:34; 14:15,21; 15:10,12). The alert biblical reader should hardly miss the force of the designation "commandment," not as a basis for legalism but in the best sense of Torah (command) as a principle for life (cf. Deut 32:46–47).[95] The New Moses had come to the world. The investigating committee had asked the Baptizer if he was the expected prophet like Moses (1:21; cf. Deut 18:15). The answer was no, but he also added that there was one standing "in their midst" whom they did not know (John 1:26). He knew the way of life!

As this centerpiece of the Gospel is concluded, therefore, the reader is also faced with the burning question: What does it mean for readers today that the sent one has come to the world, and what really is the danger of not receiving him and his commands?

I pray …

that all of them may be one, Father,
> just as you are in me and I am in you.
>> May they also be in us
>>> so that the world may believe that you have sent me.

I have given them the glory that you gave me,

that they may be one
> as we are one: I in them and you in me.
>> May they be brought to complete unity
>>> to let the world know that you sent me and have loved them even as
>>> you have loved me.

---

[95] For his views on commandment see M. J. O'Connell, "The Concept of Commandment in the Old Testament," *TS* 21 (1960): 351–403, esp. at 352. Cf. also Pancaro, *The Law in the Fourth Gospel*, 439–42.

VI. THE FAREWELL CYCLE (13:1–17:26)
  1. The Foot Washing as Preparation for Passover and Authentic
      Discipleship (13:1–38)
    (1) Jesus, Judas, and Peter at the Foot Washing (13:1–11)
Excursus 14: Foot Washings and Sacramental Interpretations
    (2) An Interpretation of Servanthood (13:12–20)
    (3) The Judas Tragedy (13:21–30)
Excursus 15: Peter and the Beloved Disciple
    (4) A Summation in Four Parts and a Preface to the Teaching That
        Follows (13:31–38)
      The Glorification of Jesus (13:31–32)
      The Shortness of Time and the Impossibility of Following
      Jesus (13:33)
      The Giving of the New Commandment to the Community
      (13:34–35)
      The Post-Passover Possibility of Following Jesus and Peter's
      Misunderstanding (13:36–38)
  2. The Great Issue of Loneliness and Anxiety for the Community—
      Part I (14:1–14)
    (1) Preparing for Both Loneliness and Ultimate Reality (14:1–3)
    (2) Loneliness and Perplexing Questions (14:4–11)
    (3) The Power of Believing (14:12–14)
Excursus 16: John's Gospel on the Trinity
  3. The Role of the Spirit: The Divine Resource for the Community—
      Part I (14:15–31)
    (1) The First Spirit Statement: The Coming of the Paraclete
        (14:15–17)
    (2) The Postresurrection Coming of Jesus (14:18–24)
    (3) The Second Paraclete Statement: Interpreter of Jesus
        (14:25–31)
  4. The *Mashal* of the Vine and the Bull's-Eye of the Farewell Cycle
      (15:1–25)
    (1) The *Mashal* of the Vine and the Branches: A Portrait of
        Discipleship (15:1–11)
    (2) The Friends of Jesus and the Love Command: Thesis
        Statements on Discipleship (15:12–17)
    (3) The Reaction of the World to Jesus and the Disciples
        (15:18–25)

Excursus 17: The "World" in John and Gnosticism
  5. The Role of the Spirit—Part II (15:26–16:15)
      (1) The Third Paraclete Statement: Witness in Persecution
          (15:26–16:4a)
      (2) The Fourth Paraclete Statement: Counselor and Judge
          (16:4b–11)
      (3) The Fifth Spirit Statement: Authentic Guide (16:12–15)
  6. Anxiety and Loneliness—Part II: The Great Reversal (16:16–33)
      (1) Confusion over Time (16:16–19)
      (2) Sorrow and Joy (16:20–22)
      (3) A New Perspective on Prayer (16:23–28)
      (4) The Forthcoming Reversal and Its Implications (16:29–33)
Excursus 18: Nonabandonment in John and the Cry of Dereliction
  7. The Magisterial Prayer as the Final Preparation for Passover
      (17:1–26)
Excursus 19: The Structure of John 17
      (1) Finishing His Mission in a Hostile World (17:1–8)
          The First Petition: Glorification in Mission (17:1–3)
          The Second Petition: The Return to Glory at the Conclusion
            of the Incarnational Mission (17:4–8)
      (2) Preparing the Disciples for Their Mission in the Hostile World
          (17:9–19)
          The Third Petition: Prayer for the Protection of God's
            Representatives to the World (17:9–15)
          The Fourth Petition: Prayer for the Holiness of God's
            Representatives in the World (17:16–19)
      (3) Looking to the Future (17:20–26)
          The Fifth Petition: Prayer for Unity in Mission (17:20–23)
          The Sixth Petition: Prayer for the Disciples to Reach Their
            Destiny (17:24)
          The Seventh and Final Petition: A Reality Prayer (17:25–26)

—————— **VI. THE FAREWELL CYCLE (13:1–17:26)** ——————

The evangelist at this point turns to a special cycle that is focused on preparing the followers of Jesus for Passover and the life of discipleship during the coming time—a time when the post-Passover community of believers would be established and sense their alienation from the world.

The Bull s-Eye or Target

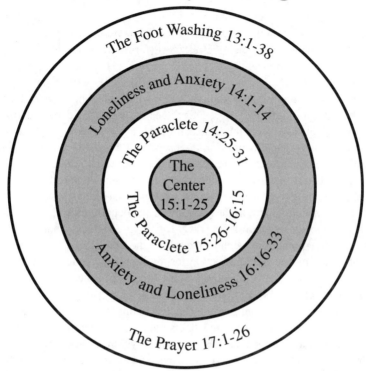

The Foot Washing 13:1-38
Loneliness and Anxiety 14:1-14
The Paraclete 14:25-31
The Center 15:1-25
The Paraclete 15:26-16:15
Anxiety and Loneliness 16:16-33
The Prayer 17:1-26

Some scholars have designated this section the Farewell Discourses,[1] but this major section, which consists of chaps. 13–17, involves far more than discourse material. Clearly there are farewell words that remind the reader of the farewell addresses by Moses and others to the people of Israel (cf. Deut 31–33).[2] But rather than simply being a farewell speech, this section (involving more than just chaps. 14–16) begins with one of the most memorable acts of Jesus. Here he vividly demonstrates a model of discipleship by

---

[1] See, for example, L. Morris, *The Gospel According to John*, NICNT (Grand Rapids: Eerdmans, 1995), 610; G. Beasley-Murray, *John*, WBC (Waco: Word, 1987), 222; and R. Bultmann, *The Gospel of John* (Philadelphia: Westminster, 1971), 522. See also D. Deeks, "The Structure of the Fourth Gospel," *NTS* 15 (1968): 119–21; F. Stagg, "The Farewell Discourses: John 13–17," *RevExp* 62 (1965): 459–72; and J. Painter, "The Farewell Discourses and the History of Johannine Christianity," *NTS* 27 (1981): 525–43.

[2] For other farewell statements see Jacob's blessings at Gen 49, David's farewell in 1 Chr 28–29, and Paul's farewell statement to the Ephesian elders in Acts 20:17–38.

washing his disciples' feet and by issuing a new commandment of love, which epitomizes that model. This major section ends in chap. 17 with a multidimensional prayer of Jesus that not only represents what discipleship dependence ought to be like but provides in prayer form a unique summation of a number of the major concerns in the Gospel.

These two bookends of the Farewell Cycle form a kind of outer ring for conceptualizing this section as a type of bull's-eye or target. The center of the bull's-eye would be the *Mashal* of the Vine and the Branches with its emphasis on abiding or remaining in the Vine and its reminder of the importance of love in the life of discipleship (15:1–17). This theme of love in the core of the bull's-eye is also a crucial aspect of the outer ring since it is introduced in chap. 13 and is reasserted in the final petition of the prayer (17:25–26). Around the core of the bull's-eye in chap. 15 and inside the outer ring are two other rings of concern. Immediately inside the outside ring of foot washing (chap. 13) and prayer (chap. 17) is a ring that treats two important issues: the disciples' sense of imminent loss or abandonment at the prospect of the departure/death of Jesus and Jesus' effort to address their fears (14:1–14; 16:16–33). Inside that ring of concern is the five-point discussion of the role of the Spirit/Paraclete in the provision of divine presence and direction for the life of the believing community (14:15–31; 15:26–16:15). Inside the Spirit ring is the center of the bull's-eye (15:1–25) described above.

If readers can conceptualize these chapters in this target fashion, they should be able to recognize that the evangelist is not simply jumping aimlessly about in the presentation of his materials. The bull's-eye image fits John's style here of employing a set of wraparound issues that lead the reader to hold together all of these matters in a united package called discipleship. The close interrelationship of these chapters is presented in words emphasizing Jesus' farewell, and the chapters are equally about challenging the community to adopt a new model of discipleship in terms of lovingly and confidently relating to one another while being effective agents for God in Christ in the midst of a hostile world.

One matter that should be mentioned here before proceeding to chap. 13 is the statement at 14:31, where Jesus tells the disciples, "Come now; let us leave," and then continues the cycle for three more chapters (15–17). Scholars frequently refer to such a statement as a "seam" in the writings of John, and some suggest that the seam is the result of bringing together what were originally two different addresses.[3] Some scholars even argue that the the-

---

[3] See R. Brown, *The Gospel According to John xiii–xxi,* AB (Garden City: Doubleday, 1966), 588–94, and esp. 582, where he states emphatically that there "can be no doubt that the chapters that form the Last Discourse were not always united." Cf. Bultmann, who argues for a significant reorganizing of the chapters to reflect the fact that "14:25–31 is obviously the conclusion of the farewell discourses" (*John*, 459). J. Bernard simply puts 15:1–16:33 between 13:31a and 13:31b (*A Critical and Exegetical Commentary on the Gospel According to St. John,* ICC [Edinburgh: T & T Clark, 1928], 2.477ff.).

ology of both sections is different.[4] However one may view the matter of sources and explain the presence of the statement at 14:31, I would emphatically argue that chaps. 13–17 of this Gospel, as we have them, now form a fully integrated line of thought; and I would strongly demur from any suggestion of a differing theological perspective in these chapters. I particularly reject Schnackenburg's suggestion that the death of Jesus has fallen out of focus in 13:12–20.[5] As I have hinted above, I believe that the argument is a brilliant literary piece of theological construction and the more one studies its bull's-eye nature, the more one should sense that whatever sources (written or oral) may have been used by the evangelist, this section in its current canonical form is a magnificently synthesized and integrated piece of work.

1. The Foot Washing as Preparation for Passover and Authentic Discipleship (13:1–38)

This chapter, which introduces the Farewell Cycle, is one of the masterpieces of Christian literature that sears itself on the mind of anyone who has heard or read it. Indeed, the foot-washing scene is a classic turnabout that is made increasingly more vivid by contrasts with the human miscues of the well-meaning Peter. It is also highlighted by the hostile action of the devilish betrayer, whose role in the events is epitomized by the evangelist's dramatic announcement at the departure of Judas that "It was night!" (13:30).[6] When one adds to these elements the fact that this chapter contains the giving of a new commandment to the Christian community (13:34), one has the basic ingredients for establishing this text as crucial in the development of Christian proclamation and liturgy. It is no surprise then that "Maundy" Thursday has been set aside in the church year to commemorate the particularities recorded in this chapter.[7]

Before proceeding to the interpretation of the various verses in this chapter, however, it is necessary to note that this chapter has been subjected to intensive source and redactional studies. Scholars from Wellhausen to more recent writers like Schnackenburg, Boismard, and Thyen have arrived at proposals in which they separate out the various strata in the text and label the original core as Gnosticizing tendencies or alternatively that later strata

---

[4] See J. Becker, "Die Abschiedsreden im Johannesevangelium," *ZNW* 61 (1970): 215–46 and *Das Evangelium des Johannes* (Gütersloh: G. Mohn, 1981), 2.477.

[5] See Schnackenburg, *St. John,* 3.23.

[6] For an interesting view see K. Hein, "Judas Iscariot: Key to the Last Supper Narrative," *NTS* 17 (1970–1978): 228–31. See also B. Gärtner, *Iscariot* (Philadelphia: Fortress, 1971), especially at 8–11, 30–31.

[7] For an interpretation of the term "maundy" see the discussion below at 13:34.

are more pastoral in perspective, and so on.[8] I have been intrigued again by retracing the steps of these scholars, but I must frankly admit that I am hardly persuaded in the promised results of their methods nor in their thesis that failure to use such methods is doomed in its understanding of the text as we have it.[9] I do not deny that the text may reflect varying historical realities experienced by the evangelist and the community over the years, but great care must be taken in dividing the text and attributing vv. 1–2,3,4–5,6–10,11,12–15, etc. to differing strata as, for example, Boismard thinks he can do.[10] What, for example, makes it possible to say with some scholars that vv. 4–5 belong to the core document when other verses do not? There is a great danger here of circularity in the arguments.

(1) Jesus, Judas, and Peter at the Foot Washing (13:1–11)

[1]**It was just before the Passover Feast. Jesus knew that the time had come for him to leave this world and go to the Father. Having loved his own who were in the world, he now showed them the full extent of his love.**

[2]**The evening meal was being served, and the devil had already prompted Judas Iscariot, son of Simon, to betray Jesus.** [3]**Jesus knew that the Father had put all things under his power, and that he had come from God and was returning to God;** [4]**so he got up from the meal, took off his outer clothing, and wrapped a towel around his waist.** [5]**After that, he poured water into a basin and began to wash his disciples' feet, drying them with the towel that was wrapped around him.**

[6]**He came to Simon Peter, who said to him, "Lord, are you going to wash my feet?"**

[7]**Jesus replied, "You do not realize now what I am doing, but later you will understand."**

[8]**"No," said Peter, "you shall never wash my feet."**

Jesus answered, "Unless I wash you, you have no part with me."

[9]**"Then, Lord," Simon Peter replied, "not just my feet but my hands and my head as well!"**

[10]**Jesus answered, "A person who has had a bath needs only to wash his feet; his whole body is clean. And you are clean, though not every one of you."** [11]**For he knew who was going to betray him, and that was why he said not every one was clean.**

13:1 The text opens with the striking note that it was just prior to Passover. The discussion should once again, therefore, be understood and inter-

---

[8] See, for example, J. Wellhausen, *Das Evangelium Johannis* (Berlin: G. Reimer, 1908), 58–61; M. Boismaid, "Le lavement des pieds (Jn XIII, 1–17)," *RB* 71 (1964): 5–24; R. Schnackenburg, *The Gospel According to St. John* (New York: Crossroad, 1987), 3.7–15; and H. Thyen, "Johannes 13 und die 'kirkliche Redaktion' des vierten Evangeliums," in *Tradition und Glaube* FS, für K. G. Kuhn (Göttingen: Vandenhoeck & Ruprecht, 1971), 343–56.

[9] See Schnackenburg, *St. John*, 3.7

[10] See Boismard, "Le lavenment," 5–24.

preted as taking place in the context of a Passover setting. Moreover, the text next relates the Passover notation directly to the arrival of the long-expected "hour" (*hōra;* the NIV translation here as "time" is surely theologically weak). The hour is that of Jesus' "departure" *(metabē)* from this world (cf. the coming of the hour of glorification at 12:23). What is more, this departure is next interpreted by John in the context of the ultimate extent of love (lit., "he loved them unto the end")[11] evidenced in Jesus' death for the world (cf. 3:16) and particularly here for those in the world who belong to him.

Accordingly, in the span of three short but incisive sentence segments this verse has spelled out the defining moment in the coming of Jesus.[12] The statement therefore is crucial for understanding the focus of both this chapter and this entire cycle. Thus the turning point has already come (12:23–26), Jesus has been prepared by having dealt with his agony (12:27–28), and has now begun the *preparation of the disciples* for the death of the Passover Lamb of God (cf. 1:29 and 19:14).

13:2 Although relating temporal markers in John to the Synoptics is often difficult, particularly in the chronology of the Passover events, the time designation at 13:1 is merely the vague "before" *(pro)* Passover, which by itself supplies little assistance in any comparison. But several matters should give some pause for reflection.

The foot washing depicted in John's (pre-Passover?) meal event (13:2, "supper") does not appear in the Synoptics, and what occurs in the Synoptics related to the institution of the Lord's Supper[13] does not occur here in John. Nevertheless, there is little reason to doubt that the meal experience should be understood to be the same meal in both John and the Synoptics.[14] One reason we can make

---

[11] I take εἰς τέλος here as both a reflection of love that carried Jesus to the end in a chronological sense, namely, to the crucifixion, and in the sense that death was the ultimate expression of love. Cf. the discussion of A. Corell, *Consummatum Est* (London: S.P.C.K., 1958), 69–73.

[12] Verse 1 according to UBS4 is a single Greek sentence, though J. Becker considers that the sentence runs through v. 3 (*Das Evangelium des Johannes* [Gütersloh: G. Mohn, 1981], 2.419).

[13] The designation the "Lord's Supper" is not found in the Gospels but is found in 1 Cor 11:20. The issue of whether the Last Supper of Jesus was, in fact, a Passover meal has been highly debated by scholars. Among the supporters is E. Gaugler (*Das Abendmahl in Neuen Testament* [1943]), but he is not prepared to argue with Jeremias, (*Die Abendmahlsworte Jesu* [Gottingen: Vandenhoeck & Ruprecht, 1935]); *The Eucharistic Words of Jesus* (New York: Scribner's, 1966), and others that the evidence is totally conclusive (24–26). Cf. M. Barth, *Das Abendmahl: Passamahl, Bundesmahl und Messiasmahl, ThST* 18 (1945), who links all three meals in an interlocking argument. On the other hand, E. Lohmeyer rejects the arguments of Jeremias as being completely unconvincing. See his reaction in "Vom urchristlichen Abendmahl," *TRu* 9 (1937): 198. Once again I would suggest that the reader should not concentrate on chronological issues in John. For a brief review of the issues see B. Klappert, "Lord's Supper," *DNTT* 2.520–38.

[14] For a discussion of the relationship of John with Luke at this point see J. A. Bailey, *Traditions Common to the Gospels of Luke and John* (Leiden: Brill, 1963), 29–31.

such an identification is that in both John and the Synoptics, Jesus announced at the meal the presence of the betrayer, which resulted in a sense of uneasiness among the disciples (13:21–22; cf. Matt 26:21–22; Mark 14:18–19; Luke 22:21–23). Moreover, Jesus also identified Judas at the meal through the event of "dipping" (*baptein* is the verb used in John 13:26; cf. Mark 14:20; Matt 26:23, where *embaptein* is used). The occasion described here, therefore, must be the so-called "Last Supper" even though the Synoptics do not speak of a "supper," and John does not speak of an upper room (cf. Mark 14:15; Luke 22:12; Matthew does not use the designation).

The dark side of the story is also introduced in this verse with the mention of the devil (see Excursus 13: "Satan and the Prince of the World").[15] Although John indicates that the devil had thrown (perfect participle of *ballein;* the NIV "prompted" is weak) "into the heart" (a nonpersonalized statement) the betraying of Jesus by Judas Iscariot,[16] the son of Simon,[17] such an idea in no way is said to excuse Judas. Rather, A. Schlatter's maxim-like explanation of a Judas-type person seems to catch forcefully the perspective of John—that the heart that is inspired by the devil wills what the devil wills (cf. also 13:18,21,27).[18] Some manuscripts read "the heart of Judas" (the genitive *Iouda*), but the nominative *Idoudas* here is to be preferred. Following the basic rules of textual analysis, the more difficult reading is to be preferred and thus can explain the others; the harder reading actually turns out here to be theologically significant because it presents Judas clearly as the responsible actor in the betrayal of Jesus and the devil as the one who inspires the evil heart.[19]

13:3 Building upon the statements concerning Jesus' knowledge of his hour in v. 1, the evangelist expands the idea here to remind the reader that Jesus was clearly knowledgeable about his origin and his goal or destiny.[20] These concerns were epitomized in the two questions of "whence?" *(pothen)* and "where?" or "whither?" *(pou)* that brought him into conflict earlier with the Pharisees (cf. 8:14ff.). The Pharisees, like most people, could not understand that Jesus was someone whose very existence defied

---

[15] I am completely unmoved by the argument that the reference to the devil here in v. 2 is a later addition to the story and is to be contrasted with the statement related to Satan in v. 27.

[16] Contrast the ideas of K. Hein, "Judas Iscariot," 228–29.

[17] The UBS text reads "Judas son of Simon Iscariot," but $\mathfrak{P}^{66}$, ℵ, B, and others read "Judas Iscariot, son of Simon," which I have used here following the NIV and against the NRSV. The weight of the manuscript evidence, however, is such that one cannot be certain.

[18] A. Schlatter, *Der Evangelist Johannes* (Stuttgart: Calwer Verlag, 1948), 279.

[19] Although I believe my analysis here is correct, I am prepared to agree that the ultimate implication of the variant reading is not radically different. There is no doubt that the devil, from John's perspective, had a part to play in Judas's betrayal of Jesus.

[20] Cr. W. Grossouw, "A Note on John xiii 1–3" *NovT* 8 (1966): 124–31.

the limitations of their time and space barriers (cf. 1:1). "Coming from" (*exerchesthai* plus *apo*) and "going to" (*hypagein* plus *pros*) was the way John here described the broad dimensions of Jesus' earthly existence and his relationship to the eternal God. But one must be careful not merely to pour these ideas into the human time restraints of past, present, and future. Of course, they are applicable to the incarnation of Jesus, but these statements are also intended to remind the reader of the divine dimension to life as well.

Moreover, these ideas form a foundation for understanding the earlier statement in this verse of the Father committing "all things" *(panta)* "into his hands." This idea, as discussed in 3:35, is a testimonial expression for Jesus acting as the agent for God. In the Prologue the *logos* was active in creation (1:3) and became flesh (1:14). There is a sense in which that special nature of Jesus impacted the way the Johannine evangelist looked at the broad scope of Jesus' *authority*. To see Jesus is to see God (12:45) or his agent on earth because he is "from above" (*ek tōn anō*, 8:23). Moreover, he has life in himself and has the authority to execute judgment because he "is" the powerful Son or Man (5:26–27).[21] But given these divinely oriented attributes, what comes next is absolutely stunning.

13:4–5 Instead of basking in the glow of power and authority, to use the Pauline image, Jesus emptied *(kenoun)* or humbled himself and adopted the form *(morphē),* here the posture or role, of a servant (cf. Phil 2:7). As indicated in connection with the story of the Baptizer (John 1:27), touching feet was regarded as menial slave work and as such was primarily an assignment given to Gentile slaves and women.[22] Students were responsible to rabbis or teachers to perform menial tasks of labor, but touching feet was clearly not expected. In a society that was very conscious of status symbols of shame and honor, such as the touching or washing of feet, was an extremely important matter. John the Baptizer had been unwilling to be categorized in the same context with Jesus, even as his lowest slave (cf. 1:27). He was viewed by the evangelist as an ideal model of a witness. But here the lowly slave was God's agent, the proclaimer of the key thesis to understanding the message of the Gospel, namely that Jesus is "the Lamb of God that takes away the sin of the world" (1:29).

But what is startling in this story is the vivid portrayal of the Messiah adopting a shameful/lowly posture in relation to his disciples. I know of no other example in the literature of the ancient world before the coming of

---

[21] See Excursus 11 on the Son of Man.

[22] See *Str-B* 1.121; *Mekhilta* on Exod 21:2; *Kethub* 96 a.

Jesus where such a foot washing by a leader occurs.[23] The evangelist makes clear that Jesus intended that he should be viewed in the posture of such a slave by removing or "laying down" (*tithēsin,* the same verb is also used of Jesus laying down his life, cf. 10:11,15,17–18; 15:13) his "outer clothing" (*ta himata,* the plural is used). Then he tied a towel around himself in the fashion of a slave and actually used *that towel* to wipe the feet of the disciples once he had washed them. The humbling or dishonoring symbolism is unmistakable.

To get the full impact of this scene one should review the setting again. The text is not unrelated to the issue of ambition among the disciples, who wanted the chief seats in Jesus' coming "kingdom" (cf. Matt 20:21; see also Mark 10:37, where the word "glory" is used instead). And since it was the sons of Zebedee who were making the request, this idea of glory probably left an indelible impression on the evangelist here and on all the disciples. These disciples undoubtedly had evidenced the human trait of ambition. Moreover, Peter was clearly convinced of his own ability to follow Jesus, as is indicated later in this chapter (cf. John 13:37). And to complete the picture of the disciples, Judas had apparently already schemed the betrayal of Jesus (13:11; cf. Mark 14:10–11; Luke 22:3–4). It was in this very human-centered context that Jesus adopted the totally different example of a humble servant to be the model for discipleship.

The picture is made more intense when one understands that at the meal they were undoubtedly reclining (not sitting) with their heads facing the center and their feet stretched out behind them. They supported themselves on one elbow (primarily the left) and reached for food with the right hand.[24] The participants at the meal could ignore the one washing their feet.

13:6–9 But it was hardly possible for the disciples to ignore Jesus. There is no reason to assume from the text that Peter was either first (Augustine) or last (Origen) in the washing.[25] But it is quite clear that Peter voiced for the disciples the sense of shock by his question, "Lord, are you going to wash my feet?" (13:6). That was not merely a question.[26] It was more like a challenge based on a confusing set of circumstances. It did not

---

[23] A familiar rabbinic story is told in *Pe'a* 1.15c.14 of Rabbi Ishmael, whose mother sought to honor him by washing his feet when he arrived home from the synagogue. After he refused her because he viewed her effort as dishonoring to her and ultimately to him, she sought a censure against him from the rabbinic court for his refusal to allow her to honor him. This story provides some insight into the perspectives of shame and honor in Judaism. For further information see *Str-B* 1.707.

[24] Readers who are able to visit Sephoris in Israel can see the partially restored home of a wealthy Jew who had an elaborate triclinium mosaic installed, which contains a number of figures of pagan deities from the ancient Greco-Roman pantheon.

[25] See R. Brown, *John,* 2.552.

[26] Contrast J. Derrett, "Domine, tu mihi lavas pedes?" *Bibbia e Oriente* 21 (1979): 13–42.

make sense to the disciples. Thus this question is like the questions asked by the Jews when Jesus spoke of their seeking him and not finding him (7:33–36) did not make sense to them, or when he spoke to them about making them free (8:31–33), or when he spoke to them about never seeing death (8:51–59).

Jesus' response in 13:7 is a direct confronting of Peter's implied challenge which had been based on his confusion. Peter did not know what was in fact taking place at that time. But Jesus said that he would realize the significance of it later. The "later" here obviously meant that Peter would understand in the post-Passover era.

Jesus' response was met in 13:8 with a forthright confrontation by Peter.[27] Peter had completely missed the point of Jesus' words about knowing; and instead of pondering them, he undoubtedly thought he understood that the issue simply involved the code of shame and honor. He was convinced he would "never" (lit. "not forever") dishonor Jesus by having him wash his feet (cf. his misguided confidence also at 13:37). The contrast between Jesus' knowledge of what was to come and Peter's lack of understanding concerning eternity should not escape the reader. Unfortunately, the English translations of "never" here, I believe, actually hide for most readers the interplay of ideas inherent in this text. Jeremias's note to the effect that Peter's statement is like an oath certainly moves in the right direction.[28]

Jesus' response was like a firm courtroom verdict that gave the offender a straightforward alternative that admits no bending. It was a strict either/or that had to be accepted or rejected, and the consequences were clearly evident. Either Peter would be washed or he would be excluded from being an heir of Jesus. The thunderous force of "no part with me" is devastating. The text here has obvious eschatological implications involving ideas of inheritance (cf. related ideas at 14:3; 17:24; cf. also Rev 20:6; 22:19; Matt 24:45–51, and note particularly the same word translated "share" in Luke 15:12).

Peter's response in 13:9 is almost hilarious. One could imagine a comic strip picture of a lightbulb flashing on over Peter's head and Peter saying something like: "Wow! If that's what it means, then do my hands and head as well!" Now he was ready for a shower or a bath! The evangelist makes clear in Jesus' reply at v. 10 that Peter's enthusiastic response missed the point completely. It is therefore a nonproductive exercise to try to make any theological distinctions about hands, head, and feet in this verse except to say that Peter was interested in obtaining a "golden blanket" insurance pol-

---

[27] See G. Snyder, "John 13:16 and the Anti-Petrinism of the Johannine Tradition," *BR* 16 (1971): 5–15, for his view of the Johannine writer. See also my views in Excursus 15. Contrast R. Brown et al., eds., *Peter in the New Testament* (Minneapolis: Fortress, 1973), 131–33.

[28] See J. Jeremias, *Eucharistic Words of Jesus* (London: SCM, 1966), 209–10.

icy to cover any concerns that might arise.

13:10–11   Jesus' reply, however, requires more attention. The first part of the reply (13:10a) involves an important contrast. Up to this point the conversation had focused on the various forms of the verb *niptein,* which has here been translated as "wash," but in this verse the verb *louein,* "bathed," occurs first. Jesus' play on words thus suggests that Peter misunderstood the meaning of the foot washing to be a mere washing of feet, whereas the washing was, in fact, much more. It actually refers to Jesus' bathing of the disciples with a new perspective (i.e., humble love). Therefore the disciples had actually been significantly bathed in the foot washing experience.

But there is also in this verse an important textual problem. The UBS text and most English translations add to the statement of "not need to wash" the words "except the feet" (*ei mē tous podas;* the NIV has reworked the words to read "needs only to wash his feet"). Codex Sinaiticus, however, omits this phrase, and the textual history might seem to indicate that the phrase was imported into the text from the eastern churches. The argument would then be that those Christian scribes may have thought that something had to be said about feet here and therefore added the phrase. It is more likely, however, that Jesus was here ignoring the issue of feet because he had proceeded to the real issue of being clean, which is the focus of vv. 10b,11. Thus the play on the verbs in v. 10a would seem to serve as the transitional statement.[29]

Washing normally makes one clean, and those who have been "bathed" by Jesus, he says, are completely or "wholly" *(holos)* clean. The NIV misunderstands the sense of the text and stays on the physical level by importing the noun "body" into the text. In so doing it does not allow the reader to sense the double-level meaning that is here once again implied in a Johannine text (cf. the "temple" in 2:19–21 and "born again/from above" in 3:3–4). The disciples may have become "wholly" clean, but the *whole* group of them (*ouchi pantes,* "not all") was not wholly clean because the group included the "betrayer" (*ton paradidonta,* 13:11).

This statement has been taken by some to suggest that Jesus did not wash the feet of Judas. But that is a misapplication of this verse and is another indication of failing to sense the double-level meaning of Johannine texts. In this case it is important to remember that the "washing" could not mean "bathing" for Judas—the devil man. Besides, one must also bear in mind that Judas did not depart the scene until later in the story (13:30), unless one unnecessarily excises the verses concerning Judas from this

---

[29] See the logic of the editors of the UBS Greek text in B. Metzger, *A Textual Commentary on the Greek New Testament* (New York: United Bible Societies, 1971), 240.

story.[30] Moreover, the text itself here indicates that Jesus was not confused about the status of the betrayer who was present at this event (13:11). The Johannine message has consistently been clear on the fact that although people like Peter and Judas may not have understood the implications of events, it is absolutely certain that Jesus understood what people were like (cf. 2:23–25). What surprised people did not surprise Jesus.

Excursus 14: Foot Washings and Sacramental Interpretations

Although foot washing has been relegated to a minor role in the worship practice of a large segment of the Christian church, there has been an effort on the part of a number of scholars to show definite links between this event in the life of Jesus and sacraments of the church, particularly baptism.[31] Brown, after surveying the early patristic evidence, concluded that besides a few vague references in Tertullian and a very few other statements elsewhere that the "external support" for foot washing being employed "as a symbol of Baptism" is "minimal." He nevertheless attempts to make a case for a linkage between foot washing and baptism.[32] In this pursuit he has been joined by others,[33] but the work of von Campenhausen is perhaps the most intriguing. He has argued, somewhat after the pattern of Peter's statement in 13:9, that early candidates for baptism probably would stand in water up to their ankles (his linkage to foot washing) and then have water poured over the rest of them.[34]

But Cullmann's probably is the strangest argument. Not only has he sought in several works to use every argument possible to make a case for infant baptism,[35] but in his work on worship he has sought to establish connections between the foot washing and the Lord's Supper. His reasoning has been that the major washing or bath is related to baptism in which the person is made wholly clean (cf. 13:10) and a follow-up washing cares for sins after baptism. This second washing (foot washing) he related to the Supper, which he thought was supported by the longer reading of v. 10.[36] J. Michl's critique of Cullmann to the effect that relat-

---

[30] See my earlier comments on the thinking of source and redaction critics in the introduction to chap. 13.

[31] Contrast J. A. T. Robinson, "The One Baptism," in *Twelve New Testament Studies* (Naperville, Ill.: Alec R. Allenson, 1962), 158–75 and "The Significance of Footwashing" in *Neotestimentica et patristica, NovT Sup* 6 (Leiden: Brill, 1962), 144–62 with E. Levine, "On the Symbolism of the *Pedilavium*," *American Benedictine Review* 33 (1982): 21– 29; cf. A. Jaubert, "Une lecture de lavement des pieds au mardimercredi saint," *Muséon* 79 (1966): 257–86. Cf. also G. MacGregor, "The Eucharist in the Fourth Gospel," *NTS* 9 (1962–1963): 113–15 for another perspective.

[32] See R. Brown, *John*, 2.567–68.

[33] See Beasley-Murray, *John*, 235; C. Dodd, *The Interpretation of the Fourth Gospel* (Cambridge: University Press, 1958), 401; C. Barrett, *The Gospel According to St. John* (London: S.P.C.K., 1956), 436; contrast Boismard, "La lavement," 13–17.

[34] See H. von Campenhausen, "Zur Auslegung von Joh 13, 6–10," *ZNW* 33 (1934): 259–71.

[35] See O. Cullmann, *Infant Baptism in the First Four Centuries* (Philadelphia: Westminster, 1962), especially at 43–58 for his valiant attempt at finding a New Testament rationale. Cf. also his statement in *Baptism in the New Testament* (Chicago: Henry Regnery, 1950) in the note at 15.

[36] See O. Cullmann, *Early Christian Worship* (London: SCM, 1953), 108–9.

ing the eating of flesh and blood to foot washing is an amazing feat. From my perspective that is about all one needs to say in response.[37]

At this point it is probably well to be reminded of the fact that some scholars like V. Eller have taken the completely opposite approach and not only have practically "demystified" Johannine mysticism but held solidly to the nonsacramental character of the Fourth Gospel.[38]

Yet how is one to interpret the foot washing here?[39] What is its significance to John? Is it about looking for baptism in this reference to water? Hardly! Of course, the act is a picture of servanthood. But in Cullmann's misguided attempt at linking the foot washing with a cleansing from sin in the Lord's Supper, there is at least a partial hint of a much more useful direction of thought. The idea of cleansing being related to human sin is certainly a familiar idea that is foundational to the entire sacrificial system of the Old Testament. Even more significant, however, is a text like Ps 51:2, which parallels the washing away of iniquity and the cleansing from sin. Such a text certainly forms a helpful background for understanding the intersection of ideas here in John.

But beyond background texts, one should not forget that an underlying concept for the entire Gospel is the humble Passover Lamb: the one who takes away the sin of the world (cf. 1:29; 19:28–31).[40] Thus it is meaningful and not a mere accident that in this Farewell context a good number of important ideas come together: the preparation for *Passover* (13:1), the *servant-like foot washing* by Jesus (13:5), the fact that he is said to have *loved* his own to the very *end* (13:1) and to have provided *cleansing* (13:10), and finally that attention should here be called to the *betrayer* (13:11), who was to be an instrument in his death (cf. 13:27; 18:2–5). The foot washing, cleansing, and presence of the betrayer are all parts of the integrated message about the Johannine Lamb of God. The foot washing, then, is to be read as the vivid beginning of the preparation of the disciples (not Jesus—that was chap. 12) for the Passover of the Lamb and the traumatic experience of the crucifixion.

(2) An Interpretation of Servanthood (13:12–20)

[12]When he had finished washing their feet, he put on his clothes and returned to his place. "Do you understand what I have done for you?" he asked them.

---

[37] See J. Michl, "Der Sinn der Fusswaschung," *Bib* 40 (1959): 697–708. The reference of the bread of the betrayer in 13:18 should not be used by anyone interested in pursuing such an idea further.

[38] See, for example, V. Eller, *The Beloved Disciple: His Name, His Story, His Thought* (Grand Rapids: Eerdmans, 1987), particularly at 110–24.

[39] For a new approach see S. Schneiders, "The Foot Washing (John 13:1–20): An Experiment in Hermeneutics," *CBQ* 43 (1981): 76–92 and *Written That You May Believe* (New York: Herder & Herder/Crossroad, 1999), 162–79, which she entitles "A Community of Friends." Contrast H. Weiss, "Foot Washing in the Johannine Community," *NovT* 21 (1979): 298–325. Cf. the helpful note of J. Dunn, "The Washing of the Disciples' Feet in John 13:1–20," *ZNW* (1970): 247–52.

[40] While R. Eisler in a much earlier article hinted at such an idea, he really did not pursue its implications (see "Zur Fusswachung am Tage vor dem Passah," *ZNW* 14 [1913]: 268).

¹³"You call me 'Teacher' and 'Lord,' and rightly so, for that is what I am. ¹⁴Now that I, your Lord and Teacher, have washed your feet, you also should wash one another's feet. ¹⁵I have set you an example that you should do as I have done for you. ¹⁶I tell you the truth, no servant is greater than his master, nor is a messenger greater than the one who sent him. ¹⁷Now that you know these things, you will be blessed if you do them.

¹⁸"I am not referring to all of you; I know those I have chosen. But this is to fulfill the scripture: 'He who shares my bread has lifted up his heel against me.'

¹⁹"I am telling you now before it happens, so that when it does happen you will believe that I am He. ²⁰I tell you the truth, whoever accepts anyone I send accepts me; and whoever accepts me accepts the one who sent me."

13:12–13 Just as the foot washing involved the rising up *(egeirein)* of Jesus from a reclining position and the laying down *(tithesthai)* of his outer garments, so in this section in which Jesus interpreted servanthood for the disciples he retook his garments and resumed his central reclining position. From that posture of one *in their midst as leader*, he began a concerted effort of preparing them. Accordingly, the general tenor of the evangelist's presentation here shifts slightly to that of Jesus as interpreter or instructor. If one were reading the Gospel of Matthew at this point, one might almost expect to find Jesus sitting down and dispensing wisdom or healing (cf. Matt 5:1; 13:1; 15:29; 24:3; 26:55,64). The sitting position in Matthew's Gospel communicated a sense of authority. Here the evangelist does not employ a physical posture to indicate such authority, but rather authority is indicated in the words of Jesus.

The disciples had called Jesus "Teacher and Lord" (*ho didaskalos kai ho kurios,* 13:12), but the way Jesus accepted that designation suggests to the reader the sense that the words are to be understood more like a royal acclamation than a mere acknowledgment of a role. Not only did Jesus accept the designation as a correct or well-stated title, but he also provided a significant rationale for this designation by announcing "for that is what I am" *(eimi gar).* The connection with the *egō eimi* ("I am") sayings should seem to be obvious, particularly since the full expression is stated at 13:19 as well. Although one could argue that "teacher" here is merely the equivalent of rabbi and "Lord" here is either a general statement like "sir" or a mere honorific title like "master," the entire mood of the text would seem to argue against it. It would seem, instead, that this double designation should be interpreted in terms of Jesus' divinely directed agency in mission and not merely as a reference to an earthly teacher (cf. Nicodemus, 3:1) or to an earthly master (cf. the nobleman from Capernaum, 4:46). Rather, this Teacher is a divine-human revealer/interpreter, and this Master is none other than the one who is one and the same with the Lord God.⁴¹

---

⁴¹ Contrast the view of G. Nicol, "Jesus' Washing the Feet of the Disciples: A Model for Johannine Christology?" *ExpTim* 91 (1979): 20–21.

Just prior to the acceptance of Jesus' "acclamation," he had started the conversation with his disciples by posing a searching question that probed their understanding of what he had just "done" to them (13:12).[42] That question was hardly intended to elicit a factual news report on the circumstances related to the foot washing episode. Rather, one senses here another double-level question in the use of the verb "understand," namely: Could they merely provide a report on the event, or did they understand the significance of what they had experienced? The way they would have answered such a question would have been extremely revealing of their perceptivity. That this question is not, in fact, answered here does not mean that we are unable to guess the way the disciples would have responded because when they did respond to Jesus in matters related to his departure (14:5,8), their response indicates a striking lack of such deep perception.

13:14–15 The foot washing of Jesus becomes in vv. 14–15 the model (*hypodeigma,* "example") for the disciples to follow. It is precisely because their Lord and Teacher (note the reversal here of the order)[43] was willing to adopt the humbling model of foot washing that Jesus' disciples cannot treat humility as merely a nice idea that is unrelated to Christian life. The actual practice of foot washing in the church is not observed widely today. The mention of the idea in connection with the enrollment of widows in 1 Tim 5:10 may possibly suggest that some practice could have been observed by the early church, though "washing the feet of saints" in that context of exhibiting hospitality and caring for the weak hardly sounds like a church rite. Rather, it seems a humble, self-giving treatment of other people without regard to shame and honor codes of society.

But the model of Jesus is not merely one of self-giving service to others epitomized in the foot washing. The model is, in fact, one that also represents the dying Lamb of God. Therefore the servant/follower of Jesus should realize that the self-giving washing of feet may be far more costly a calling than merely a matter involving a basin of water and a towel.

To follow Jesus may cost one's life (cf. 12:24–26; 21:18–19; 1 Pet 2:21), a price Peter rather glibly offered to pay (John 13:37). He soon discovered, however, that he did not realize what that offer had meant (cf. 18:17,25–27). The scene in Mark 10:32–45, which is set in the context of the third passion prediction and which deals with the ambition of the two sons of Zebedee, evidences some similar elements to this Johannine story. Although that Markan story concerns the request of the brothers for seats of honor

---

[42] Cf. the comments of A. Weiser, "Joh 13, 12–20—Zufügung eines späteren Herausgebeis?" *BZ* 12 (1968): 252–57.

[43] The reversal of the designation Teacher and Lord of 13:13 in 13:14 may be because the emphasis falls on the model of humility in the latter verse, but one cannot be certain of the reason for the change.

next to Jesus in glory, the model Jesus offered them and the rest of the disciples is the cup of death and the way of servant humility (not the way of the Gentile lords of power). Indeed, the purpose for the coming of the Son of Man was not to be served but to be a servant "and to give his life as a ransom" (Mark 10:45). The understanding of self-giving servanthood is basic to the model Jesus established here in John also.[44]

13:16 This verse is another of the Johannine double *amēn* ("truly") sayings and is almost maxim-like in its quality. It reminds the reader that the servant does not surpass the master, nor does the "sent one" (*apostolos,* the only use of this term in this Gospel)[45] surpass the sender. This agency statement here thus provides perspective on the servant's ability and responsibility in mission. Similar statements are found elsewhere in Gospel settings (cf. 15:20; see also Matt 10:24–25; Luke 6:40),[46] but the force of the statement here is to remind the followers of Jesus that there is no reason to become puffed up over their calling, accomplishments, or spirituality, a problem that plagued the Corinthians (1 Cor 4:6–7; 5:6; etc.) and is not unknown in Christian communities today.

13:17 The foot washing focus of this section is completed by means of one of the two beatitudes in the Gospel of John (cf. 20:29 and also the beatitudes of Matt 5, etc.). The Greek *makarioi* (cf. Hb. *'ašre*), translated "blessed" or "happy" in most English translations, is generally applied to humans in the sense of a positive evaluation or a judgment being rendered upon a person who meets the requirements of a situation. It is to be distinguished from the Greek *eulogētos* (cf. Hb. *bārūk*), which is applied as an ascription or benediction concerning God (cf. Mark 14:61; Luke 1:68; Rom 1:25; 9:5; etc.).

In this case Jesus (as Teacher/Lord and indeed Judge) renders a favorable verdict upon his followers who both "know" *(oidate)* and practice or "do" *(poiēte)* what he has instructed. In the teaching of Jesus there is no division between head-understanding and life-practice. Moreover, as in the case of most beatitudes, the happiness or blessedness is not to be limited to earthly well-being, for the implication is that the blessedness has eschatological ramifications.[47]

13:18–19 In contrast to his authentic servants, Jesus here noted that he was not identifying everyone in his company as genuine. Indeed, among

---

[44] Cf. D. Winter, "Motivation in Christian Behavior," in *Law, Morality and the Bible*, ed. B. Kaye and G. Wenham (Downers Grove: InterVarsity, 1978), 210–11.

[45] It is here employed in a generic sense much like our word "missionary" or "a sent one," and it is not intended by John to be viewed as a title for an "officer" in the church.

[46] Cf. C. Dodd, "Some Johannine 'Herrenworte' with Parallels in the Synoptic Gospels," *NTS* 2 (1955): 75–78.

[47] Cf. M. Smith, "The Ascending Christ's Farewell Discourse," *Worship* 34 (1960): 320–25.

those whom he chose, one was/became a traitor. The idea that Jesus chose such a one has created a problem for some interpreters. Barrett thinks that Jesus did not actually choose Judas.[48] But the statement at 6:70 would argue that even though Judas could be designated as a devil-man, he nevertheless had been chosen by Jesus as a member of the company.

On the other hand, one must not move in the opposite direction to assume that the choice of Judas by Jesus was a determination of his role as betrayer. Such a theory would be close to the harsh theory of reprobation.[49] Now the *hina* ("in order that" or "so that") here must certainly be understood either as a purpose or a result clause of fulfillment, but great care must be taken not to push the text beyond its meaning. The statement of Carson to the effect that "the reason Jesus chose one who would betray him was to fulfill Scripture" is close to the wording but not exactly the way the text is focused.[50] The text says that Jesus knew whom he chose—not that he knew who they were but that he *knew* them. The next word is "but" *(alla),* a strong adversative, which suggests that there would be a sad, negative side or implication to that choice. Nevertheless, in the working out of the events there was indeed a purpose or result in that choice, which indicated that Scripture was being fulfilled. And tying all these facts together, Jesus told his disciples that he was informing them about what would happen before it took place.

Several important ideas are present in these verses. The theme that the facts involved in the coming of Jesus actually represent the fulfillment of Scripture is repeatedly expressed in Matthew (cf. Matt 1:22; 2:17,23; etc.). That expression, however, is hardly used in Mark or Luke.[51] In John it is not used in the first eleven chapters. But at the transition to the rejection of Jesus in the Centerpiece of the Gospel, this expression is introduced for the first time (12:38), and it is employed thereafter an additional five times in the Farewell Cycle and Death Story in reference to the fulfillment of an Old Testament text (13:18; 15:25; 17:12; 19:24,36) and twice in reference to the fulfillment of Jesus' words (18:9,32). John wanted his readers to understand that the death of Jesus was no accident and that the sacrifice of the Lamb of God was God's means for dealing with the sin of the world (1:29).

The fulfillment here described is a reference to Ps 41:9 in which David bemoans the fact that a trusted friend, who shared his bread, had lifted up

---

[48] See Barrett, *St. John*, 370. Cf. R. Brown, *John*, 2.553.

[49] For a thorough analysis of the idea of reprobation within strict Calvinism see the study of former missionary H. Boer, *The Doctrine of Reprobation in the Christian Reformed Church* (Grand Rapids: Eerdmans, 1983). His critique from within his heritage is a classic study.

[50] See D. Carson, *The Gospel According to John* (Grand Rapids: Eerdmans, 1991), 470.

[51] The use is slightly different and more general in Mark 14:49 and Luke 24:44. Luke also has other ways of stating such an idea in 4:21 and 21:22.

his heel against him.[52] The long-term sharing of bread in the Middle Eastern context was normally interpreted as referring either to a family member or a permanent guest at the table. To eat at one's table was regarded as a symbol of acceptance growing out of the ancient camp context where acceptance of a stranger into the camp was symbolized by the sharing of a meal. To lift up the heel, therefore, in a culture where displaying the bottom of the foot has been regarded as a breach of honor, especially after one had enjoyed acceptance at the meal, was the epitome of shaming the host and the equivalent to being a traitorous scoundrel, after the manner of Ahithopel and his betrayal of David.[53]

The fact that Jesus predicted accurately for his disciples what was going to take place means that he fit fully the requirement for the identification of a legitimate prophet according to the test established in Deut 18:15–21, a passage that also predicted the coming of a prophet like Moses. Moreover, John 13:19 clearly indicates that the fulfillment of Jesus' prediction was to be understood by his disciples as a confirmation of his identity and mission. It was to lead the disciples to believe (cf. 20:31) that he was, in fact, none other than the *egō eimi* ("I am"), which was the name of the sending God of Exod 3:14 and the self-designation Jesus used many times in John.

13:20 At first glance the double *amēn* ("truly") saying in this verse may seem to be oddly placed, but it forms a kind of closure to the four-verse segment introduced at v. 16 with an earlier double *amēn* statement concerning the relationship of master and servant. The opening and closing verses thus form a kind of inclusio (envelope or sandwich) familiar in Mark. The focus of this sandwich is on the role of the disciple, and the statements about Judas in this section provide a clear contrast to the pattern of an authentic disciple. The statements in vv. 18 and 19 also serve as a window or introduction to the tragic story of the betrayer in vv. 21 and 30. In summary, therefore, this section presents Jesus as seeking to make evident to the disciples that he was fully aware of Judas's treachery.

In the present verse, which closes the inclusio, the evangelist completes his reflection on the disciples/servants of Jesus by developing further the model formula in the earlier twofold statement concerning "believing" and "seeing" not only "me" but "the one who sent me" from 12:44–45. Here Jesus expanded that formula by reference to the role of the disciples ("anyone I send") under the category of "receiving." Not only is Jesus an agent of

---

[52] The rabbis frequently interpreted Ps 41:9 as a reference to the betrayal of David by Ahithophel according to 2 Sam 15–17. Cf. the comments of E. Bishop, "'He that eateth bread with me hath lifted up his heel against me'—Jn xiii.18 (Ps xli.9)," *ExpTim* 70 (1959): 331–33.

[53] Having taught in both the Middle East and the Orient, I learned quickly to keep my feet on the floor and not show the bottom of my feet. Such a practice is a change of style for anyone from the West who identifies relaxation with the putting up of one's feet.

God, therefore, but the disciples also are to become agents of Jesus. As pointed out in the earlier text, the formula is used in the Gospel both in negative and positive senses (cf. Luke 10:16; Matt 10:40; cf. also Mark 9:37; Luke 9:49).[54] But the point is that the disciples as a community of faith are to be viewed as belonging to the intimate relationship of Jesus with the Father (cf. 15:20; 17:26).

(3) The Judas Tragedy (13:21–30)

[21]**After he had said this, Jesus was troubled in spirit and testified, "I tell you the truth, one of you is going to betray me."**

[22]**His disciples stared at one another, at a loss to know which of them he meant.** [23]**One of them, the disciple whom Jesus loved, was reclining next to him.** [24]**Simon Peter motioned to this disciple and said, "Ask him which one he means."**

[25]**Leaning back against Jesus, he asked him, "Lord, who is it?"**

[26]**Jesus answered, "It is the one to whom I will give this piece of bread when I have dipped it in the dish." Then, dipping the piece of bread, he gave it to Judas Iscariot, son of Simon.** [27]**As soon as Judas took the bread, Satan entered into him.**

"What you are about to do, do quickly," Jesus told him, [28]**but no one at the meal understood why Jesus said this to him.** [29]**Since Judas had charge of the money, some thought Jesus was telling him to buy what was needed for the Feast, or to give something to the poor.** [30]**As soon as Judas had taken the bread, he went out. And it was night.**

Jesus' betrayal by Judas has been noted on several occasions by the evangelist as have references concerning Judas's foul character (cf. 6:70–71; 12:4–6; 13:2,18). He has been designated as a thief, a devil man, and a traitor. There is no question that he is a villain in John, but behind him lurks the greater villain, the devil, who in this passage is for the first and only time in John designated as Satan, the accuser and enemy of God (cf. Ps 109:6; Zech 3:1–2; his description is less defined in Job 1–2). The battle here, then, is not to be viewed simply as a terrestrial conflict but as a war waged on earth (cf. Rev 12:12) between the "superpowers" (cf. Eph 6:11–12 concerning the devil and the principalities and powers). For Jesus there was no doubt about the outcome because, as Paul says, the rulers did not understand the hidden wisdom, otherwise they would not have crucified the Lord of glory (1 Cor 2:6–8).[55] But the hope of victory did not (and does not today) reduce the trauma of the battle for Jesus (or his servants).

---

[54] It is indeed interesting to note that John 12:25–26,44 and 13:16, 20 evidence similar patterns of thought to those in Matt 10:24–25,38–40. Cf. the comments of R. Brown, *John*, 2.570 on this matter. Cf. also Dodd, "Some Johannine 'Herrenworte,'" 81–83.

[55] In *The Lion, the Witch and the Wardrobe* (New York: Macmillan, 1950), C. S. Lewis portrayed this idea picturesquely in the death of Aslan on the ancient table by the servants of the white witch, none of whom understood the hidden ancient wisdom.

13:21 This section opens with a general literary connective "After he had said this" *(tauta eipōn)* and then moves directly to indicate that Jesus experienced a deep anguish *(etarachthē,* "was troubled," cf. 12:27).[56] As indicated earlier, it is important to recognize that in the incarnation Jesus experienced human senses of need (cf. his thirst 4:9; 19:28) and deep feelings or emotions (cf. 2:17; 11:33,38; 12:27). When, therefore, he was confronted with the imminent prospect of death and the traitorous Judas being present in the company, the anguish of the moment must have welled up in him. In that moment he bore witness or "testified" *(emartyrēsen,* one of the Johannine themes; cf. 3:11,32; 4:44; 5:39; 7:7; 8:14) with a solemn oathlike statement (another double *amēn,* "truly") that one of them was going to betray him (cf. Matt 26:21; Mark 14:18, which has a single *amēn*).

13:22 This announcement stunned the disciples, and they began to wonder about whom Jesus was addressing in this indictment. Jesus' trauma had thus suddenly reached the disciples, and the shock of a forthcoming tragedy, that probably had previously seemed to be somewhat futuristic and unreal, began to descend upon them. Jesus was desperately serious, and they could undoubtedly gain that sense from the troubled state of his spirit. In the Synoptics the questioning is more pointed. Matthew (26:22) and Mark (14:19) describe the disciples asking "Is it I?" whereas Luke shows them questioning one another. But the answer was not very obvious.

13:23–25 Although they all wondered, Peter in this Gospel sought the answer through a colleague. That colleague is identified in this context of the Farewell Cycle for the first time by the designation "the disciple whom Jesus loved" (13:23; 19:26; 20:2; 21:7,20, plus references in those contexts to "that" disciple).[57] That disciple is also identified by his place at the supper as lying or reclining in the bosom *(en tō kolpō)* of Jesus. The implication is obvious that just as the Son was in the bosom of the Father (1:18), so the beloved disciple was in the bosom of Jesus (13:23). That picture of the beloved disciple reclining next to Jesus at the supper (probably a Passover meal because they were not seated at a table) must have seared itself into the memory of the evangelist, who referred to that experience again at 21:20 when he and his followers write about that beloved disciple. One is also reminded of the eschatological picture in Luke of Lazarus in the bosom of Abraham, which is a symbol of being in a place of honor (cf. Luke 16:23).

---

[56] For a discussion of Jesus' deep feelings see J. Beutler, "Psalm 42/43 in Johannesevangelium," *NTS* 25 (1978): 33–57.

[57] See the views of M. Moreton, "The Beloved Disciple Again," in *StudBib II* (Sheffield: Sheffield Press, 1980), 216–18.

As noted briefly above[58] the *triclinium* was a three-sided, *U*-shaped arrangement of pillows on the floor with a low center table restocked by servants from the open side. The extant floor plans are rectangular. The beloved disciple was obviously lying in front or to the right of Jesus with his back to Jesus. Since Jesus was the host, his head would likely have been closer to the table so that when the beloved disciple rolled over (*anapēson,* lit. "fall up," but here it probably means "turned face up") to ask Jesus the question that came from Peter, his head probably would have been close to Jesus' chest. For the other disciples, including Peter and Judas, it seems impossible to know exactly their place around the table. One might be tempted, however, to guess that Peter was some distance from the beloved disciple because Peter signaled by a nod or beckon *(neuei)* for that disciple to ask Jesus who it was. On the other hand, Judas may have been close to Jesus because Jesus handed him the "dip." Thus he may even have been on the left side of Jesus.[59]

Excursus 15: Peter and the Beloved Disciple[60]

In a number of the passages in which the beloved disciple is mentioned, he is paired with or contrasted to Peter. In this chapter Peter asked that disciple to question Jesus about the identity of the betrayer (13:23–24). In 20:2–10 that disciple outran Peter to the tomb and believed first. In 21:7 it is that disciple who recognized the risen Lord and identified him for Peter at the miraculous catch of fish. Then at 21:20–23 it is that disciple who became the foil for the Lord reminding Peter that he must concentrate on his calling to serve Jesus and not compare his mission to others. One should also add the scene at 18:15–16, where Peter and the other disciple followed Jesus to the court of the high priest. In that scene, whereas that disciple, because he was known to the high priest, entered the court ostensibly to observe the trial, Peter was forced to wait outside until that other disciple made a plea with the maid to allow Peter into the courtyard. One cannot avoid the observation that in all of these cases the beloved disciple is shown to be superior to Peter in some way. But it must be stressed that in all of these comparisons there is really no degrading of Peter.[61]

---

[58] See my earlier comments at 13:4–5,12–13.

[59] If Judas were on the left side of Jesus, then such a position could be interpreted either as a place of honor, because it would have been near to Jesus and covering his back, or it could be seen as symbolic of a sinister orientation because left *(sinister* in Latin) is in some biblical texts also regarded very negatively (cf. Matt 25:41). But these ideas are completely speculative, and readers must be forewarned about such speculations. We simply do not know the positions of the other disciples, and such conclusions are at best creative.

[60] For the probable identification of the beloved disciple see Section 7 on "Authorship, Dating and Provenance" in the introduction to the first volume of this commentary.

[61] Contrast G. Snyder's views in "John 13:16 and the Anti-Petrinism," 5–15. See the various views of Peter in R. Brown, *Peter in the New Testament,* particularly here at 134–35.

Yet in all of the passages that refer to that other disciple, including what would seem to be his testimony at the cross (19:35–37), there *is not even the hint of a rebuke* concerning that disciple. The same, however, can hardly be said about Peter. In chaps. 1–11 Peter is mentioned briefly in two contexts (1:40–44 and 6:78; cf. also 6:8), and both are positive reflections. But beginning with the Farewell Cycle the situation shifts, and Peter is portrayed as a well-meaning but impetuous, misguided person who misunderstood the meaning of the foot washing and tried inappropriately to correct his error with Jesus (13:6–10). Then he misunderstood the meaning of Jesus' departure and made a misinformed offer to follow him (13:36–38). Thereafter he made a daring but foolish attempt to save Jesus through violence (18:10–11) yet collapsed under the threefold questioning in the courtyard (18:17,25–27). And even though he vowed a strong threefold "love" for Jesus, he seemed to be more concerned about how the call to Christian discipleship would affect that disciple when compared with his own call to death (21:20–22).

In these comparisons the beloved disciple is pictured as a genuine model the followers of Jesus should seek to emulate, while Peter becomes a kind of realistic picture of the many well-meaning but failure-prone persons who in general form the community of faith. Both portraits are necessary for the reader of this Gospel to contemplate. Both pictures are attached to real people. They are not mere constructs, even though their qualities may be highlighted by the writer. But the portraits are also unique in that when taken together they *epitomize the two sides of most followers of Jesus*: the side that at times can model for others the life Jesus intended for his disciples and the side that struggles valiantly to overcome failure and well-meant misunderstanding.

13:26 The answer the beloved disciple received from Jesus was that the betrayer would be the one to whom Jesus would give the dipped morsel. What was this morsel? Was it a piece of bread as in the NIV and NRSV? Perhaps. The word literally means a "little bit" of something like bread or meat; or if this was a Passover meal, it could also refer to the bitter herbs that were dipped in *harōseth* sauce and eaten during the Seder just after the second cup and prior to the meal.[62]

The dipping is also mentioned in Matthew (26:23) and Mark (14:20), though not in Luke; but in contrast to John the Synoptic accounts have the betrayer dipping *(embaptizein)* in the same bowl *(tryblion)* with Jesus. The English translations of Mark generally add the word "bread," but that addition is an assumption that may or may not be true. Yet the assumption certainly has been used to support the Eucharistic practice in some churches of dipping the bread in the cup, though the reader should be clear that it was a bowl, not a cup, in Mark. In the Matthean text the word "bread" is not generally added in translations because in that text the dipping is linked to the

---

[62] See for example the *Haggada* (Jerusalem: Koren, 1965). See also the comments of Jeremias, *Eucharistic Words*, 85–87.

hands of Jesus and the betrayer.

In putting these pieces of John together, one could conclude that Jesus and Judas were close enough to dip in the same bowl and that Jesus probably handed the dipped morsel (whatever it was) to Judas. Because of the proximity of Judas and Jesus the act did not necessarily draw the attention of the other disciples and could easily explain the comments and confusion of the rest of the disciples described in John 13:28–29. Whether the beloved disciple communicated the sign of the dipped morsel to Peter is not stated, so any conclusion about Peter's knowledge here would be built on silence.

In contrast to what was concluded at 13:2 concerning the designation of "Iscariot" being attached to Judas and not to his father Simon, here the text clearly links Simon with the term. This designation must be some identifying word such as a geographical term (see the comments at 6:71) of a town or area, but precisely what it may be is not yet clear.

13:27   The giving of the dipped morsel can be interpreted in several ways. Becker thinks that the text turns Judas into a puppet dangling on the string of Jesus' decision for his destiny.[63] Haenchen shrugs off the story as a "magical morsel with which Satan entered in Judas."[64] Schlatter considered it to be Jesus' effective termination of his relationship with Judas.[65] Bultmann sees the event as removing Judas's act from human action and placing it in the sphere of Satan.[66]

But perhaps Beasley-Murray's argument needs to be pondered. Citing Newbigin's comment that the giving of the morsel to Judas was "the final act of love,"[67] Beasley-Murray is of the opinion that Jesus' act set Judas "on the spot" to make an ultimate decision.[68] Or to put it another way, one could ask: Did Jesus, by singling out Judas with a morsel, make his final and decisive, loving offer to Judas? Was it similar to Jesus addressing Judas as "friend" in Matt 26:50? If Judas was reclining on the left of Jesus, he certainly had been given a place of honor, but he also had the potential of knifing him in the back (what a picture!). At this point the tragedy of rejecting Jesus was therefore squarely on the shoulders of Judas. If Jesus had offered him bitter herbs, symbolically one could easily see the gauntlet of pain being thrown down. But whatever Jesus offered him, Judas was hardly

---

[63] See J. Becker, *Das Evangelium des Johannes*, 2.432.

[64] See E. Haenchen, *John 2* (Philadelphia: Fortress, 1984), 111. For other views on Judas see J. Derrett, "The Footwashing in John XIII and the Alienation of Judas Iscariot," *Revue internationale des droits de l'antiquite* 24 (1977): 3–19 and K. Hein, "Judas Iscariot: Key to the Last Supper Narrative," *NTS* 17 (1971): 227–32.

[65] See Schlatter, *Der Evangelist Johannes*, 286.

[66] See Bultmann, *John*, 482.

[67] See L. Newbigin, *The Light Has Come: An Exposition of the Fourth Gospel* (Grand Rapids: Eerdmans, 1982), 173.

[68] See Beasley-Murray, *John*, 238–39. Cf. also Carson, *John*, 474–75.

a puppet, and the dipped morsel was hardly a magical potion. Satan did not need magic to enter Judas. All he needed was permission to take control.

That permission was given by Judas and confirmed by Jesus with the words "do quickly" what you are about to do (13:27). With the acceptance of the morsel and the verdict of Jesus, the tragic case was closed. The traitor had been told to leave the company of the disciples.

13:28–29 The text indicates that no one reclining at the meal "understood" why Jesus told Judas to do what he was about to do. The meaning of the verb *ginōskein* here probably does not merely mean knowing about Judas's departure from the room. They could see that fact, but the evangelist probably intended a much deeper meaning here concerning the betrayal. Accordingly, the exception suggested by Brown that the statement probably did not include the beloved disciple and Peter (may or) may not be warranted.[69] One needs to remember that the evangelist frequently thinks on at least two levels. The statement of v. 29 concerning Judas controlling the money pouch or box and their speculation that he probably left either to purchase food or to make a donation to the poor is a confirmation that most (at least) of the disciples were doing mere earthly thinking.

Some scholars have regarded this statement concerning the purchase of food for the feast to be an indication that the meal herein detailed was not a Passover supper, but such a conclusion is not necessary. As for the statement concerning a donation to the poor here, Jeremias has noted that it was the practice on the eve of Passover to provide gifts for the poor.[70]

13:30 The section concludes with the statement of the immediate departure of Judas and the striking notation by the evangelist that "it was night." The Passover meal of Jesus undoubtedly took place in the evening, and the reference in 1 Cor 11:23 confirms that it was on the "night" of his betrayal that Jesus ripped bread apart as a symbol of his broken body and spoke of the cup at the end of supper as a new covenant in his blood (1 Cor 11:24–25; Matt 26:26–28; Mark 14:22–24; cf. the order in Luke 22:17–20).

It was, indeed, night when Judas departed from the meal, just as it was "winter" when the Festival of Dedication was celebrated (cf. John 10:22). But time and temperature designations signify more than time and temperature. They are pointers to spiritual realities that the careful reader should notice. Winter had come with the attempt by the Jews to kill Jesus, and now finally darkness, about which Jesus had warned his disciples (cf. 11:9–10), had arrived. It would be dark until the dawning of the resurrection appearances began to affect the disciples (cf. 21:4).

---

[69] See R. Brown, *John*, 2.575.
[70] See Jeremias, *Eucharistic Words*, 34.

(4) A Summation in Four Parts and a Preface to the Teaching That Follows (13:31–38)

[31]When he was gone, Jesus said, "Now is the Son of Man glorified and God is glorified in him. [32]If God is glorified in him, God will glorify the Son in himself, and will glorify him at once.

[33]"My children, I will be with you only a little longer. You will look for me, and just as I told the Jews, so I tell you now: Where I am going, you cannot come.

[34]"A new command I give you: Love one another. As I have loved you, so you must love one another. [35]By this all men will know that you are my disciples, if you love one another."

[36]Simon Peter asked him, "Lord, where are you going?"

Jesus replied, "Where I am going, you cannot follow now, but you will follow later."

[37]Peter asked, "Lord, why can't I follow you now? I will lay down my life for you."

[38]Then Jesus answered, "Will you really lay down your life for me? I tell you the truth, before the rooster crows, you will disown me three times!

Segovia, Beasley-Murray, Brown, and others think that the first unit of the farewell discourses has begun at this point.[71] I prefer to see this section as a summation of the introduction to the Farewell Cycle and a preparation for the so-called discourses that are to follow.

In the sphere of law a summation brings together a number of important issues for a judge and a jury to consider. In this case the summation is like a four-point statement concluding the introductory chapter of this cycle. The statement sets before the reader important matters to remember as one moves into the further discussions that are to follow. It also calls attention to a potential misunderstanding that could occur. If one looks at this section in this manner, I believe one may more clearly perceive its function in the Farewell Cycle.

One of the genuinely intriguing facets of the Farewell Cycle and the Death Story (chaps. 13–19) is the way the evangelist, like a skillful attorney, interweaves ideas and themes from other sections. This interweaving is often very frustrating to contemporary scholars who think that they ought to straighten out the evangelist's thinking or alternatively consider that they can attribute this interweaving to different historical levels or sources in the text. But rather than following that way of scholarly thinking, it can be rather rewarding to consider the possibilities that result if one does not regard the work as a mere cut-and-paste document.

Verses 31–38 are a kind of summation to the introduction of the Farewell Cycle, which takes seriously the foot washing of Jesus and the betraying depar-

---

[71] See F. Segovia, *The Farewell of the Word* (Minneapolis: Fortress, 1991), 59; Beasley-Murray, *John*, 240–44; R. Brown, *John*, 586–605; Carson, *John*, 476.

ture of Judas as a double episode around a meal and allows the evangelist at the conclusion of these events the opportunity to stress a few salient points before turning to the longer didactic sections of the cycle. This summation, I believe, is in four parts: (1) the glorification of Jesus (vv. 31–32), (2) the shortness of the time and the impossibility of following Jesus (v. 33), (3) the new commandment to the community (vv. 34–35), and (4) the post-Passover possibility of following and Peter's misunderstanding (vv. 36–38).

THE GLORIFICATION OF JESUS (13:31–32). **13:31–32** The first part of the summation is connected directly to the previous section by the reminder that Judas had departed. In the thinking of the evangelist that event must have been a strategic moment, something like the coming of the Greeks (cf. 12:20), because he calls attention again to the theme of glorification as he did in chap. 12. It was almost as though the clock at that point had stopped ticking for Jesus and that all the actions of the Passion were to be viewed as a single event or an existential moment in the mind of Jesus. As stated in chap. 12, the reader is here once again reminded by the use of "now" that the "hour" for the glorification of the "Son of Man" had arrived (cf. 12:23 and Excursus 12 on glorification).

But beyond the "now" statement the text continues to expand on the idea of glorification by indicating that "God is glorified in him." In reviewing the various possible linguistic implications of this clause, Caird argued that it is probably best understood as "God has revealed his glory in Jesus."[72] The advantage of this suggestion is that the verb *doxazien* here being passive and intransitive does not separate the actions of Jesus from God. Indeed, if one remembers that Jesus was acting as God's agent, then it should be clear that in the legal sense God is clearly to be understood to receive the benefit of any action undertaken by his representative on earth.

The expansion of the idea of glorification in v. 32 may on first glance seem to be confusing double-talk. In fact, the conditional clause has been omitted in a number of important Greek manuscripts. Although the variant does smooth out the reading, it probably is not original and is due to a scribal copying problem *(homoioteleuton)*.[73] Nevertheless, the significance of the verse is that it presents the obverse side of the coin of v. 31. Not only is God glorified in the process but the Son is glorified in the Father's glorification, and that glorification is an immediate one.

This glorification does not require the coming of the end of time and the final victory. The glorification idea employed here is directly related to the obedience of the Son in the crucifixion and the subsequent resurrection. To

---

[72] G. B. Caird, "The Glory of God in the Fourth Gospel: An Exercise in Biblical Semantics," *NTS* 15 (1968–1969): 265–77.

[73] See Metzger, *Textual Commentary*, 242.

see God's act of glorification through the tragedy of the death of the Messiah and the victorious resurrection is a crucial aspect of the Gospel presentation. The drama of the divine reversal in history is the message of John and a basic summation thesis that is presented.

THE SHORTNESS OF TIME AND THE IMPOSSIBILITY OF FOLLOWING JESUS (13:33). **13:33** Addressing the disciples with the loving diminutive "little children" *(teknia),* used only here in the Gospel, the evangelist in the second place assumes the role of the teacher-parent similar to that of the writer of the First Epistle of John (2:1,28; 3:7,18; 4:4; 5:21) when he was speaking to the Christians in the Johannine community. Jewish teachers often addressed their learners with such kind and gentle designations.[74]

The statement that follows the address consists of several parts.[75] First, Jesus tells the disciples that he will be with them only for a "longer." The shortness of time is thus highlighted here as in 16:16. Second, the disciples are told here that they like the Jews would seek him and not be able to join him (cf. 7:34; 8:21). That statement definitely created perplexity for the hostile Jews in the Festival Cycle as they sought to determine whether Jesus was going to the Diaspora (7:35) or going to commit suicide (8:22). But in this cycle the idea of Jesus' departure was equally perplexing for the disciples (cf. also 16:17), even though they do not ultimately remain perplexed. The basic thesis here then is that the disciples had to face realistically that Jesus' time with them would be short, and that they could not join him in his Passover mission of death.

THE GIVING OF THE NEW COMMANDMENT TO THE COMMUNITY (13:34–35). **13:34–35** Many have noted that these two verses seem to interrupt the flow of the discussion in terms of Jesus' departure, which was initiated in the previous verse and will be picked up again in v. 36. But as will be indicated at that point, the focus there is different from v. 33.

In the present verses the focus is upon the community that Jesus will establish as a result of his Passover departure. Its distinctive quality was to be marked by a new commandment.[76] Like the previous summation statements, which are related to other parts of John, this statement is clearly related to verses in the central passage of the Farewell Cycle (15:12–13), where the commandment to love is reasserted.

In the establishment of communities, one of the principle factors of success is the establishing of boundaries for action, which we call laws. These laws are based on community or national covenants, whether stated or

---

[74] See *Str-B,* 2.559.

[75] Many scholars begin the discourses at this point. Cf. D. Woll, "The Departure of 'The Way': The First Farewell Discourse in the Gospel of John," *JBL* 99 (1980): 229–38.

[76] For examples of the discussion on the love command see R. Collins, "A New Commandment I Give to You, That You Love One Another ... (John 13:34)," *LTP* 35 (1979): 235–61 and J. Kelly, "What Did Christ Mean by the Sign of Love?" *African Ecclesiastical Review* 13 (1971): 113–21.

unstated. These covenants that lie behind the laws, rules, or commands are absolutely crucial. When societies go through transitions by the influx of outsiders or changes in economic or social structures, the underlying covenants are often disregarded and the society is thrown into confusion. In 1 John 2:18ff. the writer details the confusing state of affairs that apparently affected the Johannine community as some members seemed to have abandoned their earlier covenant and adopted new definitions of theology (1 John 2:22–25) and life (1 John 3:4–18). Understanding underlying covenants is therefore crucial to perceiving the significance of laws or commands.

Thus, to understand the ten so-called words or commandments of Exodus 20 one must realize that they do not start with v. 3, "no other gods." The Ten Commandments start with the presupposition of a covenant based on the liberating act of God in bringing the people out of Egypt, the house of bondage, as it is described in v. 2. It is only when one understands the foundational liberating act of God for Israel that one recognizes the responsibility to obey the divine commands. To forget the covenant is to set the commands in a sea of meaninglessness. Rules have to be contextualized to have meaning.

So it is with the new commandment of John 13:34. The commandment to love one another has almost no meaning apart from its contextual presupposition, "I have loved you." It is like commanding people to have no other gods who have not understood the meaning or accepted the exodus for themselves. Their question, "Why should I obey?" is perfectly legitimate until they recognize that the exodus is a paradigm for them as well. In the same manner, to ask people to love one another is pointless if they have not understood the love of Jesus in his Passover death for them, alluded to in the two previous summary thesis statements. Such love becomes philosophically a nice ideal without any root in reality. You can legislate "no discrimination" in the workplace based on a covenant of mutual respect, but you cannot make people love one another without the acceptance of the covenant foundation of the self-giving love of God for the world.

The acceptance of God's self-giving love for the people of the world, including each one of us as recipients of that love (3:16), and the obedient response in a derivative love enables "all people" (*pantes,* 13:35; not merely men) to recognize the accepter as a disciple of Jesus. This way of loving one another is not to be interpreted exclusively as my little in-group (as it was by many Jews; cf. the message of Jonah).[77] Instead, it was to be under-

---

[77] The Johannine community undoubtedly went through the pain of those who exited the company because of matters such as Christology (1 John 2:18–25), but one must be careful not to attribute the love command as merely applying to others in the community. For the Johannine community and concerns in the stories of Jesus see these sociological and historical studies: J. H. Neyrey, *An Ideology of Revolt* (Philadelphia: Fortress, 1988); R. E. Brown, *The Community of the Beloved Disciple* (New York: Paulist, 1979); J. L. Martyn, *History and Theology* (Nashville: Abingdon, 1979). For a helpful perspective on the extent of love see N. Lohfink, *Jesus and Community* (Philadelphia: Fortress, 1984), 3–5. For a nontechnical sociological study of John see B. Malina and R. Rohrbaugh, *Social Science Commentary on the Gospel of John* (Minneapolis: Fortress, 1998).

stood as breathtakingly explosive of old relationships and old patterns of
obedience in the way it was pointedly presented in the Sermon on the
Mount (cf. Matt 5–7 and particularly 5:43–48; cf. also 1 John 4:7–21).[78]
These two verses of John thus encapsulate the coming of the new era and
the new community. This new community, in fact, epitomized God's consistent intention in the Old Testament of calling out a people who are to be
recognized by their love for God (Deut 6:4–5; the *Shema Israel*) and their
love of neighbor (Lev 19:18) just as Jesus spelled out his model in the Sermon on the Mount. Likewise, in his first epistle (1 John 3:1–18) John articulated the fact that this new community of believers was expected to love
one another (3:11) and not act like the evil Cain (3:12) because God had
loved them and accepted them as his children (3:1–2). That thesis is basic
to this Gospel.

THE POST-PASSOVER POSSIBILITY OF FOLLOWING JESUS AND
PETER'S MISUNDERSTANDING (13:36–38). **13:36–38** The final summation is played out not in monologue but in a dialogue between Jesus and
Peter. This dialogue masterfully knits together several ideas or themes,
some of which are not unlike elements in the Synoptic portrayal of Jesus
and Peter.

Almost as though he had missed the significance of the establishment of
the new community and its mission to the world, Peter here is pictured as
returning to the issue of Jesus' departure (13:33) by his question, "Where
are you going?" Jesus' response repeats the fact that Peter is unable to follow Jesus, but he adds something new. That change did not negate the earlier statement of Jesus to the effect that Peter was not able to join him in his
Passover death. Only Jesus could die such a death for the world.

But the change in the statement was here possible because, with the coming of a new community that would follow the example of Jesus, a new element had been introduced in vv. 34–35. The "now" *(nyn)* of v. 36, however,
reminds one of the "now" of v. 31, which is related to the glorification of
Jesus in his death and resurrection. Clearly Peter was not now able to join
Jesus in that glorification, but his time would come in the era of the new
community ("later"). Jesus' prediction reminds the reader of the statements
in 21:18–19, where Peter's death as a glorifying of God is also predicted.

Unfortunately Peter misunderstood the implications of Jesus' words and
assumed that the present *(arti,* "now") also was his time. The shift here in
the Greek word for "now" may be nothing more than the evangelist's penchant for variation, or it may have been an artful variation to emphasize

---

[78] For an excellent treatment of the Sermon on the Mount and the sixth antithesis in particular
see R. Guelich, *The Sermon on the Mount* (Waco: Word, 1982), 252–55. For a helpful statement
see also D. Dockery and D. Garland, *Seeking the Kingdom* (Wheaton: Harold Shaw, 1992), 66–69.

Peter's confusion. In either case in the context of his present safe community Peter forcefully enunciated his loyalty to Jesus by boastfully proclaiming his readiness to "lay down" *(thēsō)* his life for Jesus. As P. Duke has well indicated, Peter's statement here is filled with irony.[79] Instead of Peter, however, Jesus was the one who freely (cf. 10:18) was prepared in the "now" time to lay down his life for his sheep (cf. 10:15,17; 1 John 3:16) just as he laid down his garments in the foot washing for his disciples (13:4).

Peter, on the other hand, would in the moment of trauma not lay down his life for Jesus but in fact would deny him three times (13:38; cf. 18:17,25–27). Jesus' repetition here in question form of the very words of Peter highlights the irony in Peter's words and sets the stage not only for the threefold denial of Peter but also for the threefold searing questions posed to Peter in the post-Passover period during the establishing of the community (21:15–17). The crowing of the cock *(alketor)* later became the electrifying sign that was used to remind Peter of his well-intentioned but mistaken boast.

Brown, in commenting on this passage and Peter's first question, "Where are you going?" recalls the Latin tradition in the apocryphal *Acts of Peter* that when Peter was fearful of his forthcoming death and was fleeing Rome, he was met in a vision by Jesus, and Peter asked again, *"Quo vadis?"* ("Where are you going?"). When Jesus answered that he was going to Rome to be crucified again, Peter realized that he was about to repeat his mistake and in repentance turned back to face his certain death after the pattern of Jesus.[80] Whether there is any truth in that apocryphal tradition, it is a story that vividly reminds us of this fourth thesis in the summation. Although no one could walk the lonely valley of redemption with Jesus, the disciples of Jesus do have the opportunity to follow their Lord, if they do not mistake their calling.

2. The Great Issue of Loneliness and Anxiety for the Community— Part I (14:1–14)

In contrast to a number of scholars, including Segovia, Beasley-Murray, and Carson, who view 13:31–14:31 as a unit, I regard chap. 14 as clearly

---

[79] See P. Duke's helpful work, *Irony in the Fourth Gospel* (Atlanta: John Knox, 1985) particularly at 49–52 and 96–97.

[80] See R. Brown, *John*, 2.607–9; cf. *Acts of Peter* 35. See M. R. James, *The Apocryphal New Testament* (Oxford: Clarendon Press, 1955), 333 or E. Hennecke, *New Testament Apocrypha*, (Philadelphia: Westminster, 1965), 1.317–18.

divisible after 14:14.[81] As I indicated above, I consider 13:31–38 to be a major summation or conclusion of the first part of the Farewell Cycle (13:1–38), but I also think that it serves as a preface to the discourses that follow. Since Jesus was going away and since Peter and his colleagues could not follow, at least for the present (13:36), the stage was set for a critical separation of Jesus from the disciples.

Separation naturally raises a sense of loneliness, and all sorts of questions flood the minds of those who are left behind. People experiencing the loss of a loved one and the bereavement that ensues often have difficulty integrating their state of loss with their questioning sense of what comes next. The disciples are pictured in these verses as being very human. Thus the words of Jesus that John indicates were intended to calm their anxieties turned out for the disciples to be difficult to synthesize with their earlier experience of relating to Jesus as the expected King (cf. 1:49; etc.).

It is not very different for us humans who have difficulty imagining living life on planet Earth without those who mean most to us. How do we go on in life without them? We humans do not even like to talk about death. Many people, who know better, even shy away from setting up their testamentary documents and making their wills. But death does not go away, and the potential of loneliness does not delay simply because we resist discussing it. Death is a reality we must face forthrightly because this world is not the ultimate reality.

The Farewell Cycle is intended in part to deal with our anxiety concerning such loneliness. Indeed, 14:1–14 confronts this issue squarely. As a result there is scarcely a Christian funeral conducted without some reference to John 14. The fourteen verses in this segment break naturally into three subsections: (1) preparation for the ultimate reality (14:1–3), (2) perplexing questions concerning getting there (14:4–11), and (3) the power of believing in Jesus for our life of discipleship now (14:12–14).

(1) Preparing for Both Loneliness and Ultimate Reality (14:1–3)

[1]"**Do not let your hearts be troubled. Trust in God; trust also in me. [2]In my Father's house are many rooms; if it were not so, I would have told you. I am going there to prepare a place for you. [3]And if I go and prepare a place for you, I will come back and take you to be with me that you also may be where I am.**

---

[81] F. Segovia, "The Structure, *Tendenz* and *Sitz-im-Leben* of John 13:31–14:31," *JBL* 104 (1985): 471–93 and Beasley-Murray, *John*, 243. Some scholars consider that John has in these chapters restructured earlier eschatology. See for example S. Legasse, "Le retour du Christ d'après l'évangile de Jean, chapitre 14 et 16: une adaptation du motif de la Parousie," *Bulletin de Littérature Ecclésiastique* 81 (1980): 161–74.

These verses, which are framed in homey, phenomenal language, nevertheless point to a reality concerning a Christian's ultimate relationship with Jesus. As Beasley-Murray has noted, the verbs in this passage are all in the plural form.[82] John once again is addressing the turmoil within his community of believers in a heart-to-heart manner. He does so at the same time as he portrayed Jesus addressing his disciples. Accordingly, we have another example of a double-level presentation reflecting two historical settings.

14:1 The text immediately catches the readers' attention, for it begins with a strong prohibition, a negative imperative, *mē parassesthō,* which carries the meaning of "Do not let your hearts be overcome with turmoil" or perhaps, more colloquially, "Don't allow yourself to be intimidated by the situation." This statement is immediately followed by a call to evidence confidence through the double use of the Greek *pisteuete,* which can be either an indicative or an imperative. Here the imperative is to be preferred, and while one could render the word "believe" as in the KJV, it is better translated "trust" as in the NIV.

Jesus knew that his little band could and would be shaken not only by his words concerning his departure but also by the fact that he would soon become the crucified Lamb. Accordingly, he called for them to place their "trust" not in the power evident in the world but in God and in himself. This direct linkage between God and Jesus has been a fundamental assertion of John, since he identified the Word with God (1:1–2) and later Jesus with the Father (5:17–30; see my comments at that point).[83]

The force of this verse is, in fact, a call to the disciples to follow the pattern of "trust" exhibited by Jesus (cf. Phil 2:5), who faced hostility and, indeed, abandonment by the disciples including Peter (18:17,25,27), though the beloved disciple does not ever seem to come in for criticism. The familiar cry of dereliction that is a climactic point in Mark (15:34; cf. Matt 27:46) is not present in John. Instead, there is a serenity in Jesus' words "It is finished" (John 19:30) similar to Jesus' dying declaration in Luke (23:46).

14:2 The reason the disciples should be able to evidence trust is because Jesus was going to provide preparation for them. That preparation is outlined in the metaphor of the "Father's house" *(oikia),* which undoubtedly refers to the domain of God. That domain is described as being subdivided into many *monai.*

The Greek word *monai* was rendered in the Vulgate by the Latin *mansiones,* which came down through the Tyndale version to the KJV as "man-

---

[82] Beasley-Murray, *John,* 243.

[83] Cf. the discussion in S. Schultz, *Untersuchungen zur Menschensohn—Christologie im Johannesevangelium* (Göttingen: Vandenhoeck und Ruprecht, 1957), 159–64.

sions." The use of the word "mansions" here is unfortunate because it has become infused into popular Christian culture so that one can hear some Christians speaking about the fact that they have "a mansion just over the hilltop." Such a concept, unfortunately, supports the Western economic notion that following Jesus will lead to economic prosperity either in this life or in the life to come, especially if one must suffer in this life. But such a concept fails for several reasons. First, God does not promise economic prosperity. Second, the idea is a typical Semitic word picture[84] describing a relationship of God with the people of God like the picture of heaven in Revelation 21–22. Third, and most importantly, *monai* does not mean a castle-like home anymore than *mansiones* in the Vulgate is to be interpreted in that manner. The word is derived from the Greek verb *menein,* "to remain," and *monai* means "dwelling" or "abiding" places.[85] So if the *monai* are in God's house, the NIV's "rooms," or perhaps "apartments" or "flats," would be much closer to the meaning of the text here.

But in spite of the portrayal of God dwelling in a "house," one must take great care not to visualize God in some earthlike "place."[86] Moreover, since we are bound by space-time limitations in all our thinking, we must not limit our concept of God's domain to something like our idea of a three-story universe where heaven as the dwelling place of God is "up." It is now most appropriate for Christians to begin to think in dimensional concepts that are far beyond the old three-dimensional reasoning of the previous generations (see my comments in Excursus 33). Clearly God is not running fast to catch up to our supercomputer space technologies. God is a long way ahead of us. The teacups of our thinking and language have not even yet approached the capacity of holding the ocean of divine truth. The domain of God is certainly beyond our finite thinking. The best we can do is to describe God's domain in metaphors. That is exactly what Jesus, the agent of God, did for his bewildered disciples.

Furthermore, God's domain has plenty of room, and the preparation of

---

[84] See for example M. McNamara, " 'To Prepare a Resting-Place for You': A Targumic Expression and John 14:2f.," *Miltown Studies* 3 (Dublin, 1979), 100–108.

[85] Newman and Nida (*Translator's Handbook on John,* p. 454) note that some commentators think the Greek word means "stopping place," suggesting that "heaven is a place of progression" having a multitude of stopping or resting places. But, as these Bible translators indicate, it is better to see in the word a sense of "remaining" rather than of temporary stopping. It is also important to remember that *menein,* "remain" or "abide," is an exceedingly significant idea in John (cf. 14:23; 15:4).

[86] In *The Gospel of John,* G. Turner and J. Mantey suggest that the "imagery is that of a vast palace, like that in Knossos, Versailles, or Vienna, with over a thousand rooms" (Evangelical Commentary [Grand Rapids: Eerdmans, n.d.], 280). Such a description is meaningful only if it remains symbolic. For a better perspective see R. Gundry, " 'In My Father's House Are Many *Monai*' (John 14:2)," *ZNW* 58 (1967): 68–72.

Jesus for our entrance into that domain was through his "departure" or death on the cross. Carson is surely correct when he says concerning Jesus that arriving on the scene after his departure is not the point when Jesus "begins to prepare the place," but "it is the going itself, via the cross and resurrection" that is the act of preparation.[87] The Gospel of John is not trying to portray Jesus as being in the construction business of building or renovating rooms. Rather, Jesus was in the business of leading people to God.

This preparation by Jesus is to be taken seriously because John pictures Jesus as here firmly asserting the point of his mission. And to make this point Jesus virtually uses a Jewish type of oath when he says "if it were not so, I would have told you." Like God, Jesus needed no one else to support his assertions of truth, except to refer to himself. The RSV/NRSV turns this strong assertion into a question, but that rendering of the text is unlikely since this statement is part of John's introductory announcement of Jesus concerning his purpose. An opening question here would give the impression that Jesus had opened a debate.

The text, however, does have a variant reading that adds *hoti* at this point. This reading probably is original, but the meaning is not entirely clear.[88] The *hoti* here might be either the sign of direct discourse or a causal conjunction, but it would not justify rendering the strong assertion as a question.

14:3 The promise of Jesus' return to take the disciples with him after his preparatory "going" or departure has been the subject of considerable discussion. Bultmann, relying on Dodd's view that these verses do not represent a Jewish-Christian eschatology,[89] employs his standard pattern of identifying the ideas here as focused on the individual eschatology of the Gnostic cosmological myth.[90] In that mythological message the soul that has been awakened by the divine messenger from the pleroma is challenged to make its ascent through the realm of the planets and slough off all those elements of the deficient creator as it winds its way back to the upper realm of reality.[91]

Although few scholars have been willing to follow Bultmann's commitment to a Gnostic or Mandean-like interpretation of Johannine eschatology,

---

[87] Carson, *John*, 489.

[88] See Metzger, *Textual Commentary*, 243 and Newman and Nida, *Tranlator's Handbook*, 455.

[89] See Dodd, *Interpretation*, 404.

[90] See Bultmann, *John*, 602 and the analysis of Schnackenburg, *St. John*, 3.60–62.

[91] For a discussion of the Gnostic myth see H. Jonas, *The Gnostic Religion* (Boston: Beacon, 1958) and *Gnosis und Spätantiker Geist* (Göttingen: Vandenhoeck & Ruprecht, 1964) as well as my summary in G. Borchert, "Insights into the Gnostic Threat to Christianity as Gained Through the Gospel of Philip," in *New Dimensions in New Testament Study* (Grand Rapids: Zondervan, 1974), 79–93. See also the brief introduction in the first volume of this commentary, *John 1–11*, NAC (Nashville: Broadman & Holman, 1996), 76–80.

a number have looked for other answers than the futuristic eschatology that the text seems to espouse. Some, like Dodd, have opted for a realized or inaugurated type of eschatology that regards the resurrection and the coming of the indwelling Paraclete/Spirit to be a fulfillment of these words.[92]

Brown (like Westcott[93] and others who preceded him) sees the possibility that the text could refer to several related events such as the death of Jesus, which he thinks could meet this idea because Jesus told Peter in 13:36–37 that he would follow him later.[94] Brown also affirms that the coming could be viewed as a spiritual coming.[95]

Although Gundry allows that this text may focus on the parousia, he concludes that the passage highlights the coming of the Spirit as encompassed within the idea of the coming of Jesus.[96] Employing 14:23 as a key, Gundry also connects the idea of "we will come to him" with the idea of Jesus coming in the Spirit. Moreover, he thinks it is possible to connect the idea of rooms *(monai)* with the idea of coming to "dwell" *(monēn)* with them in 14:23.[97] Although these are the only two uses of *monēn/monai* in the New Testament, it should be noted that the concept of dwelling is actually focused in two different directions: in the first the disciples are to gain their dwelling in the divine domain, and in the second the persons of the Godhead come to dwell in the disciples.

Perhaps the conclusions of L. Morris are appropriate at this point when he notes that while John does not refer as frequently "as most of the other New Testament writers" to the Second Advent of Jesus, the references, when made, "should not be missed." Clearly the details of the place are not mentioned, but the idea that Christians will dwell with their Lord is extremely significant.[98]

(2) Loneliness and Perplexing Questions (14:4–11)

[4]**You know the way to the place where I am going."**

[5]**Thomas said to him, "Lord, we don't know where you are going, so how can we know the way?"**

[6]**Jesus answered, "I am the way and the truth and the life. No one comes to the Father except through me. [7]If you really knew me, you would know my Father as well. From now on, you do know him and have seen him."**

[8]**Philip said, "Lord, show us the Father and that will be enough for us."**

---

[92] See Dodd, *Interpretation*, 404–6.

[93] B. Westcott, *The Gospel According to St. John* (Grand Rapids: Eerdmans, 1954), 2.168.

[94] R. Brown, *John*, 2.626.

[95] Ibid., 2.627.

[96] See Gundry, "In My Father's House," 68–72.

[97] Ibid., 69–70.

[98] See Morris, *John*, 568.

[9]Jesus answered: "Don't you know me, Philip, even after I have been among you such a long time? Anyone who has seen me has seen the Father. How can you say, 'Show us the Father'? [10]Don't you believe that I am in the Father, and that the Father is in me? The words I say to you are not just my own. Rather, it is the Father, living in me, who is doing his work. [11]Believe me when I say that I am in the Father and the Father is in me; or at least believe on the evidence of the miracles themselves.

14:4 This section opens with a pithy statement concerning the fact that the disciples know the way *(hodon)* Jesus is going, which can be rendered literally, "And where *[hopou]* I am going you know the way *[hodon]*." Here again is an example of Johannine shorthand that obviously moved some early copyist to expand the statement so that it would serve as a better introduction for Thomas's question: "Where I am going you know and the way you know."[99] An attempt at translating this expanded version to bring it into harmony with Thomas's question appears in the KJV, but later versions followed the shorter reading so that the strange redundancy is removed. In any event, despite the shorthand the statement seems to be clear. MacGregor's reordering of the chapters and his attempt to change this statement into a question just confuses the issue and must be rejected.[100]

14:5 Thomas's question once again identifies him as the realist of the company who wants the facts (cf. 11:16; 20:24–25), and he certainly should not merely be categorized as a doubter. In his response Thomas splits the goal as destination ("where") from the route or way *(hodon)*.[101] Thomas wanted a road map, but he did not know how to get one if he did not know "where" he was to end his trip. Thomas's problem, however, was that in the metaphor of the house and the rooms Jesus had told him the destination. But Thomas had misinterpreted the metaphor to be a statement of taking a journey. Instead, Jesus was talking about the ultimate relationship of life that humans have with God and that has implications for their eternal destiny. When one understands the metaphor from this perspective, "the way" then becomes more akin to "a way of life."[102]

This concept of a way of life was foundational not only to the proclamation of Jesus, Paul, and John but also to Israel and to the teachings of the rabbis. The Hebrew word *halak* ("walk") can provide insight to this discussion. The law or Torah was not to be understood primarily as a set of rules

---

[99] See Metzger, *Textual Commentary*, 243 and Newman and Nida, *Translator's Handbook*, 456.
[100] See C. H. C. MacGregor, *The Gospel of John* (London: Hodder & Stoughton, 1928), 305.
[101] Cf. Dodd, *Interpretation*, 412.
[102] For another view on this interchange between Jesus and the disciples see D. Wall, "The Departure of 'The Way': The First Farewell Discourse in the Gospel of John," *JBL* 99 (1980): 230–37 and his larger work *Johannine Christianity in Conflict* (Chico, Cal.: Society of Biblical Literature, 1981).

but as a walk with God.[103] Accordingly, the rabbis designated the strict commands of God as *halakah*. But interpretations and approved liturgies were designated as *haggadah*. So the celebrative ritual of Passover is appropriately named the Passover Haggadah. When Paul therefore instructs his Christian followers to live lives of integrity as Christians, he calls them to "walk not according to the flesh" (Rom 8:4, NRSV), to walk "in love" (Rom 14:15), and to walk "by the Spirit" (Gal 5:16). But many, he said, walk instead as "enemies" (Phil 3:18). Yet Christians are called to walk "worthy of God" (1 Thess 2:12). In the Gospel of John to follow Jesus is the equivalent of walking in the light or the daytime (11:9; 12:35). The Greek verb that is used in all these cases, both in Paul and John, is *peripatein,* and it means "to conduct one's life in a certain way or manner."[104]

Unfortunately, ideas of Torah, *halakah,* law, command, or instruction can all degenerate into keeping a set of rules or failing to relate directly to one who gave the rules or instructions. In such a case Torah and instruction become ends in themselves. "The way" then fades into an act of human effort so that dynamic relationship with God becomes swallowed up in keeping a set of wooden rules. Following rules is hardly what is intended in John as the "way" to the Father. Accordingly, the "way" in this verse was hardly meant to be understood as a road or pathway on which Thomas could stride or ride to get to the Father's house.

14:6 Thomas's question provides the setting for one of the most frequently quoted verses in the Gospel of John. Jesus' response is introduced by another *egō eimi* ("I am") saying. In this case Jesus asserted that he is "the way, the truth, and the life."

In previous chapters *egō eimi* has been used to indicate that Jesus is the Messiah (4:28), the bread or sustenance of the community (6:35,48,51), the light of the world (8:12; 9:5), the one who is from above and not from the world (8:23), the gate or entrance way to the sheepfold (10:7,9), the good shepherd (10:11, 14), and the resurrection and life (11:25). Here John joins three powerful ideas of "way," "truth," and "life" to produce a classic statement concerning the significance of Jesus in providing salvation.

The use of such a triad following the previous *egō eimi* statements forms a kind of summation of Jesus' mission to the world and a preparation for the integrated community statement that Jesus is the Vine and his followers

---

[103] Cf. *BAGD,* 649. For my discussions on the subject of law see G. Borchert, "Paul's Understanding of Instruction," *Biblical Illustrator* (2001). Also see my discussion on the meaning of law as "walk" and not as legalism in my commentary, *Galatians,* New Living Translation Series (Wheaton: Tyndale, forthcoming).

[104] See, e.g., *TDNT* 5.82–84 and R. Brown, *John,* 2.628. See also I. de la Potterie, "'Je suis la Voie, la Vérite et la Vie' (Jn 14, 6)," *NRT* 88 (1966): 907–42 and F. Sham, "I Am the Way, the Truth and the Life," *Neot* 2 (1968): 81–88.

are the branches. The branches, however, should never misunderstand the dependent nature of their identities (15:1,5). The concepts of these three terms are rooted solidly in the teaching of the Old Testament and in Hebrew thought. Although some might look for the background in Gnostic thought[105] concerning the ascent to the Pleroma, that quest overlooks the obvious basis of the Old Testament. For example, the Psalmist prays that the Lord would teach him the divine "way" and lead him to walk in "truth" (Ps 84:11),[106] and he contemplates the "path of life" (Ps 16:11) as his blessed hope.

For the Essenes at Qumran their hope lay in following "the way" of the teacher of righteousness. The covenanters considered his definitions or rules as the authentic interpretation of the Mosaic Torah (cf. 1 QS 9:17–21). Moreover, they regarded themselves as the true community of preparation fulfilling the instructions of Isa 40:3–5 to prepare in the desert "the way of the Lord" (cf. 1 QS 8:11–16). Both John and the Synoptic writers regarded John the Baptist as the symbolic preparation for the coming of Jesus as the Messiah (cf. John 1:23; Mark 1:1–8; Matt 3:1–12; Luke 3:2–17; cf. also Matt 11:2–15 for the interpretation of the Baptizer as the messenger according to Mal 3:1).[107]

The relationship of the words in this triad have often been questioned as to whether or not there is a subordination of "truth" and "life" to "way." I would firmly reject such an idea. But in terms of the discussion in the pericope itself the idea of "way" can naturally lead one to reflect on both the ideas of truth and life. The issue of the correct way of life inevitably raises the issue of authenticity or truth which in turn raises the issue of the consequence of accepting what is true and that involves one's life. So these ideas actually hang together in an inseparable union.

In his captivating manner Bultmann here reminded us that the ideas of "the way and the goal are not to be separated."[108] But he went further and distinguished his view from mythological thinking. Thus he regarded the idea of "I am the way" as "a pure expression of revelation" over against content.[109] In the same manner his article on *pisteuō/pistis* (believing/faith) is exemplary of a dynamic Lutheran background but the companion article on *gnōskō/gnōsis* (knowing/knowledge) leaves one wondering about the

---

[105] Cf. Bultmann's assignment of these ideas to Gnostic roots (*John*, 605–6).

[106] See my earlier discussion on "the Way."

[107] One should remember that in the Passover Haggadah the empty chair is set for the coming of Elijah, the one who is expected to precede the Messiah and prepare the way for his coming and the coming of the anticipated day in Jewish thinking. In Christian thinking that role has been assigned to John the Baptist.

[108] See Bultmann, *John*, 605.

[109] Ibid., 605–6.

nature of what is known.[110] Encountering the "I am the way" involved, for John, identifying the Jesus of history with the Christ of the disciples' faith.

But for Bultmann that combination violated the distinction between the Jesus of history and the Christ who was encountered by the disciples in their post-Easter faith.[111] Yet Christian theology or doctrine has historically united the two as Jesus Christ.[112] To view it otherwise is to miss John's affirmation. Although one can agree with Bultmann here that "one comes to him [Christ] as the truth," one does not have to agree that "truth does not exist as a doctrine."[113] The same, of course, applies to a discussion on "life." It is clear that ideas or doctrines cannot stand without a dynamic relationship to the Christ Jesus whom the early church refused to separate in the manner of Bultmann any more than that they would separate the triad here of "way," "truth," and "life" in their confession about Jesus.

The order of the triad as I have indicated above is perfectly logical. Also interesting is that these ideas are reflected in John's Prologue, though I would suggest that they are somewhat in a reverse order. There the Logos is identified as "life" (1:4), who is the "true light" (1:9) that provides the way to the Father by dwelling among us (1:14) and supplies humans with abundant grace (1:16) in order that we might receive or believe in him (1:12).

Moreover, here at 14:6 John follows the lead of the Prologue, where he already had asserted strongly that no one else has ever seen God, but the only Son has made him known (1:18). Now in this verse John concludes with an emphatic assertion that "no one comes to the Father except *[ei mē]* through me *[di 'emou]*." Any hint at universalism, syncretistic patterns of salvation, or reaching the Father through any other means than Jesus is here completely eliminated.

The issue of Johannine exclusivism is therefore placed squarely before the reader.[114] Given the fact that the Johannine church was a community struggling for its existence in the midst of powerful pressures from both its Jewish birthing setting and its Hellenistic syncretistic context, the language and antisociety stance may seem to be completely out of touch with today's

---

[110] See Bultmann's articles in *TDNT* 6.174–82, 197–228 and 1.689–719.

[111] For Bultmann the Jesus of history and the Christ of faith are not to be identified. See his discussion on "New Testament and Mythology" in *Kerygma and Myth* (New York: Harper & Row, 1961), 1–44 especially at 22ff., where he reveals how he employs the two German words for history *(Historia and Geschichte)* as the basis for separating between history as facts and history as theological/philosophical significance or existential experience and the consequent subjective conclusions that are reached.

[112] See the Apostles (Old Roman) Creed and the Nicene Creed in H. Bettenson, *Documents of the Christian Church* (London: Oxford University Press, 1956), 33–36.

[113] Bultmann, *John*, 606–7.

[114] For a helpful discussion on the Johannine view of Jesus and exclusivism here see Carson, *John*, 491–93.

adoption of pluralism. On the one hand, it is crucial to remember that this text was not written when the church represented a majority perspective. It was a small minority in which it viewed itself as under siege and its members as tempted by the threat of losing their lives, status, or possessions if they did not yield to pressure. On the other hand, it is imperative to remember that perspectives that are forged in such settings usually go to the heart of what a community is. What people are willing to die for is the measure of who they are. When such people become prosperous and respected, however, they frequently minimalize the basic reason for their existence. The Johannine concept of mission is uncompromising on the issue of the uniqueness of Jesus. For this assertion they were willing to die or be excluded from the synagogues in the pattern of the blind man (9:34).

14:7 Having stated unambiguously in the negative the assertion that "no one comes to the Father except through me," this next verse asserts positively the direct interconnection between the Father and Jesus. This direct connection is a repeated theme in the Gospel beginning in the Prologue (1:1), where the Logos is *theos* (God). It is reasserted in the fact that Jesus is equal with God (5:18) and one with the Father (10:30) and is concluded with the confession of Thomas that Jesus is God (20:28).

The form John chose to express the statement here, however, is a conditional sentence. The problem is that the textual variants at this point leave one not quite sure as to what kind of condition is involved. The UBS Greek text has the aorist *egnōkate,* which could be rendered something like "since you have really known me," but the variant reading here *(egnōkeite)* would be rendered "if you really knew me," implying you do not. The former assumes the relationship, whereas the latter assumes an acquaintance but not a real knowing. Metzger indicates that the UBS committee was in doubt about this variant and that K. Aland argued strongly that the variant was to be preferred because in the pattern of textual transmission scribes usually sought to make texts more positive.[115]

If Aland is correct here, the text is a rebuke to the disciples, who should have realized that "really knowing" Jesus would mean "really knowing" God (the NIV could be read in this way).[116] If, however, the text stands as it is in other translations, then it could mean that because the disciples "really know" who Jesus is, they would "really know" God. But it could also be argued that this verse is another instance of double-level thinking in

---

[115] Metzger, *A Textual Commentary,* 243. Cf. also the discussion in Newman and Nida, *A Translator's Handbook on John,* 458. See also the discussion in R. Schnackenburg, "Johannes 14:7," in *Studies in New Testament Language and Text* (Leiden: Brill, 1976), 345–56.

[116] While Carson (*John,* 493) and others assume that the variant is the result of the influence of Philip's follow-up question in v. 8, it is not impossible to read this text as a mild rebuke whatever one might decide concerning the textual variant.

John where the disciples who are acquainted with (know) Jesus ought to really know the Father. However one may decide this issue, the implication is that "really knowing" Jesus has a profound effect on knowing God.

In this respect John has changed from the use of the singular in v. 6 to the plural "you" in v. 7, so Jesus' statement is not merely addressed to Thomas. It is addressed as a general statement to all the disciples and thus to the Christian community. English translations like the NIV do not make that shift evident, and it can therefore be missed by many readers of the English Bible.

The question that still could be raised is, When will the disciples know him? Although the verb *gnōsesthe* is future tense, the time of their knowing is not spelled out. One could argue that the fulfillment of this statement could take place at the resurrection and the inbreathing of the Spirit (20:22), but it probably is best to leave it undefined since the concluding statement of v. 7 remains undefined. In that clause the "assuredly" of Beasley-Murray, the "henceforth" of the KJV and RSV, and the "from now on" of the NRSV and NIV are all purposely vague; but certainty is implied following the Greek *(ap'arti/aparti)*.[117] More emphatically, however, it should be remembered that the entire concept of time within the Johannine Gospel is pointed to the decisive "hour" in the life of Jesus. That hour of Jesus' glorification/death-resurrection, from Johannine perspective, had arrived (cf. 12:23; also 17:1); and Jesus was seeking to make clear to his disciples that if they have really come to see and know him, they will have come to see and know the Father also.

14:8 The focus now moves to Philip, who has been introduced earlier at 1:43–48 as being from Bethsaida and who was responsible for bringing Nathaniel to Jesus. Then he appeared in 6:5–7 offering his logical deductions concerning the impossibility of feeding the multitude with more than half a year's wages. Next he is found in 12:20–22 at the entry into Jerusalem seeking to assist the Greeks in their endeavor to see Jesus. Practical Philip in the present context is portrayed as trying to make sense out of what must have seemed to him as Jesus' ethereal talk about himself and God. So he asked Jesus to get practical and show the disciples the Father. If Jesus did that, they could dispense with any further discussion on the subject.

Philip's words here are easy to understand because they represent the general human longing to gain a firsthand personal and practical confirmation of theological ideas and assertions. The problem is that he did not realize what he was asking. He asked to see the Father, to see God.[118] In several places the Old Testament indicates that people saw God, such as in Gen 24:9–11, where Moses, Aaron, and the leaders of Israel beheld God and ate and drank (cf. also texts like

---

[117] Beasley-Murray joins the two Greek words together and correctly emphasizes the certainty of the knowledge concerning God rather than concentrating on the sense of time involved in the statement (*John*, 243). It is not specificity of time but certainty of the fact that, I believe, is the focus of this statement, whatever English words one might use to convey the idea.

Isa 33:20); but for the most part Israel took seriously the dictum that "man shall not see me and live" (Exod 33:20). Accordingly, Gideon was quite convinced that he was in great danger because he had seen the angel of the Lord (who was identified with God), and he begged the angel not to leave him until he had prepared the appropriate offering (Judg 6:18). Likewise, Isaiah was sure he was in desperate straights of woe because in the Temple he had seen a vision merely of God's trailing gown (Isa 6:1–5).

14:9 The ill-informed response of Philip elicits from Jesus a rather sharp and yet somewhat sorrowful reply. How long must it take for these well-meaning but pathetic disciples (plural "you") to catch on to who Jesus was? The picture of the disciples in each of the Gospels is that of dull, slow-learning humans. We, of course, must be careful not to judge them too quickly because if we had been walking in their sandals, we might have been even slower in perception.

But the Gospels are clear that before the resurrection, the disciples had incredible difficulty imagining that Jesus could truly have been a divine-human agent of God.[119] Yet that should hardly surprise us because scholars and others even today continually debate the question of "Who is this Jesus?" Whether it was David Fredrich Strauss of the nineteenth century or the Jesus Seminar of the close of the twentieth century, the idea of Jesus being one with the Father is rationally a hard idea for humans to accept.[120]

---

[118] See the extended discussion of T. Korteweg, "The Reality of the Invisible: Some Remarks on St. John XIV 8 and Greek Philosophic Tradition," in *Studies in Hellenistic Religions* (Leiden: Brill, 1979), 50–102.

[119] See my earlier references in this commentary to Jesus as God's agent *(shaliach)* at 5:16–18. See also P. Borgen, "God's Agent in the Fourth Gospel," in *Religions in Antiquity* (Leiden: Brill, 1968), 137–48. But it is important to realize that Jesus is actually more than a mere *Shaliach* or agent as is evident in 14:10.

[120] Scholars seem to be continually seeking to discover a historical human Jesus between the lines of the Gospel texts. See the English versions of D. F. Strauss, *The Life of Jesus Critically Examined* (Philadelphia: Fortress, 1972); W. Wrede, *The Messianic Secret* (Philadelphia: Fortress, 1971); A. Schweitzer, *The Quest for the Historical Jesus* (New York: Macmillan, 1954); followed by J. M. Robinson, *A New Quest of the Historical Jesus* (London: SCM, 1959); and then the so-called third wave in J. D. Crossan, *The Historical Jesus* (San Francisco: Harper, 1991); R. Funk, R. W. Hoover and the Jesus Seminar, *The Five Gospels: The Search for the Authentic Words of Jesus* (New York: Macmillan, 1993); and R. Funk and the Jesus Seminar, *The Acts of Jesus: The Search for the Authentic Deeds of Jesus* (San Francisco: Harper, 1998). For responses see J. Green and M. Turner, eds., *Jesus of Nazareth: Lord and Christ* (Grand Rapids: Eerdmans, 1994); B. Witherington III, *The Jesus Quest: The Third Search for the Jew of Nazareth* (Downers Grove: IVP, 1995); M. Wilkins and J. Moreland, *Jesus Under Fire* (Grand Rapids: Zondervan, 1995); M. Borg and N. T. Wright, *The Meaning of Jesus: Two Visions* (San Francisco: Harper, 1999); and J. Charlesworth, "The Historical Jesus and Exegetical Theology," *PSB* 22 (2001): 45–63. With respect to the Fourth Gospel see the discussion in Haenchen, *John*, 2.125, who represents one form of the quest when he states: "The Jesus of the Gospel of John thus already speaks as the risen Christ, and thus already with the clarity that only the spirit of truth can give to the disciples." Moreover, he continues that the Jesus of this Gospel says "what the 'historical Jesus' cannot yet say." The clear split between the Jesus of history and the Christ of the confessing church is evident in Haenchen.

Moreover, we know that we should not expect to see God. Indeed, as was explained above, the people of Israel were clearly warned about the likely fatal consequences of seeing God. Nevertheless, many people have a strong desire for a direct contact with God. They long to have a confirmation of the reality of God. They want to "see" God. In beginning his first epistle, John clearly states that is exactly what happened in Jesus, and he asserted that literally when the early witnesses both saw and touched Jesus, they touched the reality of God, who was from the beginning (1 John 1:1–3). In responding here to Philip's plea to see the Father, Jesus emphatically states that seeing him (Jesus) is the equivalent of seeing the Father.[121] So, in effect, they already had their requested encounter standing in their very midst.

14:10–11 For the disciples to ask to see the Father in the presence of Jesus, therefore, must be regarded as an indication of a serious problem. What was the problem? Jesus here in John identified that problem as an issue of "believing" *(pisteuein)*. If Paul would have been writing here, he would undoubtedly have called it a problem of "faith" *(pistis)* (Rom 4:11–20; 14:23; 2 Cor 5:7; Gal 3:22–26). Accordingly, at this point in John, Jesus asks them a follow-up question (v. 10) and then challenges them (v. 11) to believe that he is "in the Father" and the Father is in him.

Schnackenburg categorizes this dual "in-ness" of Jesus and the Father as a "reciprocal formula of immanence."[122] This close interdependent assertion is an affirmation of a close unity between the Father and the Son without assuming that the unity implies absolute identity (cf. 10:38). But such interdependent unity is far more than a mere example of the rabbinic idea of agency, where the agent is an obedient servant/envoy of the master so that the servant acts as or becomes an alter ego of the master.[123] Jesus certainly fulfills this role of agency, but he is much more than a functioning servant. The reason is that between Jesus and the Father one soon realizes that the reciprocal "in-ness" represents a kind of interpenetration of natures. Still we must also stress that, for John, Jesus is said to be obedient to the Father and not the reverse (5:30; 8:29; 14:10; etc.).

Accordingly, the works/miracles that Jesus did are in reality the works of the Father, and here Jesus told the disciples that if they had difficulty believing his "words," they should believe because of his "works" *(erga)*. Jesus earlier offered this same pattern of testing his words by his works to the Jews, who were ready to stone him (cf. 10:37–38). But the stone throwers had already rejected works as a confirmation for or against what they considered to be heretical words (10:32). For the Johannine evangelist the

---

[121] See E. Haenchen, "Der Vater, der mich gesandt hat," *NTS* 8 (1963), particularly at 211–12.

[122] Schnackenburg, *St. John*, 3.69–70.

[123] For the rabbinic idea of agency see the Mishnah *Berk* 5:5–6 and the Babylonian Talmud *Qidd* 43a.

works of Jesus were signs pointing to the reality of who Jesus was (cf. 5:20; 9:3–4; 10:25).[124] As Carson indicates, the miracles "are nonverbal Christological signposts."[125] They are, from my view, hermeneutical acts that provide keys to understanding who this Jesus really was when he was on earth.

(3) The Power of Believing (14:12–14)

[12]I tell you the truth, anyone who has faith in me will do what I have been doing. He will do even greater things than these, because I am going to the Father. [13]And I will do whatever you ask in my name, so that the Son may bring glory to the Father. [14]You may ask me for anything in my name, and I will do it.

14:12–14 The appearance of these verses strikes the reader with incredible force. In the face of loneliness and Jesus' departure, the reader is confronted with another of the Johannine strategic double *amēn* sayings ("truly, truly"; NIV, "I tell you the truth"[126]) that must always be taken as important statements of Jesus. In this case the saying provides a significant window into the postresurrection situation. Even though the disciples here may have been overwhelmed by sorrow (cf. 16:20), they are called to focus on the future rather than the present because most of the verbs are in the future tense in this section. Moreover, to highlight the postresurrection perspective the opening words "anyone who has faith" imply that the announcement is intended for many more than the present little band of Jesus' sorrowing followers.[127]

The content of the announcement is even more striking because Jesus moves the attention of the Johannine readers away from his works as a test or confirmation of who he is/was to the fact that the believer(s) "will do" "those same" *(kakeinos)* works that he has been doing. But if that statement was not sufficiently electrifying, it is then said that the believer(s) will do "greater things" *(meizona)* than Jesus has been doing because of Jesus' departure to the Father. It does not take a genius to imagine how many interpretations of this statement are possible. It should be noted at the outset, however, that "greater" can hardly here mean that believers will do more dramatic works than the raising of Lazarus (11:43–44), the changing of water to wine (2:7–11), the walking on the Sea of Galilee (6:19), the multiplying of loaves and fish (6:9–14), or any of the other amazing acts of Jesus.

---

[124] For a further discussion of signs see Excursus 10 in the first volume of this commentary, Borchert, *John 1–11*, 346–48.

[125] See Carson, *John*, 495.

[126] The NIV rendering "I tell you the truth" is a fair attempt at emphasizing the oathlike nature of the double "truly" statements in English. But most English readers generally do not recognize the force of Semitic statements like this one.

[127] Cf. Beasley-Murray, *John*, 254, who also notes that the verses here are, in fact, a single sentence.

The meaning of the statement must therefore arise out of the context of the discussion involving the fact that Jesus is speaking of his departure to the Father, namely, his death and resurrection. If that is the case, then, the basis for the "greater" is rooted in the expansive implications of Jesus' mission in light of his "glorification" (cf. 17:1–2). Jesus' departure is in effect the work of the "Lamb of God" in taking away the "sin of the world" (1:29) or the fact that he is the "Savior of the World" (4:42). Accordingly, his death and subsequent resurrection are to be seen as drawing all people to himself (12:32). But strategically this work would also require the work of those who believe because their task would be to communicate to the world the forgiveness of sins (20:23).

The works founded upon the "going" of Jesus to the Father (14:12) can, therefore, only involve the post-Easter mission of the church. To gain some insight in this matter we turn briefly to Luke. In writing the introduction to his exciting Book of Acts, in which he details the powerful works involving the early Christians, Luke also reminds us of a similar crucial perspective.[128] In the introduction to Acts he asserted that the "former book," namely, the Gospel of Luke, detailed "all that Jesus began to do and teach" until his exaltation to heaven (Acts 1:1–2). The implication of the statement in Acts is *not* that Jesus ceased to work at that point but that Luke's second volume implied that *Jesus continued to work through* the early Christians. Accordingly, when Peter heals Aeneus, Peter says, "Jesus Christ heals you" (Acts 9:34). Moreover, when the pre-Christian Saul/Paul is on the way to persecute the Christians in Damascus and he is struck blind, he hears the voice saying, "Why do you persecute me?" When he asks who the voice is, the reply comes, "I am Jesus, whom you are persecuting." Saul was in fact persecuting Christians, but the voice identified the persecuted one as Jesus (Acts 9:1–5). The conclusion can only be that for Luke, Jesus was still active in mission; but although he was with God, he was now working in and through the church.

Although John does not express himself in the same way as Luke, there is a commonality of viewpoints. John's postresurrection perspective is enunciated in the words of Jesus to the disciples, "I will do whatever you ask in my name" (14:13). These words, as Brown argued, suggest a prayer context[129] because asking either God or the departed Jesus can hardly be accomplished in a face-to-face conversation. But the coordinating idea here with Luke is that Jesus continues to act, which is expressed in the future verb "I will do" *(poiēsō)*.

---

[128] Cf. the excellent treatments of Acts in J. Polhill, *Acts* (Nashville: Broadman & Holman, 1992), 78–80 and R. Longenecker, *The Acts of the Apostles* (Grand Rapids: Zondervan, 1981), 253.

[129] See R. Brown, *John*, 2.634–35, who provides a helpful discussion related to the prayer texts of both the Gospel and the First Epistle of John.

But even more significant is the implication of v. 14. The construction here is a conditional sentence, which is not fully evident in the NIV but is much clearer in the KJV, RSV, NSRV, and others. The setting is once again to be seen as referring to a pattern of prayer, and Jesus promises to act in response to prayer ("ask"). What is most intriguing is that the most likely reading of the Greek text here would have the prayer addressed not to the Father but to Jesus.

In dealing with this anomaly of praying to Jesus, some manuscripts simply omit the entire verse whether purposefully or accidentally. If it were accidental, it would be a variant of sight whereby the scribe's eye moved accidentally from *ean* ("if") of v. 14 to *ean* of v. 15.[130] If it were purposeful, the copyist may have considered the verse to be either inconsistent with the focus of asking in v. 14 or theologically inconsistent with a church tradition concerning the one to whom prayer should be addressed. The other variant in 14:14 is merely the deleting of the Greek *mē* ("me"), which would deal with the theological idea of praying to Jesus and assume the praying is to God. Both these variants, however, are suspect. The most likely reading of the text here that can explain the presence of the other readings and has the weight of the strongest manuscript history would be "if you ask me for anything in my name, I will do it."[131] Although such a translation seems to be both a little clumsy and at variance with the way systematic theologians might wish to discuss prayer from a theocentric perspective, the style is a typical Semitic redundancy that here has been applied to asking me in my name. Such a writing style of asking God for the sake of his name is found elsewhere in the Bible (cf. Pss 25:11; 31:3), and it agrees with the Johannine idea that the Holy Spirit will be sent in the name of Jesus (cf. 14:26).[132]

This meaning of the expression here of asking me in my name, as H. Bietenhard has suggested, probably means praying both "according to his will" and "with the invocation of his name."[133]

Excursus 16: John's Gospel on the Trinity

The fact that John can here speak of praying both to Jesus (14:14) and to the Father in Jesus' name (cf. 15:16 and 16:23) would not likely trouble this Gospel writer because he would clearly see an intertwining of the two ideas in his thinking about God (cf. 1:1 and 20:28). The problem for Western Christians is that we

---

[130] See Metzger, *Textual Commentary*, 244.

[131] Cf. Newman and Nida, *Translator's Handbook*, 464.

[132] Carson, *John*, 497–98, provides a perceptive note at this point that outlines the options for dealing with the variants here.

[133] For a discussion of asking in the name see H. Bietenhard, *TDNT*, especially at 5.276. See also F. G. Untergassmair, *Im Namen Jesus: Der namensbegriffe im Johannesevangelium* (Stuttgart: Herder & Herder, 1973), 125–28.

usually define things by mean of *distinction* whereas the Semitic mind defines things by *description* or in picture-thinking. The overlap of Jesus and God in the statements of John may trouble us, but John was apparently not troubled. Therefore the Semite had no trouble in his Trinitarian formulation of speaking of God as the one who is, was, and is to come, the Spirit as the seven spirits, and Jesus as the firstborn from the dead (Rev 1:4–5)—*and in that order.*[134] But we have come to speak of Father, Son, and Holy Spirit—*and in that order.*

There is a freedom in Johannine picture-thinking that irritates our mind-set and has led to a number of church arguments. For example, in the next section on the Holy Spirit the text of 14:16 reads, "I will ask the Father, and he will give you another Counselor [Paraclete]." This text has been used by the Western church to argue that the Holy Spirit must be the *third "persona"* of the Trinity and that the Holy Spirit must have proceeded from the Father and the Son. Accordingly, the Western creed reads "and the son" *(filioque).*[135] But the Eastern church has consistently argued that the *filioque* clause is totally unnecessary. The arguments over this expression have been intense with bishops deciding to excommunicate each other from their fellowships.

Although theological formulations are intensely important, one still has to wonder whether the argument was really worth it, especially since it could be argued that the pre-Chalcedonian formulation of the Trinity in Rev 1:4–5 might not fully support such precision, to say nothing of the fact that the order of the Trinitarian formulation in 1 Pet 1:2 is exactly the same as that in the opening words of Revelation.

Matthew's order of the Godhead is Father, Son, and Holy Spirit (28:19), but the fact that there are different patterns in the New Testament should warn us against an absolutist approach to the subject. The reality of the Godhead is clear. Yet there is no question that the early Christians were struggling to describe the relationship between the members or *persona* of what we today call the Trinity. So we must be exceedingly careful in our theological formulations not to treat some inspired biblical statements as illegitimate because they do not fit our Western style of formulations. We must always remember that God is bigger than our formulations, and we will never pour the ocean of God's truth into the teacups of our minds or completely encapsulate truth in our neat little formulations about God. On the other hand, it should not stop us from trying to describe this divine reality as long as we maintain our humility concerning our attempts at comprehending the incomprehensible (cf. Paul at Rom 11:33–36).

14:14 (Cont.)   Having thus introduced the intense feeling of loss by the disciples, John has in this final subsection sought to give his readers a sense of hope in the promise of the coming power that will be experienced through the believer's relationship to Jesus. But the invitation to pray for "anything" (14:14) in this context is not, in fact, to be understood as "any-

---

[134] Note also the order in 1 Pet 1:2 as Father, Spirit, and Jesus.

[135] For discussions concerning the *filioque* clause and Chalcedon see G. Borchert, "The Spirit and Salvation," *CTR* 3 (1988): 73.

thing" in the absolute sense because the guiding principle of the believer's prayer must be the same principle that Jesus followed throughout his life. That principle was the glorification of the Father in and through everything done by the Son (14:13). To read this promise of Jesus concerning asking in any other way would be a complete misunderstanding of the promise.

Jesus lived in the will of the Father, and the Christian is duty bound to live in the will of Jesus. Appropriate praying/asking here, therefore, must follow the same model Jesus exemplified.[136] Mere reciting of the name of Jesus must not be understood as a mantra of magical power that provides the petitioner with his heart's desire. A "name" in the Semitic context carries a special sense of the nature of the name bearer. Accordingly, from Adam and Eve through Abram/Abraham to Jacob/Israel and Joshua/Jesus, names are purposive designations of important realities. So to pray in the name of Jesus implies that in the praying one recognizes the nature of the name the praying person is using.[137]

In discussing the subject of prayer in this manner as a crucial aspect of the believer's reliance on divine power, the stage is thus set for the introduction of the next major section of the Farewell Cycle—namely, Part I of the texts related to the Paraclete, or the Holy Spirit.

3. The Role of the Spirit: The Divine Resource for the Community— Part I (14:15–31)[138]

As indicated in the introduction to the Farewell Cycle, John has designed this cycle in the form of a bull's-eye composed of wraparound concentric

---

[136] Cf. Paul in Phil 2:5–11, who spelled out in the well-known *kenosis* (emptying) passage the meaning of having the mind of Christ or following the model of Jesus. As he adopted this model of copying Christ, he called on his readers also to copy him (Phil 3:17). This latter idea may seem strange to us today, but Paul is hardly enamored with himself (3:7–8) because his focus is on Christ. When one's focus is "truly" on Christ, then one can invite others to copy the one who is so focused.

[137] In addition to Bietenhard's article in *TDNT* referred to above, see his discussion in *DNTT*, especially at 2.654. For further discussions on the significance of names see A. Key, "The Giving of Proper Names in the Old Testament," *JBL* 83 (1964): 55–59; J. Barr, "The Symbolism of Names in the Old Testament," *BJRL* 52 (1969–70): 11–29; G. von Rad, *Old Testament Theology* (New York: Harper & Row, 1962), 1:179–87 and 10–11.

[138] For examples of representative perspectives on these verses see M. Carrez, "Les Promesses du Paraclet," *EGT* 12 (1981): 323–32; G. Johnston, "The Spirit-Paraclete in the Gospel of John," *Perspectives* 9 (1968): 29–37 and *The Spirit-Paraclete in the Gospel of John*, SNTSMS 12 (Cambridge: University Press, 1970); A. Leaney, "The Johannine Paraclete and the Qumran Scrolls," in *John and the Dead Sea Scrolls* (New York: Crossroad, 1991), 38–61; F. Mussner, "Die johanneischen Parakletsprüche und die apostolische Tradition," *BZ* 5 (1961): 56–70; J. Painter, "Farewell Discourses," 532–34; J. Patrick, "The Promise of the Paraclete," *BibSac* 127 (1970): 333–45; I. de la Potterie, "The Paraclete," *BBB* 2 (1976): 120–40; F. Segovia, "The Love and Hatred of Jesus and Johannine Sectarianism," *CBQ* 43 (1981): 262–69 and *Farewell of the Word*, 93–116; and D. Wenham, "Spirit and Life: Some Reflections on Johannine Theology," *Themelios* 6 (1980): 4–8.

circles with chaps. 13 and 17 forming the outside ring. Then comes the prospect of Jesus' departure (14:1–14; 16:16–33), which forms the penultimate ring. The present section, 14:15–31, the first part of the inner ring dealing with the role of the Holy Spirit, comes immediately next to the center or core of the cycle.

(1) The First Spirit Statement: The Coming of the Paraclete (14:15–17)

[15]"If you love me, you will obey what I command. [16]And I will ask the Father, and he will give you another Counselor to be with you forever— [17]the Spirit of truth. The world cannot accept him, because it neither sees him nor knows him. But you know him, for he lives with you and will be in you.

The context of this section is clearly focused on the church and not on Christians as individuals, a common misreading of these verses. The "you" in English is plural. Moreover, these verses are not to be understood as a mere subjective personal experience of the Spirit by individuals. Nor should the emphasis fall on a "personal meaning" for the word "in" at 14:17. Further, the presence of the word "world" in this text is clearly the linguistic identification that the Christian community is here set over against the world.[139] Accordingly, the passages must be viewed as a sociological defensive expression of the church against the world.

My personal encounter with this passage was brought to a focus in high school when a professional football player met with me and my brother and tried to convince us that while we may have had the Spirit "with" us that now we needed to experience the Spirit "in" us (14:17). Accordingly, he tried to convince us that we needed to be filled with the Spirit. I later realized that this misunderstands the community context of this passage (as well as the filling of the Spirit). Moreover, when I researched the concept of "filled with the Spirit," I realized he had also completely misunderstood that idea as well. But I have written on that matter elsewhere.[140]

According to Islam, "another Paraclete" was none other than Moham-

---

[139] Cf. Malina and Rohrbaugh, *Social Science Commentary on John*, 231.

[140] See Borchert, "The Spirit and Salvation," 70–71. Briefly, the idea of "filled with" is a particular Lukan expression that applies to such matters as fear, awe, wrath, madness, wonder, wine, indignation, or envy (Luke 4:28; 5:26; 6:11; Acts 3:10; 5:17; 13:45; 19:29). A house can be filled (Acts 2:2), and Jerusalem can be filled (5:28). People, such as John the Baptist, Elizabeth, and Zechariah, were filled with the Holy Spirit, according to Luke, before Pentecost and even prior to the birth of Jesus (Luke 1:15,41,67). The expression is used elsewhere *only* in Eph 5:18, and it is not used in Johannine writings. Accordingly, the idea must not be imported into John. The expression is a Lukan word picture and is hardly to be understood as an indication of the amount of the Spirit one has. It is better today to think about the Spirit controlling a person or that a person is responding to the Spirit rather than that a person has somehow been "topped off" with the Spirit.

med, the spiritual messenger of Allah, who came after Jesus.[141] There is no biblical evidence, however, for this view, nor would a reasonable hermeneutic lead to this conclusion. Of course, the Paraclete is *not* Mohammed.

Other illustrations could be added to those above. Accordingly, it is imperative to take seriously the context of the passage as we turn to the study of these verses.

14:15 This section opens with the theme of love introduced in the opening chapter of the Farewell Cycle, but here it has a slightly different focus.[142] In the earlier new commandment to love (13:34–35), the focus was on loving one another, as Jesus loved them. That idea will be repeated in the core section of the bull's-eye at 15:12–13. But here the focus is shifted in the condition to loving Jesus, namely, "if you love me." To fulfill the condition, the text specifies "you will obey [or "keep"] what I command." Although there are several variants in the Greek at this point,[143] the impact of the verse really means that obedience is a test or indication of loving Jesus. A similar connection between loving God and keeping his commands is expounded in John's first epistle (1 John 5:2–3).

"Obey what I command" *[entolas]*' is not merely to be understood as obeying a series of ethical precepts or rules of morality. For John the "commands" (John 14:17,21), "my word" (14:23–24, *logos*, the NIV has "teach-

---

[141] The view of Islam is that Mohammed is the fulfillment of the expectation of the coming Paraclete. In "A Call to the Real Salvation" (pub. by Islamic Center of Boulder, Col., n.d.) the claim is made that "Jesus (peace be upon him) further uttered words in the Bible which supports our claim that our religion is in no way different with his when he prophesied in John 16:7–14 '... *the helper will not come to you;* but if I depart, I will send him to you ...'" And after the quotation of the Johannine text the commentary continues: "This point surely proves that Jesus' (peace be upon him) teaching was not yet complete, that there was somebody to come to finalize the revelation. He is not Paul, the enemy of Jesus (peace be upon him), nor the holy spirit as some Christians believe or were made to believe. He is Mohammed (peace be upon him), the only true prophet who came after Jesus (peace be upon him)." In contrast to this view, the Johannine picture is not that the Paraclete would bring new revelation but would "remind you of everything I have said to you" (14:26). Of course guidance into the future would bring new insights (16:13), but the text there is clear that the Spirit (note the presence of the word) would glorify Jesus, not some other person. The face of Islam in North America is rather irenic and conforms to the spirit of a democratic way of life. But in other parts of the world where Islam is in control and where there are clear alliances between Islam and government, Islam is very different. Anyone who abandons Islam for Christianity will likely be found dead.

[142] K. Tomoi has raised the following question: "Is not John xiv, 15 a Dislocation?" *ExpTim* 72.1 (1960): 31, but few scholars have followed his logic.

[143] This verb in the UBS Gk. text is future, which is supported by a few manuscripts like Vaticanus and L. Our variant option is the aorist subjunctive, which is supported by $\mathfrak{P}^{66}$, $\aleph$, and the queen of the cursives (33). The other possibility is the use here of the imperative "keep my commands," which is supported by Alexandrinus and the Western reading of D. See Metzger, *A Textual Commentary*, 245. Although the manuscript evidence is widely split and the reading is therefore somewhat in doubt, the future probably is correct.

ing" and "words"), and "my words" (14:24, the NIV has "teaching") are closely related and involve the entire scope of Jesus' teaching and revelation (cf. 8:31; 12:47,50; etc.). Segovia argues that the meaning is three sided, for it includes the elements of love, practical directives (though he really defines that in terms of loving one another), and "the whole of Jesus' teaching and revelation."[144] It is perhaps sufficient to say, however, that unlike Paul, who details specific patterns of action in his epistles, John in his Gospel leaves the definition of how one obeys Jesus as rather undefined except that the "commands," "word," or "words" are to be understood as modeled on the love of Jesus and his obedience to the Father (14:21; etc.). Even in his first epistle the concept of obedience is rather generally defined in terms of rejecting sin as an attachment to the devil (1 John 3:4–10), loving and caring for the brethren/community in deed and not merely in words so as not to be like Cain the murderer (3:11–18), and believing and confessing that Jesus is the Christ (4:2; 5:1; etc.). Thus, obeying Jesus' commands in effect means to copy the example of Jesus.

14:16 Although the reader may wonder what relation there is between the discussion of love and obedience and the announcement of Jesus praying for *another* Paraclete, there is for John a clear connection.[145] Jesus knew very well that the requirement of love and keeping his commands would necessitate a resource of divine proportions and accordingly he prayed that his followers would have "another" resource. It is, however, crucial to recognize that the gift of the Paraclete it not to be understood as some kind of *quid pro quo* between Jesus and his followers, as though the market exchange for the Holy Spirit was our obedience.[146] We do not earn the Holy Spirit anymore than we can earn our salvation. But in the process of responding to the Son of God we discover that Jesus has provided a divine agent to us for living in this world.

The term Paraclete *(paraklētos)*, rendered "comforter" in the KJV, "counselor" in the RSV, NIV, HCSB, and NLT, "helper" in the TEV and NKJV, and "advocate" in the NRSV, is a verbal adjective carrying a passive force.[147] It is derived from *parakalein* and has the same meaning as *ho parakeklēmenos,* the articular perfect participle that means "the one called

---

[144] Segovia, *Farewell of the Word*, 95.

[145] Cf. J. Rieger, "Spiritus Sanctus suum praeparat adventum (Jo 14, 16–17)," *VD* 43 (1965): 19–27.

[146] Carson states that the love in this section is "not to be seen as the price paid for this gift" (*John*, 499). Cf. Barrett, who speaks of the "consequence of the disciples' love ... will be their obedience. ... Christ for his part will obtain for them the gift of the Paraclete" (*St. John*, 385). This idea is appropriate as long as one does not understand the consequence to be a deserved gift. For the helpful contrast with the perspective of Qumran see R. Brown, "The Qumran Scrolls and the Johannine Gospel and Epistles," *CBQ* 17 (1955): 403–19 and 559–74.

[147] See Westcott, *John*, 2.189.

alongside." It was sometimes used within the Greek legal system, but in the Roman legal system the comparable Latin word *advocatus* became a technical term referring to a defense counsel.[148]

The term is only used by John in the New Testament and is similarly applied to Jesus in 1 John 2:1, where Jesus is said to be the Christian's Paraclete with the Father. Also by implication John may consider Jesus to be a Paraclete here at John 14:16 because the Spirit of truth is said to be "another" Paraclete. The only other uses of the term in the New Testament are in this Gospel and refer to the Holy Spirit (14:26; 15:26; 16:7).[149] The term does not appear in the Septuagint.

Although I will discuss the various roles of the Holy Spirit in John more at length in their individual contexts, several matters may be noted here. As J. Behm argued and whose view is followed by commentators,[150] the designation "comforter" in Wycliffe and the KJV is hardly an adequate translation for the term today. The meaning "helper" certainly would be applicable to part of the function of the Spirit, but it does not generally have a sufficiently encompassing meaning, and the term does not bring out the passive nature of the Greek word adequately. Moreover, this rendering could carry for readers the misleading implication that a human could be in charge of the relationship with the Spirit and the Spirit would then be demoted to the role of an assistant. The early idea of a legal "advocate" may have some relevance to 16:8–11, but the emphasis in that context is not a "defender's" role as over against God but in a "prosecutor's" role on behalf of God and Christian witnesses as over against the disobedient in the world.[151]

As a result of such problems with the various attempts at translating the Greek term, I prefer to use the transliterated form "Paraclete." Even though it might appear to some readers that I have sought to hide in the enclaves of academic language, for the present I have yet to find an adequate English linguistic equivalent that is not encumbered with unnecessary baggage in the meaning of the options that are available.

In the present verse the impending arrival of "another" *(allon)* Paraclete who would be with the disciples (Christians) "forever" is made possible because of the asking/praying of Jesus, the first Paraclete. The context, we should remember, is that Jesus had announced his imminent departure (14:2). Thus the picture presented in this context is that of a Paraclete who will function as a replacement and a strengthening companion who will be a kind of alter ego for Jesus. Jesus had been leading them, advising them,

---

[148] Cf. *BAGD*, 618; *TDNT*, 5.800–801.

[149] Cf. Morris, *John*, 587–89.

[150] *TDNT*, 5.804. Cf. Carson, *John*, 499; Morris, *John*, 576; etc.

[151] Cf. Barrett, *St. John*, 385. For a longer discussion on the issue of meaning see K. Grayston, "The Meaning of PARACLETOS," *JSNT* 13 (1981): 67–82.

teaching them, empowering them, and critiquing them. But his time with them would thereafter be limited, and his followers needed a new companion who could function in all those ways.

14:17　The Paraclete is here given an initial identification as the Spirit of truth.[152] Among the most important attributes of Jesus for John is that he speaks the truth and that he is the truth (1:14,17; 8:30,45–46; 14:6). Followers of both Jesus and God are thus expected to follow the truth (4:23–24; 8:32; 18:37; cf. 1 John 3:18–19; Rev 14:5). But the devil is categorized as a liar, and his nature is opposed to the truth (John 8:44). For John liars and lying are to be rejected (8:55; 1 John 1:10; 2:4,22; 5:10; Rev 21:8,27). The Paraclete therefore can be nothing other than an agent of truth.

That the world would not receive or recognize such an agent of truth should not be surprising because in John's ethical dualistic thinking the two realms are poles apart. The world *(kosmos),* as Bultmann has forcefully argued, "cannot receive the Spirit; to do so it would have to give up its essential nature, that which makes it the world."[153] The Johannine picture of the world here is thus basically composed of non-Christian and anti-Christian people.[154] The social context to which John is addressing his Gospel is clearly that of a community pressured by the world, and the anti-language in the words of Jesus here would strike a responsive cord within the little community, which would see itself over against the world.[155]

Although the world cannot "accept," "see," and "know" the Paraclete, the exact opposite is true of the disciples of Jesus. The reason is that the Paraclete *menei,* "lives" (NIV and NLT), "dwelleth"/"dwells" (KJV/RSV), or "abides" (NRSV) with them and will be in them.[156] The presence of the familiar Greek verb *menein* ("to remain or abide") signals a sense of a relationship that is not merely transitory. For example, in the core section of this Farewell Cycle the disciples are instructed emphatically to abide or stay in Jesus, the true Vine (15:4,5,7), as the basis for effective living. But here it is the Paraclete who is promised to do the abiding in the community.

As I indicated in the introduction to this section, there is confusion among some Christians concerning the statement that the Paraclete is "with you and shall be in you" (KJV). The Greek prepositions for "with" and "in"

---

[152] The idea of the "Spirit of Truth" was not foreign to the Jewish way of thinking but was clearly used at Qumran (cf. 1 QS 3:16–21 and elsewhere). Cf. Beasley-Murray, *John,* 257. I do not find Johnston's analysis, in which he dissects the term, to be convincing (*The Spirit-Paraclete,* 84).

[153] See Bultmann, *John,* 616.

[154] Cf. Haenchen, *John,* 2.126.

[155] For a discussion of antilanguage see Malina and Rohrbaugh, *Social Science Commentary,* 10–11.

[156] Contrast the views of J. Morgan-Wynne, "A Note on John 14.176," *BZ* 23 (1979): 93–96 and D. Woll, "Departure," 233–34.

at this point are *para* and *en*, and they suggest a solution to the problem of the unfortunate individualistic interpretation that is frequently espoused in Evangelical, Charismatic, and other Protestant circles. The primary meaning of *para* is "alongside of," which suggests that someone has been alongside of the disciples as a group. The one who has been alongside of the disciples must in the context here mean Jesus, as Westcott many years ago argued.[157] Jesus had been their Paraclete, and in him, John states, the Spirit lived (cf. 3:14).[158] Indeed, in Jesus the Spirit existed fully (not in measure). What, then, was to happen when Jesus departed? The Spirit was to dwell personally in the disciples and become their guide (16:13). This text is not about two ways the Spirit dwells "with" and "in" Christians like a two-stage salvation process, interpreted in an individualistic way of thinking as some well-meaning people have proposed.

Today the comparison between *para* and *en* might be likened to people who have experienced a living testimony by Christians or in Christian communities and have thus experienced the presence of God's Spirit alongside of them since the Spirit is in those Christians. But when they become Christians, they discover and recognize firsthand that presence of God in themselves and in their corporate Christian communities. The reason for the change is that they are no longer on the outside of the Christian reality, but they are now inside the reality of the community because the reality of the Spirit is now in them.

Jesus' promise to the disciples was that when he departed the Spirit of Truth would come to abide in them. What a great promise! And what a great fulfillment of that promise was experienced by the early Christians and continues to be a mark of genuine Christians today (cf. 1 John 3:2,13).

(2) The Postresurrection Coming of Jesus (14:18–24)

[18]I will not leave you as orphans; I will come to you. [19]Before long, the world will not see me anymore, but you will see me. Because I live, you also will live. [20]On that day you will realize that I am in my Father, and you are in me, and I am in you. [21]Whoever has my commands and obeys them, he is the one who loves me. He who loves me will be loved by my Father, and I too will love him and show myself to him."

[22]Then Judas (not Judas Iscariot) said, "But, Lord, why do you intend to show yourself to us and not to the world?"

[23]Jesus replied, "If anyone loves me, he will obey my teaching. My Father will love him, and we will come to him and make our home with him. [24]He who does not love me will not obey my teaching. These words you hear are not my own; they belong to the Father who sent me.

---

[157] Westcott, *John*, 2.177–78.

[158] "Another Paraclete" can only mean that the disciples already had a Paraclete, and that Paraclete logically could only be Jesus, with whom the disciples were at that point speaking.

14:18–19 The words of v. 18 summarize in a poignant way Jesus' dealing with the painful feelings of loneliness in the disciples. Perhaps the most appropriate way to paraphrase these words is: "I will not leave you to be orphans. I will presence myself [come] to you [pl.]."

Standing between John's first two Paraclete sayings (14:16,26), v. 18 has created considerable scholarly debate concerning its meaning. Some like Bultmann identify this "coming" as "the primitive expectation of the Parousia, precisely in the coming of the Spirit."[159] In this statement Bultmann thus merged the two "comings," which were generally proclaimed by the early church, namely, the coming of the Spirit and the ultimate coming or Parousia of Jesus. Such a view fits both Bultmann's existentialized Christianity and his deletion of the futuristic perspective in Christianity. The probability, however, is that the coming discussed here is neither the coming of the Spirit nor the Parousia. More likely the coming here is a reference to the Easter resurrection of Jesus.[160]

The reason for making this judgment is the force of vv. 19–20, particularly the "little while" (KJV, RSV, NRSV, NLT) or "before long" (NIV) are renderings of the Greek *eti mikron,* together with the statement that the disciples would see him but the world would not. Both seem to reflect an imminent event. Besides, the "me" must refer to Jesus' presence with them and not merely some spiritual experience. But since Bultmann could not conceive of a physical resurrection of Jesus, the statement must for him be made to reflect an Easter "spiritual" encounter with God that is then identified with the experience of the Spirit.[161] Although I would clearly reject the idea that this statement refers only to some spiritual experience of the disciples, I would agree with Hoskyns and Davey that the resurrection conditions the language here "but does not exhaust its meaning."[162]

The crucifixion was the event that would separate Jesus from both the disciples and the world in general ("not see me," 14:19). The resurrection, however, was the event that divided the disciples from the world; for while the world continued in their blindness, the disciples were able at that point to see him ("you will see me"). In commenting on this passage Morris suggests that John probably intended that "we should understand the saying to look right through the crucifixion to the resurrection."[163] Although such a statement could easily be misinterpreted as diminishing the significance of the crucifixion, no such meaning would surely be intended. Rather, John

---

[159] See Bultmann's statements in *John*, 617–18.

[160] Cf. the views of Beasley-Murray, *John*, 258; Carson, *John*, 501; Morris, *John*, 578–79; etc.

[161] See Bultmann's statement in "New Testament and Mythology," 38–43 for his view of the Easter "event."

[162] E. Hoskyns, *The Fourth Gospel* (London: Faber & Faber, 1954), 459. Cf. Barrett, *John*, 387.

[163] Morris, *John*, 579.

wrote his Gospel from a postresurrection perspective.[164] John's Gospel is not a blow-by-blow television broadcast. It is a carefully constructed testimony of the significance of the coming of Jesus, as his purpose statement declares (20:30–31).

Verse 19 concludes with a powerful promise of life for the disciples based on the life of Jesus. In spite of his forthcoming death, Jesus here proclaimed, "I live." The one whose very nature is life (1:4) and who in the *egō eimi* sayings identifies himself as "the bread of life" (6:35; cf. 6:51), "the resurrection and the life" (11:25), and "the way and the truth and the life" (14:6) is the one who is able to place death in its proper perspective (5:24; 8:51; 12:31–32). Death is certainly real. But the coming of Jesus to the world, his resurrection, and his eschatological coming are all part of the great Christian affirmation that Jesus lives; and because he lives, his followers "will also live." Moreover, the interconnection of living and believing was clearly enunciated in 11:26, where the promise to the believer was made that even though such a believer dies, he or she would, in fact, never die. Although such a statement may seem to sound like double-talk to some readers of the Gospel, the evangelist has undoubtedly given us at that point another example of double-level thinking.[165] Of course, Jesus really died in the crucifixion, as Christians die. But Jesus is life in this Gospel. Moreover, life is more than a biological reality for John. It is life that reaches beyond the physical experience of the grave. It is eternal life (3:16,36, etc.), and it is life that is not merely some "spiritual" existential experience. Such life is life possessed by God (1:4; 5:26) and given to believers (6:47,63; 10:28; 17:2–3).

14:20 The expression "on that day" might seem to refer to the eschatological "day of the Lord" as in Isa 2:11 and elsewhere, which in the New Testament would point to the Parousia. But the expression here must again refer to the resurrection event, although Jesus' resurrection can also be viewed as the inauguration of Christian eschatology. On that day Jesus indicated that the connection between the Father and himself would become clear ("known"/"realized"). The "inter-indwelling" of the Father and Son would serve as the pattern of the "inter-dwelling" of Jesus and his followers. Such reciprocal indwelling does not mean that both sets of the parties are fully equal, but the latter statement must be understood to be a picture of the closest possible relationship between Jesus and his followers without any hint of equality. As a result of the death and resurrection of Jesus, those who believe "have life" through him (20:31).

---

[164] Cf. G. Borchert, "The Resurrection Perspective in John: An Evangelical Summons," *RevExp* 85 (1988): 501–13.

[165] See my comments on that verse in *John 1–11*, 356.

14:21 But believing is not merely a matter of mental assent. Being related to Jesus implies obedience, as was enunciated in 14:15. The two articular participles here, *echōn* ("has") and *tērōn* ("keep" or "obey"), imply far more than having a list of Jesus' commandments so that one can recite them or lock them in a safety deposit box for safekeeping. To have them, as Barrett states, means "to grasp fully with the mind."[166] I would suggest that the two verbs taken together mean that the commands or the expectations of Jesus for his disciples are fully integrated into the way those disciples live. It is not a matter of following a few rules. It is a way of life. That is the reason the reference to "commands" here is tied so closely to loving Jesus.

The one who loves Jesus will also be loved by the Father. But this statement must not be interpreted to imply that a believer "earns" God's love through obedience. Because love is a mark of the relationship of the Father to the Son (3:35, etc.), it also means that a loving relationship of the believer to the Son naturally implies a loving relationship of the believer with the Father. Similarly, as the Son served and obeyed the Father (5:19; 8:28–29, etc.), the disciple's life is expected to be one of service and obedience to the Son, whose commands in turn are from the Father.

This verse concludes with the magnificent promise that Jesus not only will love such a disciple but will also "show" himself to that disciple. The quest of many people from Moses to the present has been to see God. The verb *emphanisō* ("I will show myself" or "make myself manifest") is, in fact, a promise that the disciples would experience a coming appearance of Jesus. The Septuagint version of Moses' petition uses a different form of the same verb *(emphanison)* when Moses prayed "show me yourself" (Exod 33:13,18).[167]

The Old Testament is replete with theophanies, but normally they are accompanied by a sense of fear, as in cases such as Gideon and Isaiah (cf. Judg 6:22; Isa 6:5). Although there is nothing mentioned concerning fear at this point, the context here is one of distress for the disciples. Also in the context of the resurrection appearance of Jesus at 20:19–23, the disciples were already in a state of terror for their lives (20:19). The presence of Jesus in these cases, therefore, is intended to calm their fears and not to raise their anxieties about encountering the power of God.

14:22 Judas then entered into this discussion. This Judas is not mentioned before. The Gospel writer apparently here wanted to make certain that the readers did not mistakenly think Judas Iscariot was still present

---

[166] Barrett, *St. John*, 388.
[167] Cf. Beasley-Murray, *John*, 259. R. Brown also notes a similar pattern suggested in *Wis* 1:2, where the Lord states that he "will reveal Himself to those who trust Him" (*John*, 2.646–47).

since he had been dismissed earlier (13:27). The identity of this Judas, however, is not certain.

H. Koester, relying on the Old Syriac version of the text, sought to identify this Judas with Thomas the Twin (Didymus), a so-called twin brother of Jesus, according to one tradition, and another suggests that he became an evangelist in Edessa. This linkage is also thought by some to be supported by the mention of Judas as a brother of Jesus in Mark 6:3 and who is perhaps the writer of the canonical Epistle of Jude.[168] But such a view, as Brown has argued, is pure speculation.[169] A Coptic (Sahidic) variant here suggests that this Judas was a Canaanite or Cananean, which may have been part of a theory that he was to be identified with Simon the Cananean (cf. Matt 10:4; Mark 3:18); but Luke designated this Simon in the list of disciples as a zealot and mentions a second Judas in his list as well (Luke 6:15–16). Other alternatives would identify him with Thaddeus (Matt 10:3; Mark 13:18) or the son of James (Luke 6:16; Acts 1:13).[170] My inclination, however, given the thin patterns of logic, is to declare all such attempts at identification, at least for the present, to be exercises in futility.

But the message of the text itself hardly suffers the same problem. The question of Judas is clearly that of a confused person. It is hardly likely that he was asking for Jesus to expound upon the aspects of the resurrection. How could he ask such a question when that idea would hardly have crossed his mind? Was he in this story then thinking about Jesus' coming theophany (the Greek is *emphanizein,* "to show" or "make manifest")? Probably not. But such a conclusion does not mean that the evangelist was unaware of the theophanic overtones in the statement.

Here again, I believe, is another example of double-level thinking with implications far beyond the mere seeing by the disciples and the not seeing by the world. Once again the counterlanguage of a social group that here was resisting further incorporation into the mores of the society at large can be seen in John's way of expressing the situation.[171] Is Judas's question not also that of persons struggling to understand who they are, of persons who want to be able to affirm themselves and their community experience over against those who reject their Lord? It was a difficult task for the early church to take a stand against society. But their Lord had shown them that his way was one of asserting countercultural perspectives. He died to communicate the will of God, and he was raised to vindicate that way. The dis-

---

[168] H. Koester, "GNOMAI DIAPHOROI: The Origin and Nature of Diversification in the History of Early Christianity," *HTR* 58 (1965): 279–318.

[169] See R. Brown, *John*, 2.641.

[170] Cf. Morris, *John*, 580.

[171] Actually much earlier Augustine in commenting on John thought that love is the reality that divides the saints from the rest of the world. See *In Johan Tract* 76.2 (*PL* 35.1831).

ciples would be enabled to realize that fact in seeing Jesus even though the world would not be given that opportunity. But for the moment Judas was confused.

14:23–24 So Jesus had to explain the situation again. The disciples were directed to love Jesus. But loving Jesus implies obedience to his "word" (*logon,* v. 23). Although some commentators seem to make a distinction between the singular use of "word" as teaching and "words" (*logous,* v. 24) as commandments,[172] the terms are for the most part interchangeable following the patterns established in the Old Testament for understanding the references to the Ten Commandments (decalogue) and the Torah as a whole (cf. Ps 119, especially at vv. 4,25,28).[173] But keeping Jesus' word is for John not a legalism. It is rather adopting a profound sense of obedient servanthood modeled on the servant pattern of the Son with the Father (John 5:19). Loving Jesus is therefore a commitment to the "way" of Jesus.

Because of the intimate interrelationship of the Son and the Father, an obedient, loving commitment to Jesus by the disciple is recognized by the Father loving the disciple (cf. 14:21). As a result, the promise is that the Godhead would come and make their home *(monēn)* with the disciple.[174] The theological implications of this statement are extremely profound.

Clearly, John saw a direct connection between the use of *monai* ("dwelling places") at 14:2 and the use of the same noun here. The question with which this chapter began was the anxiety created among the disciples by Jesus' declared departure. Fear of abandonment (14:18) was foremost in their minds, and the promise of heavenly dwelling places did not seem to alleviate earthbound fears. So at this point Jesus employs the dwelling place motif to indicate that the disciples themselves would shortly become a dwelling place for the divine Spirit.

One of the refrains of the Old Testament was the grace-filled theme that Yahweh would be Israel's God and Israel would be his people (Ezek 34:27). This theme was connected to the idea that God would dwell with them (cf. Ezek 37:27; Zech 2:10; etc.). This idea of God dwelling with them was portrayed for them realistically in the tabernacle, which contained the mercy seat and which traveled with the people during the Exodus (cf. Exod 25:8–9; 35:7–16; 40:1–38) but was later replaced by the stationary temple. John obviously loved that idea of God dwelling with his people because in the Prologue he pictured Jesus' incarnation as "tabernacling" or "tenting" *(eskēnōsen)* among them (1:14).[175] Moreover, that theme finds its eschato-

---

[172] Cf. Carson, *John,* 504.

[173] Cf. R. Brown, *John,* 2.641–42.

[174] Cf. Carrez, "Le Promesses," 323–32.

[175] See my earlier discussion in *John 1–11,* 118–20.

logical conclusion with the idea of "dwelling" in heaven (Rev 12:12; 21:3).

In addition, the idea of the "indwelling" of the Godhead in the postresurrection period naturally raises again the question of the relationship of this idea to the Paraclete theme in the whole section. Indeed, Augustine much earlier argued that "the God of the Trinity" was here in the mind of John so that the Father, Son and Holy Spirit "come to us as we come to them."[176] For John, who was writing many years after the resurrection and who lived in the Paraclete period, the interconnection of the Godhead would surely be assumed. But the key for him was the resurrection reality. In fact, it is crucial that in the resurrection John's picture is that Jesus both breathed on the disciples, like God breathed on the dirt that became Adam (Gen 2:7), and delivered to them the Holy Spirit (John 20:22). When the full message of John is thus understood, there is little room for interpreting with Bultmann and others that the resurrection of Jesus and the coming of the Spirit are merely some spiritual experience of Easter faith that has no room for an actual resurrection.[177]

(3) The Second Paraclete Statement: Interpreter of Jesus (14:25–31)

[25]"All this I have spoken while still with you. [26]But the Counselor, the Holy Spirit, whom the Father will send in my name, will teach you all things and will remind you of everything I have said to you. [27]Peace I leave with you; my peace I give you. I do not give to you as the world gives. Do not let your hearts be troubled and do not be afraid.

[28]"You heard me say, 'I am going away and I am coming back to you.' If you loved me, you would be glad that I am going to the Father, for the Father is greater than I. [29]I have told you now before it happens, so that when it does happen you will believe. [30]I will not speak with you much longer, for the prince of this world is coming. He has no hold on me, [31]but the world must learn that I love the Father and that I do exactly what my Father has commanded me.

"Come now; let us leave.

14:25 Having reflected on Jesus' departure and the implications of his resurrection coming in the previous section, John returned to the theme of the Paraclete. But the dull, dirgelike beat of Jesus' departure continues to echo here and throughout this Farewell Cycle. As this section opens, the focus is set on the statements or teachings of Jesus during the time he "remained" *(menōn)* "alongside of them" in his role of their first Paraclete/ teacher.

14:26 But this verse obviously indicates that that time was drawing to

---

[176] See Augustine, *In Johan Tract* 76.4 (*PL* 3.1833). For a further discussion of these verses as they pertain to the Trinity see R. Gruenler, *The Trinity in the Gospel of John* (Grand Rapids: Baker, 1986), particularly at 95–107.

[177] See my comments at 14:18–19.

a close and that a new era was about to begin—the era of the Spirit/ Paraclete. Although the full designation the "Holy Spirit" appears in many other parts of the New Testament, this is the only full use of the expression in the Farewell Cycle and only one of three uses in the entire Johannine corpus (cf. also John 1:33; 20:22; none in the epistles or Revelation).

The role of the Spirit in this context is spelled out as that of instructor/ teacher but clearly *not* in the sense of a replacement for Jesus.[178] Instead, the Spirit's role is more like that of a prompter, or one who brings to memory the ideas of Jesus that one should be able to recall. The theme of "memory" or "remembrance" is certainly one reason the Gospel was written, even though the words are not frequently employed in John (*hypomnēsei,* "remind," is used only here and *mimnēskesthai,* "remember," appears only at 2:17,22; 12:16).[179] This role of prompter/teacher is crucial for John because the task of the Holy Spirit could be said to be one of confirming and interpreting the message proclaimed and demonstrated by Jesus. In his first epistle John illustrates that role when he says that it is the Spirit of God in humans who confesses or "acknowledges that Jesus Christ has come in the flesh" (1 John 4:2). Indeed, in his introduction to the epistle John himself makes that very confession (1 John 1:1–4).

Just as Jesus insisted that his teaching was not his own but represented the teaching of God (cf. John 7:17,28; 8:28), so it is here asserted that the Spirit would interpret the teaching of Jesus. As Schnackenburg has said, "the Paraclete ... simply continues Jesus' revelation, not by providing new teachings, but only by taking what Jesus himself 'taught' to a deeper level."[180]

Throughout the Gospel, Jesus has repeatedly affirmed his dependence on the Father in that he was sent from the Father (e.g., 5:30). Here the double-dependent nature of the Spirit is asserted. In the first Paraclete passage Jesus promised to pray that the Father would send the Spirit (14:16); in the present verse it is said that the Father would send the Spirit in Jesus' name. As I have indicated at 1:12, referring to a name in such a manner actually implies referring to the person's full nature as evidenced in the way the Old Testament names are used.[181] Thus the references both here and at 14:16 actually speak of the intimacy or unitedness of the Father and the Son in their joint mission of sending the Paraclete.

F. Craddock, in his usual pithy manner, summarizes four realities he sees

---

[178] Despite some claims to the contrary, R. Brown (*John,* 2.653) does not say he considers the Spirit is a substitute for Jesus. For a more detailed treatment on substitute see Schnackenburg, *St. John,* 3.84 on "in my place."

[179] See the discussion of these words in Beasley-Murray, *John,* 261.

[180] Schnackenburg, *St. John,* 3.83.

[181] See Borchert, *John 1–11,* 117–18.

in this verse. First, he reminds us that the Spirit "is given not 'gotten.'" You cannot buy the Spirit either like Simon the magician (cf. Acts 8:18–19) or in contemporary "step-by-step instruction on how to get the Holy Spirit." Second and third, having the Spirit does not "qualify one to disregard or reject the historical Jesus" because the Spirit was sent in Jesus' name and because the Spirit will bring to remembrance what Jesus said. Contemporary experiential philosophies of "just me and God" are really empty shells. The fourth reality concerns teaching. "Now conditions and circumstances call for hearing" in a fresh way the message of Jesus because the old is also new and "indigenous to every time and place."[182]

14:27 Relying on the Semitic expression of Greeting and Farewell *(shalom)*, which had come to be associated with the key Aaronic benediction (Num 6:26) and Israel's messianic expectations (e.g., Isa 9:6–7; 52:7; 57:19; Ezek 37:26), Jesus offered his "farewell" to the disciples, but it is more than a farewell. It is Jesus' version of messianic hope for his followers because they lived in a world filled with frustration, anger, violence, and death.

The Roman Empire achieved its *pax Romana* of Augustus and his successors by the sword, but here Jesus proclaims a peace far different from the way of the world. As Hoskyns and Davey have succinctly stated, Jesus was proclaiming "the new order," which "is simply the peace of God in the world."[183] It was not like the cries of "peace, peace" by Israel when Jeremiah reminded them "there is no peace" (Jer 6:14). This peace was the gift of Jesus which would calm their troubled hearts and ease their fears of his departure. It is the peace that Christians would come to experience in the postresurrection era of the Spirit, when Paul could proclaim a peace of Christ Jesus that goes beyond all human understanding and guards believers "hearts and minds" (Phil 4:7).

14:28 The first part of this verse repeats the theme of Jesus' departure and return discussed earlier in vv. 3,18. But in this case it is expanded to include the statement that the disciples' love for Jesus should issue in their joy for him because he was going to the Father. Jesus' departure/death-resurrection was part of the great mission plan of God for the world, which is focused on the great "hour" to which the initial coming of Jesus had been directed (2:4; 12:23; 17:1). It is, however, difficult for human beings to focus their attention off of themselves and on to the purposes of God. But the disciples were about to discover that perspective very soon as they became witnesses to the central events in the history of the people of God.

The concluding statement of this verse, however, has often been

---

[182] F. Craddock, *John*, Knox Preaching Guides (Atlanta: John Knox Press, 1982), 112–13.

[183] Hoskyns and Davey, *The Fourth Gospel*, 461.

wrenched out of its context concerning John's repeated proclamation of Jesus as God's agent in this marvelous event of salvation history, and it has been made to stand on its own. Thus the Arians, the Gnostics, and their modern successors have used the statement "the Father is greater than I" to make a separation in the Godhead and minimize Jesus in relation to the ultimate God.[184] As I indicated in the discussion of the Prologue, Jesus was from the beginning directly associated with God (1:1) and certainly not merely "a god," as the Jehovah Witnesses have argued.[185] Moreover, he was active in the creation of all things (1:3).

If the disciples could believe that all things were really in the control of God, whom they acknowledge as ultimate, and if they realized that Jesus was intimately involved in carrying out the wishes of the Father, who was in control of working out their salvation even if Jesus died, they would come to realize that victory was assured in God, and he would raise his Son from the grave. John knew that for Jesus the issue was never one of who was in control—that was the role of the Father. But for John the issue of the full divinity of Jesus and his equality with the Father was also never in question—that was his presupposition (1:1), his constant refrain (5:18; 10:30; 17:21; cf. Phil 2:6), and the ultimate confession of one of the disciples (20:28).

14:29–31 As this section draws to a close, the foretelling power of Jesus is once again evidenced as it was in 13:19. In both cases the purpose of Jesus' foreknowledge is identified as a means to aid the disciples in believing. In the earlier case it was to help the disciples believe that Jesus was really the *egō eimi,* the self-designation of God. Here there was no need to add that objective because the entire section had been focused on the identity of Jesus in his relationship to the Father and to the Spirit/Paraclete.

So now that the farewell *shalom* had been issued with the promise of a new peace from Jesus and the time for speaking with them, as Jesus indicated, was coming to a conclusion, there still remained a matter that needed to be addressed. That matter involved the enemy, "the prince of this world." He was the *Satan,* the adversary, the dragon, the devil (Rev 20:2), the one who had been behind the death plot against Jesus and who had gained control of Judas Iscariot when Jesus gave Judas the so-called sop or bread crust of freedom (John 13:21,26–27,30). This prince of the world, Satan, would inspire the persecution of Christians (Rev 2:13) and instigate false belief patterns (1 Tim 5:15). But he is also the same one concerning whom Jesus

---

[184] For a discussion on these issues including functional subordination see, for example, R. Brown, *John*, 2.654–55 and C. K. Barrett, *Essays on John* (London: SPCK, 1982), 19–36; Carson, *John*, 507–8.

[185] Borchert, *John 1–11*, 102–4.

had earlier announced that he would be defeated by the arrival of that dirge-like beckoning hour of the crucifixion (John 12:23,31).[186]

Being prince of the world, the world was bound to follow him in crucifying Jesus. But as Paul in his incisive critique of the Corinthian partisan Christians commented, if the servant rulers of the world would have realized what they were doing, they would never have crucified Jesus, "the Lord of glory" (1 Cor 2:8). Or as C. S. Lewis aptly put it when the White Witch's servants killed the Lion King, Aslan, they may have understood part of the mystery that they could kill the king, but they never understood the deeper mystery that this lion king would, in fact, conquer through his death.[187]

Here John pointedly sums up the situation by stating that the prince of the world "has no hold on me" (NIV) or "has no power over me" (RSV, NRSV, NLT), literally "in me he has nothing" (14:30). Morris reflects concerning the meaning of this text that "in detail it is not easy to understand" but that the overall "sense is clear enough." He then argues that although sin gives Satan his controlling power, he cannot control Jesus because "there is no sin in Jesus."[188] These statements of Morris, I suppose, are basically acceptable.

But I suggest they are not very illuminating. It would be better to remember that John often uses Jewish legal or rabbinic-type arguments in much the same way that the Old Testament prophets argued their court cases with Israel. (Concerning John's pattern of argument cf. John 5; 6; 8; etc., in which one almost has the feeling of being in a synagogue listening to a rabbinic-type debate; note 6:59.) Here at 14:30–31 the focus of the statement concerns a face-off between the prince of the world and God's agent on earth, the typical good and evil confrontation. Many in the world, even in the church, capitulate to the worldly prince, but there is no way that God's agent would ever capitulate (cf. the temptation texts in Matt 4:1–11; Luke 4:1–13). How could Jesus win the battle with Satan if he capitulated? He had to win! He would not lose because Satan could not even get a toehold grip on him since Jesus did only what the Father commanded him to do (14:31). That statement is, in fact, a coup de grâce of the argument.

As a former lawyer, I would be tempted to say that the case argument stood complete except that John needed to reassert the mission rationale for this entire discussion. That rationale involved the fundamental reason for the coming of Jesus. Clearly the great Johannine theme is that God loved

---

[186] For a brief discussion of Satan see *BAGD*, 744–45. For a longer discussion see W. Foerster's article in *TDNT*, 7.151–63, and for his particular attention to "The Prince of This World in John's Gospel and the Johannine Epistles" see 162–63.

[187] See Lewis, *The Lion, the Witch and the Wardrobe*.

[188] Morris, *John*, 585.

the world (3:16), and here it is once again indicated that the world was Jesus' missiological concern. Even though he was one with God in making the world and in spite of the fact that it did not recognize him, he nevertheless came to enlighten that same world (1:9–10). Accordingly, for the people of the world to understand his mission, they would have to realize the servant love that the Son has for the Father. Not only are Father and Son united in the acts of creation but they also are fully united in the work of redemption and in sending the Paraclete to be the companion of those who know the great love of God.

So the argument of the case is complete, and with it this section of the Gospel is finished. It is therefore time to turn to a new section as Jesus adds, "Come now, let us leave" or "Rise, let us be going" (NRSV).

These concluding words remind the reader of the Gethsemane words of Jesus in Mark 14:42, and it would not be an understatement to say they have created a good deal of speculation on the part of scholars concerning the editorial state of the Gospel. How could Jesus tell the disciples to get up and then continue teaching through chaps. 15–17 of John before actually going forth across the Kidron Valley (18:1)?

A number of proposals have been made to deal with this issue. Bultmann attempted to solve the problem by rearranging the order of chaps. 13–17, placing chap. 14 just prior to chap. 18.[189] Brown solves the problem by having chaps. 13 and 14 take place in the upper room at the Last Supper and moving the remainder of the teaching to another site.[190] The traditional theory is that the words that follow in chaps. 15–17 were spoken while they were on their way, but Haenchen argues that such an idea is "not a realistic picture."[191] Morris suggests it is possible that the group probably was slow in making its departure and so Jesus continued to teach them in the room. But he prefers the proposal of Lightfoot that it is a "stage in the teaching."[192] Hoskyns and Davey think that the statement represents a pause in the discussion.[193] A number of commentators completely avoid discussing the issue.

Whatever solution one chooses, it also brings with it unresolved problems. The views proposing that the statement represents a seam in the work of a Johannine editor who inserted a section and forgot to remove the statement when he inserted three additional chapters may appeal to some readers as the preferred solution. But that makes the editor a forgetful collector of materials and destroys the symmetry of the Farewell Cycle. The view of

---

[189] For a brief overview of Bultmann's order see his index at *John*, x–xi.

[190] R. Brown, *John*, 2.652.

[191] Haenchen, *John 2*, 131.

[192] Morris, *John*, 586–87.

[193] Hoskyns and Davey, *The Fourth Gospel*, 464–65.

speaking en route offers a difficulty that a walking band is hardly a conducive setting for communicating major segments of teaching. Total rearrangement theories make the contemporary restructuring person wiser than the original writer and means that the present order is a purposeless collection of writings. However one seeks to solve the problem, I refuse to accept any theory that proposes that the logic of this tightly knit argument is to be disturbed by rearrangement.

4. The *Mashal* of the Vine and the Bull's-Eye of the Farewell Cycle (15:1–25)

As I indicated in the opening statement to the Farewell Cycle, this section forms the core of the literary bull's-eye that contains the crucial center of the third cycle of the Gospel. This core section is composed of three parts: (1) a *mashal* portraying Jesus as the Vine and the disciples as branches (15:1–11); (2) a set of thesis statements concerning the primary responsibility that the friends/disciples of Jesus have, all wrapped in an inclusio of the love command (15:12–17); and (3) another significant Johannine saddle or linking text dealing with the reaction of the world to Jesus and the disciples (15:18–25; cf. other such saddle texts at 2:12,23–25; 5:30; 6:14–15; 10:40–42; and see on the subject my introduction to chap. 12, which also functions as a saddle).[194] The saddle in this section (15:18–25) links the Vine *mashal* and the love inclusio on discipleship (15:1–17) with the next major section on the Paraclete (15:26–16:15) by providing the framework of suffering and persecution, which required God's divine resource of the Holy Spirit for the disciples.

(1) The Mashal of the Vine and the Branches: A Portrait of Discipleship (15:1–11)

[1]"I am the true vine, and my Father is the gardener. [2]He cuts off every branch in me that bears no fruit, while every branch that does bear fruit he prunes so that it will be even more fruitful. [3]You are already clean because of the word I have spoken to you. [4]Remain in me, and I will remain in you. No branch can bear

---

[194] As Beasley-Murray notes (*John*, 269), scholars are not agreed on the parameters of this section nor where the text divides. R. Brown (*John*, 265–66) divides the passage as 15:1–6,7–17 with a new section 15:18–16:11. Carson (*John*, 510–32) divides the text as 15:1–8, 9–16 and has a new section 15:17–16:4a. Bultmann (*John*, 529–48) divides the passage 15:1–8, 9–17 and has a new section 15:18–16:4a. Beasley-Murray (*John* 271–75) merely has 15:1–17 and 15:18–16:4a. Schnackenburg (*St. John*, 96–123) has 15:1–11,12–17,18–25,26–27; 16:1–4a and then begins a new section of 16:4b–33. Morris (*John*, 592–605) simply has 15:1–16,17–25 and begins the new section as 15:26–16:15. As should be evident, I find Schnackenburg's first three segments to be convincing, but I believe Morris is correct in identifying 15:26–16:15 as a new section on the Paraclete.

fruit by itself; it must remain in the vine. Neither can you bear fruit unless you remain in me.

[5]"I am the vine; you are the branches. If a man remains in me and I in him, he will bear much fruit; apart from me you can do nothing. [6]If anyone does not remain in me, he is like a branch that is thrown away and withers; such branches are picked up, thrown into the fire and burned. [7]If you remain in me and my words remain in you, ask whatever you wish, and it will be given you. [8]This is to my Father's glory, that you bear much fruit, showing yourselves to be my disciples.

[9]"As the Father has loved me, so have I loved you. Now remain in my love. [10]If you obey my commands, you will remain in my love, just as I have obeyed my Father's commands and remain in his love. [11]I have told you this so that my joy may be in you and that your joy may be complete.

As indicated in Excursus 9,[195] a *mashal* is a powerful symbolic or figurative vehicle for communicating in an extended parabolic manner an important message concerning Jesus. This Gospel contains two such *mashals:* the *mashal* of the Good Shepherd in chap. 10 and the *mashal* of the Vine here. Also, as I indicated earlier, I have chosen the term because of the impact of Jülicher's concern that a parable has only one point, a definition I definitely regard as too restrictive.[196] I also have avoided calling it an allegory for a number of reasons including the negative associations today with the idea of allegory. If the reader prefers to refer to this text as an extended metaphor, that also seems acceptable.[197]

15:1–2 This section of the bull's-eye opens with the crucial final set of *egō eimi*[198] sayings in John (cf. 15:5; note, however, 18:5–6). But in this verse the saying is a little different. Whereas the other "I am" sayings refer to Jesus, this one refers to both Jesus and the Father. One cannot help but sense that the close association repeatedly stated between Jesus and the Father in chap. 14 has had an important impact upon the appearance of this varied form of the saying in this core chapter. What is interesting to note is that after v. 2 the Father is not mentioned as intimately involved in the metaphor of the vine. Nevertheless, the Father, as the ultimate focus of glory and the ultimate source of the commandments, does reappear in the discussion at vv. 8 and 10.

In the course of commenting on the theme of the vine, scholars continually search for the background to this *mashal.* Relying on Schweizer,

---

[195] See my Excursus 9, *John 1–11*, 329.

[196] For an excellent discussion of parables see C. Blomberg, *Interpreting the Parables* (Downers Grove: InterVarsity, 1990).

[197] Borchert, *John 1–11*, 329.

[198] For an interesting discussion of this expression related to this text see E. Schweizer, *Ego Eimi* (Göttingen: Vandenhoeck & Ruprecht, 1939), 157–61.

Mannhardt, Käsemann, Schlier and others, Bultmann thinks he finds the background for this metaphor not in the Old Testament Jewish tradition but in the Mandean myth of the tree of life.[199] Dodd sees the roots of the "true" vine in the Greek notion of the perfect ideals as over against the defective copies of the phenomenal world.[200] Both of these suggestions, however, are scarcely appropriate bases for the present text and lack the more direct connection with its closer Jewish heritage.[201]

But is the *mashal* based in any similar Jewish metaphors? The answer is that there are related ideas concerning the image of the vine, but the focus of this core *mashal* is really quite different. In the Old Testament the vine is frequently used as a symbol for Israel (e.g., Ps 80:8–9; Isa 27:2–6; Hos 10:1; etc.). Yet it is usually employed as a symbol of a disobedient Israel (Ezek 17:6–10) that has become wild (Jer 2:21) and dried up. It will therefore be burned with fire (Ezek 15:1–8; 19:10–14) because it is ripe for judgment (Isa 5:1–7). In the Old Testament texts, therefore, if Israel is the vine or the vineyard, then the Lord God is viewed as the vinedresser or gardener (cf. Isa 27:2–6). But what is totally different in the Johannine *mashal* is the role of Jesus and the disciples. In this metaphorical description the Father is still portrayed as the gardener, but Jesus is the Vine, not Israel, and the disciples, the followers of the way of God, are pictured as branches.[202] It is as though there has been an insertion into the old image that changes it radically. The "vine" in this *mashal* is hardly in any danger of judgment as in the Old Testament texts. That possible scenario is ascribed only to the branches. Jesus, the Vine, appears to stand between the vineyard keeper/gardener and the branches as a kind of "mediator" of life and sustenance.

In post-Old Testament Jewish writings the identification of the vine with Israel continued,[203] and Josephus reported that one of the significant items that adorned the Second Temple was a tall, golden cluster of grapes.[204] This ornament in the Temple has been a traditional symbol of the land of Israel, which had its roots in the report of the spies who were sent to evaluate the land. Although they brought back a huge cluster of grapes that had to be carried on a pole between two men, the pleas of Joshua and Caleb could not convince the majority to take the land (cf. Deut 13:17–14:10).

---

[199] Bultmann, *John*, 530–31.

[200] Dodd, *Interpretation*, 139. Dodd considers the concept of "time" to be borrowed from Platonic philosophy via Aristotle and sees a similar archetypal Man in Philo.

[201] See the discussion in B. Witherington III, *John's Wisdom* (Louisville: Westminster/John Knox, 1995), 255–56; R. Brown, *John*, 2.669–72 and A. Jaubert, "L'image de la Vigne (Jean 15)," in *Oikonomia*, ed. F. Christ (Hamburg: Reich, 1967), 93–99.

[202] There is in Ps 80:17 an interesting reference to man/son of man in the Hebrew poetic synonymous parallelism that is likely a reference to Israel.

[203] For further references see *Str–B*, 2.563–64.

[204] See Josephus, *Antiquities*, 15.11.3 and *Wars*, 5.5.4.

It is also fascinating that in *Sirach* (*Sir* 24:17–21) Wisdom is portrayed as a vine, but then in v. 23 Wisdom is also identified with Torah. So the metaphor is very different. In the Synoptic Gospels, Jesus uses the vine and vineyard in his parables, but none of them have the focus of Jesus as the Vine (cf. Matt 20:1–16; 21:33–46; Luke 13:6–9). This idea seems to be unique to this Johannine bull's-eye.

Following the repeated statements concerning the relationship of the Son to the Father in John 14, the designation of the Father as the gardener and Jesus as the vine (15:1) reaffirms the functional (not essential) subordination of the Son to the Father. Moreover, the role of the Father in 15:2 is that of a master gardener who is responsible for removing/trimming/cleansing the branches, both positively and negatively.

Although some commentators want to debate the issue of the status of the branches that were cut away and whether or not they were originally attached and nourished branches,[205] I would suggest that the key to interpreting this *mashal* does not lie so much in the question of status as it does in the issue of fruitfulness. The *mashal* here sets the fruitfulness of Christians as a test of belonging in the Vine. It is very likely that in the Johannine churches there were a number of people who were identified as Christians but who were not bearing fruit. The problem has only escalated in the years since that time. Sociologically speaking, the question is what constitutes the boundaries of the community?[206] That issue was a high priority matter for the evangelist.

The task of the master gardener, therefore, was one of distinguishing between productive and unproductive branches and dealing appropriately with them in both cases. The unproductive branches are eliminated/taken away/removed *(airei)* while the productive branches are cleansed/pruned *(kathairei)* so that they will become more productive.[207] The church in its humanity has generally had difficulty dealing with lack of productivity in disciples. The main reason is that it lacks the wisdom and purposiveness of God. But more importantly, it is God who does the pruning and removal. Yet the church does not usually wish removal to take place because of its attachment to numerical size and a worldly sense of what is important. In other words, the boundaries of the church have often become fuzzy today and almost nonexistent. That is not the case in some parts of the world, where it can be very costly to be a Christian—one's life can be at stake. In those places the boundary lines are much clearer.

---

[205] Contrast two opposite views in Witherington, *John's Wisdom*, 258 and Carson, *John*, 515.

[206] Cf. Malina and Rohrbaugh, *Social Science Commentary*, 233–34.

[207] For insights concerning the translations of these two verbs see *BAGD*, 24 and 386–87. The latter term is not used elsewhere in the NT. See also Newman and Nida, *Translator's Handbook*, 479–80 for an excellent differentiation between the verbs.

The question of the meaning of fruitful and unfruitful is also important. Today it is often understood primarily as how many "testimonies" can be made and how many commitment cards can be signed. For some who eschew evangelism it amounts to how consistent is one's life in caring for others. But these alternatives would have been completely foreign to Jesus, who taught and healed and who forgave sins and fed the multitude.[208] They would also have been an unreal dichotomy for John, who called readers to believe (20:30–31) and to love others as a mark of being intimately united with a genuinely loving God (1 John 4:7–8,20–21).

Accordingly, the "true" Vine, who is pictured here as steadfast and authentic,[209] expects his followers to be truly fruitful in communicating the authentic message and life to the inauthentic and hostile world.

The metaphor as described in this core passage is certainly a reflection of vineyard care in the ancient Semitic culture of the Bible lands. Even today it is intriguing to watch the vine dressers stooping over the little plants on the terraced hills of Israel. The reader of this *mashal* is quickly drawn into the picture of the involvement of both the Father and Jesus with the little twigs, just as they are concerned for their erring and developing children. But the preacher of this text is appropriately warned by Craddock not to overexplain the picture and "insult the intelligence" of listeners.[210]

15:3 Schnackenburg considers this third verse to be a gloss unrelated to the basic metaphor of the vine since it "does not come within the framework of … 'bearing fruit.'"[211] But rather than adopting this approach it seems better to recognize a transition here so that after the general opening statements of 15:1–2, which use the "first" and "third" persons in the metaphor, this verse moves to employ the second person and thus to address listeners and readers directly. Accordingly, this verse and others following serve not only as assurance texts but also as warning texts.[212] This transition to direct address in the bull's-eye was undoubtedly facilitated by the word *kathairei* ("he cleanses" and by implication "prunes") in the previous verse.

Those being addressed ("you," pl.) in this verse as the "cleansed" or "pure" ones *(katharoi)*[213] should be assumed to be the fruitful/cleansed/

---

[208] See G. Borchert, *The Dynamics of Evangelism* (Waco: Word, 1976), 20.

[209] The Hebrew background for the use of the word "truth" in the NT as G. Quell has noted is "firm" or "solid." See *TDNT* 1.232–33. For additional insights into the idea of the "true" Vine see D. Stanley, "I Am the 'Genuine Vine' John 15:1," *TBT* 1 (1963): 484–91; F. Wulf, "Ich bin der wahre Weinstock (Jo 15:1) Anleitung zur Meditation über die Selbstaussagen Jesu," *Geist und Leben* 30 (1957): 301–6, as well as J. Radermakers, "Je suis la vraie vigne. Jn 15, 1–8," *Assemblees du Seigneur* 26 (1973): 46–58.

[210] F. Craddock, *John* (Atlanta: John Knox, 1982), 114.

[211] Schnackenburg, *St. John*, 3.95.

[212] Cf. G. Borchert, *Assurance and Warning* (Nashville: Broadman, 1987), 129–31.

[213] See *BAGD*, 388.

pruned ones of the previous verse. Sociologically they are those of the faithful community who are to be contrasted with those of the world. But more significantly, they are also to be contrasted with those who have been severed from the Vine like the so-called apostates of the first epistle (1 John 2:19).[214]

The cleansing here is said to be "because of the word I have spoken to you." Bultmann, who during his life was an unbending advocate of faith, employed the present verse to texts like 13:10 of the foot washing scene and insisted that cleansing does not come by washing, including baptism, but by faith. Moreover, he likewise insisted that the "word" here does not refer to mere doctrine separated from the Jesus whom the disciples encountered.[215] Many nonsacramentalists will find this idea of Bultmann to be appealing, yet they may not relish his idea of who Jesus was. Others may find his nonsacramentalism to be highly one-sided. But one must remember that he was striking against faithless forms in the church. Koester's nonsacramental view of this text is certainly more balanced.[216]

But in the context of this passage it seems likely that the concept of the cleansing work of Jesus here does not refer to any particular words or commandments of Jesus but to his overall teaching concerning himself and salvation (cf. 14:24,26), much like the evangelist views his own writing in the purpose statement at 20:30–31.

15:4 In moving to this verse the evangelist returns to one of his basic themes, that of "remaining," "abiding," or "dwelling" (*meinate* here is the aorist imperative), which he emphasized in the previous chapter. Just as the Father abides/dwells in Jesus (14:10) and the Paraclete would abide in them (14:17), so they are commanded as his disciples to abide in the Vine. R. Boring has perceptively noted that this interabiding is a fundamental idea in Johannine thinking.[217] A branch is not a self-contained entity, and neither is the Christian disciple. And as a branch separated from the supply of nourishment cannot produce fruit, neither can the Christian. Fruit bearing for the disciple is totally dependent on a direct connection to Jesus.[218] Attachment to Jesus or abiding in him is, therefore, the *sine quo non* of Christian discipleship.

But there can be a slight problem with this verse because although the initial clause contains the verb *meinate* ("remain in me"), the follow-up

---

[214] D. Hawkin, "Orthodoxy and Heresy in John 10:1–21 and 15:1–17," *EvQ* 47 (1975): 208–13.

[215] See Bultmann, *John*, 470–72. Contrast R. Stewart, "Engrafting: A Study in New Testament Symbolism and Baptismal Application," *EvQ* 50 (1978): 8–22.

[216] See C. Koester, *Symbolism in the Fourth Gospel* (Minneapolis: Fortress, 1995), 244–46 for a more holistic interpretation of this text as well as that of the footwashing.

[217] R. Boring, *Der wahre Weinstock* (München: Kösel, 1967), 44–46.

[218] Cf. H. Bussche, "La Vigne et ses fruits (Jean 15, 1–8), *BVC* 26 (1959): 12–18.

clause contains no Greek verb (lit., "and I in you"). Therefore interpreters are left to imply what is meant. The NIV and NLT have "and I will remain in you." This idea appears to be a promise of Jesus' presence dependent on or conditioned on the action of the disciples, namely, their consistency. Such a rendering is not impossible and might be the intended sense. Yet one cannot be sure about the Greek grammar pattern here. If, however, a parallelism is implied, that would mean that Jesus would be commanding the vine to abide or remain in the branches. But this option seems more remote. The KJV and RSV do not supply a verb and leave it to the reader to interpret the meaning. The NRSV (see also NAB, REB, NJB) has "as I abide in you," which suggests that Jesus is the model for the disciples' abiding. The problem with this view is that this clause is immediately followed by *kathōs,* meaning "just as," and that sense of the double "as" seems to be less likely. Thus the first option seems to carry the balance of probabilities, but one cannot be certain. Morris attempts a paraphrase: "Abide in me, and see that I abide in you,"[219] which is not an impossible implication of the Johannine shorthand.

This verse concludes with the absolute connection between fruit bearing and abiding in the Vine. Failure to abide in the Vine cannot help but lead to failure in fruit bearing. Independence of the branches from the Vine (disciples from Jesus) necessarily means becoming fruitless. Moreover, that directive is not merely a general statement. It is addressed pointedly to the readers/disciples (*hymeis,* "you" pl.), and the remaining "in me" (cf. the Pauline idea of "in Christ") is set as the clear prerequisite to acceptable discipleship.

15:5 The reader may regard this metaphorical statement/*mashal* to be rather redundant. But the evangelist was not bothered by redundancy. He was obviously concerned that the reader recognize a core point in discipleship. That point is an age-old issue of identity that goes back to the story of the Garden of Eden, wherein the humans were tempted by the desire to become like God (Gen 3:5). The evangelist obviously did not want there to be any confusion over the issue of identity. The branches were not to be confused with the Vine, and the Vine was to be regarded as very different from the branches. The use of the Greek *egō eimi* ("I am") is undoubtedly purposeful here and is certainly to be contrasted with the pronoun *hymeis* ("you," pl.). Jesus, the one who at 20:28 will be confessed as Lord and God, is clearly to be considered as very different in essence from the disciples who are here being addressed. This identity contrast is often overlooked by commentators and preachers.

But it is the identity issue that is fundamental to the additional seeming

---

[219] Morris, *John,* 595.

redundancy concerning fruitfulness or lack thereof in this verse. The mutual abiding in Jesus, the "I am," and he (the "I") in the disciple(s) means that a disciple must be attached to the divine source in order for fruit bearing to occur. It also explains why the opposite to abiding and bearing fruit is here designated as accomplishing "nothing" *(ouden)*. The radicality of the Johannine Gospel should not be missed by familiarity with its words. Nothing is "not something" in the judgment of Jesus. It is still nothing. Such a verdict is not very popular, but it is central to this bull's-eye text.

15:6 The downside of the *mashal* here reaches its epitome. Failure to produce fruit brings a severe warning concerning the certain end of unfruitfulness. Employing the indefinite pronoun *tis* ("anyone, someone"), the evangelist separates any unfruitful person from the faithful, persevering, fruitful disciples/branches and indicates that such a person is thrown away and withers. The verbs here are in the aorist indicative. These aorists here are not primarily used in a chronological sense but as Newman and Nida have indicated, they are either used to indicate certainty of action or customary action (the gnomic sense).[220] It is almost as though the evangelist is treating unfruitfulness, either present or future, as already resolved.

Several questions may emerge from this statement: (1) Who does the handling of these unfruitful branches? Although it is not stated in this verse, the reader is likely to imply from v. 2 that it is the work of the gardener/father. (2) Does this verse refer to Judas Iscariot? The early Christians could hardly not have thought of Judas when reviewing this verse. But the application is hardly to be restricted only to Judas. Then (3) the lingering question may be: does this verse about the thrown out, withered, and finally burned up branches refer to the eschatological judgment scene? This question is a little more involved.

There is no doubt that the image of burning the dried branches is a judgment motif that goes back to the Old Testament including the plagues of Egypt (Exod 9:23) and the cities and disobedient people who are burned (Lev 10:2; Num 26:10; Deut 10:21; 12:3; Josh 6:24; 8:19; 1 Sam 30:1–3). God's anger is linked to fire (Deut 32:22), and fire is often used as a symbol of judgment both in the Old Testament (Ps 11:6; Jer 4:4; etc.) and the New (Matt 3:12; 5:22; 13:40–42; Mark 9:47; etc.). And, of course, fire is repeatedly used in the judgment scenes of Revelation (Rev 8:7–8; 11:5; 14:10; 16:8; 18:8; 19:20; 20:9–10,14–15; 21:8). But Beasley-Murray, who wrote a great deal on eschatological subjects, made a special point of stating that readers should not jump to the conclusion that fire here symbolizes the "judgment of Gehenna."[221] I would add that it is unnecessary to restrict

---

[220] Newman and Nida, *Translator's Handbook*, 482–83. Cf. also Carson, *John*, 519.

[221] Beasley-Murray, *John*, 273.

judgment here to the final cataclysmic events of the world. The *mashal* is a picture, and this verse is a vivid portrait of the significance of fruitless vine branches. Unlike olive wood, the cuttings of the vineyard are good for nothing except burning. That was the judgment of Ezekiel when he likened Jerusalem to fruitless vines (Ezek 15:1–6), and that is the judgment of fruitless disciples in this core metaphorical picture of John.

15:7 Although Brown begins a new subdivision at this point, the implications of the vine imagery are drawn out more fully through v. 11.[222] The focus of the present verse continues the theme of abiding or remaining in Jesus, the Vine, but that theme is here linked to the subject of prayer, which was discussed at 14:13–14 (cf. also 15:16; 16:23–24). The way of stating the "asking" is phrased differently in the previous chapter, but the actual implications are quite similar. Here it is unnecessary for a repetition of the discussion on asking "in my name" because if one is abiding in Jesus, it would be virtually impossible to pray in any other way than that of representing the nature of Jesus.[223]

Moreover, the condition is not only that of abiding in Jesus but also of his words *(rēmata)* abiding in his followers. As Westcott pointedly states, the "petitions of the true disciples are echoes (so to speak) of" the words of Jesus because his teaching is "transformed into a supplication, and so it will be necessarily heard."[224] There is a direct connection between how one prays and the primary commitments of one's life. Jesus in this core *mashal* demands that the fundamental commitment of a disciple's life is abiding in him.[225] That means that the model of Jesus in life and word must permeate the life and words of the disciple. When this happens, praying ceases to be selfish asking and becomes aligned with the will and purposes of God in Christ.

15:8 At this point the twofold purpose or result of fruit bearing is specifically articulated. In the first place, the verse begins literally "By this my Father is glorified." The aorist passive here probably is similar to the uses of the aorist in the previous verse. It emphasizes either the certainty or customariness of an action (here glorification). The NIV has restructured the statement.

In the Johannine Gospel the verb *doxazein* ("to glorify") is usually employed in two ways: to refer to the hour of Jesus' glorification (namely, his death and resurrection) and its result, the Father's glorification in the

---

[222] R. Brown, *John*, 2.679. Although Brown ends the *mashal* at v. 6, he entitles the new subdivision that begins at v. 7 as "Development of the *Mashal* in the Context of the Last Discourse."

[223] See the discussion in chap. 14 and the views of F. Untergasmair, "Im Namen Jesu," 140–46.

[224] Westcott, *St. John*, 2.201.

[225] For the relationship of Jesus' words to the idea of commands or law see S. Pancaro, *The Law in the Fourth Gospel* (Leiden: Brill, 1975), 414–20.

Son (7:39; 8:54; 11:4; 12:16,23,28; 13:31–32; 14:13; 16:14; 17:1, 4–5). But here the Father is glorified through the disciples. This text, however, must not be understood as implying that the disciples glorify the Father directly as the result of their own actions. It is because they abide in Jesus, the Vine, and are obedient to him in the bearing of fruit that they bring glory to the Father.[226] This derivative relationship of the disciples to the Father is a significant point in this bull's-eye *mashal*. The primary task of the disciple is to glorify Jesus (cf. 17:10; 21:19), who glorifies the Father. This bearing of fruit, therefore, not only indicates that the followers are true disciples *(mathētai)* of Jesus but also that God is glorified in their discipleship.

15:9   In this verse the focus turns again so that the theme of abiding merges into the crucial Johannine theme of love. Here some of the elements of the circle of love are enunciated. They are as follows: the Father loves the Son (cf. 3:35; 17:23), and the Son obediently loves the Father (cf. 10:17; 14:31); the Son loves his followers, and they are to love and obey him (cf. 13:34; 14:15,23); loving and obeying the Son means being loved by the Father (cf. 14:21,23; 17:23); being loved by the Son also implies loving one another (cf. 13:34; 15:12,17); God not only loves the disciples but loves the world and gave his Son for its people (cf. 3:16); but many in the world love darkness and do not do the will of God (cf. 3:19; 14:24). In his first epistle John carries the theme of love further and insists that the disciple must not love in words only but in actual deeds of love (cf. 1 John 3:18) and that hating one's brother is actually an indication of not loving God (cf. 3:15) because love is the sign of knowing God (cf. 4:7).

Bearing fruit therefore means loving others as God loves them and giving witness to the world.[227] Such fruit bearing is possible only by abiding in Jesus, the Vine.

15:10   In 14:15 it was said that loving Jesus would result in obeying or keeping *(tērēsete)* his commands *(entolas,* cf. 14:21; and "word," *logos,* 14:23). But in the present text the order is completely reversed. Accordingly, here obeying/keeping his commands results in abiding in Jesus' love. The only natural conclusion from these virtually reversible statements, therefore, is that they are so interrelated and inseparable that you cannot have one without the other. Moreover, once again the relationship of the disciple to Jesus in terms of obedience and love is modeled on the relationship of the Son to the Father.

15:11   Ridderbos correctly categorizes this verse as simultaneously a

---

[226] Cf. C. Barth, "Bible Study IV. The Disciples of the Servant. John 15:1–11," *SEAJT* 6 (1965): 7 and 7 (1965): 14–16.

[227] Cf. Witherington, *John's Wisdom,* 257.

recapitulation and a climax.[228] As this core *mashal* comes to its final stage, it focuses our attention on a wonderful capstone promise of joy. Obedience, love, fruit bearing, being pruned could all be viewed as rather painful and demanding ideas that scarcely suggest excitement or desirability. But that is hardly the goal of the *mashal*. The purpose of abiding in the vine is to provide the sense of delight to those who are authentic disciples of Jesus, even though they may face pain or persecution.

The noun for joy *(chara)* has been used only once in the Gospel prior to this verse, and that was in the Baptizer's metaphor of the bridegroom (3:29). But from this point forward in the Farewell Cycle it appears at 16:20,21,23,24; 17:13. The verb *chairein* ("rejoice"), however, was used four times prior to the Farewell Cycle: in the bridegroom text (3:29), the harvest metaphor (4:36), the expectation of Abraham (8:56), and Jesus' statement concerning Lazarus (11:15), all of which except the Lazarus text are metaphors pointing to the meaning of the coming of Jesus. The verb appears twice in the Farewell Cycle at 14:28 and 16:20. Besides this present verse, all the uses of the noun and the verb concerning the theme of joy in the Farewell Cycle are directly focused on Jesus' departure from the world and his desire to provide his beloved followers with a sense that they must not fear the future but rejoice in what is being done through him. They must look beyond their anxieties.

Accordingly, it could be legitimately concluded that one of the major purposes of the Farewell Cycle and particularly of this core *mashal* is to help Christian readers glimpse the perspective of God concerning the death/departure of Jesus and thus to view their own pain in light of the divine perspective. Such a perspective will not produce a superficial, fairy tale-like "happily-ever-after" attitude but a deep sense of well-being and joy that their lives are united in the vine of Jesus and thus in his self-giving death and powerful resurrection (cf. the disciples' reaction of joy at the resurrection in 20:20).

(2) The Friends of Jesus and the Love Command: Thesis Statements on Discipleship (15:12–17)

[12]My command is this: Love each other as I have loved you. [13]Greater love has no one than this, that he lay down his life for his friends. [14]You are my friends if you do what I command. [15]I no longer call you servants, because a servant does not know his master's business. Instead, I have called you friends, for everything that I learned from my Father I have made known to you. [16]You did not choose me, but I chose you and appointed you to go and bear fruit—fruit that will last.

---

[228] H. Ridderbos, *The Gospel of John: A Theological Commentary* (Grand Rapids: Eerdmans, 1997), 519.

Then the Father will give you whatever you ask in my name. [17]This is my command: Love each other.

15:12–13 The "commands" required by Jesus for abiding in his love (15:10) are in v. 12 encapsulated in *one* core command or order.[229] That command is a restatement of the new command that was presented in 13:34–35 as the mark of authentic Christian discipleship. And here again it is founded on the previous exemplary love of Jesus for them. The verbs for love are significant here in that the love of the disciples is in the Greek a present continuing tense whereas the love of Jesus is stated in the aorist or past tense. It is obvious that John has the crucial event of the death and resurrection of the Lord in mind as he states this major discipleship thesis from a postresurrection perspective.[230]

These verses immediately call to mind the double command discussed in the Synoptic Gospels wherein the summary of the law is stated in terms of loving God and loving one's neighbor (cf. Mark 12:29–31). The dialog of Jesus with the rich young man who wondered how true obedience could be summarized (Matt 19:16–30; Mark 10:17–22; Luke 18:18–30) begins with a discussion concerning the second register of the Decalogue. But Jesus moved the discussion quickly to the first register and the subject of Israel's daily affirmation of the *Shema* (Deut 6:4–5). Here the pattern of thinking is reversed, for the *mashal* began with a major focus on a relationship to Jesus, the Vine, and moved to obedience, which in this section is focused on love for others (cf. also Matt 5:44–45).

But Brown correctly reminds us that in our lives we have come to know real love because Jesus laid down his life for us (cf. 1 John 3:16).[231] As a result we are to follow his example. Judaism, however, generally has rejected such self-sacrifice as an unnecessary and inappropriate pattern for life.[232] Moreover, in commenting on the subject of friendship, Stählin, after reviewing the writings of the Greek philosophers, argues that John has clothed ancient ideas concerning true "friendship in biblical speech"[233] and applied them to Jesus in the giving of a model for the disciples. Whatever may be any literary antecedents for such self-giving in terms of friendship, however, it is clear that self-sacrifice as understood by John did not arise

---

[229] Cf. Morris, *John*, 598. Contrast V. P. Furnish, *The Love Command in the New Testament* (London: SCM Press, 1972), 132–43.

[230] For further details on the postresurrection perspective in John see Borchert, "Resurrection Perspective," 501–13.

[231] R. Brown, *John*, 2.682.

[232] For the distinction between Jewish and Christian perspectives on this subject see L. Jacobs, "'Greater Love Hath No Man …': The Jewish Point of View of Self-Sacrifice," *Judaism* 6 (1957): 41–47.

[233] *TDNT*, 9.146–71, especially at 165–66.

from a philosophical ideal but from the actual self-giving death of Jesus. Such a death is the ultimate measure of love, and thus Jesus indicated that no other love surpasses such love *(meizona tautēs agapēn).*

Although some might argue that such love for friends is not the ultimate love in comparison to love of enemies,[234] the thesis here concerns the basis for discipleship in its reference to the death of Jesus. It would be illegitimate in such a context to argue that either John or Jesus would be making a case that the sacrificial death of Jesus was for friends and not for the world (cf. John 3:16; cf. also the Sermon on the Mount at Matt 5:43–45, where Jesus completely rejected such an improper interpretation of Lev 19:17–18). Indeed, Paul in Romans (Rom 5:10) argued that Christ died to reconcile *us* while *we* were still enemies.

15:14 Having introduced in the previous verse the subject of genuine friendship by means of an articular participle *(tōn philōn),* lit. "the ones he loved"), John now employs the noun *philoi* to spell out the implications or basic requirements of such friendship. They are exactly the same obedience requirements as those (15:10) for abiding in his love *(agapē).* It is therefore imperative to avoid making the frequent mistake of highlighting differences between *agapan* and *philein* in John.[235]

The point of the verse is that obedience to the commands of Jesus defines what it means to be his friends.[236] The concept of being a friend of God is applied in the Old Testament to Abraham (2 Chr 20:7; Isa 41:8; cf. Jas 2:23) and implicitly to Moses (Exod 33:11). Likewise, Jesus can refer to Lazarus as "our friend Lazarus" (John 11:11). But neither in the Old Testament nor the New Testament is God or Jesus referred to as the friend of humans in the manner of the gospel song "What a Friend We Have in Jesus." Such a thought probably would be regarded by the biblical writers as too debasing of God or Jesus.[237] The biblical writers like John already

---

[234] Morris, *John,* 598–99; Barrett, *St. John,* 397; and Carson, *John,* 522. But Dibelius argues that this verse is part of a midrashic argument that breaks up the logic of the Johannine message ("Joh. 15:13 Eine Studie zum Traditionsproblem des Johannesesvangeliums" in *Botschaft und Geschichte* [Tübingen: Mohr, 1953], 1.204–20).

[235] Readers who have heard frequent sermons on the difference between *agapē* and *eros* may have been led astray by A. Nygren's *Agape and Eros* (Philadelphia: Fortress, 1953), a motif distinction used inaccurately by many as a linguistic biblical distinction. They are forewarned here that *eros* never appears in the NT and that John has no difficulty in switching from the *agapan* word family to the *philein* word family without making much distinction. This forewarning especially applies to the use of the "love" words in chap. 21 of the Gospel.

[236] See the note on this verse by G. Lee, "John xv 14 'Ye Are My Friends,'" *NovT* 15 (1973): 260.

[237] For the Jewish idea of Israel as the friend of God derived from being followers of Moses see *Mek. Exod* 11:33. Also see *Str–B,* 2.564–65. For a discussion of Philo's ideas of friendship see Schnackenburg, *St. John,* 3.111.

understood that Jesus was not a mortal to be treated as any other mere
human. The evangelist was not in danger of confusing Jesus, who is the
Vine, with a mere branch (cf. 15:5 and the comments there on identity).
Clarity on this issue goes to the very heart of discipleship.

15:15   Jesus for John remains Lord and God (20:28), but the Johannine
Gospel asserts that in discipleship the relationship has been altered for the
disciples. They have not lost their subordinate role, as Ridderbos has aptly
stated.[238] But instead of Jesus referring to them as servants or slaves *(dou-
lous),* he refers to his followers as friends *(philous).*

The concept of humans as slaves of the deity was a common concept in
the ancient world. But for all practical purposes the Hebrew writers rejected
the idea that the people of Israel were slaves of God. Moreover, that perspective undoubtedly impacted their staunch rejection that in Jesus the truth
would set them free (John 8:32). Their view was that as children of Israel
and servants of God they had not ever really been in bondage (8:33, see my
earlier comments on these verses), in spite of the fact that they had been
human slaves in Egypt.[239]

But the idea of being the friends of Jesus in this verse is attached to the
important Johannine theme of knowing. Slaves are expected to obey even
though the master does not explain the reason for any given order. But the
friends of Jesus, according to this text, are viewed in a completely different
light. They are the objects of divine revelation because Jesus has communicated to them "everything I learned from my Father." That they did not
understand everything (or even much) prior to the resurrection is clear from
16:29–32, but such understanding would come. The point of this passage in
the bull's-eye is that servants/slaves are not expected to understand God's
will, but disciples are not regarded as mere slaves. They are being offered
the understanding that comes from a different relationship—the relationship
based on knowing and accepting the divine purpose in the coming of Jesus.

15:16   The disciples' acquisition of this knowledge from the Father,
however, is not based on earning the right to such understanding. Obedience to Jesus by his friends is expected (15:14), but they were not the
authors or initiators of this discipleship to Jesus. They did not choose him.
He both "chose" and "appointed"/set apart them for a purpose.

It is absolutely crucial whenever one discusses the subject of election to
realize that election is not about privilege but purpose. As early as the summons of Abram to leave his home and receive the blessing of God, to
receive a new name and become a great nation, that blessing was accompa-

---

[238] Ridderbos, *John,* 520.

[239] A. Böhling pursues the matter further in "Vom 'Knect' zum 'Sohn,'" in *Mysterion und
Wahrheit* (Leiden: Brill, 1968), especially at 63.

nied by a divine purpose—to be a blessing to all the people of the earth (Gen 12:2–3). Similarly, the promise of the presence of Jesus in the conclusion of Matthew is intimately united with the command/commission to go and disciple the world (Matt 28:18–20). Likewise, in the Johannine imparting of the Spirit by Jesus there is a purposeful task assigned to the disciples—namely, communicating the forgiveness of sins (John 20:22–23). So here also the "choosing" and "appointing" of the disciples is not merely for some privilege of being selected to an elite group but for the specific purpose of bearing fruit.

Communicating the knowledge of the Father's will, which was made known to them as friends of Jesus in the previous verse, becomes in this verse the disciples' assigned responsibility as fruit bearers for Jesus. In making this connection with fruit bearing, the evangelist has recaptured the metaphor of the vine in this crucial thesis statement on discipleship. Schnackenburg seems to make a special effort here to expand the purpose beyond mission and thus reduce the force of this verse,[240] but it would seem better to recognize that mission is the primary focus of such statements in the Bible and that fruit bearing in this verse involves communicating the entire message of the Gospel.

Yet the disciples/friends of Jesus are not left on their own without a resource. The text returns to the subject of prayer (introduced in the *mashal* at 15:7) and dependence on abiding in the Vine. This text also restates the thesis of 14:13–14 that such prayer is to be made in Jesus' name. As indicated in comments related to those earlier texts, prayer in Jesus' name is not merely a simple using of the name of Jesus. Abiding in Jesus, the Vine, and praying in his name implies that the petitioner has become aligned with the spirit and nature of Jesus so that requesting something out of line with the nature of Jesus would here be completely excluded from consideration. Such praying receives the anticipated results not because of the petitioner's worthiness but because of the intimate relationship of the petitioner to Jesus.

15:17 This section concludes with a restatement of the love command and thus forms an inclusio with 15:12.[241] As such it reenunciates the thesis that loving one another is the mark of Christian discipleship (cf. 13:34–35). It is always important when discussing such inclusions to recognize their encompassing nature. The opening and concluding statements are intended

---

[240] Schnackenburg, *St. John*, 3.112.

[241] Carson, along with many commentators, does not recognize the inclusio at this point and thus begins the section on opposition from the world a verse too soon (*John*, 524). He also continues the next section into the discussion of the Paraclete, failing to recognize the shift at 15:26. Morris likewise misses the inclusio and hesitantly begins the next section here, though he does conclude it appropriately at 15:25 (*John*, 601).

to be bookends that hold together the statements between them so that they are not treated as isolated verses. In other words, this section must be seen as part of a unit of crucial theological thesis statements at the heart of the Johannine Farewell Cycle.

To summarize, authentic discipleship in this bull's-eye segment is evidenced and encapsulated in love for one another (15:12,17) that has been epitomized by Jesus, who died for frail human beings (15:13). This model of self-sacrifice is recognized by those whom Jesus called his friends, for they do what he commands (15:14). But their obedience is not the result of some sort of slavery, since as his friends they have learned from Jesus about the will of God (15:15). This knowledge did not result from their own capabilities. It was given to them because they were chosen and appointed to bear fruit or spread the wonderful Gospel to others as their mission (15:16). They were given the resource of prayer because to accomplish God's will one needs God's resources (15:16). And finally, God's will is exemplified in a living community of disciples who love one another (15:17).

But the world does not easily accept such a community or its theses commitments. Therefore in the next section the world's reaction is discussed.

(3) The Reaction of the World to Jesus and the Disciples (15:18–25)

[18]"If the world hates you, keep in mind that it hated me first. [19]If you belonged to the world, it would love you as its own. As it is, you do not belong to the world, but I have chosen you out of the world. That is why the world hates you. [20]Remember the words I spoke to you: 'No servant is greater than his master.' If they persecuted me, they will persecute you also. If they obeyed my teaching, they will obey yours also. [21]They will treat you this way because of my name, for they do not know the One who sent me. [22]If I had not come and spoken to them, they would not be guilty of sin. Now, however, they have no excuse for their sin. [23]He who hates me hates my Father as well. [24]If I had not done among them what no one else did, they would not be guilty of sin. But now they have seen these miracles, and yet they have hated both me and my Father. [25]But this is to fulfill what is written in their Law: 'They hated me without reason.'

Having laid out some fundamental principles concerning discipleship in both the *mashal* of the vine and the inclusio on the love command, John details in this section Jesus' perspective on the forthcoming reaction of the world to the disciples. Simply stated, it will parallel the world's reaction to Jesus. The theme of the world's hatred permeates this entire section, and the contrast with the previous section therefore is exceedingly vivid.

If Christians think that the message of love in Christ will generally be well received by the world, they are in for a big surprise, just as the disciples had to learn. Love is not the usual pattern in social orders where power and domination are rampant and where the Good News runs counter to cultural commitments. The love of Jesus does not sell well on Madison Avenue and Times Square in New York or Whitehall and Piccadilly Circus in London any more that it did on the Via Dolorosa in first-century Jerusalem or in the central Forum of Ancient Rome. Disciples of Jesus are, accordingly, advised to take this section very seriously as they contemplate their relationship to the world.

Excursus 17: The "World" in John and Gnosticism

The Johannine view of the world *(cosmos)* is radically different from that of Gnosticism. In the Syrian-Egyptian Gnostic theological structure, the ultimate *syzygy* (divine union) of "Bythos" ("depth") and "Sige" ("silence") were responsible for producing an array of deities known as the "Pleroma" ("fullness of the godhead").[242] Briefly stated, then, each of the subdeities were in turn assigned to a similar *syzygy* or union so that each union was composed of both a male and a female counterpart. But the last of the deities, named "Sophia" ("wisdom"), rejected her consort and sought union with Ultimate Depth. She was naturally rejected. Her "desire," which was judged totally inappropriate for a divine being, was separated from her, and she was excluded from the Pleroma. This excluded part of Sophia is referred to as the little Sophia or Achamoth (from the Hb. *ḥokmâ,* "wisdom") and is linked to the act of creating the world by the Cosmocrater or Demiurge. This Demiurge likewise created planetary deities who are set against any interference from the outside. They entombed their human subjects in earthly bodies which forced humans to respond to them. Thus death for Gnostic devotees meant escape from bodily entombment and the shedding (purging) of created aspects in their ascent beyond the sphere of the planets to the divine realm. Such, briefly stated, is the structure of this type of Gnosticism.

Although all of this mythological construct may seem strange to contemporary readers, the main purpose of the myth was to explain the Gnostic opposition to the world and to define Gnostic salvation as an escape from both the world and the restrictive bodily tomb.

Fresh from the Mandean fervor that stalked the scholarly halls during the nineteenth century and the first half of the twentieth century, a number of commentators sought to suggest that John's Gospel breathed Gnostic overtones.[243] But at its very heart the perspectives of John's Gospel are totally opposed to

---

[242] See G. Borchert, "Insights into the Gnostic Threat to Christianity as Gained Through the Gospel of Philip," in *New Dimensions in New Testament Study* (Grand Rapids: Zondervan, 1974), 73–93. For a review of Gnostic Systems see H. Jonas, *The Gnostic Religion* (Boston: Beacon, 1958).

[243] See Bultmann's commentary, *John,* 7–9, etc.; Dodd, *Interpretation,* 10–53. For an evaluation see E. Yamauchi, *Pre-Christian Gnosticism: A Survey of the Proposed Evidence* (London: Tyndale, 1973). Also see my analysis: G. Borchert, "Is Bultmann's Theology a New Gnosticism?" *EvQ* 36 (1964): 222–28, which was my first attempt to confront this issue. For this reason in my doctoral studies I purposely undertook the investigation of Gnosticism. G. Borchert, "An Analysis of the Literary Arrangement and Theological Views in the Coptic Gnostic Gospel of Philip" (Ph.D. diss., Princeton Theological Seminary, 1967).

Gnostic views. The so-called savior of Gnosticism, the alien messenger from without, was not sent by the Pleroma to save the world but to proclaim a rejection of the world and all those who are not predestined to be saved because they do not have their origin in the escaped light particles from the Pleroma.

John, however, is not against the world per se. For him God loved the world and gave his Son so that the people of the world might believe in him and escape the clear judgment for sin (3:16–18). But John claims that the world has been in rebellion against God. Its people have walked in darkness (8:12) and have not generally recognized or accepted the Son and his "truth" (8:32; cf. 1:9–10; etc.). Instead, the people of the world have chosen to follow the devil and have accepted his lies (8:44). The world therefore is viewed by John not as essentially evil but as potentially transformable. This distinction is absolutely crucial to any comparison with Gnosticism.

Yet disciples must understand clearly that the world is a hostile place and that while it is potentially transformable, it will generally resist such transformation because of its rebellion and sin (8:21–24; 15:22–24).

15:18 With the above stated picture of their world in mind, it is not difficult to understand the clarity with which Jesus details the hatred of the world. Jesus modeled the standard of God (15:10; etc.), and that meant his very presence in the world was a reminder to the world of its evil works and God's resultant judgment (7:7; a pattern that will likewise shortly be stated concerning the presence of the Paraclete; cf. 16:8).

As this section opens, therefore, it begins with a condition that is assumed to be true ("If the world hates you"). The situation was, for the recipients of this Gospel, not some distant possibility. The Christian community had already been excluded from the synagogues and had suffered martyrdom throughout the Roman Empire. For them to read these words struck a painful cord of realism. They were in the midst of suffering. But they were also reminded that their resurrected Lord had also walked the way of being hated. The "before you" in the text is important here (the NIV fails to use the personal pronoun but simply says "first"). They had been informed of what was to come. But hearing about and experiencing persecution are not the same. Jesus knew that hatred was the mark of the world just as love was to be the mark of the authentic Christian.

15:19 Although the previous verse involved a condition assumed to be true, this verse involves a condition assumed not to be true. The world, of course, evidences a kind of love; so "if" the disciples "belonged to the world," they would experience that kind of love the world offers to its devotees (its own, *idion*). But the disciples did not belong to the world because Jesus chose (*egō exelexamēn*, "I chose"; the expression is emphatic) them out of the world. Thus they had to be informed that they would be hated.

To speak of being chosen or elected here is very different from the ontologically predestined view of Gnosticism, but it reminds one of the fact that the disciples were chosen for the purpose of bearing lasting fruit (see my comments at 15:16). Yet the idea of being chosen, as Brown notes, is here strangely linked to the idea of separation.[244] But as John later clarified, Jesus' intention was not to remove the disciples from the world; it was to protect them from evil or the evil one who dominates most of the world (cf. 17:15).

The concept of the separation of the disciples, accordingly, is not to be viewed in terms of copying the pattern of a Simeon Stylites, who sat for thirty-six years on a pillar to keep himself from the contamination of the world.[245] Such a pattern would impede the disciple's fruit-bearing election or calling. Moreover, the disciple of Jesus was never to forget that, having been called "out of the world," one was not in a position to boast about one's status because, as Paul pointedly told the Corinthians, we are only earthen pots that contain the marvelous treasure of God's gracious gospel (2 Cor 4:7). Elected separation then is not a chosenness to be vaunted before others. Rather, it entails the privilege of being hated and persecuted for bearing fruit on behalf of Christ (cf. also Matt 5:10–11).

15:20 This verse opens with a maxim that a servant is "not greater" than the master, an idea also used in the foot-washing scene to emphasize the necessity of humility (13:16). A parallel idea is also used in the Q (or sayings) material of the Synoptic Gospels, where the comparison is between disciples and their teacher rather than servants and their master. In Matthew the context is one of persecution, where the disciples are maligned falsely as devil-type people (10:24), while in Luke the phrase is used in a context of teaching (6:40). The varied uses of the statement gives credence to the fact that it probably was a popular maxim used in Jesus' time to clarify roles of a leader and the devotees of that person.

The maxim here is followed by two conditional sentences that illustrate what the disciples should expect in their relationship to the world. The first involves persecution and is clearly assumed to be true. They should expect persecution because that is the way it was with Jesus. The sense of the second condition, however, is not quite so clear. From the construction of the statement "If they obeyed my teaching" one might assume it to be true, but that presents a significant reality problem. One possible solution could be to apply the facticity of the statement to the minority, who did obey, and thus to separate them in our thinking from the majority, who did not obey. This

---

[244] R. Brown, *John*, 2.686, 696.

[245] The early Christian ascetic monks believed they could escape contamination by the world if they would observe austere self-disciplinary practices and if possible exclude themselves from contact with the world. Simeon Stylites was the extreme example of hermits. Of course his success in exclusion required that someone else had to supply him with the essentials of life. Cf. K. S. Latourette, *A History of Christianity* (New York: Harper, 1953), 228, 298.

option emphasizes the potentiality of the disciples' teaching being accepted in the same manner as happened with Jesus. Such a solution seems close to Carson's view.[246] But Dodd merely comments that such a view of the condition was "impossible!"[247] Lagrange followed a similar line of thought when he distinguished between the potentiality of the world obeying and the actual sad reality of the situation.[248] The NIV here seems to favor the first solution, but the NLT seems to move a little closer to the second perspective when it has "if they had listened to me, they would listen to you." The rendering of the NLT is to be preferred because it does not deny the viability of the mission perspective here. It also recognizes the reality of the situation and is certainly in line with the following verse.[249] The related idea in 1 John 4:6 offers a more positive perspective about obedience to God, but both texts make it clear that the world is not waiting with baited breath to follow God's will.

15:21 This verse is introduced in Greek with the strong adversative *alla*, "but," which brings the reader to realize clearly that the world does not follow the way of obedience. Indeed, the world persecutes Jesus and the disciples because the world does "not know the one who sent me." Throughout this Gospel, Jesus has asserted that he was the agent *(shaliach)* of the Father (cf. 5:30,36,38; 6:29,57, etc.). Unfortunately, the people to whom he was sent did not receive him (1:11). Morris here suggests that "the root cause of persecution is now traced to the world's ignorance of God."[250] This statement is technically and linguistically correct; but in the Western world, where ignorance is basically understood in mental, informational categories, ignorance, like knowledge in John, is not merely a matter of the head. It involves the whole person. To know God is to know God with one's whole being.[251] Likewise, not to know God is akin to disobedience, as is suggested by the next verse.

15:22 The meaning of the so-called ignorance of the previous verse now becomes evident. The world's lack of knowledge is not because the people did not see or hear Jesus. If that had been the case, it would be somewhat conceivable, as the verse indicates, that they would not be judged as "guilty." But such was not the case because, as Paul argued in Romans,

---

[246] Carson, *John*, 525–26.

[247] C. H. Dodd, *Historical Tradition in the Fourth Gospel* (Cambridge: University Press, 1963), 409.

[248] M. J. Lagrange, *Evangile selon Saint Jean* (Paris: Gabalda, 1948), 411.

[249] R. Brown correctly recognizes that the negative perspective in the following verses argues against a positive perspective in this verse (*John*, 2.687).

[250] Morris, *John*, 603.

[251] See my comments on "knowing" elsewhere in this commentary but particularly at *John 1–11*, 116, where I have discussed "believing" in relation to John 1:12.

even the pagans have enough knowledge to be condemned for sin (1:18–32). The argument here, therefore, is a reduction of the issue to a basic alternative, which might offer a slight loophole for escape. But since the facts are totally different, even that alternative is not possible. The verdict is absolutely clear. Jesus did come, the gospel was presented, the people have been disobedient, and therefore they are guilty of sin. Mark this conclusion well because it does not merely apply to Jews!

15:23 The implication of their action is also clear because hating "me" means nothing less than hating "my Father." The pronouns here stress the great divide between Jesus and the world and thus between the Father/God and the world.

15:24–25 Now comes the climax of the argument. If the issue is the great divide between humans and God, the natural question is, How does one bridge the gap? The good news answer is that Jesus, himself God's agent, is the bridge across the chasm. The indication that he serves as the bridge is to be found in the theme of his "works." This theme was offered repeatedly in the earlier Festival Cycle that emphasized the hostility of the Jews to Jesus. They rejected his words and refused to recognize the connection between his words and his works as being from the Father (5:36; 6:29; 7:3–5; 10:24–25,32–33,38; etc.). But even the disciples in this present Farewell Cycle had difficulty connecting words and works (14:10–11). The works are signs for the world to see that in Jesus divine glory was vested (2:11; cf. 1:14).

Again the argument is here reduced to a minimal alternative that might offer a slight hope of nonjudgment. But the possible condition of his not having done such works is closed almost as soon as it is opened because Jesus did come and Jesus did do the works *(erga);* and they have seen *(heōrakasin,* the perfect here used to indicate its continuing impact). Still they have hated not only him but by implication the Father also. The verdict is therefore certainly "Guilty!"

To this verdict is added a powerful scriptural footnote of proof or legal dictum, "They hated me without reason" (cf. Pss 35:19; 69:4).[252] This Old Testament citation is set in the context of a crucial statement, namely, that these things happened to fulfill "the word *[logos],* which stands written *[gegrammenos,* perfect tense of something with continuing significance] in their *[autōn]* law *[nomō]*." The importance of this statement should not be missed, for each element is significant. The use of "law" here reflects the general meaning of Torah, not merely as a set of rules and not only as the

[252] See E. Freed, *Old Testament Quotations in the Gospel of John* (Leiden: Brill, 1965), 94–95. See also A. T. Hanson, *The New Testament Interpretation of Scripture* (London: S.P.C.K., 1980), 158–59.

first five books of the canon, but as Scripture as a whole, which spells out the way one must walk in the will of God. The emphasis on "their" law is because the Jews who opposed Jesus did not actually obey God and their own Torah (cf. 7:19,23,51; 8:17; 10:34–38; 19:7–11). Finally, the idea that they were "written" emphasizes that these words continue to be the authoritative word for the people of God.

When John had thus penned these words, it was almost as though he could say, Case closed! The constructional logic in this Gospel is impressive. Although this logic may not convince those who stouteartedly refuse to be convinced, the Gospel makes a sound case for the Good News in Jesus on behalf of those who believe while they live and seek to bear fruit among those who are opposed to the wonderful message of life (20:31).

The core or the bull's-eye of discipleship in the Farewell Cycle is thus complete. It has involved the fascinating *mashal,* which sets forth the necessity of abiding in the Vine, Jesus, in order to be authentic fruit-bearing disciples. It then clarifies that love is the encompassing mark of the obedient friends of Jesus, who have been ordered to go and bear the fruit of discipleship. And it concludes by detailing for the faithful disciples the nature of the hostile world in which they live and are called to follow their master.

Having thus finished the core, attention is turned to moving back out through the rings of the bull's-eye and first turning to Part II of the discussion on the role of the Spirit, or Paraclete.

5. The Role of the Spirit—Part II (15:26–16:15)

B. Metzger regularly delighted to tell his students that the chapter and verse divisions as they appear in our Bibles today are often about as logical as someone putting a mark in their text every time a rider bounces on a trotting or galloping horse. The beginning of this major section is frequently not marked in Bibles, even with the start of a new paragraph, let alone with a new chapter (such as 16) or a new section heading. But there is little doubt in my mind that at 15:26 the focus of concern shifts dramatically and returns to the subject of the Paraclete/Holy Spirit.

In this return to the inside ring of the bull's-eye that was begun in 14:15–31, the evangelist completes his strategic interpretation of the role of the Paraclete in the life of the disciple. This major segment of the Farewell Cycle breaks naturally into three distinct sections: (1) the third Paraclete statement (15:26–16:4a) draws attention to the role of the Spirit as witness in the midst of persecution, (2) the fourth statement (16:4b–11) treats the Spirit's role as court counselor and judge on behalf of the disciples, and (3) the fifth Spirit statement (16:11–15) concludes this ring with the Spirit's role as a guide for the disciples.

(1) The Third Paraclete Statement: Witness in Persecution (15:26–16:4a)

[26]"When the Counselor comes, whom I will send to you from the Father, the Spirit of truth who goes out from the Father, he will testify about me. [27]And you also must testify, for you have been with me from the beginning.

[1]"All this I have told you so that you will not go astray. [2]They will put you out of the synagogue; in fact, a time is coming when anyone who kills you will think he is offering a service to God. [3]They will do such things because they have not known the Father or me. [4]I have told you this, so that when the time comes you will remember that I warned you.

15:26–27 Having concluded the previous section on the hatred of the world, the focus shifts to Jesus' concern for the disciples and the supplying of the divine resource of the Spirit to assist them in coping with the hostility they are to experience. Although some commentaries consider these two verses to be a later insertion into the subject of persecution, Barrett finds this idea to be improbable since the argument bears the clear marks of unity.[253]

The coming of the Paraclete is based on the sending of the Spirit from the Father by Jesus.[254] The pronoun used of the Spirit here is the masculine case *(ekeinos),* which might normally seem to be unusual because its referent noun, *pneuma,* "spirit," is neuter. But John undoubtedly considered the Spirit as a personal being and not as something impersonal, a mere force.

Moreover, as indicated earlier (see my comments on 14:16,26) the theologians of the Eastern Greek Church have refused to accept the *filioque* ("and son") clause in the historic creeds because they have stoutly argued that the text here pointedly says that the Spirit "proceeds" from the Father and not from both the Father *and the Son.* But, as Brown indicates, these verses are about the Spirit's mission in the world and not about the nature of the Trinity or about "the eternal procession of the Third person" of the Godhead.[255] This argument is an excellent example of how early Christian theologians argued for the exactness of the words of the text and missed the basic meaning of the passage. Such a hermeneutical pattern of interpreting texts is not limited to early exegetes of the Bible. Accordingly, we must continually guard ourselves against such misreading of words in our desire

---

[253] Barrett, *St. John,* 402. For another view see U. Wilckens, "Der Paraklet und Die Kirche," in *Kirche,* ed. D. Lührmann and G. Strecker (Tübingen: Mohr-Siebeck, 1980), 185–203.

[254] The identification of the Paraclete with the Spirit of Truth has already been made in 14:17. For a fuller discussion on the Spirit in this chapter see E. Bammel, "Jesus und der Paraklet in Johannes 16," in *Christ and the Spirit in the New Testament* (New York: Cambridge University Press, 1973), 199–217. For a Gnostic interpretation see H. Becker, *Die Reden des Johannesevangeliums und der Stil der gnostischen Offenbarungsrede* (Göttingen: Vandenhoeck & Ruprecht, 1956), 96–105.

[255] R. Brown, *John,* 2.689.

to be faithful to Scripture. To separate Jesus from the Father in theological interpretations of John runs counter to Jesus' insistence on his identification with the Father (1:1; 10:30; 17:21; etc.). Besides, it is making too fine a distinction to separate sending and proceeding.[256]

The role of this helper is to testify or witness concerning Jesus. But the disciples are also given the same task of witnessing. So it is imperative to note with Hoskyns and Davey at this point that the work of the Spirit (v. 6) is "not for one moment thought of as independent of the disciples of Jesus" (v. 27).[257] The point is not that there are two different patterns of witnessing. The Spirit works in the disciples (cf. 14:17), and they have the same mission: namely, giving witness to Jesus. The Spirit therefore does not operate independently of the Gospel concerning Jesus because the Spirit has been sent from the Father by Jesus.[258] Moreover, it is not that the Gospel message is incomplete and that the Spirit needs to complete it. The basic message of the gospel is available, and both the Spirit and the disciples are together agents of communicating the same gospel. The role of the Spirit here, then, is likened to that of a supporter for the disciples in witnessing to a hostile world. This statement, of course, does not mean that where there are no disciples present the Spirit is unable to work. Such a suggestion would mean that God is bound totally by human frailty. Rather, the meaning of these verses points to the intended harmony of humans and the Spirit working in mission.

The two uses of the verb for "testify" here are intriguing. It is said that the Spirit (v. 26) "will testify," which undoubtedly reflects the perspective of Jesus' original promise related to the expected coming of the Paraclete. But the present tense (either indicative or imperative) is used in reference to the disciples (v. 27). Translators usually choose the imperative because it represents a continuing command to the followers of Jesus. The disciples who are here in mind are those who have been with Jesus "from the beginning," which is not a reference to the beginning of time or creation as in John 1:1. It might, however, mean from the beginning of Jesus' ministry (cf. Luke 1:2) or, by context and implication, from the day when the disciples joined in following Jesus.

16:1 With both the hostility of the world and the presence of the helping Paraclete in mind, John turned to a defining subject for the disciples: the threat of falling away (NLT and RSV), stumbling (NRSV), being offended (KJV), or going astray (NIV). The Greek verb *skandalizō,* from which we get the English words "scandal" and "scandalize," is in the pas-

---

[256] Indeed, Schnackenburg argues correctly, I believe, that "the double statement" concerning sending and proceeding is an example of "synonymous parallelism" (*St. John*, 3.118).

[257] Hoskyns and Davey, *The Fourth Gospel*, 481. Cf. also Carrez, "Les Promesses," 323–32.

[258] Johnston, *The Spirit Paraclete*, 32–34.

sive voice and means "to give up one's faith" or "fall into sin." It is used earlier in John 6:61 (in the active voice), where Jesus' followers begin to murmur and turn away from him (6:66). They are like the people who were with Moses in the wilderness and who did not make it into the promised land. It also reminds one of Paul's warning to the Corinthians not to grumble and turn against God like the people of Israel who died in the desert because they entered into idolatry and immorality (1 Cor 10:6–10),[259] two prohibited activities for the church (cf. Acts 15:20,29; and see Rev 2:14,20).

Many Christians have great anxieties with warning texts like those here, in 1 Corinthians 9–10; and Hebrews 6; 10. They would prefer to read over them and treat them as though they did not exist in the Bible. Indeed, they probably would be willing to reduce them to a subcanonical category that does not relate to theology. But it is absolutely imperative for contemporary disciples to remember that the goal of Jesus and of the New Testament writers was not divine condemnation. These texts are instead intended to be warnings, as Paul says, for our benefit to prevent us from falling (1 Cor 9:27; 10:11). Moreover, within almost every warning context there is either a statement of assurance or encouragement for Christians to succeed in faithfulness (cf. in addition to 1 Cor 10:11; John 16:4; Heb 6:17–18; etc.).

16:2 A basic reason for Jesus having given the warning in 16:1 is now spelled out in this verse. Persecution is a major threat to the Christian community's well-being and the continuing faithfulness of its people. Moreover, as part of the world's culture, we often think that our well-being and prosperity are regarded as a mark of our obedience to God and of our divine approval.[260]

But that was not the perspective of Jesus, who in this Gospel is said to have lived with his "hour" (death) relentlessly approaching (cf. the move from 2:4 to 12:23 to 17:1 and to 19:30). Now the term *hōra,* "hour" (the NIV has the less adequate "time"), is applied to the disciples. Not only was persecution to be expected, but for many death was to be their assignment (cf. 21:18–19).

Moreover, the persecutors would actually think that they were serving God by seeking to stamp out what they considered to be the Christian error. The expression translated "offering a service to God" clearly carries a sense of holy zeal, a jihad (a holy war), or a worshipful commitment on the part of the persecutors. It is with this type of understanding that the "Curse

---

[259] See Borchert, *Assurance and Warning,* 56–57.
[260] Morris, *John,* 614.

on the Heretics" was inserted into the daily Jewish prayers known as the Eighteen Benedictions.[261]

Such was likewise the perspective of Paul, the persecutor, before he became a Christian (cf. Acts 26:9). Paul's teacher, Gamaliel (Acts 22:3), was said to be of quite a different spirit (Acts 5:33–39), but apparently the evangelist encountered more Jews like pre-Christian Paul than those like Gamaliel. His picture of the Jews in the story of the blind man certainly reflects the type of hostility described here, for they would excommunicate anyone from the synagogue who gave a positive witness concerning Jesus (cf. John 9:22,34). Excommunication, exclusion, and arranging for the death of such rebels was an approved pattern (cf. Acts 20:3; 23:12–14).[262]

16:3　The root cause of the hostility is again articulated (cf. 15:22) as a failure on the part of the Jews in "knowing" the Father. But here the failure of knowing Jesus is added to the cause of the persecution.[263] Indeed, in the letters to the seven churches of Revelation, John goes far beyond saying that the Jews did not know God. He called the Jewish assemblies synagogues of Satan (Rev 2:9; 3:9). Persecution can draw strong reactions, and it did so in the Johannine community.[264]

16:4a　This section concludes with a reminder that when the "hour" comes they should remember that Jesus had told them what was to happen.[265]

With these stern words of warning concerning the immanent arrival of their "hour" of persecution, John concluded this section. Persecution is certain, but there is not the slightest hint that the disciples should retreat into safe havens and cease witnessing about Jesus. In fact, just the opposite is expected. And to make their witnessing effective the Paraclete, the Spirit of truth or authenticity, is promised to them to support them in their witnessing.

---

[261] For the curse of the *minim* (heretics) in the Twelfth Benediction see C. K. Barrett, *New Testament Documents* (New York: Harper & Row, 1961), 166–67. The curse was added at least by the mideighties of the first century, and by the nineties under Rabbi Gamaliel II exclusion was added to excommunication as a means of attempting to control those who did not follow the revisions of Jamnia. For further information see W. D. Davies, *The Setting of the Sermon on the Mount* (Cambridge: University Press, 1964), 274–76. For Jewish sources see *m. Sanh* 9.6, and for an intriguing rabbinic interpretation of Num 25:13 see *Midr. Rab.* 21.3, where shedding the blood of a rebel/heretic was viewed as an offering. See also Josephus, *Ant.,* 20.9.1 for the killing of Christians.

[262] See the previous footnote.

[263] Some manuscripts read "do these things *to you*," but this addition is probably the result of the influence of 15:21 and is not likely original. Cf. Metzger, *Textual Commentary,* 246.

[264] For a helpful sociological discussion concerning in-groups and out-groups and how they pertain to this section of John, see Malina and Rohrbaugh, *Social Science Commentary,* 238–40.

[265] There is a rather unusual double use of the Gk. for "them" (referring to the warnings Jesus gave) in several significant ancient Gk. manuscripts, which argues that the reading probably was original, though it does not alter the meaning substantially.

(2) The Fourth Paraclete Statement: Counselor and Judge (16:4b–11)

I did not tell you this at first because I was with you.
⁵"Now I am going to him who sent me, yet none of you asks me, 'Where are you going?' ⁶Because I have said these things, you are filled with grief. ⁷But I tell you the truth: It is for your good that I am going away. Unless I go away, the Counselor will not come to you; but if I go, I will send him to you. ⁸When he comes, he will convict the world of guilt in regard to sin and righteousness and judgment: ⁹in regard to sin, because men do not believe in me; ¹⁰in regard to righteousness, because I am going to the Father, where you can see me no longer; ¹¹and in regard to judgment, because the prince of this world now stands condemned.

16:4b–6 The second part of v. 4 serves as a link to what has gone before and connects with what is said in this section. The evangelist alludes to the previous Paraclete statement in 15:26–27 by returning to the idea of "from the beginning" *(ex archeēs),* but there is here a slight change of focus. In the previous chapter he referred to the fact that they had accompanied Jesus from the beginning. But here Jesus provides the rationale for not telling them earlier about the Paraclete: namely, he was still with them.

Now *(nyn)* everything was about to change. Jesus' role as the incarnate agent *(shaliach)*[266] of the one who sent him was coming to an end, and that meant a shift in relationships for the disciples. He was leaving them to be with the divine sender. This first part of v. 5 is quite clear.

The second part of v. 5, however, has created major problems for commentators. These words seem to be in direct contradiction to the questions of Peter (13:36) and Thomas (14:5). As such they led Bernard to a realignment of the chapters by inserting chaps. 15–16 after 13:31.[267] Bultmann followed this lead but also moved chap. 17 before 13:31–35 and then inserted chaps. 15–16 before 13:36.[268] But as I suggested in the discussion related to Bultmann's moving of chap. 5 after chap. 6, such restructuring of the Gospel treats John as a poor historian who has little understanding of what he was doing in his organization.[269] On the contrary, the organization of the pericopes in John serve his theological goal of communicating the vivid message of Jesus. The solutions of Brown, Schnackenburg, and Beasley-Murray reject structural reorganization but blame such poorly aligned statements on a forgetful editor who failed to remove such inconsistencies.[270]

---

[266] See my notes on "agency" in chap. 5 (Borchert, *John 1–11*, 236) and elsewhere throughout this commentary.

[267] Bernard, *St. John*, 1.xx.

[268] Bultmann, *John*, x–xi.

[269] Borchert, *John 1–11*, 224–25.

[270] R. Brown, *John*, 2.710; Schnackenburg, *St. John*, 3.126–27; Beasley-Murray, *John*, 279.

The alternative is to explain why such noticeable inconsistencies remain. That task may not seem to be an easy one. Lagrange sought to explain the situation by emphasizing the *nyn* ("now") and thus to focus on the current situation over against the earlier references so that the disciples did not need "now" to ask those questions because they were further informed.[271] Dodd argued similarly but restructured the statement at 14:4 to imply that the disciples do know the way but not the goal.[272] But such a manipulative rendering has inadequate support.

From my point of view, part of our problem is tied into our human commitment to read John within sequential time and space frames. That does not work with the cleansing of the Temple or the relationship of chaps. 5–6, and it certainly does not work in the Farewell Cycle. One must read each section of John's Gospel for what it says, not what we readers might want the text to say. The issue here is not where Jesus is going; the issue is that he *is* going to the one who sent him. He is leaving them, and they unhappily saw no benefit accruing to their messianic hopes. They were clearly filled with sorrow (v. 6). Morris says here that "the perfect is somewhat strange since sorrow was to give way to joy (16:20)."[273] But that again is a time-oriented sequential statement. It is true, however, that the word for grief or sorrow *(lypē)* here occurs both in vv. 20 and 22, thus linking it verbally with the next section of the Gospel. In contrast to that section, Jesus is here trying to help them understand the nature of the spiritual resource that will be supplied to them. But their minds have become stuck on the physical presence of Jesus in the midst of the hostile world. Therefore the task was to help these disciples realize that another powerful resource would be made available to them in the coming of the Paraclete.

16:7   Here is the crucial statement for understanding the previous verses. Using the equivalent of an oath, "I tell you the truth," the "I," Jesus, asserts the authenticity of what follows. Jesus' assertion is that their concern for benefit or advantage will be realized by his departure. The coming of the Paraclete will benefit or be good for the disciples, even though they had no understanding of the significance of this statement at the time. But when John wrote the Gospel, he understood fully the significance of that statement. Moreover, he understood the reverse side also. Fulfilling the condition for the coming of the Paraclete necessitated both Jesus' going and his sending the Paraclete to them.

Although theologians might wish to discuss the issue, the question of whether Jesus and the Paraclete could be present together "with" and "in"

---

[271] Lagrange, *Saint Jean*, 417–418.

[272] Dodd, *Interpretation*, 412–13, n. 1.

[273] Morris, *John*, 617.

the disciples (cf. 14:17) is not treated here.[274] Nor is the issue one of determining the relative merits of the presence of the Spirit as over against the bodily presence of Jesus.[275] Instead, the issue here involves what would trigger the Spirit's coming to the disciples. The answer is the departure or the atoning death of Jesus. This act of Jesus' glorification set in motion a number of significant consequences, among them the inauguration of the era of the Spirit/Paraclete and the dawn of Christian discipleship. The Lamb of God would have to die before the new era would come. In the new era of the resurrection Jesus would breathe on them as God breathed on Adam in creation (Gen 2:7), and the Spirit era would begin (John 20:22).

16:8 The following verses spell out in detail the threefold role of the Paraclete in terms of the legal image of counselor and judge.[276] Büchsel notes that in early Greek writings the verb *elenchein* meant "to scorn" and later "to shame," but in the New Testament it "almost always ... means 'to show someone his sin and to summon him to repentance.' "[277]

In these verses, however, I believe the meaning of the verb is even more focused so as to suggest something akin to a courtroom procedure. It is a fascinating picture in which one can imagine three elements of the procedure being presented. The first appears to be like a charge for which the defendant has been indicted. The second can be envisioned as the standard to which the defendant is required to conform, and the third can be viewed as the rationale the presiding judge uses to render the verdict. All of these elements can come within the basic meaning of this Greek verb, which is "bring to light, expose, set forth."[278]

Although Carson has provided at least five basic options for the meaning of *elenchein,* it is my opinion that one does not need to press for a precise meaning from among the suggested specific meanings of "prove," "convict," "prove wrong," "expose as guilty," or Carson's own "convict in a personal sense."[279] John's Semitic type of word-picture thinking would allow for more breadth in the definition. It is because of such breadth that translators have struggled to find the right word to render this Greek verb in John (e.g., note the following: "reprove," KJV; "convince," RSV/NLT;

---

[274] See Carson, *John,* 533. Also see W. F. Howard, "John," *IB,* 7.730–31.

[275] F. Porsch, *Pneuma und Wort: Ein exegetischer Beitrag zur Pneumatologie des Johannesevangeliums* (Frankfurt: Knect, 1974), 279–80.

[276] G. Behler has identified several aspects of the Spirit's work, but the ideas need to be expanded as done here ("La double fonction de l'Esprit. Advocat et guide," *Vie Spirituelle* 102 [1960]: 614–25).

[277] See Büchsel, *TDNT,* 2.473–74.

[278] See *BAGD,* 249. See also R. Brown, *John,* 2.705.

[279] See D. Carson, "The Function of the Paraclete in John 16:7–11," *JBL* 98 (1979): 547–66; and in *John,* 535–37.

"prove," NRSV; "convict," NIV; "prove wrong," TEV, none of which carries the full meaning).[280]

16:9 As John turned to the specific features of this triad,[281] he first considered the Paraclete's role in regard to the issue of sin. The basic reasons for the overall charge of sin here is that the people of the world "do not believe" in Jesus. As I indicated as early as the Prologue, to "believe" is set in apposition with "receive" (1:12), which means that not to believe means rejecting Jesus. Such a charge of rejecting Jesus would be regarded by John as the equivalent of Israel's rejection or rebellion against God in the Old Testament (cf. Exod 32:1–8; Num 25:1–9).

The idea of sin here is not merely conceived in terms of a listing of erroneous acts but of the fundamental act of choosing another god. Such an act of rejection means that one stands above God in the way in which Adam and Eve first rebelled against God in the Garden (Gen 3:5; cf. John's evaluation concerning the people's rejection of Jesus at 12:37; 15:24; etc.). Morris is certainly correct when he states, "The basic sin is the sin that puts self at the center of things and consequently refuses to believe."[282] If one were to relate this idea to a political system, it would be the equivalent of registering a charge of treason against a ruler, and there is no question that John regarded Jesus as the Lord (20:28).

16:10 The second element of the triad is the standard against which the charge is leveled. That standard is righteousness.[283] It is none other than the standard expected by God because the judgments of God are both true and righteous (cf. Ps 19:9). Here and in the prayer of 17:25 are the two places in the Farewell Cycle where the *dikaios* family of words is used. The only other places in the Gospel are in the Festival Cycle where Jesus emphasizes his own righteous standard for judgment (5:30) and questions his critics' ability to apply the same righteous standard (7:24). In the First Epistle, John expanded the theme by not only stating that both God and Jesus are righteous/just (1 John 1:9; 2:1) but that everyone who *does* "right" is from God and those who do not do "right" are like Cain the murderer and are from the devil (2:29; 3:7,10,12).

The addition of the causal statement "I am going to the Father, where you can see me no longer" is a clever formulation of the crucial nature of the death and resurrection of Jesus. It also serves as God's confirmation of

---

[280] See also the struggle for meaning in Newman and Nida, *Translator's Handbook*, 503.

[281] The triad is united by the familiar Greek pattern of using μεν, δε, and δε in vv. 9–11.

[282] Morris, *John*, 619.

[283] For a different view that has been influenced by a Pauline interpretation see W. Stenger, "*Dikaiosunē* in Jo. xvi 8.10," *NovT* 21 (1979): 2–12. Contrast B. Lindars, "*Dikaiosunē* in Jn 16 and 10," in *Mélanges bibliques en hommage au R. P. Béda Rigaux* (Gembloux: Duclot, 1970), 275–86.

this standard in Jesus. Barrett also reminds us pointedly that the death and resurrection must be understood as a "compound event" in the New Testament.[284] Thus what seemed to be the world's victory over Jesus was, in fact, a clear Johannine example of the divine reversal because Jesus did not decay in the tomb. Rather, his exaltation to the Father vindicated his presence among them. Blank portrays this idea beautifully when he states that their rejoicing at being finished with Jesus (16:20) turned out to be the rejoicing of the damned.[285] It reminds one of the vivid picture of the two slain witnesses in Revelation where the world was rejoicing over their death for three and a half days until God took them up to heaven and then sent the great earthquake (11:4–13). Humanity is not in control either of the future or of setting the standards for life. That is the work of God.

16:11 Now the case is completed. The verdict of the court can be rendered. It is "Guilty!" But the guilty verdict did not merely apply to the opponents of Jesus—the world. John saw the bigger picture. There has been an evil hand at work in the world, and any modern attempt to demythologize this prince of the world will receive the same verdict as the evil ruler. This prince of the world, the devil, Satan, may well have won Judas in his attack on Jesus (13:27). He may also have taunted Jesus through the Jews, who charged Jesus as having a demon (7:20; 8:48–52), but in the crucifixion and resurrection the prince of the world lost (12:31) because of his insufficient power (14:30). The Johannine visions in the apocalypse vividly portray not only the great power of evil (12:3–4) and its seductive ways (13:1–18; 17:1–14) but also its unambiguous defeat (14:17–20; 19:11–21; 20:7–10).

The Paraclete's forensic task here then is portrayed in the presence of the disciples and in the Johannine court of God like a counselor and judge in bringing to just judgment the world and its rebellious prince. This section then is not unrelated to the way Jesus had earlier been pictured as having been given the authority to render all judgment by the Father (cf. 5:22). In the midst of a hostile world, therefore, the disciples are clearly shown that to take the side of the world is hardly a viable option because of its dire consequences. The prince of the world and all who side with him stand condemned.

(3) The Fifth Spirit Statement: Authentic Guide (16:12–15)

[12]"I have much more to say to you, more than you can now bear. [13]But when he, the Spirit of truth, comes, he will guide you into all truth. He will not speak on

---

[284] See Barrett, *St. John*, 407. Cf. also Paul's view of the work of Jesus in Rom 3:21–31.

[285] Cf. J. Blank, *Krisis: Untusuchungen zur johanneischen Christologie und Eschatologie* (Freiburg: Lambertus, 1964), 337–38. Cf. also Beasley-Murray, *John*, 282.

his own; he will speak only what he hears, and he will tell you what is yet to come. [14]He will bring glory to me by taking from what is mine and making it known to you. [15]All that belongs to the Father is mine. That is why I said the Spirit will take from what is mine and make it known to you.

The Five Portrait Statements concerning the roles of the Spirit in the community life of Jesus' disciples are brought to an appropriate conclusion by picturing the Spirit as a guide.[286]

Those who have trekked through wildernesses, as I have done in the Sinai desert and elsewhere in the world, know that the role of a guide is crucial to one's survival. Without a guide, everything in the vast unpopulated expanse seems to be unwelcoming. The guide is the security blanket. Your guide is a resource of information and insight when there are no roads and the faint trails that are there seem to crisscross without rhyme or reason. In situations like that, one knows the ultimate significance of a guide.

Perhaps one illustration will suffice. When the Israeli army first took the Sinai, one of the now famous military archaeologists took his assistants on the hunt for the stone-carved records of the ancient turquoise campaigns of the Egyptians in the Sinai. They flew over the area at a low altitude in a helicopter for several hours searching and searching for the site they knew was there in the region. Finally, in desperation they landed in a group of Bedouins and asked them if they knew where the site was. One agreed to show them the place in exchange for the lunches of the general and his assistants. As they once again circled over the wilderness region, the Bedouin calmly ate the lunches. When the Israeli archaeological/military men became perturbed at not finding the place, they prodded the Bedouin; but he said nothing until he took the last bite. Then they said, "Well, where it is?" He pointed down below them. There it was! With all of their sophisticated equipment, they still needed a guide.

Without a guide, wilderness landscapes are often seemingly devoid of reality. When you ponder this image of the Spirit, remember the significance of a guide in an unknown territory. That is where the disciples were headed as Jesus was departing.

16:12–13 Jesus knew their situation, and he knew they were totally confused. He knew they could not handle much more in the way of up-front instruction, so although he had more to add, he would wait until the coming of the Spirit (v. 13).

This statement has created scholarly debate, and for Becker this verse seems to stand in direct contradiction to the second Paraclete saying, where the role of

---

[286] For A. George's views of the Spirit as a guide to all truth see "L'Esprit, guide vers la vérité plénière. Jn 16, 12–15," *Assemblées du Seigneur* 31 (1973): 40–47.

the Spirit is to "remind" them of "everything" Jesus had said (14:26).[287] Was there or was there not more revelation to be communicated? The answer, it seems, is that Becker has interpreted the "more to say" as more "revelation" needed; or perhaps for him v. 12 could mean an addition to the Gospel. But that is not the necessary meaning of the words. To people in anxiety, comfort and direction probably are the more likely meaning of this expression. This meaning, I suggest, would seem to be supported by the unusual use of *bastazein* ("to bear") here. In the three other uses of the verb in John it can mean "take up" stones (10:31), "take" money referring to Judas (12:6), and "take away" the body of Jesus (20:15). Here, however, whatever Jesus still had to say would have been too much for them to accept at the time (*arti,* "now"). Such further information would more naturally be information about their forthcoming unbearable persecution and even death (cf. Peter's reaction to Jesus' prediction of his death, and that came after Jesus' resurrection; 21:21). It is hardly necessary, therefore, to suggest that this verse reveals the hand of a different editor of the Gospel or that the Spirit was to bring a major addition to the basic message of salvation.

Indeed, the role of the Spirit of truth (see my comments at 14:17; 15:26) is precisely defined here in v. 13 as not being independent of Jesus (cf. 14:16; 15:26). Harmony in the Godhead concerning the gospel message is a basic assumption of John. Moreover, the role of the Spirit as guide "into all truth" *(en tē alētheia pasē),* as Barrett suggests, involves "guidance in the whole sphere of truth."[288] Such an expression is not primarily focused on the context of communicating pedantic secular knowledge or even sophisticated astrophysical and microprocessed genetic information. But the focus is upon one's life-defining orientation with God and in turn how that affects the way one is guided and related to the various information highways of life.

Like Jesus, who was the obedient agent of the Father (cf. 5:19,30), the Spirit's role is also one of agency—namely, to communicate (*lalēsei,* "speak") to the disciples what he receives (*akousei,* "hears"). That communication, or messaging (*anangelei,* "tell"), of the Spirit is here said to involve "what is yet to come."

One does not have to be a brilliant interpreter to guess that this last clause has led to a great deal of speculation concerning its intended meaning. Is the role of the Spirit to provide predictions concerning future events?[289] Or is the role one of simply providing perspective for the future

---

[287] J. Becker, *Das Evangelium des Johannes* (Gütersloh: G. Mohn, 1979–1981), 2.498.

[288] Barrett, *St. John,* 407.

[289] Some scholars have even suggested that this idea could be related to messages such as the ones evident in the Book of Revelation or other predictions concerning the coming kingdom of God. See Bernard, *St. John,* 2.511; Johnston, *The Spirit–Paraclete,* 38–39 and the earlier comments of A. Schlatter, *Das Evangelium nach Johannes* (Stuttgart: Calwer, 1928), 314.

in light of the already revealed message of the Gospel?[290] These two poles of opinion reflect the two sides of the way people speak of prophecy in terms of "foretelling" and "forthtelling." The former can be as radically expansive and lacking in controlled guidelines as the latter can be restrictive.

The appropriate meaning is undoubtedly to be found in a synthesis of both, wherein wide-ranging speculation is eliminated by remembering that these words were written as a Farewell message to anxious disciples who feared the imminent loss of Jesus, their physical companion and guide. But the future was also an unknown page for them, since these Paraclete passages indicate that the coming times would be traumatic for them and that in such times the disciples would need the truthful and authentic Spirit to guide them through their forthcoming wilderness. It is in this combination of farewell and hope of guidance that contemporary readers can find this passage to be of great significance for their lives of discipleship.

16:14–15   This section and the Paraclete passages end with a reaffirmation of the centrality of Jesus in all our thinking concerning the Spirit. Once again the identity of the Spirit as personal and not as a vague material or immaterial force is emphasized by the masculine pronoun rather than by the expected neuter pronoun to agree with the nonpersonal gender of the noun "Spirit" *(pneuma)*. The Godhead is both unified in purpose and avowedly personal.

In this setting the theme of glory is once again brought to the forefront of our thinking. Just as the disciples witnessed the glory of Jesus in the incarnation (cf. 1:14; 2:11; etc.), and just as Jesus' mission was to bring glory to the Father (cf. 7:18; 12:28; 17:4), so his death and resurrection are designated in this Gospel as the hour of his glorification (12:23; 13:31–32; 17:1,5). Accordingly, just as Jesus' mission was to glorify the Father, so here the mission of the Spirit will glorify Jesus.

This spiritual guide's task then is pointedly summarized as receiving that which comes directly from Jesus and passing it on or messaging it (cf. vv. 13–15 for a communication triad)[291] directly to the disciples. This type of passing on of significant information reminds me of the rabbinic concept of the passing on of tradition and assuming that such tradition has been unaltered in the process. Reflections of this type of Jewish thinking can be found in Paul's use of the verbs *paralambanein* ("receive") and *paradidonai* ("deliver") in 1 Cor 11:23; 15:3. The Spirit then is the deliverer of the saving message, which the world received through the disciples.

---

[290] Cf. W. Thüsing, *Die Erhöhung und Verrherlichung Jesu in Johannesevangelium* (Münster: Aschendorff, 1960), 149–53, who limits the reference to the upper room scene and the immediate death and resurrection of Jesus. Contrast E. Bammel, "Jesus und der Paraklet," 207–10, 214–16.

[291] Cf. Morris, *John*, 622, n. 35, who identifies this phenomenon as a threefold repetition.

Finally, John concludes this section on the Spirit by reminding everyone that his theology is not Christocentric (as Morris suggested).[292] John's theology is uncompromisingly theocentric because Jesus has received his mission from the Father, and it is the Spirit's task to communicate what comes from Jesus to the disciples.

To be authentically Christian in a hostile world, according to John, is not to be pneumatically centered nor Christocentric but theocentric. The Spirit serves the mission of Jesus, just as Jesus served the will of the Father. The Godhead is united in purpose and mission. Thus Christians never speak of there being three Gods. Disciples are called to follow in communicating the saving mission of Jesus to the hostile world that killed Jesus. They will not escape the wilderness of hostility and persecution, but they will have (1) another Paraclete, (2) one who will teach them, (3) one who will witness with them, (4) one who will serve as their attorney and judge in the world, and (5) one who will guide them authentically in truth.

Clearly this message was intended primarily for the anxiety filled disciples who knew Jesus firsthand and were troubled by his imminent departure. But John was not writing merely for the first group of disciples.[293] His intention was that this fivefold message concerning the Paraclete would have continuing implication for his own readers and, therefore, derivatively for us today. The divine resource of the Spirit is the gift Jesus sent from the Father to Christian disciples in a hostile world so that they could cope effectively with the anxiety that is inherent in living in a life-context that openly resists the proclamation of the Gospel.

The two parts of the inner ring around the core of the bull's-eye that deal with the divine resource of the Spirit are thus complete. Attention is now returned to the penultimate ring and the issue of the disciples' anxiety in light of Jesus' imminent departure.

6. Anxiety and Loneliness—Part II: The Great Reversal (16:16–33)

In this Gospel the anxieties that accompany discipleship are taken very seriously. There is here no attempt to ignore pain. There is here no suggestion of a Gnostic escape plan to a heavenly counterworld. There is here not even the hint that Jesus will rescue them out of their sufferings. About all he does is pray for them to be kept wholesome and untainted by the clutching attacks of evil/the evil one (17:15). The presence of the disciples in the world, even though it would be difficult for them, is a necessary part of

---

[292] Ibid. I believe Morris missed the role of the Father here.

[293] I find Carson's logic (*John*, 541) of applying these texts to the first disciples to be too restrictive. He fails to recognize the readers to whom the Gospel is addressed, and so he jumps from Jesus to today and misses the middle step of John's early audience.

God's plan for communicating the Gospel, just as it was in God's great saving purpose through the genuine incarnation and death of Jesus. Christians do not run from the hostile world. They are God's witnesses to the world. But that means that they do not quite fit the world just as Jesus did not quite fit the world. So the world treats them as it treated Jesus. And when Jesus announced his departure, the anxiety level of the disciples became intense.

In this second part of the anxiety circle, John treats four important issues. In the first segment he focuses on the disciples' bewilderment with Jesus' references to time (16:16–19). In the second he deals with the relationship of sorrow to joy (16:20–22). In the third he provides perspective on the disciples' petitions (16:23–28). And in the fourth he presents a surprising reversal and its implications (16:29–33).

(1) Confusion over Time (16:16–19)

16"In a little while you will see me no more, and then after a little while you will see me."

17Some of his disciples said to one another, "What does he mean by saying, 'In a little while you will see me no more, and then after a little while you will see me,' and 'Because I am going to the Father'?" **18**They kept asking, "What does he mean by 'a little while'? We don't understand what he is saying."

19Jesus saw that they wanted to ask him about this, so he said to them, "Are you asking one another what I meant when I said, 'In a little while you will see me no more, and then after a little while you will see me'?

Time is a difficult factor for humans to integrate fully into their understanding of the perspectives of God. It was no different with the disciples. Jesus was somehow able to stand above time as he did when he told the Jews "before Abraham was I am" (8:58). That statement for mere humans was not only illogical but bordered on being for the Jews both sacrilegious and crazy. In this section the discussion is not quite so radical, but it created for the disciples a sense of complete bewilderment that necessitated an extended explanation from Jesus that reaches beyond this current segment.

16:16 The transitional double use of the "little while" here undoubtedly refers to the events of the forthcoming death and resurrection of Jesus, the departure of which had been alluded to using similar words in 7:33; 12:35; 13:33.[294] Although the allusion to these two events is here made in a successive manner, it is crucial to recognize the perspective of Jesus at this point. His perspective is that he could visualize both events as a united whole, inseparably bound together in God's plan for salvation. That capacity to see related events together enabled him to view events in their totality.

---

[294] For a two-sided perspective see C. Dietzfelbinger, "Die eschatologische Freude der Gemeinde in der Angst der Welt. Joh 16, 16–33," *EvT* 40 (1980): 420–36.

Accordingly, he could see pain, hurt, and tragedy in the full perspective of God's work without minimizing the reality of their hurtful impact. So, although this verse might not be said to focus precisely on eschatological events,[295] this unified perspective enabled Jesus to view these events in the overall work of God in the history of the world.[296]

But one must not overlook the fact that the phrase a "little while" was used by the prophets with respect to both the coming judgment on Israel (cf. Hos 1:4) and its deliverance (cf. Isa 10:25; Jer 51:33). Of particular note is the promise of an eschatological nature when the deaf would hear and the blind would see (Isa 29:17–18). That perspective is certainly suggested in the next verse, where the disciples in fact conclude that this statement must be linked to Jesus' earlier repeated remarks concerning "going to the Father" (16:17; cf. 16:5; 14:1–11; 13:33,36).[297]

16:17–18 These verses now highlight the disciples' perplexity concerning Jesus' departure and his seeming double-talk to them about the repeated "little while." Conversations like this one often go on for some time when people are confused and hurting. In such situations ideas seem to run together because anxiety and confusion are often partners in the thinking of those who are grieving and hurting. However long such a conversation with Jesus may have lasted, these verses can represent only a Johannine summary of what might have occurred. But they are enough to indicate that the disciples' understanding of time and its relation to any coming events was in complete disarray. They did not comprehend at the time what Jesus was saying (16:18).

16:19 Even though the disciples were in a state of confusion, Jesus understood the situation and its implications. Indeed, Jesus "knew" (not "saw" as NIV) their reasoning and the nature of their questions. In contrast to the way the Synoptic Gospels sometimes speak of Jesus' knowledge, Brown correctly notes that in "John the special knowledge attributed to Jesus seems to be consistently presented as supernatural" (cf. 2:24–25; 4:17–18).[298]

These verses set the stage for Jesus' explanation concerning their sorrow and future joy, which is the focus of the next subsection.

---

[295] Cf. Carson, *John*, 542–43 for a narrow interpretation.

[296] Schnackenburg (*St. John*, 155–56), relying on Augustine's comments *On John* (101.5–6), sees post-Easter implications as well. Beasley-Murray (*John*, 285–86) correctly, I believe, sees similarities with the prophets. Cf. also Barrett, *St. John*, 411.

[297] Several manuscripts actually lengthen 16:16 with the words meaning "because I go to the Father" in order to prepare for the disciple's question. But this addition is undoubtedly a scribal attempt to make the transition to v. 17 easier. See Metzger, *Textual Commentary*, 247.

[298] See R. Brown, *John*, 2.721, but for the opposing view see Carson, *John*, 543. Contrast the Synoptic presentations to John at Mark 5:30; Luke 7:39–40 but the opposite at Matt 12:25; Luke 11:17.

(2) Sorrow and Joy (16:20–22)

[20]I tell you the truth, you will weep and mourn while the world rejoices. You will grieve, but your grief will turn to joy. [21]A woman giving birth to a child has pain because her time has come; but when her baby is born she forgets the anguish because of her joy that a child is born into the world. [22]So with you: Now is your time of grief, but I will see you again and you will rejoice, and no one will take away your joy.

16:20 In this verse, which is introduced by a familiar Johannine double *amēn* ("truly, truly") oathlike statement, the coming twofold experience of the disciples is clearly set out by Jesus, who understood the imminent future. There would first be a period of sorrow for the disciples while the world rejoiced, but that period would give way to a period of rejoicing for them. This coming twofold experience that was here predicted is not only illustrated beautifully in the next verse but is also similarly exemplified forcefully in the eschatological vision of the two witnesses of Revelation (11:3–13).

The idea of sorrow is indicated by the use of two Greek verbs: *klausete* ("weep" or "wail") and *thēnēsete* ("mourn" or "lament"). These verbs represent the usual Semitic grief process (suggested by the Greek verb *lypēthēsesthe*, "grieve," and the noun *lypē*, "grief") wherein the survivors would openly "wail" (cf. 11:31–33 as well as 20:11–15) and express their "laments" (cf. Luke 23:27; this verb is not used elsewhere in John).

16:21 In a typical Semitic type of picture thinking, a strategic brief parable is next included to illustrate the relationship of the disciples' forthcoming experiences. The disciples and the readers of this Gospel are reminded that normally the severe labor pains and anguish experienced prior to the delivery of a baby usually retreat from memory with the joyous arrival of the newborn.

This figurative image of birth pangs followed by joy in the arrival of a child was not a new image in the Bible. It was used in the Old Testament to refer to the painful experiences of Israel in awaiting the coming of their deliverance in the messianic era. Isaiah particularly employs this image in the suffering of Israel and the promise of hope when the dead will live (Isa 26:17–19; cf. 66:7–9; cf. also 21:3 in his prophecy of the defeat of Babylon). But Micah (Mic 4:9–10), Hosea (Hos 13:13), and Jeremiah (Jer 13:21) also use the image as both an indication of Israel's suffering for disobedience and as a window of hope. Similarly the image was apparently used by the Dead Sea Convenanters (cf. 1 QH 2:8–10)[299] and was important in the

---

[299] See remarks by J. Price, "A Light from Qumran upon Some Aspects of Johannine Theology," in *John and the Dead Sea Scrolls* (New York: Crossroad, 1991), 34–35; and W. Brownlee, "Messianic Motifs of Qumran and the New Testament," *NTS* 3 (1956): 29–30.

vision of the woman and the dragon in the Apocalypse, but there after the birth the dragon seeks to devour the child (Rev 12:1–4).

In this text the joyous birth must surely be a reference to the expected resurrection of Jesus, but because it was used in connection with Israel's messianic expectations, it could quite possibly also have had some eschatological overtones for the early readers of the Gospel. Such overtones seem to be suggested in the next verse.

16:22 This verse represents the typical application of a parabolic message to the listener or reader. "So with you" followed immediately by the emphatic "now" (lit. "therefore now") leaves no question that the listener/reader is being addressed with an important message for the present situation. Then the Greek construction sets in bold relief the alternatives in the message. On the one hand the disciples are currently experiencing "grief" *(lypēn),* while on the other hand Jesus promised "I will see you again." The shift in the focus from the disciples to Jesus is significant. It should remind readers that they do not pull themselves up by their own bootstraps. The gaining of hope is not ultimately a result of our own efforts. Transforming hope comes because of divine action.

The resulting action is literally expressed by the statement that "your hearts will rejoice." For the Hebrew/Jewish writers, who loved to think in pictorial words, the heart was frequently regarded as the seat of the will (see Paul's threefold analysis of the fallen human person in Rom 1:24, 26,28; cf. Gen 6:5–6; Pss 7:10; 10:6–17; 14:1). Thus the transforming of the heart is regarded as crucial in gaining wholeness or salvation (cf. Jer 31:33; Ezek 11:19; 36:26). Here transformation is exemplified in the rejoicing heart.

It is also significant to remember that the rejoicing heart could be seen as a sign of the messianic era for Isaiah (Isa 66:14). Here this Johannine verse seems to suggest a similar understanding when it points to the fact that with the coming of the resurrection of Jesus "no one will take away your joy."[300] Joy, then, is multidimensional and can have eschatological overtones. It also clearly reminds us that there are those who would try to scuttle the disciples' joy. The resurrection brings the beginning of a new age.[301]

(3) A New Perspective on Prayer (16:23–28)

[23]In that day you will no longer ask me anything. I tell you the truth, my Father will give you whatever you ask in my name. [24]Until now you have not

---

[300] See C. Dietzfelbinger, "Die eschatologische Freude," 420–36 and B. Schwank, "Sieg und Friede in Christus: Jo 16, 16–33," *Sein und Sendung* 28 (1963): 388–400.

[301] Cf. Morris, *John,* 626–27 and Carson, *John,* 544–45 but contrast Schnackenburg, *St. John,* 3.159.

asked for anything in my name. Ask and you will receive, and your joy will be complete.
²⁵"Though I have been speaking figuratively, a time is coming when I will no longer use this kind of language but will tell you plainly about my Father. ²⁶In that day you will ask in my name. I am not saying that I will ask the Father on your behalf. ²⁷No, the Father himself loves you because you have loved me and have believed that I came from God. ²⁸I came from the Father and entered the world; now I am leaving the world and going back to the Father."

16:23–24 The coming new age would also bring a new perspective on prayer. Verse 23 says that at that time the disciples would no longer be seeking their clarifications or "asking" anything of Jesus (the Greek is actually an emphatic double negative). Carson thinks the two verbs for "asking" here have different meanings, but the distinction may be too refined for a Jew like John.[302]

The death and resurrection of their Lord, however, would clearly bring a phenomenal change to their lives. Such a change is also emphasized by another of the familiar Johannine double *amēn* (truly, truly) oathlike statements. Whenever these doublets occur in the Gospel, they signal crucial statements of Jesus. This double *amēn* statement is particularly significant because it confirms the coming of a new era for the disciples. It would bring a new way in which they would relate to the Godhead and thus to Jesus. Although at this stage they may have been confused and sorrowing, the situation was about to change radically, just as the birthing parable had indicated (16:21). Their requests either for clarification or something particular would no longer be directed to the incarnate Jesus who had walked and talked with them on earth (cf. 1 John 1:1–3). They would then have entered the new era of "joy" (cf. 1 John 1:4), and they would direct these requests to the Father (John 16:23).

The "in my name" of v. 23 appears in some Greek manuscripts with the verb "ask" (cf. NIV, NRSV) and in other manuscripts with the verb "give" (cf. RSV).[303] The Egyptian manuscripts primarily support the latter reading. But the former reading seems to be more consistent with the Johannine pattern of prayer in Jesus' name (cf. 14:13–14; 16:15,24,26).[304]

These texts have led to Protestant patterns of praying in the name of

---

[302] I would not argue that these verbs per se must be distinguished in this way at all times as seemingly suggested by Carson, *John*, 545, but I would agree to some extent that in this context the verbs for asking at v. 23 (first time) and in vv. 23 (second time), 24,26 probably have that effect. The problem with making such a firm distinction as Carson does is that vv. 23 (second reference) and 24 follow directly on the first asking in v. 23. Moreover, those familiar with John's writing habits soon recognize that he can shift words easily without making major distinctions in meaning. Cf. also the discussion of R. Brown, *John*, 2.722–23.

[303] See the discussion of Untergassmair, "Im Namen Jesus," 163–66.

[304] Cf. Metzger, *Textual Commentary*, 248.

Jesus. The mentioning of his name in prayer, however, is not meant to be a magical formula for assuring a desired answer to a request, nor is it to be viewed as a cure-all for poorly expressed or formulated prayers. Rather, it should be a reminder that prayer is to be offered in the nature or spirit of the Lord Jesus, whose name is being used.

The "until now" of v. 24 again signals the inauguration of the new era of prayer, which is once again linked with the postresurrection promise of joy (cf. the rejoicing heart of v. 22). But the promise of receiving the answer to one's requests, as indicated earlier (see my discussions at 14:14; 15:7), is premised not on using a correct verbal formula such as "in the name of Jesus" but on asking in the spirit of Jesus. Because of the promise of divine answers, one can expect to experience the "fulfillment" of joy. The perfect passive participle (translated "complete") here emphasizes the continuing impact of such a fulfilling joy. Such an encompassing joy should be a mark of a vital Christian.

16:25 The new era will likewise bring a new way in which Jesus will communicate with the disciples. Although he was with them in the flesh, he sought to communicate his divinely inspired message in a way they could understand. The Greek *paroimiais,* which can be rendered "figuratively" (NIV) or "in figures of speech" (NRSV), is undoubtedly an attempt to communicate to earthbound humans ideas of the reality of God and of salvation. The word does not need to imply that Jesus constantly spoke to them in parables, as is suggested by the NLT.[305] Thus one does not need, as some have done, to set this statement over against the one in Mark 4:33–34 in which Jesus spoke in parables to the crowd, but to the disciples he "explained everything." The issue here is one of human capacity to receive divine truth. This fact is forcefully underlined in the next section when the disciples mistakenly think that the new era has already arrived, that Jesus can already speak to them in plain terms *(parrēsia),* and that they will understand before the resurrection (cf. John 16:23,29). The new era would provide the key to communication, but that era had not yet arrived. So Jesus still had to provide illustrations of what he meant, such as the picture of childbirth in v. 21. This text also stresses the new era, which will be marked by a new understanding of the work of God. This work will be interpreted and clarified by the Paraclete, as was emphasized in the previous Farewell sections.[306]

16:26–27 To emphasize this point, the text in these verses returns to the subject of prayer and reiterates that "in that day" praying or asking "in

---

[305] *BAGD,* 629 suggests that for Johannine usage the word παροιμια means "a figure of speech" and can have both positive and negative implications. See John 10:6 and 16:25,29.

[306] Cf. Newman and Nida, *Translator's Handbook,* 516.

my name" will be a sign or evidence of a new relationship with the Father. These verses do not denigrate the mediatorial work of Jesus in making intercession for us (cf. Rom 8:34; Heb 7:25) or in being our Paraclete (cf. 1 John 2:1), but they emphasize the wonderful postresurrection access Christians have with the Father through prayer.[307] Because of the new access the followers of Jesus have with the Father in the spirit (name) of Jesus, postresurrection disciples do not need to wait for Jesus to connect them with the Father like some overseas, long-distance operator. Connection is assured because the Father loves *(philei)* the disciples since they have loved and believed in Jesus.

Several important points need to be underscored here. The first involves the use of the verbs for love. As I indicated in connection with 15:14, because of the motif study of *Agape and Eros* by A. Nygren, many preachers have been led astray to believe that the verbs for "love" in the New Testament have special meanings. It is important to remember that *eros* never appears in the New Testament, but that does not mean that inadequate love cannot be expressed by the word *agapē*. Moreover, the distinction that is often made by preachers between *agapan* and *philein* just cannot be supported. As I will indicate in the discussion of John 21, the distinction between the statements of Peter and Jesus can still be made in John 21 but for very different reasons. In the present context (16:17), because the verb is *philein* and not *agapan,* the reader must not suppose here that either the Father's love or the disciple's love is to be understood as inadequate or merely friendship love. The love of the disciple for Jesus here is expected to reflect the love of God.

But there is an additional potential problem for interpreters and that involves the so-called causal particle *(hoti)* in v. 27. Its use in this context does not mean, as Morris states, that the disciples' love "merits the Father's love, or that he loves them *because* of their prior love for Jesus."[308] In the Gospel of John the love of God is prior to and exemplary for any love the disciples exhibit toward the Godhead. It is not a case of the exchange of loves in which humans gain access to God and God therefore responds in an accepting manner. God and Jesus are the prime movers in our relationships, and humans respond to the movements of God. Moreover, Gods' loving openness to our prayers is in fact the outworking of God's prior love to us in "giving" Jesus (cf. 3:16). Our prayers, based on our having entered a state of loving *(pephilēkate,* perfect) and believing *(pepisteukate,* perfect), are therefore premised on God's prior loving and Jesus' self-giving implied in the important words "I came from God." These concluding words of

---

[307] See Beasley-Murray's helpful discussion on this subject in *John*, 287.

[308] Cf. Morris, *John*, 630. The italics are here added for emphasis.

v. 27 are absolutely crucial for a correct understanding of this verse. The coming of Jesus (aorist tense reflecting the incarnation) is a precondition to our loving and believing Jesus.

The unity of the Godhead is once again stressed in the fact that Jesus did not come on his own but came from God/the Father,[309] which is similar to the fact that the Spirit/Paraclete proceeded from the Father (cf. 15:26).

16:28 This verse draws the incarnational picture into a unified whole and summarizes in a brief span the mission of Jesus. Thus (1) it encapsulates his *coming* as the incarnate representative of the Father (1:1,9,14) and (2) his *entering* the world to serve as the unique agent of God in communicating God's message to humans (5:19–30). In addition, (3) it highlights the traumatic *departure* of Jesus in the arrival of that fateful but purposeful hour of the crucifixion/death of Jesus (12:23–24,27; 19:30), and (4) it culminates in his victorious *going back* to the Father and preparing a place for his followers (14:2).

(4) The Forthcoming Reversal and Its Implications (16:29–33)

[29]Then Jesus' disciples said, "Now you are speaking clearly and without figures of speech. [30]Now we can see that you know all things and that you do not even need to have anyone ask you questions. This makes us believe that you came from God."

[31]"You believe at last!" Jesus answered. [32]"But a time is coming, and has come, when you will be scattered, each to his own home. You will leave me all alone. Yet I am not alone, for my Father is with me.

[33]"I have told you these things, so that in me you may have peace. In this world you will have trouble. But take heart! I have overcome the world."

This subsection concludes the Anxiety Circle with a masterfully constructed, ironic great reversal.[310]

16:29–30 Obviously Jesus had earlier told them that the time would come when he would no longer have to speak to them figuratively but would then be speaking plainly or clearly to them (*parrēsia*, 16:25). John, however, details here the irony of the disciples' statements in that they thought they knew the meaning of what Jesus was saying. Unfortunately, they misunderstood both in terms of their time ("now") and their "clarity" (*parrēsia*) of perception. Their theological statements were quite good, if they had understood what they were saying.

They were partly correct in their assumption that Jesus had great knowl-

---

[309] Although there is strong support for "the Father" here from manuscripts like Vaticanus and some Western readings, the most likely reading here is "God." Cf. Metzger, *Textual Commentary*, 248.

[310] See P. Duke, *Irony in the Fourth Gospel* (Atlanta: John Knox, 1985), especially at 48–51, 56–59.

edge ("we know," *oidamen,* "that you know," *oidas;* the NIV has "we can see that you know"). Their generalization of how much knowledge Jesus had ("all things," *panta*) was, however, a typical human overstatement that was far beyond their actual capacity to comprehend. It was merely one of their assumptions. Such an assumption has often become part of our theological assumptions about the incarnate Jesus' knowledge, even though elsewhere, for example, he states that he did not know the time of the end (cf. Mark 13:32). Moreover, Paul states that he "emptied himself" ("made himself nothing," NIV; *eauton ekenosen,* Phil 2:7), although we are not quite sure of the full implications of that statement.

Their next statement that they did not need to probe his mind *(erōta)* to gain further information or confirmation that he "came from God" is likewise a theologically correct assumption. Yet practically or existentially at this time it was for them an unfulfilled claim. Their statement at that point went far beyond their personal understanding and commitments. Theologically they were correct: Jesus did come from God.[311] Yet what did that statement actually mean for them?

Their understanding of reality was sadly skewed so badly that their words were almost meaningless. Accordingly, they could make theologically significant statements such as Martha made (cf. 11:22,24,27). But like Martha, whose life responses were not actually coordinated with her words (11:39), the disciples' actions would later prove the clear disconnection between their words and their lives (John 16:32; cf. Peter's role at 18:10, 17,25–27; 21:15–21).

16:31 The follow-up statement of Jesus is definitely ironic, whether it is rendered as a question (KJV, RSV, NRSV, NLT, HCSB) or as an exasperated statement (NIV).[312] That Jesus came from God has been his consistent affirmation throughout the Gospel. He was God's special agent (cf. 5:19–30). The disciples had arrived at the point of a "belief" that they could express. But typical human words and adequate believing may be far apart in real life. People may say they believe in Jesus, but that does not mean they have arrived at the point where their life patterns follow their beliefs. Jesus was not confused by statements of belief or about stages of believing. He knew how to evaluate human believing (cf. 2:23–24; 12:42–43).

16:32 The reality bomb then was dropped by Jesus in the great reversal

---

[311] Cf. the *Gos. Pet.* 6:69, which has a similar statement to John 16:30. The basic difference is that there the disciples are convinced that Jesus is "God's Holy One." Cf. also the comments of Dodd, *Interpretation,* 392.

[312] Readers should remember that punctuation marks in Greek are generally part of the translation process as well as part of the developing of adequate Greek texts for contemporary translators from unpunctuated early Greek manuscripts, where letters are all in capitals and words are undivided. Cf. the comments also of Newman and Nida, *Translator's Handbook,* 520.

statement of this section. Their hour (*hōra*, the NIV has the less adequate "time") would soon be coming, and it would bring a dramatic shift. The Anxiety Circle began with the disciples' concern about Jesus' departure (14:1) and their obvious feelings of abandonment (14:18). But while the disciples' fears were real, Jesus made it clear that in the forthcoming scattering of the disciples they would "abandon" Jesus ("leave me all alone," *kame mono aphete*), not the reverse.

This statement structures the connections within this two-part section on anxiety and loneliness and in fact illuminates the entire Farewell Cycle. It is a masterpiece of literary construction, a fact overlooked by most commentators as they quickly move to discuss his nonabandonment by God. The *glue of Christianity is not the disciples; it is Jesus, who will not abandon the disciples* or let them become orphans (14:18) even though they would leave Jesus when the pressures came to them (16:32).

Persecution and societal pressure do strange things to people. Both Jesus and John understood this reality. John had witnessed the abandonment of Jesus by the disciples, and the Christians of the late first century were faced with similar pressures to abandon their relationship with Jesus (cf. 1 John 2:19).

Such pressures have been repeated continually in history. Throughout the church's history those who call themselves Christians have even pressured others who call themselves Christians to conform to their views. Indeed, they have pressured them to the point of killing them or burning them at the stake prior to coming to North America. My own ancestors were persecuted by Roman Catholics, Lutherans, and Russian Orthodox before finally fleeing to the so-called western haven of religious liberty. The sad stories of the past are unfortunately being repeated throughout the world even today. But of one thing we can be sure, even though we are tempted to abandon our loyalty to Jesus: Jesus will not abandon his people. But what of the abandoned Jesus? This text makes clear that the *Father did not abandon his Son!*

Excursus 18: Nonabandonment in John and the Cry of Dereliction

The statement concerning Jesus' not being abandoned in 16:32 immediately brings to mind the well-known Cry of Dereliction in Mark 15:34 and Matt 27:46, "My God, my God, why have you forsaken me?" which is not mentioned in either Luke or John.

Brown, in his major treatment of *The Death of the Messiah*, concludes that the Death Cry is a transliteration of an Aramaic free rendering of the Hebrew of Ps 22:2 and not a direct transliteration of the Hebrew itself.[313] Accordingly, it would probably be hard to argue strictly that the cry is basically a victory cry and not a

---

[313] R. Brown, *The Death of the Messiah: From Gethsemane to the Grave*, Vol. 2 (New York: Doubleday), 1051–53.

cry of agony. Sometimes preachers and theologians have sought to protect Jesus in such arguments by pointing to the fact that Psalm 22 ends not merely with a prayer for deliverance (Ps 22:19–21) but also with a strong affirmation of praise to the Lord for such an anticipated deliverance (Ps 22:23–31).

On the other hand, several points can certainly be made concerning this cry. In the first place, such cries, shouts, or loud screams should be understood as quite consistent with the terrible suffering that persons experienced in crucifixion.[314] Although many victims cursed their crucifiers, judges, and betrayers, it is important to recognize that there is not the slightest hint of any such attitude on the part of Jesus in any of the four Gospels. Instead, there is a clear proclamation of forgiveness of his crucifiers on the part of Jesus because they did not understand the real meaning of what they were doing (Luke 23:34; cf. also the statement of Stephen in Acts 7:60). Cries in death and suffering are a very human phenomenon (cf. Ezek 11:13), and it is important not to remove Jesus from the realm of suffering as a human in the horrible death of crucifixion.

It is likewise crucial not to think of God the Father, as some passionless stoic-type deity who had no understanding or feelings for the pain of his Son. That may be the God of some theological constructions, but that is hardly the God of Israel, who showed his incredible patience and mercy time and again to his erring children. To be a "person" means to be able to ache when things seem to be going other than one wishes, even when one knows they may go differently in the long run. God is not some stone-deaf idol carved by human hands. God is the caring Creator of people into whom he breathed the breath of life (Gen 2:7). And Jesus, the one who became the incarnate Word (John 1:14), was one with God in the creation of the world (1:3).

Holding together in the teacups of our little minds the humanity and deity of Jesus has always been difficult. That is especially true when it comes to the suffering of Jesus. Although it is inappropriate since Schweitzer to attempt to psychoanalyze Jesus,[315] it is certainly appropriate to recognize the reasonableness of Jesus' question "Why?" in the midst of his suffering. That is a very familiar question of all humans. It is actually the same question as that of the martyrs of Rev 6:10 when they asked "how long?" That question is, in fact: "Where are you God, right now?" or "God, are you really involved with us in our suffering?"

It is especially significant that in the Gospels the prayers of Jesus are addressed to the "Father" *(pater,* cf. John 11:11; 12:27; 17:1,5,11,21,24,25; also cf. 16:23; for the Synoptics cf. Matt 6:9; Mark 14:36; 11:25–26; 26:39; Luke 10:21; 11:2; 22:42; 23:34,46) and not to God. Accordingly, the Cry of Dereliction is certainly not a prayer; so although it may seem to be a direct statement addressed to God, it probably is more of a human cry of agony in the midst of tremendous pain.

The suffering and death of Jesus was of course very real. But both John and Luke were more concerned to show that the death of Jesus was the ultimate vic-

---

[314] See J. Blinzer, *The Trial of Jesus* (Westminster: Newman, 1959), 261.

[315] A. Schweitzer, *The Psychiatric Study of Jesus* (Boston: Beacon, 1948) and *The Quest for the Historical Jesus* (New York: Macmillan, 1954), 345, 386, 399–401.

tory rather than to concentrate on the painfulness of the death. In Luke, Jesus prays, "Father, into your hands I commit my spirit" (Luke 23:46), and John brings the glorification of Jesus to a climax with the words "It is finished" (John 19:30). Therefore it is not surprising that the Father for whom Jesus had been faithfully serving as a special agent throughout the Gospel of John would be powerfully pictured at 16:32 before the resurrection as not abandoning Jesus in the same manner as Jesus was portrayed as being unwilling before the resurrection to abandon his disciples, in spite of the fact that he was speaking forcefully of his own departure (14:2–3,18).

The Johannine portrait of Jesus is focused a little differently from that of Mark and Matthew, but in spite of the differences Jesus is both God's divine Son as well as a human being. In contrast, Schweitzer's view sees Jesus in the Cry of Dereliction as merely a human eschatological dreamer who misunderstood his mission in Mark and elsewhere. Thus he died a disillusioned prophet. But Schweitzer's way of explaining the cry is a complete misunderstanding of both Jesus and Mark.[316] Likewise, those who argue from the ending of Mark at 16:8 that Mark did now envision a resurrection or that the lost ending of Mark was heretical[317] do not, I believe, fully sense the force of the resurrection perspectives in the passion predictions (e.g., Mark 8:31; 9:31; 10:33–34) as well as the transfiguration and post-Last Supper statements (9:9; 14:28) in addition to the postresurrection instructions to the women (16:7). Jesus' suffering and in agony in death both in Mark and John was *not* that of a disillusioned dreamer but represents genuine human agony.

16:32 (Cont.) The scattering of the disciples could here easily reflect the idea in the prophecy of Zech 13:7, where the striking of the shepherd is said to result in the scattering of the sheep.[318] That text probably became a familiar kerygmatic passage in the early church, for it also appears in Mark 14:27 (cf. Matt 26:31) after the Last Supper. In the Markan text the regathering in Galilee in the postresurrection era is also mentioned, but Schnackenburg thinks that the positive regathering in Mark, which could be suggested in the conclusion to the prediction of Zechariah at 13:9, was not used in the Johannine text because of the disciples' misguided "self-confidence" and the need to focus on their failed understanding.[319]

16:33 On the other hand, this next verse does provide a positive conclusion to the discussion because Jesus is able to look beyond the situation of the bewildered disciples and provide them with a sense of encourage-

---

[316] Ibid., 225, also 392–94, 396, 398.

[317] See T. Boomersheim, "The Narrative Technique of Mark 16:8," *JBL* 100 (1981): 213–25 and the follow-up article at 225–39; cf. R. Fuller, *The Formation of the Resurrection Narratives* (Philadelphia: Fortress, 1980), 64–70. Contrast Peterson, "When Is the End Not the End?" *Int* 34 (1980): 151–66. Cf. C. Moule, "St. Mark 16:8 Once More," *NTS* 2 (1955): 58–59.

[318] For the view of suffering in Qumran see R. Brown, "The Scrolls and the Johannine Gospel and Epistles," *CBQ* 17 (1955): 403–19, 559–74.

[319] See Schnackenburg, *St. John*, 3.165.

ment. But that encouragement is not predicated on their own understanding. The promise of peace, or Shalom *(eirēnē)*, which is foundational to the Semitic understanding of wholeness and satisfying life, is here clearly dependent on the little phrase "in me." This idea that peace and wholeness of life or salvation were to be found fully "in Jesus" or "in Christ" became one of the most significant aspects of Pauline theology. So strategic are these phrases that it would be impossible to write a theology of Paul without references to "in Christ" or "in him." But Pauline mysticism is not a flight to be alone with Jesus. As S. Cave has well stated, it is a community idea wherein Christians share with each other the experience of being in Christ.[320]

The world, Jesus said, is not an easy place in which to live. In Johannine thinking the world is in the hands of an evil ruler *(archōn;* cf. 12:31; 14:30; 16:11). As a result the followers of Jesus are subject to "tribulation" (RSV), "trouble" (NIV), "persecution" (NRSV), "trials and sorrows" (NLT). The word *thlipsin* (singular, but undoubtedly with a collective sense) appears only here and at 16:21 to refer to pains in childbirth and is undoubtedly used to suggest serious difficulties for Christians.

But in spite of such predicted troubles in the world, the followers of Jesus were called to encouragement because Jesus had "overcome" the world. The use of the perfect *nenikēka* was obviously intended by John to communicate a proleptic sense of victory even before the crucifixion. It is the only use of this battle term in the Gospel, although it is used a number of times in 1 John, where the stress is on winning the victory against both the evil one and the inauthentic ways of the world (2:13–14; 4:4; 5:4–5 plus the noun *nikē*, "victory," at 5:4; cf. also the many uses of the term in the Apocalypse).

The Gospel of John and 1 John are not books that proclaim a defeatist attitude. They are realistic in that they take suffering, persecution, and martyrdom very seriously, just as the Book of Revelation takes them seriously. They are books of encouragement in the face of anxiety and genuine concern. They do not call the followers of Jesus to superficial discipleship but to a self-giving obedience modeled on the life, death, and resurrection of Jesus. The Shalom they offer is not the peace of the world (14:27) because that peace is not peace, for it ends in violence (Rev 6:4). So in spite of all the concerns of the disciples, this ring of anxiety begins and ends with a message of hope—an ultimate hope to be with Jesus in his specially prepared place (14:1) and a hope of victory for living in a world of hatred and trouble (16:33).

---

[320] For a discussion of the community idea of mysticism see S. Cave, *The Gospel of St. Paul* (New York: Doubleday, Doran & Co., 1929), 50.

7. The Magisterial Prayer as the Final Preparation for Passover (17:1–26)

Unlike the Synoptic Gospels, which highlight the Prayer in the Garden of Gethsemane as the final preparation of Jesus before his arrest (cf. Matt 26:36–46; Mark 14:32–43; Luke 22:39–46), the Gospel of John does not include that pericope but has instead this magnificent prayer of chap. 17. This chapter has been labeled with many titles such as "The Consecration Prayer," or "The Prayer of Consecration" (Westcott, Hoskyns and Davey, Beasley-Murray),[321] "The Prayer of the Departing Redeemer" (Schnackenburg),[322] "The Farewell Prayer" (Bultmann, Ridderbos),[323] "The Sage's Prayer" (Witherington),[324] "The Prayer"/"Final Prayer of Jesus" (Barrett, Carson),[325] "Jesus Prays for His Disciples" (Newman and Nida),[326] and "The High Priestly Prayer" (Agourides, Haenchen, Morris).[327] Brown designates the chapter merely as "The Last Discourse,"[328] and Segovia does not even include the prayer in his Farewell study.[329]

Although there are a few manuscript variants, the chapter is surprisingly free of debatable textual issues.[330] Instead, the attention given the chapter has focused on theological concerns and more recently on structural issues.[331]

Excursus 19: The Structure of John 17

In dealing with the chapter's structure many scholars have developed their analytical patterns based on theological and linguistic considerations and have divided the chapter into three, four, or more subsections. Westcott argued for three sections based on the petitions of Jesus for himself (vv. 1–5), his immediate disciples (vv. 6–19), and the later community of followers (vv. 20–26).[332] Schnackenburg, in his 1973 article on structure, further subdivided vv. 6–19 into

---

[321] Westcott, *St. John*, 2.238; Hoskyns and Davey, *The Fourth Gospel*, 494; Beasley-Murray, *John*, 291.

[322] Schnackenburg, *St. John*, 167.

[323] Bultmann, *John*, 486; Ridderbos, *John*, 546.

[324] Witherington, *John's Wisdom*, 226.

[325] Barrett, *St. John*, 416; Carson, *John*, 550; D. A. Carson, *The Farewell Discourse and Final Prayer of Jesus* (Grand Rapids: Baker, 1980).

[326] Newman and Nida, *Textual Commentary*, 523. They also refer to the chapter as the traditional "high-priestly prayer."

[327] S. Agourides, "The 'High Priestly Prayer' of Jesus," *SE* 4 (1968): 137–43; Haenchen, *John* 2, 147; Morris, *John*, 634.

[328] R. Brown, *John*, 2.739.

[329] Segovia, *The Farewell of the Word*, vi.

[330] Metzger, *Textual Commentary*, 249–50.

[331] G. Borchert, "The Prayer of John 17 in the Narrative Framework of the Johannine Gospel," in *Gemeinschaft am Evangelium* (Leipzig: Evangelische Verlagsanstalt, 1996), 7–18.

[332] Westcott, *St. John*, 2.240.

three parts related to a direct personal concern for the disciples (vv. 6–11a), a concern for their protection in the world (vv. 11b–16), and a concern for their consecration or sanctification (vv. 17–19). Furthermore, he divided vv. 20–26 into two parts related to the concern for oneness (vv. 20–23) and the concern for the community's fulfillment (vv. 24–26). As a result he ended up with six basic subsections.[333]

This basic pattern of dividing the chapter has been followed substantially by others such as Beasley-Murray and Carson.[334] Moreover, D. A. Black has since attempted to support this division through a linguistic analysis.[335]

Brown, however, turned away from Westcott's threefold pattern and its revisions and chose another three-part division of vv. 1–8,9–19,20–26, although he adds the following subdivisions: vv. 1–5,6–8,9–16,17–19,20–23 and 24–26, thus ending with a slightly different six-part subdivision.[336] Barrett, Lagrange, and others have employed a four-part division,[337] while Dodd decided to alter Westcott's second section of vv. 6–19 by dividing it into vv. 6–8 and 9–19.[338] Malatesta decided on a five-part structure he developed from an overly complex chiastic pattern that he thought he found in the Gospel.[339]

My own structure is based on what I think is a clearly defined seven-part subdivision of the chapter based on the content, the petitional divisions, and the relationship of these petitions to the overall structure of the book. It is my hope that the reader will therefore once again be led to realize that this Johannine writer had an amazing organizational ability for developing his themes and integrating them into the rest of the book.

Before I turn to the specific structure of this chapter, it is important to note that the major section in which this chapter has been located is the conclusion to the Farewell Cycle. The designation "Farewell Discourses" that has been used by a number of scholars is a deceptive misnomer because chaps. 13–17 include far more than discourses. I have instead likened this Farewell Cycle to a bull's-eye or target with concentric rings and a center that moves the reader's thinking from the outside and a readiness for the strategic Passover (13:1) in the life and ministry of Jesus, introduced with the arrival of the "hour" at 12:23, to the core of what it means to be a disciple. Then the Cycle moves back again to the outer ring, where the toll of the dominating hour is once again sounded (17:1). In this Cycle the first

---

[333] R. Schnackenburg, "Strukturanalyse von Joh 17," *BZ* 17 (1973): 67–78, 196–202.

[334] Beasley-Murray, *John*, 295–96; Carson, *John*, 553.

[335] D. A. Black, "On the Style and Significance of John 17," *CTR* 3 (1988): 141–59. Cf. also A. Laurentin for his earlier analysis in *"We 'attah-Kai nun. Formule caracteristique des textes juridiques et liturgieques* (à propos de Jean 17, 5)," *Bib* 45 (1964): 168–97, 413–32.

[336] R. Brown, *John*, 2.738–81.

[337] See Barrett, *St. John*, 416–17; M. Lagrange, *Evangile selon Saint Jean* (Paris: Gabalda, 1925), 436.

[338] Dodd, *Interpretation*, 417.

[339] E. Malatesta, "The Literary Structure of John 17," *Bib* 52 (1971): 190–214.

half of the outer ring or circle involved a footwashing act that modeled for the disciples the meaning of discipleship in love. But in closing that ring Jesus' departure was clearly announced.

The first part of the next ring therefore involved the introduction of the Circle of Anxiety and the promise that Jesus' departure to the Father was purposeful. Inside that ring came the first part of the divine answer to the disciples' distress in the first segment of the Paraclete sayings. That, in turn, led to the core involving the necessity of abiding in Jesus to assure authentic discipleship. As we moved out from that core again to the inner ring, new Paraclete sayings were introduced to deal with the hostility in the world. That, in turn, led back to the Circle of Anxiety and the promise that like the pain of childbirth, the disciples' anxiety would turn to joy; and even though they would abandon Jesus, he would bring them peace.

Now as we return to the outer ring and chap. 17, the focus is once again fully on Jesus. As Jesus modeled for them in chap. 13 the nature of community discipleship through love, here he modeled for them his concerns for the community's mission and well-being through prayer. This Farewell Cycle is like a beautiful symphony that integrates an amazing interplay of ideas into a priceless work of art.

But chap. 17 is also an intriguing work itself, and it serves as a magnificent conclusion to this Farewell Cycle. Encapsulated within this concluding chapter are a series of seven distinct petitions that for the most part invoke the name "Father" and are like flashing signals notifying the reader of changing emphases in this great prayer. As I have indicated earlier, the three previous petitions in the Gospel all use this same signal (11:41; 12:27–28). In learning about prayer from the Lord, John also learned from Jesus that God was not some abstract force in the universe but was like a personal Father.

Jesus came into a Jewish world that had developed a remote view of God, one that needed angels to carry messages. The people had ceased to use the name of God for fear of taking his name in vain, just like the Prodigal Son, who could speak of "heaven" but not use the name of God (cf. Luke 15:18,21). Into this context of speaking of God by means of surrogate titles Jesus came and called God his Father. But what was even more astounding was that he taught his disciples to pray "Our Father" (cf. Matt 6:9).[340] For the Jews of that day such a personal view of God was very degrading of God and akin to blasphemy (cf. John 5:18). Yet in spite of his

---

[340] See G. Borchert, "The Lord of Form and Freedom: A New Testament Perspective on Worship," *RevExp* 80 (1983): 5–18.

personal sense of the Father's presence, Jesus modeled for his disciples how to honor and glorify God through consistent obedience to the will of the Father. It is this wonderful sense of Jesus' personal relationship to God that John captured in this magisterial prayer of John 17. Few passages of Scripture come so close to revealing the heart of God's special agent as these magnificent twenty-six verses.

Using the key of *pater* (father), it immediately becomes evident that there are at least six petitions in this chapter (vv. 1,5,11,21,24,25). To these six petitions is added a seventh petition using an implied *pater* in v. 17. What is even more intriguing is that these seven petitions seem to connect with seven aspects of the Gospel theologically and linguistically in a way that stretches the mind because of how these connections were so artfully designed.

But the structure is not merely developed in terms of the seven petitions. There also seems to be another structural marker, *erotō*, "I pray" or "I ask" at 17:9 and 17:20 that seems to signal major shifts in the petitions and therefore to divide the chapter into three major sections, as was suggested by Brown.[341] But I would entitle these three sections (1) Finishing the Mission in a Hostile World (17:1–8), (2) Preparing the Disciples (17:9–19), and (3) Looking to the Future (17:20–26).

In concluding these introductory remarks, I must also mention another important fact with respect to two verbs that are used repeatedly throughout this chapter. They are *didonai* ("give") in 17:2,6,7,8,9,11,14,22,25 and *apostellein* ("send") in 17:3,8,18,21,23,25. In using these verbs John was highlighting the fact that the main focus of the chapter was not to be put on Jesus but on his mission in the establishment and confirming of a community that would believe and obey him, God's agent or *shaliach*.[342]

An understanding of this fact is absolutely crucial in expounding this chapter because many commentators have argued that the first part of this prayer concerns Jesus' self rather than his work of establishing a community of disciples for the continuing divine purpose of mission. By missing this crucial element of the prayer interpreters can easily turn the prayer into a model for a mystical experience with God that neglects its overarching mission incentive. The same can be said of much of the preaching and debate concerning the use of the strategic verses on oneness in 17:21–22 during the last century, for they have often failed to recognize the centrality

---

[341] R. Brown, *John*, 2.750–51.

[342] For a discussion of agency in John see J. A. Bühner, *Der Gesandte in sein Weg im vierten Evangelium* (Tübingen: Mohr/Siebeck, 1977 and J. P. Miranda, *Die Sendung Jesu im Vierten Evangelium* (Stuttgart: Katholisches Bibelwerk, 1977).

of mission in the quest for unity.[343]

With these extended introductory remarks on John 17 in mind, attention is now directed to an analysis of the chapter.

(1) Finishing His Mission in a Hostile World (17:1–8)

¹After Jesus said this, he looked toward heaven and prayed:

"Father, the time has come. Glorify your Son, that your Son may glorify you. ²For you granted him authority over all people that he might give eternal life to all those you have given him. ³Now this is eternal life: that they may know you, the only true God, and Jesus Christ, whom you have sent. ⁴I have brought you glory on earth by completing the work you gave me to do. ⁵And now, Father, glorify me in your presence with the glory I had with you before the world began.

⁶"I have revealed you to those whom you gave me out of the world. They were yours; you gave them to me and they have obeyed your word. ⁷Now they know that everything you have given me comes from you. ⁸For I gave them the words you gave me and they accepted them. They knew with certainty that I came from you, and they believed that you sent me.

This section of chap. 17 includes two significant petitional subsections (vv. 1–3 and vv. 4–8), which are directed to the conclusion of Jesus' earthly mission and return to the Father as he prepared to turn over the Gospel task to his designated human agents, the disciples.

THE FIRST PETITION: GLORIFICATION IN MISSION (17:1–3). **17:1** This chapter and the first petition begin with several important noteworthy markers. The first is that by beginning with the words *tauta elalēsen,* Jesus "said these things," it implies that Jesus had completed speaking and was turning to something else, namely, to the prayer. Agourides, however, argues that the prayer was actually a "consolatory discourse" or teaching mechanism itself.[344] Although the prayer undoubtedly has didactic implications, it reveals something far more of what John sensed was the driving force of the mission of Jesus,[345] in a similar way to that which the Song of Moses (Deut 32) encapsulated Moses' concerns in the long farewell to his

---

[343] For some works on the subject of John 17 and Unity see J. Cadier, "The Unity of the Church," *Int* 11 (1957): 166–76; D. M. Lloyd-Jones, *The Basis of Christian Unity: An Exposition of John 17 and Ephesians 4* (Grand Rapids: Eerdmans, 1963); P. Minear, "Evangelism, Ecumenism and John Seventeen," *ThTo* 35 (1978): 5–13; T. E. Pollard, " 'That They All May be One': John xvii 21 and the Unity of the Church," *ExpTim* 70 (1958–59): 149–50; J. F. Randall, "The Theme of Unity in John 17:20–23," *ETL* 41 (1965): 373–94; and W. Thüsing, *Herrlichkeit und Einheit: Eine Auslegung des Hohepriesterlichen Gebetes Jesu (Johannes 17)* (Düsseldorf: Patmos, 1962).

[344] Agourides, "High-Priestly Prayer," 137, etc.

[345] Cf. M. Cressey, "In the World Not of It: New Testament Perspectives on World, Church and Mission," *IBS* (1979): 227–41 and C. Morrison, "Mission and Ethic: An Interpretation of John 17," *Int* 19 (1965): 259–73.

people in Deuteronomy.

The second marker involves the fact that Jesus (lit.) raised "his eyes to heaven." This act is to be understood as a symbolic gesture of prayer (cf. 11:41). In advising translators concerning this expression Newman and Nida assert that "it is important to avoid the impression that Jesus looked into heaven in the literal sense."[346] That this act was viewed as directing one's full attention to God should here be understood, and heaven is not to be thought of as "sky" but as the abode of God. In that day it was viewed as "up," whereas today one might think of God as existing in another dimension.

The third marker, "Father," has been discussed at length in the introduction to this chapter as an indication of a petition for both Jesus and subsequently for his followers.

The fourth marker is the familiar word "hour" (NIV "time"), which provides the presupposition to the entire prayer: namely, that the crucial Passover death of Jesus was at hand and everything in this chapter presupposed Jesus' imminent departure.[347]

The petition itself is fully purpose driven. It is not self-oriented. Jesus' petition for the Father to "Glorify your Son" cannot be understood apart from the goal that the Father would be glorified through the Son's glorification.[348] Moreover, it cannot be understood apart from the fact that the "hour" of the Son's glorification was premised on the death of the Son. It is essential, therefore, not to assume that glorification implies only bright lights and victory because Jesus' resurrection cannot in John be separated from the death of God's Son, his special agent. Thus, honoring/glorifying the Son in his mission to the world actually honors the Father (cf. 5:21–23).

17:2–3 In like manner the rationale continues in that the giving of power/authority to the Son was for the purpose of bestowing/giving eternal life to all. But the parameters for the giving of this eternal life are clearly established by the stated mission of Jesus to the effect that "they may know … the only true God" and his specially sent agent.

Suffice it to state briefly that while God's intention is that everyone or all people should be given eternal life, receiving this bestowal is inseparably linked to knowing God and his special Son. Moreover, the God about whom the prayer speaks is not some generally defined "god" within the world of many gods. God here is defined by two specific adjectival limitations. God is, first, the one and only God; and, second, God is absolutely genuine or authentic.

---

[346] Newman and Nida, *Translator's Handbook*, 525.

[347] See A. George, "'L'Heure' de Jean XVII," *RB* 61 (1959): 392–97.

[348] Cf. the view of B. Schwank, "Vater, verherrliche deinen Sohn?: Jo 17, 1–5," *Sein und Sendung* 28 (1963): 436–49.

In addition, the mission of the Son is defined in close connection to the overall purposes of God because his giving of eternal life to people is further explained as given to those whom God had given to him. The Son's saving activity, therefore, is directly related to the will and purposes of God. But great care must be taken in not overinterpreting the words in this passage to limit the number God has given to the Son because the point of the prayer is not to categorize people as those who are to be "in" and those who are to be left "out" of the divine mission. The point of this petition and its explication is that Jesus submitted and was obedient to God's purpose for him.[349] That purpose in his life, death, and resurrection (his glorification) was to glorify God and to bring the promise of eternal life and salvation to the world. His mission was good news, not limiting bad news.[350] But at the same time he took seriously evil in the world as the context for both *his* mission (highlighted in the Passover events) and for the *disciple's* mission (as evidenced later in the fourth petition).

As one reflects on the words in this subsection concerning Jesus' purpose in giving eternal life to all, one is not merely drawn to the great assertion of John 3:16, wherein God and the Son are joined together in the purpose of bringing eternal life to all who believe. One is equally drawn to the fact that this petition of Jesus actually reflects the purpose statement for the entire Gospel (20:30–31). There it is said that many other signs could, in fact, be given that are not included in this book, but those that have been selected are chosen to promote believing in the intimate relationship of Jesus, the Son, and God the Father in order that the believer might experience dynamic new life because of him.

THE SECOND PETITION: THE RETURN TO GLORY AT THE CONCLUSION OF THE INCARNATIONAL MISSION (17:4–8). **17:4** This verse provides the transition from the purpose statement concerning the coming of Jesus to the incarnational work of Jesus. The link is provided by the extended use of the concept of glory. This verse is both reflective of the past and serves as the basis for the prospect of the future in the petition of the next verse. As Jesus anticipated the cross, he could review his incarnation and speak of bringing glory to God by completing or fulfilling his assigned work.

17:5 As Jesus looked back before the incarnation, he voiced his second petition with the standard marker "Father" and prayed that his mission would be *fully completed* by the sign of his return to the glory he had before creation. The connection between this verse and the Prologue of John has

---

[349] Contrast the argument of D. Wenham, "Spirit and Life. Some Reflections on Johannine Theology," *Them* 6 (1980): 4–8.

[350] Cf. the discussion in A. Laurentin, "Jean XVII, 5 et le prédestination du Christ á la glorie chez S. Augustin et ses predecisseurs," in *L'Evangile de Jean* (Paris: Cerf, 1958), 225–48.

been often noted by commentators. But I should add that just as in 1:1–2 it was said that the Word was in the beginning with God and yet the two were distinguishable, so there is here no attempt made for the Son to pray for the merging of the two or for the Son's absorption into God or the divine mind/ soul as might have been proposed by Plato and the Greek philosophers. The Godhead in John is very personal and identifiable both before the incarnation (1:1), in the incarnation (1:14), and thereafter in the postresurrection return.

Käsemann had argued that the idea of Jesus possessing glory in the incarnation (as in 1:14) was a contradiction of ideas.[351] Haenchen, however, countered by stating that the prayer of Jesus for a restoration of the former glory here "presupposed" that he did not possess that type of glory in the incarnation. Accordingly, Jesus was hardly Käsemann's docetic "god walking about the earth."[352] Schnackenburg posited that while both John here and Paul in Phil 2:6–11 may have been seeking to assist believers to understand the greatness of the Redeemer in his effective work, the perspective is slightly different in that for Paul, Jesus has an enhanced status after the emptying and subsequent exaltation whereas in John, Jesus "regains the glory that was previously his."[353] Yet these ideas seem to make overly fine distinctions, and perhaps it is best not to concentrate on the temporal issues such as the premundane existence of the Logos but to focus on his supermundane nature and thus emphasize "his transcendence over the world."[354] But I would insist that however one might describe the transitional nature of Jesus, there is no question that the present statements are to be linked with the description in the Prologue of the Word *(logos)* and God *(theos)*.

17:6–8 These verses form another of the Johannine saddle texts, which here relate both to the petition in v. 5 and the petition introduced in v. 9. These verses are again like the saddle of a mountain range that enables climbers to move from one peak to another without returning to the base of the mountain. The two previous verses involved a reflection on the past ministry of Jesus as well as the prospect for completion of his mission and return to his former glory.

These three verses continue the reflective process of Jesus' incarnational work, but here the focus is particularly with his disciples.[355] This work of Jesus is described as revealing (lit.) "your name." The NIV has "you,"

---

[351] E. Käsemann, *The Testament of Jesus According to John 17* (Philadelphia: Fortress, 1968), 8–26.

[352] Haenchen, *John*, 2.152.

[353] Schnackenburg, *St. John*, 3.174.

[354] Ibid. Cf. Beasley-Murray, *John*, 297–98.

[355] B. Rigaux, "Die Jünger Jesu in Johnnes 17," *TQ* 150 (1970): 202–13.

which omits the powerful Semitic word picture that implies Jesus' work involved revealing the very nature of God (cf. 14:9–10).

Those disciples to whom Jesus revealed God's name or nature belonged to God[356] (the Greek uses the idiom "they were to you"), and God in turn gave them to Jesus. They did not have any special origin as Jesus did because they came "out of the world." Yet they had become special to God because when God gave them to the incarnate Jesus to reveal his own name/nature, they would become important to God's strategy of mission. In analyzing 17:6 the interpreter should avoid jumping into the predestination/prestatus argument like Carson and not attempt to bisect words in terms of time.[357] The issue is not the previous status of the disciples but their role in God's mission strategy through the coming of the incarnate Jesus.

The importance of v. 6 is that the disciples have become a strategic link in God's work. The text states that they have kept/obeyed "your word." The verb is in the perfect tense, indicating the continuing implications of their obedience. The singular of "word" *(logon)* is to be understood as a collective for God's message, the good news or the gospel, and not as a reference to individual commands of God or to the teachings of Jesus.

Although some commentators are tempted to discuss the anachronistic nature of this statement, such a discussion is unnecessary. Of course, John was writing after the resurrection and understood that the disciples had been failures and were later restored. But that does not mean that Jesus could not have proleptically viewed the disciples as fulfilling God's intention for them in spite of their failures. All one has to do is read the incredible statement of Paul concerning the pathetic Corinthians in 1 Cor 1:4–9 and to wonder if Paul was talking about the same group of people that he writes about in the rest of the epistle.

The disciples of Jesus had not been and would not be perfect models of consistently following Jesus, but Jesus knew their hearts. Peter is a good example of inconsistency in the sword episode (18:10–11), the denial (18:15–27), and the recommissioning (21:20–22). Yet in his heart he had committed himself to Jesus (6:67–69), was willing to lay down his life for Jesus (13:37), jumped overboard to be with Jesus (21:7), and three times affirmed that he loved Jesus (21:15–17). The disciples were merely human beings, but just think of what God was about to do with them!

As we move to v. 7, the word "now" signals the fact that Jesus turned his thinking from the past experiences with the disciples to the current situation. He was about to depart from the world, and he was confident that the

---

[356] G. Quispel seeks for the background to this idea primarily in Gnosticism ("Qumran, John and Jewish Christianity," in *John and the Dead Sea Scrolls* [New York: Crossroad, 1991], 149–51).

[357] See Carson, *John*, 558–59.

disciples would fulfill God's goal of mission for them. The reason was that they had come to know (the Greek is perfect)[358] that Jesus was the special agent of the Father because everything associated with Jesus had actually been given (another perfect tense) by God. The use of the perfect tenses here indicates that a stage had been reached in the disciples' lives that (although they would fail) still gave Jesus the sense that the mission of God would go forward when he departed. Not only had he been given by the Father everything/everyone pertaining to his work, but these disciples had come to know that the source was the Father.

The statements in 17:8 then tie together the various ideas in a closing unified incarnational perspective. First, Jesus had been transferring (the perfect of "give") to the disciples the "words" he was given by God. The implication is clearly that the words of Jesus were revealed words from the Father (cf. 3:34; 6:63,68; 14:10; 15:7). Second, the disciples had received or accepted these revealed words. Third, the disciples "knew with certainty" that Jesus came from God. And fourth, they believed that he was on a mission, sent directly by the Father.

This subsection involving the second petition for a return to Jesus' former glory (17:5) thus reflects the focus of the Prologue (1:1–18), in which at the beginning *(en archē)* the Word was not only directly related to God *(pros ton theon,* 1:1) but in his incarnation he revealed God's glory (1:14). It also completes the logic of the Prologue concerning the children of God who have received or "accepted" *(elabon,* cf. 1:12; 17:8) both him and his words. Moreover, this section (17:8) is also clearly reminiscent of the focus of the Cana Cycle, the stories of which were directed to engendering authentic knowing and believing (at Cana, 2:11; after the Temple scene, 2:23–25; in the Nicodemus context, 3:16–18,36); with the Samaritan woman, 4:42; and with the official, 4:48,53).

As this section draws to a conclusion, the introduction of the disciples in connection with the incarnational mission of Jesus actually sets the stage for the next several petitions, which focus on the disciples in a hostile world. In concluding this section, therefore, it is appropriate to reiterate what I have stated elsewhere concerning these first two petitions in contrast to what Brown, Käsemann, and others have said, that "what may seem to be a personal petition" on the part of Jesus "must not be understood in any way as self-serving because Jesus in no way sought to escape death."[359] Instead, his death was "in fact the way to glory in the mind of the evange-

---

[358] Although there is some significant support for the first person aorist singular here, the third person perfect plural is most likely. See Metzger, *Textual Commentary,* 249.

[359] See Borchert, "The Prayer of John 17," 15.

list."[360] It was for John as for Jesus the clear means of the Lord "completing his mission as God's agent."[361]

(2) Preparing the Disciples for Their Mission in the Hostile World (17:9–19)

⁹I pray for them. I am not praying for the world, but for those you have given me, for they are yours. ¹⁰All I have is yours, and all you have is mine. And glory has come to me through them. ¹¹I will remain in the world no longer, but they are still in the world, and I am coming to you. Holy Father, protect them by the power of your name—the name you gave me—so that they may be one as we are one. ¹²While I was with them, I protected them and kept them safe by that name you gave me. None has been lost except the one doomed to destruction so that Scripture would be fulfilled.

¹³"I am coming to you now, but I say these things while I am still in the world, so that they may have the full measure of my joy within them. ¹⁴I have given them your word and the world has hated them, for they are not of the world any more than I am of the world. ¹⁵My prayer is not that you take them out of the world but that you protect them from the evil one. ¹⁶They are not of the world, even as I am not of it. ¹⁷Sanctify them by the truth; your word is truth. ¹⁸As you sent me into the world, I have sent them into the world. ¹⁹For them I sanctify myself, that they too may be truly sanctified.

The appearance of the verb *erōtō* ("I pray") signals the first major shift in the chapter to a direct concern for the disciples in the hostile world. It is parallel to the shift in focus from the Cana Cycle to the Festival Cycle in the Gospel itself.

THE THIRD PETITION: PRAYER FOR THE PROTECTION OF GOD'S REPRESENTATIVES TO THE WORLD (17:9–15).   This third subsection not only takes seriously the hostile nature of the world but also the need of the disciples for protection or security in the context of their mission to the world.

17:9   In this verse Jesus prayed specifically for the disciples and not for the world. This distinction, as Morris indicates, does not mean that Jesus was unconcerned about the world or that the world was "beyond God's love."[362] The exact opposite is actually the case (cf. 3:16), and the preparation of the disciples is directed ultimately to the goal that the world might believe (17:21) and realize that God sent Jesus (17:25).

But Jesus' task included the protection (17:12) of those whom God had given to him. In this verse John has captured an extremely significant insight into the mind and heart of Jesus because in this prayer Jesus did not

---

[360] Ibid.
[361] Ibid.
[362] Morris, *John*, 642.

claim ownership of the disciples. Instead, he said that they belonged to the Father: "They are yours." If we had the same perspective as Jesus, we would not make statements such as "my church," "my people," and "my things"; but we would be speaking about "God's church," "God's people," and "God's things," which the Lord has loaned or given to us. When Christians start to reflect this spirit, their lives actually begin to evidence the transformation about which they so often glibly speak.

17:10 The missiological implications of the above perspective followed quite naturally for Jesus. Since "his" disciples actually belonged to the Father and the Father's disciples were also his, then what brought honor and glory to God through them actually also brought glory or honor to Jesus. But the christological implications are also extremely important in this verse. Throughout the hostile Festival Cycle, Jesus reasserted time and again the affirmation of the unity of Jesus (the Word) and God proclaimed in the Prologue (1:1; cf. 5:18–23; 6:29; 7:16–17; 8:18; 9:33; 10:30,37–38; 11:27,51–52).[363] That Jesus' own people repeatedly refused to accept his divine calling and reacted with hostility is also confirmed in the judgment of the Prologue at 1:11 and prepares the reader for the departure and petition of Jesus in the next verse.

17:11 In the first part of this verse Jesus sets out the immediate rationale for the petition stated in the second part of the verse. The reason for the necessity of the petition is Jesus' imminent departure from the world and his coming to the Father. His departure is emphasized by the strong Greek word *ouketi* ("no longer"). The dynamics of this situation, however, are greatly intensified by the fact that the disciples will remain in the world. This separation of Jesus from the disciples clearly raised concern because of the world's hostile context.

In the second part of the verse the petition therefore matches the intensity of the situation because the marker or address is not merely "Father" here but "Holy Father." Beasley-Murray and others have shown that the use of "holy" in this verse points to the otherness or awesomeness of the Father.[364] I would add that there is something more involved here as well because in the midst of the forthcoming trauma there was a pressing need for the disciples to experience a calming sense of security. It is exceedingly significant, therefore, that the linguistic family of *hagios,* "holy," and *hagiazein,* "make holy, consecrate, sanctify," is very rare in this Gospel, appearing only in this section of the Great Prayer (17:11,17) and in the hos-

---

[363] Schnackenburg reminds the reader that in the Shepherd *Mashal* of chap. 10 Jesus identifies the sheep as belonging to the shepherd on the one hand (10:4,12,14,27) but also notes that they are protected by being in the Father's hand and that "I and the Father are one" (10:30) (*St. John*, 178–79).

[364] Cf. Beasley-Murray, *John*, 298; Morris, *John*, 643; etc.

tile context of the Festival Cycle (10:36). Can this be merely by chance? The awesomeness and power of God provides the basis for the sense of security that is necessary for the disciples to face the hostile world. Moreover, it will also become the unique and transforming characteristic of the disciples in the world that will be strategic in their mission when we reflect on the next petition (17:17).

In the present petition, however, the focus is on the strong protecting power or name of God in preserving and keeping the disciples safe while they are in the world. The Old Testament theme of the name of God as an instrument of power (e.g., Ps 54:1; cf. also Ps 20:1; Prov 18:10) undoubtedly lies behind this petition as Bruce, Schlatter, and others have noted.[365] The NIV rendering here of "protect them by the power of your name" is a slightly expanded interpretation of the Greek *tērēson autous en tō onomati*, which may be rendered "you kept them in/by your name." As Brown suggested, the *en* could be both locative and instrumental,[366] which means that the name could here be understood as both a context of protection and a means of protection.

The next clause, "which you have given me" (RSV, NRSV), contains a textual variant in the pronoun "which" that is of some import. The best manuscripts have the dative, which would refer to the name and not to the disciples as the KJV and NLT have in their translations.[367] The NIV makes the antecedent clear.

The final clause of the sentence refers to the oneness of the disciples, which is based on the unity of the Godhead. Barrett argues that the disciples are "kept by God not as units but as a unity" and refers to the fact that the neuter for "one" is used rather than the masculine for persons.[368] Carson thinks that Barrett misses the point because the "unity is the purpose of their being kept."[369] In some sense they are both correct at this point, but both are also far too restrictive. This text cannot be understood fully without reference to the later petition at 17:21, where the purpose of unity is spelled out more fully. It is imperative to remember that throughout this prayer the overarching concern is not status but mission and that much of the discussion that has taken place in the last century on oneness or unity is truncated because it neglects to emphasize mission. Accordingly, because

---

[365] Cf. A. Schlatter, *Der Evangelist Johannes* (Stuttgart: Calwer Verlag, 1948), 321; and particularly F. F. Bruce, *The Gospel of John* (Grand Rapids: Eerdmans, 1983), who noted that in quoting Ps 54:1 the concept of "name" stands in direct poetic parallelism with the concept of "might" in that text. Cf. also Bultmann, *John*, 503; Hoskyns and Davey, *The Fourth Gospel*, 503; etc.

[366] R. Brown, *John*, 2.759.

[367] For a discussion of this variant here see Metzger, *Textual Commentary*, 249–50.

[368] Barrett, *St. John*, 424.

[369] Carson, *John*, 562.

we Christians continue to focus our attention on internal issues of similarities and differences rather than looking out on the hostile world and concentrating efforts on mission, we continue to divide rather than to assume as
contemporary disciples of Jesus the strategic calling and purpose of Jesus.
We all usually have reasons for acting contrary to Jesus' wishes, but in the
process we usually diminish mission.

17:12   This verse turns our attention away from internal concerns to the
hostile world, which is both the traumatic context in which Christians are
called to live but is also the unfriendly context for their mission. Prior to his
departure Jesus had protected/kept safe the disciples in/by[370] the name of
the Father. This name or power of God in the world was God's divine gift,
and it reflected a much earlier Mosaic experience on the mountain when
God discussed his name with Moses (Exod 3:13–15). It was not to be used
as a magical formula, but that name, Yahweh, represented the powerful personal presence of God in Israel.

This God of the name protected Israel in the wilderness and guarded the
disciples in and by the presence of Jesus while he was on earth. Indeed,
none of the disciples was lost/perished except Judas Iscariot. In this verse
he is called the son of perdition, the one doomed to destruction, the one
destined for perishing or lostness. There is at this point an important Greek
wordplay in *apōleto* (the verb for "perish") and *apōleias* (the noun for
destruction/perdition). In other words, the perishing one perished. It is clear
that John regarded Judas as thoroughly villainous, and as an evangelist John
took pains to point out his wicked character. Even though Judas's name is
not always used, his evil nature lurks in the background of the Gospel. So
as early as 6:70 John already called him a devil; then at 12:6 Judas is
regarded as a thief; at 13:27 he is an instrument of Satan, and here John
sees Jesus dismissing him as the perishing one, the bad egg, or the weak
link in the chain of the disciples.

Not only was Judas the weak link, but he was an evil instrument in his
fulfillment of Scripture. Although at this point it would be difficult to tell
which Scripture was in the evangelist's mind, other New Testament texts
related to Judas's actions seem to suggest more specific references such as
Matt 27:3–10, which probably refers to Zech 11:12–13 and Acts 1:16–20,
which contains a free rendering of Ps 69:25.[371] Beasley-Murray sees in

---

[370] Carson is very forceful in his opposition to the locative statement "in the revelation of God
mediated in the person of Jesus," but the instrumental use is just as plausible, as is evident in the
NIV rendering (*John*, 563). Protection is not merely achieved through theological formulations.
The power of God was evident in and by the agency of Jesus' mediatorial work.

[371] Cf. R. Brown's discussion in *John*, 2.760. For further discussions on possible OT references
see Freed, *Old Testament Quotations*, 96–98 and Hanson, *The New Testament Interpretation of
Scripture*, 158–59.

John's statement concerning Judas some similarity to texts like Ps 57:4 and Isa 34:5, but they are a little distant in comparison.[372] The title "son of perdition" is also used in 2 Thess 2:3, but there it refers to the eschatological man of lawlessness. For John, Judas probably was viewed as an early example of such an evil figure.

17:13 The contrast in this verse with what has come before and what comes after is fascinating. The texts on either side are filled with trauma and concern, but this verse is very different. The emphasis is not on the departure of Jesus but on the coming of Jesus to the Father. To speak of that imminent occurrence later must have brought a smile to the face of Jesus and to the faces of the disciples. Crucifixion must have brought concern and sadness, but not the resurrection and exaltation. The glory of the Father was a joyous thought for Jesus, and to speak of it must have been contagious because the text says that his joy filled them. This thought picks up the other references to joy in the Farewell Cycle like the joy related to the birth illustration in the Anxiety ring (16:20–22; cf. 14:28) and the joy the disciples can experience when they abide in Jesus and obey him (15:11). It also reminds us of the friend of the bridegroom who rejoices in the fulfillment of the wedding (3:29) and the rejoicing at harvest (4:36). More particularly, it reminds us of the resurrection, when the disciples finally realized that Jesus fulfilled his promise to bring them joy after sorrow (20:20).

17:14 But that joyful experience was not yet a reality for them, so the text returns to a different "word" *(logon),* one that provided the reality check and the reason for the petition of protection in 17:11. The reality is that "the world hated them" because they were on a totally different wavelength from the rest of the world's population.

They did not belong to the world and did not think like the rest of the world because they were not *ek kosmou* ("out of the world"). The preposition *ek* in Greek is basically the preposition of "origin" or "source," which leads to a concept of "separation."[373] Accordingly, it would be appropriate to say that even though the disciples were human, their orientation or source of thinking and action was to be viewed as very different from that of the world. They had become attached to Jesus, who was "not out of the world." Therefore the world could hardly accept them as being "their kind of people." They were in some sense aliens in the world.

It is imperative, however, when reflecting on this idea not to create the impression that Christians are to be different for the sake of being different. The intention of God is that they are to be like Jesus. Paul expresses this

---

[372] See Beasley-Murray, *John,* 299.
[373] See *BAGD,* 234–35.

idea masterfully through his use of the idea of imitation.[374] He calls the Philippians to imitate him (Phil 3:17), but he is not the ultimate model of imitation. That model is Christ Jesus, and Christians are to think and act as Jesus did (2:1–8) while he was on earth. Then, like Jesus, they are to leave the results of their lives to God (cf. 2:9–11; 3:20–21). They are not to boast about themselves or focus attention on themselves (3:4–11) because the goal of their lives is to honor God in Christ Jesus (3:12–15).

17:15 The prayer of Jesus was not for God to send something like "rescue planes" to evacuate the disciples from their hostile setting in the world. Such a plan would destroy God's mission through them. Nor was it to wrap them in some plastic, danger-free safety casing where they would never encounter evil. But the prayer of Jesus was to protect them from succumbing to the onslaught of evil or the evil one.

Jesus was not under any delusion concerning the power of evil or of the enemy. John was clear that Jesus understood the nature of the battle, which Paul elsewhere explained is not merely against flesh and blood but is at the core of a spiritual battle (Eph 6:12). This battle requires not merely spiritual weapons (6:13–17), for both texts recognize the crucial nature of prayer in this hostile world setting (John 17:15; Eph 6:18).

The Greek *ek tou ponērou* can be translated as "from evil" in the abstract sense of a force in the world, but probably here it should be rendered "from the evil one" as a reference to the devil (John 8:34; 13:2), Satan (13:27), or the prince of the world (12:31; 14:30; 16:11), who stands behind the evil activities of humans. To understand the hostility of the world from the perspective of a personal power set against God, the work of Jesus, and the mission of Christians is both sobering and yet much closer to the view of Jesus and the early disciples than contemporary ideas that demythologize evil into some vague natural set of counter forces in the world. The devil was not some medieval imp dressed in red or black with a pitchfork and tail. The devil in the New Testament is a powerful force like a roaring lion (1 Pet 5:8) bent on destroying both God's work and God's people.

In 1 John this confrontation with the evil one in the life of Christian followers is further emphasized. The world in which the disciples live and work is both theologically and sociologically an alien place for Christians, one set against or oriented quite counter to the followers of Jesus (cf. 1 John 2:15–17). It is dominated by antichrist perspectives that are also enfleshed in humans (2:18–22; 4:3) and evidenced in the works of the children of the devil. These devil people like Judas imitate their Devil master,

---

[374] For a thorough discussion of imitation in terms of the background in the Mystery Religions, Greek Philosophy, and Jewish Thought see M. E. Hopper, "The Pauline Concept of Imitation" (Ph.D. diss., Southern Baptist Theological Seminary), 11–96.

who has been opposed to the way of God from the beginning (3:8–10). There is to be no compromise with such works and perspectives because Jesus came to call a people who would overcome the evil one (2:14) and gain victory through faith over the ways of the world (5:4).[375]

THE FOURTH PETITION: PRAYER FOR THE HOLINESS OF GOD'S REP-RESENTATIVES IN THE WORLD (17:16–19). **17:16** Although most scholars place this verse within the previous subsection, it actually forms a linking text not only to what has gone before but also to the fourth petition in the next verse. With a minor exception it virtually is a repetition of the concluding part of v. 14.[376] But that is just the point. The repetition of the alien statement provides for the introduction of another aspect of preparing the disciples for their mission in the world.

In the former subsection the need for unity in mission is stressed in the context of an alien society from which protection is necessary. Jesus knew that lonely and insecure people have great difficulty in working together in the mission of Christ. They tend to compare themselves with one another and emphasize one another's faults. Yet when mission in the context of a hostile world is foremost, perceived faults do not mean quite as much to them.

There is in this section a second aspect of crucial importance to the mission of Jesus that is fundamental to a sense of trust and security in the Christian community. Without it doubts of all sorts will arise, and the mission of God will be put in jeopardy. That aspect is holiness, which forms the subject of the next petition (17:17). Holiness is a way of life that is completely foreign to the way of the world. In the minds of many, holiness sets the disciple of Jesus over against the world as an alien because the world follows the ways of sin, hatred, immorality, and idolatry (cf. Rom 1:24–32). Thus, just as the world was alienated from God and hated both the Father and the Son (John 16:23–25), so the world likewise hates and persecutes the followers of Jesus (16:18–20).

Yet because the world is a tempting place in which to live, holiness is not always evident in Christian disciples and even in the clergy. I have talked with a number of ministers who have slipped from the standard of holiness, and their responses sound as though the standards of God do not apply to them. I remember vividly one pastor who tried to explain to me after an immoral affair that his wife no longer fulfilled his needs. I finally asked him as a minister: "What do you do with sin? Doesn't holiness mean anything?" The world rejects the standards of God as absolutely applicable. Even Christians are tempted to fudge on the standards. Jesus understood the

---

[375] Cf. Schnackenburg, *St. John*, 3.184.
[376] Cf. R. Brown, *John*, 2.761.

problem of living in the world, and that is the reason for the petition in the next verse.

17:17 Unlike the six other petitions in this chapter, this petition does not contain the usual *pater* ("Father"). But there is no question that this verse contains a direct petition to the Father for the disciples.

It seems quite evident that the address used in the previous petition, "Holy Father," would also be exceedingly appropriate for this petition since Jesus here prayed for the sanctification *(hagiason)* or holiness of the disciples. As I indicated in connection with 17:11, the use of the *hagios* family of words is very rare in John, appearing only in these petitions and in the earlier Festival Cycle. In the context of the *Mashal* of the Shepherd, Jesus confronted his opponents with the vital question not merely of why they did not accept him but why they did not accept the sanctified/consecrated/holy, set-apart One sent by the Father. The Festival Cycle is the cycle that emphasizes the *hostility* of God's people (the Jews) to God's special Son. It climaxes with the never-to-be-forgotten council of the high priest, the one who bore the insignia of holiness/set-apartness to God. But this high priest, who was supposed to represent holiness and authenticity as it pertains to God, instead, in what I have called his *ex cathedra* statement,[377] settled for an unholy compromise to kill Jesus in order to calm religious renewal and zeal and to maintain his own status and position (11:48–52). That temptation to yield to unholy compromises can also be present in the Christian church. But what seems even more ironic in that text is the way the Festival Cycle ends with people going up to Jerusalem in order to purify *(hagnisōsin)* themselves for Passover and at the same time acceding to murder (11:55).

It can hardly be an accident, therefore, that this petition, "sanctify them in/by the truth,"[378] is a prayer for the holiness of the disciples premised on *truth*. Jesus understood inauthenticity in religion, and he prayed that such a lack of integrity might not be present in his disciples. Accordingly, when one tries to communicate the meaning of this text, it is important not merely to remain on the intellectual level of discussing consecration and truth. It is also important to recognize that those statements are purposely gathered together by the Johannine writer as a stark closing to the Farewell Cycle. Together with the other petitions, these words are the haunting echoes of someone who was about to die himself and who is pictured as vitally concerned about the disciples' holiness and integrity with God. Truth is here

---

[377] See Borchert, *John 1–11*, 365.

[378] A number of scholars have pointed to the parallelism between the petitions of "sanctify them in [by] the truth" at 17:17 and "keep [protect] them in [by] your name" at 17:11. Cf. Beasley-Murray, *John*, 300 and Schnackenburg, *St. John*, 3.185. For the interpretation of "in"/"by" see my discussion at 17:11.

related to the word *(logos)* of God.[379] But truth and the word in John are not merely ideas. They are to be embodied in people in the same way that the word became flesh (1:14).[380] As such, John is very Semitic in his thinking. Since God is holy, God's people are to be holy (cf. Lev 11:44; 19:2; 20:26; cf. also 1 Pet 1:15–16).[381]

But holiness is not merely a human achievement; it is to be understood as an act of God in setting apart a people to be like God. Therefore Jesus' petition is for the Father to sanctify the disciples just as he earlier sanctified and sent Jesus (cf. John 10:36). For the disciples to be holy necessitated the work of God.

17:18 This verse confirms the fact that the main focus of this section of the prayer is on the preparation of the disciples for mission. The disciples, like Jesus, would experience the sense of being aliens in the hostile world (17:14), but this prayer does not advocate abandoning the world to the devil. Quite the opposite is true because just as it has been repeatedly said throughout this Gospel that the Father sent Jesus into the world, so it is here clearly asserted that Jesus has sent his followers into the world. The Greek verb *apostellein* occurring twice carries the idea of being sent for a purpose or being sent on a mission.[382] The English word "apostle" is obviously derived from this Greek word family, and apostleship must accordingly be understood not so much as a status but as a purposeful calling to a mission by Jesus.

17:19 This subsection of the disciples' preparation for mission concludes with a statement that for some readers may seem to be quite shocking in its implication. They may ask, How can the Son of God who is holy sanctify himself? But such a question is, in fact, misconceived. The New Testament writers would readily assert not only the holiness of God but also by implication the holiness of the Son who was sent by God (10:36) and marked out by the spirit of holiness (cf. Rom 1:4).

But here *hagiazō ematon* ("I sanctify/consecrate myself") is to be understood as an act of committing himself to the holy will of the Father and in dedicating himself to Calvary, as Morris states, "with all that Calvary means."[383] In this sense to consecrate himself meant to be set aside for God's special purpose. Consecration is also identified in the Torah with sacrifice (Deut 15:19), a sacrifice that usually implied the death of the offering.

---

[379] R. Brown reminds the reader that when one thinks about holiness and the word of God, these ideas are to be understood as very Jewish in perspective (*John*, 2.765).

[380] W. Brownlee considers that these verses reflect messianic motifs. See "Messianic Motifs of Qumran and the New Testament," *NTS* 3 (1956): 28–29.

[381] Cf. Carson's analysis in *John*, 566–67.

[382] For the use of this word family in John see K. H. Rengstorf's discussion in *TDNT*, 1.403–6.

[383] Morris, *John*, 648.

In consecrating himself, Jesus modeled for his disciples what is meant to be both alien from the world and yet committed to a mission in and to the world, even to the point of death.

To follow the way of the Lord and die as the ultimate sacrifice for the salvation of humanity was Jesus' mission. The disciples were likewise called to a mission of not only proclaiming this truth but also of living and dying for this truth in their own consecrations.[384] For Jesus holiness/set-apartness to the point of personal sacrifice was the key to an effective mission in a hostile world. That example is not passé today.

In this section of the prayer John has beautifully brought together the model of how Jesus handled hostility in his own life through the references to the Festival Cycle and Jesus' strategic concerns for the disciples' protection and holiness in their preparation for ministry.

(3) Looking to the Future (17:20–26)

[20]"My prayer is not for them alone. I pray also for those who will believe in me through their message, [21]that all of them may be one, Father, just as you are in me and I am in you. May they also be in us so that the world may believe that you have sent me. [22]I have given them the glory that you gave me, that they may be one as we are one: [23]I in them and you in me. May they be brought to complete unity to let the world know that you sent me and have loved them even as you have loved me.

[24]"Father, I want those you have given me to be with me where I am, and to see my glory, the glory you have given me because you loved me before the creation of the world.

[25]"Righteous Father, though the world does not know you, I know you, and they know that you have sent me. [26]I have made you known to them, and will continue to make you known in order that the love you have for me may be in them and that I myself may be in them."

The second appearance of the verb *erōtō* ("I pray") signals another major shift in the concern of Jesus for the disciples. In this case the perspective turns to the concern Jesus had for the disciples as they faced their future mission and their ultimate destinies. The shift in focus is similar to that of the move evident as one turns from the Festival Cycle to the Farewell Cycle in the Gospel itself. This interplay between this magisterial prayer and the Gospel as a whole is extremely fascinating and certainly marks the Gospel of John as one of the most intriguing works of artistic and spiritual inspiration in the entire Bible.

THE FIFTH PETITION: PRAYER FOR UNITY IN MISSION (17:20–23). These verses have been the subject of a great deal of explication at least

---

[384] For a discussion of Chrysostom's views of these verses as referring to sacrifice see J. Creham, *The Theology of St. John* (New York: Sheed & Ward, 1965), 92–93.

since the fourth century, when the discussion focused on the nature of the unity between Jesus and the Father. The Arians employed this text (especially 20:21) to argue for a moral or ethical unity between the Father and the Son rather than an essential unity (cf. 10:30).[385] The issue involves the pattern of John's argument. It seems certain that he does not argue from human relationships to the divine but from the divine to the human. Therefore one cannot legitimately propose that human experiences of unity, even in the best ecclesiastical situations, are the pattern for divine relationships in the Godhead.[386] The task of formulating an adequate Trinitarian understanding will continue to remain a difficulty for the human mind, but the Arian attempt was hardly satisfactory.

In the twentieth century these verses became the basis for biblical support to the modern ecumenical movement. Many scholars, including J. Cadier, D. M. Lloyd-Jones, P. Minear, T. E. Pollard, J. F. Randall, W. Thüsing, and others, have attempted to expound these verses in terms of the need for unity among Christian churches.[387] I personally have been involved in many discussions with other church bodies when serving as the chair of both Study and Research and the Commission on Doctrine and Interchurch Relations for the Baptist World Alliance, but it has always been with the understanding that my efforts have been focused where the text is focused, which is on the mission of Jesus and not on discussions of unity or cooperation for their own sakes.[388] Mission must be central to all discussions of oneness.

Before turning to these verses directly, it is important to notice the interweaving of the references to the first disciples of Jesus in vv. 20,22–23 and references directly or implied to future disciples in vv. 20–21, etc. It is also significant, as Randall has noted, that there is a parallelism in the construction of these verses.[389] Clauses in v. 21 are introduced by *hina,* "that," *kathōs,* "just as," *hina* (untranslated), and finally *hina,* "so that." The same connectives occur then in the same order in vv. 22–23. But the two final

---

[385] Cf. Brown, *John,* 2.769.

[386] Cf. T. E. Pollard, "'That They All May Be One' (John xvii 21)—and the Unity of the Church," *ExpTim* 70 (1958–1959): 149–50.

[387] J. Cadier, "The Unity of the Church," *Int* 11 (1957): 166–76; D. M. Lloyd-Jones, *The Basis of Christian Unity in John 17 and Ephesians 4* (Grand Rapids: Eerdmans, 1963); P. Minear, "Evangelism, Ecumenism and John Seventeen," *ThT* 35 (1978): 5–13; Pollard, "That They All May Be One," 149–50; J. Randall, "The Theme of Unity in John 17:20–23," *ETL* 41 (1965): 373–94; and W. Thüsing, *Herrlichkeit und Einheit; Eine Auslegung des Hohepriesterlichen Gebetes Jesu (Johannes 17)* (Düsseldorf: Patmos Verlag, 1962).

[388] Cf. G. Borchert, *Today's Model Church* (Forest Park, Ill.: Roger Williams Press, 1971), 52–54 and "The Nature and Mission of the Church: A Baptist Perspective," *PRSt* 20 (1993): 19–41.

[389] See Randall, "The Theme of Unity," 141.

clauses in the parallelism argue for the point that oneness is to be understood as directed to "believing" or "knowing" by the world to which "you sent me" (17:21,23) because you love "me" and "them." This is the message that the disciples both then and now are to present to the hostile world. God sent Jesus. And Jesus sent us to the world.

With these important introductory remarks in mind, attention is directed briefly to the verses in this fifth petition.

17:20 The thrust of Jesus' prayer is that disciples are to communicate the saving message to those who would come after them ("believe in me through their word"—*logos*). The good news was not intended to be held exclusively (*monon*, "alone") by the first disciples. It was to be shared with succeeding generations of disciples. The prayer therefore is also a mandate to mission and to making new disciples (cf. Matt 28:19).

17:21 The divided and hostile world desperately needs the unifying power of the good news of love (cf. 3:16; 13:34; 17:26). Oneness in the community of believers is modeled on the interrelationship of the Father and the Son ("you are in me and I am in you").[390]

The fifth petition in this verse once again employs the distinctive address *pater* ("Father") and is a prayer for the unity of believers. Beasley-Murray suggests that the evangelist may have had the Qumran community's concept of "unity" in mind and may have been polemicizing against their concept of a unity with the heavenly host.[391] Whatever may have been their idea, it is clear that the idea of unity here is modeled on the unique interrelationship of the Father and Son (Word) vividly portrayed in both the *pros ton theon* ("toward God") and the *theos ēn ho logos* ("the Word was God") of the Prologue (1:1–3).

But what becomes exceedingly striking here is the significant clause in the petition *hina kai autoi en hymin ōsin* ("may they also be in us"). The petition thus suggests that the oneness of the community is predicated on a direct relationship of the believers with the Godhead.

The oneness or unity here in this fifth petition is rooted in the idea of "indwelling" in the Godhead and calls to mind the major focus of the indwelling pictured in the vine and branches core text of the Farewell Cycle (15:1–11). The world is certainly a hostile place in which Christians live (cf. 15:18–25). Yet they are still called to be fruitful in this environment (cf. 15:5) because they are sent on mission to this world (cf. 15:20), which hates them as it hated Jesus (cf. 15:18).

---

[390] M. Appold, *The Oneness Motif in the Fourth Gospel: Motif Analysis and Exegetical Probe into the Theology of John* (Tübingen: Mohr, 1976), 157–93.

[391] See Beasley-Murray, *John*, 302; cf. M. Boismard, "The Epistle of John and the Writings of Qumran," in *John and the Dead Sea Scrolls* (New York: Crossroad, 1991), 160–61.

This oneness with the Godhead is not to be viewed as a mystical flight of the hermit to be alone with God or to be mystically absorbed into the divine. Nor is this relationship to be understood as an individualized self-centered salvation that has developed in many churches as a result of the subjective individualistic philosophies of the nineteenth and twentieth centuries. This relationship of believers with God is premised on a community who together experience a oneness with God.

This oneness of the community of believers with God is to be viewed as a kerygmatic vehicle in the context of a divided world. When the world sees the church in harmony with God and with each other, the point of Jesus' petition may be realized, namely, "that the world may believe that you have sent me." Does this petition of Jesus not judge our church disputes as detrimental to the task of mission? The ancient Romans had a classic maxim that they used in teaching. It is *verbum sap sapietia* ("a word to the wise is sufficient").

17:22 The surprise continues, for the next aspect of this fifth petition suggests that Jesus gave the disciples his "glory." The meaning of this text has created a good deal of debate. Bultmann linked this idea to the name of God (v. 6) and the words of God (v. 8).[392] Schnackenburg favors a view that is related to the future glory yet to be experienced[393] and also links it with the cross and resurrection, as in Barrett.[394]

Although the meaning is not totally clear here and commentators have struggled to make sense of the words, several ideas seem to be fairly certain. The disciples' glory must be understood as derivative of the glory of the Godhead. This glory is not something innate in them. That is the reason the petition continues to assert that "they may be one as we are one." Moreover, Morris is probably correct in pointing to the contrast of the little band that seemed insignificant to the world;[395] yet in following the pattern of the cross, which Jesus continually holds up as the way to glory, the disciples would in their humility find the reality of Jesus' gift of glory (cf. Phil 2:6–11). This verse would seem, therefore, to be proleptic or forward looking in its meaning and include not merely the early disciples but also later Christians who were to come after them (John 17:20). John, therefore, saw in these words of Jesus the great postresurrection perspective that has been evident throughout the Gospel since 2:22.[396]

---

[392] See Bultmann, *John*, 515.

[393] See Schnackenburg, *St. John*, 3.191–92.

[394] See Barrett, *St. John*, 428.

[395] See Morris, *John*, 650.

[396] See Borchert, *John 1–11*, 166 and "The Resurrection Perspective in John: An Evangelical Summons," *RevExp* 85 (1988): 501–13.

17:23 This fifth petition concludes with a strategic step-ladder statement concerning this indwelling of Jesus in the disciples and the parallel indwelling of the Father in Jesus. The point of this indwelling is that the disciples might be brought to "complete oneness." The Greek construction here produces an emphatic statement that the NLT renders as "all being perfected into one" and the NIV renders as "may they be brought to complete unity."

But unity is neither self-generated in the disciples nor their ultimate goal. Oneness is a means to enable the world to realize what God has been doing. The marvelous message is that God sent Jesus on an important mission to the world and that he not only loved his beloved Son but that he also loved the train of disciples who are fulfilling that continuing mission to the world. Accordingly, this verse reflects the significance love plays in the Farewell Cycle (cf. 13:34–35) and particularly in the core at 15:12–17.

THE SIXTH PETITION: PRAYER FOR THE DISCIPLES TO REACH THEIR DESTINY (17:24). **17:24** The word *pater* ("Father") again initiates the sixth petition. In this petition Jesus expresses his heart longing (*thelō,* "I want").[397] That longing is for the disciples, those whom (the Greek is a singular collective) the Father gave him, to witness firsthand the ultimate reality of who Jesus is. To do that, the disciples would also have to reach their ultimate destiny of being where Jesus would be and now is since the resurrection. That destiny, which was described elsewhere in the Farewell Cycle at 14:2 as the Father's house, is the destiny Jesus is said to be preparing for his followers.

Although it is here referred to as a place where Jesus is *(eimi egō),* the focus of this verse is actually on the experience of seeing the glory of Jesus. This Jesus of the petitions was not one of those periodic Jewish messianic figures like Bar Kochba (Son of the Star) who appeared and gained a following of Jewish loyalists and then passed off the scene. Instead, when the disciples would reach their destiny, they would realize more completely the incredible nature of this person they had been following. His "star" would not fall like a messianic pretender because his glory was linked to the Father's love before creation (cf. 17:5). This glory of Jesus, which is already apparent in some of its unveiled splendor, as Paul began to envisage it after the resurrection, will later be even more magnificently transformative of mere human beings (cf. 2 Cor 3:18) because in that ultimate encounter, when we will be "like him," we will behold him "as he is" (1 John 3:2).

---

[397] Although one could translate this verb as "I wish," there is not the least hint that Jesus' desire is a mere wish or that the will of Jesus is unrelated to the will of the Father. Throughout this Gospel, Jesus' will has been one with the will of the Father (cf. 4:34; 5:30; 6:38; etc.).

Unlike the postresurrection Paul, who could at least glimpse a little of the reality of this ultimate destiny as in a dim reflective mirror (cf. 1 Cor 13:12), the disciples in this Farewell Cycle were in a fog. As a result they debated with Jesus where he was going and how he was related to the Father (John 14:5–8). But when he penned this petition, John recognized that the fogginess would lift after the resurrection, and he understood that the followers of Jesus would one day see him in his divine glory (not the veiled glory of the incarnation, cf. 1:14). The birth pangs of the Messiah (cf. 16:21) would then have given way to a very different reality, and the disciples would behold him in his full glory.[398]

THE SEVENTH AND FINAL PETITION: A REALITY PRAYER (17:25–26). The address *pater dikaie* ("Righteous Father") announces the seventh and final petition in this magnificent prayer. Morris, however, is representative of scholars who seem bewildered by this segment. Indeed, he thinks "there is no petition in" these verses but they are merely "something of a retrospect."[399] There is a reason for this confusion because the petition is more implied than it is stated. The evangelist has supplied the introductory form for the petition in the use of the vocative *pater.* Moreover, he has also supplied Jesus' logic for the petition in these verses. Our task then is to infer the sense of the petition.

Note that the modifying adjective in this address is "righteous." It is crucial in this discussion to recognize that while Paul employs the "righteousness" family of words (*dikaios/dikaioun,* etc.) frequently, this evangelist uses this family of words only twice in the entire Gospel: here and in only one other place in the Farewell Cycle (16:8).

I have tried in brief to point out how the various segments of the prayer are tied to the various sections of the Gospel. In this third major segment of the prayer, petitions five and six can easily be linked to the Farewell Cycle. It seems quite natural, therefore, to find that this seventh petition would likewise be so linked.

What then is the focus of this final implied petition? It seems rather obvious that it is a reality prayer. The use of "righteous" here reminds the reader that the role of the Paraclete in the life of the disciples was meant to provide the standard of righteousness by which the world would be judged. But how was that about to happen? It would be accomplished

---

[398] While Bultmann (*John,* 519–21) and others struggle to give an existential focus to this passage, it seems clear to me that not only does the evangelist look back to Jesus' glory before creation but also to an eschatological glory that is beyond this world. Cf. Beasley-Murray, *John,* 304 and Carson, *John,* 569–70.

[399] See Morris, *John,* 652.

when the disciples would represent their self-giving, loving Lord in a sat-isfactory manner. Hostility in the world would be the context of mission. Self-giving love would be the righteous means God would continue to use in achieving his goal. The way of Jesus would therefore have to be the way of the disciples. But that is no surprise because that has been the focus of this entire segment of the prayer. The disciples are to be deriva-tively in parallel with Jesus. To put it another way: as Jesus lived and acted, so he prayed the disciples might live and act.

17:25 This verse spells out clearly the context of the disciples' future mission. It is a fallen world, one that has turned its back on God (cf. Rom 1:18), so it does not really know either God or his will. And since it does not know God, it hardly could know that God sent Jesus as his agent in sal-vation. But this verse makes clear that Jesus knew the Father intimately (cf. John 1:18; 14:10) and that the disciples recognized that Jesus was on a mis-sion directly ordered by God.[400] Although they may not have fully under-stood the implications of that mission, they soon would (cf. 14:20; 15:15).

17:26 As this prayer draws to a close, Jesus' concern becomes quite clear. He has given the disciples a divine revelation: he has made the name (*onoma,* the NIV omits this important idea) of God known to them (cf. 17:6,11; cf. also 5:43; 10:25; 12:28).[401] In a time when the Jews had adopted a remote and highly transcendent view of God and likewise had been avoiding the name of God for fear of taking it in vain, Jesus reintro-duced the necessity of direct encounter with God and reverently referring to God as Father, not some mysterious unapproachable deity.

But Jesus has also made known to the disciples the nature of God as a caring God of love. The God of Jesus was actually the same God as the God of the Old Testament who, although he demanded obedience, time after time showed the erring people of Israel his gentle forgiveness and loving kindness and offered comfort to them in their brokenness (cf. Isa 40:1–11).

Now Jesus was coming to the end of his time with them. The prayer was drawing to a close. The Farewell Cycle was ending. The next chapter was to begin the death story of Jesus. What was left to say? The heart of Jesus has been opened by John. What impression was to be left? What was the point?

The world is a hostile place, and the disciples were now to be sent to that world. With what spirit should they go? And what would be their model and resource? Those questions are answered in the concluding

---

[400] The construction is a little unusual here, but the NIV probably is correct in rendering it "though the world ..., I know ... and they know ..."

[401] Cf. Untergassmair, "Im Namen Jesu," 70–81.

words of the prayer, which are both an affirmation and a petition. The spirit of the disciples was to be that of love, not the love of which the world speaks but the kind of love God had for the Son. May that kind of love be in us! And the model and resource of the disciples? Surely not the power structures of the world. It must be Jesus himself. Jesus would act in them after the resurrection through the agency of the Paraclete. That is the reason he breathed on them as God breathed on Adam (cf. John 20:22; Gen 2:7). Jesus himself through the Spirit would be the focal resource of Christians, even though such a resource may seem foolish and weak to the world (cf. 1 Cor 1:22–25). The way of God in Christ Jesus is neither foolish nor weak because, as Pilate would learn, ultimate power is not in the world. It is from above (John 19:11).

VII. THE DEATH OF THE KING (18:1–19:42)
   1. The Garden Arrest of the King (18:1–12)
      (1) The Fateful Meeting in the Garden (18:1–3)
      (2) The Confrontation of the Arresting Band with the King (18:4–9)
      (3) Peter's Misdirected Attempt at Defense and the Arrest of the King (18:10–12)
Excursus 20: The Political and Judicial Situation in Israel During the Time of Jesus
   2. The Jewish Hearings and Peter's Denials (18:13–27)
      (1) Introduction to the Hearing before Annas (18:13–14)
      (2) Peter's Entrance into the Courtyard and His First Denial (18:15–18)
      (3) The Hearing before Annas and Its Disposal (18:19–24)
      (4) Peter's Second and Third Denials (18:25–27)
   3. The Roman "Trial" of the King (18:28–19:16)
      (1) Delivering Jesus to Pilate and the Opening Charges (18:28–32)
      (2) The First Interrogation of Jesus in the Praetorium (18:33–38a)
      (3) Pilate's First Verdict and the Jewish Reaction (18:38b–40)
      (4) The Scourging and Mock Crowning of the King (19:1–3)
Excursus 21: The Roman Scourging of Jesus and His Condition
      (5) Pilate's Declaration and Presentation of the Innocent King (19:4–5)
      (6) The Jewish Reaction to the Verdict (19:6–7)
      (7) Pilate's Retreat to the Praetorium and His Review of the Case (19:8–11)
      (8) Pilate's Vanquished Verdict and the Delivery of Jesus to Be Crucified (19:12–16)
   4. The Crucifixion of the King (19:17–27)
      (1) To Skull Place and the Crucifixion (19:17–18)
Excursus 22: The Site of Golgotha
Excursus 23: The Crucifixion of Jesus
      (2) The Royal Entitlement on the Cross (19:19–22)
      (3) The Clothes-Collecting, Lot-Casting Soldiers and the Faithful Friends around the Cross (19:23–27)
Excursus 24: On Allegorical Interpretations
   5. The Death of the Lamb/King (19:28–37)
      (1) The Last Moments of the Dying King (19:28–30)

(2) The Piercing of the Lamb (19:31–37)
Excursus 25: On the Reality of Jesus Christ's Death
6. The Burial of the King (19:38–42)
Excursus 26: Archaeology and the Tomb of Jesus
7. Concluding Reference in the Death Story (19:42)

―――――― **VII. THE DEATH OF THE KING (18:1–19:42)** ――――――

The death story of Jesus in John is a most fascinating piece of literature. The evangelist has wonderfully woven together the positive subplots in a synthesizing manner and has integrated in a masterful way the harsh notes of the negative subplots in a magnificent literary framework. The result is that he has created a skillfully constructed symphony on death. These two chapters are a model of clever artistry, to say nothing of the theological finesse exhibited in the development of the argument.[1] I am constantly amazed at the gifted inspiration in this Gospel, and I understand why some scholars wonder how a rough Galilean fisherman could ever pen such a marvelous document. I also recognize their desire to attribute this masterpiece to a person educated in the finest traditions of literary artistry. But I am also still surprised today how God can do amazing things with mere human beings, and this Johannine death story is certainly a wonderful example of it.

Throughout this story Jesus is shown to be completely in control of the events, even though he apparently possessed no earthly political or economic power. Indeed, he stunned Pilate, the symbol of Roman power, by reminding him of the actual source of power (19:11). Moreover, the arresting band that possessed the symbols of earthly force were rendered helpless in the face of Jesus' divine serenity (18:6), and it was he who appeared to be in charge of the arrest, not those who were carrying the weapons of force (18:8–9).

The actors in this death story all seem to be hollow, spineless, weak, or perverted people when they are compared to the unruffled dying King of Israel. Although they are all willfully directed people: from the traitorous Judas, to the misguided Peter of the puny sword and the fearful denials, to the treacherous Annas of the mock Jewish trial, and to the seemingly helpless Pilate of Roman power, who apparently could muster a backbone only when he correctly represented Jesus in the official charge on the cross, they

―――――――――――――――――――――――

[1] For a helpful analysis of the weaving together of the various story segments see J. P. Heil, *Blood and Water* (Washington: Catholic Biblical Quarterly Monograph Series, 1995).

come across as tragic, pawnlike figures in comparison to the dignified and authentic Jesus. All, however, move the story forward with a measured cadence of a dirgelike march in a military funeral.

But there are also in this death story some missing subplots of the other Gospels that the harmonizing reader might consciously expect to appear in this narrative. Yet they are clearly omitted in this Johannine death story of Jesus. There is here no kiss of Judas (cf. Mark 14:45), no washing of the hands of Pilate (cf. Matt 27:24), no assistance in carrying of the cross by Simon of Cyrene (cf. Mark 15:22), no special recognition of the two who were crucified at the same time as Jesus except for their mere mention (cf. John 19:18 with Luke 23:32,39–43 and Mark 15:27; Matt 27:38), no further recognition by Judas of his sin and no mention of his death (cf. Matt 27:38 with Acts 1:16–20), no cry of abandonment by Jesus, no ripping of Temple's veil (cf. Mark 15:33–38 and parallels), no confession by the centurion that Jesus was the Son of God (cf. Mark 15:39), and no guard at the tomb to prevent some unlikely escape or theft by the bewildered disciples (cf. Matt 27:65–66).[2]

Although the harmonizing reader might imagine that these details are present in the story or may be troubled by their absence, such a reader must remember that John was not writing an on-the-spot news report for the twenty-first century or producing a contemporary blow-by-blow video of the death story. Instead, readers are reminded that this evangelist has made a conscious choice of the events he has included in the story (John 20:30). The events that have been selected are to further his purpose of presenting a convincing and authoritative testimony concerning the King so that these same readers might come to believe in Jesus and receive the gift of eternal life (20:31).

The events chosen in this death story focus on the commanding nature of Jesus' presence even in his march to death. He is not surprised by the events or shaken by their implications that they could mean his execution. Throughout the Gospel, John has presented Jesus as moving quite consciously toward the hour of his glorification (cf. 2:4; 4:21; 5:25; 12:23,27; 17:1). The serenity he therefore exhibited was built upon a knowledge of his own destiny with God (14:2; 17:5,24). He was fully the King of Israel (2:29; 12:13; 19:19), even in dying. At the same time he was and is the sacrificial Lamb of God (1:29,36; cf. 19:14,31) who determined the moment of his own death when his work was "finished" (19:30) and delivered over his own spirit in the climactic act of dying to the surprise of his crucifiers (19:32–27; cf. Mark 15:44–45).

---

[2] Cf. my reflections on these topics in G. Borchert, "John," in the *Mercer Commentary on the Bible* (Macon, Ga.: Mercer University Press, 1995), 1075.

The way the story is presented is both exceedingly heroic and filled with irony. It ends with Jesus' burial not as a criminal in a pauper's tomb but as a king, fully spiced and entombed in a newly carved vault that was located in a garden (19:39–41). The story is a priceless piece of literature that warrants a much closer look.

1. The Garden Arrest of the King (18:1–12)

This section of the death story deals with three particular topics: (1) the fateful meeting in the garden (18:1–3), (2) the confrontation with the arresting band (18:4–9), and (3) Peter's misdirected attempt at defense and the arrest of the king (18:10–12a).

(1) The Fateful Meeting in the Garden (18:1–3)

¹When he had finished praying, Jesus left with his disciples and crossed the Kidron Valley. On the other side there was an olive grove, and he and his disciples went into it.

²Now Judas, who betrayed him, knew the place, because Jesus had often met there with his disciples. ³So Judas came to the grove, guiding a detachment of soldiers and some officials from the chief priests and Pharisees. They were carrying torches, lanterns and weapons.

18:1 This verse reminds the reader of the text in 14:31, where Jesus says, "Come now; let us leave" but then continued his instructions and prayer through 17:26. The present verse, however, notes that the Farewell Cycle had now closed and that Jesus had finished his speaking and praying (lit., "after having said these things").

Then Jesus and the disciples crossed the Kidron Valley. This valley or ravine was a typical Middle Eastern wadi that carried water during a rainy period but was basically dry during most of the year. It lies east of the Old City of Jerusalem and separates the city from the Mount of Olives. Into this wadi or valley ran the fluids from the Temple sacrifices.

At the foot of the Mount of Olives is the traditional site of Gethsemane. The Synoptics indicate that this was the place where Jesus was troubled and prayed his agonizing prayer (Matt 26:36–46; Mark 14:32–43; Luke 22:39–46). Indeed, it is noted in some texts of Luke that Jesus' sweat at this time was like drops of blood (Luke 22:44).[3] John does not here include this

---

[3] Although some early manuscripts include Luke 22:43–44, the likelihood is that they are an early addition to the text by scribes and writers who sought to explain the suffering passion of Jesus at this point. Cf. B. Metzger, *A Textual Commentary on the Greek New Testament* (New York: United Bible Societies, 1971), 177. For comments on the "sweat like drops of blood" see R. Brown, *The Death of the Messiah* (New York: Doubleday, 1994), 2.181, 184–86.

prayer experience. Instead, he has noted earlier a similar agony of Jesus in facing death after his dramatic entrance into Jerusalem (John 12:27), and instead of a final prayer here he included his great summarizing prayer in the previous chapter, prior to crossing the Kidron.

Only John among the Gospels tells us that there was a garden in this place. For several scholars the mention of the garden here suggests to them that John was comparing this event of betrayal by Judas in the garden with the temptation of Adam and Eve in the Garden (paradise) of Eden.[4] But that seems to be more a work of moralizing than exegeting the actual text of John.

18:2–3 Judas, the betrayer, is introduced again here and in v. 5 for the last time in this Gospel.[5] In contrast to the Synoptic Gospels, mention of him or allusion to him is made with much more regularity in John. Like the reverberating of the fateful "hour," the references to Judas, particularly from chap. 12 on (John 6:71; 12:4; 13:2,26,29; 17:12; 18:2,3,5), are a constant reminder that Jesus' life was moving with inevitability to the death of the Lamb of God.

This fateful, final earthly meeting of Judas with Jesus is almost presented by John as a clash between good and evil, where the traitor knows and violates the sacred place of retreat for his blameless victim.[6] Judas's knowledge is clearly portrayed as the special knowledge of an insider who breaks a trust and shares that knowledge with the enemy. The violating enemy is represented by the "detachment" of soldiers, the "officials" of the high priests (pl.), and the Pharisees.

The Greek text merely says that Judas "took" or "received" this band of captors and they all came to the set place. The statement hardly needs to imply that Judas was in charge of this band[7] as might be suggested from brief English translations using words such as "procuring" (RSV), "given" (NLT), or even "receiving" (KJV). The NIV "guiding" here seems to render the idea a little better.

Concerning the various aspects of this band, first, the Greek *speiran*, rendered "detachment" in the NRSV and NIV, is normally used to refer to a cohort of six hundred Roman soldiers who would usually be under the command of a senior officer such as a *chiliarchos* (note 18:12), but it could also

---

[4] Cf. B. P. Robinson, "Gethsemane: The Synoptic and Johannine Viewpoints," *CQR* 167 (1966): 4–11 and D. M. Stanley, "The Passion According to John," *Worship* 33 (1958–1959): 210–20.

[5] B. Gartner likens Judas to an Ahithophel type (*Iscariot* [Philadelphia: Fortress, 1971], 13–14, 25–27, 30).

[6] For a discussion of Jesus' meeting often with his disciples in this place see H. Rynen, "Synagesthai, Joh 18,2," *BZ* 5 (1961): 86–90.

[7] P. Winter, *On the Trial of Jesus* (Berlin: de Gruyter, 1974), 62.

refer to a smaller band such as a *maniple* or detachment of about two hundred soldiers.[8] It is not likely, however, that John was attempting to be technical concerning the number of soldiers present here. Their presence at this point may have been summoned by the Jewish authorities to ensure that there would be no uprising during the arrest of Jesus by any segment of the multitudes of celebrants in the city of Jerusalem for the great festival of Passover. The Roman procurators or prefects would always come to Jerusalem from Caesarea Maratima with reinforcements during major festivals. The soldiers would be housed in the Tower of Antonia next to the Temple during the feast times to guarantee that the peace would be kept.

Second, the Jewish members of the arresting band are here designated as *hypēretas,*[9] a general term that can mean assistants or officials. In this case it could legitimately be interpreted as the arresting police or Temple guards under the control of the high priestly family.

Third, the use of the plural as in high priests here, which may seem strange, is quite in order since the Romans deposed Annas and set up his son-in-law Caiaphas as the high priest. But Annas continued to maintain that designation and, in fact, was the power behind the throne, functioning like a "godfather" figure for the entire family. This ruling family was hardly regarded as saintly by many of the Jews, and during the siege of Jerusalem by the Romans the Jews themselves killed the then reigning high priest, Ananias, because they interpreted the siege in part as God's judgment on Jerusalem as the result of the desecration of the holy office. Although this priestly family was aligned with the Sadducees, the term is never used in John probably because by the time the Gospel was written the Sadducean party had disappeared following the destruction of the Temple. To refer to them by name would have been meaningless in John's day.

Finally, the fact that they were carrying lanterns, torches,[10] and weapons

---

[8] Cf. C. H. Dodd, *Historical Tradition in the Fourth Gospel* (Cambridge: University Press, 1963), 73–74. J. Bernard had already noted that there is no mention in the Synoptics of soldiers being present at the arrest and that John certainly did not have to mean that an entire Roman regiment was meant by the reference to soldiers here (*A Critical and Exegetical Commentary on the Gospel According to St. John,* ICC [Edinburgh: T & T Clark, 1928], 2.584). The same would probably be true of the reference to the soldiers at the crucifixion in Mark 15:16. Although some scholars might argue that the Romans would not be involved in such an arrest, L. Morris seems to argue plausibly when he writes: "It is likely that the Jewish authorities would have brought in the Romans as soon as possible in view of their ultimate aim" and because of their earlier failure to arrest Jesus (cf. John 7:44–49; *The Gospel According to John,* rev. ed., NICNT [Grand Rapids: Eerdmans, 1995], 657). Cf. also R. Schnackenburg, *The Gospel According to St. John* (New York: Crossroad, 1987), 3.222–23.

[9] For a discussion of this term see K. Rengstorf's comments in *TDNT* 8.537–40.

[10] These two terms are very similar in meaning, but R. H. Smith argues for the above distinction in the Johannine usage ("The Household Lamps of Palestine in New Testament Times," *BA* 29 [1966]: 2–27).

certainly must have seemed ironic for the evangelist. This huge band had to come at night (cf. 13:30) to arrest a peaceful preacher-miracle worker whom they probably thought might stir up a violent crowd. But it is exactly this contrast between peaceful means and force that was an important contrast for John. It was certainly one that Peter obviously did not understand when he later sought to disrupt the arrest with his puny action. Here the "Light of the World" (8:12; 9:5) was being seized by those in darkness carrying puny little torches and weapons. Matthew even makes more of this contrast when he rebukes Peter with the reminder that Jesus had the heavenly army at his disposal if he needed to be defended (Matt 26:53). But for John the contrast of power is described differently in the next section.

(2) The Confrontation of the Arresting Band with the King (18:4–9)

[4]Jesus, knowing all that was going to happen to him, went out and asked them, "Who is it you want?"

[5] "Jesus of Nazareth," they replied.

"I am he," Jesus said. (And Judas the traitor was standing there with them.) [6]When Jesus said, "I am he," they drew back and fell to the ground.

[7]Again he asked them, "Who is it you want?"

And they said, "Jesus of Nazareth."

[8] "I told you that I am he," Jesus answered. "If you are looking for me, then let these men go." [9]This happened so that the words he had spoken would be fulfilled: "I have not lost one of those you gave me."

18:4–7 The picture of Jesus presented in this part of the story is one of a commanding figure who was in charge of the events that were transpiring. John states with unreserved confidence that Jesus knew everything that was about to happen. This statement is not merely a postresurrection perspective on the part of John as in 2:22 and elsewhere. Rather, it is meant to assert Jesus' understanding ahead of time concerning the events that were moving inevitably to his determined "hour."

The fact is that Jesus stepped forward ("came forth") from among the disciples and asked the probing question, "Who are you seeking?" This question is undoubtedly meant as an indication that John was highlighting "the *voluntariness*" of Jesus in accepting his arrest.[11] John does not mention Judas's identification by means of a kiss (cf. Matt 26:49; Mark 14:45; Luke 22:47). Instead, when Judas has done his traitorous deed, John dismissed him (18:5). The identification of Jesus here is done by Jesus himself through the dynamic self-disclosure statement, *"Egō eimi"* ("I am"), which mirrors the great self-disclosure statement of God to Moses in Exod 3:14. That John intended such a connection with the Old Testament is clear from

---

[11] Cf. Bernard, *St. John*, 2.586.

the fact that the arresting band is forced to the ground as if in obeisance to deity.

Lindars suggests that this experience is like a theophany,[12] but if anything it is more like a negative theophany. Beasley-Murray[13] correctly identifies this experience with a confrontation of what philosophers refer to as the *mysterium tremendum,* or what I call the terrifying mystery of the ultimate reality. And I would add that I heartily advise no one to encounter the wrong side of this mystery, for if the incarnate mystery could render an arresting band prostrate, what can the ultimate mystery do to mere disobedient humans? God did not and does not play games concerning his Son.

The name used by the arresting officers here in their search for Jesus was "Jesus of Nazareth." This designation is used only four times in the Gospel of John: first, in the context of the third cameo of witnesses that brought to a conclusion the opening identifying references to Jesus as the "King of Israel" and the "Son of God" (1:45–49); then, second and third, here two references at the arrest (18:5,7); and fourth, in the official charge or verdict by Pilate against Jesus as the "King of the Jews," which Pilate had attached to the cross (19:19). These strategic events, which focus on the fact that Jesus, who was a historical figure and was the King of Israel, was also the one who fulfilled God's mission for him to be the dying Lamb of God who takes away the sin of the world (1:29).

18:8–9 Jesus' answer to their second quest for Jesus of Nazareth was once again *egō eimi* ("I am"), yet here in addition to the self-identification and self-yielding by Jesus to the arresting band there is now added a stern imperative: "Let these men go!" The picture presented by John is once again very clear. The arresting band may have been a strong human force armed with weapons, but the person being arrested is here clearly represented as being in charge of the entire process. The King was not being captured; he was giving himself over to his enemies.

This event is of such significance for John that he added one of his rare proof texts or fulfillment statements. But rather than quoting an Old Testament text here, the evangelist cites an earlier statement by Jesus as an authoritative declaration equal to divine revelation or Scripture that Jesus had not lost one of those whom the Father had given him (cf. 17:12). In that earlier prayer text, however, there was an exception added concerning Judas, the doomed one. Here there was no need to add the exception clause because Judas, the deliverer (cf. 18:2), now stood side by side with the enemies of Jesus. The statement was fulfilled.

---

[12] See B. Lindars, *The Gospel of John* (Grand Rapids: Eerdmans, 1972), 541. Cf. R. Bultmann, *The Gospel of John* (Philadelphia: Westminster, 1971), 639, where he relates the idea to some Old Testament texts related to theophanies. He questions whether everyone fell down.

[13] See G. Beasley-Murray, *John*, WBC (Waco: Word, 1987), 322.

(3) Peter's Misdirected Attempt at Defense and the Arrest of the King (18:10–12)

[10]Then Simon Peter, who had a sword, drew it and struck the high priest's servant, cutting off his right ear. (The servant's name was Malchus.)
[11]Jesus commanded Peter, "Put your sword away! Shall I not drink the cup the Father has given me?"
[12]Then the detachment of soldiers with its commander and the Jewish officials arrested Jesus. They bound him

18:10–11   Schnackenburg thinks these verses disturb the natural flow of the story after Jesus had virtually released the disciples.[14] Although I do not totally agree, there is a sense in which Peter's action is almost ridiculous, if it were not so tragic. I find him to be a comic-tragic figure who often lacks a perspective of realism about a given situation. In that sense he is like many humans who blunder through life without taking time for reality checks. What could Peter's puny sword do against the force of a Roman "detachment" (18:3) led by a chiliarch (the usual commander of a thousand soldiers, 18:12)?

But the evangelist was making an important point that should be recognized by well-meaning Christians who often think that everything depends on them and their own actions. Jesus had already shown that he could control the arresting band, if he wanted to do so. Yet that was not what the Father chose for the Son's mission on earth (the cup the Father had given him to drink). Doing God's work in God's way is absolutely crucial. That is the very point of the temptation stories in the Synoptics (cf. Matt 4:3–10; Luke 4:3–12).

The perspective in these two brief verses together with their Synoptic parallels was extremely important for the early Christians because they were faced with issues of how to deal with force. Should they join the Jewish revolt of "God's chosen people" against the Romans, or was there another way? The way they chose when the Romans were marching south was to leave Jerusalem and the provinces of Israel and flee to Gentile territories: to Pella and the cities of the Decapolis, following the eschatological instructions of their Lord (cf. Mark 13:14–18; Luke 21:20–24) as the new people of God.

A comparison of the present Johannine verses with parallels in the Synoptics has led some scholars to think that John was adding names to more general statements about the "ear-cutting" episode to enhance the historicity of the text, but such a view is unnecessarily skeptical. Only in John do you find that the ear cutter is Peter, but that action is certainly not out of line with his blundering style elsewhere. Only in John do you also discover

---

[14] Schnackenburg, *St. John*, 3.226.

that the person who was attacked is Malchus, but both Matthew and Luke also indicate that the man was the servant of the high priest. Luke, who seems to have some interest in physical aspects of people, notes along with John that it was the right ear that was severed, which some scholars have argued rendered the servant of the high priest unworthy for Temple service.[15] But one wonders if that is the point of the statements in the Gospels. Moreover, Luke also adds with the rebuke of Peter that Jesus restored the ear (Luke 22:51). Matthew, with his typical interest in angelic and spiritual forces, includes a different focus to Jesus' rebuke by informing Peter that he could counter the arrest with twelve legions of angels, if that was his will (Matt 26:53). Clearly the focus of the three rebukes (Mark does not have this story) is different in each Gospel. But the rebuke is similar in each Gospel, although each evangelist chooses an aspect of the rebuke that is in conformity to his own interests and his own particular way of testifying to the basic concern of Jesus. Bloodshed is not the mission of Jesus.

18:12 Verses 12–13 form another of the typical linking texts in John. Verse 12 marks the conclusion to the arrest, and v. 13 introduces the Jewish hearing. Although they are inseparably connected in the story, they are here divided for purposes of this commentary.

For Haenchen this verse reveals some of the tension in the narrative.[16] Who was in charge of the arrest? Was it the Jews or the Romans? Obviously Pilate was in control of the Roman leader (a Chiliarch or Tribune, but hardly a *decurio*).[17] And what was a Roman commander doing turning over a prisoner to the Jews? That would mean that the Jews were responsible for the arrest and condemnation of Jesus. Such a perspective seems to be quite clear as the story in John progresses.

But in the postholocaust era scholars react negatively to such ideas.

---

[15] Hobart earlier had argued that one could prove from the language of Luke that he was a physician (W. Hobart, *The Medical Language of Luke* [Dublin: Hodges, Figgis & Co., 1882]), but H. Cadbury (*The Style and Literary Method of Luke* [Cambridge, Mass.: Harvard University Press, 1920]) showed that such an argument could only prove that Luke was an educated person. Cadbury's antithesis does not mean Luke was not a physician as stated in Col 4:14. D. Daube argued in his article, "Three Notes Having to Do with Johanan ben Zaccai," *JTS* 11 (1960): 59–61, that the severing of the ear was an effort not to kill the servant of the high priest but to render him deformed and thus unworthy of serving in the Temple. But such an argument is a little too speculative and an overtheologizing of an incident in the narrative. There is no hint in any of the Gospels that such was the point, even though such an injury would have that effect. Cf. D. Garland, who argued similarly in "Malchus," *ISBE*, 3.229 and in "John 18–19: Life Through Jesus' Death," *RevExp* 85 (1988): 487. Contrast N. Krieger, Der Knecht des Hohenpriesters," *NovT* 2 (1957): 73–74.

[16] E. Haenchen, *John 2* (Philadelphia: Fortress, 1984), 166–67.

[17] Winter argues that John has here mistakenly used the term for a major Roman commander when the leader was an official in charge of ten soldiers (*The Trial*, 29). The problem with such a view is that it is a speculative opinion supported by what one would think took place many years after the event.

Accordingly, John has either been dismissed as unhistorical[18] or termed an anti-Semitic document (see my earlier excursus on anti-Semitism).[19] It is absolutely clear that the holocaust was an unmitigated horror and an inexcusable tragedy in which not only Jews but also gypsies and other people were systematically eliminated. That should not happen, but in parts of the world such purgings still continue to occur despite all the pleas in the United Nations and official condemnations by various governments. My ancestors came out of places where they were vigorously persecuted by others. But that does not mean that I should either despise those persecutors today or deny the reality of what happened in the past and in some cases has actually reemerged today.

John was not anti-Semitic; he was being honest as a Jew himself. The Jewish establishment was bent on eliminating Jesus, and it was clearly also intolerant of his Jewish (as well as his Gentile) followers after the resurrection. There is no point in avoiding this fact or trying to suggest that the curse of the heretics[20] was not primarily directed at Christians. Carson is correct[21] when he suggests that S. Sandmel's approach is better when he admits that "some Jews, even leading Jews, recommended the death of Jesus to Pilate."[22] And "Christians" must likewise be willing to admit that if they would have been there, some of them might also have been tempted to recommend the death of this disturbing Jesus, who consistently inserted God's will into matters of human life and relationships.

The Romans and their commander were involved in this event, but it was the Jews, not the Romans, whom John says actually arrested Jesus. Or better still, it was the incarnate King Jesus who identified himself and thereby allowed the Jewish servants to take, seize, or arrest him and put him in bonds.

Before proceeding further with the hearings, or so-called trials, of Jesus,

---

[18] Many years ago J. Wellhausen took this approach to the Johannine story (*Das Johannesevangelium* [Berlin: Reimer, 1908], 105–6.

[19] I have been disturbed by the anti-Semitism charges leveled at John's Gospel in the John sections of the Society of Biblical Literature and elsewhere. See G. Borchert, *John 1–11*, NAC (Nashville: Broadman & Holman, 1996), 227–28. For some examples of the polemics in scholarship see J. Sizoo, "Did the Jews Kill Jesus? Historical Criticism in the Pulpit," *Int* 1 (1947): 201–6; K. Ernst, "Did the Jews Kill Jesus? A Reply," *Int* (1947): 376–78; and L. Johnson, "The New Testament's Anti-Jewish Slander and the Convention of Ancient Polemic," *JBL* 108 (1989): 419–41. See also the 2000 Leuven Colloquium papers *Anti-Judaism and the Fourth Gospel*, ed. R. Bieringer et al. (Assen, Netherlands: Van Gorcum, 2001), which includes essays by J. D. G. Dunn, R. A. Culpepper, S. Motyer, S. Lieu, S. Schoon, etc.

[20] For the curse of the Christians/*Minim* in Benediction 12 see C. Barrett, *The New Testament Background* (New York: Harper & Row, 1961), 166–67.

[21] D. Carson, *The Gospel According to John* (Grand Rapids: Eerdmans, 1991), 575.

[22] S. Sandmel, *We Jews and Jesus* (Oxford: Clarendon Press, 1965), 56–58.

it is crucial at this point that there be some overall understanding of the political and judicial situation in Israel during the late second Temple period of the time of Jesus. Therefore I have included a brief overview of that historical setting in an excursus to ensure that there is a better understanding of that somewhat confusing context.

Excursus 20: The Political and Judicial Situation in Israel during the Time of Jesus[23]

In broad strokes the Romans entered the political scene in Israel in 63 B.C. during the internecine battle between the Hasmonean rivals (the successors of the Maccabees), Aristobulus II, who was trying to unseat his brother Hyrcanus II. When Pompey arrived in the land, he finally rejected the claims of Aristobulus II, but he also wanted to see the famous God of these Jewish people. Rejecting the pleas of the Jews, he strode into the Temple precincts and the Most Holy Place to catch a glimpse of the statue of their "god." When he emerged from the empty shrine (the ark had long since been lost) in astonishment, he labeled the Jews as atheists who had NO GOD! The Jews never forgot this desecration of their sanctuary, and when Crasus later (54 B.C.) robbed the Temple treasury to pay the tribute rather than collecting it by more tedious means, the die was cast in hatred against the defiling pagan Romans.

After Pompey and his cohorts exited the scene, Julius Caesar entered the stage of Jewish history. Along with him the Idumean family of Antipater rose to greater power as governors, with the Hasmoneans having to settle for the high priesthood. But when Caesar was murdered, Antipater was likewise eliminated by the Jews. The stage was then set for one of the major battles in the history of the Roman republic. Octavian and Mark Antony joined forces to defeat Brutus and Cassius at the battle of Philippi in 42 B.C.[24] Although Antony was probably the most capable military leader in the winning triumvirate, his escapades with Cleopatra caused him to lose support among the rank and file of his Roman legions. Herod had been appointed by Antony as governor, similar to his father, but when

---

[23] For more detail I would recommend interested readers might consult: J. Jeremias, *Jerusalem in the Time of Jesus* (London: SCM Press, 1969); R. Brown, *The Death of the Messiah,* 329–97; E. Schürer, *The History of the Jewish People in the Age of Jesus Christ (175 BC–AD 135),* 4 vols., rev. ed. (Edinburgh: T & T Clark, 1973–1987); various articles in *ISBE* on the "Hasmoneans," 2.621–27, "Israel, History of the People of," 2.918–24, "Roman Empire and Christianity," 4.207–16; A. Sherwin-White, *Roman Society and Roman Law in the New Testament* (Oxford: Clarendon, 1963); R. Martin, *New Testament Foundations,* vol. 1 (Grand Rapids: Eerdmans, 1975); and E. Sanders, *Jesus and Judaism* (Philadelphia: Fortress, 1985). For further information on the "trials" of Jesus see J. Blinzer, *The Trial of Jesus* (Westminster: Newman, 1959) as well as his fuller treatment *Der Prozess Jesu* (Regensburg: Verlag Pustet, 1969); F. Bruce, "The Trial of Jesus in the Fourth Gospel," in *Gospel Perspectives: Studies of History and Tradition in the Four Gospels* (Sheffield: JSOT, 1980), 1.7–20; D. Hill, "Jesus Before the Sanhedrin—On What Charge?" *IBS* 7 (1985): 174–86; P. Winter, *On the Trial of Jesus* (Berlin: de Gruyter, 1974).

[24] For a discussion of the crucial role of Philippi in the history of the Roman republic see G. Borchert, "Philippi," *ISBE* 3.834–36.

Antony lost to Octavian at the strategic battle of Actium in 31 B.C., Herod had to flee for his life.

With his strategic victory Octavian moved quickly to eliminate from the Senate any opponents to his complete power. Although for a time he was reappointed annually as emperor, he was awarded by the Senate the auspicious title of Augustus, and he was praised by many as a divine savior in Rome. Even Virgil penned a most honoring poem to him in his Sixth Eclogue.

Herod the Great charmed Octavian with his political abilities, and in an unusual act Octavian appointed him king of the entire area, which virtually approximated the size of the kingdom of David and Solomon. Herod returned to Israel and ruthlessly secured his position by conquering the territory and then building fortresses throughout the land so that he would have places of protection wherever he went. He eliminated anyone whom he thought might pose a threat to his status. Although the Jews despised him because of his harshness and because he was an Idumean, Herod won for the Jews some significant rights. Among those rights was the declaration that the Jews were regarded as an official *ethnos* within the Roman Empire. They thereby gained some significant privileges, including some tax relief and the right to be a *religio licita* (licensed religion), which excused them from worshiping the Roman gods on the condition that they would offer daily prayers and sacrifices on behalf of the Roman imperium.

When Herod died, he sought to have his most ruthless son Archelaus enthroned in his place (cf. Matt 2:22), but the Romans did not honor his will because such rights of succession did not accrue to conquered peoples and because of complaints by the Jews concerning him (cf. Luke 19:12,14,27).

To understand the post-Herodian period and the time of Jesus requires some clarity concerning the Roman provincial system. Rome had two types of provinces: senatorial and imperial.

Senatorial provinces were basically peaceful provinces governed by a senior senator/proconsul who generally held office for one year at a time. During that period the senator was expected to keep the peace and to collect money for his retirement by skimming off a portion from the taxing process. This brief pattern when senators were for a short time proconsuls in the provinces provides an excellent way of gaining time frames of events. For instance, because of the Gallio inscription found at Delphi, we are able to date Paul's time in Corinth to the beginning of the fifties (approximately 52–54; cf. Acts 18:12,17). Senators were permitted to succeed themselves but normally for only one year. In unusual circumstances some senators were given a second assignment in another province, as was the case with Marcus T. Cicero. But such a senator would have to have been deemed very significant to gain such a privilege.

Imperial provinces, however, usually created problems for Rome, and therefore they were in imperial times under the direct supervision of the emperor. The governors were usually termed legates or what we would term generals, as was the case with Vespasian before he became emperor. They had major armies under their control. Some of the legates served in more general capacities to assist in the collecting of taxes or tribute (cf. Luke 2:2). They held office at the discretion of the emperor. Where there was need for closer supervision in smaller areas, such as Judah, within a larger imperial province, such as Syria, then prefects or procurators such as Pilate would be appointed by the emperor for as long as he felt they were useful. Normally these subprovinces were not desirable postings, and often they would either ruin a military man's career or be given to less respected commanders.

In terms of the judicial system in the empire, those city states that were granted colonial status, such as Philippi,[25] had all the privileges of Roman law that were enjoyed by Rome itself. Those provinces governed by proconsuls had a modicum of independence in matters of civil law, but criminal matters were under the jurisdiction of the proconsuls. For example, during the time of Jesus and Paul, Ephesus was not the capital of the Roman province of Asia and was under the jurisdiction of Asiarchs (local authorities) in civil matters (cf. Acts 19:30). But riots and grounds for disruption were another matter because they threatened the *pax* (peace) and would come to the attention of proconsuls (cf. Acts 19:38). Two decades after Paul, the proconsulship for Asia was shifted from Pergamum to Ephesus.[26]

What, then, was the situation in the subprovince of Judea in the time of Jesus? Archelaus was removed in A.D. 6 because he was such a ruthless ethnarch (a local ethnic governor, one stage below a tetrarch, which was the status given to Herod Antipas in Galilee and Philip in northern Caesarea). When Archelaus was removed, the Romans were not ready (until Herod Agrippa I) to have a Jewish ruler in charge of this volatile area. Therefore they appointed a procurator/prefect to govern Judea and Samaria. The Roman governor was clearly in charge, but the legal system was a little confused because under Herod the Great the Jews had been granted the rights of an *ethnos* and along with that status went certain rights of punishment, although in general capital punishment was reserved for the Roman governor. Nevertheless, the Jews sometimes took stoning into their own hands in matters of blasphemy (cf. Stephen in Acts 7:58 and the attempted stoning of Jesus in John 10:31–33). But official declarations of death belonged to Rome.

With these brief remarks concerning the political and judicial situation in Israel in the time of Jesus, attention is returned to the text of John and the hearings or trials of Jesus.

2. The Jewish Hearings and Peter's Denials (18:13–27)

As one turns to the postarrest narrative in John, one encounters a fascinating literary style in which the evangelist interweaves the stories of the Jewish hearings and Peter's denials.[27] This phenomenon continues into the Roman hearings, where he interweaves Pilate's conferences with the Jewish

---

[25] Ibid., 834–35.

[26] For a discussion of the history of Ephesus and the commonly misunderstood dating when it became the capital see G. Borchert, "Ephesus," *ISBE*, 2.115–17.

[27] Cf. Heil, *Blood and Water*, 16–42.

leadership and Pilate's interrogations of Jesus.[28] The result of this interweaving process produces a skillfully executed piece of literature in which the varying parts of the narrative are molded into an integrated story.

This particular segment of the death story involves four night scenes as the evangelist alternates our attention between the interrogation that takes place inside the high priests' residence and outside in the courtyard, where Peter is challenged and denies being associated with Jesus.

(1) Introduction to the Hearing before Annas (18:13–14)

[13]**and brought him first to Annas, who was the father-in-law of Caiaphas, the high priest that year. [14]Caiaphas was the one who had advised the Jews that it would be good if one man died for the people.**

18:13 Jesus was first brought bound before Annas. John is very specific here, which some find difficult to reconcile with the Synoptics. Annas was appointed high priest by the legate Quirinius[29] in A.D. 6, approximately at the same time Archelaus the ethnarch was removed from office and sent into exile. Normally Annas should have held that office for life, but the procurator Valerius Gratus, Pilate's predecessor, found him intolerable and deposed him in A.D. 15.[30] Nevertheless, Annas simply became the power behind the throne of his son-in-law Caiaphas and five other family members who also held that position. Brown[31] is undoubtedly correct in concluding that although it was unusual, Annas was still called high priest because Josephus had no difficulty referring to him by that designation in describing events in which he was involved long after being deposed.[32] There is therefore no reason to think that Annas would not be involved in such a hearing, as some scholars have thought. Even a few manuscripts sought to alter the presence of such an early hearing before Annas, but these are later attempts at unnecessary harmonization with the more general statements in the Synoptics.[33]

The statement that Caiaphas was the high priest "that year" is not meant to suggest that the high priesthood changed every year. Rather, for John it meant that in the determinative year of salvation and world history Caiaphas was the high priest. He would be remembered for what he said and did.

---

[28] Ibid., 45–74.

[29] See Josephus, *Antiquities*, 18.2.1.

[30] Ibid., 20.9.1.

[31] R. Brown, *Death of the Messiah*, 1.405.

[32] Cf. Josephus, *Antiquities*, 18.4.3 and 20.9.1. Cf. also Luke 3:2 and Acts 4:6 for combinations of Annas and Caiaphas.

[33] Metzger, *Textual Commentary*, 251–52. A. Mahoney also proposed a comparable type of emendation but that is hardly necessary when one understands the role of Annas in the high priestly family ("A New Look at an Old Problem (John 18:12–14)," *CBQ* 27 [1965]: 137–44).

18:14   However one might regard the role of this hearing, as far as John was concerned it was fundamentally a sham because a verdict had already been rendered by Caiaphas to the effect that Jesus had to die as an expedient sacrifice (John 11:49–51). This event, therefore, hardly began as anything akin to a fair trial. The way the evangelist presents the story, it is more like a biased police investigation or witch hunt from which most decent people would recoil in horror. Yet the ancient Middle East was not necessarily known for fairness, even though among the Jews the judicial procedures of the Sanhedrin were supposed to be weighted in favor of innocence.[34] But John notes that Nicodemus earlier had complained that such procedures were not being following in the council (cf. 7:50–51).

(2) Peter's Entrance into the Courtyard and His First Denial (18:15–18)

[15]Simon Peter and another disciple were following Jesus. Because this disciple was known to the high priest, he went with Jesus into the high priest's courtyard, [16]but Peter had to wait outside at the door. The other disciple, who was known to the high priest, came back, spoke to the girl on duty there and brought Peter in.

[17] "You are not one of his disciples, are you?" the girl at the door asked Peter.

He replied, "I am not."

[18]It was cold, and the servants and officials stood around a fire they had made to keep warm. Peter also was standing with them, warming himself.

18:15–16   The focus of attention here switches from the hearing scene to the courtyard outside the priestly residence, which Josephus[35] states was on the hill west of the Temple Mount and which today is erroneously known as Mount Zion. An ancient large structure today known as the House of Caiaphas is identified with an earlier Hasmonean palace that overlooked the entire valley and which once may have included the *xystos* (a covered colonnade) or gymnasium. Recently the ancient steps leading down to the valley and up to the Temple have been uncovered next to this palace. Within the palace is a deep pit guides suggest could have served as a dungeon for holding prisoners and which might have held Jesus during the Jewish hearings by Annas and Caiaphas.[36] Whether Annas and Caiaphas would have lived in different sections of the same building may be a little doubtful for

---

[34] For a thorough discussion of the Jewish hearing or trial see R. Brown, *Death of the Messiah*, 1.340–64. One of the problems one faces in evaluating Jewish procedures with Jesus is that it is difficult to be sure of the rules that were in effect prior to the restructuring that took place at Jamnia and thus in the Mishnah itself. For a brief statement see Bruce, "The Trial of Jesus," 8–10.

[35] Josephus, *Wars*, 2.16.3.

[36] Whether the building now known as Peter-in-Gallicantu ("the place of the crowing cock"), the traditional site of the high priest's place, was actually the palace of the Jewish leadership is an open question, but the ancient steps nearby would provide easy access to the Temple. See R. Mackowski, *Jerusalem, City of Jesus* (Grand Rapids: Eerdmans, 1980), 145, 164.

some, yet others have employed this idea to assist in synthesizing the various Gospel accounts.[37]

The use of the term *aulēn* ("courtyard") here implies a fairly substantial building. The fact that a woman was guarding the door would indicate that the hearing did not occur at the Temple but at the home of the high priest.

To this setting Peter and "the other disciple" came following Jesus and the arresting band. This verse indicates that the other disciple was "known" to the high priest. Who this disciple was has been debated much by scholars. Of particular significance in the debate is the issue of whether or not the unnamed disciple could have been John and whether this John, a Galilean fisherman, could have been known to the high priest. The fact that the evangelist refers to almost everyone else in his Gospel by name suggests that the early readers must have had no difficulty identifying who this person was. Moreover, it is highly unlikely that the so-called beloved disciple who was commissioned to care for Jesus' mother (19:25–27) and who was reclining next to Jesus at the supper (13:23) would be different from this "other" disciple here or the witness at the cross (19:35).[38] As I indicated in my introduction to this commentary, the likely person would have been the one who stands behind the basic text of this Gospel, John the son of Zebedee.[39]

But could a Galilean fisherman have had access to the residence of the high priest, and could such a person have persuaded the female guard to let a companion outsider into the courtyard? The answer to that question relates to one's view of fishermen.

Peter and John in Acts 4:13 are called *agrammatoi eisin kai idiōtai*. The KJV had referred to them as "unlearned and ignorant," but more recent renderings have modified that to "unschooled, ordinary" (NIV), "uneducated and ordinary" (NRSV), and "ordinary men who had no special training" (NLT). But to understand the situation better one needs to get into the minds of those Pharisees who regarded themselves as elite and the people of the land or the people who worked with their hands as basically ignorant. The stories of the rabbis are filled with condemnations of such people, and even this Gospel has one such castigation (7:49). But if Mark 1:19–20 is any indication of John's family, he was not a pauper. The scepticism I find in some comments that the son of Zebedee could not have had access to the high priest's residence is based on an unproven premise that he must have been both illiterate and unconnected. I would stoutly challenge that

---

[37] Cf. R. Brown is very skeptical of such an argument (*Death of the Messiah*, 1.404).

[38] For a review of the issues involved see F. Neirynck, "The 'other disciple' in John 18:15–16," *ETL* 51 (1975): 113–41. He considers it to be quite feasible that the 'other disciple' is the beloved disciple.

[39] See my views in *John 1–11*, 89–90.

premise. Morris posits a fascinating suggestion that John was of the priestly class, relying on a reflection from Polycrates and a construct of verses from the Gospels. Although the idea is very intriguing, the loose chain of connections back to this verse hardly provides a secure argument.[40]

18:17 In this story Peter may have gained access to the courtyard, but that was the beginning of his problems. The maid servant who guarded the door asked him a very pertinent question. The form of the question in Greek (cf. also 18:25) normally expects a negative answer. It is different from the third question in v. 26, which clearly expects a positive response. Did the maid then merely ask a question without barbs attached to it? I will discuss another aspect of the question below, but this question certainly put Peter in a defensive posture.

Peter's answer was a sharp *ouk eimi* ("I am not!"). For the evangelist, who has focused repeatedly on the affirmations of Jesus as *egō eimi* ("I am") and most immediately at the arrest (18:5,8), the contrast here is very striking. The denial is especially significant in light of Peter's earlier forceful statement that he would be willing to die for Jesus (13:37) and his impulsive attempt to defend Jesus (18:10). When Jesus was present, Peter was filled with boldness and sought to interfere in Jesus' mission. But when he was alone and challenged, he lost his courage and abandoned his discipleship.

A number of scholars have followed Culpepper's lead in seeking to move the focus away from the denials of Peter to the assertion of his discipleship, but this shift hardly does justice to the evangelist's presentation here.[41] Of course, Peter's discipleship is important, as is his reinstatement, but that is not the point here. The point is that in spite of his brashness and self-confidence he failed Jesus and as such his story is a warning to all who would claim self-confidently that they would follow Jesus "wherever he leads them." Boasting of our abilities is an invitation to failure. That is exactly what Peter discovered.

But the presence of *kai* ("also, too") is a little strange and requires some comment. Although it may be nothing significant, it may help to explain the form of the question. Could Brown be on the right track when he suggested

---

[40] Morris suggests that it is possible that Salome, who was at the cross (Mark 15:40), could have been the mother of John (cf. also Matt 27:56), the sister (?) of the mother of Jesus who was also at the cross (John 19:25), who could have been related to Elizabeth, the wife of Zechariah the priest (cf. Luke 1:36), who was a descendant of Aaron (Luke 1:5; *John*, 666, n.37). A letter of Polycrates referred to in Eusebius (*HE*, 3.31.3) states that John "was a priest" and that he wore a *petalon*, whatever that might be. For further reflection on this argument see R. A. Culpepper, *John, Son of Zebedee: The Life of a Legend* (Columbia, S.C.: University Press, 1994), 61–63.

[41] See R. A. Culpepper, *Anatomy of the Fourth Gospel* (Philadelphia: Fortress, 1983), 120. Cf. Beasley-Murray, *John*, 324 and Carson, *John*, 581.

the possibility that the maid was wondering if Peter was not "also" one of his disciples?[42] The NIV conveniently omits reference to the *kai* here and thus eliminates the issue. But if this was the case, perhaps the maid was expecting a negative answer, and that is exactly what she received. The problem with making too strong a case for this suggestion is that while the Greek construction with initial *ouk* was clearly used to imply a positive answer, the construction with initial *mē*, often implying a negative answer, was a little more slippery. But the above suggestion also raises a number of intriguing questions itself, the answers to which seem to be hidden in silence. Yet it is only fair to ponder them: Did the woman know that the "other" disciple was a follower of Jesus? If she did, then the next question follows: Did the high priest knowingly permit friends of Jesus into that setting and even into the hearing? Would Nicodemus have been there? If the high priest would have done so, then one might ask: Was the high priest's motive for expediting the hearing at night so crucial that he needed Roman support to protect himself against the popularity of Jesus? And did he need to do it hastily at the festival time both to prevent Jesus' escape and at the same time to demonstrate publicly the powerlessness of Jesus to resist political force and thus quash what he viewed as a mistaken messianic movement? I have my doubts.

18:18 Jerusalem is built on a mountain and is on the edge of the desert. That means when the sun goes down, it gets chilly. In the month of Nisan it gets rather cold at night, and Jerusalem can also be windy. This verse is an excellent climatic description of Jerusalem at Passover time. But time and temperature statements in John are often theological statements as well. Night with Nicodemus (3:2) and Judas (13:30) and winter in the Shepherd *Mashal* (10:22) are not merely physical descriptors. They are also theological descriptors of the situation in these texts. So also here the cold is indicative of the conditions in the story. Not until the resurrection stories will the night ultimately give way to daybreak.

But there is also one other feature in this verse that is absolutely crucial for understanding the significance of this event here. That feature is the "charcoal fire," which appears in the New Testament only here and in 21:9 at Peter's reinstatement. That double use of the word is not just a coincidence. These two events are directly connected in the mind of the evangelist. Accordingly, any attempt to remove the Epilogue (chap. 21) from the rest of the Gospel is basically ill conceived. But for the interrelationship of these two events the reader should turn to chap. 21.

---

[42] See R. Brown, *The Gospel According to John (xiii–xxi),* AB (Garden City: Doubleday, 1970), 824. Contrast the work of R. Fortna, "Jesus and Peter at the High Priest's House: A Test Case for the Question of the Relation Between Mark's and John's Gospels," *NTS* 24 (1978): 371–83, who focuses on the differences in the accounts and their literary constructions.

(3) The Hearing before Annas and Its Disposal (18:19–24)

[19]Meanwhile, the high priest questioned Jesus about his disciples and his teaching.

[20] "I have spoken openly to the world," Jesus replied. "I always taught in synagogues or at the temple, where all the Jews come together. I said nothing in secret. [21]Why question me? Ask those who heard me. Surely they know what I said."

[22]When Jesus said this, one of the officials nearby struck him in the face. "Is this the way you answer the high priest?" he demanded.

[23] "If I said something wrong," Jesus replied, "testify as to what is wrong. But if I spoke the truth, why did you strike me?" [24]Then Annas sent him, still bound, to Caiaphas the high priest.

18:19–20 This segment opens with the statement that "the high priest questioned Jesus." This statement raises two questions. The first relates to the fact that Caiaphas was actually the high priest but, as I have indicated above, Annas continued to be called the high priest much the same as a former president or general continues to be called by those designations, except that Annas continued to exert real power after being deposed.

The second question involves the legitimacy of the high priest questioning a defendant. Certainly by the time of Maimonides it was clearly established that a defendant according to the Mishnah *Sanh.* 6.2 was not required to testify but that charges had to be made and supported by witnesses. Although Danby[43] argued that such a perspective did not apply to the Second Temple period, Barrett citing Abrahams[44] for support countered that such an interpretation was still a "legitimate inference" from the early texts.[45]

The particular focus of the high priest's question here seems to be directed both at the disciples and at Jesus' teaching. Concerning the first issue, Jesus said very little as though he were ignoring any suggestion of sedition, but his closing words in v. 20 were clearly aimed at denying any hidden secret plot against the ruling authorities. That statement does not mean that he never had any private conversations with people but that he was not double-tongued or two-faced in what he said.

The point of the second issue was apparently directed by Annas at seeking information concerning Jesus' teaching itself. This is the issue that is the primary concern in the Jewish trial before Caiaphas in the Synoptic Gospels. The hearing described here in John is not mentioned in the Synop-

---

[43] See H. Danby, "The Bearing of the Rabbinical Criminal Code on the Jewish Trial Narratives in the Gospels," *JTS* 21 (1920): 51–76.

[44] I. Abrahams, "The Tannaitic Tradition and the Trial Narratives," *Studies in Pharisaism and the Gospels* (Cambridge: University Press, 1924), 2.129–37. Cf. also Bruce, "Trial," 1.7–20.

[45] C. K. Barrett, *The Gospel According to St. John* (London: S.P.C.K., 1956), 441.

tics. Some scholars faced with the differences between John and the Synoptics suggest that John may have been confused about the order of the events, and they propose various alternatives, such as a rearranging of the Johannine text to conform to the Synoptics, emendations of the text, or insertions into the original story of some material that does not fit.[46] But I agree with Brown in distrusting all of these suggestions.[47]

Jesus' response to the high priest's questioning is not really to answer the high priest's question, as will become clear in the next verse. Jesus' response is to remind the high priest that he had plenty of opportunity to gather the information he wanted in using against Jesus because Jesus was a very public figure and spoke openly to the world. Indeed, Jesus boldly asserted that he had taught in both synagogue and the Temple itself, the special domain of the high priests. When this statement of Jesus is read in the context of Annas's peremptory show of authority, it comes across clearly as a verbal challenge to the high priest by Jesus. There is here no sense that Jesus is threatened by this human authority figure.

18:21–23   Indeed, Jesus parried the high priest's question with one of his own. His response basically was to ask the high priest for his witnesses. Jewish trials patently demanded witnesses. Where are the witnesses? The challenge of Jesus was thus a direct rebuke of the procedure being employed by the high priest in this hearing that resembles an interrogation more than a formal trial. The fact that Jesus had pointedly confronted the high priest is clearly supported by the reaction of one of the assistants of the high priest, who gave Jesus an insulting open-handed slap on the face.[48] The assistant followed this demeaning slap with a questioning demand for Jesus to be more humble in answering the high priest. This servant reminds us of contemporary assistants to important people who often take it as their duty to make people cringe before their bosses. It is their way of displaying their derivative sense of power.

Jesus, however, did not back down to this minor official. Instead, he challenged the man to be a witness *(martyrēson)* himself to how Jesus was wrong or pernicious. But if Jesus was correct, in terms of his rights in such a hearing, then the man himself needed to answer to the question of why he struck Jesus.

---

[46] Although Bultmann proposed some insertions, even he found rearrangement theories to be unlikely since he regarded John's source to be an independent tradition unrelated to the Synoptics (*John*, 643). A. Mahoney chose the route of textual emendation, but he leaves many unanswered questions in the process ("A New Look at an Old Problem (John 18:12–14, 19–24)," *CBQ* 27 [1965]: 137–44). Readers should understand that the relationship of John here to the Synoptics was recognized many years ago as a possible concern, and several minuscule Greek manuscripts 225 and 1195 from the Middle Ages actually rearrange the verses. For further details see Metzger, *Textual Commentary*, 251–52.

[47] R. Brown, *Death of the Messiah*, 1.407.

[48] See *BAGD*, 734.

Accordingly, from my legal perspective in reading this segment of the story, it seems quite evident that John was seeking to make a point that Jesus stood completely within his rights and also that people of power like Annas (and later Pilate) hardly unnerved Jesus. Annas's goal was obviously one of questioning Jesus, and in so doing he attempted to reduce Jesus to a whimpering defendant. But that procedure did not work with Jesus. In John it is clear that Jesus stands serene throughout the entire story as the legitimate Messiah or King of Israel (cf. 1:41,49; 18:33–37).

18:24 Because the hearing from the high priest's perspective did not seem to accomplish anything except call into question his own procedural irregularities, the reader gets the impression that Annas turns the task of trying or interrogating Jesus over to his son-in-law, Caiaphas. This verse thus basically concludes the Jewish hearing in John.

When one compares the Gospel accounts on this portion of the Death Story, it becomes apparent that John focuses his story on a failed hearing before Annas that is not mentioned in the Synoptics. But Mark and Matthew focus on a Sanhedrin (Council) hearing, probably chaired by Caiaphas (cf. Matt 26:57). In all three Synoptic Gospels, Jesus is also struck and in Mark (14:65) and Matthew (26:67) even spit upon in the convened night session. Such a spitting was a degrading and condemning act rendered against someone regarded as guilty in Jewish tradition. But this incident is missing in the Johannine portrait. Neither included are any conflicting testimonies given by witnesses, some of whom claimed that Jesus would destroy "this man-made temple and in three days build another, not made by man" (Mark 14:58; cf. Matt 26:61). Nor is the high priest's frustration after he could get little conclusive agreement from the witnesses or his questioning of Jesus about whether he was the Son of God/Son of the Blessed One/Christ and received Jesus' response concerning being seated at the right hand of power (cf. Matt 26:63; Mark 14:61–62; Luke 22:67–69). Likewise missing in John is the tearing by the high priest of his robe (Matt 26:65; Mark 14:63) and his condemnation of Jesus to death for blasphemy (Matt 26:65–66; Mark 14:64). The frustration of the hearing before Annas and Jesus' commanding serenity is the focus of John.

Although briefly mentioned in this verse is the fact that Jesus is sent to Caiaphas, the presence of the word "bound" is intriguing here. Jesus may be bound, but he is hardly cowed by the events. It reminds one of the closing word in Acts 28:31, where Paul is a prisoner but the gospel is unbound. The images of victory in spite of bondage were very important to the early Christians, who had little power in the face of Imperial Rome and who suffered condemnation in Jewish synagogues. They are no less significant for Christians who suffer today.

The next stage in this sham process of condemning Jesus that is reported by John would be to turn Jesus over to the Roman governor. But before that occurred, John returned to the conclusion of Peter's denial outside the hearing chambers in the courtyard of the high priest.

(4) Peter's Second and Third Denials (18:25–27)

25As Simon Peter stood warming himself, he was asked, "You are not one of his disciples, are you?"

He denied it, saying, "I am not."

26One of the high priest's servants, a relative of the man whose ear Peter had cut off, challenged him, "Didn't I see you with him in the olive grove?" **27**Again Peter denied it, and at that moment a rooster began to crow.

18:25–27 Not only does Annas emerge in this story as incapable of dealing with Jesus, but Peter in this section is portrayed as weak in the face of calls for his integrity. The opening words of v. 25 concerning Peter's need for warmth is John's way of indicating the chilling fact of Peter's failure to live up to his earlier boast of following Jesus even to the point of his own death (13:37).

At this stage in his commentary Haenchen included a long essay concerning Peter's denial and scholarly views related to these verses. G. Klein had earlier argued that the entire story of Peter's denials was the result of a very strong resentment on the part of an opposition to Peter in the church which was then read back into the preresurrection stories as a threefold denial of Jesus by Peter.[49] But Haenchen understandably finds no evidence for such a hostility that would create this story.[50] In an early article E. Linnemann countered that the source for the story was not some hostility to Peter but the distress of the disciples. Thus, because Peter was held in such esteem, he became a symbol of their regret. Although Linnemann has since moved away from that view, it nevertheless indicates how scholars wrestle with historical issues in the Gospel stories.[51] Haenchen's own view is not unrelated to this idea because he was attracted to the thesis of the literary creativity of the Gospel writers. Accordingly, he sees the allusion in Mark 14:27 to Zech 13:7 as one source for the development of the traditions concerning the denials.[52] Beasley-Murray[53] is undoubtedly correct in suggesting that much of such scepticism concerning these events has its roots in Bultmann's conclusion that the story is both "legendary and literary."[54]

---

[49] G. Klein, "Die Verleungnung des Petrus. Eine traditionsgeschichtliche Untersuchung," *ZTK* 58 (1961): 285–328.

[50] Haenchen, *John*, 2.171.

[51] E. Linnemann, "Die Verleugnung des Petrus," *ZTK* 63 (1966): 1–32.

[52] Haenchen, *John*, 2.171–74. Cf. Fortna, "Jesus and Peter," 371–83.

[53] See Beasley-Murray, *John*, 325.

[54] R. Bultmann, *The History of the Synoptic Tradition* (New York: Harper & Row, 1963), 269.

Specifically it may be said, therefore, that John's particular description of these events is slightly different from those in the Synoptics. For example, the maid seems to be responsible for Peter's second denial in Mark 14:69, yet another maid seems to take on that task in Matt 26:71, while in Luke 22:58 it is another man who confronts Peter, whereas here in John it is a collective "they." Moreover, Peter simply is said to deny his relationship to Jesus in Mark, whereas in Matthew he denies it with an oath and with the statement "I don't know the man!" In Luke he says, "I am not" *(ouk eimi)*. John, of course, happily uses these same words because of his theological attachment to "I am" *(egō eimi)*. Similar differences can be found with the third denial, particularly in Matthew and Mark, where Peter is said to have invoked a curse upon himself to prove his negative assertion, whereas in John special mention is made of the fact that the third interrogator was identified as a relative of the high priest's servant who had his ear cut off. Although these differences are rather significant, they are actually part of the unique way the dynamic story involving a group campfire event is told by the various evangelists.

The point of all the narratives, however, is virtually the same. Peter failed at this stage of his discipleship. He was merely a fallible human whom the church must not remake into something more than a human. Clearly, sometimes he was a miserable failure as a follower of Jesus. But that fact helps us as human failures to realize that we do not have to be perfect to become followers of Jesus or to be accepted by God. Jesus knew Peter's good intentions, but he also recognized his human insecurities and his resistance to full commitment, even after the resurrection (cf. John 21:21–22). That reality ought to help us find acceptance when we like Peter hear the trumpet blow or the cock crow[55] and we are alerted to our failures.

---

[55] The Romans divided the night watch into four segments for guard duty: the third was between midnight and the change of duty at 3:00 a.m., which became known as the "cock crow" *(alectrophonia* or *gallicinium)*. This fourth segment was still night but known as early morning *(prōi)* and ran between 3:00 a.m. and 6:00 a.m., at which point the Romans regarded the time as the dawning of a new day. The change of watches was signaled by the blowing of a Roman trumpet. The idea of the cock crow following Peter's denials fits perfectly the Johannine theology that evil, lack of understanding, and rejection of Jesus are all linked to "night" (cf. John 3:2; 13:30). Cf. R. Brown, *Death of the Messiah*, 1.606 as well as *John*, 2.844. Concerning "night" cf. Bultmann, *John*, 651. That the Romans had a specific time designated as the "cock crow" does not mean a rooster could not have crowed at this point, but the classic arguments over whether or not there could have been roosters in Jerusalem at that time is rendered moot concerning the prohibition against foul in Jerusalem in the Mishnah (*B. Qam.* 7.7; cf. *Str-B* 1.992–93) if one recognizes the segments of Roman time. Cf. J. Jeremias, *Jerusalem in the Time of Jesus* (Philadelphia: Fortress, 1969), 46–48 for his earlier discussion. It is also appropriate to recall the somewhat strange logic of J. Cheney, which was followed partly by H. Lindsell in *The Battle for the Bible* (Grand Rapids: Zondervan, 1976), 174–75. In an attempt to take seriously all the biblical texts, Cheney added together all the Gospel accounts of the crowing of the cocks and in weaving them together actually arrived at six denial segments—a phenomenon that is in no biblical text.

The integrated nature of this part of the Death Story, which interweaves the Jewish hearing statements and Peter's denials, provides a theological reality check concerning how the unbelieving world can challenge commitment and faith.

3. The Roman "Trial" of the King (18:28–19:16)

Following the pattern from the previous section of interweaving stories in order to produce an integrated picture of the dynamics involved in interrogative hearings and trials, the evangelist in this section skillfully balances Pilate's interrogation of Jesus with the Jewish charges and indictments leveled against Jesus. The means John uses is to alternate the scenes once again in a repeated pattern but this time from outside to inside Pilate's hearing chambers.

(1) Delivering Jesus to Pilate and the Opening Charges (18:28–32)

[28]Then the Jews led Jesus from Caiaphas to the palace of the Roman governor. By now it was early morning, and to avoid ceremonial uncleanness the Jews did not enter the palace; they wanted to be able to eat the Passover. [29]So Pilate came out to them and asked, "What charges are you bringing against this man?"

[30]"If he were not a criminal," they replied, "we would not have handed him over to you."

[31]Pilate said, "Take him yourselves and judge him by your own law."

"But we have no right to execute anyone," the Jews objected. [32]This happened so that the words Jesus had spoken indicating the kind of death he was going to die would be fulfilled.

18:28 The transfer of Jesus from [the place] of Caiaphas (the Greek here is not specific but probably refers to his palace) to the praetorium probably took place sometime during or at the end of the fourth night duty watch (the Greek is *prōi*). The transferring of Jesus to Pilate was done by the vague "they" in Greek, even though the NIV states that it was "the Jews."

The *praetorium* where they led Jesus was the official headquarters, judgment seat, and command center of the military leader in an area. In the subprovince of Judea and Samaria the governor's headquarters was normally at Caesarea Maratima (by the sea), but during festival periods, which attracted flocks of visitors to Jerusalem, the governor moved his command center to Jerusalem, either to the Antonio Fortress north and next to the Temple or to the site of Herod's palace with its three great towers that served as part of the defense system for the Western (Jaffa) Gate. The most likely site for this stay by Pilate was not the Antonio (and the Lithostroton) but the great triple tower fortress palace.[56]

In the second half of this verse the evangelist provides an ironic contrast between the Jews who were seeking Jesus's death and their unwillingness to enter the praetorium for fear of defiling themselves lest they would not be able to eat the Passover.[57] The Mishnah *Ohol.*, 7–10 suggests that court-yards and some other outlying buildings did not always come within the definition of Gentile places where Jews would be contaminated and ren-dered religiously unclean. Although the laws of clean and unclean in respect to eating the Passover were complex, it seems that entering the resi-dence of a Gentile would have been a major problem and would likely have rendered a Jew unclean for at least seven days and required the postpone-ment of eating Passover for a month. The basic logic seems to have grown out of an interpretation of the rule of contamination from the dead in Num 19:11–13. It was widely believed that Gentiles aborted babies in their homes and either buried them within their homes or ran them down through their sewers.[58] The uncleanness here was hardly the usual uncleanness of public encounter that could by sunset have been removed through a regular lustration or bath as an appropriate purification rite (cf. Lev 15:5–11).

18:29–30 In "delivering" or handing over Jesus to Pilate, the Jewish authorities would have been expected to provide a charge or accusation *(katēgorian)* against Jesus. The use of this term by John probably strength-ens the view that the "hearing" by Annas served to provide an indictment, although it is not clear, according to John, what may have occurred with Caiaphas (but contrast the reference to Caiaphas in Matt 26:57 at the begin-ning of the hearing scene in that Gospel).

In Luke the earlier hearing is clearly defined as a meeting of the Sanhe-

---

[56] For varying opinions see examples in R. Brown, *Death of the Messiah*, 1.706–10; Schnack-enburg, *St. John*, 3.243; Carson, *John*, 586; etc. Emotionally I would probably be attached to the Antonio and the Sisters of Zion site, but intellectually I would have difficulty not choosing the old Herodian palace. But that phenomenon of heart and mind preferences often affects people who know Jerusalem well because "tradition" is deeply imbedded into the ancient sites. For some sup-port of the view here see Philo, *Legatio ad Garium*, 299; and Josephus, *War*, 1.21.1; 2.14.8. For an excellent summary of the issues see P. Benoit, "Praetorium, Lithostraton and Gabbatha," in *Jesus and the Gospels* (New York: Herder, 1973), 1.170–76.

[57] See P. Duke, *Irony in the Fourth Gospel* (Atlanta: John Knox, 1985), 127–28. C. Story, in attempting to make sense of the confusing dating in John, argued that Jesus had eaten the Passover meal on the Thursday but that the arresting Jewish officers had not yet eaten the meal. So, using Exod 12:10, he proposed that they had until the conclusion of the fourth night watch (6:00 a.m.) to do so, and they still had the time to eat the meal. But such an argument seems to me to stretch all logic. The issue in John is not time but their possible defilement. See C. Story, "The Bearing of Old Testament Terminology on the Johannine Chronology of the Final Passover of Jesus," *NovT* 31 (1989): 316–24.

[58] For further references see *Str–B*, 1.838–39. Cf. Beasley-Murray, *John*, 327.

drin (22:66), and the charge in that scene would be akin to blasphemy (Luke 22:70–71; cf. Matt 26:65). But then Luke says the whole Sanhedrin came over to Pilate, and there they introduced the entire situation with a shift in the charge to treasonable offenses (Luke 23:1–2).

In John the story seems to be crafted by the evangelist in stages so that the reader is engaged by the movement of the story. Pilate in this Gospel asked for the charge. The immediate response is not a statement of the charge but an accusation of Jesus being a criminal or literally "one who does evil."

18:31 Obviously the prefect Pilate was aware of the fact that the Jews were upset, otherwise why would they disturb him at a high feast time? But John seems to picture Pilate as not wanting to get involved in a mere Jewish problem. Could Pilate have been trying to "toy" with the Jews? We know from Josephus and others that Pilate and the Jews were not on very friendly terms.[59] So Pilate tried to deflect their concern by reminding them that they were given the rights of an *ethos* during the time of Herod and that they could handle most criminal cases. Therefore his opinion was to let them follow their legal system with this apparent Jewish misfit in their society. The Jewish leaders probably expected that if the Romans had helped in Jesus' arrest (cf. 18:3,12) Pilate would accept any decision they would make concerning him and "rubber stamp" their views.

Accordingly, the Jewish leaders would not be put off by this dismissive attempt of Pilate. Instead, they called for dealing with Jesus by means of Roman law because their hostility against him could only be assuaged by a sentence of death. Although Barrett seems to have little regard for the historicity of the Johannine account of Pilate in relation to Roman court rules of the time, his views have been followed only by the most skeptical scholars.[60] Moreover, while some have attempted to argue that the Romans gave the Jewish leadership powers to execute even Gentiles, this rule was hardly the situation in effect during the period of the prefects and procurators of Judea and Samaria.[61]

---

[59] Pilate was appointed by Tiberius as Prefect of Judea and Samaria in A.D. 26 shortly before the death of Jesus (cf. Tacitus, *Annals*, 15.44) and frequently had difficulties with the Jewish leadership. They finally petitioned to have him removed. For further references see B. McGing, "Pontius Pilate and the Sources," *CBQ* 53 (1991): 416–38; E. Smallwood, "The Date of the Dismissal of Pontius Pilate from Judea," *JJS* 5 (1954): 12–21. See Josephus, *War*, 2.9.1–4 and *Ant*, 18.3.1. See also J. Blank, "Die Verhanlung vor Pilatus Joh 18, 28–29, 16 im Lichte johanneischer Theologie," *BZ* 3 (1959): 60–81.

[60] Barrett, *St. John*, 443.

[61] Josephus, *War*, 2.8.1. For a helpful review see Blinzer, *Trial*, 157–63; see also Sherwin-White, *Roman Society*, 25–39 for a strong affirmation of the Johannine understanding of the situation. For a confirmation of the death penalty in the hands of the Romans at this time see the Jerusalem Talmud, *Sanhedrin* 1.1 and 7.2. For a counterargument see Barrett, *St. John*, 445–46.

18:32   This verse brings to a conclusion the initial encounter of Pilate
with the Jewish leadership outside the praetorium. It concludes with one of
the few Johannine fulfillment sayings. Although this statement could well
refer to verses like John 3:14 and 12:32, where Jesus predicted that he
would be lifted up, the Old Testament reference behind it, Beasley-Murray
and Morris think, could easily have been Deut 21:23, where it is said that
anyone who was hung on a tree would be under the curse of God.[62] The
idea of lifting up and hanging on a tree would obviously be interpreted in
reference to the Roman punishment of crucifixion rather than the Jewish
punishment of stoning.

(2) The First Interrogation of Jesus in the Praetorium (18:33–38a)

[33]Pilate then went back inside the palace, summoned Jesus and asked him,
"Are you the king of the Jews?"
[34] "Is that your own idea," Jesus asked, "or did others talk to you about me?"
[35] "Am I a Jew?" Pilate replied. "It was your people and your chief priests
who handed you over to me. What is it you have done?"
[36]Jesus said, "My kingdom is not of this world. If it were, my servants would
fight to prevent my arrest by the Jews. But now my kingdom is from another
place."
[37] "You are a king, then!" said Pilate.
Jesus answered, "You are right in saying I am a king. In fact, for this reason I
was born, and for this I came into the world, to testify to the truth. Everyone on
the side of truth listens to me."
[38] "What is truth?" Pilate asked.

The direct examination of Jesus by the Roman governor focuses attention on one of the major themes of the Death Story in John: the fact that
Jesus is the King of the Jews. The Johannine Death Story brings together
the two ideas of this King of Jews dying as the Lamb of God.

18:33   All four Gospels indicate that Pilate's opening question to Jesus
was: "Are you the king of the Jews?"[63] So deeply imbedded into the traditions of the early church was this question that it could hardly be omitted
from a legitimate canonical testimony of the Death Story of Jesus. While
this question had not been noted earlier in the Jewish hearing reported by

---

[62] See Beasley-Murray, *John*, 328 and Morris, *John*, 677. Some scholars have argued that the
Jews used crucifixion as a means of execution; but when Alexander Jannaeus, the Sadducee, used
this means during the Hasmonean period against the Pharisees, he was severely castigated (cf.
Josephus, *War*, 1.4.6), and there is no further record of such use by Jews.

[63] The idea of the kingship of Jesus is a major theme in the Johannine Gospel. The term is used
twelve times in the Death Story, whereas it appears four times in Matthew and Mark. The expression "King of the Jews" is clearly a non-Jewish, Roman way of speaking. The Jews would have
used the expression "King of Israel." Cf. Garland, "John 18–19," 489–90, 498.

John, it must be assumed that this was in fact the charge or indictment the Jews leveled against Jesus. Such a charge was undoubtedly intended to gain the attention of the Roman governor. Messianic claims swirled around Israel in the post-Maccabean period and were only put to rest after the second Jewish uprising with the defeat of Simon Bar Kokhba (A.D. 135).

In each Gospel the question begins with the emphatic Greek *su* (you!): "Are you ...?" which suggests that Pilate could well have been astonished that Jesus was claiming such a title. Jesus hardly had an army, and he certainly had not led an uprising against the Romans as a rebel king might have been tempted to do. What kind of a king was this?

18:34–35 With v. 34 there begins an interplay of questions that reveals the genuine skill of the evangelist in presenting the story of the interrogation. Jesus parried the opening question of Pilate with his own question concerning the source of Pilate's question. A journalist learns to look behind people's questions for the reasons they are asking them. That is exactly what Jesus was doing when he questioned Pilate about the source of his question. As a result Jesus' question was not basically a question for information. It was actually a challenge concerning the basis for the interrogation.

Pilate's response indicates that as a governor, who was responsible for the "just" conduct of trials, he recognized he was being challenged by the defendant. He was disturbed by the way the interrogation was going; and he replied sharply, "Am I a Jew?" Such an idea was obviously from Pilate's point of view unthinkable.

Moreover, he countered with an additional statement of fact to the effect that Jesus' own people and leadership had "delivered" or "handed over" *(paredōkan)* Jesus to him. By now readers should be realizing that in John "handing over" is a recurrent theme that includes Judas's "betraying" *(paradidous)* of Jesus (18:5). It will conclude with Pilate "handing over" Jesus to be crucified (19:16). The progression to death involves a series of people who participate in this great conspiracy.

Finally, Pilate is forced to ask the question he should have asked at the outset of the interrogation. It is only fair to ask: Why are you here? Or, what have you done? Coming where it does in this investigation, however, it seems to be less of a genuine question of seeking the facts and more of a question of why there is so much pressure to dispose of this case.

The way the questioning proceeded, however, indicates that Pilate did not simply rubber stamp Jewish hostility. He did seek for some answer to this Jesus that might satisfy the logic of his judgment.

18:36 Pilate's statement attached to the question in the previous verse certainly warranted a response, and thus Jesus departed from countering question with question. He answered Pilate's concern by introducing the concept of his kingdom. The fundamental attribute of Jesus' kingdom is that it is not derived from or out of this world. Accordingly, it would not do battle with the Romans by means of earthly weapons. Jesus' kingdom had its origin and strength external to the world, and therefore his followers would not take up arms to prevent his being "handed over." Peter's way in 18:10 was not the way of Jesus. Jesus' kingdom is not a piece of land on earth or involved in earthly power and domination. Schnackenburg argued further that *basileia* here does not even refer to kingdom but is "a designation of function ('kingship')." Thus he proposed that it should be distinguished from the concept of kingdom in John 3:3,5 and generally in the Synoptics.[64] But Beasley-Murray is undoubtedly correct that the concept of kingdom includes kingship and the kingly reign of Jesus similar to the concept of *malkuth* in the Hebrew Bible.[65] Jesus' kingdom is directly related to the concept of the kingdom of heaven and the reign or authority of God. It is both a proleptic reality now and a future expectation yet to come in its fullness.[66] Although this kingdom does not have its source in the world, it is nonetheless active in the world. But since it is related to God, it draws its power from a source external to the world. Moreover, its task is one of transformation in the world (cf. 20:31) so that its citizens will authentically represent God or Heaven here on earth.

18:37 This answer of Jesus elicited from Pilate an ensuing reply: "You are a king, [then! or?]," which might be a statement as in the NIV or more likely a summarizing question as in the KJV, RSV, NRSV, and NLT.

Pilate's question went to the heart of John's proclamation of who Jesus is, and therefore Jesus did not parry the question. Instead, he thrust his response directly at Pilate. The response literally is: "You say that I am a king," which Dodd reshaped and interpreted as "king is your word, not mine."[67] Dodd's influence was very strong, and his rendering was followed in both the NEB and NAB. Newman and Nida, therefore, consider there to be "no scholarly consensus" on the meaning,[68] but the point is certainly clarified in Jesus' next statement.

There was no doubt what Jesus' answer was intended to be. He certainly was a king! Indeed, he was born to be a king, even though he was not a king

---

[64] See Schnackenburg, *St. John*, 3.249.

[65] See Beasley-Murray, *John*, 330–31.

[66] For further discussion of kingdom see G. von Rad, *TDNT*, 1.565; Kuhn, *TDNT*, 1.571–74 and K. Schmidt, *TDNT*, 1.579–90. See also G. Beasley-Murray, *Jesus and the Kingdom* (Grand Rapids: Eerdmans, 1986).

[67] See Dodd, *Historical Tradition*, 99. F. F. Bruce, *The Gospel of John* (Grand Rapids: Eerdmans, 1983), 353–54, employs this rendering, but he clearly does not intend it to mean that Jesus was evading the question. Cf. also Morris, *John*, 680–81.

[68] Cf. B. Newman and E. Nida, *A Translator's Handbook on the Gospel of John* (London: United Bible Societies, 1980), 571.

in the earthly sense. But his kingship was intimately tied to his mission. His coming into the world was to be a witness or testifier to the truth.

The theme of truth is a foundational idea in John. For Jesus and for John truth is not merely some intellectual concept of correct facticity. It also involves life-oriented integrity. Accordingly, we misunderstand Johannine truth if we merely speak of the truth about Jesus or doctrinal formulations about Jesus. Jesus is himself truth as he states: "I am the way, the truth and the life" (14:6). Jesus was not proposing to give the disciples a map or "triptik" to heaven or a theological description about himself. Jesus gave them himself. There is no doubt that truth is related to ideas and matters of facticity, but Jesus' mission was to bring people to himself and to God and in the process thereby bring them to integrity of life. It is clearly possible to be academically right and theologically correct but still lack integrity in life.

Jesus' mission was to integrate truth into life. That is the reason the text here defines people who are of truth as those who hear the voice of Jesus. Hearing or obeying Jesus is not the same as affirming correct ideas. The Pharisees and legalists in Jesus' day were very precise in their theological formulations, but God was remote for them. Moreover, they schemed his crucifixion in their correctness because they missed hearing the voice of God. That can still happen today. What Jesus did in this story was confront Pilate with himself and with the genuine nature of truth.

18:38a For politically motivated people, truth is frequently sacrificed on the altar of expediency. Many politically oriented people pretend they are interested in truth. But Pilate summarizes his politically oriented life pattern with the haunting question: "What is truth?" The implications of that question are exceedingly far reaching for any person.

For Pilate that question was an attempt to resist taking Jesus' statement seriously in his own life,[69] but it did make an initial impact on his view of Jesus during this first interrogation session.

(3) Pilate's First Verdict and the Jewish Reaction (18:38b–40)

With this he went out again to the Jews and said, "I find no basis for a charge against him.

[39]But it is your custom for me to release to you one prisoner at the time of the Passover. Do you want me to release 'the king of the Jews'?"

---

[69] Haenchen concludes that by his question Pilate reveals that he is not one of Jesus' elect people (*John*, 2.180). He has been often referred to as a sceptic, yet E. Hirsch argued that Pilate was not the usual type of sceptic, but a clear pagan who was driven by the desire to succeed and not by inner motivations of some undisclosed power *(Das vierte Evangelium in seiner ursprünglishen Gesalt* [Tübingen: Mohr-Siebeck, 1936], 416).

40They shouted back, "No, not him! Give us Barabbas!" Now Barabbas had taken part in a rebellion.

18:38b Strategically John does not include any response on Pilate's part. Pilate has revealed himself by his question in the last exchange of 18:38a to be an advocate of expediency, just as the Jewish high priest Caiaphas had done earlier (cf. 11:49–50). Whether to outfox the Jewish leadership or because he actually believed Jesus to be innocent, Pilate developed what he thought would be a successful plan to release Jesus and dismiss the interrogation. Accordingly, he went outside the Praetorium (judgment hall) and rendered his verdict of Jesus' innocence.

Pilate probably recognized that the Jewish leaders were simply trying to use him to dispose of someone who threatened their religious prestige (cf. John 12:18–19). It is also highly unlikely that Pilate would have been uninformed about Jesus' popularity with the people. But it is also most probable that he was at that point convinced that this Jesus offered no threat to Roman political authority in that region. That was hardly the point of the Jewish leadership's concern.

18:39–40 Instead of simply dismissing the case as a good judge interested in integrity should have done following his verdict of innocence, Pilate devised a scheme using Barabbas to deal with any potential fallout he thought might occur as a result. It may be that Pilate thought he could gain popularity points with the Jewish people and at the same time score a blow against the manipulative Jewish leadership. Whatever he may have thought, it is obvious that he had not judged the situation correctly. Pilate's scheme involved giving the people a predetermined choice he thought they could not refuse. Matthew (27:15) and Mark (15:6) indicate that the governor had developed a custom of releasing a prisoner to please the crowd.[70] Mark indicates it was at "the feast." John here identifies the custom with Passover and indicates that it was their [Jewish?] custom, but it is difficult to know when such a custom arose or its source.[71]

So Pilate offered a choice that seemed obvious, yet even the choice contained a hook that clearly would have irritated the Jewish establishment. The choice was either to release Jesus, whom he knowingly called "the

---

[70] A similar statement in Luke 23:17 is obviously a later insertion into the text in a harmonizing attempt to explain the cry for the release of Barabbas. Cf. Metzger, *Textual Commentary*, 179–80.

[71] C. Chavel thought he had located the tradition in the Mishnah *Pesah.* 8.6. It may have been adopted from the post-Maccabean Hasmonean rulers, but the sources and connections in such arguments are very tenuous ("The Releasing of a Prisoner on the Eve of Passover in Ancient Jerusalem," *JBL* 60 [1941]: 273–78). Cf. also "The Pardoning of Prisoners of Pilate," *AJT* 21 (1917): 110–16 and R. Merritt, "Jesus, Barabbas and the Paschal Pardon," *JBL* 104 (1985): 57–68.

King of the Jews," or the scoundrel and thief, Barabbas.[72] Mark goes further in 15:7 and identifies Barabbas as a murderer and an insurrectionist.
This Barabbas was hardly the kind of person Pilate thought the Jews would
desire to have loosed on their society.[73] The obvious alternative from his
point of view was the healer, wonder worker, and prophet-type king. He
must have smirked at the choice he gave to the people. But Pilate had not
calculated on the scheming way in which the Jewish leadership had readied
the group outside the Praetorium to answer him. Pilate's shrewd plan was
undone by the leadership when the people chose the scoundrel and rejected
the King.

(4) The Scourging and Mock Crowning of the King (19:1-3)

**[1]Then Pilate took Jesus and had him flogged. [2]The soldiers twisted together a
crown of thorns and put it on his head. They clothed him in a purple robe [3]and
went up to him again and again, saying, "Hail, king of the Jews!" And they struck
him in the face.**

19:1 Pilate next returned to the inside judgment hall since he had
failed in his manipulative attempt to release Jesus. There he apparently
devised yet another plan to deal with this bothersome situation. The Jews
normally railed on the Romans for their harsh treatment of Jews. So the
next stage was to have Jesus whipped. Luke supports the factualness of
Pilate's plan to have Jesus whipped and then released (Luke 23:16).

The purpose of such a whipping would, according to John 19:4, here
seem to have been not as a preparation for death but a means to attain the
placation of the Jews and the justification for Jesus' release by Pilate.
Accordingly, it would seem that the type of beating described here would
not have been a *verberatio* (see the discussion in Excursus 21). But soldiers may not have always been technical in the severity of their whippings.[74]

---

[72] Scholars have tried to identify Barabbas. Some have suggested he was the son of a "rabban"
or esteemed rabbi. Others have proposed that his name merely is an illusive designation "son of the
father," whoever that might be. R. Brown thinks that he was the son of someone named Abba
(*Death of the Messiah*, 2.799–800). But we really do not know much about him.

[73] In his article on thief or robber K. Rengstorf, *TDNT*, 4.258 notes that Josephus used the term
to refer to Zealots whose aim was to remove the Romans and their collaborators from the land. In
an oppressed society scoundrels often gain a hearing and support from people when those who are
not oppressed would never give them the time of day.

[74] The term *phragellōsas* in Mark 15:15 normally rendered "flogged" as in *verberatio* is probably not used in the technical sense. John's description is probably more precise, since Mark is
basically a brief summary statement. See my discussion in Excursus 21. For a contrary view see
Blinzer, *Der Prozess*, 321–22.

Excursus 21: The Roman Scourging of Jesus and His Condition

The Romans devised three forms or patterns of bodily whipping or scourging in their repertoire of corporal punishments.[75] The least severe was *fustiagatio,* which was a lashing for less serious offenses. This lashing was usually accompanied by a stern warning against any repetition of such an offense. A more serious stage was *flagellatio,* which was a flogging or beating that was severe and was intended to be sufficiently punitive to bring the victim into a state of full submission without execution, something like the so-called thirty-nine stripes. The third and most severe form of this type of punishment was *verberatio,* which was extremely brutal. In this form of punishment the victim was forcefully brutalized with rods or whips that frequently contained leather thongs fitted with spikes, bones, or scraps of metal. When used, these whips tore pieces of flesh from the victim's body. Sometimes a recipient of such cruel punishment actually died while tied to the flogging block, and then the corpse was simply hung on the cross. The severity of such a beating depended on the ruthlessness or blood thirstiness of the officer in charge. Whether such a victim lived or died at the block mattered little since death was usually the expected end of this type of punishment process.

Generally, Roman citizens were not subject to whippings without a formal trial according to strict judicial rules of order (cf. Acts 16:37–39), and in capital cases citizens were executed by beheading and not by crucifixion.

The Gospels do not provide us with specific statements concerning which type of punishment was used on Jesus. Accordingly, scholars have attempted to piece together the nature of Jesus' punishment from statements connected to the punishment itself or from the condition of Jesus after the whipping or scourging. As might be expected, opinions differ depending on which expressions or Gospel descriptions are chosen as the basis for developing such speculations. The statement in Luke 23:23 suggests that the whipping would have been more of a *fustiagatio* because the statement is made in the context of Pilate's desire to release Jesus. But then why was Simon of Cyrene seized to carry the cross? Was Jesus too weak to do it? The descriptive statements concerning beating in Mark 15:15 and Matt 27:26 are made following the release of Barabbas and are often taken to mean that the beating or flogging was done in connection with the delivering of Jesus over to be crucified. Such an order of events is then thought to suggest a *verberatio* as part of the execution process. But in John 19:1 the whipping, in fact, takes place prior to Pilate's attempt to release Jesus and as such it would hardly seem to be a *verberatio.*

Now the reason I have provided such a comparison is to illustrate the kind of problem in which it is very easy to become enmeshed when one seeks clarity in comparative arguments of precision related to the Gospels. For example, Blinzer argued that the beating of Jesus and the condemnation to death were not two sep-

---

[75] For a fuller description of such corporal punishments based on Justinian's code see Sherwin-White, *Roman Society,* 26–28. For the code of Justinian see T. Mommsen, ed., *The Digest of Justinian* (Philadelphia: University of Pennsylvania, 1985), at 40.19.7.

arate events but that the beating actually was an announcement or declaration of his forthcoming death by crucifixion.[76] But what does that have to do with the attempted declaration of innocence in connection with the whipping on the part of Pilate in Luke and John? Dodd concluded that the solution to such an issue was that the Gospels preserved "more than one tradition" concerning this event.[77]

Perhaps a little light on the subject can be found in something like the reversal of Blinzer's argument, namely, that the brief statements in Mark and Matthew are not intended to be more than summation notes and as such do not provide the precision concerning these events we might think they ought to detail. That view could mean that Luke's statement, written in typical Lukan fashion, was a description of what he viewed was Pilate's desired effect that such a whipping of Jesus might have. John's statement then could be a typical Johannine way of expounding through his inside/outside literary presentation a genuine historical reminiscence concerning Pilate's attempt to manipulate the Jews.

But this suggestion still leaves hanging the issue of Simon of Cyrene mentioned in all three Synoptic Gospels (Matt 27:32; Mark 15:21; Luke 23:26). Was Jesus so beaten and weak that he could not carry his cross? Yet John says that Jesus carried his own cross (John 19:17), lending some credence to Dodd's view of two traditions in the Gospels. This contrast in John and the Synoptics is not easy to resolve, given the summary nature of the accounts. One popular solution to the situation has been to suggest that there were two beatings. Brown argues strongly that such a conclusion does not solve the problem.[78] Bruce, however, takes the opposite point of view.[79]

Although implications derived from the various accounts in the Gospels leave scholars with quite differing opinions on the issue of the beatings and Jesus' condition, several matters need to be noted here. Despite the fact that in the Synoptics Simon is said to have been compelled to carry the cross, there is no mention of Jesus' being in a totally exhausted condition. That is an assumption that may or may not be correct, but it is an assumption that often presupposes Jesus suffered the punishment of *verberatio*. It is also an assumption that is often justified as being a fulfillment of Isaiah 53.

This idea has then been further developed and enshrined in the following assigned stations of the cross on the Via Dolorosa in Jerusalem: Station 3, the first fall of Jesus; Station 4, Mary meets Jesus; Station 6, Veronica wipes Jesus' face; Station 7, the second fall of Jesus; Station 9, the third fall of Jesus.[80] These enshrined "stations" are all traditional enhancements to the Gospel accounts that have served to support a theology of intense suffering and agony by Jesus. Although agony is certainly present in the Gospel accounts of the Death Story of

---

[76] See Blinzer, *Der Prozess*, 334.

[77] Dodd, *Historical Tradition*, 103.

[78] See R. Brown, *Death of the Messiah*, 1.852.

[79] See Bruce, "Trial," 7–20.

[80] For a brief statement on each of these stations and their traditional locations see works like H. Bishko, *This Is Jerusalem* (Tel Aviv: Heritage, 1973), 28–29.

Jesus, it is important to remember that the Gospel writers desire to point readers beyond agony to resurrection. The church often is obsessed with Jesus' death and blood, yet John, like Paul, wants Christians to see beyond the death to the resurrection and life (cf. John 11:25; 1 Cor 15:12–22).

In making these comments, I have sought to be clear that the Johannine evangelist is a brilliant literary figure who organizes events to make important theological points. Yet to be a literary artist does not mean that historicity has to be sacrificed. Historical reliability, theological clarity, and literary astuteness can all be partners in a work of art. But the interpreter is then duty bound to try and understand what the artist is seeking to communicate and not merely describe what it means subjectively to the reader.

This latter subjective approach is the pattern many reader-response critics are now following, since they have given up on seeking to discover both historical reliability and authorial intentions. But neither historical scepticism nor existential relevance-reading are fully adequate ways of interpreting a text such as this story of the beating of Jesus.

19:2–3 Turning Jesus over to the soldiers for their "gaming" with him would have been a welcomed release from their frustrations of being assigned to duty in hostile Israel (see Excursus 20). Jewish *sicarii,* assassins or knife-men, stalked the cities and towns of Israel and loved to come up behind the Romans or their sympathizers and jab them in the back with their sharp knives (cf. the vow of such assassins to the high priests concerning Paul and the response of the Tribune in Acts 23:12–23).

The number of soldiers involved in this gaming is not stated in John, but Mark 15:16 (cf. Matt 27:27) suggests it was an entire *speira* (cohort of six hundred men). Yet that may be another case of a Markan generalization without any desire to be precise. On the floor of the Antonio Fortress visitors to the Sisters of Zion Convent in Jerusalem can still see deeply imbedded scratchings of games that were played by Roman soldiers. Although this site may or may not be the exact place of the "gaming" with Jesus, it provides a testimony in stone from that time of the type of gaming that occurred among the soldiers.

The crown of thorns the soldiers forced on Jesus' head may have been woven from the long spikelike thorns of the date palm, which are exceedingly sharp to the touch and can easily puncture thick plastics, to say nothing of flesh.[81] It has even been suggested that these long spiked thorns would give the impression of radiance coming from the crown of the emperor or an Eastern ruler as portrayed on ancient coins.[82] Although such an idea is not stated in our Gospels, the suggestion would not be inappropri-

---

[81] For a fuller discussion of the crown see H. Hart, "The Crown of Thorns in John 19:2–5," *JTS* 3 (1952): 66–75.

[82] See, for example, ibid.; R. Brown, *John,* 2.875; and Beasley-Murray, *John,* 336.

ate for the Roman attempt at caricaturing Jesus as a king.

The purple (John 19:2), or dark red (Matt 27:28), robe that was put on Jesus then was undoubtedly some old cloak or rug grabbed by a soldier and flung around Jesus to give him the comic appearance of being clad with an emperor's robe.

To the robe and crown they added their verbal taunts: "Hail, King of the Jews!" These taunts were likewise a caricature of their revered address to the emperor: "*Ave, Caesar!*" Moreover, instead of the homage paid to Caesar by the bended knee and in some cases the kiss of fealty, the soldiers administered on Jesus the slap of rebuke or challenge. This gaming by the soldiers was intended to be a complete mockery of Jesus based on his supposed offense. That charge amounted to treason against Rome.

(5) Pilate's Declaration and Presentation of the Innocent King (19:4–5)

[4]Once more Pilate came out and said to the Jews, "Look, I am bringing him out to you to let you know that I find no basis for a charge against him." [5]When Jesus came out wearing the crown of thorns and the purple robe, Pilate said to them, "Here is the man!"

19:4–5 No indication had been given earlier in John concerning the release time of Barabbas, but if he was still in custody at that time of the call to "crucify" Jesus (cf. the brief summary statements in Matt 27:21–22; Mark 15:11–13; Luke 23:18–21), then the contrast of the villain Barabbas and the nonviolent, mocked king here would have been exceedingly ironic.[83]

When Pilate came out of the Praetorium again to face the crowd of Jews who did not want to defile themselves, he must have thought that the sight of the emaciated looking Jesus would have been sufficient to justify his desire to release Jesus. What problem could such a pathetic figure engender among these rebellious Jews? Surely he was harmless. Pilate's forceful introduction of Jesus in "Here is the Man!" is therefore loaded with sarcasm toward the Jews.[84] Undoubtedly, however, John found this statement to be a powerful, ironic theological announcement that Christianity has preserved

---

[83] For a further discussion of the situation see A. Bajsic, "Pilatus, Jesus und Barabbas," *Bib* 48 (1967): 7–28 especially at 10–12.

[84] Bultmann is undoubtedly correct that Pilate's purpose was "to make the person of Jesus appear to the Jews as ridiculous and harmless, so that they should drop their accusation" of him (*John*, 658–59). Haenchen seems to catch part of the sense here when he says that Pilate's intention was to portray Jesus as "no dangerous revolutionary, but a poor, powerless sufferer, for whom his worst enemies should have compassion" (*John*, 2.181). But Schlatter concluded that there was probably no hint that Pilate was desirous of arousing sympathy for Jesus. Cf. A. Schlatter, *Der Evangelist Johannes* (Stuttgart: Calwer Verlag, 1948), 343–49.

in its Latin form of *Ecce Homo*.[85] As such it is also a theological affirmation that Jesus was indeed "the man," the second Adam, God's Son, who
dealt with the sin of the world introduced through the first Adam (cf. Rom
5:12–21; 1 Cor 15:22).

Pilate's second verdict was once again a declaration of innocence,
namely, "I find no legal ground for the charge against him!" Case closed?
Not quite.

(6) The Jewish Reaction to the Verdict (19:6–7)

**⁶As soon as the chief priests and their officials saw him, they shouted, "Cru-
cify! Crucify!"**

**But Pilate answered, "You take him and crucify him. As for me, I find no basis
for a charge against him."**

**⁷The Jews insisted, "We have a law, and according to that law he must die,
because he claimed to be the Son of God."**

19:6 The Jewish reaction was swift. Pilate had shown them the beginning of blood, and they wanted more. His demeaning strategy against the
Jews was shattered in their cries to "Crucify!" The Jewish leadership was
undoubtedly provoked, but they also knew how to unnerve Pilate and to
control those who were outside waiting for his verdict.

Riots were something that Rome could not tolerate, so many leaders
were removed from their posts if they failed to keep the Roman peace.
Pilate must have known that they would not give up easily. Thus to avoid
turmoil he toyed with them by offering them their wish but rejecting their
desired verdict. It was another demeaning strategy: offer them what they
wanted but then hold them responsible for executing an innocent man. This
verse contains Pilate's third statement of Jesus' innocence (18:38; 19:4,6).
But this offer was not what the Jewish leadership wanted. They were used
to bargaining (even Abraham bargained with God; cf. Gen 18:22–33), but
this bargain could come back to haunt them.[86] They could not accept the
conditions.

19:7 In complete frustration with Pilate's manipulation, the Jews
blurted out their real concern. It reminds one of Adam's impulsive admis-

---

[85] See the following discussions: R. Marcus, "A Note on Origen in Ev. Joannis xix, 5 (*PG* XIV,
586 b–c)," *HTR* 47 (1954): 317–18. See also J. Houlden, "John 19:5: 'And he said to them, Behold
the man,'" *ExpTim* 92 (1981): 148–49.

[86] H. Schlier thinks that Pilate was no longer able to control the Jews at this point ("Jesus und
Pilatus nach dem Johannesevangelium," in *Die Zeit der Kirche* [Freiburg: Herder, 1956], 56–74 at
67–68). R. Brown thinks that Pilate was not serious with them (*John*, 2.877). I am of the opinion
that Pilate was both uneasy with the potential Jewish problem and was struggling in a face-saving
action to withdraw from the situation without capitulating to the Jewish pressure. But I think his
bargaining chips were almost gone at this point.

sion to God that he knew he was naked and thus his disobedience was uncovered (cf. Gen 3:10). The charge of treason against Jesus was a Jewish sham, created to obtain a Roman sentence of death against him. But now their real concern was clear.

The Jews refused to accept the fact that Jesus claimed to have a direct relationship with God, and therefore they interpreted his statements as though he "made" himself the Son of God. The nuance in the meaning is slightly different. There is no doubt that Jesus made such a claim, but the evangelist would never say that Jesus made himself the Son of God because his repeated claim was that he served God as God's agent (cf. John 5:30, etc.).

This new charge was the actual one the Synoptic Gospels (cf. Mark 14:61–64) indicate was leveled against Jesus in the hearing before Caiaphas: a charge of blasphemy and not a charge of treason. But it clearly reflects the Jewish concern with Jesus not only of working on the Sabbath but more pointedly of being "equal with God" (John 5:18). In Lev 24:16 blasphemy against the name of the Lord was regarded as extremely serious and punishable by stoning. For the Jews, Jesus had violated the law even though he had earlier countered their charges by calling Moses to his defense (John 5:45–47; 7:17). But they were not receptive to his arguments earlier, and they continued adamant here. They had earlier tried to stone Jesus for what they considered to be the current charge (cf. John 10:31–33), but he had escaped from them (10:39). They were obviously determined that it would not happen again.

But the new charge had a striking affect on the governor.

(7) Pilate's Retreat to the Praetorium and His Review of the Case (19:8–11)

8When Pilate heard this, he was even more afraid, 9and he went back inside the palace. "Where do you come from?" he asked Jesus, but Jesus gave him no answer. 10"Do you refuse to speak to me?" Pilate said. "Don't you realize I have power either to free you or to crucify you?"

11Jesus answered, "You would have no power over me if it were not given to you from above. Therefore the one who handed me over to you is guilty of a greater sin."

19:8 Although there had been no indication of Pilate having fear prior to this verse, there was obviously still something that had been unsettling in the entire event for him. Now the words "Son of God" produced a much more disturbing feeling. These words might not have put fear in the heart of a Jew, but for a superstitious Roman the situation may have been radically different. Indeed, Matthew apparently delighted in detailing elements of the *mysterium tremendum* in his testimony concerning Jesus, for he includes details like the opening of the tombs when the bodies of holy people rose after the death of Jesus (Matt 27:52–53), the great earthquake, and the descent of a lightning-like angel at the opening of Jesus' tomb (28:2–3). In his parallel account of the hearing, Matthew included an intriguing note concerning Pilate's wife warning her husband to cease and desist from his judgment of this righteous or innocent man because of an unsettling dream she had (Matt 27:19).

Although John does not detail the full causes leading up to Pilate's greater fear here, the fact that Jesus could have been some sort of divine man obviously further unnerved him. Like all Romans, whose lives were bound up with the *Pantheon* and who had heard of stories about the gods visiting the earth in human form, the thought of a god-man in his presence would not have been welcomed for Pilate, even if he was not a religious person.

19:9 The possibility that Jesus was some sort of divine person accordingly required another review of the case. So Pilate retreated to the Praetorium for a reconsideration. The natural question was no longer who he was but whether he was some sort of divine visitor. Pilate's interrogative term *pothen* ("where?" "from where?") is a common one in John (cf. 2:9; 3:8; 4:11; 7:27,28; 8:14; 9:29,30). Throughout the Gospel double-level thinking has been utilized to identify misunderstandings, particularly in the first two cycles of the Gospel. Pilate's question actually was used by the evangelist here to bring those two levels together, even though Pilate would hardly believe that Jesus was actually God in human flesh (cf. 1:14).

Given Pilate's Roman perspective, the question was quite legitimate, but it was hardly a question that ultimately made a difference in the outcome. Instead of getting into a philosophical discussion about the possibility of Jesus actually being a divine person, however, Jesus remained completely silent. The evangelist understood the dramatic power of silence, which is modeled also in the breaking open of the great seventh seal of the Book of Revelation (8:1).

19:10 The impact of Jesus' silence was very effective because it greatly irritated Pilate. In this face-off of two wills there is no question that the will of Jesus is portrayed as much stronger than that of Pilate, who was like a reed blown in the wind.

The governor probably had never encountered anyone of such moral strength before, and Jesus' refusal to answer him elicited from Pilate a harsh defensive retort concerning his status and role as a representative of Roman power and judicial authority (cf. Jesus' authority in 1:12).[87] Pilate's

---

[87] I frankly find Carson's, *John*, 600, comment that Pilate interpreted "Jesus silence as at best stupidity, at worse a baiting sullenness" to miss the point of a confrontation of wills rooted in a fundamental difference of understanding power.

answer to Jesus' lack of response reminds one of a dictator who sees his empire on the verge of collapse and cries out defensively "I have power!" Of course, like Hitler of Germany he could kill a Bonhoeffer, or like Milosovic of Yugoslavia and others he could thunder that he was in control. But the die had already been cast not only for Jesus' death but also for Pilate's ultimate removal from office.[88]

19:11   Although Jesus had remained silent concerning Pilate's probe of "whence," he was fully ready to respond to Pilate's claim of authority over him. Authority over Jesus was hardly given to a mere human governor like Pilate. Moreover, it could not even be dispensed by the emperor who made Pilate's appointment. Authority in this event of the Roman hearing was vested only in the one who was here designated by the word *anōthen* ("from above"; cf. the use of the same word in 3:3 in the statement "born from above"). The expression "from above" is clearly a reference to God.

Thus, although Pilate claimed authority over Jesus, that authority resided in God alone. Pilate was not in control of Jesus, and Jesus was not ready to let Pilate think he was. Indeed, despite the fact that Pilate believed he was the presiding judge, the evangelist makes it clear that Jesus was doing the judging. Furthermore, Jesus knew exactly where to lay the blame for the incidents leading up to and including this so-called trial. The prisoner was actually the judge, and the judges were in fact the defendants.[89]

The issue of relative sin or blame in this verse has been the subject of considerable discussion among scholars. Who is the "deliverer," and how should one regard Pilate? Although the "deliverer" is regarded as more guilty than Pilate, Pilate is hardly excused or exonerated in his involvement in the trial of Jesus. Although he may have sought to free Jesus, he was hardly an authentic judge. He had whipped an innocent man, allowed him to be subjected to humiliating actions by the soldiers, and would finally himself "deliver" Jesus to be crucified (19:16). The verdict on Pilate as on the other "deliverers" must surely be "Guilty!"

But what of the deliverer who is judged by Jesus to be guilty of an even greater sin? Who is he? Some might suggest Judas was the one. Yet Judas— although he certainly was a "deliverer" (12:4; 18:5), a devil-man (6:70; 13:27), and a thief (12:6)—did not technically deliver Jesus to Pilate. Bernard notes that it is remarkable that it is not told anywhere that Judas bore "witness" against Jesus and that after Gethsemane he no longer is part of the story.[90] That deliverance was technically done from Annas (18:24) to

---

[88] While Pilate had the mantle of Roman power, the Jews and Samaritans continued to make his life utterly miserable. He was removed from office and exiled to Vienna on the Rhone, where he apparently committed suicide. Cf. A. Sherwin-White, "Pilate, Pontius," *ISBE*, 3.867–69.

[89] Cf. I. de la Potterie, "Jesus King and Judge According to John 19:13," *Scr* 13 (1961): 97–111. For the French version see *Bib* 41 (1960): 217–24.

[90] See Bernard, *St. John*, 2.620.

Caiaphas and on to Pilate (18:28,30). Moreover, it was Caiaphas, the "high priest that year," who issued the judgment following the popular raising of Lazarus that Jesus had to die and who also plotted to have him killed (11:49–53). Given this Jewish conspiracy, a number of commentators have argued that the deliverer must have been the Jewish hierarchy.[91] Brown considers that John attributes the "greater sin" to "the Jewish nation and the chief priests," and Haenchen joins him in assigning guilt more generally to "the Jews."[92] Beasley-Murray, Morris, and Carson argue that the deliverer is singular and should refer to Caiaphas.[93] In selecting this option they are following a long tradition that includes Westcott, who opined that while Pilate was guilty, the high priest was "doubly guilty, both in using wrongfully a higher (spiritual) power and in transgressing his legitimate rules of action."[94] Some may tend to disagree on the issue of legitimate priestly procedure for the Sanhedrin,[95] but the probability is that the deliverer referred to here is the high priest.

The impact of Jesus upon Pilate must have been considerable because with some degree of emboldened determination Pilate returned to the crowd outside the praetorium.

(8) Pilate's Vanquished Verdict and the Delivery of Jesus to Be Crucified (19:12–16)

[12]From then on, Pilate tried to set Jesus free, but the Jews kept shouting, "If you let this man go, you are no friend of Caesar. Anyone who claims to be a king opposes Caesar."

[13]When Pilate heard this, he brought Jesus out and sat down on the judge's seat at a place known as the Stone Pavement (which in Aramaic is Gabbatha). [14]It was the day of Preparation of Passover Week, about the sixth hour.

"Here is your king," Pilate said to the Jews.

[15]But they shouted, "Take him away! Take him away! Crucify him!"

"Shall I crucify your king?" Pilate asked.

"We have no king but Caesar," the chief priests answered.

[16]Finally Pilate handed him over to them to be crucified.

So the soldiers took charge of Jesus.

---

[91] For the idea of a collective Jewish guilt see Bultmann, *John*, 662; Schnackenburg, *St. John*, 3.261–62; B. Lindars, *The Gospel of John* (Grand Rapids: Eerdmans, 1981), 569. Bernard seems to consider that this guilt belongs to the Sanhedrin, but his argument is focused on Caiaphas (*St. John*, 2.620).

[92] See R. Brown, *John*, 2.879. Haenchen merely states that "the Jews" bear "the real guilt" (*John*, 2.183).

[93] Beasley-Murray, *John*, 340; Morris, *John*, 705; Carson, *John*, 601.

[94] See B. Westcott, *The Gospel According to St. John* (Grand Rapids: Eerdmans, 1954), 2.302.

[95] See Abrahams, "Tannaitic Tradition," 2.129–37; Danby, "Rabbinical Criminal Code," 51–76.

19:12 As a result of his encounter with Jesus, Pilate was determined to release Jesus. But his determination was short-lived because this time the Jews were ready for him with an argument that could easily have placed Pilate's head on the chopping block. The Roman successors of Augustus clearly permitted no challenge to their authority. Indeed, their military appointees, like Pilate, were allowed no latitude in respect to acknowledging the supremacy of Caesar.

The Jewish leadership could not have chosen a more forceful argument to melt Pilate's opposition to their demands than the challenge that Pilate was not absolutely loyal to Caesar. It was an insidious argument, used by a people who hated Caesar, but it was a wedge that was powerful and could be used later to remove the governor when he became overzealous in his treatment of Jews and Samaritans.[96]

The expression "Friend of Caesar," according to Bammel, was bestowed on an elite group in Roman society who gained special privileges because of their undoubted loyalty to the emperor.[97] There is no indication that Pilate ever attained such a status, but he was a member of the equestrian class, and it was undoubtedly one of his goals, as it was for most Romans.[98] But it is also quite possible, as Sherwin-White suggests, that the expression was used here more generally to designate any leading representative in the provinces of the Roman emperor.[99]

In any case, an astute politician like Caiaphas would hardly have been unaware of this type of designation and undoubtedly was fully prepared to use any such argument to gain his goal. The Jews had reported to Pilate, and Jesus himself had admitted, that Jesus was a "king," albeit a totally different kind of king. Therefore Pilate could not deny this fact (cf. 18:33–37). How then could he explain to his superiors that if Jesus was a king, he did not make himself a king or that he was not a challenger or opponent to Caesar? In any possible subsequent defense the Jews would appear absolutely

---

[96] See, for example, Blinzer, *Der Prozess*, 336–38; Sherwin-White, "Pilate," 868–69.

[97] See E. Bammel, "*Philos tou Kaisanos* (John 19:12)," *TLZ* 77 (1952): 205–20. The view of Bernard that the designation "Friend of Caesar" was introduced with Vespasian is certainly no longer adequate (*St. John*, 2.621).

[98] Some have sought to argue that since Pilate was an equestrian and an associate of Aelius Sejanus who was an influential leader of the equestrians and since any friend of Sejanus was, according to Tacitus (*Annals* 6.8), likely to be a friend of Caesar, then it is posited that Pilate was probably a "Friend of Caesar." But Sejanus fell out of high regard and was executed by order of Tiberius in the fall of A.D. 31; and depending on when one dates the crucifixion of Jesus, this event could be telling on such a reconstruction of Pilate's status. Cf. R. Brown, *John*, 2.879–80; Sherwin-White, "Pilate," 867–69. See also P. Maier, "Sejanus, Pilate and the Date of the Crucifixion," *CH* 37 (1968): 3–13. For a similar story of insecurity on the part of a Roman governor in Alexandria when his patron died see Philo, *In Flaccum*, 1–4.

[99] See Sherwin-White, *Roman Society*, 47.

correct, and Pilate would be judged by his superiors to be incompetent if not stupid. His grounds for dismissing the case against Jesus were gone. Self-preservation demanded that he grant the Jews their desire.

19:13–14 The Jews had won the case, but Pilate was still shrewd. With all the pomposity he could muster he brought Jesus out to face the Jewish accusers, and he sat down[100] on the judgment seat *(bēma)* to render his verdict. This concept of *Bema,* or judgment seat, is used elsewhere in reference to the proconsul or senator Gallio at Corinth, but there Paul was acquitted of all charges, and the Jews were punished (cf. Acts 18:12,16,17). Likewise, it is used to refer to the judgment seat of the procurator/prefect Festus in the hearing at Caesarea, but there Paul also identified his trial as taking place before the tribunal, or seat, of Caesar (cf. Acts 25:6,10). In the Corinthian correspondence Paul also employs the term in reference to Christ before whose judgment seat everyone will ultimately appear (cf. 2 Cor 5:10). A *Bema* was a raised platform in a public place where the governor would be elevated above the masses and would render his verdict in the open before the gods and in the presence of his subjects. The stone Bema in Corinth can still be seen by visitors to the ancient Corinthian agora or forum.

John here describes the *Bema* as located at the Stone Pavement in Jerusalem, which in Hebrew/Aramaic was in John's mind linked to a place known as *Gabbatha.* The stone pavement would have been a public place where persons could gather to witness the governor's judgments or hear his important proclamations. Visitors to Jerusalem today can visit a site in the basement of the Sisters of Zion Convent, which has been designated by pilgrims as the "Lithostratos." This site may go back to the time of the Antonio Fortress but most likely to the postdestruction period of Hadrian's reconstructed Aelia Capitolina (A.D./C.E. 129–130).[101] This courtyard was paved with large flat paving stones and was apparently at least twenty-five hundred square feet in size.[102] It is close to the so-called "Ecce Homo" arch, which is clearly from the time of Hadrian. The more likely site would have been near the western or Jaffa Gate in the vicinity of the triple tower complex, little of which actually remains today. The term *Gabbatha* was, as Brown observed, undoubtedly developed from the Aramaic root *gbh* or *gbʾ*

[100] Some scholars, relying on the fact that the verb ἐκάθισεν ("he sat") should be transitive here rather than intransitive, have Jesus sitting down on the Bema and thus they think he is presented by John here as a sitting king. For the best example of this argument see I. de la Potterei, "Jesus roi et juge d'après Jn 19, 13," *Bib* 41 (1960): 217–47. For an English translation see *Scr* 13 (1961): 97–111. Such a view, however, focuses on the theology of John and gives little credence to the historical realities in the narrative.

[101] See the discussion of Aelia Capitolína in *NEAEHL,* 2.759.

[102] For further details on the sites in Jerusalem see Mackowski, *Jerusalem,* 96–97 and *NEAEHL,* 2.765 for the dating of the pavement to the time of Hadrian.

and means something "high," such as a high promontory.[103] This meaning could readily be applied to either the Antonio Tower area or the Herodian palace area on the western hill near the western gate.

Not only does the evangelist supply the reader with specific details of the place where Pilate's verdict is delivered but he also includes specific details concerning the time of this event. Unlike Luke's attention to chronological details, the Gospel of John is primarily focused on literary organization and theological implications. So the presence of such specificity is indeed worthy of special attention. These details can only mean that for the Johannine evangelist this event was absolutely crucial for understanding his Gospel.

The day stated here is the Day of Preparation, the day before Passover. That day has been hauntingly mentioned throughout the entire Gospel in a dirgelike repetition of the day of Jesus' glorification. That day was the day when the Lamb of God would be sacrificed for the ultimate Passover. That day was the same day when the people of Israel slaughtered their lambs in preparation for their celebration of Passover. The symbolism is so powerful that it is almost overwhelming in its implications.[104]

The time is stated as the sixth hour. Much had taken place since the early morning of the night watch and the cock crow when Peter's denials occurred. What time was the sixth hour? Some have argued that the reckoning was according to Roman time, which would have the day marked from midnight and thus make it about six a.m. But if the time was reckoned by Jewish standards, and thus counted from dawn, it would place the time about noon. The problem with the latter reckoning for those who would synthesize all of the Gospel accounts is Mark 15:25, which states that Jesus was crucified at the "third" hour. Some therefore have resorted to adopting the Roman reckoning method with respect to John. Early scribes found this temporal problem to be disturbing, so they altered the texts of both Mark and John in several different attempts to remove the problem.[105] The alteration option is, of course, hardly viable. The former option was chosen by Westcott and is sometimes followed today.[106] Mahoney tried another approach by arguing that the stripping of Jesus for whipping was what was meant in Mark by the "third" hour.[107] But scholars

---

[103] See R. Brown, *Death of the Messiah*, 1.845.

[104] For a discussion on this aspect of John see C. Koester, *Symbolism in the Fourth Gospel* (Minneapolis: Fortress, 1995), 193–200.

[105] Cf. the discussions concerning textual corruptions in Metzger, *Textual Commentary*, 118 and 252.

[106] Cf. Westcott, *St. John*, 326, who admits this is not a satisfactory solution.

[107] Cf. A. Mahoney, "A New Look at 'The Third Hour' of Mark 15:25," *CBQ* 28 (1966): 292–96.

on both sides of the theological spectrum have generally agreed that such solutions do not work.[108]

After a full review of the situation L. Morris concluded that modern readers are expecting from the biblical writers more chronological exactitude than should be expected of people who "did not have clocks or watches, and the reckoning of time was always very important."[109] I would add that even today I have experienced this same phenomenon as a missionary among people who do not wear watches and for whom a designated meeting time of 10:00 a.m. means sometime in the middle of the day, and it can actually take place not in the morning but in the early afternoon. The missionary must then learn to adjust expectations because people without watches are not oriented to minutes and hours, even if you give them a watch.

But I believe there is more to this "sixth" hour than mere chronology. The designation the "sixth" hour was absolutely crucial for John because this was the time on the Day of Preparation when the Jews began their preparations for Passover in earnest. Any leaven in the house had to be collected and burned; labor stopped at this time, and the major task of slaughtering the lambs in preparation for the Passover meal began.[110] This would be an appropriate general time designation for the sentencing of the Passover Lamb in keeping with the way John has presented his major theme of the Lamb of God and Passover throughout his Gospel (cf. 1:29; etc.). The new Exodus, God's deliverance, was about to begin. The sacrificial lamb was being sentenced.

Pilate must have known the anxiousness of the Jews to get this hearing concluded so that they might not miss the Preparations for Passover. Therefore what he did next was an evidence of his sarcastic shrewdness. Seated on his judicial chair, he presented Jesus to the Jews with the words "Here is your king!" Pilate may have lost the argument, but he did not go down without antagonizing the Jews further by stating his decision in a way the Jewish accusers could hardly stomach. "Your king" was for them a completely intolerable statement.

19:15   The reaction of the Jewish accusers was immediate, but their responses were both predictable and quite unexpected. Their first response was the rather predictable "Away! away!" together with "crucify him!" which was to be anticipated following their earlier outcry for his crucifixion

---

[108] Cf. Carson, *John*, 605; Beasley-Murray, *John*, 341; R. Brown, *Death of the Messiah*, 1.846–47.

[109] Morris, *John*, 800–801.

[110] See, for example, the details concerning those matters in J. Bonsirven, "Hora Talmudica: La notion chronologique de Jean 19, 14 auraitelle un sens symbolique?" *Bib* 33 (1952): 511–15; cf. the Mishnah, *Peshah*, 1.4; 4.1–5.

in 19:6. But here "him" is added to the cry of "crucify!"

The subsequent question of Pilate was in part a continuation of his toying with the Jews. He knew they refused to acknowledge Jesus as their king, yet almost insidiously he asked them, "Shall I crucify your king?" But Pilate's insistent reference to Jesus as their king was more than just playing a game with them. He was also obviously aiming at removing from himself responsibility for any perceived wrongful death of Jesus. Although the Gospel writers picture Pilate as weak, they also portray him as ingenious in his dealing with the manipulative Jews. It reminds one of the well-known hand-washing episode in Matt 27:24, where more clearly he is portrayed as seeking to escape any accountability.

The reply of the chief priests who here are pictured as representing the Jewish people is astounding, given Israel's history. God wanted to be the King of Israel (Judg 8:23; Isa 26:13), but the people had demanded a king so that they could be like the surrounding nations. Israel's demand for a king irritated Samuel, and he tried hopelessly to argue for the kingship of God in Israel. Finally, however, God conceded to the people's wishes, but God also let the people experience the consequence of rejecting the Lord as their king (1 Sam 8:4–9).

In this present text the religious leaders, who were charged with the responsibility of representing God, actually committed the ultimate hypocrisy by responding to Pilate with the blasphemous words "we have no king but Caesar." In doing so they verbally removed God from any role in the kingship of Israel. Perhaps some Jews were tired of the messianic pretenders arising in their midst who claimed to be the "new David,"[111] but to eliminate God from ultimate kingship was astonishing. The Jews in the Eleventh Benediction prayed, "May you be our Ruler, you alone!"[112] But it only proves again the thesis that, according to John, the chief priests followed the political pattern of the end justifying the means (cf. Caiaphas at 11:49–50), even when the means and end involved lying, cheating, and murder. But I have often wondered: How does God react to such a statement? Does God grant us our wishes? And what would that mean in this case?

19:16 Thus, with the hypocritical acknowledgment of the Jewish leadership that Caesar was their only king, the case was closed. Although John did not here detail either the verdict or the sentence, both can be assumed. The verdict of Pilate was obviously "treason," namely here the treasonous rising of an opposition king to Caesar (cf. the charge on the cross at 19:19).

---

[111] See R. Brown, *John*, 2.884.

[112] See *Shemoneh Esreh* (The Eighteen Benedictions); cf. Schnackenburg, *St. John*, 3.266; R. Brown, *Death of the Messiah*, 1.849.

Moreover, the sentence must have been: Death by Crucifixion.

The present verse merely states that "he handed him over to them to be crucified." The generalized nature of this verse can easily be a problem. Indeed, Brown categorized the statement as "an example of careless narrative style."[113] Although Sherwin-White indicated that it was "entirely within the scope of the procurator's imperium" to adopt the sentence of the Sanhedrin,[114] that does not mean that the governor in fact also turned Jesus over to the Jews for execution. The expression *paredōken auton autois* ("he delivered him to them") is clearly the way John has of completing his theme of "deliverance." The "them" is obviously vague, and it becomes evident in the next verse that it was not the Jews but the soldiers who were given the task of crucifying Jesus. Indeed, if the Jews had been given the task, the charge on the cross would never have been stated in the way it was (cf. 19:19). Nevertheless, the early Christians held the Jews responsible for the crucifixion of Jesus (cf. Acts 2:36; 3:15; 10:39).[115] But the New Testament must not be viewed as anti-Semitic in our contemporary sense. It must be remembered that the early conflict involved Jewish Christians suffering at the hands of the Jewish establishment and not Christian Gentiles being hostile to a Jewish minority. But to conclude the "trial," the sentence was rendered, and Jesus, the condemned one, was "delivered" to those who would execute him.

4. The Crucifixion of the King (19:17–27)

This section of the Gospel breaks naturally into three parts. It begins with the scene on the way to skull hill and the crucifixion itself (19:17–18); then it deals with the kingly entitlement of Jesus on the cross (19:19–22); thereafter it contrasts the clothes-collecting, lot-casting soldiers with the faithful observant friends of Jesus around the cross (19:23–24).

(1) To Skull Place and the Crucifixion (19:17–18)

[17]Carrying his own cross, he went out to the place of the Skull (which in Aramaic is called Golgotha). [18]Here they crucified him, and with him two others— one on each side and Jesus in the middle.

19:17 This description is brief compared to the longer scenes in the Synoptic Gospels dealing with the so-called Via Dolorosa (Way of Sorrows) of tradition. Indeed, there is here no wailing of the women as in Luke

---

[113] Ibid., 1.855.

[114] See Sherwin-White, *Roman Society*, 47. Cf. also p. 35.

[115] See also Justin, *Apology*, 85.6 and Tertullian, *Apology*, 21.18.

23:28–31.[116] There is also no mention of Simon of Cyrene, who was forced to carry the cross as in the Synoptics (Matt 27:32; Mark 15:21; Luke 23:26).[117] Instead, Jesus here is said to have carried/borne his own cross to "the Skull." Faced with the concern that there seems to be a direct contradiction between John and the Synoptics, Dodd argued that Jesus first carried his own cross and broke down under its weight. At that point Simon being pressed into carrying the cross for him was "a perfectly reasonable interpretation of the evidence."[118] Certainly Dodd's explanation is reasonable.

But there is much more to this statement than an issue of historical reporting, which was Dodd's concern. The scene John wants us to focus on is Jesus on his way to the cross. Although Jesus has been whipped and condemned as a criminal, he is not a helpless victim but the Shepherd-King laying down his life for his sheep (10:11,15,17; 15:13). The King was carrying his own cross to crucifixion and to his glorification. This carrying of his own cross may be reminiscent of the story in Gen 22:6, when Abraham laid the wood on Isaac which the boy carried and which was to be the means of his own sacrifice. The rabbis loved this story, which is reflected in the Jewish Haggadah and in the Genesis Rabbah 56 concerning the above text.[119]

Condemned persons were generally weakened but were still required to carry their own crosses on the way to execution.[120] The Roman action referred to in the Synoptics of pressing someone else from a conquered nation to carry the cross of a weakened victim was, however, not out of pity. It was to insure that the victim would not die on the way to the place of execution. That would be intolerably anticlimactic. Roman justice was harsh, and "cruel and unusual punishment" was hardly frowned upon as it is in the contemporary Western democracies. Beating, mocking, cursing, taunting, and painful suffering were all regarded by the Roman administrators and their lackeys as justifiable parts of deserved punishment for condemned, noncitizen criminals and revolutionaries, especially in the provinces.

---

[116] Cf. M. Soards reviews this text in terms of a Lukan theological construct in the light of the fact it is only in Luke ("Tradition, Composition and Theology in Jesus' Speech to the 'Daughters of Jerusalem' (Luke 23, 26–32)," *Bib* 68 [1987]: 221–24).

[117] For an analysis of Simon of Cyrene see the discussion in R. Brown, *Death of the Messiah*, 2.911–17.

[118] See Dodd, *Historical Tradition*, 125.

[119] For a further discussion of these texts see G. Vermes, *Scripture and Tradition in Judaism* (Leiden: Brill, 1961), 193–227. See also J. Wood, "Isaac Typology in the New Testament," *NTS* 14 (1968): 583–89.

[120] For ancient accounts of cross carrying see Quintilian, *Decl.*, 274; Plutarch, *Sera,* 554; Plautus, *Mil. glor.* 2.4.5–7; etc.

But it is also important to note that the cross the condemned Jesus carried was hardly the type of full cross that is often portrayed in pictures of the event or in religious plays. The upright piece normally was stationed at the execution site, and the victim would then carry the heavy cross piece to which he would later be attached at the site. This cross piece with the victim attached to it would then be raised and fixed or dropped onto the upright pole through a slot in the cross piece.[121]

The soldiers and their victims, according to the Synoptics, probably moved through the city amid both jeers and weeping to a point outside the city wall (*exēlthen;* "he went out") known as "the Skull" *(kronion).* Crucifixions by Romans were normally set on major traffic routes in and outside of cities and towns where many would witness the horrible execution events and be forewarned not to follow the same path of disobedience. In Jewish tradition stonings took place outside the cities so as not to contaminate the cities or camps of the people of Israel (cf. Num 15:35–26 and the stoning of Stephen in Acts 7:58).

Excursus 22: The Site of Golgotha

Although it is impossible to be certain of the exact site of "skull place" *(Golgotha),* it has traditionally been identified with a hill now enshrined in the upper chapel in the Church of the Holy Sepulcher. The site of Gordon's Calvary and the Garden Tomb, however, while being a peaceful setting in an otherwise overcrowded, busy city has little historical support for its authenticity, not even having the support of traditional recollections from the period of Queen Helena following the so-called Christianization of the empire under Constantine. This church lies within the current walls of the Old City of Jerusalem, but a major segment of these walls are from Islamic times. This church lies outside the old Second Temple wall with its exit from the Gennath Gate, east and north of Herod's palace and the current Jaffa Gate. But it was still inside the so-called third wall that protected the expanded new city. This third wall was at first hastily constructed in the late Hellenistic Period to protect Jerusalem from its various enemies.[122] The pockmarked hill next to Gordon's tomb, which is behind the crowded bus station in East Jerusalem, however, does provide a vivid example of what a "skull" hill could have looked like. But the importance of the crucifixion event can hardly be fully encapsulated in a precise site. Such sites may enhance our spiritual sense of the event, but the reality of the event is not dependent on the authenticity of a specific site.

19:18   The description of the crucifixion in John is brief and states merely that Jesus was crucified between two others. But by piecing together

---

[121] For a fuller explanation of crucifixion see M. Hengel, *Crucifixion in the Ancient World and the Folly of the Message of the Cross* (Philadelphia: Fortress, 1977).

[122] For a detailed study of Jerusalem see *NEAEHL* 2.718–20, 779–81, 802.

various references in ancient literature and in the Gospels themselves, it is possible to present a picture of the crucifixion of Jesus.

Excursus 23: The Crucifixion of Jesus

Although crucifixion seems to have been used by the Persians and the Greeks and included both the execution of the living and the hanging of dead bodies in an act of warning or desecration,[123] the Romans particularly employed crucifixion as a severe public punishment for slaves, conquered peoples, and lower class serious criminals and rebels. Crucifixion could be done in a variety of ways, such as on (1) an X-shaped cross where the victim's limbs would be stretched and fastened on each segment of the cross; (2) a single pole where the victim's arms would be stretched and fastened about the head; (3) a T-shaped cross where the crosspiece would be set in a notch on the top of the upright; or (4) a pole on which the crosspiece would be dropped in a notch a short distance from the top and thus form the shape of the cross most familiar in art and in other representations with the charge fastened to the top section.[124]

The arms would be fastened along with the legs, and the body would normally fall forward, creating great difficulty in breathing.[125] The fastened legs would enable the victim to push up on the body and gasp for breath. Without the fastened legs the victim would die. The breaking of the legs of those crucified with Jesus would quickly hasten death, but since Jesus was already dead, that was, according to John 19:32–33, unnecessary.

The way the hands and legs were fastened was normally either by tying the limbs with ropes or by fastening the limbs with nails. None of the crucifixion stories in the Gospels actually indicate how Jesus was attached to the cross, but in the postresurrection appearance stories there is more specificity. In the Thomas pericope there is a clear indication of the presence of nail marks in Jesus' hands (John 20:24–27). In the general reference that the disciples should look at Jesus' hands and feet in Luke 24:39 it must mean that they were clearly torn. The nail marks in the hands were probably not in the palms but likely in the wrists, which would hold the weight of the body more securely. If the feet were nailed, as seems to be suggested by Luke, then they could be nailed on either side of the upright pole and less likely by a single spike penetrating both feet/legs, as indi-

---

[123] See M. Hengel, *Crucifixion in the Ancient World*, 18–40. R. Brown, *Death of the Messiah*, 2.945–46. Cf. Tacitus, *Hist.*, 2.72.1–2. See also J. Collins, "The Archaeology of Crucifixion," *CBQ* 1 (1939): 154–59. Josephus (*War*, 1.4.6) indicates that Alexander Janaeus, the Hasmonean king, crucified eight hundred persons in an attempt to subdue his own Jewish subjects.

[124] For statements respecting the various types of crucifixion see Josephus, *War*, 5.11.1; Seneca, *Marc.*, 20.3. Some were indeed crucified upside down. For an excellent summary see R. Brown, *Death of the Messiah*, 2.948.

[125] See G. Borchert, "They Broke Not His Legs," *Christianity Today* 6 (1962): 572, for a summary statement of crucifixion.

cated in later artistic representations that were enamored with the idea of three nails being used to attach Jesus to the cross.[126]

The struggle for breath from the stretched arms and extended rib cage, together with the pain from the nails and the earlier whipping, must have combined to create excruciating suffering. Yet pain is hardly the focus of the Johannine Gospel.

19:18 (Cont.)   Although he was repeatedly declared innocent, Jesus was consigned to a torturous death. His companions in death were "criminals" *(kakourgous)* according to the Synoptic Gospels (Luke 23:33). They are more specifically identified as "robbers" *(lēstai)* in both Matt 27:38 and Mark 15:27. But Jesus was scarcely a criminal in the plain sense of the term. He was not even treasonous in that sense. Yet he died rejected and condemned by those who should have accepted him (cf. John 1:11) and betrayed and delivered to outsiders/Romans who would have released him. The death story in John is filled with irony.

(2) The Royal Entitlement on the Cross (19:19–22)

[19]**Pilate had a notice prepared and fastened to the cross. It read: JESUS OF NAZARETH, THE KING OF THE JEWS.** [20]**Many of the Jews read this sign, for the place where Jesus was crucified was near the city, and the sign was written in Aramaic, Latin and Greek.** [21]**The chief priests of the Jews protested to Pilate, "Do not write 'The King of the Jews,' but that this man claimed to be king of the Jews."**
[22]**Pilate answered, "What I have written, I have written."**

19:19   The irony in John continues as the reason for the death of Jesus received its official entitlement or "notice" *(titlon)*. Frequently persons condemned to death had their offense written on a placard and either hung on their bodies or carried before them as they were paraded to the execution site.[127] Thereafter it was in this case apparently fixed to the cross for all to read. The execution styles of the Romans were clearly designed for publicity in addition to retributive suffering.

The title attached to the cross was "Jesus of Nazareth, the King of the

---

[126] There is little evidence in the ancient writers for the nailing of the feet, but there has been serious discussion over whether the bones in the tomb at Giv'at ha-Mivtor near Jerusalem represent a person crucified by nailing the legs. Cf. the discussion in V. Tzaferis, "Crucifixion—The Archaeological Evidence," *BAR* 11.1 (1985): 44–53 and 11.6 (1985): 20–21; H. Kuhn, "Zum Gekreuzigten von Giv'at ha-Mivtar.Korrektur eigenes Verschens in Erstveröffentlichung," *ZNW* 69 (1978): 118–22.

[127] Cf. Eusebius, *Hist. ecc.*, 6.44. Suetonius (*Col.* 32) also reports an example of such a public display during the reign of Caligula, but in that case the hands of the poor victim were hung around his neck, and his crime was placarded before him. Blinzer (*Trial*, 254) suggests that the lettering would be in bold black or red letters that would stand out on a white gypsum colored board.

Jews." John here indicates that Pilate wrote *(egrapsen)* the offense. Most translations treat the verb here as causative and assume that Pilate was the authority behind the inscription *(epigraphē,* the term used in Mark 15:26; Luke 23:38), though it is not impossible that in disgust with the Jews he may have written it himself (cf. John 19:22).

The record of the inscription is slightly different in the various Gospels, with John being the longest. Such a fact may create a problem for some contemporary readers who are word-oriented rather than meaning-oriented. But that would hardly be a concern for the Johannine writer who was not oriented to tape recorders and video cameras. He would probably shake his head at such a concern and ask the contemporary reader, "What is the difference?" The inscription in all four Gospels asserts that the so-called treasonous offense was that Jesus was "the King of the Jews."

19:20 Since crucifixion was a public execution rather than a privately held termination of life by lethal injection, hanging, or electric chair, John makes it clear just how public the event was intended to be. The place was near the city so that many persons had the opportunity to see the victim and read the charge. Moreover, only John indicates that the entitlement was written in Hebrew or Aramaic (the language of the general populace), Latin (the language of the army and the presiding government), and Greek (the universal language of commerce in that time).[128] There is little doubt that John saw in this entitlement an ironic declaration that Jesus was in death being declared universally the expected Messiah, the King of the Jews.

19:21–22 The Jewish religious hierarchy was plainly offended by the charge and, according to John, sought to have the entitlement altered to read that it was merely a personal claim on the part of Jesus or that he was merely a kingly pretender. Yet it was the Jewish leaders themselves who had obviously brought the charge on which he was arraigned as a treasonous king (cf. 18:33–35). But Pilate realized that it was a trumped up charge (18:38) and taunted the Jewish leaders with repeatedly designating Jesus as the King of the Jews (18:39; 19:5,15). In spite of the hypocritical allegiance to Caesar (19:15) through which the Jewish leaders won their legal goal, John portrays Pilate as manifestly realizing that they had used a legal ploy to beat him. The title was his legal way of countering their hoax. Accordingly, he responded curtly to their challenge for a change of inscription with

---

[128] The major Greek manuscripts have the order as in the text, but in a few manuscripts the order is changed for political or missionary development purposes. For an example of such a change see Metzger, *Textual Commentary,* 253. Such multilanguage or polyglot statements in execution charges or on tombstones were not uncommon in the Hellenistic world and are noted by various authors who are dependent on the work of W. Bauer, *Das Johannesevangelium* (Tübingen: Mohr, 1925), 222, etc.

the harsh words, "What I have written, I have written."[129]

There is little doubt that John saw in this final declaration of Pilate a fascinating phenomenon. The Pilate who seemed throughout the trial to have little backbone in following through on his decisions finally gains a backbone against the manipulating Jewish leadership. It is almost as though the story affirms in capsule form the earlier statement of Jesus that power or authority is given from above. Two major themes throughout this Gospel are thus brought together: that Jesus was going to the hour of his glorification (cf. 2:4 to 17:1) but that he was also the expected King of Israel (cf. 1:49 to 12:13 and to the present verses). For John nothing could change these realities. Jesus' kingship was certified by both God and Rome.

(3) The Clothes-Collecting, Lot-Casting Soldiers and the Faithful Friends around the Cross (19:23–27)

23When the soldiers crucified Jesus, they took his clothes, dividing them into four shares, one for each of them, with the undergarment remaining. This garment was seamless, woven in one piece from top to bottom.

24 "Let's not tear it," they said to one another. "Let's decide by lot who will get it."

This happened that the scripture might be fulfilled which said,

"They divided my garments among them
and cast lots for my clothing."

So this is what the soldiers did.

25Near the cross of Jesus stood his mother, his mother's sister, Mary the wife of Clopas, and Mary Magdalene. 26When Jesus saw his mother there, and the disciple whom he loved standing nearby, he said to his mother, "Dear woman, here is your son," 27and to the disciple, "Here is your mother." From that time on, this disciple took her into his home.

The Johannine writer is a master of picturing contrasts, and none is more stark than the contrast between the soldiers and the friends of Jesus. Moreover, this section contains the first of four key scriptural references in a short space used as fulfillment statements to indicate to the reader that these closing events of the Death Story are, in fact, authenticated by reference to texts from the earlier canon of the Hebrew Bible. Since the use of such proof texts or fulfillment passages are rather limited in John, as compared for example to Matthew, their multiple use at this point in the Gospel bears special consideration.

---

[129] In the ancient world what an official wrote was almost sacrosanct, and when a ruler in the Roman Empire wrote a declaration, it was assumed to be carried out. The royal cliché "Let it be written" implied that "It would be done!" Accounts of such official declarations, however, did not carry quite the same weight of inviolability. The Jewish objection to Pilate's declaration could have been viewed as a direct challenge to the governor's authority, and as such, according to the text, it was sternly rebuffed.

19:23–24 In comparison to the Synoptic reports (Matt 27:35b; Mark 15:22b; Luke 23:34b) the narrative concerning the soldiers dealing with Jesus' clothing in John is much longer and more specific. The picture presented is one of a squad (or quaternion) of soldiers completely unconcerned about the dying victims on the crosses and instead engrossed in dividing the spoils of the event. It is a stark reminder of pictures of a conquering army picking through the belongings of dead opponents to acquire booty for the personal enrichment of the victors. Crucifixion was for this squad of soldiers a business enterprise. Dividing the clothes was a matter of sharing the basic garments, undoubtedly like sandals, a belt, and perhaps a head scarf, and so forth. But the seamless tunic *(chitōn)* caught their attention, and they agreed that rather than ripping it into four pieces, they could enjoy a game of chance and see who could win the prize by challenging each other in "casting lots."[130] Clearly each of the four evangelists noted the fact that those who crucified Jesus were involved in gaming for his clothing, but John saw in the two lines of the synonymous parallelism at Ps 22:18 a distinction between dividing the garments and casting lots for the clothing, and he viewed these acts by the soldiers as a clear fulfillment of Scripture.

Excursus 24: On Allegorical Interpretations

It seems necessary at this point to comment very briefly on the fact that since the days of Cyprian[131] this text has been subjected to a significant amount of typological and even allegorical speculation so as, for example, to identify the seamless robe or tunic of Jesus with the unity of the church. But such speculations are part of patterns of interpretation which were regarded as illegitimate in the more reasoned interpretive patterns of the Protestant Reformation. Although the reformers sought to do away with the so-called fourfold sense of Scripture,[132] allegory periodically raises its head in a concern to find spiritual interpretations that can enhance the biblical texts and impress the uninformed. Advocates of such patterns often parade their interpretive skills among the less knowing and appear to reveal unknown mysteries where they do not seem to be present. Accordingly, it is imperative for those seeking to be faithful in the pur-

---

[130] The NLT rendering "threw dice for my robe" would be a contemporary equivalent for the casting of lots. For the basic meaning see *BAGD*, 462.

[131] Cyprian, *Unit. eccl.*, 7; cf. E. Hoskyns, *The Fourth Gospel*, ed. F. Davey (London: Farber & Farber, 1956), 529. See also the view of Schnackenburg, *St. John*, 3.274. Carson, *John*, 614 includes an erroneous reference to Hoskyns and Davey but see his helpful comparison to Philo, *Fug.*, 110–12.

[132] For an explanation of what was called the Quadriga see W. Pauck's *Introduction to Luther: Lectures on Romans* (Philadelphia: Westminster, 1961), xxvii–xxviii and R. Grant, *The Bible in the Church* (New York: Macmillan, 1960), 101–2. 'The Quadriga was usually expressed as *"Littera gesta docet, quid credas allegoria, Moralis quid agas, quo tendas anagogia,"* which was the justification for the fourfold pattern of interpretation as employed in the Middle Ages, namely, literal, allegorical, moral, and anagogical.

suit of the genuine meaning of a biblical text, like the present one, to avoid the pitfalls of proposing generalized allegorical meanings that have very little relation to the plain meaning of the text.

19:25 The first part of this verse[133] serves as a transitional comparison to the second part and as a consideration of the friends of Jesus. The soldiers were involved in their profiting from the victim's few possessions. The friends, however, offer a significant contrast.

These friends of Jesus are described as observers who were standing near the cross. The question, however, is, How many women were there? As Newman and Nida ask, "Are there two, three, or four?"[134] Two seems to be illogical because the mother of Jesus is not likely Mary (the wife) of Clopas. Three is also unlikely because that would make Mary of Clopas the sister of Mary the mother of Jesus, resulting in two Marys in the same family. Although such is possible, it seems unlikely.[135] The most likely scenario is that there are four women mentioned: the mother of Jesus, her sister, Mary (the wife) of Clopas, and Mary Magdalene.[136] Only two of these women appear elsewhere in John: the mother of Jesus (2:1–5) and Mary Magdalene (20:1–2,11–18).

19:26–27 In addition to the women, one man is also mentioned as a friend of Jesus standing near. That man is identified as the disciple whom he loved and who was so designated earlier (cf. 13:23–25). That disciple is then linked to the mother of Jesus both by the fact that the Johannine evangelist identified them as standing together in Jesus' sight and by the testamentary-type disposition that follows.

Jesus' statement "Woman,[137] here is your son!" spoken to his mother

---

[133] The NIV follows NA27 (see also KJV, NAB, NJB, REB, NLT, TEV, HCSB) in beginning v. 25 not with the soldiers (see NRSV, NASB) but with the women.

[134] Newman and Nida, *A Translator's Handbook*, 589. Cf. also Beasley-Murray, *John*, 348. For some representative views on the women here see F. Wulf, "Das Marianische Geheimnis der Kirche im Licht des Johannesevangeliums," *Geist und Leben* 50 (1977): 326–34; E. Bishop, "Mary Clopas–Joh 19, 25," *ExpTim* 65 (1954): 286–87 and D. and F. Stagg, *Women in the World of Jesus* (Philadelphia: Westminster, 1978), 238.

[135] Herod the Great had ten wives and a number of sons who were given first names of Herod such as Herod Archelaus, Herod Antipas, Herod Philip, etc. because Herod was a megalomaniac. It is certainly possible for sisters to be called Mary, but it is highly improbable that such would have occurred.

[136] Among the many scholars who favor this view are Beasley-Murray, *John*, 348; R. Brown, *John*, 2.904; Carson, *John*, 615; Hoskyns and Davey, *The Fourth Gospel*, 530; Morris, *John*, 717; Newman and Nida, *Translator's Handbook*, 589; Schnackenburg, *St. John*, 3.276–77; etc. It seems that the first two are not named, and the second two are Marys but are distinguished from each other and from the mother of Jesus by the additional designation "of Clopas" and "Magdalene."

[137] The NIV translators in rendering the text "Dear woman" were obviously attempting to indicate that Jesus was not being impolite to his mother. The TEV completely omits the vocative "Woman" for the same reason. Cf. Newman and Nida, *Translator's Handbook,* 589.

and the subsequent one spoken to the disciple, "Here is your mother," are undoubtedly intended to be testamentary formulas.[138] The statements are also akin to common practice, nonlegal adoption formulas such as in *Tob* 7:12.[139]

The significance of those statements is further defined by the evangelist's editorial note that "from that time on this disciple took her into his home." The traditional role of the oldest son in a Jewish family was to provide for the care of the mother when the husband or father of the house was no longer around to care for the mother. It seems clear that Jesus here fulfilled his family responsibility as a dutiful son.

But, as Beasley-Murray has indicated, some traditional Roman Catholic interpreters have turned this idea on its head and viewed the testamentary statements as placing the disciple under the care of Mary. Thus the church was so assigned as well.[140] This ecclesiastical reassignment to Mary has thus been viewed as the final task of Jesus (rather than his redemptive death); and having finished his work (19:28), he was ready to die. Thus Brown stated: "We suggested [in connection with the Cana story] that if Mary was refused a role during the ministry of Jesus as it began at Cana, she finally received her role in the hour of Jesus' passion, death, and resurrection."

Moreover, he continued, "In becoming the mother of the Beloved Disciple (the Christian), Mary is symbolically evocative of Lady Zion, who after the birth pangs, brings forth a new people in joy."[141] But Schnackenburg may signal a less doctrinaire and more satisfactory, although not official, Roman Catholic perspective when relying on Schürmann he links Mary at Cana and at the cross as one who "stands for those begging for Jesus' gift," the gift symbolized in the wine as pointing to a future fulfillment.[142]

The contrast between the goods-seeking soldiers and the observant friends at the cross is thus complete. Jesus, who was concerned to care for the disciples at the time of his arrest (18:8), was likewise concerned to care for his mother at the time of his death while the soldiers played their game for his clothes.

---

[138] Cf. E. Stauffer, *Jesus and His Story* (New York: Alfred Knopf, 1960), 113; R. de Vaux, *Ancient Israel* (New York: McGraw-Hill, 1961), 112–13.

[139] The statement in Ps 2:7 is not unrelated to such formulas though there the statement is a divine decree.

[140] See Beasley-Murray, *John*, 349–50. Contrast D. Unger, "The Meaning of John 19, 26–27 in the Light of Papal Documents," *Mirianum* 21 (1959): 186–221.

[141] R. Brown, *John*, 2.925.

[142] Schnackenburg, *St. John*, 3.278. See also H. Schürmann, "Jesu letzte Weisung Jo 19, 26–27a," in *Ursprung und Gestalt* (Düsseldorf: Patmos Verlag, 1970), 13–28.

5. The Death of the Lamb/King (19:28–37)

This section of the Death Story unites the themes of the dying King with the Lamb of God. It divides naturally into two parts: the last moments of the dying King (19:28–30) and the piercing of the Lamb (19:31–37).

(1) The Last Moments of the Dying King (19:28–30)

[28]Later, knowing that all was now completed, and so that the Scripture would be fulfilled, Jesus said, "I am thirsty." [29]A jar of wine vinegar was there, so they soaked a sponge in it, put the sponge on a stalk of the hyssop plant, and lifted it to Jesus' lips. [30]When he had received the drink, Jesus said, "It is finished." With that, he bowed his head and gave up his spirit.

19:28–29 The end of Jesus' earthly life was at this point imminent. To highlight this fact the Johannine evangelist used the strategic word *tetelestai,* by which he meant that the life of Jesus was coming to its intended end or goal. Indeed, within the space of the three verses (vv. 28–30) the verb family of *telein/teleioun* is used three times, whereas all words associated with this word family are used only six additional times in the rest of the Gospel, and two of those times appear in the summary of chap. 17 (17:4,23). The intended hour of Jesus' glorification had finally fully arrived (cf. 12:23; 17:1). The King had been crucified, and he was dying.

Jesus understood the implications of this moment, and although he had earlier been troubled by what they would involve and thought seriously of calling on the Father to save him from this hour, he refused to abandon the purpose or goal for which he came (cf. 12:27). Now the conclusion to the life of God's unique agent had arrived. He had been beaten, mocked, been burdened with his heavy crosspiece, been nailed to it, and then hoisted on the pole. According to Mark 15:23 he had earlier refused to accept the dulling sedative of wine mixed with myrrh during the painful march with the crosspiece, but now his body craved something to drink. So he cried, "I am thirsty" *(dipsō).*

The evangelist then added that Jesus said this "in order that the Scripture would be fulfilled." This statement, however, raises two questions: (1) What Scripture was intended? and (2) To what was the fulfillment referring? As indicated in reference to the previous verse, it is hardly likely that it was referring to the mother of Jesus. Nor is it likely to be referring to the fact that everything is brought to its complete goal.[143] Thus it must refer primarily to the thirst experienced by Jesus. If so, it might be viewed as a state-

---

[143] For a helpful discussion of this issue see D. Moo, *The Old Testament in the Gospel Passion Narratives* (Sheffield: Almond, 1983), 275–78.

ment of an intention on the part of Jesus to fulfill Scripture[144] or more probably as the evangelist's insight (as a commentator) concerning the fact that he viewed this cry of Jesus for something to drink as a fulfillment of Scripture.

Although in Mark 15:34–36 the giving to Jesus of a drink of cheap sour wine/vinegar is linked to the cry of desolation in that Gospel, there is here in John no such cry. For Mark that cry clearly reflected a scriptural allusion to Ps 22:1, and the same psalm alludes to the dividing and casting of lots for the victim's clothing (22:18). Moreover, it is interesting that the same psalm also alludes to the dehydrated state of the victim, for his strength is dried up like a broken "potsherd" and his "tongue sticks to the roof of [his] mouth" (22:15).

The connection of the Markan Death Story, and to a lesser extent the Johannine Death Story, with Psalm 22 is unmistakable. But the Death Stories in both Mark and John can likewise be linked to statements in Psalm 69, where the victim's "throat is parched" (Ps 69:3) and he is given "vinegar for [his] thirst" (Ps 69:21). In John the drink offered to Jesus is also here identified as a cheap sour wine/vinegar *(oxous)*, which "was cheaper than regular wine, [and] was a favorite beverage of the lower ranks of society."[145]

Although there is in John no cry of desolation, as indicated above, the reader must not assume that John completely avoided the sense of Jesus experiencing suffering. His entire life was pictured as directed to the hour of his glorification (cf. 2:4,11; 12:27; etc.). His statement "I am thirsty," therefore, as Dodd has indicated, must be understood in this context of hanging on a painful cross and must be viewed in light of the allusions to sufferings in Psalms.[146]

This cheap sour wine was given to Jesus in a soaked sponge *(spongon)* from a nearby jar/container/object. The sponge was put on/placed around hyssop and brought to his mouth. The problem is to understand how a small rather flexible bush like hyssop could hold a soaked sponge (cf. 1 Kgs 4:33). This problem probably led to a variant being introduced in several later cursive Greek manuscripts from *hyssōpō* to *hyssō* ("javelin"; Latin

---

[144] If Jesus was fulfilling Scripture by this act, Carson, *John*, 619, observes that it does not mean that it "was a bit of manipulative histrionics" on the part of Jesus. See also J. Spurrell, "An Interpretation of 'I Thirst'," *CQR* 167 (1966): 12–18.

[145] See *BAGD*, 574.

[146] Cf. Dodd, *Historical Tradition*, 42. See also A. Dauer, *Die Passionsgeschichte im Johannesevangelium* (Munich: Kösel, 1972), 209–10. Beasley-Murray's summation (*John*, 351) is pertinent here: "One may no more assume that John's emphasis on the cross as the exaltation of Jesus excludes his desolation of spirit than his emphasis on the deity of the Son excludes the Son's true humanity."

peticae), which is the rendering in the NEB version. Other recent translations have attempted to solve the problem by adding a qualifier not present in the Greek such as "branch" (NRSV, NLT) or "stalk" (NIV, TEV). The problem may be alleviated by remembering that the crucifixion pole probably was not very tall and Jesus was certainly not lifted as high as is pictured in most art devoted to the cross. All that would be required was that his feet were above the ground. As a result the soldiers could probably have washed his mouth without too much difficulty by putting the sponge on a small plant that could easily be ripped from the nearby rocks.[147]

19:30 When Jesus had thus tasted the sour wine, he was ready to die. But before Jesus died, John records the third and final statement of Jesus from the cross. That word, *Tetelestai* (Greek), *Consummatuum est* (Latin), "It is finished" (English), has reverberated down through Christian history and theology as an expression of the finished work of Christ.[148] As Paul and the Preacher of Hebrews stated, Jesus' death took place "once" for everyone (Rom 6:10; Heb 7:27; 9:12; 10:10). Moreover, the Johannine seer echoed this expression of the end of time when he wrote in his visions "It is done!" (Rev 16:17; 21:6).

With this statement John declared that Jesus bowed his head and "delivered" *(paredōken)* his spirit. For the Johannine evangelist this picture of the dying Jesus is extremely powerful. Jesus, the obedient agent of God, died in a spirit of reverence with the bowed *(klinas)* head.[149] In contrast with the fact that throughout the Death Story Jesus had been repeatedly "delivered," first from Judas, the deliverer," then to Annas and Caiaphas, then to Pilate, and finally to the soldiers to be crucified, at this point Jesus delivered his spirit. The force of these repeated deliverances should not be missed. Although Bultmann sees little difference between the Synoptics and John in the death of Jesus, he (along with others) has often missed the point of the Johannine progression in the Death Story.[150] But Schnackenburg is absolutely correct in linking the death of Jesus here with Jesus' earlier statement that he had the personal "authority to lay [his life] down and authority to take it up again" (John 10:18).[151]

Jesus is portrayed as totally in control of the time of his dying, just as he had been pictured as in control of his arrest, his appearance before Annas, his trial before the spineless Pilate, and the carrying of his own cross. For

---

[147] See R. K. Harrison, "Hyssop," *ISBE*, 2.790.

[148] Cf. the discussion in A. Corell, *Consummatum Est* (London: S.P.C.K., 1958), 105–7, 201–7.

[149] Of course the use of the bowed head can be used as an expression of both sleep (cf. Matt 8:20; Luke 9:58) and death but the order in death would normally be breathing the last breath and bowing the head. Cf. Morris, *John*, 721.

[150] Bultmann, *John*, 675.

[151] See Schnackenburg, *St. John*, 3.284. Cf. also Beasley-Murray, *John*, 353.

his readers John was illustrating in bold letters that even what seems to be tragedy was still not out of God's control. The focus in this story, therefore, must not be lost because the evangelist is continually both a reporter and a theologian. The two cannot be separated as some have tried to do in seeking for a historical Jesus apart from John's confession of faith. For John the point of the story is not just that Jesus was killed but that he died in accordance with God's appointed hour.

(2) The Piercing of the Lamb (19:31–37)

[31]Now it was the day of Preparation, and the next day was to be a special Sabbath. Because the Jews did not want the bodies left on the crosses during the Sabbath, they asked Pilate to have the legs broken and the bodies taken down. [32]The soldiers therefore came and broke the legs of the first man who had been crucified with Jesus, and then those of the other. [33]But when they came to Jesus and found that he was already dead, they did not break his legs. [34]Instead, one of the soldiers pierced Jesus' side with a spear, bringing a sudden flow of blood and water. [35]The man who saw it has given testimony, and his testimony is true. He knows that he tells the truth, and he testifies so that you also may believe. [36]These things happened so that the scripture would be fulfilled: "Not one of his bones will be broken," [37]and, as another scripture says, "They will look on the one they have pierced."

19:31 As indicated in 19:14, it was the day before Nisan 15, the day before Passover; it was the day of Preparation, the day on which the lambs were slaughtered.[152] But at this point in the Gospel the evangelist makes a special note because in that year Nisan 14 was also the day before the Sabbath, as though to emphasize the irony of the fact that it was to be the high day of Passover week. The Lamb of God (cf. 1:29,36) had died along with the Passover lambs, and that confluence of events must have seared itself into the mind of John.

But there was more that impressed itself on his theological consciousness. The Romans normally left victims on crosses until they were sure they had died, so flesh-eating animals could chew at their feet, and birds of prey could pick at them even while they were still living. Therefore, given the high celebration of the Jews, who were concerned about the land being cleansed of its contamination for Passover, they asked that the bodies be removed from the crosses by sunset (cf. Deut 21:22–23). Usually in such cases, to hasten death, as indicated in the Excursus 23 on the subject of crucifixion, the leg bones were broken so that the death of the victim would be hastened from this *crucifragium*. This act would quicken death because of

---

[152] Cf. R. Brown, *John*, 2.934.

an inability to breathe.[153] The story of this final request of the Jews is dripping with irony. With this final desire for ritual purity noted, the Jews fade from the picture in this Gospel.[154] Their role was finished, but little did they know that this petition to Pilate was unnecessary.

19:32–33 The soldiers followed their instructions and broke the legs of the two who had been crucified at the same time as Jesus. When they came to Jesus, the central figure in our story, they found that the Lamb of God was already dead. Accordingly, it was not necessary to break his legs.

It is almost as though John wanted this readers to know that this Lamb of God died complete and unblemished because the broken legs might not have provided the church with such a wonderful picture of the perfect lamb (cf. 1 Pet 1:19; cf. also the inauguration of Passover and the unblemished lamb in Exod 12:5).[155] This righteous Jesus, John would later proclaim, died as the atoning sacrifice for the whole world (cf. 1 John 2:2). Although Passover and Yom Kippur (the Day of Atonement) are different events in the Jewish calendar, in Johannine theology they have been merged in the death picture of Jesus Christ.

19:34 The soldiers' task was to make sure that the victim on the cross was dead before removing the body. The Johannine Gospel provides an interesting assurance of the reality of Jesus' death in the account of the piercing of Jesus' side. Obviously the use of the spear was more than a mere probe to see if the victim was still alive because the result of the jab opened a wound in the side of the corpse from which blood and water immediately came out.

Theories concerning the nature of this blood and water abound. Some medical theories have argued that instead of the side being punctured the upper pericardial sac was pierced, which resulted in the separated blood and

---

[153] The *crucifragium* or breaking of the legs was done with a heavy iron mallet like a sledge hammer and was intensely traumatic to the weakened victim. If death did not result from the blow, it would quickly follow because the rib cage would slump forward and the victim would no longer be able to gasp for breath. See also Excursus 21. See also F. Zugibe, "Two Questions about Crucifixion: Does the Victim Die of Asphyxiation? Would Nails in the Hand Hold the Weight of the Body?" *BibRev* 5 (1989): 34–43. D. Daube argued that the Jews may have wanted to disfigure the body to prevent resurrection, but that is hardly the point here (*The New Testament and Rabbinic Judaism* [London: Athlone, 1956], 325–28). Cf. R. Brown, *The Death of the Messiah*, 2.1176,

[154] There is no hint in John of a guard being set to watch the tomb as in Matt 27:62–66. There is also no mention of the curtain at the entrance to the Most Holy Place (Holy of Holies) being torn (Mark 15:38; Matt 27:51; Luke 23:45) or of the earthquake and the bodies of former holy ones walking about (Matt 27:52–53). There also is no mention of the Roman centurion speaking of the dying Jesus as the Son of God (Mark 15:39; Matt 27:54) or "innocent" (Luke 23:47).

[155] Bultmann viewed the nature of the story as a theological construction (*John*, 676, 651, 664).

water flowing out.[156] Others have suggested that the separated mixture filled the lungs and rib cage and then the lower membrane containing the separated mixture was punctured.[157] Whichever medical explanation may be correct, it is highly unlikely that the idea of a bleeding heart is the most adequate representation of the picture here presented.[158]

Still others would argue that the statement is a highly developed Johannine symbolic representation of the Eucharist or communion. One of the most novel symbolic representations was a film portrayal of the crucifixion of Jesus in which when he died, it began to rain. Thus, after the soldier pierced his side, blood flowed down and mixed with rain water. Of course, this latter view hardly represents the meaning of the text. On the other hand, the symbolic Eucharistic view hardly provides an adequate explanation for the origin of the story.[159] C. Koester, whose major work is on symbolism, notes the connection to communion through John 6:51–55;[160] his major focus on water as a Messianic theme is connected with the Spirit.[161] But given the symbolic nature of the Gospel, this statement in John must have given rise to the development of the practice in some traditions where the Eucharistic drink element is enacted as a mixture of wine and water.

The basis for such an identification is undoubtedly to be found in the symbolic statements of John 6:53–55, where the drink is identified with Jesus' blood and the bread with Jesus' flesh (6:51).[162] But this blood/drink symbolism may not be viewed as fully dealing with the inclusion of the water. So when one enters the realm of symbolic speculation, I have heard it argued strongly that the water here could equally represent the water of baptism, and some have suggested that it should be linked to such ideas in John 3:5,[163] though the statement of "blood and water" would here seem to imply a reverse order. But note the order of "water and blood" in 1 John 5:6.[164]

---

[156] Cf. P. Barbet, *A Doctor at Calvary* (Garden City: Kennedy/Doubleday, 1953); Carson, *John*, 623. Cf. also W. Edwards, et al., "On the Physical Death of Jesus," *Journal of the American Medical Association* 25.11 (1986): 1455–63.

[157] Cf. A. Sava, "The Wounds of Christ," *CBQ* 19 (1957): 343–46.

[158] Cf. the earlier discussion of A. Simpson, The Broken Heart of Jesus," *Expositor*, 8th Series, 2 (1911): 310–21. For other interpretations see A. Sava, "The Blood and Water from the Side of Christ," *AER* 138 (1958): 341–45; J. M. Ford, " 'Mingled Blood' from the Side of Christ (John xix.34)," *NTS* (1969): 337–38 and J. Wilkinson, "The Incident of the Blood and Water in John 19:34," *SJT* 28 (1975): 149–72.

[159] C. Koester indicates that the appearance of water is "remarkable" here although it "could be explained as a natural occurrence according to the canons of ancient physiology" (*Symbolism in the Fourth Gospel* [Minneapolis: Fortress, 1995], 181).

[160] Ibid., 99.

[161] Ibid., 14, 184, 204, etc.

[162] See my earlier discussion on these texts in Borchert, *John*, 1.270–72.

[163] See my comments at ibid., 1.174–76.

[164] For a discussion of the various interpretations of this text see the major work on the Johannine letters in R. Brown, *The Epistles of John*, AB (Garden City: Doubleday, 1982), 575–85.

Nevertheless, it is probably best to curtail such unrestricted symbolic speculation because it can quickly lead to allegorizing the text.[165] It is perhaps sufficient to note here that for John this story was obviously quite significant theologically and historically because of his special footnote concerning the witness and his authenticity in 19:35.

Excursus 25: On the Reality of Jesus Christ's Death

The inclusion of the statement concerning "blood and water" in this context raises the bigger issue of the legitimacy or reality of Jesus as a truly divine-human figure. Soon after the death of Jesus various theories concerning the nature of Jesus Christ began to emerge. The Gnostic-type, Greek-oriented persons within the Christian community began to deny the humanity of Jesus and assert a clear division between flesh and the spirit or of materiality and the spirit. Accordingly, for John the focus was not merely on living or authentic life in following the pattern established by Jesus. But for him nonauthentic living was rooted in a false dichotomizing of Jesus, namely, denying that the human Jesus was also the divine Christ (cf. 1 John 2:22).[166] Or more precisely it was a refusal to accept that Jesus Christ had come in the flesh. Thus in his first epistle John declared persons who confessed the incarnation/enfleshment of Jesus "of God" (1:14). But those who denied this confession John judged endued with the spirit of antichrist (1 John 4:2–3).[167]

The early proclaimers of Christianity realized that the well-known Platonic separation of the ideal and phenomenal worlds could not apply to Jesus. Moreover, flesh was not of itself inherently evil. Yet when a person's mind was set on fleshly concerns rather than on God, then such a mind-set or perspective of Jesus was inherently negative or evil (cf. Rom 8:5–8; John 1:11). The Platonic and Gnostic view of hope was linked to escape from the flesh (the body). Such a view did not affirm the body as created by God, but it asserted that the body resulted from the work of negative forces in the cosmic order that was usually attributed to the Demiurge or evil creator.[168] For Jesus to become flesh meant in some sense the affirmation of the flesh or the created order. Such a view is affirmed in Genesis when God said he created all things "good" (cf. Gen 1:31). But such a view was rejected by the Gnosticizing proponents within the overall context of Christianity.

Among their schemes was a "docetic" Christ, one who *appeared* in the body of Jesus but was not really flesh and blood. One of the theories was that the divine Son "adopted" the body of Jesus at the baptism and departed before he suffered and died. This split between the human Jesus and the divine Christ has continued to invade formulations of Christian theology throughout the centuries. Among its

---

[165] See my comments on allegory in Excursus 21.

[166] See S. Smalley, *1, 2, 3 John*, WBC (Waco: Word, 1984), 110–15 for another discussion of the heretical tendencies in the Johannine community.

[167] See ibid., 220–25.

[168] For the Gnostic work of the Demiurge see, for example, H. Jonas, *The Gnostic Problem* (Boston: Beacon, 1958). See also my earlier discussion in Borchert, *John*, 1.76–80.

most recent forms was Bultmann's division between the Jesus of Nazareth and the Christ of faith. Bultmann regarded the confession "Jesus Christ" as merely a theological construct and not a factual reality.[169]

The early church fathers struggled repeatedly to articulate the dimensions of the incarnation of Jesus Christ during the first three centuries. It was in the fourth century, however, that the issue reached its zenith, when the debate with Arius argued that Jesus was not God but only a son of God. Athanasius[170] and the Nicene Creed (A.D. 325) asserted that such a view was unacceptable and declared among other matters that Jesus Christ was "eternally begotten," "true (very) God from true God," "begotten not made," "one being with the Father," and "incarnate from the Virgin Mary."[171] In this statement the creed affirms the Johannine thesis statements that the Word was with God and was God (John 1:1), that the Word became flesh (1:14), and that Jesus was confessed as truly God (20:28). From the Apostle's Creed onward the great confessions of Christianity declared that this incarnate Jesus clearly suffered under Pontius Pilate, was crucified, and really died.[172]

There seems to be no doubt then that whatever symbolism may be implied in John's mentioning of the blood and water, the death of Jesus, the incarnate Son of God, was in this statement declared to be a genuine death and not some docetic ruse on God's part.[173]

19:35 In contemporary writing this verse would be the equivalent of a footnote supporting the statements made in the previous verses. The import of this verse is that the one who saw was also the one who stood behind (bore witness to) the details enunciated in this pericope, which appear only in John. This witness, moreover, is clearly asserted to be true or authentic. The reason for confidence in the witness is given as "that one knows he speaks the truth." The purpose for detailing this information is then defined emphatically as being in order for "you" to believe. This emphatic "you" is obviously to be understood as the reader. Indeed, this purpose statement is parallel to the main Johannine purpose statement in 20:30–31.

---

[169] For a brief outline of Bultmann's views on myths about Jesus and his distinction between the Jesus of history and the Christ of faith see "New Testament and Mythology," in *Kerygma and Myth*, ed. H. Bartsch (New York: Harper & Row, 1961), 22–44. Cf. also my earlier review of Bultmann in G. Borchert, "Is Bultmann's Theology a New Gnosticism?" *EvQ* 36 (1964): 222–28.

[170] For his views see Athanasius, *On Incarnation* (Crestwood, N.Y.: St. Vladimir Orthodox Theological Seminary Press, 1993).

[171] For the Nicene Creed see H. Bettenson, *Documents of the Christian Church* (London: Oxford University Press, 1956), 34–37. For an excellent interpretation see B. Marthaler, *The Creed: The Apostolic Faith in Contemporary Theology* (Mystic, Conn.: Twenty Third Publications, 1996).

[172] For the Apostle's Creed see Bettenson, *Documents*, 33–34.

[173] By making this statement I am not suggesting that the "blood and water" statement was for John merely a statement of a human death. For example, see G. Richter, "'Blut und Wasser' aus der durchbohsten Seit Jesu (Joh 19, 34b)," *MTZ* 21 (1970): 1–21.

But who is this true witness? Brown concludes: "There can be little doubt ... this witness was the Beloved Disciple" and is the same authentic witness as in 21:24.[174] The theme of truthful witness is a key idea in this Gospel, which begins by focusing on John, the witness, who was doing the baptizing (1:6,24). But the model witness must be the beloved disciple.

The identity of the one who "knows" has raised some questions. Carson recognizes that while it could even be Christ, or some other witness than the evangelist, the statement probably is an elliptical reference to himself.[175] Some scholars would follow this quest for identity with the suggestion that the verse is an editorial insertion into the text, but the style seems to be completely Johannine. Accordingly, even if the verse were a later insertion,[176] it seems to come from the same pen as the one who wrote the rest of the Gospel.[177]

19:36–37 These verses contain the final fulfillment statements in the Death Story (cf. 19:24 and 19:28).[178] The obvious implication is that for the evangelist both the breaking of the legs (19:33) and the piercing of his side (19:34) are to be understood as fulfillments of Scripture.

For John one of the governing themes in the Gospel has been the death of the Lamb of God (1:29,36). When this theme is linked with the controlling idea of Passover, which has appeared in every section of the Gospel to this point, it is not difficult to understand why the image of the paschal lamb would come immediately to John's mind and the fact that in both Exod 12:10 and Num 9:12 no bone of the Passover lamb should be broken. But beyond these direct references to the paschal lamb, it is interesting to recall that the concept of the Lord's preservation and care for his righteous people is expressed in Ps 34:19–20 in terms of the Lord persevering or delivering the bones of his faithful ones from being broken. And who for John would represent the righteous one more than Jesus?

The second scriptural referent is taken from Zechariah's long reflection on the state of Jerusalem and the fact that in the future there would come a day when a fountain of cleansing would be opened in Jerusalem and the people would be purified from their sin and uncleanness (Zech 13:1). But prior to that statement the Hebrew text says that the citizens would look on

---

[174] R. Brown, *John*, 2.936. See also his summary of the various possibilities in *The Death of the Messiah*, 2.1183–84.

[175] Carson, *John*, 625–26.

[176] See Haenchen, *John*, 2.201. See also Beasley-Murray, *John*, 354–55 for a review of the situation.

[177] See R. Brown, *John*, 2.936–37; Carson, *John*, 626.

[178] See E. Freed, *Old Testament Quotations in the Gospel of John* (Leiden: Brill, 1965), 108–16 and A. Hanson, *New Testament Interpretation of Scripture* (London: S.P.C.K., 1980), 158–59.

him (the representative of the house of David) "whom they had pierced" (12:10).[179]

The Johannine renderings of these Old Testament texts are not exact quotations as though he had a copy of the Hebrew or Greek Scriptures in front of him, but in substance they certainly represent accurately the meanings of those cited texts. Moreover, they provide valuable insight into the fact that the early Christians were not attempting to create a Christianity separated from its Jewish roots, as Marcion tried to do in the second century. Although the early Christian *kerygma* (preaching) clearly recognized the evil actions of the Jews in the death of Jesus (cf. Acts 10:39), it did not reject its Jewish heritage. The God of the Hebrew patriarchs, kings, and prophets was the same God who sent Jesus to fulfill the hopes and dreams of the people of God in the earlier covenant. The use of these quotations by John was thus a forceful testimony to the fact that even the Death Story of Jesus, God's only Son, was to be viewed as having taken place within the permissive will of the God of Abraham, Isaac, Jacob, Moses, David, Isaiah, Jeremiah, and Zechariah. For the evangelist nothing was more certain than that Jesus was the special agent of God who died according to the Scriptures.

6. The Burial of the King (19:38–42)

[38]Later, Joseph of Arimathea asked Pilate for the body of Jesus. Now Joseph was a disciple of Jesus, but secretly because he feared the Jews. With Pilate's permission, he came and took the body away. [39]He was accompanied by Nicodemus, the man who earlier had visited Jesus at night. Nicodemus brought a mixture of myrrh and aloes, about seventy-five pounds. [40]Taking Jesus' body, the two of them wrapped it, with the spices, in strips of linen. This was in accordance with Jewish burial customs. [41]At the place where Jesus was crucified, there was a garden, and in the garden a new tomb, in which no one had ever been laid. [42]Because it was the Jewish day of Preparation and since the tomb was nearby, they laid Jesus there.

19:38 The picture of Joseph from Arimathea in the various Gospel accounts provides a fascinating collage. He was said to be rich (Matt 27:57), an important member of the Sanhedrin (Mark 15:43; Luke 23:50) who apparently was both a good and righteous person (Luke 23:50) and one who lived with the expectation of God fulfilling the promise of the coming of the kingdom (Mark 15:43; Luke 23:51). But beyond these descriptions he was also said to be a disciple of Jesus (Matt 27:57; John 19:38), whom John adds was a closet or secret disciple because he apparently feared reprisal from the Jews (John 19:38).

---

[179] The LXX at this point has a very different reading concerning the people sporting or dancing in a reviling manner before him.

Perhaps because of his wealth or standing in the community, Joseph was able to gain access to Pilate. Having gained an audience with Pilate, he asked leave to bury the body of Jesus. According to the comments of Ulpian and the code of Justinian, the bodies of those executed by the state were to be released to relatives or others who were willing to provide them with burial.[180] Brown indicates that such leniency can be traced back via Ulpian to Augustus, but the major exception was in the case of *maiestas* or treason.[181] The reason for that rule was obviously because treason was regarded as a supremely odious crime against the state by the Roman curia. The probability is that Jesus was crucified for *maiestas,* but, since it was a trumped-up charge, Pilate apparently did not think that rule would apply.

Blinzer argued that the Jewish petition to remove the bodies of those who had been crucified would also contain the acknowledgment that they would provide a common burial site for the body. This would mean Jesus' body would normally have been buried among the bodies of those who were rejected and shamed.[182] Joseph's request thus meant that by taking control of the body he in fact was being very courageous. The reason for such an evaluation is that in doing so he could hardly be a closet disciple any longer.

19:39   Not only did Joseph become involved in the burial, but according to John he was joined by Nicodemus. Nicodemus had also earlier moved from being a closet inquirer (3:1–9) to a council member who sought to be fair in judgment (7:50). At this point he is also portrayed as a person who was willing to make a declarative statement through the burial of Jesus' body. To facilitate this task, he brought a mixture of myrrh and aloes.[183] Bernard argued at this point that Nicodemus must have had at his home these spices because he would have hardly had time to collect or purchase them.[184] But perhaps Joseph and Nicodemus divided their tasks, one

---

[180] For the applicable legal prescriptions see *The Digest of Justinian*, ed. T. Mommsen (Philadelphia: University of Pennsylvania, 1985), 48.24. See also T. Mommsen, *Römisches Strafrecht* (Leipzig: Duncker, 1899), 986–90 for his comments on these prescriptions.

[181] R. Brown sees the literal view going back through Ulpian to Augustus in *Vita Sua*, Book 10 (*The Death of the Messiah*, 2.1207).

[182] See Blinzer, *Der Prozess*, 385–95.

[183] Myrrh was a typical Egyptian preparation used in their embalming process. It comes from a small thorn tree found in southern Arabia and Ethiopia that is very fragrant and produces an aromatic resin. It was also used in cosmetics and was one of the gifts Matthew indicates was brought by the star gazers to the baby Jesus and his family (2:11). For further details see R. K. Harrison's article in *ISBE* 3.450–51. Aloe was also used by the Egyptians in embalming. Most of the references in the OT to this item are, according to Harrison, general references to a sweet fragrant powder (e.g., Num 14:6; Ps 45:8; Prov 7:17; *Cant* 4:14) probably derived from a sandalwood or eaglewood tree found from India through Malaysia. The reference in John to aloes is probably from a small plant, *aloë succotrina,* used in embalming. For further information see Harrison's article in *ISBE* 1.99. Most commentators fail to make this distinction.

[184] Bernard, *St. John*, 2.653–54.

going for the spices and the other seeking the release of the body.[185] Both suggestions, however, are speculations.

The amount surely is surprising—about a hundred Roman "pounds" *(litas)* of spice. That amount would be roughly the equivalent of sixty-five pounds of spice or nearly thirty kilograms in terms of modern weights.[186] It was truly an immense amount of spice. Indeed, it was enough spice to bury a king royally. The Johannine Death Story thus makes clear that Jesus was a King. He acknowledged that fact before Pilate (18:37). He died enthroned on a cross with his title placarded in three strategic languages announcing his kingship (19:19–20). And finally, he was here appropriately buried as a king.[187]

In the Synoptic Gospels it is said that the women watched the hasty burial (cf. Matt 27:61; Mark 15:47; Luke 23:55), and Luke adds that they departed to prepare the spices or aromatics and myrrh. The NIV has "perfumers" (Luke 23:56), but there is no mention of the women in John at this point of the story. For John the women have faded from the picture with the exception of the important role played by Mary Magdalene in two of the early resurrection pericopes (John 20:1–2,11–18).

19:40 This verse raises some problems when compared with the Synoptics, particularly when related to the well-known issue concerning the legitimacy of the Shroud of Turin.[188] The Johannine text indicates that the body was wrapped in spices by bandages or linen cloths *(othoniois)*[189] similar to the picture presented of the bound-up body of Lazarus (11:44). In the Synoptics the term used is *sindona/sindoni* (Matt 27:59; Mark 15:46; Luke 23:53), which can be translated as a linen sheet or even a tunic.[190] As such

---

[185] This suggestion made by M. Lagrange, *Évangile selon Saint Jean* (Paris: Gabalda, 1948), 503, has been followed by most later commentators. See R. Brown, *John*, 2.940; Beasley-Murray, *John*, 359; Carson, *John*, 629–30; etc.

[186] The NIV rendering of seventy-five pounds or thirty-four kilograms may be slightly generous. The NLT footnote of 32.7 kilograms is a little closer. But these translations indicate the difficulties one encounters in translating ancient approximate measurements into contemporary equivalents. Schnackenburg's *St. John*, 3.297, equivalent of 65.45 pounds may be more realistic.

[187] At the death of Rabbi Gamaliel I approximately ten to twenty years after the death of Jesus, Onkelos, the well-known targumist who regarded Gamaliel as his model, left an account of Gamaliel's funerary rites, which included the burning of some eighty pounds of such spices. In his comment concerning this event he asked: "Is R. Gamaliel not much better than a hundred kings?" (see *Str–B*, 2.584).

[188] For a series of articles related to the recent analyses done on the Shroud of Turin see the Nov/Dec issue of *BAR*, 24.6 (1998). For further comments see also *BAR* 25.2 (1999): 16–18, 20, 66 and 25.4 (1999): 10, 12. For a general article see W. H. Gloer, *ISBE*, 4.494–96. For an earlier perspective see W. Bulst, "Novae in sepulturam Jesu inquisitones," *VD* 31 (1953): 257–74 and 352–59 or *MTZ* 3 (1952): 244–55.

[189] For the meaning of this term see *BAGD*, 555.

[190] For the meaning of this term see *BAGD*, 751.

it might more easily support the idea of a shroud. Brown tries valiantly to bring these two ideas together by diminishing the meaning of *othoniois* in John so as to support the idea of a shroud, but Schnackenburg (along with the present writer) is unconvinced by Brown's labored logic.[191] Indeed, one could even argue that *sindōn* is a more general term than the plural of *othonion*. Besides, one still has to deal with the issue of head/face wrapping in 20:7 and 11:44.

The crux of the issue might be thought to be resolved by the concluding words of this verse, "in accordance with Jewish burial customs." But we cannot establish that a single burial custom was observed in Judea at this time. We are quite certain that the internal organs were not removed and treated before placing them in funerary jars after the fashion of the Egyptian preparation of mummies. The burial procedures were much less involved, and the bodies normally began to decompose rather quickly (cf. the statement concerning Lazarus's body at John 11:39), which accounts for the fact that higher class burials generally involved the use of sweet smelling spices. Yet the body wrappings were not consistent in Judea during this time. Some bodies were buried in tunic-type wrappings, and others were buried in other wrappings.[192]

19:41–42 The new tomb where Jesus was laid, John indicates, was in a garden in the vicinity of both the place of the crucifixion and the place of preparation for burial. Accordingly, the Church of the Holy Sepulcher in Jerusalem contains a special elevated chapel to mark the site of the crucifixion and a lower benchlike memorial to mark the place of preparation for burial. Both are a short distance from the traditional site of the tomb.[193] Whether all of these places were actually that close together may be open to question.

Mark refers to the tomb as one that was "cut out of rock" (Mark 15:46). Matthew (27:60) and John (19:41) indicate that it was a new tomb, and

---

[191] See R. Brown, *John*, 2.941–42, who attempts to discount the linguistic concept of linen strips as the meaning of the burial clothes. Since the Shroud implies a long narrow sheet folded over the body and loosely tied but not bound with a series of bound strips, the Johannine idea of strips might argue against the concept of a shroud. Schnackenburg is hardly convinced by this manipulation of Brown and states that the "apparently divergent details ... do not allow for any certain conclusion" (*St. John*, 3.297–98). Brown's subsequent reflections on the topic (*The Death of the Messiah*, 2.1264–65) are more balanced, but he continues to argue for a generalized Johannine interpretation. See also my comments in connection with John 20:7.

[192] But particularly note *Sir* 38:1b. For a discussion concerning Jewish burial customs see J. Blinzer, *Der Prozess*, 385–415 and the earlier studies of A. Bender, "Beliefs, Rites and Customs of the Jews, Connected with Death, Burial and Mourning," *JQR* 6 (1894): 317–47, 664–71; 7 (1895): 101–18, 259–69. See also the helpful work of J. Payne in *ISBE*, 1.556–61, especially at 557.

[193] For a discussion and plan of the Church of the Holy Sepulcher see *NEAEHL*, 2.779–81.

Luke (23:53) states that no one had been buried in it. Matthew (27:60) adds that it was Joseph's own tomb. To understand these statements, particularly that of Luke, one must realize that tombs were valuable pieces of property and were used repeatedly by families. A person was placed on a burial slab in the tomb until the flesh decomposed, then the bones were collected and put in an ossuary (a small box), which was kept in another part of the tomb. Then the burial slab could be reused. According to Matthew's account the tomb was apparently a new tomb for Joseph and his family. For a longer discussion of the tomb see Excursus 26 below.

Excursus 26: Archaeology and the Tomb of Jesus

Until recently the site and nature of the tomb of Jesus seemed to be quite settled. The place itself became debated when Gordon selected an alternative site to that remembered by tradition while he was sitting on the present Muslim wall looking over the city of Jerusalem.[194] More recently, however, the question of the form and nature of the tomb has also been raised because of archaeological research on tombs in the region.

Tourists who visit Jerusalem and the Garden Tomb, which is outside the current walls of the city, are not only shown a rock outcropping with cavelike gashes in the face of it near the bus station in East Jerusalem, but they are also informed by the caretakers that the place is certainly Golgotha or the hill of Calvary. More impressively, they are also shown a large tomb with an entry room and a side room where Jesus is said to have been laid after his crucifixion. The opening to the tomb is replete with a trough for a huge rolling stone that would have been rolled in place to cover the entrance. For most Protestants unaccustomed to the smell of incense, elaborate ornaments, and liturgical accouterments, this place seems to be much more appealing than the cavernous building with its numerous chapels known as the Church of the Holy Sepulcher, especially since today it lies within the Islamic walls.[195]

If tradition since Queen Helena (see below) is reliable, however, the latter place might be the site of the tomb, and perhaps the nearby chapel at the top of the narrow steps might be close to the place of the crucifixion. The attempts to confirm the location of the wall of the Herodian city have yielded some positive results, but the excavations under the nearby Lutheran church have not been absolutely conclusive about the site of the tomb itself even though the location of the old wall is now probably not greatly in dispute.

The identification of the tomb with the site of the Church of the Holy Sepulcher was made during the church building period of Queen Helena, the mother of Constantine. It was her goal to gather the most reliable information she could at the time and to preserve the historic sites of Christianity by marking them with

---

[194] For a helpful discussion on Gordon and the Garden Tomb see J. Rousseau and R. Arav, *Jesus and His World* (Minneapolis: Fortress, 1995), 104–9.

[195] See *NEAEHL*, 2.779–81 and J. Prewitt's brief article in *ISBE*, 2.730. See also the diagrams and notes in Rousseau and Arav, *Jesus and His World*, 112–18.

worship or remembrance centers for pilgrims.[196] The stone outcroppings that would have been the original tomb have suffered devastation during the many battles and religious disputes that have ravaged the area through the centuries so that the site hardly resembles a tomb today. Yet this church may be close to the site of the tomb because the Romans tended to vilify or desecrate places of meaning for those they considered enemies by erecting pagan shrines on those sites— witness the building of a temple to Jupiter on the site of the Jewish Temple by Hadrian sometime after the destruction of Jerusalem in A.D. 70. Such may be one reason that Helena was able to mark the Church of the Holy Sepulcher as the site of Jesus' burial.

We can be absolutely sure about some locations, such as the Sea of Galilee, the ancient tels with their gates and water sources, the hill of Gilead, and the Temple Mount. There are other sites that are "traditional" and may have significant support, but we may not be able to say with absolute certainty that they go back to Jesus, David, or Abraham.

On the morning of the resurrection the women came to the tomb and found the stone rolled away (cf. Matt 27:60; 28:2; Mark 16:3–4; Luke 24:2). There are in Israel a number of tombs that have been sealed with round rolling stones. Some that are shown to tourists are from a later time than the time of Jesus. Some are exceedingly large and are likely to be family tombs of the high priests or nobles. The tombs of ordinary citizens are usually much smaller, and many are constructed quite differently. As A. Kloner has indicated, most of these tombs (98 percent of them) have the more typical square type blocking stones, which are shoved into the openings. These square blocking stones have a larger ridge to prevent the stone from going completely into the tomb entrance and enables them to be dragged out again for further use.[197]

What was the form of the stone that blocked Jesus' tomb? Was it round or square? We cannot be sure, but the Greek term *kulio* could possibly be rendered either "rolled" or "moved." The interesting fact is that the Gospel of John concentrates on the bending down of both the other disciple and Mary to look into the tomb, where they saw either the linen wrappings or the angels sitting where the head and feet of Jesus would have been laying (cf. John 20:5,11–12). Such a notation seems to reflect a smaller tomb of the style used by the general citizenry of Israel closed by either a round or square stone and having a bench or benches for holding bodies. As indicated earlier, when the flesh decomposed the bones would then be collected and placed in small boxes called ossuaries, which were stored appropriately in another part of the tomb, and the slab could then be reused. The Gospel texts indicate that the family tomb of Joseph of Arimathea (Matt 27:60) was new and had not been used for burial previously (John 19:40–41). What kind of a tomb was it in which Jesus was laid?

---

[196] See Eusebius, *Vit. Const.*, 3.25–40 for Queen Helena's work in the fourth century. Cf. also Rousseau and Arav, *Jesus and His World*, 113, 117.

[197] For a discussion of the square type openings in most tombs see A. Kloner, "Did a Rolling Stone Close Jesus' Tomb?" *BAR* 25.5 (1999): 22–29, 76. See also *NEAEHL*, 2.747–57 for a discussion of tombs in general around Jerusalem.

It is possible that the tomb might have been one of the rarer tombs that was sealed with a round stone. It is also possible that it was one of the more customary types of tombs with a square blocking stone. Whichever kind it was and whatever was its location, Jesus occupied an earthly tomb for an incredibly short period of time. The reason is that God raised him from the dead.

7. Concluding Reference in the Death Story (19:42)

[42]Because it was the Jewish day of Preparation and since the tomb was nearby, they laid Jesus there.

19:42 (Cont.) So important has Passover been to the Johannine evangelist that he cannot end the Death Story without another mention of the fact that the Day of Preparation was closing and the Passover was about to begin. It is important at this stage to reflect on the fact that the Passover, Day of Preparation, and the Death of the Lamb have been present in every major narrative section of the Gospel from the introduction of the Lamb in the Three Cameos of Witness (1:29,36), to the Cana Cycle (2:13,23), the Festival Cycle (6:4; 11:55), the Centerpiece of the Gospel (12:1), the Farewell Cycle (13:1), and the Death Story (18:28,39; 19:14,31,42). And these references do not include the repeated mention of the hour of his destiny.

With all of these references in mind, the reader should pay particular attention to the fact that in the next major section, the Resurrection Stories, there is no mention of Passover. The death of the Lamb will then be in the past tense. The wounds are still evident (20:20,27), but the Passover has taken place. It was a once-for-all event, to quote other New Testament writers (cf. Heb 9:28; 1 Pet 3:18; Jude 3). This sacrifice of Jesus is nonrepeatable. Therefore we must take it extremely seriously (Heb 6:4–6). Clearly this singular sacrifice of Jesus has provided God's answer, according to John, for the expiation or removal of our sins (1 John 2:2; 4:10). The death of Jesus may not be how we would choose to be reconciled to God, but the basis of reconciliation is the work of God, not the work of human beings. Our task is to accept Jesus Christ (cf. 1 John 1:2–3; 2:23; 4:2,14–15) and follow his model of love in the world (John 13:34–35; 15:12; 1 John 3:11; 4:7–9,16–21).

VIII. THE RESURRECTION STORIES (20:1–21:25)

Excursus 27: The Resurrection Perspective and the Purpose of the Gospel

1. Chapter 20: The Resurrection and the First Conclusion to the Gospel (20:1–31)

(1) Mary Magdalene at the Tomb—Part 1 (20:1–2)

(2) Peter and the Beloved Disciple at the Tomb (20:3–10)

(3) Mary Magdalene—Part 2: The First Appearance (20:11–18)

(4) Jesus Appears to the Disciples behind Closed Doors in the Evening (20:19–23)

(5) The Thomas Story in Two Parts (20:24–29)

Excursus 28: The Twelve

(6) The Main Purpose Statement of the Gospel and the Initial Conclusion (20:30–31)

2. The Epilogue (21:1–25)

(1) The Revelation to the Seven by the Sea of Tiberias (21:1–14)

Excursus 29: Jerusalem and Galilee

Excursus 30: The Sons of Zebedee, the Beloved Disciple, and Oblique References in John

Excursus 31: John 21:1–14 and Luke 5:1–11: A Form and Redactional Note

(2) The Three-Part Conversation between Jesus and Peter (21:15–23)

The Reinstatement of Peter Following His Denial (21:15–17)

The Prediction of Peter's Martyrdom (21:18–19)

The Prediction Concerning the Beloved Disciple (21:20–23)

(3) The Authentication and Conclusion to the Epilogue and the Gospel (21:24–25)

Excursus 32: The Community "We" and Their Confession

─── VIII. THE RESURRECTION STORIES (20:1–21:25) ───

Excursus 27: The Resurrection Perspective and the Purpose of the Gospel

The hinge point of Christianity is the resurrection of Jesus, the Christ.[1] The resurrection is the authentic foundation for Christianity, for the church, for Sun-

---

[1] See G. Borchert, "The Resurrection Perspective in John: An Evangelical Summons," *RevExp* 85 (1988): 502; and "The Resurrection: 1 Corinthians 15," *RevExp* 80 (1983): 401.

day worship, for Christian colleges and seminaries, and for the Christian proclamation of the forgiveness of sins. Without the resurrection Christianity would be
an empty shell (cf. Paul's strategic statements in 1 Cor 15:14–19).

Christianity and the Gospel of John are hardly based on nonmaterial visions
and the removal of the body from the ancestral tomb by Joseph of Arimathea, as
was argued by J. Klausner.[2] Neither is Christianity merely built on faith in the
mythologically conceived Easter faith of the early disciples so as to be just faith
in faith as was proposed by R. Bultmann.[3]

Obviously the resurrection accounts in the Gospels may not convince those
who are committed to the rationalistic perspectives of theologies and philosophies of suspicion. But this commentary is not written from that perspective. Nor
is it the intention of this writer to engage in the fruitless apologetic task of seeking to convince the unconvinced that a resurrection is rationally and scientifically
possible. That approach basically convinces the convinced, which as a young
lawyer this writer sought to do when he read every conceivable apologetic work
available to him. Nor does this work aim to harmonize all of the resurrection
accounts in the Gospels as though they were mere historical reports, for this strategy fails to give adequate attention to the particular theological purposes of each
evangelist. Such was the method this writer used in his first theological thesis on
the resurrection accounts many years ago in which he followed a similar style to
Tatian's Diatessaron (composed in the second century).[4]

The Gospels are not mere history books. They are testimonies concerning the
life, death, and resurrection of the most unique person ever to set foot on planet
Earth. Moreover, especially the Johannine evangelist did not write his Gospel to
give a mere blow-by-blow account of all that Jesus did, as is stated clearly in the
Gospel itself (cf. 20:30; 21:25). This evangelist purposely wrote his work to
bring people to believe in Jesus so that they might experience the marvel of a new
way of life (20:31). Furthermore, he wrote his first epistle to spell out the implications of that life (1 John 1:1–4; 5:20). The Johannine evangelist was an evangelistic theologian, not a mere newspaper reporter. But he used the facts he
selected to present the exciting message about Jesus.

Finally, before turning to the specific analysis of these two chapters, it is well
to be reminded of what I have stated in connection with John 2:22, namely, that
this entire Gospel is written from a postresurrection perspective.[5] *Everything* that

---

[2] See J. Klausner, *Jesus of Nazareth* (London: George Allen & Unwin, 1925), 356–59 as an
example of this approach. See also the skeptical reviews of P. Gardner-Smith, *The Narratives of the
Resurrection* (London: Metheuen, 1926) and W. E. Bundy, *Jesus and the First Three Gospels*
(Cambridge, Mass.: Harvard University Press, 1955), 557–73.

[3] See R. Bultmann, "New Testament and Mythology," in *Kerygma and Myth*, ed. H. Bartch
(London: S.P.C.K., 1953), 39.

[4] See G. Borchert, "An Investigation of the Biblical Records of the Resurrection of Jesus
Christ," a thesis submitted to the faculty of Princeton Theological Seminary, 1961.

[5] Ibid., *John 1–11*, NAC (Nashville: Broadman & Holman, 1996), 166.

had been *stated* in the Gospel *assumes that Jesus,* the Son of God, *is no longer dead.* Every word is based on the fact that he is alive and has ascended to the Father (20:17).

This Gospel is a proclamation of victory over the forces of evil. Even the death of Jesus and the themes of the hour and of glorification that point to his death are all to be read in the context that Jesus is alive and victorious. He is God's answer to the plight of humanity. He is King Jesus, the Lord!

This section involving the Resurrection Stories naturally falls into two major parts according to the chapter divisions. Chapter 20, forming the first set of resurrection stories, was the original ending of the Gospel, and it contains six segments. Chapter 21 is either an epilogue or a long postscript to the Gospel and contains three segments. Together these chapters provide some theologically significant testimonial statements concerning the resurrection and the impact it had upon followers of Jesus. It also offers concluding statements to the Gospel.

1. Chapter 20: The Resurrection and the First Conclusion to the Gospel (20:1–31)

This major section of the Resurrection Stories may be divided easily into six parts: (1) Mary Magdalene at the Tomb, Part 1 (20:1–2); (2) Peter and the Beloved Disciples at the Tomb (20:3–10); (3) Mary Magdalene at the Tomb, Part 2 (20:11–18); (4) Jesus' Appearance to the Disciples Behind Closed Doors (20:19–23); (5) The Thomas Story in Two Parts (20:24–29); and (6) The Main Purpose Statement of the Gospel and the Initial Conclusion (20:30–31).

(1) Mary Magdalene at the Tomb—Part 1 (20:1–2)

[1]Early on the first day of the week, while it was still dark, Mary Magdalene went to the tomb and saw that the stone had been removed from the entrance. [2]So she came running to Simon Peter and the other disciple, the one Jesus loved, and said, "They have taken the Lord out of the tomb, and we don't know where they have put him!"

The reader who has carefully studied the fascinating interweaving of the segments of the Death Story will be familiar with the brilliant way in which the Johannine evangelist is able to carry multiple stories and combine them to produce a single message. Here the pattern continues briefly for three segments so as to produce an envelope affect or sandwich pattern of thinking. Such a pattern of writing will be recognized by those familiar with the

Gospel of Mark.[6] The effect is that the Mary Magdalene stories provide an outer casing for the important faith statement concerning the beloved disciple, who is able to believe without seeing the risen Lord.[7]

20:1 The Synoptic accounts of the resurrection story include several women coming to the tomb: three in Mark 16:1 ("Mary Magdalene, Mary the mother of James, and Salome"); two in Matt 28:1 ("Mary Magdalene and the other Mary"); and according to Luke 24:10 there were more than three ("Mary Magdalene, Joanna, Mary the mother of James, and the others). The purpose for their coming was apparently the bringing of spices to anoint the body (Mark 16:1; Luke 24:1) or to see the tomb (Matt 28:1).[8]

The Johannine story focuses on Mary Magdalene, who is mentioned only in this chapter of John and at the cross in 19:25. In Johannine fashion she serves as a model or representative of a type of person, here the women. This evangelist is interested in painting word portraits of people such as John the witness, Andrew, Nathaniel, Nicodemus, the Woman of Samaria, the Blind Man, Thomas, Martha, Mary the sister of Lazarus, the High Priest, Pilate, Peter, and so on. As such these people are not to be viewed merely as exclusive units/persons but as identifiable representatives of their kind of people.

We may not be happy unless we can detail the exact number of women who came to the tomb. We might prefer at least the general type of statement in Luke rather than the singular representative type of statement in John. But the Johannine writer was in a different time and place. The "we" in 20:2 at least forewarns the reader against a misreading of the evangelist's intention.[9]

We may also inquire concerning the time when Mary came to the tomb. All the Gospels indicate it was about dawn, but Mark 16:2 notes that the sun had risen. Yet John states that it was still dark *(prōi skotias)*. Both Gos-

---

[6] My former colleague James Blevins, who dedicated much of his life to reflecting on Mark, loved to speak of the Markan sandwiches. I usually have used the expression "envelope effect" to explain how the two outside parts of a story encase the inside portion of another message and give focus to the letter or words inside.

[7] Cf. the helpful interpretation of R. H. Smith, *Easter Gospels* (Minneapolis: Augsburg, 1983), 156–57.

[8] L. Morris's attempt to harmonize the Gospel accounts by saying that "Nicodemus was not able to use all the spices he had brought" fails to be convincing (*The Gospel According to John*, rev. ed., NICNT [Grand Rapids: Eerdmans, 1995], 733). Contrast his work with the segmented views of R. Fortna, *The Gospel of Signs* (Cambridge: University Press, 1970), 134–44, especially at 135. See the alternative view of E. Ruckstuhl, *Die literarische Einheit des Johannesevangeliums* (Freiburg: Paulus, 1951), 130–34. See also his "Johannine Language and Style: The Question of Their Unity," in *L 'Evangile de Jean*, ed. M. de Jonge (Leuven: University Press, 1977), 125–47.

[9] R. Bultmann considers the plural here not to be genuine (*The Gospel of John* [Philadelphia: Westminster, 1971], 684). But for the opposite view see E. Hoskyns, *The Fourth Gospel*, ed. F. Davey (London: Faber & Faber, 1956), 540.

pels, however, use the term *prōi,* "early," and "dark" is a relative term. Also Mark's "very early" suggests that that sunrise had barely occurred. More important, the reader should remember that time and temperature readings in John are also theologically oriented statements (cf. 3:2; 10:23; 13:30). It was indeed early morning when Mary Magdalene saw a sign of the resurrection—the removed stone—but she was still in the dark concerning its significance.[10]

Although Matthew had been interested in justifying the physical security of the tomb (cf. Matt 27:62–66) and in stressing that the resurrection was a powerful act of God accompanied by an earthquake and an angelic removal of the stone (28:2–4),[11] John just assumed that the resurrection was a miracle and that the removed stone was an evidence of that miracle.

It is significant that John along with the rest of the Gospel writers designated the day of the resurrection as the "first day of the week" rather than the third day after the crucifixion. Although the death of Jesus was absolutely crucial for salvation and the forgiveness of sins, as I have indicated above, "the hinge point of Christianity" is the resurrection. Indeed, on the basis of the resurrection Christians have established their day of worship and praise to God (John 20:19,26; cf. Rev 1:10).[12] Brown is probably correct in suggesting that the shock of the resurrection seared itself into the memory of the early Christians before they went back to reflect on the fact it was the third day after the crucifixion and formulated the implications of that fact for their theologies.[13]

20:2 Obviously the evangelist regarded Mary Magdalene as completely bewildered by the sight of the empty tomb. Accordingly she ran to tell Peter and the beloved disciple about her concern for the removal of the body of "the Lord." When she said, "They have taken," she could only have referred to the crucifiers of Jesus (the Jews and/or Romans). Her second statement

---

[10] R. Brown discusses the time sequences here at length with just a mere hint that there might be some theological significance involved (*The Gospel According to John xiii–xxi,* AB [Garden City: Doubleday, 1970], 980–81). Of course the time was early, but there is no point in suggesting that there is a reason to set John over against the Synoptics as though there was a chronological discrepancy here any more than that one needs to attempt (cf. p. 981) a harmonization of the names or number of women at the tomb. But see the reflections of D. Carson, *The Gospel According to John* (Grand Rapids: Eerdmans, 1991), 635.

[11] The apocryphal *Gospel of Peter,* 39–42, elaborates greatly on the Matthean story and imagines how Jesus emerged from the tomb.

[12] It was not until much later that Dionysus Exeguum recalculated the calendar to the birth of Jesus and unfortunately miscalculated so that Anno Domini (A.D. or 754 A.U.C.) occurred after the death of Herod the Great, which took place according to correct calculations in 4 B.C./ B.C.E. or 750 A.U.C. (A.U.C. stands for *Ab urbe condita* or the Roman calculations "from the founding of the city" of Rome).

[13] R. Brown, *John,* 2.980. Cf. G. Beasley-Murray, *John,* WBC (Waco: Word, 1987), 370–71.

indicates that the early Christians had no sense that the tomb would have been empty.[14] The contemporary thought that they could create a resurrection hoax or experience a joint encounter with some mystical Christ as some have suggested is absurd, given the defeatism that enveloped Jesus' followers after they realized Jesus was truly dead. The only possibility that crossed Mary's mind was that the body must have been stolen in clear violation of Jewish burial integrity and of Roman practice.[15]

(2) Peter and the Beloved Disciple at the Tomb (20:3–10)

[3]So Peter and the other disciple started for the tomb. [4]Both were running, but the other disciple outran Peter and reached the tomb first. [5]He bent over and looked in at the strips of linen lying there but did not go in. [6]Then Simon Peter, who was behind him, arrived and went into the tomb. He saw the strips of linen lying there, [7]as well as the burial cloth that had been around Jesus' head. The cloth was folded up by itself, separate from the linen. [8]Finally the other disciple, who had reached the tomb first, also went inside. He saw and believed. [9](They still did not understand from Scripture that Jesus had to rise from the dead.) [10]Then the disciples went back to their homes,

20:3–5 John has inserted into the story of Mary Magdalene the story of Peter and the beloved disciple. This shift of focus was facilitated by Mary's bewildered cry in v. 2. The cry for help met with a prompt response on the part of the two disciples.

In the second half of this Gospel, Peter and the beloved disciple are frequently set in sharp contrast to each other. Here they both ran to the tomb, but the beloved disciple was the first to reach the tomb. Earlier the beloved disciple had been identified as lying in the breast of Jesus while at the meal and serving as the conveyer of Peter's question to the Lord (13:23–24). Likewise, the beloved disciple had first gained access to the court of the high priest and had served as a mediator to assist in Peter's gaining access as well (18:15–16). Later at the sea he would recognize the Lord first and report that fact to Peter (21:7). Finally, when Peter was informed that he too

---

[14] Cf. P. Minear, "'We don't know where ...' (John 21:2)," *Int* 30 (1976): 125–39.

[15] For the imperial edict concerning stolen bodies that must have been promulgated no later than Emperor Claudius (A.D. 41–54) but undoubtedly was a concern much earlier see C. K. Barrett, *New Testament Background: Selected Documents* (New York: Harper, 1956/1961), 15. Indeed, I find Brown's rationale in *The Death of the Messiah* (Vol. 2 [New York: Doubleday, 1994], 1310–13) for the historicity of even the setting of the guard story in Matthew to be much more compelling than most views that conceive of the story as a created tale by early Christian apologists. Contrast the views of K. Smyth, "The Guard at the Tomb," *HeyJ* 2 (1961): 157–59; G. Lee, "The Guard at the Tomb," *Theology* 72 (1969): 169–75; W. Craig, "The Guard at the Tomb," *NTS* 30 (1984): 273–81. For an analysis of the Nazareth Inscription on this matter see B. M. Metzger, "The Nazareth Inscription Once Again," *NTS* (Leiden: Brill, 1980), 75–92. The point of the inscription referring to Caesar is that graves should not be disturbed in perpetuity.

would be stretched out, Jesus needed to tell Peter that it was none of his business to ask about the beloved disciple's mission (21:20–23). But in this present context the beloved disciple was not merely swifter in running; he was also more sensitive to believing the reality of the resurrection (20:8). As indicated in Excursus 15, this contrast is obviously intended to show the significance of the beloved disciple. Peter's role in early Christian tradition was firmly established as a primary witness to the resurrection (cf. Mark 16:7; Luke 24:34; 1 Cor 15:5), but that did not mean that the priority of his role was unchallenged by the Johannine community[16] or, for that matter, by Paul when in writing to the Galatians the Apostle to the Gentiles regarded Peter as following an erroneous path (cf. Gal 2:11–16).[17]

In this story, when the beloved disciple arrived at the tomb, he bent down to look into the tomb at the linen bandages.[18] The sight of those linen strips must have left an indelible impression upon his sensitive mind because they are mentioned both here and at v. 6. That sight was apparently enough to stop his progress. It is doubtful that he merely stopped to wait for Peter as Beasley-Murray suggested.[19] Body robbers leaving body wrappings? Do those ideas connect? They must have started his mind into a computing mode that ended in believing.

20:6–7 Before long, however, the slower running Peter arrived at the tomb "following" him.[20] Carson perhaps states what others have thought

---

[16] R. Smith, in *Easter Gospels* (159), seeks to distinguish the nature of priorities with respect to Peter and the beloved disciple, but in doing so he seems to play down the message of the Johannine Gospel in favor of the traditions in other NT texts. Cf. M. Moreton, "The Beloved Disciple Again," in *Text and Interpretation*, ed. E. Livingstone, StudBib 2 (Sheffield: University Press, 1980), 215–16. Contrast the report of the symposium *Peter in the New Testament*, R. Brown, K. Donfried, and J. Reumann, eds. (Minneapolis/New York: Augsburg/Paulist, 1973), 137–39. Carson, however, finds the idea that this verse could suggest "greater preeminence than Peter" for John in this verse to be "repulsive," given the model of Jesus in 13:12–17 (*John*, 637). But he has offered no explanation for such a repeated contrast between the two in the Fourth Gospel. Moreover, why is Peter not mentioned at the cross, and why is the beloved disciple given the special privilege of caring for Jesus' mother? Why, indeed, is John seen as lying in the breast/bosom of Jesus (13:23) as Jesus was in the Father's breast/bosom (*kolpos*, the only two uses of the term in the Gospel; cf. 1:18)? Carson's view is definitely truncated at this point. But his rejection of Bultmann's (*John*, 685) thesis that Peter is here representative of Jewish Christianity and John is representative of Gentile Christianity is certainly well taken (Carson, *John*, 637). I would add that Bultmann has read into John the distinction between Peter and Paul made in Gal 2:7 as well as the comparison intended by the emphasis given to Peter and Paul in Acts.

[17] See my discussion on this text in the previous footnote.

[18] See my earlier comments at 19:40 concerning the linen wrappings.

[19] Beasley-Murray, *John*, 372.

[20] C. K. Barrett posits the possibility that the use of the "following" motif, which is usually significant in John, might be used here "to subordinate Peter to the Beloved Disciple (*The Gospel According to St. John* [London: S. P. C. K., 1956], 468). Cf. also R. Smith, *Easter Gospels*, 159. But that suggestion is probably reading a little too much into the word. Cf. Brown, *John*, 2.985–86.

when he says that "true to his nature," Peter "impetuously rushed right into the tomb."[21] The reader will remember with a smile that when Peter finally recognized he needed to have his feet washed, he asked for a shower (13:8–9); but much more seriously the reader will recall that after Peter professed a willingness to lay down his life for Jesus (13:37), he denied Jesus three times (19:17–27); that in the face of the arresting band, he sliced off the ear of Malchus (18:10) but then backed down to a servant girl (18:17); and that at the sea when he learned it was the Lord on the land, he hastily jumped off the boat and sprang into the water (21:7). As one searches the Gospels, the examples continue to multiply.

While the beloved disciple paused outside the tomb to view the scene, Simon Peter entered. What Peter saw inside the tomb was intriguing because the burial wrappings were separated from the head/face covering *(soudarion)*.[22] This separation of the grave wrappings may give some reason to question the shroud theory. On the other hand, the term *soudarion* is a general word that is something like a handkerchief or facecloth.[23] How it was employed is not clearly defined in antiquity. It could have been used as a means for holding the mouth/chin closed.[24] But the Johannine idea of a separate face wrapping for Lazarus (11:44) or head covering on Jesus (20:7) seems to be slightly at odds with the shroud concept.[25]

20:8–10 Apparently the reason for the beloved disciple's hesitancy was removed when Peter went into the tomb. Accordingly, the evangelist reported that he also entered, viewed the situation, and believed.

The question has often been asked: What did he believe? That question is especially significant in view of the fact that John added a footnote in v. 9 to the effect that they still did not realize the implications of what they were witnessing in terms of the Scripture.

Bultmann concluded: "It is presupposed that Peter before him was likewise brought to faith through the sight of the empty grave." Therefore, he argued, both disciples simply left for home.[26] He then assigned the note in v. 9 to an "ecclesiastical redactor" as an unnecessary "gloss" and spiritual-

---

[21] See Carson, *John*, 637.

[22] For discussions on the wrappings see W. Reiser, "The Case of the Tidy Tomb: The Place of the Napkins in John 11:44 and 20:7," *HeyJ* 14 (1973): 47–57 and B. Osborne, "A Folded Napkin in an Empty Tomb: John 11:44 and 20:7 Again," *HeyJ* 14 (1973): 437–40.

[23] See *BAGD*, 759.

[24] Brown argues for such a use of the napkin as a kind of chin strap which enables him to maintain the view of a loose type of burial cloth such as a shroud (*John*, 2.985). Such a view, however, is hardly certain.

[25] See my extended discussion and notes on the burial clothes in connection with John 19:40.

[26] Bultmann, *John*, 684. Cf. F. Neirynck, "*Apēlthen pros heauton.* Lc 24, 12 et Jn 20, 10," *ETL* 54 (1978): 104–18. The clause in the title focuses on the Lukan text, but the idea of returning to their places is in both Gospels.

ized the story to mean that since Peter represented Jewish Christianity and the beloved disciple represented Gentile Christianity both groups would come to faith following their representatives. He also added that the story "does not signify any precedence."[27]

Hoskyns and Davey provide a solid answer to the question when they argued that the "preeminence of the faith of the Beloved Disciple is the climax of the narrative." They summarized the sense of the text when they asserted that in the case of the beloved disciple, "His faith was not derived from ancient prophetic texts; the fact of the empty tomb illuminated the sense of scripture (Ps xvi.10 ...)."[28]

Although it would be difficult to say for certain what level of believing is here envisioned, it certainly marks an example of the fact that the beloved disciple is a symbol of those who at this stage had not seen an appearance of the risen Lord and yet believed (cf. 20:29). It must be remembered that the combination of seeing and believing has been a repeated theme in John (cf. 2:23; etc.). Many had seen his signs and had failed or refused to believe (cf. 6:30; 9:38–41; 12:27; etc.). But to believe without seeing the actual reality was marked by the evangelist for special note (cf. 4:50; 9:35–36; 20:29). Accordingly, one must tend to agree with Schnackenburg that the believing was "according to the context, undoubtedly, to the full faith in the resurrection of Jesus." Moreover, he added that "any kind of diminution, with a view to v. 9, is ruled out."[29] Furthermore, it is particularly noteworthy that the beloved disciple is the only person in the Gospels who is recognized as having reached a point of believing as the result of seeing the empty tomb. Given the trauma of the crucifixion, the fear and bewilderment of most of the followers of Jesus was not allayed by the sight or reports of the empty tomb (cf. John 20:1–2; Matt 28:5; Mark 16:8; Luke 24:11,17). It took the appearances of the risen Lord himself to convince most followers that the resurrection was a reality. The beloved disciple, however, is here viewed as the model for the believing community.

This pericope ends with the brief statement that the disciples returned home. But that is not the end of the story because this pericope was inserted by the evangelist into the account of Mary Magdalene to provide perspective or give an envelope/sandwich effect to the story. The creative literary style of this presentation produces a powerful testimony especially for early readers who might have wondered about the reliability of the testimony of a

---

[27] See Bultmann, *John*, 685.

[28] Contrast Hoskyns and Davey (*The Fourth Gospel*, 540), who rely on the earlier logic of B. Westcott, *The Gospel According to St. John*, Vol. 2 (Grand Rapids: Eerdmans, 1954), 341. Cf. also Morris, *John*, 736. Cf. Luke 24:25,45.

[29] R. Schnackenburg, *The Gospel According to St. John*, Vol. 3 (New York: Crossroad, 1987), 312.

woman (women) concerning the empty tomb.[30]

For the conclusion to this envelope we turn to the next subsection.

(3) Mary Magdalene—Part 2: The First Appearance (20:11–18)

[11]but Mary stood outside the tomb crying. As she wept, she bent over to look into the tomb [12]and saw two angels in white, seated where Jesus' body had been, one at the head and the other at the foot.

[13]They asked her, "Woman, why are you crying?"

"They have taken my Lord away," she said, "and I don't know where they have put him." [14]At this, she turned around and saw Jesus standing there, but she did not realize that it was Jesus.

[15]"Woman," he said, "why are you crying? Who is it you are looking for?"

Thinking he was the gardener, she said, "Sir, if you have carried him away, tell me where you have put him, and I will get him."

[16]Jesus said to her, "Mary."

She turned toward him and cried out in Aramaic, "Rabboni!" (which means Teacher).

[17]Jesus said, "Do not hold on to me, for I have not yet returned to the Father. Go instead to my brothers and tell them, 'I am returning to my Father and your Father, to my God and your God.'"

[18]Mary Magdalene went to the disciples with the news: "I have seen the Lord!" And she told them that he had said these things to her.

It is intriguing, indeed, that John opens his appearance accounts not with well-known male disciples but with a woman at the tomb. Yet that is the point of the envelope. The evangelist wrapped the Mary Magdalene story around Peter and the beloved disciple and thus creatively focused on bringing the two stories together in such a way that he could highlight two people, the beloved disciple and Mary (a man and a woman). The beloved disciple believed without an appearance, and Mary Magdalene recognized the Lord, as will soon become evident, when her name was called (20:16). Thus, in his creative way the evangelist has continued to highlight the presence of both men and women in the company of Jesus. (For other stories of

---

[30] Luke 24:12 has a similar statement concerning the visit of Peter to the tomb and his return home in bewilderment. It has often been thought following the categorizations of Westcott and Hart that verses such as this one in Luke were to be categorized as later "Western noninterpretations," which should be omitted (cf. B. Westcott and J. Hort, *The New Testament in the Original Greek: Introduction, Appendix*, Vol. 2 [Cambridge: University Press, 1896], 175–77). As a result of this view some have argued that the Lukan text was not an independent corroboration of Peter visiting the tomb and leaving bewildered but merely an insertion from John. The discovery of Papyrus #75, however, has cast grave doubts on this thesis and strongly argues against its omission. The Lukan statement is none-the-less hardly as creatively presented. For an analysis of the textual implications see B. M. Metzger, *A Textual Commentary on the Greek New Testament* (New York: United Bible Societies, 1971), 184, 191–93.

women see the woman of Samaria, 4:7–26, and Mary and Martha, the sisters of Lazarus, 11:1–40; cf. also the story of the woman in adultery, 7:53–8:11.)[31]

In a patriarchal society where a woman's testimony to the resurrection of Jesus would not be valued highly (cf. the way women's statements were regarded in Luke 24:11,24–25; Acts 12:15), the length of this story in the evangelist's selection of materials is rather striking. It is all the more striking when one compares the accounts in John with those of the Synoptic evangelists and with Paul. It is further significant when one notes that J. Klausner categorized Mary Magdalene as "a woman who had suffered from hysterics to the verge of madness."[32] But concerning the New Testament texts themselves, it is noteworthy that Matthew and Luke focus the appearance stories on men with the exception of a brief appearance to the women that concentrates on calming them and delivering to them a message for the men while they were on their way from the tomb. They were thus basically messengers who had been experiencing mixed emotions (Matt 28:8–10). Mark records no appearances of Jesus in its truncated ending although a later editor added an ending after Mark 16:8 with a brief reconstructed account of an appearance to the women (Mark 16:9–11).[33] Paul lists a series of appearances but makes no mention of women in his list (cf. 1 Cor 15:5–9). Accordingly, the sheer length of this account is significant, and here Mary is also commissioned to carry a message to the community of believers (John 20:17), the point of which is slightly different from the brief encounter with the women in Matthew. But more of that interpretation is treated below.

20:11–12 This pericope opens with Mary once again at the tomb. When she returned is not stated, but what is noted by the evangelist is that she was "crying." The verb *klaiein* appears eight times in this Gospel, three times in the Lazarus death scene (11:31,33[2x]), once in the prediction of lament that would come to the disciples with the death of Jesus (16:20), and four times in Mary's lament here (20:11[2x],13,15). The term is used for the anguished crying or wailing associated with mourning as at funerals and

---

[31] See Borchert, *John 1–11*, 369–70.

[32] See J. Klausner, *Jesus of Nazareth*, 358. During my early years of dealing with these stories I was greatly disturbed by Klausner's evaluation of Mary Magdalene in the Johannine story since I thought it was a Jewish biased dismissal of Christianity, especially since he linked the aside in Luke 8:2 with the judgment statement of Matt 12:45 as his support for this conclusion. But I had to admit that his proof-texting method was not much different from the way many Christians join together texts and draw conclusions favorable to their own purposes. For a more balanced Jewish view see P. Lapide, *The Resurrection of Jesus: A Jewish Perspective* (Minneapolis: Augsburg, 1983).

[33] For a detailed discussion of the later Markan endings see Metzger, *A Textual Commentary*, 122–28.

in times of bereavement.[34] Morris adds that it would hardly be viewed as "a quiet, restrained shedding of tears, but the noisy lamentation typical of Easterners of that day."[35]

Obviously Mary's lament was not merely over the death of Jesus but because she was sure that the body had been violated as well. Proper burial was regarded by the Jews as an inherent part of their faith. That is the reason the heroic men of Jabesh in Gilead risked their lives to rescue and bury the bodies of Saul and his sons from the desecration to which their decapitated corpses were being subjected (1 Sam 31:8–13).

In this state of lament Mary stooped to look into the tomb,[36] and through her tears she saw an incredible sight: two angelic beings clothed in white sitting on the burial slab where Jesus previously would have been lying, one at the head position and the other at the place where the feet would have been. The presence of such mysterious visitors at the tomb is included in each of the Gospels, though not described the same way in all of them. Mark has a young man in a white robe seated at the right of the tomb (Mark 16:4); Matthew has a powerful angel in a snow white robe who appeared like lightning and who rolled away the stone and sat on it as a conqueror (Matt 28:3). Luke has two men in gleaming clothing come and stand by the women (Luke 24:4). The apocryphal *Gospel of Peter* has an expanded account of two angels escorting Jesus out of the tomb to heaven as well as a young visitor in a shining robe seated on the burial slab (36:55). Although the accounts are not identical, the point of the mysterious visitors is the same. The tomb was no longer in the hands of humans; it was at that stage enveloped in the *mystery* of God!

20:13–15 Moreover, the implication was the same: Jesus was alive! He was not in the tomb (Matt 28:7; Mark 16:6; Luke 24:5; cf. the Gospel of Peter as above). The message of the Johannine Gospel is the same except for the fact that the evangelist divides the communication of the message. In 20:13 the angels asked Mary why she was crying or wailing.[37] Then that question is followed by the "gardener" asking the same question and adding a second question which in fact is the focus of this pericope: "Who are you seeking?" (20:15). Mark and Matthew have the angelic messenger making announcements to the women, but the Lukan statement is in the form of a question concerning the women's search, after which the messengers

---

[34] See *BAGD*, 433.

[35] See Morris, *John*, 739.

[36] See the discussion in R. Collins, "The Search for Jesus: Reflections on the Fourth Gospel," *LTP* 34 (1978): 27–48.

[37] Schnackenburg thinks the "scene with the angels is secondary" because no reason is provided for Mary's turning around to see the gardener (20:14). Thus it appears as though two unrelated stories have been joined together (*St. John*, 316). But this is an unnecessary conclusion.

review Jesus' earlier statement concerning the coming crucifixion and resurrection (Luke 24:5–6).

Mary's answer to the angelic visitors was that her wailing was because
she thought the burial tomb had been violated and the body had been
removed. It seems apparent that her presence at the tomb was to get close to
the corpse as though in revering the tomb the presence of the dead person
might seem close at hand. In ministry one frequently encounters people
who have lost their spouses, parents, or children, and the grieving person
visits the tomb to "talk" to the person who is buried there. Or the bereaved
person may sit at the kitchen table and "speak" with the person who used to
sit there.

The intimacy of the statements in this Johannine pericope led the later
Gnostics to theorize that Mary Magdalene had been the consort of Jesus.[38]
That scenario, of course, is hardly biblical and is part of the sexual philosophic orientation of Gnostic thought, where the bridal chamber became the
symbol of a heavenly, pleromatic paradise.[39]

Mary's response in John to both the angelic visitors and the so-called
gardener are substantially the same with one exception. In the first case she
gives the visitors her reason for weeping: she does not know where "they"
have put the stolen body (20:13). In the second case she pleads with the
"gardener" in the general term "sir" (not implying "Lord") that if he has
taken the body, she would take care of it if he would only tell her where it
was laid.

This Johannine story contains some interesting features concerning the
angelic visitors and the nonrecognition of Jesus. Westcott suggests that "the
vision of angels makes no impression on her." He then adds that, preoccu-
pied with her own reflections, "she was typical of us who see only that for
which we have the inward power of seeing."[40] Morris thinks concerning her
not recognizing Jesus that it "is possible that tears were blurring her vision,
but tears are not usually the reason for failing to recognize someone well

---

[38] For examples of Gnostic views of Mary Magdalene see the "Gospel of Mary" in R. Grant,
ed., *Gnosticism* (New York: Harper & Brothers, 1961), 66–68, in statements such as: "Sister we
know the Savior loved you more than other women," and in contrast to Peter and the disciples it is
said "Surely the Savior loved her more than us." Cf. *The Gospel of Philip* for the concept of Mary
as companion of the Lord and the concept of the Holy Kiss for perfect conception in J. M. Robinson, *The Nag Hammadi Library* (San Francisco: Harper & Row, 1977), 134–36 text section 2.3 and
plates 55–60. But note also the intriguing idea that the Lord will turn Mary into a male in the final
saying of the *Gospel of Thomas*. See ibid., 130.

[39] For an example of the Gnostic view of the bridal chamber as the Gnostic sacrament of union
see G. Borchert, "An Analysis of the Literary Arrangement and Theological Views in the Coptic
Gnostic Gospel of Philip" (Ph.D. diss., Princeton Theological Seminary, 1967), especially at 290–
314 and 491–97. The Muslim view of heaven for the hero is similarly sexually oriented.

[40] Westcott, *St. John*, 2.343.

known to us."[41] Brown suggests that it might have been "still too dark to see clearly."[42] Beasley-Murray posits that "she assumed that at so early an hour during the Feast only the gardener would be there."[43] The possibilities of explaining the situation are almost endless. But one must at least be careful not to think one can analyze and reach clear conclusions on unstated parts of a story. One must also be careful not to attempt the psychoanalyzing of a person in a story.

The nonrecognition theme concerning the risen Lord, however, does seem to be a significant feature in the Johannine presentation of the appearance stories because such nonrecognition reports are included in the Gospel not only here but also in the story involving the miraculous catch of fish at 21:4. Luke also reports a similar phenomenon of nonrecognition in the Emmaus story (Luke 24:16; cf. 24:31). This nonrecognition theme, as U. Enyoiha has well argued, appears to have had both apologetic and evangelistic significance for the early Christians as a means of explaining their pattern of coming to faith.[44] Brown earlier had suggested that this nonrecognition may have been related to the Pauline idea of the transformation of the body when Paul discussed at some length the nature of the resurrection body (1 Cor 15:35–50).[45]

20:16 The transforming process of Mary coming to recognize the risen Lord took place when Jesus called her name, "Mary," or more precisely at this point *"Miriam."* It is fascinating to note that the Johannine evangelist has described transformative recognition occurring through the use of *one word* at this point. In the sea story it occurred when the disciples responded obediently to the stranger on the shore and cast their nets (in what seemed to be a foolish act) on the other side of the boat (21:6–7). In the Lukan Emmaus story the recognition occurred in the breaking of bread. What should be concluded from these examples is that recognition of Jesus does not need to follow a single pattern. Coming to the point of conviction that Jesus is alive is probably as varied as the nature of the people who believe.

Mary's response was immediate, for her cries of sorrow turned to a word of exclamation and personal association. The evangelist captured the interchange in two singular statements. For Jesus it was *"Miriam"*; for Mary it

---

[41] Morris, *John*, 740.

[42] R. Brown, *John*, 2.989.

[43] Beasley-Murray, *John*, 375.

[44] For a full discussion of this subject see B. U. Enyoiha, "Nonrecognition as a Motif in the Post-Resurrection Appearance Narratives" (Ph.D. diss., Southern Baptist Theological Seminary, 1985). R. Bultmann, in reflecting on this story, concluded that "it is possible for Jesus to be present, and yet for a man not to recognize him until his word goes home to him" (*John*, 686).

[45] R. Brown, *John*, 2.1009.

was "*Rabbouni*" (my dear Rabbi).[46] In his concern for Greek-speaking readers, unfamiliar with Aramaic, however, the evangelist clarified the term by adding another of his linguistic interpretive footnotes (cf. 1:41–42) to identify the term as meaning "teacher," although the Greek hardly carries the same personal impact as the Aramaic word.

20:17–18   Jesus' response in this verse is encrusted with a series of problems, which for some may resist full certainty. In an effort to gain some clarity on the issue of touching Jesus, several manuscripts (including the first hand of Sinaiticus) added an interpretive note that "she ran forward to touch him." This addition is obviously a later interpretive gloss and can be dismissed.[47]

Jesus' initial statement, *me mou haptou,* which was rendered "touch me not" in the KJV but better "do not hold on to me" in the NIV and other later versions, probably is the more natural use of a present imperative to indicate a prohibition against fastening oneself to the physical Jesus.[48] The NASB rendering "stop clinging to me" may be a little too harsh. The NLT "don't cling to me" seems to be a little more nuanced. The statement does not seem to be a rejection of touching Jesus because that would vitiate against the invitation to touch or handle him in Luke 24:39 and the invitation to Thomas to touch his hands and his side (John 20:27; cf. also the women touching his feet in worship at Matt 28:9).

The more difficult issue involves Jesus' statement concerning the fact that he had not yet ascended to the Father/God. In trying to deal with this issue some have suggested that Jesus must have ascended between the story of Mary and then returned to earth in time for the following stories involving the disciples and Thomas in order for Jesus to be touched. Such a suggestion, however, is a misunderstanding of John and is based on the translation of *haptou* as "touch" in the KJV and elsewhere.

The purpose of this ascent statement must have been to indicate to Mary that the way of relating to the resurrected Lord would no longer be through the physical senses because the ascent would terminate such encounters. Accordingly, clinging to the physical patterns of the preresurrected Lord was no longer possible. Even her efforts at revering a body in a tomb were gone because the tomb was empty.

Nevertheless, the physical reality of both the preresurrected and resur-

---

[46] The Greek is normally rendered in English "Rabboni," which in this diminutive form of the term does not imply "little" but is a term of acknowledging personally the honor due the rabbi such as "my beloved rabbi" or "my dear rabbi." See *BAGD* 733 and W. F. Albright, "Recent Discoveries in Palestine and Jerusalem" in *The Background of the New Testament and Its Eschatology* (Cambridge: Clarendon Press, 1956), 158.

[47] See Metzger, *Textual Commentary,* 255.

[48] Cf. D. Fowler, "The Meaning of 'Touch Me Not' in John 20:17," *EvQ* 47 (1975): 16–25.

rected Jesus was according to John an absolutely crucial part of the Christian confession about Jesus. Moreover, in his first epistle John makes it clear that the early Christian witnesses had heard, seen, and touched or handled this Jesus ("the Word of life"), that he unmistakably appeared to them, and that this living Jesus was the basis for eternal life (1 John 1:1–3). The physical reality of the resurrection is therefore fully asserted in the Gospels, and one must not use the Pauline appearance references as the basis for interpreting the Gospel resurrection stories as involving merely "spiritual" appearances.[49] Even Paul recognized that his experience of the risen Lord was out of the temporal pattern (1 Cor 15:8). But when John wrote the Gospel, he asserted that the physical touching and seeing of Jesus had at that time ceased on earth and that confession of Jesus had to be made without seeing or touching him, as Mary, the disciples, and Thomas had been able to do (John 20:29).

On the other hand, it is interesting to view the glorification of Jesus, which was expressed in terms of the "lifting up" of Jesus (John 3:14–15; 12:32; etc.) as not merely focused on Jesus' death but also as a return to glory in the presence of the Father (cf. 17:5). When one sees the glorification of Jesus in this perspective, Johannine theology tends to merge the resurrection and ascension into a single concept, even though it may not have been a single event as in the Lukan writings (Luke 24:50–51; Acts 1:9–11).

The story concludes in a typical biblical fashion of a theophany in which the one who receives an experience of God or the angel of the Lord is usually also given some form of commission (cf. Judg 6:25–26; Isa 6:8–13). In this case Mary was instructed to communicate to the brethren (the nascent Christian community) that the final stage of the lifting up of Jesus was being accomplished. Instead of speaking of the ascent, however, she reported to the disciples: "I have seen the Lord." Thus concludes the first appearance story in the Gospel of John. It is a detailed, fascinating story of a grieving woman whom the evangelist chooses to be the first one to report as seeing the risen Lord.

Carson concludes his analysis of this story with the note that "there is no reason to think that they [the disciples] reacted any better than they did to the women's report of the empty tomb (Luke 24:9–11),"[50] but the Johannine Gospel is not merely about an empty tomb. John may have started his account at 20:1–2 in this manner, but 20:3–10 led the beloved disciple to believing, and this story at the tomb moves the reader's attention from the tomb to the living Jesus.

---

[49] R. Fuller is an example of one who builds his view of the resurrection on Paul's experience of the resurrection (*The Formation of the Resurrection Narratives* [New York: Macmillan, 1972], 9–49). See also his note "John 20:19–23" in *Int* 32 (1978): 180–84.

[50] See Carson, *John*, 646.

Thus the evangelist has a very different focus in telling his stories. In John people become models of experiences with Jesus, and Mary is a model of someone who comes to see but at first has to react inappropriately until Jesus corrects her reaction. The Mary story has a message for every Christian. You cannot take control of Jesus! But you can acknowledge him.[51]

(4) Jesus Appears to the Disciples Behind Closed Doors in the Evening (20:19–23)

[19]On the evening of that first day of the week, when the disciples were together, with the doors locked for fear of the Jews, Jesus came and stood among them and said, "Peace be with you!" [20]After he said this, he showed them his hands and side. The disciples were overjoyed when they saw the Lord.

[21]Again Jesus said, "Peace be with you! As the Father has sent me, I am sending you." [22]And with that he breathed on them and said, "Receive the Holy Spirit. [23]If you forgive anyone his sins, they are forgiven; if you do not forgive them, they are not forgiven."

20:19–20 This story continues the unfolding of mystery. It begins with the notation that the time was evening. In other words, there was still darkness gripping the disciples. On the other hand, it was the first day of the week, the day that would become their day of rejoicing. That unbelievable day would change the way they would view everything. It was a new day for worship and remembrance. That day would become known throughout Christian history as the "Lord's Day" (cf. Rev 1:10). This remarkable day would foreshadow the coming eschatological "Day of the Lord," a day predicted in the prophets (cf. Isa 2:11–19; 11:11; 12:1,6; Jer 31:6,27–34; Ezek 34:11–12; Joel 2:1–2,11,31; Amos 5:18–20; etc.) and reaffirmed in the New Testament (cf. John 6:39–40; 12:48; Matt 24:22,36; 26:29; Rom 2:5,16; Eph 4:30; 1 Thess 5:2–4; Heb 10:25; 2 Pet 2:9; 3:10–11; Rev 6:16–17; 16:14; etc.). This first day of the week became the dividing day in history, the day when God revealed his power in an unmistakable manner.

But the disciples at this point of the story were still gripped with fear. They were still terrified that security forces would find them. After all, their enemies found Jesus at night and came after him with torches and weapons (18:3). Now they were locked in a room and undoubtedly were reviewing

---

[51] Morris reaches the conclusion that because Mary calls him her teacher, her "understanding of Jesus' person is not complete" (*John*, 741). When compared to Thomas's confession, Mary's confession here certainly expressed a lower Christology. But John's Gospel is written to encourage everyone to greater confessional positions, and one could probably even add Thomas, who confessed because he saw (cf. John's added comment at 20:28b).

their uncomfortable situation.[52] It was somewhat reminiscent of the fear they expressed when they had been up north in Galilee and Jesus told them he was going back south to Judea to wake Lazarus. It was then that Jesus gave them his sermonette on stumbling in the night and Thomas volunteered to go south and die with him (11:8–16). Fear of world forces can often seize Christians who focus not on God's power but on worldly might (cf. Acts 12:1–16).[53]

The disciples would indeed be found that night, but not by their enemies. Jesus appeared in the locked room! Readers of this story are often tempted to ponder what kind of body Jesus could have that passed through walls or doors and yet was physically present so that he could be touched (cf. not only John 20:27 but also Matt 28:9; Luke 24:39) and even eat physical food (cf. Luke 24:41–43). The Gospel writers did not and undoubtedly could not explain such a mystery. What the early followers of Jesus did was witness to what they saw and touched (cf. 1 John 1:1).

For some contemporary readers trained in scientific rationality, such testimonies may not suffice. But divine mystery can hardly be grasped fully by human minds and certainly cannot be analyzed by the computer or other mechanisms of mere humans. Apparently the brilliant apostle Paul struggled with the phenomenon of the resurrection body, and the best even he could do was to conclude that while there is a connection between mortal bodies and immortal bodies (1 Cor 15:35–36), the nature of the new body and the change is a mystery (1 Cor 15:51).

The appearance of Jesus in their midst was accompanied by the words of Jesus, "Peace be with you!"[54] Those familiar with theophanies in the Old Testament will soon recognize the various elements of a theophany/Christophany (an appearance of God or Christ) here but with a slight variation. The basic elements of a theophany are (1) fear, (2) the calming word of "peace" or "do not be afraid" from God or Christ, and (3) a word of commission for the task to be performed.[55]

---

[52] Although some scholars have proposed that the locked doors are an attempt on the part of the evangelist to prove Jesus' ability to go through locked doors, R. Brown argues properly that the reason is related to the fear that held the disillusioned disciples (*John*, 2.1020). Indeed, that is exactly what the text of 20:19 says.

[53] Note the similar fear that gripped the disciples after Herod Agrippa I killed James and seized Peter. Locked in Mark's home the disciples were praying for Peter but hardly were expecting his release (Acts 12:14), even though Peter had been miraculously released once before from prison (cf. 5:19–26). Debilitating fear often seizes Christians when they focus on the world rather than on Christ.

[54] J. Suggit, "The Eucharistic Significance of John 20:19–29," *JTSA* 16 (1976): 52–59, finds eucharistic overtones in this story.

[55] For a discussion of such theophanies in the OT see E. Thornton and G. Borchert, *The Crisis of Fear* (Nashville: Broadman, 1988), 75–80 and 87–89 and my comments in *John 1–11*, 258–59.

In most theophanic reports the fear is engendered by an appearance of the divine. In this case the fear had already gripped the followers of Jesus. What was necessary was the calming word of "Shalom!" (cf. Luke 24:36 for the same greeting). Normally the term *shalom* (Hebrew)/*Salam* (Arabic)[56] is the common Semitic greeting to others in the community. The context of a theophany, the divine appearance, was expected to strike terror in the life of a human because of the common Semitic belief that to see God would mean that one would die or be "undone" (cf. Judg 6:22–23; Isa 6:5; 8:13; cf. also Rev 1:17; Heb 10:31). To have God say "fear not" or to place a hand on the person indicated that the appearance did not bring with it judgment (cf. Rev 1:17–18).

The final element of the Christophany, the commission, is articulated in 20:21–23. But before detailing the commission, the evangelist wanted to stress for his readers that in this Christophany or appearance the risen Jesus made sure his followers understood that he was the very same Jesus (20:20) who had been their earlier Paraclete, or companion (cf. John 14:16). They needed to be sure that he was the same Jesus who was attached to the cross by nails through his hands (there is no mention of feet in John as in Luke 24:39) and that he was precisely the same Jesus who was pierced in the side by one of the soldiers (cf. John 19:34).

The disciples' reaction when they realized that Jesus was alive was obviously one of great rejoicing. The evangelist added the editorial note that their rejoicing was because "they saw the Lord."

The use of the term *kyrios* is fascinating in this Gospel. Sometimes it merely seems to mean "sir" (cf. 4:11,15,19; 5:7; 9:36). At other times it seems to be used to address Jesus as an important leader or rabbi (cf. 6:31; 11:3,12,21,27,32,39; 13:6,25,36,37; 14:5,8,22; 20:2,13). At one point Jesus accepts for himself their use of the term "Lord" (13:13–14). But as one moves through the resurrection stories, the term begins to take on a much clearer identification and has a divine confessional ring, as it appears here in 20:20 and in 21:7 (also apparently in Mary's report at 20:15). But the term reaches the confessional epitome with the formulaic announcement of Thomas in 20:28. The editorial statements of the evangelist concerning the Lord in 4:1; 6:23; 9:38; 11:2; 12:21 must therefore imply significant theological weight as well.

But in commenting on 20:20, Haenchen considers it to be an editorial insertion into the story since the verse contains the confessional "Lord."[57] My view is that if one is focused on seeking historical kernels in the Gos-

---

[56] For a discussion of the concept of peace in the OT see the discussion of G. von Rad in *TDNT*, 2.402–6. It is important to note in this context that Islam does not, as sometimes stated, mean "peace" in the usual sense of the term. It means basically "submission" to Allah.

[57] See Haenchen, *John 2*, 210–11.

pel, apart from the evangelist's confessional statements, one is in fact in pursuit of an elusive goal. From my perspective of this Gospel, it is virtually impossible to strip away the confessional elements in the story because it is like peeling an onion, since there is confession implied in every sentence and phrase of the book (cf. 20:31). Bultmann, likewise, seeks for a rationale of bewilderment to explain the need for Jesus showing his hands and side, but I submit again that his quest is an example of the Western mind-set imposing itself on the powerful, biblical story line.[58]

These verses are an assertion that the disciples' mourning for Jesus and "fear of the Jews" gave way to the surprising revelation that the very Jesus who had been crucified was indeed alive and standing in their presence. And just as he promised before his crucifixion, their weeping and mourning turned to an effervescent experience of joy (cf. 16:20). Although the appearance stories on the road to Emmaus and the meeting in Jerusalem in Luke (24:13–35,36–42) are quite different, the experience patterns in that Gospel are quite similar. A surprised identification of the physical Jesus with the risen Lord that results in an enthusiastic response at the realization that he was alive is a common characteristic of the Gospel witnesses.[59]

20:21 This verse introduces the commission associated with the Christophany. The next verse (v. 22) defines the resource for carrying out the commission, and the subsequent verse (v. 23) outlines the nature of the commission.

It is frequently asserted by scholars that the repetition of the giving of peace is an editorial addition to the source or notes the evangelist was using. Whatever may be the truth in that suggestion, it is clear that the point of the repetition was to focus the reader's attention on the fact that the commission is not to be understood in terms of a harsh assignment given by a noncaring tyrannical dictator who is unconcerned about the welfare of his slaves but only in the completion of the tasks he assigned. That is hardly the picture of either the Father or of Jesus in this Gospel. In sending Jesus, God made it eminently clear that Jesus was to be the Savior of the world (cf. 4:42). Moreover, Jesus' loving concern for his followers is repeatedly expressed in the Farewell Cycle, and his love was to be duplicated in the Christian community (cf. 13:34–35; 14:18–21; 15:12–17; 16:23–24; 17:25–26).

His "sending" (*pempō,* present tense) of his followers was to be patterned on the fact that the Father "sent" (*apestalken,* perfect tense) him. No major distinction should be made here in the use of two different verbs. The use of the perfect rather than the aorist in reference to the commission of

---

[58] Bultmann, *John,* 691.

[59] Contrast the interpretation of C. Dodd, "The Appearance of the Risen Christ: A Study in Form-Criticism of the Gospels," in *More New Testament Studies* (Grand Rapids: Eerdmans, 1968), 102–33.

Jesus should be understood to indicate that the mission of Jesus still continues and that the divine mission is not merely in mortal hands.[60]

Furthermore, there is no warrant for assuming that the "disciples" who were given the peace and likewise commissioned in this story are to be limited to "ten" (namely, the twelve less Judas and Thomas). The common words for followers of Jesus, believers and disciples, are not exclusive terms in John (cf. 2:23; 3:22; 4:1; 6:61,66; 12:42; 19:38–39). There is a great possibility that women could also have been present. R. Brown concludes that this verse "probably does reflect the commissioning of the apostles," and he adds that "an earlier understanding of 'apostle' did not confine that term to the twelve."[61] Luke is at times more specific in his designation of groups, and in another such meeting he lists those present as the eleven, women, including Jesus' mother, together with his brothers (see Acts 1:12–14).

20:22 This verse has created a good deal of concern on the part of readers of both Luke and John, since in Acts Luke assigns the experience of receiving the Spirit to Pentecost or fifty days after the Passover (Acts 2:1–3) while John in this verse links the gift of the Holy Spirit to the Easter events. Westcott argued that because there was no article attached to *pneuma hagion* this event marked a spiritual endowment given to the disciples in order to prepare them for the Pentecost event. In this way he distinguished between the work of new birth and the Spirit's work in empowering believers for ministry.[62]

Bruce considers the breathing of Jesus and the imparting of the Spirit an empowerment for ministry.[63] He rejects as "precarious" the alternative view that the lack of an article in effect depersonalizes the Spirit and turns him into a spiritual gift or endowment.[64] In John 7:39 the Spirit is also mentioned without using an article in Greek. In fact, "the Holy Spirit" is referred to over fifty times in the New Testament without the article, three of them being in John's Gospel (1:33; 14:26; 20:22).

In an extended argument Carson substantially adopts the old view of Theodore of Mopsuestia that the statement concerning the Spirit in 20:22 "is to be regarded as a symbolic promise of the gift of the Spirit later to be given." Even though Theodore's view was condemned as heretical by the

---

[60] Cf. Westcott, *St. John*, 2.349–50 and Beasley-Murray, *John*, 379–80.

[61] See Brown, *John*, 2.1022.

[62] Westcott, *St. John*, 2.350–51. J. Calvin developed a somewhat similar idea in which he argued that the disciples were sprinkled with the Spirit at this stage and at Pentecost were filled with the Spirit (*The Gospel According to St. John* [London: Oliver & Boyd, 1961], 2.204–5). Contrast these views with the radically opposite perspective of F. Beare, "The Risen Jesus Bestows the Spirit: A Study of John 20:19–23," *CJT* 4 (1958): 95–100.

[63] F. F. Bruce, *The Gospel of John* (Grand Rapids: Eerdmans, 1983), 392.

[64] Cf. G. Johnston, *The Spirit Paraclete in the Gospel of John* (Cambridge: University Press, 1970), 11, who depersonalizes the Spirit when it is anarthrous.

Council of Constantinople (A.D. 553), Carson argues for this view because it harmonizes John and Acts.[65]

From my perspective, however, the arguments offered by Beasley-Murray and Burge are to be preferred because they fit more faithfully into the style and logic of the writings by the Johannine evangelist.[66] As I indicated in connection with the discussion on the cleansing of the Temple pericope and the resurrection perspective throughout the Gospel, the evangelist views the life of Jesus as a whole. Therefore chronological sequences are not of primary concern to him.

Accordingly, he can speak of the next day in three successive pericopes (1:29,35,43) and then move immediately in the next pericope to speak of "on the third day" (2:1). But the point of the third day is not primarily a reference to sequence. It is, rather, the theological significance as the beginning of Jesus' signs and the fact that the third day is the preferred day for Jewish weddings because of its attachment to the God of creation and the double blessing associated with that day (Gen 1:9–13).

John viewed the resurrection, the gift of the Spirit, and the ascension of Jesus as a unified event. Does that mean it is impossible to harmonize/reconcile the Johannine and Lukan (Acts) texts, as Barrett has stated?[67] Or does it mean that the Johannine writer played loose with history or created the stories to suit his own purposes or was polemicizing against Acts, as J. Koehler argued?[68] The answer to these questions must be a resounding no!

To view events holistically means that the story is told in such a way that the end is already part of the beginning. That also means that time sequences are not as important as meaning sequences, and it certainly does not imply that if someone writes in this manner he is polemicizing against someone who writes sequentially or that he creates the stories to provide the meanings. For example, simply because John places the cleansing in chap. 2 does not mean he is polemicizing against the late position of the cleansing in the Synoptics. Neither does it mean that he has created a second cleansing at the beginning of Jesus' ministry, something that is done by many Christians today. There is only one cleansing in any Gospel, but John uses the cleansing at the beginning of his Gospel to indicate the concluding

---

[65] Carson concludes his detailed exegetical argument by drawing an example from a similar pattern in the Azusa Street Meetings, which gave impetus to the contemporary Pentecostal/ Charismatic movement (*John*, 651–55).

[66] Cf. Beasley-Murray, *John*, 380–82 and G. Burge, *The Anointed Community: The Holy Spirit in the Johannine Tradition* (Grand Rapids: Eerdmans, 1987), 114–49. Cf. also G. Johnston, *The Spirit-Paraclete in the Gospel of John* (New York: Cambridge University Press, 1970), 49–51.

[67] See Barrett, *St. John*, 475.

[68] See Bultmann, *John*, 692–93 and J. Koehler, *Erfücht von dem Leben*, 75–76.

situation from the beginning.

The same can be said of the giving of the Spirit and commissioning of the disciples. There is only one giving of the Spirit. It can be described from various points of view. Indeed, John described the promise of the coming Spirit in various ways in chaps. 14–16. Yet the one thing that becomes absolutely clear is that the Spirit is not merely given by the Father but also by the Son. That idea of a joint procession or sending is a major assertion of the Fourth Gospel, and if there is any polemicizing going on in that statement, it is not against Acts; it is against those who deny the Son's role in the coming of the Spirit. Obviously there were theologians and preachers around in John's day who were already developing strange ideas concerning Jesus, as is evident in our first epistle of John. John was totally unwilling to accept any reduction of Jesus as equal to God (John 10:30; 5:18; 1 John 4:14; 5:20) or as God who had truly come in the flesh (John 1:1,14; 1 John 4:1–3). It is Jesus, indeed, in union with God who has sent the Spirit (John 15:26).

So, just as God, who in Gen 2:7 (cf. also Ezek 37:9) breathed into man the breath of life and he became a "living being" *(nephesh hayyah),* Jesus also breathed into his followers the new breath and let the Spirit loose among his followers so that they might be empowered to do his will.

20:23 This verse focuses on the commission of the risen Jesus concerning the forgiving and retaining of sins. As a result it has also been the subject of considerable debate. At the outset it should be emphasized that the overall contextual framework undoubtedly involves the followers of Jesus in their mission and evangelistic task within the hostile world. Forgiveness of sins is directed to a right relation or standing with God, a concern that in the Pauline letters would be called to justification, as for example in Rom 3:21–5:11. Accordingly, it is imperative to recognize that while Christians are involved in mission, it is God who ultimately does the forgiving.

Christians who are thus involved in the forgiveness of sins do so as agents of the Holy Spirit and never as independent actors in this process. It is equally important to recognize that the Gospel of John, like the first epistle, is addressed to the church (the Christian community) and not simply to individuals. Moreover, it is extremely difficult to agree with R. Brown when he said that "the power to absolve and to hold men's sins is explicitly given to (ten of) the twelve in 20:23."[69] Morris is quite correct when he says he finds no evidence for such a limitation to the ten.[70]

---

[69] Cf. R. Brown, "The Kerygma of the Gospel According the John: The Johannine View of Jesus in Modern Studies," *Int* 21 (1967): 391.

[70] Cf. Morris, *John,* 748–49.

Now the concept of forgiveness and retention of sins is not unrelated to the binding and loosing texts of Matt 16:19; 18:18, which must be understood in the context of rabbinic legal thought as the obligation to communicate correctly the requirements of the law so that those who are obedient to God's will would be accepted, and those who are disobedient would be judged. The obligation on the part of the rabbis was very weighty because the people's well-being was clearly at stake. But to carry the point further, the terms are patently legal terms that also relate to a judge's task of discerning legitimacy or illegitimacy of given patterns of behavior. The Semitic style of stating issues in clearly defined opposites is evident in both the Johannine and Matthean texts.[71]

Thus one could say that Jesus' followers are to make the Gospel so clear that it is evident where people stand on the nature of sin. When these texts are understood in this perspective, it should become clear that Jesus' commission to his followers is not one of privileged judgment but of weighty responsibility to represent the will of God in Christ with extreme faithfulness and to be honest and authentic about their evaluations or judgments.

With these basic remarks in mind, several comments can be made. It is obvious that this verse contains a two-sided condition. The use of the perfect tenses in the two apodoses (concluding parts of the conditions) have essentially the same meaning as the present and future."[72] Thus the argument of J. Mantey that these perfects were simply to be understood as past events and his thesis that the variant readings in the present and future were later priestly scribal attempts to sacramentalize the texts is really wrongly conceived.[73]

Moreover, the focus is, as Barclay notes, not on giving individuals the power to forgive sins" but rather on the church's duty "to proclaim that forgiveness" and "to warn the impenitent that they are forfeiting the mercy of God."[74] From these verses the Roman Catholic church developed the sacrament of penance from which most Protestants shrink in horror.[75] In spite of such revulsion on the part of Protestants to the sacramental nature of pen-

---

[71] See A. Schlatter, *Der Evangelist Mattäus* (Stuttgart: Calwer Verlag, 1948), 511 and J. Jeremias, *New Testament Theology* (New York: Scribner, 1971), 23. Cf. Beasley-Murray, *John*, 383.

[72] Newman and Nida, *Translator's Handbook*, 615–16.

[73] See J. Mantey, "The Mistranslation of the Perfect Tense in John 20:23; Matt 16:19 and Matt 18:18," *JBL* 58 (1939): 243–49. See also the critique of H. Cadbury, "The Meaning of John 20:23; Matt 16:19 and Matt 18:18," *JBL* (1939): 251–54. Conditional sentences do not follow the pattern of purely temporal models, but in any case a perfect has a present continuing sense built within it. For a discussion of the variants see Metzger, *Textual Commentary*, 255.

[74] W. Barclay, *The Gospel of John* (Philadelphia: Westminster, 1956), 2.319.

[75] Cf. Martin Luther's forceful statements against the sacrament of penance in his Ninety-Five Theses of 1517 in H. Bettenson, *Documents of the Christian Church* (London: Oxford University Press, 1956), 260–68.

ance, however, there needs to be a recognition of the significant role that declarations of forgiveness can have in freeing people to set aside their past sins and feelings of guilt and turn their attention to the joy of living with the risen Christ under the direction of the Holy Spirit.

(5) The Thomas Story in Two Parts (20:24–29)

[24]Now Thomas (called Didymus), one of the Twelve, was not with the disciples when Jesus came. [25]So the other disciples told him, "We have seen the Lord!"

But he said to them, "Unless I see the nail marks in his hands and put my finger where the nails were, and put my hand into his side, I will not believe it."

[26]A week later his disciples were in the house again, and Thomas was with them. Though the doors were locked, Jesus came and stood among them and said, "Peace be with you!" [27]Then he said to Thomas, "Put your finger here; see my hands. Reach out your hand and put it into my side. Stop doubting and believe."

[28]Thomas said to him, "My Lord and my God!"

[29]Then Jesus told him, "Because you have seen me, you have believed; blessed are those who have not seen and yet have believed."

20:24 It now becomes clear that one of the Twelve—Thomas, the twin—was not at the empowering commissioning meeting with the risen Lord. Newman and Nida suggest that this statement indicates the size of the group (20:19), but such a conclusion is unwarranted. The statement merely indicates that one of the Twelve had been noticeably absent.[76]

Excursus 28: The Twelve

The designation "the Twelve" was obviously viewed as a technical term for Jesus' close group of followers and was undoubtedly understood to stand in parallelism to the expression the twelve sons of Jacob/Israel, the designation for the people of God. In Rev 21:12–13 these two groups are placed in parallel, but it is significant to note there that in a surprising statement the apostles are designated as the foundations of the walls and not the gates. Clearly the concept of the people of God in the Apocalypse was being reinterpreted in light of the coming of Jesus. Accordingly, the twelve tribes are listed as beginning with Judah rather than Reuben, and other adjustments are likewise made, including the omission of Dan, the deviant (Rev 7:4–8; cf. Gen 49:17; 18:30–31).

It is important to recognize that Judas, like Dan, who was replaced in the Apocalypse text, was replaced by the early assembly of the believers in Acts 1:15–26. Judas was replaced not because he died in a kind of successionist pattern but because he was unworthy. When James, the brother of John, was killed, he was not replaced (cf. Acts 12:2). The Twelve are historic standard bearers, symbolic representatives of the new people of God. The whole people of God are their successors.

---

[76]Newman and Nida, *Translator's Handbook*, 617.

20:24 (Cont.)   Thomas has often been vilified by Christians because of his early doubts expressed in these verses. But throughout this Gospel he has been presented as a realist, a person who evaluated situations on the basis of what he could perceive. He understood the dangers of going south to Judea (11:16), and he wanted more than words in order to follow Jesus to his place of preparation (14:5). But he was willing to take risks for Jesus (11:16), and in these verses he is also capable of reaching magnificent conclusions. Thomas is not merely a pathetic doubter. He is a paradigm of many Christians who are capable of great possibilities as well as hesitations in faith.

Bernard's categorization of Thomas as a "pessimist," which led to his absence from the meeting because "such gatherings were futile," is a bold assumption.[77] Moreover, the homiletical suggestion that since Thomas is called a twin, it symbolically represents his double-mindedness must be judged irresponsible exegesis.[78] I therefore appeal to the reader to reflect on the insights of Thomas in connection with these verses and see the message in them from Jesus to contemporary people.

20:25   The disciples who had experienced the surprising appearance of Jesus and his empowering commissioning were apparently enthusiastically ready to share the details of their postresurrection experience of "the Lord." But like many of us who have experienced the marvel of transforming grace and are desirous of sharing it, these disciples were met with a cold, skeptical face. Thomas had not been at the meeting, and he had no immediate sense of the significance of the miracle that had occurred, an event that had begun to change the course of history and would soon change his life as well.

His only reaction at that in-between state was the human tendency to demand proof of such an incredible fact. His demand was for some assurance to connect in a reliable manner the physical Jesus of the crucifixion (his hands and his side) with the experience of the other disciples. After all, that is what they said they had been able to do (cf. 20:20). Therefore Thomas's demand was to have virtually the same experience that they had received, only in his case he wanted to "shove" *(balō)* his finger into the place or holes made by the nails and likewise to "shove" his hand into Jesus' side where the spear had been stuck. These were his nonnegotiable bases for accepting the reversing of his mind on that event. Unless he had such physical proof, he stated, "I will not believe [what you are saying]." Although this statement of Thomas may seem to be quite obstinate, there is a sense in which contemporary believers ought to thank God that someone

---

[77] Bernard, *St. John*, 681.

[78] Cf. the critique of Brown, *John*, 2. 1024 in respect to such thinking.

like Thomas was there to do the reality check for us.

20:26 The next Lord's Day, or as John says (lit.) "eight days later" (according to ancient reckoning, which began counting with the current day),[79] Thomas was also present in the community meeting. The liturgical emphasis on meeting the first day of each week is obviously in focus (one week after the previous first day of the week, 20:19).

The doors were once again shut tight. The early readers of John's Gospel must have clearly felt a kinship with the first believers since they also were a marked group of people, excluded from synagogues and undoubtedly seized and imprisoned, like the seer of Revelation, who was sent to the prison island of Patmos (Rev 1:9).

Into this community meeting Jesus once again made his appearance. Bernard argued that Jesus was "expected" to reappear at this meeting,[80] but I find his view to be unconvincing. With the many years intervening between the death and resurrection of Jesus and the later community of John, one can easily agree that in the later time the Lord's Day was regarded as the regular time for meeting the Lord in a church assembly. But could such a possibility have been an expectation of the first believers? I very much doubt it. The fear and surprise probably were similar among the group to that of the earlier appearance experience (20:19–20). Besides, the address of "peace" is most likely again included to indicate the presence of another Christophany. What can be said is that these addresses of "peace" undoubtedly gave rise to the development of the "giving of peace" in the later liturgy of the Lord's Supper or Eucharist.[81]

20:27 As R. Smith has noted, this pericope highlights "the gracious condescension of the resurrected one who will not be hindered or put off" by human demands. Jesus' response is to give Thomas what he in his humanness required "point for point."[82] Schnackenburg compares this story at the end of the Gospel to the Nathaniel story in the first chapter. In both cases the result is a powerful confession from both.[83] In the Nathaniel story, however, Jesus informs the confessor that he will take the novice far beyond mere Jewish expectations of the coming of the Messiah (John 1:50–51). In the closing response of Jesus to Thomas he will likewise take this novice disciple far beyond his human demands to a new view of believing.

It is most probable then that when Thomas made his demand for proof,

---

[79] But note that the *Epistle of Barnabas* (15:9) has a celebration on the eighth day. Cf. also Ignatius, *Magn.* 9.1 for the Lord's Day as the resurrection day, the eighth day. For a further discussion see Schnackenburg, *St. John*, 3.331.

[80] See Bernard, *St. John*, 2.682.

[81] Cf. *Did* 14:1. Note that Acts 20:7 links the breaking of bread with the first day of the week.

[82] See R. Smith, *Easter Gospels*, 169.

[83] Schnackenburg, *St. John*, 3.333.

he hardly expected to have his material proof met. Similarly, when the early church prayed for Peter's release from prison, their reaction to the report of Rhoda (Rose) clearly indicates their doubts about their own prayers (Acts 12:13–15). These stories indicate that what often is viewed as believing and praying is, in fact, not much more than human wishful thinking.

This story is particularly captivating. Imagine for a moment Thomas the realist coming to the community meeting on Sunday after having made his firm demands. Into that meeting Jesus materialized. Then, having given the "Peace," Jesus looked around and his eyes fastened on Thomas. Then he said something like: "Hello, Thomas! Fancy meeting you here." After Thomas had taken a big gulp, Jesus continued, "Oh, Thomas, I think I heard you say something this past week about needing to touch my hands and my side." After a brief but interminable pause, Jesus continued. "Well, come here Thomas and bring your finger!" By this time Thomas was almost completely undone (to use an expression from Isaiah 6). But Jesus continued. "No, Thomas, put your finger right here!" "And now your hand, Thomas, put it right here in my side."[84] Can you feel the churning that must have gone on in the whole psyche of this early disciple? Authentic believing was the issue. Thomas was now prepared to make his unforgettable declaration. But Jesus was also prepared to set the parameters of his requirements for believing.

20:28 Thomas's response forms the high point of confession in the Gospel. What it does is bring the Gospel full circle from the Prologue, where it is emphatically said that the "Word was God" (1:1) to this confession, "My Lord and my God."[85] In the process of writing this Gospel the evangelist has proclaimed that Jesus was active in creation (1:2), the Word who became incarnate/enfleshed (1:14), the sin-bearing Lamb of God (1:29,36), the Messiah (1:41; 4:25–26), the Son of God (1:48), the King of Israel (1:48), the new Temple (2:19–21), a teacher sent from God (3:2), a

---

[84] K. Kastner argued that the fact that Jesus told Thomas to touch his side meant that Jesus was naked ("Noli me tangere," *BZ* 13 [1915]: 344–53). This speculation has led to some other intriguing theories, but such ideas are purely hypothetical constructs about the bodily resurrection appearances of Jesus. Bultmann (*John*, 695–96) argues that the touching of Jesus was purposeful and led to Thomas's believing. Thus he turns the "and" *(kai)* before "stop doubting," which is not translated in the NIV, into a purpose conjunction. Brown (*John*, 2.1026) argues that "if Thomas had accepted the invitation to examine and touch him, Thomas would not have been a believer." I find little support for either conclusion since the first view is reconstructive and the second is at best an argument from silence. To see Jesus is at least the first stage of examination. But why Brown negates the explicit instructions of Jesus by his firm argument the other way is for me a bewildering, unnecessary conclusion.

[85] For an interesting commentary on this exclamation from a historical comparison see B. Mastin, "The Imperial Cult and the Ascription of the Title *theos* to Jesus (John 20, 28)," *SE* 6 (1973): 352–65.

new symbol of God's power exhibited through Moses (3:14), the evidence
of the love of God (3:16), the Savior of the World (4:42), equal with God
(5:18), the authority in judgment (5:27), the agent of God (5:30), the fulfillment of Scripture (5:39), the expected prophet (6:14), the "I am" (6:35,
etc.), the supplier of living water (7:38), the one who was from God (9:31–
33), the Son of Man (9:35), the consecrated/Holy one (10:36), the lifted up
one (4:14; 12:32–34), the glorified one (13:31), the preparer of his followers' destiny (14:2), the nonabandoning one (14:18), the one in whom we
must abide and who is the basis for the fruitfulness of his followers (15:5–
7), the sender of the Paraclete (15:26), the bearer of truth (18:37), the crucified King (19:15), the risen Lord (20:20) *and God* (20:26). The list can be
expanded greatly, but the point is that when this list is compared to the designations of Jesus in the Synoptic Gospels, the other presentations of Jesus
pale in significance before these magnificent confessions about him in John.
In the years of contemplating the significance of Jesus, the Johannine evangelist in the context of that early community has supplied for the church of
all ages a truly masterful statement about Jesus—Jesus is indeed Lord and
God![86]

Although the statement in 1:1 is nonarticular (does not have an article
before God, *theos*), here in 20:28 both words Lord and God have articles in
addition to the possessive pronoun "my" *(mou)*. Interpreters, however, are
advised against seeking to make a distinction in the statements or to reduce
the import of the first statement, as I indicated in my earlier commentary.[87]
Both statements carry a similar theological force. Neither should interpreters seek to reduce the high Christology of the present text by following
some sort of slippery logic like that of Theodore of Mopsuestia, who
claimed that Thomas was exclaiming a praise to God rather than speaking
to Jesus. As I indicated earlier, his views were forcefully condemned by the
fifth ecumenical council at Constantinople in A.D. 553.[88]

The confession of Thomas is not unlike the attribution to "my God and
my Lord" in Ps 34:23 and to a lesser extent is somewhat similar to Pss 29:3
and 86:15. But more pointedly it also touches directly upon the daily Jewish reciting of the *Shema*, "Hear, O Israel, the Lord our God, the Lord is
one" (Deut 6:4). The early Christians thus claimed for Jesus attributes akin
to Yahweh, the God of the Old Testament. To suggest that such a confession
might go unnoticed by the Jews would be highly naive. Moreover, since the
Roman Emperors took to themselves designations of divinity, it meant that

---

[86] K. Matsunaga, "The 'Theos' Christology as the Ultimate Confession of the Fourth Gospel,"
AJBI (1981): 125–28.

[87] See Borchert, *John 1–11*, 103–4.

[88] See *Enchiridion Symbolorum*, ed. H. Denzinger and C. Bannwart, rev. A Schönmetzer
(Freiburg: Herder, 1963), 434. Cf. Brown, *John*, 2.1026.

the early Christians were caught in a grip between two hostile forces. Indeed, Suetonius, the Roman historian, reports that Domitian claimed the title *"Dominus et Deus noster"* ("Our Lord and God," *Dom.* 13).[89] This confession epitomizes the highest declaration Christians could make concerning Jesus and brought them into a direct challenge with their contemporaries.

20:29   But the evangelist was unwilling to conclude this pericope with the climactic confession of Thomas. He was writing to a community who had never seen the risen Lord and whose witnesses to the historical presence of Jesus had for the most part died or were about to die. Therefore there was one last part of the exchange between Thomas and the risen Jesus that needed to be communicated. It was in the form of both a rhetorical question and a concluding beatitude.

Although many translators and commentators tend to view this initial statement as a rebuke,[90] Carson's view is a more adequate evaluation, namely, that Jesus' first remark was to be understood as a question.[91] But I would add that it is rhetorical in nature. Of course, Thomas had seen him. Indeed, he may have also touched the old wounds because John in the first epistle alludes to the disciples' both seeing and touching Jesus (1 John 1:1). But this question, rather than being a rebuke of Thomas, provides the evangelist with the opportunity to call for believing that is not based on sight or touch but on the message of the witnesses. The Gospel and this pericope itself is intended to engender such believing that is parallel to that of the early witnesses without the benefit of tangible evidences.

To this rhetorical question the evangelist added that Jesus pronounced a beatitude upon those who were able to believe without such first-hand support or proof. The term *makarios* (blessed), which is the sign of a beatitude, appears in only one other place in John where the precrucified Jesus bestows a blessing upon those who know or experience what he means (13:17).

As in the case of the Matthean and Lukan beatitudes (cf. Matt 5:3–12; Luke 6:20–23) the biblical beatitudes imply that the benefit accrues to those who meet the conditions. The Synoptic beatitudes are rather intriguing because they present a set of conditions that are usually rejected by the world. Accordingly, one might get the point much better if he renders *makarios* in those texts as "congratulations!" rather than merely saying "happy." For example, the world despises being poor, but Jesus says "congratulations" and then he proceeds to tell them why.

---

[89] For further references see W. Foerster, *TDNT*, 3.1054–58.

[90] Cf. the KJV, RV, NEB, NIV, NLT, etc. Cf. also Beasley-Murray, *John*, 386; R. Brown, *John*, 2.1019; etc.

[91] See Carson, *John*, 659. Cf. also the RSV.

In many biblical examples of the beatitudes, however, the concluding bestowal is left unstated or remains a generalized blessing. In Rev 1:3 the reader and listeners of the community are to be blessed if they participate in the joint reading of that book. Similarly, those who participate in the first resurrection are blessed, but in this case it states that they do not need to be concerned about judgment (Rev 20:6). In the present case the blessing remains generalized, but it is assumed that believing without tangible support will be rewarded.[92] A similar idea is expressed in the introduction to 1 Peter at 1:8–9, which states that although the believers "have not seen him," because they love and believe in him they "are filled with an inexpressible and glorious joy" and receive their goal, which is "the salvation of [their] souls."

This beatitude is both a striking challenge and a powerful promise of divine blessing upon our authentic lives as believers who wait for the coming *eschaton* to witness first hand the unseen reality of the risen Lord Jesus.

(6) The Main Purpose Statement of the Gospel and the Initial Conclusion (20:30–31)

[30]Jesus did many other miraculous signs in the presence of his disciples, which are not recorded in this book. [31]But these are written that you may believe that Jesus is the Christ, the Son of God, and that by believing you may have life in his name.

When Loisy reached this stage in commenting on the Gospel, he penned these unforgettable words: *"Le Livere est fini, tres bien fini!"*[93] Although the statement can be rendered in English as "the book is complete (or finished), very well finished!" it hardly carries the grand force of the French words. Finished was the original plan, and what a finish![94]

---

[92] Commentators often quote a Midrashic statement in *Str-B*, 2.586 from a third century (A.D.) Rabbi Simeon ben Lakish. He praises the proselyte as being dearer to God than all the people of Israel at Sinai who witnessed the powerful acts of God because although the proselyte has seen none of these wonders, yet he gives himself to God and regards his rule as authority. There are, of course, some similarities in this later rabbinic statement with the earlier Johannine text, yet Jesus does not play down Thomas's believing as the rabbinic statement does of the Sinai witnesses. But Jesus uses Thomas's experience to challenge future believers to a new perspective on believing.

[93] A. Loisy, *Le quatrième evangile* (Paris: Emile Nourrey, 1921), 514.

[94] I do not find acceptable the argument of those few who think chap. 21 was not originally intended to be part of the Gospel and who, like M. J. Lagrange (*Évangele selon Saint Jean* [Paris: Gabalda, 1948], 520) displace these two verses to a point in chap. 21 after v. 24. Cf. also L. Vaganay, "La finale du quatrième Evagile," *RB* 45 (1936): 512–28, who places these verses after 21:23. There is absolutely no textual warrant for such displacements. Instead, I agree with Westcott (*St. John*, 2.359) that chap. 21 was written by the same evangelist as an afterthought. It is like a postscript (ps.) in a modern letter. But, as far as we know textually, the first twenty chapters never circulated without chap. 21.

These twenty chapters of John are a masterpiece of literary construction. They are artistically designed like a symphony yet pointedly focused; simplistically worded for the reader yet intensely complex in meaning; and dramatically engaging in the stories yet very deliberate in the speech presentation. The Gospel is a marvel of inspired writing. And its concluding two verses sum up its purpose in what has to be one of the great classic summations of biblical literature.[95] Although the evangelist acknowledged that much had been left untold, the reader would have to be exceedingly dense if he or she were unable to perceive the point of the work.

20:30–31 This statement is both pithy in expression and exceedingly precise in meaning. As might be expected of such a concise statement, several of the phrases are not the more typical expressions of the Johannine evangelist. Indeed, a number of writers have recognized that a couple of the phrases are more akin to Luke than John, but most are hesitant to see the Lukan hand here.[96]

Other scholars see the use of "signs" here as one indication that the statement originally was part of an earlier Signs Source.[97] Indeed, Bultmann found such an idea attractive because of his view that signs involved almost every aspect of the Gospel.[98] But while some scholars may lean toward accepting a Signs Source for part of the Gospel, few would accept Bultmann's broadening of the meaning of *sēmeia* (signs).

The issue comes down to whether one thinks that the "many other signs" stated in 20:30 has a meaning akin only to the signs recorded in chaps. 2–11 or whether the evangelist included in his view of signs the crucifixion and resurrection, which constitute a major portion of the last part of the Gospel. Most scholars would tend to limit the concept of signs to acts of power that point beyond themselves to who Jesus is. But while I do not agree with Bultmann that the signs include the words of Jesus, in contrast to Brown and Beasley-Murray[99] I am of the opinion that signs may have

---

[95] There are certainly other similar concluding statements such as *Sir* 13:28 and *1 Macc* 9:22, but these are merely summary statements and lack the depth of this Johannine conclusion.

[96] Cf. M. Boismard and H. Lamouille, *L'Evangile de Jean* (Paris: Cerf, 1977), 1033 and H. Boismard, "Saint Luc et la rédaction du Quatrième Evangile," *RB* 69 (1962): 200–203, who consider that Luke wrote these verses. This view has not been accepted by most scholars, even though they would recognize some kinship with Lukan style. Among the similarities to a Lukan style are the expressions μεν ουν, which can be rendered "now" or simply left untranslated, and ενωπιον, which means "in the presence of." But this later term is also used in the Book of Revelation as well as in the first epistle (1 John 3:22).

[97] For the most complete discussion of the Signs Source see R. Fortna's expanded treatment, *The Fourth Gospel and Its Predecessor* (Philadelphia: Fortress, 1988). For my discussion on sources see Borchert, *John 1–11*, 42–50.

[98] See Bultmann, *John*, 698.

[99] See Brown, *John*, 2.1058–59 and Beasley-Murray, *John*, 387. But contrast their view with Carson, *John*, 661.

included other pointers to Jesus as well. Indeed, in his answer to the Jews when they requested a sign at the cleansing of the Temple, Jesus responded by speaking of his body (2:18–21). I suspect it was texts like this one that convinced R. Lightfoot and C. Barrett to view the crucifixion and resurrection as a sign.[100]

It is certainly not difficult to realize that Jesus must have provided other signs than those presented in the Johannine Gospel. Clearly this Gospel contains a small portion of the acts and works of Jesus contained in the Synoptic Gospels.[101]

But in spite of a different pattern in the selection of materials for inclusion, the Johannine evangelist has made it eminently clear in 20:30 why he chose to include those pericopes. As I indicated in my Introduction, the purpose for writing this Gospel was not meant to be "a mere academic exercise." The selection was clearly made with a view to engendering a life-transforming response.[102] Thus the purpose can be interpreted as both evangelistic and instructional in nature.[103] It can be viewed as focused on both those within the community who need to have a more dynamic life of believing (or to use the Pauline term "faith") and on those outside the community who need to be persuaded and discover for themselves the genuineness of Christian life in Jesus.

But transformation of life for the evangelist is not based on mere acceptance of creedal formulations.[104] That is the reason the evangelist completely avoided the use of the nouns for faith *(pistis)* and knowledge *(gnōsis)*. Instead, his summary again contains only the verbal form for believing. Thus nothing less than a dynamic believing in the person of Jesus, who is both Christ and Son of God in the highest meaning of those terms, will be adequate for John. Moreover, nothing less than genuine believing that issues in life transformation will satisfy the evangelist's goal for writing this Gospel.

With such an initial summation this work of John reaches its powerful conclusion. The evangelist has indeed achieved his desire of presenting a captivating picture of the divine Word become flesh (1:14) so that humanity

---

[100] See R. H. Lightfoot, *St. John's Gospel* (Oxford: University Press, 1956), 336. Cf. Barrett, *St. John*, 65, who does not merely call them a sign but the "supreme sign."

[101] All one has to do in order to realize how few stories overlap between John and the Synoptics is to study a copy of parallel texts in the Gospels. In particular, of those stories frequently designated as powerful acts of Jesus, when one excludes the passion and resurrection narrative, only the feeding of the five thousand and the walking on the water in John are to be regarded as overlapping stories.

[102] See Borchert, *John 1–11*, 30–31.

[103] Ibid.

[104] Contrast the theological emphasis in E. Groenewald, "The Christological Meaning of John 30:31," *Neot* 2 (1968): 131–40.

could behold the glory of the Father's/God's only Son (1:14,18). And from the incredible *plerōma* (fullness) of this Son we all have become the recipients of overwhelming grace (1:16).

2. The Epilogue (21:1–25)

As I indicated in the conclusion of chap. 20, the original intention of the evangelist for writing the Gospel was brilliantly concluded with the gripping story of Thomas and the classic summation in 20:30–31. The work was magnificently finished.

What, then, is to be said of the presence in this Gospel of this chapter, which I, along with many other commentators, have designated as an Epilogue? A number of alternative terms could be used, such as appendix, postscript, or addendum, but I prefer the term epilogue. It is imperative, however, to understand that various commentators imply different things by the use of the term. R. Smith, for instance, sees the chapter as a collection of disparate pieces of tradition woven together by a single editorial hand.[105] Beasley-Murray, Bultmann, Brown, Schnackenburg, and others view the chapter as the work of a Johannine ecclesiastical redactor.[106] Boismard removes it entirely from the Johannine tradition and attributes it to Luke.[107] Carson, on the other hand, sees the work as originally intended to be part of the Gospel like the Prologue.[108] But he does not go as far as Lagrange in restructuring the text so that 20:30–31 stood after 21:23.[109]

I prefer Westcott's view that the epilogue was written after the Gospel was completed, basically by the same hand,[110] with the exception of the authentication by the community (21:24). I would, however, not be greatly surprised if the evangelist was supported or assisted in this effort by others in the community, just as I think there is some evidence of such assistance in a text like 19:35.[111]

But what was the reason for this Epilogue? It seems clear that some matters were left unsaid that really had to be treated. Among those matters was

---

[105] See R. Smith, *Easter Gospels*, 171–76.

[106] See, for example, Beasley-Murray, *John*, 395–96; Bultmann, *John*, 700–701; R. Brown, *John*, 2.1080; Schnackenburg, *St. John*, 3.341–45.

[107] M. Boismard, "Le chapitre xxi de saint Jean: essai de critique littéraire," *RB* 54 (1947): 473–501.

[108] Carson, *John*, 665–68.

[109] Lagrange, *Saint Jean*, 502.

[110] Westcott, *St. John*, 2.359–60.

[111] The presence of texts like 19:35 and 21:24 were undoubtedly the underlying reason that R. A. Culpepper proposed his view of a Johannine school in his dissertation. See his work, *The Johannine School: An Evaluation of the Johannine School Hypothesis Based on an Investigation of the Nature of Ancient Schools* (Missoula, Mont.: Scholars Press, 1975).

the role of Peter. He had been clearly marked in the Gospel as one who denied Jesus, and although he was a part of the resurrection stories, chap. 20 hardly provided a sufficient rationale for his prominence within the other parts of the church beyond the Johannine community. Accordingly, Peter needed to be restored to prominence in this Gospel, but not so as to eclipse the importance of the beloved disciple. Chapter 21 thus supplies such a restoration of Peter.

Another reason for the need of this chapter was to explain to the community that in spite of their having the witness of the beloved disciple, he would not forever be present to lead them. So in order to make clear to the community that he would not be around indefinitely as their resource, this chapter indicates that they probably had not been surprised at the death of the early disciples, including the martyrdom of Peter. The reason is that Jesus had already predicted the death of Peter. Likewise, therefore, they should also not have expected that their beloved disciple would continue endlessly in their midst. Any such notion was a wrong conclusion from Jesus' relationship to him. Disciples, even the most revered of them, are only human beings and subject to death. Furthermore, they needed to realize that the *eschaton* and the coming of Jesus was not something in their control or subject to the time span of their lifetimes.

This Epilogue was thus a necessity to ensure that misunderstandings and misconceptions in the community would not develop and persist. And even though it appears as an afterthought to the Gospel, it is clearly a necessary addition. Moreover, as Westcott noted, there is no textual evidence that the Gospel ever circulated without it.[112] And as E. Ruckstuhl has convincingly detailed, there are no adequate linguistic and stylistic grounds for arguing that this chapter was written by anyone other than the writer of the rest of the Gospel.[113]

As for the organization of this chapter, it falls naturally into three segments with the middle section also conveniently being subdivided into three subsections. Thus I would accept an organization for the chapter that is somewhat comparable to that of Beasley-Murray.[114] The three major segments of this Epilogue are: (1) the revelation to the seven by the Sea of Tiberias (21:1–14), (2) the three-part conversation between Jesus and Peter (21:15–23), and (3) the authentication and conclusion to the Epilogue and

---

[112] See Westcott, *St. John*, 2.359. About the only possible indication otherwise is a fifth or sixth century Syriac manuscript, but in this case it appears that the concluding chapter has been lost. Cf. Brown, *John*, 2.1077.

[113] For a thorough linguistic and stylistic analysis see E. Ruckstuhl, *Die literarische Einheit des Johannesevangeliums* (Freiburg: Paulus, 1951). Many of his approximately fifty literary aspects that mark all the major segments of John are related to this chapter.

[114] See Beasley-Murray, *John*, 398 for a similar outline.

the Gospel (21:24–25). The middle segment I would divide into: (i) the reinstatement of Peter following his denial (21:15–17), (ii) the prediction of his martyrdom (21:18–19), and (iii) the prediction concerning the beloved disciple in response to Peter's question (21:20–23).

(1) The Revelation to the Seven by the Sea of Tiberias (21:1–14)

[1]Afterward Jesus appeared again to his disciples, by the Sea of Tiberias. It happened this way: [2]Simon Peter, Thomas (called Didymus), Nathanael from Cana in Galilee, the sons of Zebedee, and two other disciples were together. [3]"I'm going out to fish," Simon Peter told them, and they said, "We'll go with you." So they went out and got into the boat, but that night they caught nothing.

[4]Early in the morning, Jesus stood on the shore, but the disciples did not realize that it was Jesus.

[5]He called out to them, "Friends, haven't you any fish?"

"No," they answered.

[6]He said, "Throw your net on the right side of the boat and you will find some." When they did, they were unable to haul the net in because of the large number of fish.

[7]Then the disciple whom Jesus loved said to Peter, "It is the Lord!" As soon as Simon Peter heard him say, "It is the Lord," he wrapped his outer garment around him (for he had taken it off) and jumped into the water. [8]The other disciples followed in the boat, towing the net full of fish, for they were not far from shore, about a hundred yards. [9]When they landed, they saw a fire of burning coals there with fish on it, and some bread.

[10]Jesus said to them, "Bring some of the fish you have just caught."

[11]Simon Peter climbed aboard and dragged the net ashore. It was full of large fish, 153, but even with so many the net was not torn. [12]Jesus said to them, "Come and have breakfast." None of the disciples dared ask him, "Who are you?" They knew it was the Lord. [13]Jesus came, took the bread and gave it to them, and did the same with the fish. [14]This was now the third time Jesus appeared to his disciples after he was raised from the dead.

21:1   The Epilogue opens with the general Greek phrase *meta tauta* (lit., "after these things"), which does not provide any specificity as to time. Rather, it is primarily a literary logical connector, as for example in 6:1. Immediately thereafter it is said that Jesus revealed or showed himself *ephanerōsen* (the NIV has "appeared") to the disciples.[115] Although the verb is used nine times in both John and 1 John, Schnackenburg and Beasley-Murray point out[116] that this is the only pericope in the Gospels where it is used to speak of the resurrection appearances (except for the later addition to Mark at 16:12,14). The term is used here at the beginning

---

[115] See *BAGD*, 853.

[116] See Schnackenburg, *St. John*, 3.351 and Beasley-Murray, *John*, 398.

of the pericope two times and at its conclusion (21:14).

The place of the appearance is at the Sea of Tiberias, the Roman designation for the Sea of Galilee (cf. 6:1), a place also called the Sea of Genessaret as in Luke 5:1 and the Sea of Chinnereth (Num 34:11), from the Hebrew *kinnerot/kinneret* meaning "harp."

Excursus 29: Jerusalem and Galilee

Although Jesus undoubtedly provided the disciples with a number of resurrection appearances, this pericope is the only appearance beside the Sea in Galilee. Matthew presents a resurrection appearance on a mountain in Galilee (Matt 28:16), and although there are no extant accounts in Mark of an appearance in Galilee except for the later constructed ending, the women are instructed to inform the disciples and Peter that Jesus was going to Galilee and there they would see him (Mark 16:7).

Luke has only resurrection appearances in the south around Jerusalem. There are no Galilean appearances in Luke's resurrection stories, but there is a unique statement in Luke from the two radiant men (angels) to the effect that the women are told to remember what Jesus said to them "while he was still in Galilee" (Luke 24:6). So Galilee is mentioned but only as an aside. When these resurrection texts are set alongside the Johannine stories of the Jerusalem appearances in chap. 20 and a Galilee appearance in chap. 21, an interesting phenomenon results.

It is clear that in early Christianity there were two resurrection appearance traditions concerning Jesus. One is related to Jerusalem (Luke 24; John 20 as well as a brief statement in Matt 28:9–10), and the other is related to Galilee (most of Matt 28; John 21; and the brief statement in Mark 16:7). The presence of these two traditions has, as might be expected, led to a good deal of scholarly debate concerning the historical reliability of one or the other of the traditions.[117] Indeed, the question was raised by Lohmeyer about whether it was Jerusalem or Galilee and the implications of each.[118] Although it is impossible to summarize here the major aspects of the debate, it remains a difficult task to sort out the relationship between and within the various resurrection accounts.

Since John contains both traditions, harmonizers tend to favor John in their syntheses. But as I have noted in connection with the Temple cleansing, such a procedure may be questionable since chronology is not John's primary goal and especially here, since we have already learned that the "third" day in the initial sign may not be primarily sequential but related to Jewish practice (John 2:1).[119]

---

[117] See R. Fuller, *The Formation of the Resurrection Narratives* (Philadelphia: Fortress, 1980); K. Lake, *The Historical Evidence for the Resurrection of Jesus Christ* (New York: G. Putnam's Sons, 1907); E. Bode, *The First Easter Morning* (Rome: Biblical Institute, 1970); C. Moule, *Resurrection* (Atlanta: John Knox, 1978); N. Perrin, *The Resurrection According to Matthew, Mark and Luke* (Philadelphia: Fortress, 1977); G. Ladd, *I Believe in the Resurrection* (Grand Rapids: Eerdmans, 1975).

[118] E. Lohmeyer, *Galiläa und Jerusalem* (Göttingen: Vandenhoeck & Ruprecht, 1936).

[119] See Borchert, *John 1–11* for comments on the third day as the special day for Jewish weddings. But the third day is also important in Christian tradition because of the resurrection.

Moreover, in light of the idea that divine messages are often given three times (cf. Acts 10:16; Rev 4:8; 8:13), this fact should give one pause to reflect on the significance of the statement in John 21:14.

21:2 In this verse seven disciples are mentioned. This is a representative number like twelve, which here represents a full or complete chosen group. Seven and twelve, of course, represent two different combinations of the divine number (3) and the number of the world (4).[120]

The seven persons included are (1) Simon Peter, who is typically listed first among the disciples; (2) Thomas, the one referred to as the twin and who was highlighted in the closing pericope of chap. 20, thus linking the two closing chapters of John together; (3) Nathanael, the one identified in the opening chapter of John at his first meeting with Jesus as an Israelite in whom there was no guile/falseness (1:47) but who is not mentioned in the Synoptic lists of the twelve;[121] yet he is here specifically listed as being from Cana in Galilee (a feature not stated previously); (4 and 5) the [sons] of Zebedee, who are not mentioned otherwise in this Gospel either with the designation of their father or by their names James and John (cf. Mark 3:17); and (6 and 7) two unnamed disciples.

Excursus 30: The Sons of Zebedee, the Beloved Disciple, and Oblique References in John

Because the sons of Zebedee are mentioned with the two unnamed disciples, it has been popular among some scholars to argue that the beloved disciple could not be one of the sons of Zebedee but must be one of the unnamed seven.[122] This assumption, however, is another argument from silence and implies that the evangelist was trying to hide the identity of the beloved disciple/the one whom Jesus loved rather than assuming that everyone knew him. Although the identification with John is also an argument from textual silence, as I have stated at length in the Introduction to my first volume, tradition is hardly silent on this issue.[123] Moreover, to speak about the sons of Zebedee is just about as oblique a reference to John as to speak of the beloved disciple. Neither designations were unknown to the early readers, but the use of oblique references in literature enables one to speak of oneself without using the personal pronoun "I." Until recently in the West it was customary to refer to oneself in literature by an oblique reference such as "the writer" or by using an impersonal statement such as "it is submitted," but today that pseudocustom is disappearing, and the "I" is appearing in scholarly literature.

In the case of the Gospel of John, the writer was faced with an additional problem. Much of the Gospel involves the speeches of Jesus. Not only does he

---

[120] Ibid., 254–56.

[121] It is popular among some ecclesiastical traditions to identify Nathanael with Bartholomew, but there is no textual support for such an identification.

[122] See for example Bultmann, *John*, 707.

[123] See Borchert, *John 1–11*, 86–91; for internal evidence see ibid., 83–86.

speak in the first person singular, but Jesus' self-designation in John is the "I am." Accordingly, if the evangelist was to be inserted into the Gospel, it would be most appropriate to use an oblique designation for himself to distinguish him from Jesus.

Furthermore, it is often thought that a reference to oneself as the beloved disciple would be extremely presumptive, but this perspective is based on a false humility. Such language was hardly a problem in a Semitic culture, which clearly understood the special role of standing given to some people, such as the eldest son in a family. To see an example of a lack of concern about a person's special regard for himself, one merely has to read Paul's own seemingly high regard for himself in such places as Gal 1:13–15 or Phil 3:4–6. The statement of Paul that he was "blameless" (Phil 3:6) may seem to the Western mind to be extremely presumptive, but for Paul it was merely regarded as a statement of fact based on his pattern of obedience. Such judgments are typical Semitic evaluations that go back in the Old Testament to Noah and his successors (Gen 6:9; 17:1; cf. 2 Chr 15:17; Job 1:1 and especially 9:20–21). One should also note Paul's opinion of his own work in 1 Cor 15:10 and 2 Cor 10:21–23, but these references are to the Western mind slightly modified and probably would also be to the Corinthian converts because of Paul's admission that such boasting was in the context of service to God. Yet in the Jewish mind, at its best, personal standing has been assumed to be reckoned as dependent upon God's will.

21:3 Having thus introduced this account, the stage is set for Peter's announcement that he was going fishing and the other six agreeing to accompany him. Despite trawling during the night, the fishermen caught nothing.[124] A number of commentators have seen in this verse either an indication of the disciples turning their backs on Jesus and getting back to their role as fishermen[125] or of entering into "aimless activity in desperation," to quote Brown.[126] But such remarks amount to a psychoanalyzing of people in a story, which since A. Schweitzer should be recognized as totally illegitimate.[127] Accordingly, I am quite in agreement with Beasley-Murray's critique of Brown when he questions "how the learned professor knows" what he says since there is no "hint of 'aimlessness' or 'desperation' in the text."[128] But he then adds his own conclusion to the effect that "the disciples must still *eat!*"[129] I must admit that sometimes it is intriguing

---

[124] Loisy considers this setting to be rather an artless and pedantic creation of the writer (*La quatrième evangile*, 515).

[125] See the remarks of M. Tenney, "The Gospel of John," EBC (Grand Rapids: Zondervan, 1981), 9:199. Cf. Hoskyns and Davey (*The Fourth Gospel*, 552), who in fact carry the idea further and charge the disciples with apostasy. But Bruce sees absolutely no warrant for the view that they had abandoned their commission (*John*, 399). Cf. also Barrett, *St. John*, 481.

[126] Brown, *John*, 2.1096.

[127] Schweitzer, *The Psychiatric Study of Jesus*.

[128] Beasley-Murray, *John*, 399.

[129] Ibid.

to read the banter among scholars.

But the question that remains is a haunting one, and it is the reason I have included Excursus 29 on Jerusalem and Galilee and added a discussion on the third time. In spite of all the attempts at harmonization, this story reads like an initial encounter with the risen Lord. It is a truly captivating story and an inspired part of John's Gospel. But it seems to be out of chronological sequence. Yet as far as the message is concerned, it truly belongs at this point. It introduces an excellent Epilogue to the Gospel because it leads beautifully into the meaning of commissioning by Jesus. Accordingly, it basically acts just in the reverse of the Temple cleansing pericope, which as I noted has been moved forward in sequence. Thus, as far as this pericope is concerned, it seems to have been moved backward in sequence to accomplish the evangelist's purpose.

21:4–5 Verse 3 ends with the Johannine notation of an experience at night (cf. other night statements such as Nicodemus coming at night [3:2]; Judas leaving at night to do his evil work [13:30]; the resurrection morning when it was still dark [20:1]; the gathering of the disciples on the first day in the evening and the doors being shut for fear [20:19]). Night and darkness are symbolic in John.

But with v. 4 the day has finally broken into reality. Morning has come. This story, then, is about a new morning having arrived not only physically but also as a Johannine theological symbolization of the arrival of a new era.

Into this new morning Jesus appeared on the shore, but the disciples did not seem yet to understand the significance of this new morning because they did not recognize that the person on the shore was Jesus. This stranger, Jesus, called out to them "children" (*paidia,* the NIV and NLT have the less satisfactory "friends"). This term, *paidia,* can at times be an expression of intimacy as between a parent and children or a leader and followers. John will later use it when he addresses his young Christian community in his special letter to them (cf. 1 John 2:18). Although the term does not always necessarily carry such intimacy, it may be that the evangelist here remembered it with a sense of fond intimacy.

The question Jesus asked them is initiated with a *mē,* which probably indicates he expected a negative response concerning their catching of fish. Their response, true to form, was no. Brown notes at this point that in the Gospels the disciples never catch fish without Jesus' assistance.[130] Although this phenomenon may be correct, it should not be taken to mean that they were poor fishermen. It merely means that fishing for people is more significant to the evangelist than fishing for fish.

---

[130] See R. Brown, *John,* 2.1071.

The term translated "fish" here is *prosphagion,* which actually means "something you eat." It originally stood for a side of relish and paste, often involving fish eaten with some form of bread/pita, familiar in Mediterranean countries. But the term later came to apply to the main course and thus to fish.[131]

21:6 The stranger on shore responded to the disciples' negative reply by telling them to "throw your net on the right side of the boat and you will find." Why the disciples, who were seasoned fishermen, obeyed an apparent stranger on the land, especially since it is assumed they had been up and down working the sea during the night, remains an unstated mystery.

When some aspect of a story pertaining to Jesus remains unstated, speculation runs high. But it is unlikely that the right side of the boat is better than the left for fishermen.[132] Bernard posits that Jesus may have seen a shoal of fish off the right side of the boat and informed the fishermen to this effect,[133] but that is again a rationalistic attempt to make silence speak. Did the disciples sense something supernatural about the stranger?[134] We do not know, but later that fact becomes clear. Whatever may have been the reason for their willingness/desperation in moving their net, it soon becomes evident that these disciples were in for a huge surprise. The net caught so many fish that the seven were not strong enough *(ischyon)*[135] to haul the catch into the boat.

21:7 At this point another contrast between the beloved disciple and Peter is introduced into this Gospel. To recall, it was the beloved disciple who was nearest Jesus at the supper and who mediated Peter's request for information (13:23–25); it was also the other disciple who gained access to the court of the high priest and arranged for Peter to enter (18:15–16); it was likewise he who was at the cross and into his care that the mother of Jesus was given (19:25–27); and it was the other disciple who outraced Peter to the tomb, and he both saw it empty first and believed (20:4–8).[136] Now it is the beloved disciple who first recognized the risen Jesus and exclaimed to Peter, "It is the Lord!"

Simon Peter required nothing more than these words to respond in action. Before he jumped *(ebalen eauton,* "threw himself") into the sea,

---

[131] See *BAGD,* 719. Schnackenburg thinks the stranger on the shore seems to be asking for fish trimmings *(St. John,* 3.554).

[132] R. Smith wonders whether the right side implies "good fortune" *(Easter Gospels,* 158).

[133] Bernard, *St. John,* 2.696.

[134] Beasley-Murray, *John,* 400.

[135] The verb is used in each of the other Gospels more frequently and especially in the Lukan writings, but it is only used here and in Rev 12:8 in the Johannine corpus.

[136] See Excursus 15: Peter and the Beloved Disciple. See also the discussions at 18:15–27 and 20:3–10 as well as Excursus 30.

however, he tied up (*diezōsato;* cf. 13:4, where Jesus tied the towel around himself) his garment *(exendytēn).* Since this is the only use of the word for this garment in the New Testament, we can only surmise that it refers to Peter's outer robe.

The text also indicates that during his fishing activity Peter had been stripped (*gymnos,* or "naked," but see below.)[137] This term for "naked," as one can easily guess, is the root for our English word "gymnasium." In the Greek athletic houses activities were practiced in the nude, which is the reason most Greek statues portray male athletes nude. There are remains of a few gymnasia in Israel, but one reason for the intense Jewish antagonism against the Seleucid rulers is that they insisted on installing Greek cultural patterns in Israel, including the gymnasium, to the dismay of Jewish religious sensitivities.[138] Uncovering oneself in public was viewed as a breech of Jewish morality (cf. Gen 9:22–27). Accordingly, the term *gymnos* in this verse can hardly mean that Peter was completely naked. He would undoubtedly have worn at least a loin cloth.

But why does the verse also add that Peter tied up his robe before jumping into the water on his way to meet Jesus? Would not this addition of clothing weigh against swimming or sloshing in the water?[139] The answer, as most commentators agree, is of course![140] Barrett responds by noting that for religious people they do not pass the greeting to another without being dressed.[141] How, then, can Peter greet Jesus without being clothed?

21:8 The six remaining disciples came in the boat towing or dragging the net full of fish.[142] It is fascinating to note that the NIV translates *ēlthon* here as the disciples "followed" but that Hoskyns and Davey argue that the boat arrived first.[143] Both statements are in fact assumptions because the text merely says "they came" and is unclear on this point. What is clear is that the boat was "not far from the land," namely, about "two hundred cubits" (which is a hundred yards or not quite ninety meters).

21:9 This verse provides an important key to understanding the role of this story in the evangelist's mind. When they arrived/embarked on the land,

---

[137] See *BAGD*, 167.

[138] For a further discussion of the Seleucid pressure to Hellenize the Jews and their rebellion, see *1, 2 Maccabees* and R. Martin, *New Testament Foundations: Vol 1 The Four Gospels* (Grand Rapids: Eerdmans, 1975), 53–57.

[139] This event certainly was not a case of Peter walking on the water. Cf. Matt 14:28–33.

[140] See, for example, Carson *John*, 671 and R. Brown, *John*, 2.1072.

[141] Barrett, *St. John*, 482.

[142] The story in Luke 5:6–7 has the disciples filling two boats with the large catch of fish. For comments on this event see G. Osborne, "John 21: Test Case for History and Redaction in the Resurrection Narratives," in *Gospel Perspectives* (Sheffield: University Press, 1981), 2:293–328. Cf. S. Smalley, "The Sign in John xxi," *NTS* 20 (1974): 275–88.

[143] See Hoskyns and Davey, *The Fourth Gospel*, 555.

an important sight met them. It was none other than a charcoal fire *(anthrakian)*. This word appears only in two places in the entire New Testament, and both of them are related to Peter in the Gospel of John (18:18; 21:29). The first forms a setting for Peter's denial and the second for his reinstatement; the first concerns the darkness of an evil night and the second the morning of new possibilities. Although this chapter is a later Epilogue added to the Gospel, it becomes an integral part of the message of the Gospel when one sees its purpose in the work of the evangelist. Although the earlier fire marked the symbol of an uninviting situation of cold, hostile questioning, this second fire with its fish and bread must be seen as an inviting setting of a new round of penetrating questions that are the complete opposite of hostility and are aimed at providing a new commissioning for Peter.

Some have argued that since *opsarion* (fish) and *arton* (bread) are singular here, they are indicative of the fact that John was intending the story to be a proclamation of the sacred meal (i.e., one fish and one bread).[144] This interpretation probably will extend the meaning unnecessarily for many, but there are some interesting examples of this idea in art.[145]

21:10–11 Morris regards this event as breakfast for the disciples but then finds the supply not abundantly sufficient. Accordingly, Jesus tells the disciples "to supplement" his preparation.[146] This statement in John has created considerable discussion among scholars and has been used to support theories of editing and several sources for this pericope.[147]

Peter reappears in the story. Did he then just arrive?[148] Probably not. But however one may answer that question, it raises another question. Did Peter take upon himself the major task of hauling the catch to land? Or one may ask of the story, did the other disciples actually leave the fish in the sea? Or perhaps one should ask, did Peter just drag the net to a place where he could count the fish rather than assuming he was the one who secured them from escape? Clearly it is impossible to answer these and a number of other questions. The story simply does not provide the answers. But such unresolved questions are fertile grounds for both speculation and editing arguments.

---

[144] For this interpretation and others see R. Brown, *John*, 2.1073. See also C. Dodd, *Interpretation of the Fourth Gospel* (Cambridge: University Press, 1953), 431, who reminds us that fish and bread has been pictured as an alternative to the eucharistic meal in some examples of Christian art.

[145] Those who visit the site of Tabgah, which is remembered as one of the traditional sites for this event, will see an example of such artwork. Cf. also A. Shaw, "The Breakfast by the Shore and the Mary Magdalene Encounter as Eucharistic Narratives," *JTS* 25 (1974): 12–26.

[146] See Morris, *John*, 763–64.

[147] See, for example, Schnackenburg, *St. John*, 3.345–47 and especially 356–57 and Loisy, *Le quatrième evangile*, 519–20.

[148] So Loisy and others have suggested. See ibid.

But beyond these matters, the report of the number of fish as 153 has raised a great deal of speculation. Among the most well-known ideas was the one spelled out by Jerome in his comment on Ezekiel 47 that deals with the stream flowing from the temple eastward that brings life to the Dead Sea (cf. Ezek 47:9–10). In this interpretation he thought that the Greek zoologist Oppianus Cilex considered that there existed 153 species of fish (but in reality it was for that early scientist 157 species).[149] Augustine developed another argument based on the sum of all the numbers from one to seventeen.[150] Then, in recent times, Hoskyns and Davey[151] followed by R. Smith[152] altered Augustine's view and formulated an idea based on an equilateral triangle starting at the top with one digit and proceeding down, adding a digit for each new row until the base had seventeen digits in it. The reason for choosing seventeen is that it produces a symbolic meaning by adding ten and seven.[153] Other patterns could be listed here, but these are sufficient to illustrate the imaginative ideas that have been developed not merely by moderns but by the Latin Fathers as well.

Of course, it is just possible that the number 153 might not be primarily a symbolic number. It could, in fact, be an actual reminiscence of an event. But for some readers that idea might not be an acceptable option. It may be too literal for them.

21:12–13 The words of these verses sound strangely similar to some words in the institution of the Lord's Supper (or Eucharist) recorded in 1 Cor 11:23–26. They include an invitation, the knowledge of the postresurrection presence of "the Lord," and the distribution of the elements. The difference in the elements, however, is that they are bread and fish rather than bread and wine. In this respect it should also be recalled that Luke focuses two of his resurrection pericopes on eating. In the Emmaus story Jesus took bread, blessed it, and gave it to the tired travelers. They then recognized him in the breaking of bread (Luke 24:30–31,35). In the Jerusalem appearance Jesus evidenced that he was not a mere spiritual apparition by eating some cooked fish in their presence (Luke 24:41–42). Schnackenburg suggests that the absence of prayers in the Johannine verses "could be an indication against the eucharistic understanding."[154] But is that aspect

---

[149] See Jerome's Commentary on Ezekiel in Migne, *PL*, 25.474c.

[150] See Augustine's comments on John in section 122.8 in Migne, *PL*, 35.1963–64.

[151] Hoskyns and Davey, *The Fourth Gospel*, 553–54.

[152] R. Smith, *Easter Gospels*, 180.

[153] See Excursus 6 on Numbers in Borchert, *John 1–11*, 254–56. For additional reflections see J. Emerton's discussions on numbers in *JTS* 9 (1958): 86–89. See also J. Emerton, "The Hundred and Fifty-Three Fishes in John xxi.11," *JTS* 9 (1958): 86–89; P. Ackroyd, "The 153 Fishes in John XXI.11—A Further Note," *JTS* 10 (1959): 94; and N. McEleney, "153 Great Fishes (John 21,11)–Gematrical Atbash," *Bib* 58 (1977): 411–17.

[154] See Schnackenburg, *St. John*, 3.359.

determinative?[155] Bultmann carries the reverse view to its opposite conclusion by arguing that the risen Lord does not need to give thanks in the same way the earthly Jesus did,[156] but that is because of his absolute separation between the Jesus of history and the Christ of faith.

Excursus 31: John 21:1–14 and Luke 5:1–11: A Form and Redactional Note

The relationship of these two pericopes has often been debated and therefore requires a brief comment. A miraculous catch of fish appears in only two places in the Gospels: once at the beginning of Jesus' ministry at Luke 5:1–11 in the context of the two sets of brothers prior to the choosing of the twelve in Luke 6:12–16 and once in John 21:1–14 following the resurrection in the context of the seven disciples and prior to the recommissioning of Peter (21:15–23).

The similarities between the two stories are quite significant although there are also significant differences as well. In both stories the fishermen have spent the night on the Sea of Galilee, referred to as the Sea of Genessaret in Luke and the Sea of Tiberias in John. In both cases they have caught nothing. In Luke two boats are mentioned, but in John there is only one boat. In both stories, however, only one boat made the catch, though in Luke the second was called on to assist in completing the catch. In the Johannine story Jesus was on the land in the morning calling to the fishermen who had been out all night. In Luke the fishermen had returned to land and were cleaning their nets prior to Jesus entering the boat and teaching from it. Then Jesus told Peter to push out into the deep part of the water and let down the nets. In John, however, Jesus called from the shore to the disciples to let down the net on the right side of the boat. In Luke, Peter complained that they had already been out all night, but they acquiesced according to Jesus' instructions. But in John there was no complaint, just mere acquiescence. In both stories there was a great catch of fish, and the net began to break. In Luke the fishermen signaled to their colleagues in the second boat to help, while in John there were no colleagues to help. In John they towed the net to land because the fish were not taken into the boat. Yet in Luke they filled both boats with the catch of fish to the point that both were on the verge of sinking. In the Johannine story the beloved disciple recognized the Lord and informed Peter, who jumped into the water to get to Jesus quickly. In Luke, on the other hand, Jesus was in the boat, and Peter was awed by the event. Then he fell down before Jesus confessing that he was a sinful man and asked Jesus to depart from him (an indication that he has experienced a Christophany). In John, Peter pulled the catch up and counted the fish. They numbered 153 fish. In Luke the fish were apparently not counted. In John the reader must await the next pericope to learn of Peter's encounter and questioning by Jesus, but in Luke there is no questioning. There is also no indication in Luke of Peter having gone overboard since Jesus was in the

---

[155] Carson cannot see any eucharistic symbolism here or in John 6. He considers the determinative issue is that "there is no hint that Jesus gives *himself* in the bread and fish" (*John*, 674). But even if the issue here is or is not one of the eucharist, biblical interpreters in this postmodern era should become more sensitive to the power of symbolism in Scripture, and John is quite symbolic.

[156] See Bultmann, *John*, 550.

boat. There is, however, in Matt 14:28–33 a story in which Peter went overboard and walked on the water in response to Jesus' invitation. But that is in a different story form.

What, then, should one make of these two stories? To begin with, it should be recalled that there are a number of sea stories in the Gospels. Indeed, Mark has two (4:35–41; 6:45–52), Matthew has two (8:23–27; 14:22–32), Luke has two (5:1–11; 8:22–25), and John has two (6:15–21; 21;1–14); but the stories have different forms, and the events do not easily coordinate into a single form. Indeed, there seem to be a minimum of three or four stories among these Gospels, depending on how one interprets them. And there may have been more.

Concerning the present two stories that have been detailed above, if one holds that they reflect the same event, then one has to decide whether the locus of the event is primarily Lukan or Johannine and whether it reflects a preresurrection life of Jesus event or a postresurrection appearance event. What is most interesting in this discussion is the fact that of those who think that the two events reflect a single tradition, there is little consistency in their conclusions. For example, Brown favors a Lukan tradition in John,[157] and Bultmann argues that the event in Luke is a displaced resurrection account.[158] The examples can be multiplied. But it is probably unlikely that there will develop a consensus of opinion.

The reason for the problem is that while form and redactional methodologies can define possible patterns of form development, similarities in base stories, and editorial enhancements, they are actually rather ineffective in defining the actual historical realities of those stories. Moreover, they usually concentrate on similarities within patterns and assume that differences are the result of editorial or community alterations and interpretations. But not all differences can be so easily assumed, and that is the reason I have detailed not merely the similarities but also the differences.

The issue then comes down to the question of whether the two stories in this case actually point to a single tradition in which the differences can be explained in terms of form and redactional developments. The answer to that question is not, as is frequently assumed, a scientific one but is really quite a subjective one, enhanced by some detailed comparisons but for the most part based on the sensitivities of the interpreter. Although I recognize that not all will agree with my perspective, I find that those who claim to regard the stories as arising from a single tradition have a significant burden of proof to contend with, and I am convinced that they have not proven their case, since I find the differences still quite striking and not explained by either form developments or editorial enhancements.

21:14   In the case of the third time Jesus appeared, I think this could

---

[157] See, for example, Brown's extended discussion on this text in *John*, 2.1085–92.

[158] See, for example, Bultmann, *John*, 705, but note that in *The History of the Synoptic Tradition* ([New York: Harper & Row, 1963], 217–18), Bultmann states that the Johannine story "derives from Luke." In any case, however, he thinks that the story is a legend "adopted from Pagan Hellenism" (ibid., 304). Cf. F. Beare, *The Earliest Records of Jesus* (New York: Abingdon, 1962), 51, who calls both stories a "legend."

well be a matter of Johannine literary purpose and, as I have indicated in the discussion of Excursus 29: Jerusalem and Galilee, the nature of sequencing throughout the Johannine Gospel, particularly in relation to the resurrection accounts in the Gospels.

(2) The Three-Part Conversation between Jesus and Peter (21:15–23)

¹⁵When they had finished eating, Jesus said to Simon Peter, "Simon son of John, do you truly love me more than these?"

"Yes, Lord," he said, "you know that I love you."

Jesus said, "Feed my lambs."

¹⁶Again Jesus said, "Simon son of John, do you truly love me?"

He answered, "Yes, Lord, you know that I love you."

Jesus said, "Take care of my sheep."

¹⁷The third time he said to him, "Simon son of John, do you love me?"

Peter was hurt because Jesus asked him the third time, "Do you love me?" He said, "Lord, you know all things; you know that I love you."

Jesus said, "Feed my sheep. ¹⁸I tell you the truth, when you were younger you dressed yourself and went where you wanted; but when you are old you will stretch out your hands, and someone else will dress you and lead you where you do not want to go." ¹⁹Jesus said this to indicate the kind of death by which Peter would glorify God. Then he said to him, "Follow me!"

²⁰Peter turned and saw that the disciple whom Jesus loved was following them. (This was the one who had leaned back against Jesus at the supper and had said, "Lord, who is going to betray you?") ²¹When Peter saw him, he asked, "Lord, what about him?"

²²Jesus answered, "If I want him to remain alive until I return, what is that to you? You must follow me." ²³Because of this, the rumor spread among the brothers that this disciple would not die. But Jesus did not say that he would not die; he only said, "If I want him to remain alive until I return, what is that to you?"

THE REINSTATEMENT OF PETER FOLLOWING HIS DENIAL (21:15–17).   Among the three crucial matters the evangelist obviously considered had been left untreated in the earlier part of the Gospel was the status of Peter following his threefold denial of Jesus before the crucifixion (18:17,25–27). That this matter was of importance to the Johannine community is highlighted by the fact that the stage is prepared for the encounter with the corresponding set of three questions concerning Peter's love of Jesus and by the presence of another charcoal fire being introduced at 21:9 (cf. the charcoal fire in 18:18).[159] It is almost as though the evangelist is affirming the well-known concept that for a person to become right with God and gain a sense of release from the past sense of rebellion that that person should face the reality of where the deviation or sin occurred.

---

[159] See the comments concerning the use of the concept of the charcoal fire at 21:9.

The issue of denying the Lord became a significant problem in the early church during times of persecution, and processes of reinstatement were debated. Hardliners were often not willing to accept those who denied their Lord while others may have tended to accept such deviants too easily. This pericope of the questioning of Peter must have served as a model of a median position willing to reestablish deviants but not without testing their commitment.[160]

21:15–17 With these next three verses the focus of the text turns from Jesus and the seven to concentrate particularly on Peter. He had been extremely sure of himself that he and his colleagues would not go back on their loyalty to Jesus (cf. 6:66–68) and that he particularly would follow Jesus, even to the point of death (13:37). In a sense one really has to like Peter for his good intentions. Indeed, he, among the disciples, was the one who ventured to defend Jesus with his sword, even though he misunderstood the situation (18:10–11). And he at least made an attempt to follow Jesus after his arrest (18:15). But in this Gospel it is clear that Peter denied Jesus three times and that he is not mentioned at the cross when others were there. It is almost as though he disappeared from sight for a time, only to reappear after the resurrection (20:2).

It was to this well-intentioned but frail disciple that Jesus pointedly asked, "Do you truly love me more than these?" (21:15). The "these" here must of necessity mean loving Jesus more than the other disciples did rather than focusing on Peter preferring Jesus to other people or to his general love of fishing. Peter obviously had had a high opinion of his loyalty and probably had regarded himself as the model of love and respect for Jesus. But he had hardly lived up to his own view of his loyalty or in comparison to others. So Jesus confronted Peter's own high opinion of himself and in so doing made Peter face his own frailty head-on.

The threefold questioning of Peter by Jesus concerning his love brought the disciple from a response of something like "of course!" concerning the first question, to a sense of grief with the third one.[161] But Jesus would not let him go with offering an easy response. Instead, Jesus probed him until he opened the wounded heart of this would-be follower. Off-the-cuff replies and well-meaning superficial responses to the risen Lord will not work in the call of Jesus to the life of discipleship. Jesus forced Peter to learn the hard lesson of a changed life. Everyone who follows Jesus must learn what real believing and loving Jesus means. To be clear on this perspective about

---

[160] For a discussion of the issue of persecution and its effects on the church see H. Workman, *Persecution in the Early Church* (Oxford: University Press, 1981). The text in 1 John 2:19 concerns theological deviants John considered apostates and not genuinely part of the community of faith.

[161] See P. Trudinger, "Subtle Word-Plays in the Gospel of John and the Problem of Chapter 21," *JRT* 28 (1971): 27–31.

the story is absolutely crucial before turning to specific words and phrases in the verses, which are often poorly interpreted by preachers, priests, and teachers. To whatever denomination one belongs, this encounter of Jesus with Peter can provide a salutary message.

To begin with the misunderstanding of many Protestants concerning this text, these verses are not about a change in the use of the Greek verbs for love. The motif study of A. Nygren entitled *Agape and Eros* has led many to incorrect conclusions about the use of Greek verbs in the New Testament and particularly in John. For example, it is crucial to understand that *eros* never appears in the New Testament, but that does not mean inadequate love is not present. Just glance at 12:43, where it is said that the Pharisees "loved the praise of men" and realize that the verb there is *agapan!* That verse alone should dispel poor exegetical patterns of interpretation among preachers!

But to be more specific with the use of the verbs for "love" in this passage, Carson is absolutely correct when he says that the two verbs *agapan* and *philein* "are used interchangeably in this Gospel" and that from the fourth century B.C. forward in Greek literature *agapan* became "one of the standard verbs for 'to love.'"[162] He then refers to Demas loving this present age (2 Tim 4:10),[163] a reference not in John but the point is the same as in John 12:43 and elsewhere.[164]

Why, then, was Peter "grieved" (*elupēthē*, the NIV "hurt" just does not catch the pathos of this statement)? It was hardly because of the change in the Greek verbs. Besides, that argument would hardly be viable if the original conversation would have been in Aramaic. A mere glance at the text tells the reader the reason. Peter experienced a major "undoing" (cf. Isa 6:5, KJV) of his self-assertiveness because Jesus asked him "the third time" (21:17) about his love. The third time did it. Imagine again the scene as the evangelist framed it: a charcoal fire and three questions about Peter's relationship to Jesus. It hardly takes a genius to relate this event to that of the denial. Facing up to oneself is a traumatic experience.

Did Peter learn from this experience? Well, maybe not immediately, as the following verses seem to indicate. But ultimately? If the first letter of Peter is any indication, there seems to be little doubt that this experience seared itself into the consciousness of this well-meaning disciple because in

---

[162] See Carson, *John*, 676.

[163] Ibid., 677.

[164] In the case of the Johannine use of the words for *love* and *shepherding,* the reader should not focus on the change of the Greek words but concentrate on the growing impact of Jesus' statements. For discussion on the use of words such as *love, sheep,* and *pasturing* see L. Morris, *Studies in the Fourth Gospel* (London: Paternoster, 1969), 293–319 and the important work of J. Barr, *The Semantics of Biblical Language* (Oxford: University Press, 1961), especially at 216–17.

that letter there is an instructive message for the leaders of his missionary churches. In the three responses of Jesus to Peter's assertions of love Jesus said, "Feed ["tend," *boske*] my sheep ["lambs," *arnia*]" in 21:15; "Pasture ["tend," *poimaine*] my sheep *[probata]*" in 21:16; and "feed ["tend," *boske*] my sheep *[probata]*" again in 21:17. Then in his epistle Peter in turn told the leaders of the churches to "pasture ["tend," *poimanate*] the flock *[poimnion]* of God" appropriately (1 Pet 5:2).[165] Leadership in the Christian church should not be a matter of obligation or oughtness but of a willing desire. It should likewise not be from a goal of achieving personal gain but from a sense of calling to serve others. And it should not be because one wishes to dominate others but because one is willing to model the way of Christ in serving God's flock (cf. 1 Pet 5:3).[166] Seeking power and personal aggrandizement should not be any part of the goals among Jesus' disciples.

These texts also should speak to some Roman Catholic concepts of Peter and the role of shepherding. Stählin argues that the three questions reflect a liturgical pattern leading to the establishment of Peter's pastoral ministry,[167] but this notion surely has to be read into the text, as Beasley-Murray has correctly noted.[168]

But more to the point is the fact that Vatican I in its concern for the papacy quoted these three verses together with Matt 16:16–19 in making its dogmatic statement that "Peter the Apostle was constituted by Christ the Lord as chief of all the apostles and as visible head of the Church on earth."[169] As a result of this statement many other comments have since been made by Roman Catholic scholars. Among them Lapide's declaration is worthy of note. He opines that "on his departure into heaven Christ here designates his Vicar upon earth and creates Peter the Supreme Pontiff, in order that one Church may be governed by one Pastor."[170] The concept of the pastor/shepherd in this type of argument is rooted in the idea of the shepherd king like David who was a ruler over Israel (cf. 2 Sam 5:2). The question, of course, that can be raised is whether that is the meaning of the present text. But this commentary is hardly the format to discuss the papacy or whether whatever might be implied concerning Peter applies to those who claim to be his successors.

Fortunately, current biblical scholars on both sides of the papacy issue

---

[165] See the previous footnote.

[166] For a discussion of these instructions in 1 Peter see G. Borchert, "The Conduct of Christians in the Face of the 'Fiery Ordeal' (4:12–5:11)," *RevExp* 79 (1982): 451–62 at 456.

[167] See *TDNT* 9.134.

[168] See Beasley-Murray, *John*, 405.

[169] See *Enchiridion Symbolorum*, 3053–55.

[170] See C. Lapide cited in Hoskyns and Davey, *The Fourth Gospel*, 557.

have become a little more irenic than those of previous eras.[171] Brown, for example, who was a revered member of the Pontifical Council before his death, not only argued that Peter's authority was hardly absolute[172] but he clearly disagreed with those who considered that these three verses meant that Peter was "made shepherd over the other disciples or over the other members of the Twelve."[173]

Perhaps it is sufficient to conclude at this point that whatever one has to say here about Peter, it is clear that Jesus had a task for him, but not for the Peter of the preresurrection. It was a Peter who needed to be sifted by the penetrating questioning of Jesus in order to do the work of the risen Lord and be reinstated after his devastating fall.[174] God/Jesus does not bless human beings primarily to provide them with status but to carry out the divine purposes in the world. Thus mission is inseparably linked to the calling and blessing of God. This inseparable linkage was evidenced as early as the call of Abraham (Gen 12:2–3) and has been repeated many times in history, including to Peter and to all who are likewise called by God in Christ.

THE PREDICTION OF PETER'S MARTYRDOM (21:18–19). The second crucial issue that was left untreated in the earlier part of the Gospel is the risen Jesus' understanding of Peter's end on earth.

There is no doubt that by the time these verses were written Peter had suffered martyrdom. One question that would have been on the minds of some was the issue of whether Peter's death was known and understood by the risen Jesus. Death was taken very seriously by the early Christians, as is evident from the questions raised by the believers in Thessalonica when their hope was at stake (cf. 1 Thess 4:13–18). Why were the leaders dying before the Lord returned? Was the God of the resurrection really in control? The answer to the last question was a resounding yes. Jesus knew Peter would suffer martyrdom. Therefore, do not worry! The church and history are in the hands of God. That is the basic message Peter himself delivered to the church in 1 Pet 4:12–14.[175]

21:18–19 The significance of these verses for the early church is marked by the fact that these words of Jesus are introduced by the well-known double *amēn* (truly, truly) expression found repeatedly in the rest of the Gospel.

Some scholars, such as Bultmann and Bernard, have considered v. 18 to

---

[171] The acidic remarks of Lagrange (*Saint Jean*, 528–30), who attacked Protestants as narrow and out of touch, are probably no more acidic than many Protestant pulpiteers who consider the Roman Catholics unbiblical.

[172] See Brown, *John*, 2.1115.

[173] Ibid., 2.1116.

[174] Bultmann does not consider that Peter needed to be reinstated or rehabilitated (*John*, 551).

[175] See Borchert, "The Conduct of Christians," 451–54.

be a Johannine construct (even a reconstructed ancient proverb) contrasting the freedom and alertness of youth with the helplessness of old age.[176] But early in the twentieth century Bauer had already argued that it was a fitting description of the ancient custom of crucifixion.[177] Hengel confirmed that this statement was an accurate description of the ancient tortuous execution procedure of crucifixion.[178] The victim would be forced to carry the heavy *patibulum*, or cross beam, over his shoulders and behind his neck, and his arms and hands would be stretched out and tied to the cross beam. His midsection would normally be covered with a loin cloth, and he would be led like an animal to the place of execution.[179]

The Johannine editorial aside in v. 19, therefore, was undoubtedly intended to make certain the reader understood that Jesus was clearly addressing the concern about Peter's death.[180] Literary asides in stories are vital because they provide the insurance that readers will not misunderstand the writer's intentions for inclusion of certain materials. They also provide windows of insight into the concerns of writers. In this case the aside reveals that Peter's death was a concern to the community. But it was also a way of preparing the community for an even more significant concern, the death of the beloved disciple.

The section ends with Jesus' words to Peter, "Follow me!" Carson concluded an otherwise appropriate analysis of this section with what I consider to be a rather sentimental ending that seems to miss the theological point of the section. He proposed that Jesus then invited "Peter for a private walk along the beach."[181]

The point of this section is, I think, quite different in the way John has set up this three-part literary piece. In the first part of this presentation related to previously untreated issues Peter is reinstated and rehabilitated after an intensive set of questions. Then in this second part Jesus informed Peter that he must suffer martyrdom as an aspect of his discipleship. That

---

[176] See Bultmann, *John*, 713, and Bernard, *St. John*, 2.708. Cf. also J. Elliott, who regards the statement as a contrast between a recent and a mature convert ("Ministry and Church Order in the New Testament: A Traditio-Historical Analysis," *CBQ* 32 [1970]: 383).

[177] See W. Bauer, *Das Johannes-Evangelium* (Tübingen: Mohr-Siebeck, 1933), 232. See also the references to ancient crucifixion in Haenchen, *John 2*, 590.

[178] See M. Hengel, *Crucifixion* (Philadelphia: Fortress, 1977).

[179] For some reason Schnackenburg (*St. John*, 3.482 n.75), quoting Wellhausen, considers such an explanation as "antiquarian sophistry." Beasley-Murray, normally very reserved in his comments, responded: "Antiquarian sophistry indeed!" (*John*, 408). He then proceeded to detail the fact that Roman crucifixion customs were well known.

[180] Peter's martyrdom is briefly addressed in the letter of *1 Clem* 5:4 from the midnineties, but no details are mentioned. The theory that he was crucified upside down in order not to appear competitive with Jesus is a much later accretion to the story and has little historical significance.

[181] See Carson, *John*, 680.

meant that he was obliged to "follow" Jesus, even to the point of crucifixion. In this way he would also glorify God, not in the theological impact and significance of Jesus' death (cf. 12:27–28; 13:31–32; 17:1) but as a faithful disciple who was willing to follow his master to death (cf. 1 Pet 4:16). The final part, to which we now turn, involves the typical Peter who was concerned about someone else's life and who needed to hear *again* the emphatic words of Jesus: "Follow me!" (21:22).

THE PREDICTION CONCERNING THE BELOVED DISCIPLE (21:20–23). **21:20** This verse, in terms of literary flow, is attached to the previous section by the notation that as Peter turned, he saw the beloved disciple. The word "following" *(akolouthounta)* stands in a somewhat nonconnected fashion to the rest of the sentence and probably refers to the beloved disciple, but one should not overpress its significance in relation to Jesus' command to Peter to follow him.[182] The verse serves as a basic literary connective.

This verse also contains another Johannine editorial aside, supplied to the reader to connect the beloved disciple with the incident at the supper when he leaned on Jesus' chest (cf. 13:25) and acted as an intermediary for Peter to Jesus (13:24). The verse is also reminiscent of the close connection between Jesus and the Father in the closing verse of the Prologue (1:18).

21:21 Having focused on the beloved disciple, Peter asked his gnawing question: "And what about this one?" "What about someone else?" is a very human question. We tend to focus on comparisons. That is usually the way we try to understand whether we are okay. But that is not the way it works with God. God is concerned about us personally. Of course, God is concerned about our community, our brothers and sisters, our friends, the world. But these can stand in the way of our confronting our own individual responsibilities before God. Our concern for others can actually sidetrack us from facing God's personal demands on us. That was the problem with Peter in this verse, and Jesus was prepared to confront him with this sidetracking of his personal calling.

Unfortunately, most commentaries concentrate on the rivalry between the followers of Peter and John[183] and avoid discussing this aspect of the story. The reason, I suspect, is that biblical scholars are fearful of psychologizing texts. But where such an interplay is obvious, it is only proper to discuss these matters as well.

21:22–23 Jesus' answer to Peter involves the third basic concern that

---

[182] Bultmann seems to be quite correct in not pushing the significance of the use of the word here (*John*, 553). Cf. R. Brown, *John*, 2.1109. But as the tradition developed, the contrast with Peter in the Johannine community may have heightened.

[183] Cf. for example R. Brown, *John*, 2.1117–22; Beasley-Murray, *John*, 410; Schnackenburg, *St. John*, 3.368–70; etc. Carson, *John*, 680–81, moves a little further in this direction.

had not been addressed. The answer was, basically, Concentrate on your relationship to me and your own life and death and do not be concerned about his! That was the clear message to Peter.

But there was more to Jesus' answer than a direct response to Peter. And it was the additional statement with respect to the beloved disciple that was of significant concern to the community. That part of the answer was in the protasis of a conditional sentence: "If I want him to remain *[menein]*[184] [NIV adds "alive"] until I come *[erchomai]*." Apparently that part of the statement led to a good deal of speculation in the Johannine community to the effect that their beloved leader would continue to live until the *eschaton,* the end of time and the "coming" of Jesus.

The editorial comment of the evangelist/writer that follows, therefore, supplies us with an important insight into this community. It apparently expected the imminent return of Jesus, so as they saw their leader nearing death, it must have greatly shaken their sense of hope concerning their eschatological expectations. Not only was Peter dead, but now their beloved leader was either dead or dying. The one death they probably could and did accept, but the reality of the second must have caused great trauma in the community.

Accordingly, the writer made a special effort to explain precisely what Jesus *did* and *did not* say. That type of precision is a clear indication of a real existing problem in the Johannine community that could not go unaddressed.

Indeed, the community and the Johannine writer both seemed to believe they were living in the last "hour" (cf. 1 John 2:18).[185] But in spite of the fact that in each era the church considers its people to be living in the last days, the time of the Lord's coming is not in human hands. That time is in the hand of God and even the earthly Jesus did not know that time (cf. Mark 13:32).

It is clear in John that pain and persecution will touch believers (cf. John 16:2), but Jesus did not give the calendar date for the end. Nor did he plan to remove Christians from this world (cf. 17:15). Instead, he promised to keep his people in his own care (cf. 10:28) and provide the Paraclete to keep them from becoming scandalized or falling away (cf. 16:1). Tribulation and turmoil would certainly come in the world, but Jesus told his disciples not to give up or abandon hope. Rather, they were/are to live with a positive perspective because he had indeed overcome all that the world could muster against him (cf. 16:33).

---

[184] E. Schwartz's suggestion in "Noch einmal der Tod der Söhne Zebedäi" (*ZNW* 11 [1910]: 89–104) that "remain" here meant remain in the tomb is interesting but hardly acceptable.

[185] Cf. the view of J. A. T. Robinson, who sees the Gospel as an example of early eschatology (*The Priority of John* [London: SCM, 1985], 70–71). While I would not date the Gospel as early as Robinson, his point about eschatology is relevant here.

The end of this Epilogue is therefore an implicit warning against chronologizing the *eschaton*. Just as the risen Jesus did not promise the beloved disciple control of the calendar of his lifespan, neither does he offer readers such insight. That knowledge belongs only to God.

(3) The Authentication and Conclusion to the Epilogue and the Gospel (21:24–25)

24This is the disciple who testifies to these things and who wrote them down. We know that his testimony is true.

25Jesus did many other things as well. If every one of them were written down, I suppose that even the whole world would not have room for the books that would be written.

21:24 As I have indicated in the Introduction within the section on authorship, this verse has been the subject of varying views. From my perspective the witness who stands behind this Gospel is John. The "we," who knew that the testimony was authentic, however, must refer to a community prepared to assert the legitimacy of that disciple's witness.[186] This view is close to that of Westcott, who regarded the "we" as the elders of the church at Ephesus. Dodd proposed that the "we" was an indefinite way of writing something by an author who did not want to be identified, but that thesis runs afoul on the "I" mentioned in v. 25.[187] Schlatter and others have suggested that the "we" involved the writer and his colleagues who knew him and encouraged him and may even have contributed to his work as he wrote on their behalf.[188] This view is somewhat similar to that espoused in the Muratorian Canon (11:11–15) and to that of Clement of Alexandria, but such a joint type of effort is difficult to substantiate.[189] For some more recent commentators it would be difficult to pinpoint who that writer was.[190] But Morris would favor apostolic authorship similar to that held in the Patristic period.[191]

The meaning of "wrote them down" has also led to differences of opinion. Did it mean the writer actually wrote down the words, caused them to be written down, as was probably the case with Pilate (19:19), or did he use a more free style amanuensis (scribe)? Whether it was the first or second, the difference would be minimal, though the second option might explain the references to the witness as the beloved disciple. But it is very unlikely

---

[186] See the Introduction in Borchert, *John 1–11*, particularly at 89–90.

[187] See C. Dodd, "Note on John 21:24," *JTS* 4 (1953): 212–13.

[188] Cf. A. Schlatter, *Der Evangelist Johannes* (Stuttgart: Calwer Verlag, 1975), 376.

[189] For Clement's view see Eusebius, *Hist. eccl.* 6.14.7.

[190] See, for example, Bultmann, *John*, 717–18.

[191] See Morris, *John*, 776.

that any such scribe who penned the Gospel would be at liberty to edit freely the work or to put the document in his own form, as in the third case after the pattern of an official business letter or legal document. Such an edited document might well be acceptable in the business world, but how would such a document as a Gospel relate to its authentication? Truth is a primary theme in John, and truth of witness is a particular emphasis of this verse.

Excursus 32: The Community "We" and Their Confession

Whoever the ultimate scribe may have been, the message of this Gospel reflects the encompassing testimony concerning Jesus by their "towering" disciple who was known as the beloved disciple (13:23; 19:26; 20:2; 21:7,20), the other disciple (18:15–16; 20:8; etc.), and the witness at the cross (19:35).[192] It is he upon whom the Johannine community relied for its authentic view concerning the crucified-risen Jesus Christ, the genuine Lamb of God who takes away the sin of the world because that Lamb obediently gave himself on the cross as the true servant of the Father.

The disciple who stands behind this Gospel is the one whom the church has called John. It is the testimony of this disciple that was crucial for the Johannine community. They affirmed his testimony with their authenticating colophon and signified their community confession by the presence of the word "we." This "we" appears not only here at 21:24 but significantly also in the Prologues of both the Gospel at 1:14 and of the first Johannine epistle at 1:2, both of which assert the inseparability of Jesus with the Father as the human-divine one who provided eternal life for all who accept Jesus Christ, the Son of God.

This assertion of the "we" must have stood over against other people of that time who were making statements about Jesus and about the nature of the Gospel that deviated from the statements asserted by the evangelist and the Johannine community. Whether these opponents would have been different in the case of the Gospel (outsiders) and 1 John (separatists), as was argued by R. Brown in his intriguing studies is a matter of speculation.[193]

But what seems fully evident is that those who represented the faithful in the Johannine community were prepared to take a firm stand on the correct nature of the Johannine proclamation of Jesus. This proclamation included the fact that Jesus was the preexistent one, the one who revealed the Father, and the one whose death and resurrection bring salvation. This Jesus is indeed none other than the Lamb of Rev 5:6, who is "standing" even though he "had been slain!" It was against all who would deny the complex unity in the divinity and humanity of the crucified-resurrected Son of Man/Son of God that this "we" stood. The evangelist and the Johannine community were prepared to assert their clear con-

---

[192] See Borchert, *John 1–11*, especially at 86 and 90.

[193] See R. Brown, *The Community of the Beloved Disciple* (New York: Paulist Press, 1979), especially at 27–58, 59–91, 103–23; and *The Churches the Apostles Left Behind* (New York: Paulist, 1984), 84–123.

demnation of anyone who denied that God in Jesus Christ had come in the flesh (John 1:14; 6:51; 10:33; 1 John 2:22; 4:2–3). For them his atoning death and resurrection were the basis for their confession and for their believing that they were participants in the victory that overcomes the world (John 1:12; 3:16; 6:68–69; 10:27–30; 11:25–26; 12:23–24,32; 14:28–30; 16:22; 17:24; 1 John 4:4,14,17; 5:4–5).

21:25 This final verse brings the Epilogue and the Gospel to a conclusion. Although there is not doubt that it was written to complement the original conclusion of the book at 20:30–31, it does not really possess the theological summarizing force of the earlier conclusion.

Instead, it focuses primarily on the expansiveness of the reservoir of materials that would be available if one desired to add to this amazing Gospel.[194] But in spite of the fact that this ending does not quite possess the theological depth of the earlier conclusion, it clearly does complete the Epilogue on an exalted note. It calls on the reader to recognize the immeasurable greatness of the Jesus who touched the world in human form and left an indelible impression on human lives and history.

Finally, as this verse speaks of many books that could be written, it is appropriate to recognize here that among these many books and pages that have been written about Jesus and this strategic Gospel of John, the present work is, in fact, many times the length of this wonderful Gospel. But in spite of its two-volume length, it is the prayer of the present writer that the many words in this work will honor both the Lord and the evangelist who so perceptively wrote about him.

May each of us, therefore, in studying this Gospel perceive more fully the preexistent and risen glory of God's only Son (1:14). But may each of us also recognize that that glory involved the self-giving death of the Lamb of God who takes away the sin of the world.

Soli Deo Gloria

---

[194] This verse, as Beasley-Murray (*John*, 416) suggests, reminds the reader of statements like the one attributed to Johanan ben Zakkai, who was reputed to have imagined that even if the heavens were parchment, the trees were quills, and the seas were ink, they could not suffice to record all of his wisdom or learning that he received from his rabbinic instructors (cf. *Str–B*, 2.587). This statement, of course, also reminds one of the final stanza that was added to the gospel song, "The Love of God," which basically uses the imagery of ben Zakkai.

A SUMMARY OF JOHANNINE THEOLOGY

1. Introduction
2. One Possible Approach: A Systematic Pattern
3. Another Option: Affirming the Story Nature of the Gospel in Theology
   (1) About God in John
   (2) About Human Weakness and Sin
   (3) About Human Hostility
   (4) About Satan, the Ultimate Enemy
   (5) About Jesus
   (6) About Believing and Life
   (7) About Love
   (8) About the Community
   (9) About Prayer
   (10) About the Holy Spirit and the Divine Presence
   (11) About Destiny and the Ultimate Hope
Excursus 33: Questions of Eternity—Where Is the Place? What Is It Like?
   How Do We Get There?

A SUMMARY OF JOHANNINE THEOLOGY

---

1. Introduction

The Gospel of John is an amazing theological document. Its verses have been used repeatedly by the Church Fathers and successive Christian formulators of varying doctrinal views. Its texts have also been manipulated by a host of deviants who have departed from historic Christianity, such as the Gnostic mythologists[1] and outright opponents of Christianity such as the followers of Islam, who have employed the Paraclete passages to proclaim the foretelling of Mohammed.[2]

To supply a brief theological summary of Johannine thought, therefore, is no mean task. In this summary I will not attempt to re-present the

---

[1] For example the *Gospel of Truth* as well as many other Gnostic documents show a knowledge of the canonical Gospel of John. For the *Gospel of Truth* see J. M. Robinson, ed., *The Nag Hammadi Library* (New York: Harper & Row, 1977), 37–49. For a commentary on this work see K. Grobel, *The Gospel of Truth* (Nashville: Abingdon, 1960).

[2] For a brief review of this interpretation see my comments in connection with "The First Spirit Statement" at 14:15–17 and particularly at n. 146.

detailed arguments in the commentary or repeat the footnotes included in the various sections. Rather, an effort will be made to provide an overview of some striking theological features in John's Gospel.

In this effort one is faced with a decision with the way one should design such a summary. In recent times a number of significant theological studies have appeared. After discussing the various settings in which the Gospel took shape, M. Smith concentrated on discussing the Johannine themes.[3] In this process he was clearly aided by the earlier work of R. Brown, who detailed a number of the Johannine themes in appendices to his commentary.[4] Earlier E. Lee and J. Crehan also followed a similar pattern to that of Smith and Brown.[5] And prior to these writers A. Corell had focused on this style in terms of Johannine eschatology and ecclesiology.[6]

More recently Beasley-Murray sought to summarize Johannine theology in terms of the concept of life as it relates to the Son of God/Son of Man, the Holy Spirit, and the church and ministry, including what he refers to as the Sacraments in the Fourth Gospel.[7] In the present study I will not attempt to replicate these earlier studies. Instead, I will attempt to provide a brief summary of some theological perspectives I find emerging from the Gospel.

2. One Possible Approach: A Systematic Pattern

In this effort of arriving at a reasonable summary, I have struggled with how to begin such a summary and maintain a sensitivity to the approach of John's Gospel presentation. Of course, one obvious option was to employ the categories of systematic or dogmatic theology. Such an option can be very appealing to readers who tend to think in deductive categories. The result of such an effort would be to supply readers with what might be a brief handbook of Johannine theology. This handbook could serve as a teaching aid by setting forth in a logical manner the Johannine perspectives on such matters as revelation, God (including the possible triune formulations), humanity, and the subsequent relationships between God and humanity in terms of creation, sin, salvation, and the processes of bringing about both judgment and blessing in the present world and in the hereafter,

---

[3] See D. M. Smith, *The Theology of the Gospel of John* (Cambridge: University Press, 1995).

[4] See R. E. Brown, *The Gospel According to John (i–xii)*, AB (Garden City: Doubleday, 1966), 497–538.

[5] See E. Lee, *The Religious Thought of St. John* (London: S.P.C.K., 1962) and J. Crehan, *The Theology of St. John* (New York: Sheed & Ward, 1965).

[6] A. Corell, *Consummatum Est* (London: S.P.C.K., 1958).

[7] G. Beasley-Murray, *Gospel of Life: Theology in the Fourth Gospel* (Peabody, Mass.: Hendrickson, 1991).

including, of course, the nature and role of the church in that process.

Such a pattern usually requires constructing a theological statement through the extraction of the Johannine ideas and theological themes from the stories and the dialogical pericopes in the Gospel. The resulting construct might be quite helpful if one would pursue it in something like the following manner.

Beginning with the concern for revelation, one could naturally detail the fact that God made known his divine purposes with humanity at a strategic point in history through the unique *(monogenes)* WORD *(logos)* that for a brief time became flesh and tented/dwelt among us (John 1:14).

In this section one would certainly want to include a discussion of the meaning of terms such as "knowing" *(ginōskein)* and "believing" *(pisteuein),* which are only used in their verb forms and never in their noun or substantive forms in this Gospel. Such a restriction to verbs is certainly of critical importance in understanding this Gospel. The reason, of course, is that the evangelist has purposely drawn attention to the fact that it is not "what" you know or believe that is the foundation of this revelation but "who" you know that is the focus of this Johannine message. The use of the verbs clearly emphasizes the dynamic nature of believing and knowing, and readers should pay particular attention to this fact. Thus, while doctrinal formulations were certainly important to the Johannine community, as is evidenced by the arguments in the first epistle (cf. 1 John 2:22; 4:2–3), nevertheless even in that epistle the dynamics of "living" and "loving" (2:24–25; 4:7–23) are just as significant as the centrality of the new commandment is in the Gospel (cf. John 13:34–35).

As with Nicodemus, who thought he could categorize Jesus (3:2–4), and the woman of Samaria, who had neat little packaged ideas about the Messiah and worship (4:19–26), so the reader of John should soon realize that such ideas when presented primarily in terms of formulations can easily miss the living reality of the revealing Word who tented among humans like the tabernacle that moved around the wilderness with the people of Israel (cf. John 1:14).

Formulations and idea constructs can often fail to represent John adequately. Thus the Jews of Jesus' day had many ideas about God and the way God worked in the world. Like the Prodigal Son in Luke 15:18,21, the Jews avoided using the name of God and spoke of God in surrogate ways such as "heaven" because they feared taking the name of God in vain and in so doing violating God's holiness. Even more recently the followers of Islam set in single moveable script for print the entire name of Allah rather than in separate moveable type for fear that the letters of their God would be used elsewhere in unholy words and thus take the name of God in vain. But Jesus entered this world scene and fearlessly called God his "Father," a fact that clearly angered the theologically sensitive Jewish leaders of his day (cf. John 5:18). And what was even more startling is that he had the audacity to teach his disciples to call God their Father also (cf. Matt 6:9,14–15; John 16:23,27).[8] Therefore what Jesus actually did was to upset the Jewish finely tuned theological base system. He summoned people to view their relationship to God in a very different manner from the harsh way the rabbis did.

Misguided views about the way the ancients thought God related to the world were common. Among those misguided humans the man who had been paralyzed for thirty-eight years is a prime example. In his wrongly conceived mythological mind-set he pictured God as dealing with humans on a "first come, first served" basis (John 5:7) so that he could not conceive of God acting in Jesus outside the boundaries of his set perception. Likewise, the Jews argued that Moses was the dispenser of manna or bread in the wilderness (6:30–31). They were also certain that "when Christ would appear" no one would know where he came from (7:27); and that since they were Abraham's descendants they had never been in bondage (8:33). Moreover, in their commitments to their doctrinal "correctness" they clearly instructed the healed blind man to give praise to God but also to admit that Jesus must be a sinner because he healed on the Sabbath (9:24). But their "ideas" about God and Jesus were patently incorrect according to John.

It should be apparent that the wonderful stories of the Johannine Gospel do not fit nicely into the specific divisions of systematic or dogmatic theology. Of course, one can extract verses from the stories to fit the categories, as was done most notably in past generations by renowned writers such as A. H. Strong and C. Hodge.[9] But that method, helpful as it may be for some readers, really employs categories that are external to the Gospel stories and pericopes in a deductive manner as a means for organizing idea segments presented by the evangelist for the purpose of developing a holistic system or structure. In a sense we all import structure in the task of writing theologies. My goal, therefore, is not to condemn structure nor to provide this brief theological summary without a structure.

3. Another Option: Affirming the Story Nature of the Gospel in Theology

My purpose in this summary is to affirm the story nature of this Gospel and to focus on the primary aspects of theology that are related to the Gospel stories. Besides, anyone reading my commentary will sense immedi-

---

[8] For my comments on the Lord's Prayer and the use of "Father" see G. Borchert, "The Lord of Form and Freedom: A New Testament Perspective on Worship," *RevExp* 80 (1983): 15–16.

[9] See A. H. Strong, *Systematic Theology: A Compendium* (1907; reprint, Philadelphia: Judson, 1957) and C. Hodge, *Systematic Theology* (1871; reprint, Grand Rapids: Eerdmans, 1989).

ately that I think the Gospel has a definite structure of its own, and I have sought to elucidate that structure in the commentary and the earlier "triptik," or map, which I have provided in both volumes of this study. My goal at this point, however, is not to repeat that structure but to reaffirm the story nature of John's theology.

(1) About God in John

The stories in this Gospel do tell us some very important ideas about God: who was in the beginning (1:1; 17:5); whom no one has seen (1:18; 6:46); who loves the world (3:16); and more specifically loves the *obedient* followers of Jesus (14:21; 17:26); who sent the Son to save the world (3:17); who is Spirit (4:26); who raises the dead (5:21) and does not need to judge because he has committed that role to Jesus (5:22), who in turn uses the Scriptures and Moses to judge (5:45–46); who draws people to himself and is the source of authentic teaching (6:44–45; 7:16) who speaks and his people hear (8:47); whose "realm" is the consummate destiny of his people (14:1–3; 17:24); who with Jesus sends the Paraclete/the Spirit (14:26; 15:26); who is the ultimate protector of his people (17:11); and is the one to whom Jesus "delivered" his spirit when he died (19:30), an idea that is a deduction to avoid Jesus' delivering his spirit to the devil.

(2) About Human Weakness and Sin

These stories and pericopes also tell us about the other side of reality, namely human weakness, sin, hostility to God and the penchant for human misunderstanding. Even those who were supposed to be God's own people refused to receive God's sent Word (1:10). Since they had turned God's house into a place of business (2:16), they hardly were able to recognize his messenger, who embodied in himself the sanctuary of God (2:18–19). As a result Jesus was unwilling to accept the integrity of their believing because he knew the real nature of humanity (2:23–25) and understood the lack of commitment on the part of some of the leaders in their believing patterns (12:42–43).

The misunderstanding of the people who are out of harmony with God is a constant refrain in this Gospel: whether it is Nicodemus, who thinks he knows the nature of Jesus (3:2–4); the woman of Samaria, who represents the perspective of the rejected ones (4:15,19–22,25–26); the disciples themselves, who often seem to live in a fog (4:27,31–34; 11:8–14; 12:16; 16:29–32); the well-intentioned Peter (13:36–38; 21:20–22); the realist Thomas, who made intriguing statements (11:16; 14:5–7; 20:25); the sidekick Philip (14:8–9); Martha, who could parrot typical Jewish theology (11:21–27,39–40); the doubting brothers of Jesus (7:3–9); the Jews, who waited for the coming of the Messiah (7:25–28; 12:12–13); or the grieving Mary

Magdalene (20:13–17). Confusion concerning Jesus and his work reigned supreme.

(3) About Human Hostility

But this Gospel also presents pictures of those whose misunderstanding merges into rejection of Jesus and outright hostility and enmity toward him. Among those who could be included in this negative group are those who refused to accept him (1:11); the paralytic, who blamed others for his situations in life and testified against Jesus to save his skin (5:6–7,10–15); the parents of the blind man, who did not want to become involved in a problem with their rejected son in order to maintain their status in the synagogue (9:20–23); the leaders, who believed but refused to acknowledge Jesus openly because of their desire for human praise and affirmation (12:42–43); the Pharisees and Jews who refused to accept Jesus and became part of the growing opposition to Jesus (2:18–20; 5:16; 6:41–42,52–59; 7:25,32,45–49; 8:13,39–44,48; 9:13–16,34,39–41; 10:31–33; 12:19); the scheming Caiaphas and Annas and their obedient council members and followers (11:47–53,57; 18:3,13,19–24,28; 19:6–7,15,21); and of course Judas, the betrayer, thief, son of doom, and devil man (6:70–71; 12:4–6; 13:2,26–30; 17:12; 18:3–6).

(4) About Satan, the Ultimate Enemy

To this negative category one must also add the ultimate enemy of God and Jesus, the one who is called the devil, Satan, and the prince of this world (12:31; 13:27 and perhaps 17:15). He is, in fact, the major force in the world behind the hostility against Jesus and his followers. He is portrayed as the one who instigates opposition directly or indirectly through knowing or unknowing devotees (8:44; 10:35–39; 12:31–35; 14:30; 15:18–25; 16:2,11). The hostility against the followers of Jesus resulted in all forms of persecution epitomized in hatred (17:14), excommunication of Jesus' followers from Jewish synagogues (16:2; cf. 9:22,34), and the killing of Jesus' followers (16:2; 21:18–19).

(5) About Jesus

Having thus detailed several general theological issues in this Gospel, it is imperative at this point to recognize that the Gospel of John is focused primarily on the person and work of Jesus. Everything that is written by the evangelist is intended to provide the reader with an adequate theology concerning the significance of Jesus in order that the reader might believe that Jesus is indeed the expected Messiah/Christ, the Son of God, and through authentic believing in him gain "life" (20:31).

This Jesus was none other than the Word *(logos)* who was *sui genesis* with God. Even though a distinction is made between the *logos* and *theos* (God) on the one hand, the evangelist, as I have indicated in the commentary at 1:1, immediately adds that the *logos* was also *theos*. This Word that was also God became flesh *(sarx)* and lived or tented among humans as God's special agent or gift to the world. He was indeed the unique revealer of the nature of God to humans (1:18). Here then is the manner in which John describes the incarnation of Jesus and the way in which the evangelist presents his high Christological formulation concerning the person of Jesus. Elsewhere in the Gospel he sets out repeatedly in narrative fashion that Jesus is both equal with God and the obedient agent of the Father (e.g., 5:18–19,30; 6:38; 8:14,23–24; 10:29–30; 14:8–9,20; 17:5).

For John, Jesus epitomized Yahweh, the God who revealed himself to Moses as the great "I AM." Thus in this Gospel, Jesus proclaimed himself as *ego eimi* to the Samaritan woman in her expectation of the Messiah (4:26) and to the disciples when he walked on the water (6:20). Moreover, he concluded the use of this form of self-reference by employing it during his arrest, after which his opponents fell helplessly to the ground before the serene divine-like figure of Jesus (18:4–6; cf. 13:19).

In addition to the above unexpanded, bold *ego eimi* references to Jesus, John includes a number of expanded "I am" sayings of Jesus that help to define for the reader both Jesus' nature and his work. Jesus is "the bread of life" (6:35,48), "the light of the world" (8:12; 9:5), "the door" for his sheep (10:7,9), "the good shepherd" (10:11,14), "the resurrection and the life" (11:25), "the way, the truth and the life" (14:6), and "the true vine" (15:1,5). Each of these "I am" descriptions, as I have indicated in the commentary, present Jesus as the epitome of some aspect of Israel's heritage with Yahweh, whether it was from the time of the Exodus, or the entry into the Promised Land, or the symbol of faithful Israel, or the replacement for the false shepherds, or Israel's eschatological hope. Jesus is the symbol and embodiment of true Israel.

But even in those chapters of John where the "I am" formula is not used or expanded, the reader is led step by step to recognize that Jesus is represented as bringing a replacement or fulfilment to Israel's heritage. He is the new Bethel for (Jacob) Israel (1:51); the new wine of celebration (2:10); the new sanctuary of God (2:19); the new birth from above (3:3); the new lifted-up one who like Moses brings healing to the people who believe (3:14–15); the new salvation for the Samaritan rejects of society (4:42); the new way of believing without seeing (4:48–50; cf. 9:11,35–38; 20:29); the new hope for those who have despaired as the people in the wilderness for thirty-eight years (5:5); the fulfillment of the messianic expectations at Tabernacles (7:2–3,27) and the replacement for the Water ceremony (7:37–39); the new freedom from slavery (8:31–34); the "I am" of time before Abraham (8:58); the new answer with the blind man to theodicy (9:2); the fulfillment of the "winter" festival of Dedication/Hanukkah (10:22); the new interpretation of Passover (11:50–52); the new meaning of Hosanna, the King of Israel and the parade into Jerusalem (12:7,13,24); the new perspective on being the teacher and Lord (13:4–5,12–14); the giver of the new commandment for God's people (13:34–35; 15:12); the provider of a new understanding of God's "place" or "realm" (14:1–3); the sender of a new Paraclete/Companion (14:16); the initiator of a new relationship of the Lord with his people (15:14–16); the one who brings a new joy (16:20–22; cf. 15:11); the petitioner for new perspectives among the people of God including security, holiness, oneness, hope, and love (17:11,15,17,21, 24,26); the new day of Preparation (19:14,31); the new peace (20:21–22); and the presenter of a new commission (20:23,21:15–17,22). In spite of the length of this list, it is hardly exhaustive.

On every page of the Gospel, Jesus is "exegeting" God and God's intention in the world (1:18). Moreover, for John, Jesus is the completion or fulfillment of authentic Israel. For him, therefore, after the resurrection there is no longer a need for Passover or Sabbath. As I have indicated repeatedly in the commentary, Passover is a factor in every section of the Gospel up to the death of Jesus. But with the coming of the resurrection (which was in the background repeatedly and acknowledged as early as 2:22), everything changed for John. Everything became new. The resurrection of Jesus brought a new day. Worship became focused on the first day of the week (20:19,26),[10] the Lord's day (cf. Rev 1:10). The seventh day was no longer viewed as the day of the Lord. It was changed to celebrate the day of the victory over death,[11] which the *logos* (the Word) had brought to the people of God.

This victory over death was absolutely strategic in the thinking of both the Johannine and Pauline churches because the "last" enemy was not regarded as the devil but *death* (cf. Rev 20:14; 1 Cor 15:26). When Jesus conquered death, he evidenced for the early Christians the greatest power known to humanity. Because of the resurrection power of God, Thomas, the realist of the disciples, was able to make the most significant confession in any of the Gospels, namely, "My Lord and My God!" (20:28).

This confession of Thomas encapsulates Johannine Christology about Jesus, who was God (cf. 1:1). Moreover, according to John, Jesus invited

---

[10] For a discussion on "eight days later" see my commentary on John 20:26.

[11] For Paul the hinge point of Christianity is also the resurrection of Jesus Christ (cf. 1 Cor 15:12–17). For my comment on this passage see G. Borchert, "The Resurrection: 1 Corinthians 15," *RevExp* 80 (1983): 401–15.

those who would hear or read about him (receive the testimony) to make the same confession as Thomas, even though they would not have the same opportunity to see the resurrected Lord. Remember that the Gospel of John was written very late in the first century to readers who would, like us, never have the opportunity to see the risen Lord. Therefore for John the accompanying blessing of Jesus on such believers (20:29) was extremely significant. And this statement leads us to return to the pervasive Johannine themes of "believing" and "life" (20:30–31).

(6) About Believing and Life

The gaining of eternal life is for John the strategic purpose of God in giving his Son to the world (3:16). God's purpose was hardly condemnation (3:17), but the reality of human disobedience, which would in John be united with not believing, meant that judgment was a consequence of human behavior (3:18,36; cf. 1:11; 5:23–24). To gain life in John necessitates accepting, receiving, and obeying Jesus (1:12; 3:36; 4:14; 5:24; 6:51; 8:51; 10:27–28; 11:25; 12:36; 17:2–3).

For the disciples in the time of Jesus before the resurrection, the expectation was probably that if people would see Jesus and his signs then they would believe in him (6:40; cf. 2:11). But not all who "saw" and "believed" were regarded by Jesus as authentic believers (2:23–24). Indeed, the ultimate goal of this Gospel was not a believing that was based on seeing. It was a believing that was based on accepting the testimony of the witnesses without seeing (20:29).

Thus the trusting official in the second Cana sign, who believed the word of Jesus concerning his ill son without seeing the healing take place, is a model for Christian believing (4:46–53). But since this second sign forms an inclusio with the first Cana sign (cf. 2:11), the believing official (4:53) serves as an introductory comparison to the disciples who were present at the changing of water to wine and who believed when they saw the sign performed by Jesus (2:11). To believe is certainly a focal theme in John, but to believe without seeing is the overall point of this inclusio (4:48).[12] And the reader should remember that an inclusio encompasses not merely the beginning and end of a comparison but all parts of the comparison contained within the unit (cf. for example the first eight statements of

---

[12] Remember that no other signs are numbered in John even though readers often try to count the signs with a view to reaching the number seven. The point of the numbering of the Cana signs is to communicate that the two signs form a unit on the issue of believing. But the strategic difference is that the official was not present to see the healing taking place.

the Beatitudes in Matt 5:3–10).[13]

Another model of this nonseeing and believing is the blind man who acted on Jesus' command to wash (9:7) and then defended Jesus, the healer, even though he had not seen Jesus (9:17,25,27,30–33; cf. 9:36–38). Still another example would be the Beloved (other) Disciple, who saw only the grave clothes and believed (20:8).

Of course the question readers tend to ask is: How much believing would constitute adequate believing, especially in light of the statement at 20:9, which indicated that the disciples "did not understand the Scripture" concerning the necessity of Jesus' resurrection? Great care, therefore, must be taken not to concentrate on the amount of believing involved in the stories. For example, readers may be tempted to rate the amount of believing associated with the disciples in the first Cana story (2:11) because of the contemporary desire to identify what is often called "saving" believing. Obviously some believing in the Gospel is classified as inadequate or inauthentic by the evangelist and Jesus (cf. 2:23–25). It becomes clear that Martha's powerful believing confession that Jesus is the Christ, the Son of God, at 11:27 later proves to be primarily mere words when she comes with Jesus to the tomb of her brother and warns Jesus that her brother stinks (11:39–40)!

The best way to understand the evangelist's stories, however, is to realize that he is not satisfied with achieving a set level of believing. Rather, John, like Jesus, would constantly push the reader and the believer to more intense stages of believing. Accordingly, a follower of Jesus should never be satisfied with having attained to a *stage* of belief *(a noun)*. Instead, the believer's life should be constantly more integrated into the life of the Lord as branches are called to abide *(a verb)* in the vine (15:4–5).

Abiding in Jesus, therefore, would be a better way of interpreting for contemporary readers what believing implies for John. Accordingly, those who "turned back" and ceased following Jesus were inadequate believers (cf. 6:66). Also the Scripture's as well as the Paraclete's role in the lives of Christians is to bear witness to Jesus (15:26) in order to keep us Christians from "falling away" or "going astray" (16:1).

---

[13] Interpreters of the Sermon on the Mount and especially the Beatitudes should pay particular attention to the nature of an inclusio in communicating its meaning. In the Beatitudes it is absolutely crucial because the eight Beatitudes (Matt 5:3–10) are not merely to be understood as separable characteristics of individual Christian lives but more pointedly as a composite of a Christian life. Then the ninth Beatitude, with its conclusion of rejoicing (5:11–12), is the application of all of the earlier Beatitudes as the shift is made from generalized statements (Blessed are those …) to particularized application (Blessed are you …!). Many teachers and preachers of the Beatitudes often miss this important fact in their presentations.

Most Christians, as I indicated in my study on *Assurance and Warning,*[14] devour the assurance texts in the Bible but hardly resonate with any texts that suggest that a sense of warning is being given (e.g., 1 Cor 10:6–12; Heb 6:4–6). Yet even where there are indications of warnings the reader should note that there are usually assurances connected with those warnings (e.g., 1 Cor 6:13; Heb 6:18). The reason is that the Gospel is "good news," not "bad news." But it also serves notice to readers that they should accept the reality checks on believing and obeying that are in Scripture (e.g., John 3:18,36). It should also be remembered that while the texts of the New Testament advocate an evangelistic message for unbelievers, they were first and foremost written to instruct Christian believers in the authentic nature of the Gospel.

This later point is absolutely crucial to recognize because it affects the way we interpret not only the theme of believing/obeying but also the crucial theme of life in John. The theme of life is not merely about beginning new life with Jesus, the Lord, but equally, if not more, about living life with the living Jesus. That is the reason why the central idea of the Farewell Cycle is focused on "abiding" in Jesus, the Vine. But it is also imperative for those who were brought up on older English versions of the New Testament to understand that the Greek verb *menein* is best translated "remain" or "continue" in the vine (15:4,6,7,10). Starting life with Jesus is very important; continuing to live with Jesus and obeying his directions in life are crucial (15:10).

(7) About Love

Although the Johannine Gospel does not spend much time outlining the characteristics of the Christian life and ethical behavior, it epitomizes the transformed life in the commandment "to love" (13:34–35; 15:12). Because love is not self-oriented and indeed transcends the self, it reflects the nature of the divine perspective, namely, the God who loved the world and gave his Son to provide eternal life for the people of the world (3:16; 1 John 4:9). And since the Father loved the Son (10:17; 17:24), Jesus modeled the Father's love while he was on earth (13:34; 15:9). Moreover, he summoned his followers to love him as the basis for their lives (14:21).

Loving also means keeping Jesus' commandments, which are epitomized in loving one another (13:34; 14:15,21,23; 15:12,17). Loving others means caring for them, as Peter came to understand (21:15,16,17; cf. 1 Pet 5:2).

In directing the community to further recognize the meaning of this love, John in the first epistle reminded Christians that love does not merely involve words but includes deeds of love (1 John 3:18). Loving God implies

---

[14] See G. Borchert, *Assurance and Warning* (Nashville: Broadman, 1987).

loving others also. Therefore John enunciates clearly the fact that God-talk (namely, saying one loves God) without concrete loving action is inauthentic speech that can be categorized frankly as lying (1 John 4:20–21), and lying is in essence the characteristic of the devil (cf. John 8:44). But among the basic characteristics of both Jesus and God are truth (1:14; 14:6) and love (John 5:42; 15:9–10; 1 John 4:16). Jesus modeled that love in action through exemplifying the pattern of servanthood during the foot-washing scene that begins the Farewell Cycle. John introduced this entire cycle by stating that in the foot washing Jesus showed the disciples "the full extent of his love," an idea that reflected his willingness to love them to the ultimate level—namely, his death (John 13:1; cf. 15:13).

(8) About the Community

The modeling of the divine pattern of life for his disciples in foot washing presupposes that Jesus intended to establish a believing community that would follow his pattern and represent him in the world after his death and resurrection. Jesus was not a mere solitary voice "crying in the wilderness" like John the baptizer and witness (John 1:23–27). Moreover, Jesus was not a leader seeking to establish an alternative community in the desert like the Qumran covenanters. Although his community undoubtedly was intended to provide an alternative life pattern to the way of the world, Jesus did not intend for his community to be removed from the world but to be kept holy and pure in the midst of the world (17:15).

Because Jesus' community was to be established in the very heart of the world, the world would hate and kill his followers just as they hated and killed him (15:18–25; 16:2–3; 17:14). Accordingly, they needed to be protected by the power of God so that their witness might not be squelched (17:11–14). They certainly would abandon him in his hour of death (16:32), but he would never abandon them in their days of tribulation (14:18; 16:33).

Furthermore, in spite of the fact that this new community of Jesus would be hated, as I have indicated above, they were not to be known as a people of hate (cf. 1 John 4:19–20). Instead, they were to be characterized by love, the exact opposite of hate (John 13:34–35; cf. 1 John 3:13–17). And this community was to be marked by obedience to the commands of Jesus (John 14:15; 15:10). Thus the community was to reflect the very nature of Jesus because their members would be like branches that were attached to the parent vine that is Jesus. And it is only because of this attachment that the branches can bear the authentic fruit of the vine (15:1–5).

One of the most fascinating assertions in the Gospel is the statement that these believers (followers of Jesus) would later do even greater works than Jesus had done (14:12). This statement can easily be misunderstood to imply that the community would be able to perform more spectacular signs than the raising of Lazarus (11:43–44), the walking on the water (6:19), or the healing of the official's son at a distance (4:50–53). Can you imagine your Christian community outdoing these amazing acts? This idea may be difficult to accept, but Jesus' statement correctly understood is quite legitimate. There are works done by the Christian community that do exceed anything Jesus did while he was on earth. For example, in terms of the extent of the Christian mission, the sheer number of people who are confronted with the Gospel during any given week far exceeds anything Jesus did while he was on earth. Yet the followers of Jesus do not do this work in their own strength. They do their effective work only when they are attached to the Vine (15:5). If they do not continue to be attached to the Vine, that incisive pericope indicates they are dead wood and might as well be burned (15:6).

But Jesus was not interested in the destruction of his followers. He wanted them to be preserved and to prosper in their representation of him. Therefore he not only prayed for their protection but also for their holiness (17:11–15,17). Moreover, he was clearly concerned for their unity because communities of faith can easily fragment, and in so doing the mission purposes of our Lord are devastated (17:11,20–21). In addition, Jesus wanted his faithful communities to sense that they had a destiny to meet their Lord where he is in all his splendor (17:24). But while they are still on earth, they are to model the love of God in their lives.

(9) About Prayer

While they are on earth, members of the Christian community maintain their relationship with God in Jesus through prayer and the presence of the Holy Spirit. Concerning prayer, Christians are to remain attached to the Vine, who is Jesus, in order for the resources of God to be available to them (15:4). In this relationship they can petition God concerning their needs. As I indicated in the commentary on the texts about "asking" or praying to God, it is absolutely essential that Christians have the correct understanding about prayer and petitioning God. It may seem like the Johannine texts at 14:14; 15:7; 16:23 mean that the Christian community can ask of God anything the people desire and as long as they accompany the request with the name of "Jesus," God will do it. With such a perspective God would thus be like a jolly, old Santa Claus dispensing any presents we might wish, as long as we repeat the magical formula of Jesus' name. But instinctively we know that such an interpretation cannot be the correct meaning of these texts. Instead, when we ask in the name of Jesus, we must remember that "name" implies "nature," so we must ask not in our sinful, selfish natures but in the nature or spirit of Jesus. When we pray the way Jesus would pray, our prayers are no longer formulated as selfish statements of our desires enhanced by a magical mantra of reciting a mysterious name that assures us of results. Rather, prayers become, like those of Jesus in the Garden of Gethsemane, great experiences of agonizing wrestling with God's will (Luke 22:42–44). Similarly in John 15:7 asking presupposes both abiding in Jesus and obeying or embodying his self-giving pattern of living (his words) in our lives. When such an obedient pattern becomes our way of life, our prayers can hardly be self-centered petitions. Prayer then becomes a reflection of our authentic worship of God and a genuine response to God's presence in our lives.

(10) About the Holy Spirit and the Divine Presence

The Johannine sections concerning the Paraclete (14:25–31; 15:26–16:15) are crucial to the message of the Farewell Cycle and to our understanding of the Christian community are. When Jesus announced his departure from the world, he promised his grieving followers that they would be given another Companion/Paraclete to replace him (14:16). They would not be orphaned or left without the divine presence in their lives (14:18).

The Holy Spirit would be for them their resource of authenticity or truth, guaranteeing them that they would have within them the perspectives of God in direct contrast to the perspectives of the world (14:17). The Paraclete would serve as their divine teacher, reminding them of the way of Jesus (14:26). And the peace *(shalom)* of God would touch their troubled hearts so that they would not need to fear living in the world (14:27). Even though the world was a hostile place, their new companion would be their present witness to Jesus, and this word of comfort and resource would keep them from being a victim of scandal and falling from God's way (16:1).

But the role of the Holy Spirit was not merely for protection and preservation. The Paraclete would also serve as an attorney and judge on their behalf and through them charge the world with sinfulness and set clearly before the world God's standard of righteousness. The result would be that judgment would be rendered on the world because the world and its prince, the devil, fail to meet the divine standards (16:8–11). But positively the companion Spirit would act as an authentic truthful guide in leading the followers of Jesus in the way of Jesus (16:13). In this role the Spirit would bring glory to Jesus (16:14).

Although the disciples did not fully understand the implications of these promises concerning the Spirit before the death and resurrection of Jesus (cf. 16:31–33), these words became a reality in the postresurrection era. During the resurrection appearances Jesus breathed on the disciples (20:22), just as God breathed on the dust called Adam (Gen 2:7), and in that act Jesus told them to "receive the Holy Spirit" (John 20:22).

In addition, he gave them their commission concerning the forgiveness of sins (20:23). That commission in effect summarized the church's role as Jesus' agents in the proclamation of salvation. But that commission presupposed the presence of the Spirit in the lives of the members of the Christian community to supply them with the authority to communicate the Gospel both positively and negatively in the power of God (20:23; cf. Matt 16:18; 18:18; cf. also 1 Cor 5:3–5; 2 Cor 2:10–11).

The reception of the Spirit thus brings to a fulfillment the expectation of the Tabernacles' water festival in John (7:37–39). And in harmony with the fact that God is Spirit (John 4:24) and Jesus has been given the Spirit without limits (3:34), the true followers of Jesus are born of the Spirit (3:5). But since there are many spirits in the world, as the first epistle of John makes clear, the people of God must exercise discernment and test the spirits to determine whether people are truly of God. To have the Spirit of Truth one must be a living example not only of active love (1 John 4:7–21) but also of one whose theology is solidly built on the incarnation of Jesus (1 John 4:1–6). The overall task of the Spirit within Christians and the community of faith is to reaffirm and witness to the person and way of Jesus (14:26; 15:26) and to glorify him on earth (16:14).

(11) About Destiny and the Ultimate Hope

The message of John, however, does not end with an earthly destiny and death. While the focus of the Gospel is on the time of Jesus and the implications for the present earthly world, there is another order that provides perspective to everything that takes place in this world. That other order is briefly mentioned in a few places in John's Gospel.

The coming of Jesus affects the horizons of our thinking and our theology. His coming brought a new dimension in thinking about the hour. Although the hour pointed most consistently in John to the hour of Jesus' glorification in the death on the cross (e.g., 2:4; 12:23–24), that hour also pointed to the opening of the tombs (5:28) and the time when the dead would come forth to the great divide: the resurrection to life on the one hand and the resurrection to condemnation on the other (5:29). Clearly then John does not regard this era to be the final stage of reality. Although the reader would need to consult the Book of Revelation for more details on blessing, judgment, and condemnation in the thinking of the Johannine community, the negative aspect of ultimate destiny is briefly but certainly asserted in the Gospel.

Yet the concern of the Gospel is not so much with the bad news as it is with the good news and the hope of the Christian community. The departure of Jesus made it imperative for him to provide his disciples with some hints concerning the destiny and hope of his followers. Thus he spoke to them of going away to prepare a special place for them in the Father's realm (14:1–

2) even though they could hardly integrate his ideas into their thinking (14:3–9). Moreover, he prayed to the Father that they would be able to see his place of destiny and recognize his glory (17:24). Further, he indicated that the Spirit would help them to understand what would take place in the future (16:13). But beyond these verses and a few references to the fact that Jesus was "going back to the Father" (16:28) and would regain the glory he had "before the world began" (17:5), the perspective of the future hope of Christians is gained in John from our sense of the meaning of resurrection faith.

Rather than pursuing the matter of destiny further in this context, therefore, I have opted to close this theological summary with an extended excursus on the question of human destiny from various perspectives so that the reader will have a larger framework into which the ideas of time, space, and the future may be placed, particularly in light of our new concepts of dimensional thinking. The reason for adding this excursus is to help the reader realize that some of the ideas are rooted not in the Bible but in cultural views that may now be quite passé. Accordingly, it is imperative, from my point of view, to release our biblical texts like John from the bondage of inadequate philosophical perspectives and allow those texts to speak freely and unchained in the second millennium.

Excursus 33: Questions of Eternity: Where Is the Place? What Is It Like? How Do We Get There?

The text of John 14:1–9 and others in the New Testament raise some extremely important questions for Christians. Many assumptions are made concerning these texts that affect our theological commitments. Indeed, among some of the most misunderstood concepts in Christianity are popular folk ideas about the afterlife, heaven, and the soul. The task of a biblical commentator is to try to interpret biblical texts within their contexts and relate them to contemporary understandings of reality.

Many thoughts go through our minds about what happens to people who die. Our questions are like those of the recipients of 1 Thess 4:13. Of course we have learned in Sunday School that these people are with Jesus, but some may wonder what they were doing without a body since they were in caskets. Some well-meaning people tell us about the soul and about the fact that dead Christians do not need bodies any longer. But usually their explanations leave us with many more questions. These questions stir in our minds as we seek to understand the mystery of death and life with Jesus, a mystery that many people call immortality.

The little book by Oscar Cullmann on immortality *or* resurrection[15] can be helpful in rethinking our views concerning immortality because it forces us to

---

[15] O. Cullmann, *Immortality of the Soul or Resurrection of the Dead? The Witness of the New Testament* (London: Epworth, 1958).

think in an alternative way. And what of space? The British astronomer Sir James Jeans caused a stir a number of years ago when he said that "space was expanding." That is hardly a shock today, but if space is expanding, one can ask, Where is heaven, and what is happening to it during this expansion?

Now we know that heaven is not merely up and hell is not merely down. So when Nikita Kruschev declared that his cosmonauts could not find heaven or God as they went up in their space ship, it hardly made a ripple in most people's thinking.

Of particular significance for this present issue is Lewis's *The Great Divorce,* which is a story of a bus ride between earth, hell, and heaven. In that story people wanted to go to heaven, but when they arrived in heaven, some of them felt totally out of place. The reason was that they could not walk in heaven because of the substance in their feet. Every step was painful. Other people, however, could walk without any trouble because their bodies were of a different composition. Accordingly, those who could not walk in heaven got back on the bus and went to what we would call hell, where their feet would allow them to walk again.[16]

How much that idea of different substances in bodies is reminiscent of John 20:20,26, where the nature of Jesus' resurrected body allowed him to go through walls and doors that were shut while mere humans like the disciples could hardly do the same. We would surely bang our noses. Now both Jesus and humans have bodies, but the compositions of those bodies are radically different. If such bodies are vastly different (that surely is what Paul says in 1 Cor 15:35–44) and if the ideas of "up-ness" and "down-ness" are quite inappropriate in thinking about God and God's realm, then perhaps our reasoning about the nature of "whereness" with respect to God might be rather misconceived. It would also follow that our understanding of heaven and hell might be quite skewed and still built upon a presupposition of a three-storied universe—an idea that is totally inappropriate in the context of a spherical cosmos. A contemporary view of time and space might offer a very different scenario if one was willing to engage in dimensional thinking rather than thinking that is rooted in plane geometry.

Let me therefore lead your thinking in a different direction. As I have often asked my students to do, I now ask my readers to think about space—not space of astronauts but the mere space occupied by a chair. When I sit on a chair, my wife cannot sit on the space of the chair where I am sitting. She would have to sit on my lap because both of us cannot occupy the same space on the chair. Yet when I sit on a chair, the Bible implies, it is very possible for God to sit on that chair with me. Indeed, *God is not only with me but in me* (John 14:17)!

But what have I now done in thinking? I have made a shift to a belief statement. Indeed, I believe that God comes and lives in us and challenges us to be our very best, authentic selves. God is *not* a far-off *deus absconditus* (hidden god) of rationalism and deism. God is personal and very present. Is such thinking real or merely subjective, wishful thinking? Is this God who is very present with us the God of Abraham? Is the Jesus who died on the cross and was raised about two millennia ago the same Jesus who confronts us today? The answer to these ques-

---

[16] C. S. Lewis, *The Great Divorce* (New York: Macmillan, 1946.)

tions is: I absolutely believe them to be yes! So when I speak of God being on the chair in me, my thinking has crossed into a different dimension—a dimension that is difficult to test by the measuring tools of science that are normally applied to human space.

Now move slightly with me to think about the biblical idea of time. Does the Genesis introduction (chaps. 1–3) and the Johannine Prologue (1:1–18) announce that in the beginning there was God *and* time? You know that the answer must be no. Is *chronos*/time then eternal, or must it be an element of the created activity of God? Does not Genesis imply that there was a start not only to creation but also to time (whatever time that might have been)? And what did John mean when he said "before Abraham was, I am" (John 8:57)? Is that just a nice theological statement about a thematic idea of "I am-ness" in John? Or is it telling us something more about God and his Son Jesus? Jesus certainly had a beginning in the incarnation *ginomai* (John 1:14), but John implies also that the Word *(logos)* does not have a beginning *(eimi,* John 1:1; see my discussion of these Greek verbs in the first volume of my commentary). Time and creation for John are not of the same nature as the reality of God's being and presence.

If our realm of time and God's reality of existence are radically different from each other, how much more is the difference between created space and the nature of how we ought to think about the "whereness" of God. To imagine God dwelling in a far-off abode, in fact, succumbs to the fallacy inherent in the idea of the three-story universe. But how could Jesus, two millennia ago, speak about the realm of God to humans who were tied to concepts of time and place in every aspect of their thinking? Indeed, the "when" and "where" issues like those in John 8:14,23,58 even encumber all of our thinking about God today. Notice that when we think of God we usually conceive of God being in some place.

Yet place itself is a confining or limiting concept. But the biblical notion of God is that God is not limited by human understandings of space. That is what the Book of Jonah tried to teach the people of Israel when Jonah thought he could flee from the face (presence or place) of God (Jonah 1:3). Jonah learned to his amazement that God was present and could control the sea or the deep. Moreover, God was even in Sheol, the place of the dead, which Israel did not usually associate with God. Israel had to learn like Jonah that they could not run away from God (Jonah 2:2,6; cf. Pss 18:4–6; 139:7–12).

When Jesus tried to comfort his sorrowful disciples at his departure, therefore, he told them according to John that God had plenty of room for all of them (John 14:2). He said that his departure was, in fact, a preparation (14:3). When Jesus added that they knew the place (14:4), Thomas responded that they had no idea of the place and accordingly they had no idea of the road or path they should use to get to that place. In response to Thomas, Jesus switched the base system of the total conversation and indicated that *he* was the route or way (14:6). To make things even more complicated Jesus added to Philip that since they had seen Jesus, they had also seen the Father (14:9). These responses really must have confused both Thomas and Philip. It has confused many later Christians, even those scholars of the early church who were struggling to formulate the early Christian creeds. How could Philip, who was looking at Jesus standing in a place right in front of him, be looking at the Father? Of course, the formulators of the early creeds knew that John the Evangelist was trying to inform his readers concerning the reality of the close tie between Jesus and the Father (cf. John 14:10,11). Yet what Jesus was also saying to both Thomas and Philip was that their thinking was stuck in the wrong dimension.

The same problem has affected Christian thinkers throughout the centuries. They have tried to resolve the relationships within the Trinitarian Godhead through the concept of the Latin idea of *persona*. But when it really comes down to evaluating our church formulations, we must admit that we never really could decide how three so-called "persons" could still be one. Our problem is that as long as the parameters of our thinking are confined to earthly space and time dimensions, *our human minds cannot tolerate a space overlap.* Our thinking about heaven is often likewise stuck in the wrong dimension.

Now, to be frank, most of our ideas of "heaven" are rooted in Greek and even Gnostic concepts of escape from this current space. At the heart of our thinking is the fact that we usually regard the world, Earth, or the cosmos as unworthy of God's concern and a place from which we should flee to the safer place called "heaven." Yet the first chapter of Genesis boldly and repeatedly proclaims that God created the world and that it was "good." To proclaim otherwise is to agree with the Gnostics that the world is the creation of the enemy and that salvation implies a rejection of the Creator and an escape from the creation.

Of course, Genesis 3 announces that because of sin, the creation is subject to a sense of futility, producing thorns and thistles (Gen 3:18). But that is not God's intention for the world. His intention for the creation is that it should be liberated from its bondage of thistles and decay (e.g., see Rom 8:21; Isa 55:13). Moreover, the apocalyptic writer, in attempting to describe his vision of the future with God, reminds his readers that there will be a new heaven *and* a new earth, not just a new heaven (Rev 21:1).

The biblical idea of heaven and earth envisages an inseparable linkage between the two. It was so in the mind of the writer of Gen 1:1 when he described creation, and it was so in the mind of the Johannine seer in his presentation of the last two chapters of Revelation. In that final book of the Bible this linkage of the new heaven and the new earth is described as a city—the new Jerusalem, which comes "down" from God (Rev 21:3,10). Even though the Johannine Christians were living with concepts of time and space conceived in terms of a three-story universe, they knew that their ideas of God and the eternal reality had to extend beyond their limited concepts.

It seems then that the John of the Gospel and of Revelation accepted the task of moving the first-century readers from their narrow thought patterns to grasp a vision beyond the dimensional thinking of the first century. The styles of the communication in the Gospel and the Apocalypse are certainly very different, but the goal of stretching perspectives is identical.

What then of Christians in the third millennium? In spite of the fact that we live in the space age and watch movies like *Star Wars, Star Trek,* and their successors, the question must be asked: Is our theology of heaven and earth still rooted in a Platonic and/or Gnostic dualism, developed in the context of a three-story or a later Ptolemaic concept of the world? Is it possible for us to envision an idea of heaven not as a place far off from earth and merely in the future but rather as a realm of God existing in a dimension that is beyond time and even co-existing with the "present"? If Christians today could conceive of such a reality, then they might also be able to accept the idea that time is, in fact, only a created element within the broader reality of nontime or what we often call eternity. The Bible is very clear that God is to be understood as the God of the present, but God's presentness is not to be confused with our sense of presentness, which is rooted in the context of time (cf. the way the seer of Revelation speaks of God in relation to time as "who is, and who was, and who is to come" at Rev 1:4 and the way the four living creatures who represent the world speak of time as "who was, and is, and is to come" at 4:8).

If the reader has followed my thinking thus far and remembered what I said about my wife and God occupying my space, then it is a minor conceptual move to imagine that God exists in a dimension that overlaps with our created dimensions of time and space. This idea has tremendous implications for understanding the reality of life and death and the crucial biblical concept of resurrection.

The age-old query of people at funerals is, in fact, related to the concern of the disciples in John 14. The usual resolution is customarily phrased in terms of either the Greek/Gnostic ideas of immortality or the generally regarded abhorrent idea in Christianity known as "soul-sleep." Neither view adequately reflects the biblical perspective.

The first issue, the Greek view of immortality, is rooted in the idea that the soul alone is eternal and the body is part of this world that can be left behind as unnecessary. Accordingly, in his essay on the soul Plato pictures the soul at death as having wings that allow it to leave this burdensome corporeal world and fly up to join the great eternal soul.[17] The Gnostic idea is even more negative in respect to the goodness of God's creation.[18]

The problem with both Platonic and Gnostic ideas is similar to the problem of early twentieth-century liberalism in that they all advocate a divine spark in humans. But human beings are not divine, not even a small part of them. They are created beings, and even when they join God in his presence they are still not divine. They are still his creations. There is a basic qualitative difference between God or Jesus and humans, and it will remain so. Nevertheless, humans can experience life that is eternal, but it is not part of their essence; it is a gift given by God (John 3:16; 10:27–28).

It is at this very point that the significance of the resurrection must be understood. The resurrection does not make us divine; it is God's gift of life after death. Paul, writing to the Greek recipients who were used to regarding death as an escape to the eternal realm, emphasized in 1 Corinthians 15 that the resurrection

---

[17] See Plato, *Phaedrus*, 246–54 for his dialogue on the winged soul and the comparison of the soul to a charioteer. Note that he divided the soul into three segments at 254.

[18] See Excursus 16: "The 'World' in John and Gnosticism" above. See also G. Borchert, "Insights into the Gnostic Threat to Christianity as Gained through the Gospel of Philip," in *New Dimensions in New Testament Study* (Grand Rapids: Zondervan, 1974), 88–91.

was the key to the Christian proclamation. Indeed, he thundered that if Christ was not raised, then the Christian message was empty (1 Cor 15:14). Christ in effect modeled for Christians the way through death to resurrection so that when Christians die they can expect to be raised by God. They will have a body, but the body that will be raised will have a very different composition (15:35–44), just as Christ's body was very different in the resurrection. To affirm a view of immortality without a resurrected body is therefore a totally foreign idea to the Christian view of life following death.

The second issue, the concept of soul-sleep, was undoubtedly developed as an attempt to explain what happens to a person between death and resurrection. It has the advantage of taking the idea of resurrection seriously, but it is usually viewed by most Christians with disdain because it leaves most people with an empty feeling about death and dead bodies. It certainly seems to be a far cry from Paul's positive view of death when he said that if he were to be absent from the body he would be present with the Lord (Phil 1:22). One would hardly wonder why Paul would be hard pressed in deciding between living and dying (1:23) if he believed in soul-sleep. Yet here again I believe that a concept of being in the presence of Christ in a different dimension seems to fit Paul's thesis in Philippians.

So let us return to the question of what happens to people when they die? Better still, let us first ask what happened to Jesus when he died? I have often startled my students by saying that Jesus was "dead, dead." Why would I say that? Now be careful and consider the reason. The reason is that people often do not take death seriously—neither our death nor the death of Jesus. They think that death is just a mere transition in which part of the person continues to exist on its own, and they usually fail to understand that life is a gift of God. We do not naturally possess life as God does. Moreover, life after death is equally a gift of God. Usually, when speaking of the resurrection of Jesus, the New Testament writers prefer the expression that "God raised him from the dead" or the passive expression "that he was raised" rather than that Jesus rose (cf. Acts 3:15; 4:10; 5:30; 13:30–37; Rom 4:24; 8:11; 1 Cor 6:14; 15:15; 1 Pet 1:21). The point is that the writers of the New Testament took the death of Jesus very seriously and left his resurrection in the hands of God. Am I making a distinction between Jesus and God? The answer is that Paul made the same incarnational distinction as John (1:14; cf. 1 John 1:1–2; 4:2) when he said that during his time in the flesh ("of being born") Jesus emptied himself of various facets of his divine nature so that he could enter humanity. Moreover, Jesus actually died the ugly death of the cross (Phil 2:6–8; cf. John 1:29; 1 John 4:9–10). It was God who then reversed the terminal expectations of humanity and who exalted his Son with a name that is superior to the entire created order (Phil 2:9–11; cf. John 1:14,18; 1 John 4:14–15).

But what of the so-called postdeath places designated in the Bible? In the developing of their theologies the people of Israel did not at first have a concept of resurrection. Their early view was rooted in their basic idea of the people of God. It was a corporate idea. So the future was a future shared by the living and the dead. Inheritance was therefore extremely important since in some sense the dead lived on in their children. When people died, they were viewed as going to

Sheol, the place of sleep from which they did not wish to be disturbed—witness Saul's attempt through the medium/witch of Endor to call the sleeping Samuel back from Sheol in order to give him insight into his hopes in battle (1 Sam 28).

As Israel's theology developed away from thinking about a mere Sheol, a concept of a general resurrection began to emerge, and with it a Jewish party called the Pharisees developed. Yet even at the time of Jesus there were doubters such as the Sadducees, who argued that the Pharisaic ideas were revisionist and could not be found in the teaching of Moses (cf. the questions of the Sadducees to Jesus in Matt 22:23–33; cf. also Acts 4:1–2; 23:6–8). Because the Sadducees were so aligned with the institution of the Temple and the high priesthood (cf. Acts 5:17–18), however, when the Temple and Jerusalem were destroyed in A.D. 70 the influence of the Sadducees waned, and they died out. Accordingly, by the time of the writing of the Gospel of John the Sadducees are not even mentioned in the entire book. They are simply included among the references to Jewish authorities.

In the development of Israel's faith the Pharisaic ideas of individualism began to take hold and undoubtedly contributed to the refinements in later Phaisaic ideas of a personal resurrection.[19]

These Jewish ideas of resurrection clashed directly with Greek ideas of the immortality of the soul, as Paul is reported in Acts to have experienced in his Aereopagus/Mars Hill address. The city counselors and philosophers were apparently ready to debate most issues, but the thought of a resurrection left them in a complete stir (Acts 17:32). Some of the Athenians apparently even thought that Paul might be trying to add a new syzygy (couple) of gods (namely, Jesus, the masculine one, and *anastasis*/resurrection, the feminine one).

The Johannine teaching of resurrection is not merely to be understood as a resuscitation of the soul into the body, as the Greek Aeropagites might have thought. John certainly was not proposing that the resurrection was akin to some-one coming back to life in this body. He knew what that type of resuscitation was, as was evident in the case of the miraculous raising of Lazarus (John 11:44; 12:9). In that story Martha certainly expressed the typical developed Jewish idea of resurrection in terms of the end time (11:24). But notice in that story Jesus pointed her beyond a mere final time designation and challenged her to consider the fact that *he* is the resurrection (11:25). Such an idea blew a hole in all of her popular Pharisaic, carefully constructed ideas of resurrection, just as Jesus demolished Thomas's idea of finding a "road" to the place called heaven. Accordingly, Jesus actually proclaimed that he is both the answer to questions of time (resurrection) and place (way) as they relate to the issues of our ultimate hope. To encounter Jesus means to discover an entirely new way of thinking about God and eternity.

Yet what did/does such a new perspective on eternity mean for disciples of Jesus? To follow Jesus means that one does not really need to fear falling into the

---

[19] For a discussion of the Pharisees in terms of their social and cultural context see L. Finkel-stein, *The Pharisees: The Sociological Background of Their Faith* (Philadelphia: Jewish Publication Society of America, 1962).

hands of the living God (Heb 10:31; cf. Exod 3:6). It means hearing the gracious words from God or Jesus, "Peace be with you," and "Do not be afraid" (cf., for example, John 6:20; also Judg 6:23; Matt 14:27; 17:7; 28:10; Mark 6:50). It means knowing that we will have a destiny with Jesus where he is (John 17:24). It means having a personal invitation to be with Christ in his realm (14:3), even though we do not know how to diagram his "place" or draw the blueprints of heaven.

Thus assurance of God's resurrection gift to us and of being continually in Christ's presence thus should be the focus of our thinking concerning the future. We should not be seeking to define the dimension or construction of some "mansion" (a poor translation of John 14:2) that we think might be given to us in heaven. Any such speculation can only be a poor approximation of the eternal reality by the human mind, which is limited in terms of human conceptions of time and space. Moreover, such speculation actually diminishes the focus of our wonderfully inspired biblical texts to a physical and finite perspective on God's magnificent messages of love and hope for us.

But it is also imperative to realize that Christ's message of the future is a two-edged sword (Rev 1:16) that on the negative side is symbolized in the Apocalypse of John by the Lake of Fire (Rev 20:10,14; 21:8) and in the Gospel of John by the theme of judgment, wrath, and exclusion (e.g., John 3:19,36; 5:29; 12:31). There is a dark side to the love of God that is just as certain as the blessings of God. But it is likewise unnecessary to speculate concerning its dimensions. We really do not know the temperature of hell (cf. Matt 25:41; Luke 16:24) or the components of that existence. For example, C. S. Lewis imagined hell to be a place of noise— a problem for a writer who loves quietness.[20] But it is important to recognize the great tragedy of such a state that is outside the presence of Christ (John 3:20; 8:20; 12:31). That state will indeed be a realm of neither happiness nor joy (contrast John 15:11). In biblical terms it will be a painful experience (cf. Mark 9:48) of weeping and gnashing of teeth (cf. Matt 24:51) from which John says that the Son is the only way of escape (John 10:26–28; 11:49–52; 12:32).

Ultimate joyous hope and tragic judgment are both proclaimed in the Gospel of John. The gift of God's love in Jesus is probably God's most serious act. To receive that loving act is the beginning of a new life that will lead to a resurrection of life (John 3:16; 5:29). But to reject that love means nothing less than judgment "already" (3:18) and the state of ultimate tragedy (5:29; 15:6).

---

[20] See C. S. Lewis, *The Screwtape Letters,* rev. ed. (New York: Macmillan, 1982) for a series of concepts of hell from noise to stupor.

APPENDIX 2

CHARACTERIZATION IN THE GOSPEL OF JOHN

1. The Nature of Characterization
Excursus 34: Characterization in Literature
2. The Characters
   (1) John the Witness
   (2) The Beloved Disciple
   (3) Judas
   (4) Nicodemus
   (5) Peter
   (6) Thomas
   (7) Other Characters
3. Conclusion

—— **1. CHARACTERIZATION IN THE GOSPEL OF JOHN** ——

1. The Nature of Characterization

The Johannine evangelist is a magnificent model of a character writer. In the Johannine presentation the people become for the reader not only figures in the story of Jesus but also examples of types of human beings. Some are presented in a way that they appear to be rather single focused or one dimensional, while others are what narratologists regard as multidimensional or more fully developed in character.

Excursus 34: Characterization in Literature

Although it is beyond the scope of this commentary to enter into the complex study of literary characterization discussions today, a brief statement concerning this field may be helpful for the reader who then may find further direction from the attached bibliographical references in the accompanying footnotes.

As N. Frye indicated, character may refer to a persona in a work, personality traits in a real or fictive person, or a description concerning a type of a person.[1] Character studies usually concentrate on two primary areas: a character's way of being and a character's relationship to the plot.[2] Much of the contemporary literature deals with fiction, but the methodology for studying characters in literary

---

[1] See N. Frye, *The Harper Handbook to Literature* (New York: Harper & Row, 1989), 178.

[2] See S. Rimmon-Kenan, *Narrative Fiction: Contemporary Poetics* (New York: Methuen, 1983), 31–41.

works is applicable to historical works that relate to actual figures. Observations concerning character analysis, however, are not merely part of the modern study; and, as W. H. Frye indicates, it goes back to Aristotle's analysis that character writing should be good or authentic *(chrēstos)*, fitting or appropriate *(harmonzō)*, like reality *(homoios)*, and consistent *(homalos)* even if it is consistent in its inconsistency.[3]

In his classification of characters E. Forster proposed that figures in literature should be regarded as either round or flat.[4] But his classification has since been criticized for being too simplistic and reductive.[5] W. Harvey suggested that characters in literature could be divided into three groups: protagonists, choric figures or background characters, and intermediate characters of which he says some are dynamic and some are mere cards.[6] B. Hochman greatly expanded the study of characters by positing eight sets of polar opposites in the analysis of literary figures.[7] Although such a classification may be helpful in major character analyses, it is far too fine and complex a system for our current analysis of Johannine characters. Our purpose will be to focus primarily on Harvey's last two types in this present overview without making too many distinctions between the two. The reader will be able to judge easily whether the figures are presented in a fuller sense or serve primarily as mere cards introduced for one major purpose in this drama of Jesus, the Son of God. Some figures, like the "people," the "crowd," and the "Jews," are usually background figures in the Gospel, though sometimes they emerge beyond the scope of the background.

S. Chatman was one of the significant writers who helped establish the pattern for interpreting the roles of supporting characters. He concentrated on viewing such characters in literature in terms of traits, and he suggested three important criteria to aid literary analysts in identifying the roles played by supporting characters in a story. They are biological personhood (does the figure have a persona?), identity (is the figure named?), and importance (does the figure have significance in the plot or subplot?).[8]

R. A. Culpepper took the insights of Chatman and others and applied the methodologies of the literary critics to an analysis of some of the characters and groups in the Gospel of John.[9] The purpose of the present section on characterization is briefly to pursue the matter further and identify the basic traits and roles that the subordinate characters in the Gospel evidence.

---

[3] See W. H. Frye, *Aristotle: The Poetics,* LCL (Cambridge: Harvard University Press, 1932), 55.

[4] See E. M. Forster, *Aspects of the Novel* (New York: Penguin, 1962), 67–78.

[5] Cf. Rimmon-Kenan, *Narrative Fiction,* 40–41.

[6] W. J. Harvey, *Character and Novel* (Ithaca: Cornell University Press, 1966), 56–58.

[7] B. Hochman identifies the following eight pairs of polar opposites in his study of character: stylization/naturalism, coherence/incoherence, wholeness/fragmentariness, literalness/symbolism, complexity/simplicity, transparency/opacity, dynamism/staticism, and closure/openness (*Character in Literature* [New York: Cornell University Press, 1985], 89).

[8] See S. Chatman, *Story and Discourse: Narrative Structure in Fiction and Film* (New York: Cornell University Press, 1978), 125–40.

[9] See R. A. Culpepper, *Anatomy of the Fourth Gospel: A Study in Literary Design* (Philadelphia: Fortress, 1983), 101–48.

As indicated in the final sentence of the above excursus, the purpose of this section is to focus on the subordinate characters and groups with a view to identifying the particular traits they exhibit as a means for further establishing their roles in this Gospel. As an adjunctive goal it is hoped that by gaining insight into the characters and groups in this Gospel the reader may also gain further perspective on human characteristics.

No attempt is made in this study to psychoanalyze Jesus or any other figure because, as indicated several times in the commentary, A. Schweitzer, in his attempt to do so, only proved that such a task was impossible.[10] Furthermore, because the portrait of Jesus is covered in more detail in the theological summary, I have elected to focus on the subordinate characters rather than reanalyzing the Johannine picture of Jesus at this point. He, of course, is the central character in this Gospel story. He is, for John, the King of Israel, the Son of God, the one and only God-man, the divine Word who was from the beginning (e.g., 1:1,18,49). All human characters pale in significance before him.

Of the other figures, some appear only in one brief or extended pericope, such as Nathaniel, the woman of Samaria, the paralytic, the blind man, Martha, and Mary Magdalene. Then they fade from the dramatic stage. Others are introduced and their character presentation is tweaked slightly by further encounters. These include John the Baptizer/Witness, Nicodemus, Peter, Judas, Thomas, Mary of Bethany, and the high priest family.

Because of the way the narrative is woven in terms of its characters, the reader is easily drawn into the story and quickly identifies with certain figures while rejecting others. Accordingly, the Gospel can serve the function of a kind of mirror so that the reader can identify personality traits in oneself and in one's associates.

It is therefore not merely because of memorable verses like John 3:16–19 as well as 1:12; 6:35; 8:32; 10:27–28; 11:25–26; 13:34–35; 14:1–3; 15:7–8; 17:20–21; and 20:28–29,30–31 that this Gospel is loved by a countless number of Christians. But it is also vividly remembered because the characters in this inspired work are truly captivating.

2. The Characters

These characters offer intriguing insights into personality traits. When understood in their narrative contexts and their imbedded theological presuppositions, they provide some revealing perspectives on humanity and the ways we mortals both reach the heights of authenticity and the depths of vacillation and incongruity.

---

[10] A. Schweitzer, *The Psychiatric Study of Jesus* (Boston: Beacon, 1948).

To reflect on the Johannine skill of character writing does not mean that the narratives are merely Johannine creations, however, or that they are not based in events from the life and ministry of Jesus. Instead, it means that the evangelist was artfully able to analyze and portray the characters in such a way that they represent models or examples of recognizable characteristics in people. When these characters are set together in a side-by-side fashion, they provide a fascinating collage on human nature. Although it is impossible here to reflect on all of the Johannine characters in detail, I will describe a few of them as examples. The reflection on Jesus, the Son of God, however, I have, as indicated above, discussed at length in the theological summary.

(1) John the Witness

Although John was a baptizer (1:25,28,33), his primary function in this Gospel is that of a witness (1:7). He is clearly distinguished from Jesus/the Word/the Light by his assignment to bear witness to the Light. Unlike the presentation in the Synoptics, this Gospel tells the reader nothing about his appearance, clothing, or eating habits (cf. Matt 3:4–6; Mark 1:5–7). Here John is presented merely as a voice with a message to give (John 1:23). His primary message is to announce the strategic fact that Jesus is the "Son of God" (1:34) and the "Lamb of God" (1:29,36) whose role is to "take away the sin of the world" (1:29). There is in this Gospel no hint that John has any doubt about Jesus (cf. Matt 11:2–6; Luke 7:18–23). And even when John's disciples are concerned that Jesus was gaining more attention than their teacher, John responded that he was perfectly ready to decrease in terms of popularity and standing in the eyes of the people (John 3:30) since he recognized that such a reduction of his role was God's will ("given from above," 3:27). He knew he was not to be identified as the center of attention as was Jesus, the bridegroom, but he was like the witness (3:29) at a wedding. As a result John can be categorized in this Gospel as an ideal witness who knew his God-given role and who was not tempted to think more highly of himself than he ought (cf. Rom 12:3; Gal 6:3–4).

(2) The Beloved Disciple

When John the witness faded from the picture (John 3:30), the beloved disciple emerged as the subsequent witness. The description of him as reclining on the breast of Jesus at the dinner (13:23) mirrors a similar statement made concerning Jesus in relation to the Father at the conclusion of the Prologue (1:18). This beloved disciple is thus characterized as the mediator of information for Peter at the meal (13:24), the one who believed at the tomb (20:8), and the one who first recognized Jesus and again mediated information when he informed Peter in the resurrection appearance at the

Sea of Galilee (21:7).[11] In fulfilling the duty of eldest son, Jesus entrusted the care of his mother to this same disciple (19:26–27). And only in this Gospel is it said that he served as the authentic witness to the fact that in the crucifixion at the time of the slaughter of the Passover lambs that the dead Jesus was pierced and bled both blood and water from the Roman spear wound (19:34–35). In the presence of this true witness, therefore, the Passover death of Jesus, the perfect Lamb whose legs were not broken (19:37), brought to fulfillment the prediction of beholding the pierced one (Zech 12:10) and of the baptizer's earlier witness that Jesus was indeed the "Lamb of God" who was designated to take away the sin of the world (John 1:29).

For the Johannine community this beloved disciple thus epitomized the authentic messenger/representative of Jesus who himself modeled for them the nature of abiding in Jesus, the Vine (cf. 15:4). Moreover, it is certainly no accident that his first designation as the disciple whom Jesus loved (13:23) and the great command of love (13:34–35) that should be the epitome of the Christian community both appear in the same chapter. Christian tradition has identified this one whom Jesus loved as the evangelist who proclaimed most clearly the gospel of love.

(3) Judas

Diametrically opposed to the model of love and authenticity is Judas, the exemplar of a devil man (6:70), who is called the son of perdition or destruction (17:12). Not only was he a thief (12:6), but his statement concerning Mary's anointing of Jesus (12:5) is a clear indication that he was a manipulative liar and therefore truly a son of the devil (cf. 8:44). He, like some of the Jewish Pharisees and high priests, conformed to the murderous pattern of the devil (8:44) when he betrayed/delivered Jesus to the Jewish hierarchy. Therefore when Jesus gave Judas the dipped morsel at the supper as the sign of treachery, in so doing Jesus also gave Satan permission to take control of him. In this act Jesus was also patently confirming Judas in his devilish ways (13:2,26–27). Judas's role in the arrest of Jesus and his alignment with those who fall before the presence of the powerful Jesus, the "I am," mark his condemnation along with the others in the arresting band (18:5–6).

Furthermore, while Nicodemus may have at first come to Jesus by night out of concern for exposure (3:2), Judas's character can be symbolized at the end by the sheer darkness of night that enveloped the scene (13:30). As a result, when architects later constructed early churches that employed twelve pillars to symbolize the twelve original disciples, sometimes they

---

[11] See my discussion concerning Peter and the beloved disciple in Excursus 14 as well as my comments in the commentary at the appropriate verses.

would use one black pillar among the white ones to represent Judas, as was done in the early, well-known Coptic church of Cairo. For the Johannine evangelist the character of Judas was as dark as the night he entered in his betrayal. The reader gains the sense that for this Gospel, Judas is completely lost (17:12). He is the villainous traitor who sides with the enemies, the high priests, and the devil.

(4) Nicodemus

In contrast to Judas, Nicodemus is represented in this Gospel as a transitional figure. Although he began his relationship to Jesus in a night experience, representing the state from which he emerged (3:2), he did not remain there. As a member of the Jewish Council (Sanhedrin), the determiners of Jewish theology, Nicodemus approached Jesus with a sense of confidence that he knew that Jesus was a God-endowed man sent to Israel like one of their earlier prophets (3:2). He soon discovered that his knowledge of Jesus was as infantile as his understanding of the ways of God and of new birth (3:4,9). The teacher needed to be taught, and the theologian needed to learn the higher theology of the spiritual realm.

The initial inoculation of spiritual wisdom given by Jesus (3:3–8) had a profound affect upon the reasoning pattern of Nicodemus because the next time he was introduced by the evangelist he no longer assumed his earlier know-it-all, Pharisaic teacher perspective. At the subsequent council meeting he argued that Jesus ought to be given a fair hearing (7:51). But his openness was dismissed by his colleagues as theologically naive and unacceptable (7:52).

The third and final appearance of Nicodemus marks a significant change. No longer fearful of what others may have thought of his spiritual pilgrimage when he came to Jesus at night, he joined Joseph of Arimathea in providing a kingly burial (19:39–40) for the very person the Council had condemned (11:49–53; 18:19–24,28–30). To act in such a manner was tantamount to opening himself to the charge of being linked directly with Jesus as his disciple (cf. the Council's earlier statement at 7:52 and the fact that Joseph was also a disciple of Jesus, 19:38).

In this Gospel, Nicodemus, the seeker, undoubtedly is represented as having become a follower. As a character figure he is like many who since that time have walked the path of transition from outsider to insider in the Christian community.

(5) Peter

Among the followers of Jesus few were more well intentioned than Peter, yet few have been presented as more inconsistent than this disciple. In reflecting on both John and the Synoptics, Protestant readers who have not been socialized to view him as a pope may be tempted to shake their heads in amazement and criticism at the foibles of this well-meaning spokesman for the community.[12] Yet hardly should most humans shake their heads too vigorously in judgment at his words and actions because Peter is so human that he seems to be like most of us. Perhaps that is the reason he emerges in the Gospels as such a striking figure. He reminds one of David the king who could fall so low and yet be called a man after God's heart (1 Sam 13:14; Acts 13:22). When Peter was good and on track, he seemed to be "very, very good," but when he was off track in his words and actions, "he was horrid," to employ the categories of a famous nursery rhyme.

In the Synoptics he could make the strategic confession at Caesarea Philippi that Jesus was the Christ/Messiah and soon thereafter be like the tempter, Satan, in rebuking Jesus for choosing the way of the suffering servant (cf. Matt 16:13–23; Mark 8:27–33). In John, Peter faithfully refused to entertain leaving Jesus "the Holy One of God" (John 6:68–69), at the time others were rejecting the Lord because Jesus had identified himself as the Bread of Life and called his followers to digest him inwardly (6:35,53–56,60,66). Similarly, when Jesus announced that his departure was at hand and that the disciples could not follow him (13:33), Peter jumped to a hasty conclusion concerning his own ability and at that point confidently asserted that he would be willing even to die for Jesus (13:37). But Jesus knew that Peter's good intentions would fizzle into a threefold denial (13:38; cf. 18:17,25,27) at the challenge around the charcoal fire (18:18). Peter had to learn that words were scarcely a measure of reality.

This characteristic of jumping to hasty conclusions and actions certainly is a repeated pattern in the portrait of Peter that John developed. When Peter realized that Jesus, their Lord, was about to wash his feet as a way of modeling for the disciples the spirit of humble service performed by a slave, Peter quickly concluded that such an activity was inappropriate for a Messiah and therefore asserted that Jesus would never wash his feet (13:8). But when he discovered that he would not be considered part of Jesus' community unless he experienced the humbling lustration event, he quickly

---

[12] It is important to recognize with A. T. Robertson in his appendix to *A Harmony of the Gospels* ([New York: Harper & Brothers, 1922], 271–73) that in the lists of the Twelve in the Synoptics and Acts, Peter appears first and is part of the inner group of the disciples. But while he continually expresses his opinion as a spokesperson for the disciples, it is a far cry from making him the continuing spokesperson for the church, to say nothing of arguing that the church leaders of Rome held that position. Indeed, the Gospel of John and the Johannine community would undoubtedly challenge such an idea directly since it was the beloved disciple who reclined on the breast of Jesus. But to assert this challenge does not mean that Protestants should dismiss Peter's importance or his contribution to Christ's church, as is often done by those who are anti-Catholic. He was a significant disciple of Jesus, especially once he learned to deal with his denials and self-assertiveness.

responded by wanting a complete shower (13:10). No washing first, but a total bath later were the two completely opposite responses of the well-meaning Peter.

This jumping to conclusions can also be seen in Peter's attempt to defend Jesus before the arresting forces in the garden when he cut off the ear of Malchus, the high priest's servant (18:10). Defending Jesus by violence was his early macho means of displaying loyalty to Jesus. But this show of courage was followed by the first of his denials when his courage collapsed in the presence not of an army but before a mere maid who was in charge of the entrance to the courtyard of the high priest (18:17).

Then at the tomb when he was outrun by the other disciple who had paused before entering and contemplated the empty tomb with the linen wrappings that formerly had bound Jesus, Peter acted very differently (20:5,8). Instead, Peter, who came up later, entered directly into the tomb (20:6). When afterwards they both left the tomb scene, this Gospel indicates that it was the other disciple who believed as a result of encountering the empty sepulcher (20:8), even though they did not yet fully comprehend the significance of what they beheld (20:9–10).

Then in the Epilogue this picture of Peter is expanded. Although the beloved disciple first recognized Jesus from the boat and told Peter concerning the Lord (21:7), it was none other than Peter who responded by jumping overboard in an effort to get to the risen Jesus before the others (21:7–8). But when he then encountered Jesus, he had to face the trauma of the second charcoal fire and the second set of three challenges in order to be restored (21:15–19). And then after he received his final commission to serve his Lord and he learned of his forthcoming death as a martyr, he probed Jesus not merely about his own death but also about that of the beloved disciple (21:21). The response of Jesus, however, was to tell Peter to concentrate on his own commission and not to be concerned about that of someone else.

Although one could view Peter as a hopelessly confused follower of Jesus, that view would be a very unfortunate conclusion. After all, his enthusiastic reactions provide a contrast to much of the placid faith that is seen in Western Christianity today. As J. A. MacKay, the former missionary and president of Princeton Seminary, used to say: if you send blasé students to seminary, we can do very little with them; but if you send us enthusiastic, faithful people, even if they are slightly misdirected, we can help them to become powerful servants of God. That is the way I would characterize Peter in this Gospel: well-meaning and enthusiastic but greatly needing direction. He was hardly either a perfect human capable of enunciating "perfect" theology or a misguided misanthrope. Both designations are theologically incorrect. He was fully human, and to his dying day he remained merely human. But along with the beloved disciple, with whom he is constantly compared in this Gospel, he served God as a wonderful messenger of the Lord Jesus. In God's good time the well-meaning Peter became a faithful follower of Christ who was able to advise other followers of Jesus on the nature of authentic servanthood (cf. 1 Pet 5:1–11).

(6) Thomas

Thomas is among the most misunderstood characters in the Johannine Gospel. He is frequently remembered as a doubter, a designation that is both unfortunate and myopic. In the three major appearances of Thomas he emerges most clearly as a realist who sought clarity in his understanding of Jesus and his mission. He was fully aware that the province of Judea was a hostile territory for Jesus, and he recognized that to reenter that part of Israel would likely mean death. But *he was willing to die* with Jesus if Jesus was determined to return to the south (John 11:16). Thomas's problem was that he was more sensitive to human realities (the political conditions of the time) than to the fact that while Jesus was alive (it was still the day, 11:9) he would not have to fear the politically charged situation.

His realism is again evident in the discussion concerning the fact that Jesus was going to prepare a "place" for them (14:2). But despite the fact that Jesus told them they knew where he was going, Thomas voiced for the disciples a sense of bewilderment. Not only did they not perceive where he was going, but they had no idea of how to get there. And so Thomas virtually asked for a road map, a "triptik," to Jesus' place (14:5). In response Jesus informed the disciples that he was both "the way" and one with the Father (14:6–7), to which answer Philip, his colleague, continued the discussion by requesting to see the Father.

With these perspectives in mind, we turn to the crucial resurrection appearance text. Thomas had missed the first Lord's Day meeting with Jesus, so when he heard that the other disciples had seen the Lord, he expressed his doubts as to the actuality of such a resurrection appearance (20:25). Being a realist, he wanted proof that what his colleagues experienced was not some ghost or apparition. To touch the wounds of the crucified Jesus was what he wanted as proof. When he met with the disciples the following Lord's Day (a week later or eight days later by Jewish calculation; 20:26), the risen Jesus offered him the proof he required. What followed from the lips of this realist was the greatest confession in the Gospels—"My Lord and my God!" (20:28).

The realist Thomas was not afraid to take a stand on who Jesus is, just as he was not unwilling to join Jesus in a death march to Judea. Of course, the model for Christian believing must be believing without seeing, and for such believing Jesus promised a special blessing to all who would believe and assert the confession of the early disciples (20:29). But Christian acceptance of the resurrection is not based on a "faith in mere faith," as Bultmann argued.[13] It is a believing based on the actual encounter of the early disciples with the risen Jesus, whom we proclaim as both Lord and God.

In the confidence that the early disciples like Thomas were absolutely certain that Jesus had been raised from the dead, we take our stance and make our proclamations that Jesus lives and because he lives we too shall live. I thank God for realists like Thomas, and I am grateful that he wanted to make sure that his believing was not a dream and that the risen Jesus was not an apparition.

(7) Other Characters

Among the other figures that appear in this Gospel, Nathanael represents a true Israelite in whom there is no fraudulent or manipulative pattern of life (1:47). Nathanael is represented as authentically seeking for the coming of God's fulfillment (1:48), as a serious student of God's promised word.

Andrew is represented as the one who is a symbol of being a helper among the inner circle of the Twelve (1:40; 12:22). It is probably for this reason that when churches today develop helping or assistance groups, they often call them Andrew fellowships, committees, or groups.

Of the other male characters, the paralytic represents the depressed of the world who have lost hope (5:5) and tend to blame others for their sad state (5:7,11,14). The blind man, by contrast, symbolizes the helpless of the world who welcome grace in their lives (9:30) and are willing to recognize the work of God. Even though they may not see fully the source of the help, they still understand it comes from God (9:32,35–38).

Among the groups, the brothers of Jesus are portraits of those who rely on privileged relationships but do not really believe in the work of God (7:3–5). The Pharisees represent the religious leaders who are more concerned with their own theology, status, and self-preservation. Even though they are institutional leaders, they often fail to accept the dynamic presence of God in their midst (7:32,47; 8:13,33,39; 9:16,40; 12:19). The chief priests represent the religious leaders who use their power to force conformity and who are willing to lie and manipulate the truth to serve their own ends (11:49–50; 18:19–24,28; 19:6–7,12,21). The "Jews" is usually a negative designation in this Gospel. The general designations the "people" and the "crowd" are represented as sometimes confused and lacking perception (e.g., 7:25–26). Sometimes they praise Jesus (e.g., 12:12–13), but many

---

[13] See R. Bultmann, "New Testament and Mythology," in *Kerygma and Myth* (New York: Harper & Brothers, 1953), especially at 38–43.

times (along with the "Jews") they are pawns of the Jewish establishment, who are set in opposition to Jesus (e.g., 7:15–20).

Among the women Martha represents those who can mouth their theology but are not really able to integrate their theological views into the working of God in their midst (11:21–27,39). Mary of Bethany represents one who both loves deeply (11:32) and was willing to sacrifice her economic and (probably) marriageable future for Jesus (12:3–7). The woman of Samaria symbolizes the ethnic and moral rejects of society (4:9,17–18) who nonetheless can come to know the Savior of the world (4:42). The mother of Jesus represents both a woman who seeks to use her Jewish motherly relationship to get her out of a problem (2:3) and who quickly had to learn that Jesus was not answerable to her but only to God, the Father (2:4–5). The term "woman," which is used both at 2:4 and 19:26 in conversation, is not to be interpreted as a word of disrespect. Finally, Mary Magdalene represents those who mourn, grasp for solace, and appear to have lost hope. But like many others, she discovered that Jesus can turn mourning into joy through the power of the resurrection (20:11–18).

3. Conclusion

As should be evident from the above brief review of the Johannine figures, the personalities in the Gospel provide a rich variety of characteristics. They serve the evangelist in creating a very dynamic presentation in their relationship to Jesus, *the central character* of the Gospel. He is the God-man who stands between the Father and the Satan in the cosmic drama of salvation.

Although neither the Father nor the devil appear, with the exception of the voice of God from heaven at John 12:28, their presence in the drama is clearly perceived. The battle between good and evil is not merely a human face-off. Behind the human protagonists on earth there exist both God and *the* enemy. And in the midst of the battle Jesus (the agent/messenger of God, the Word who became flesh) stands as the symbol of the fact that God loves the people of his creation and will never cede the victory to the devil. Even in dying on the cross, Jesus is not pictured as the loser because there he "finished" (19:30) the divine commission as the Savior of the World (4:42).

Moreover, the crucifixion and the burial of Jesus were not the end of the drama. Although it ended the need for Passover, it began a new era. The resurrection is the guarantee that the ultimate victory belongs to God. In the resurrection event the Christian church asserts boldly with Thomas that Jesus is not merely some prophet (like Mohammed or Joseph Smith), but he is indeed with the Father both "Lord and God" (20:28). And in this resurrection era the risen Jesus blessed the church by breathing on his followers (20:22; as God breathed on the dirt called Adam, Gen 2:7), and he gave to them the Holy Spirit, the Divine substitute/Paraclete for his personal presence (John 14:16).

> Thus, for God, who truly loved the world,
>> And sent to us his only Son;
> And for the gift of God in Jesus Christ,
>> The crucified-risen Savior, our Lord and God:
> And for the gift of God and of Jesus in the Divine Holy Spirit;
>> The constant Paraclete of the believing Church;
> Together with the representatives of heaven we joyously sing:
>> To God be all glory, honor, thanksgiving, and power (cf. Rev 4:9,11).

In conclusion, I join with John in praying that all who read this magnificent Gospel might come fully to believe that Jesus is the only and authentic Son of God, the promised Messiah, and that believing they might experience the transforming life that is in Christ (John 20:31).

Selected Bibliography
John 1–11 and John 12–21

Included in this list are the most frequently quoted books. References to most specialized articles are cited at the appropriate places in the footnotes.

Appold, M. *The Oneness Motif in the Fourth Gospel: Motif Analysis and Exegetical Probe into the Theology of John.* Tübingen: J. Mohr-Siebeck, 1976.

Ashton, J. *Understanding the Fourth Gospel.* Oxford: Clarendon, 1991.

Bailey, J. A. *Traditions Common to the Gospels of Luke and John.* Leiden: Brill, 1963.

Barrett, C. K. *New Testament Background: Selected Documents.* New York: Harper, 1961.

————. *The Gospel According to St. John.* London: S.P.C.K., 1956.

Bauer, W. *Das Johannesevangelium.* Tübingen: Mohr, 1925.

Beasley-Murray, G. *Jesus and the Kingdom.* Grand Rapids: Eerdmans, 1986.

————. *John.* WBC. Waco: Word, 1987.

Becker, H. *Die Reden des Johannesevangeliums und der Stil der gnostischen Offenbarungsrede.* Göttingen: Vandenhoeck & Ruprecht, 1956.

Becker, J. *Das Evangelium des Johannes.* Gütersloh: G. Mohn, 1981.

Bernard, J. *A Critical and Exegetical Commentary on the Gospel According to St. John.* ICC. Edinburgh: T & T Clark, 1928.

Bettenson, H. *Documents of the Christian Church.* London: Oxford University, 1956.

Bieringer, R. et al., eds. *Anti-Judaism and the Fourth Gospel.* Assen, Netherlands: Van Gorcum, 2001.

Blinzer, J. *The Trial of Jesus.* Westminster, Md.: Newman, 1959.

————. *Der Prozess Jesu.* Regensburg: Pustet, 1969.

Blomberg, C. *Jesus and the Gospels.* Nashville: Broadman & Holman, 1997.

Boismard, M. E. *St. John's Prologue.* Westminster: Newman, 1957.

Boismard, M. E. et al., eds. *L'Evangile de Jean.* Paris: Cerf, 1958.

Boismard, M. E. and H. Lamouille. *L'Evangile de Jean.* Paris: Cerf, 1977.

Borchert, G. "An Analysis of the Literary Arrangement and Theological Views in the Coptic Gnostic Gospel of Philip." Ph.D. diss., Princeton Theological Seminary, 1967.

————. *Assurance and Warning.* Nashville: Broadman, 1987.

————. "Insights into the Gnostic Threat to Christianity as Gained Through the Gospel of Philip." In *New Dimensions in New Testament Study.* Edited by R. Longenecker and M. Tenney. Grand Rapids: Zondervan, 1974, 79–93.

————. "Passover and the Narrative Cycles in John." In *Perspectives on John: Method and Interpretation in the Fourth Gospel.* Edited by R. Sloan and M. Parsons. Lewiston, N.Y.: Edwin Mellen, 1993, 303–16.

————. "The Resurrection Perspective in John: An Evangelical Summons." *RevExp* 85 (1988): 501–13.

————. "The Spirit and Salvation." *CTR* 3 (1988): 65–78.

Borg, M. and N. T. Wright. *The Meaning of Jesus: Two Visions.* San Francisco: Harper, 1999.

Borgen, P. *Bread from Heaven: An Exegetical Study of the Concept of Manna in the Gospel of John and the Writings of Philo.* Leiden: Brill, 1965.

Boring, R. *Der wahre Weinstock.* München: Kösel, 1967.

Bowman, J. *The Fourth Gospel and the Jews: A Study in R. Akiba, Esther and the Gospel of John.* Pittsburg: Pickwick, 1975.

Braun, F. *Jean le Théologien et son évangile dans l'église ancienne*. Paris: Gabalda, 1959.

Brown, R. E. *The Community of the Beloved Disciple*. New York: Paulist, 1979.

———. *The Death of the Messiah*. 2 Vols. New York: Doubleday, 1994.

———. *The Gospel According to John i–xii and John xiii–xxi, 29 and 29a*. AB. Garden City: Doubleday, 1966, 1970.

Brown, R., K. Donfried, and J. Reumann, eds. *Peter in the New Testament*. Minneapolis/New York: Augsburg/Paulist, 1973.

Bruce, F. F. *The Gospel of John*. Grand Rapids: Eerdmans, 1983.

Bühner, J. A. *Der Gesandte und sein Weg im Vierte Evangelium: Die Kultur - und religionsgeschichtliche Grundlagen der Johanneischen Sendungschristologie sowie ihre traditionsgeschichtliche Entwichlung*. Tübingen: Mohr-Siebeck, 1977.

Bultmann, R. *The Gospel of John: A Commentary*. Philadelphia: Westminster, 1971.

———. *The History of the Synoptic Tradition*. New York: Harper and Row, 1963.

———. "New Testament and Mythology." In *Kerygma and Myth*. Edited by H. Bartsch. New York: Harper & Row, 1961, 1–44.

Burge, G. *The Annointed Community: The Holy Spirit in the Johannine Tradition*. Grand Rapids: Eerdmans, 1987.

Carson, D. *The Gospel According to John*. Grand Rapids: Eerdmans, 1991.

Charlesworth, J., ed. *John and the Dead Sea Scrolls*. New York: Crossroad, 1991.

Corell, A. *Consummatum Est*. London: S.P.C.K., 1958.

Craddock, F. *John*. Knox Preaching Guides. Atlanta: John Knox, 1982.

Crehan, J. *The Theology of St. John*. New York: Sheed & Ward, 1965.

Crossan, J. D. *The Essential Jesus: Original Sayings and Earliest Images*. San Francisco: Harper, 1994.

Cullman, O. *Early Christian Worship*. London: SCM, 1953.

Culpepper, R. A. *Anatomy of the Fourth Gospel*. Philadelphia: Fortress, 1983.

———. *John the Son of Zebedee: The Life of a Legend*. Columbia, S.C.: University of South Carolina, 1994.

———. *The Johannine School: An Evaluation of the Johannine School Hypothesis Based on an Investigation of the Nature of Ancient Schools*. Missoula, Mont.: Scholars Press, 1975.

Daube, D. *The New Testament and Rabbinic Judaism*. London: Athlone, 1956.

Davies, W. D. *The Gospel and the Land: Early Christianity and Jewish Territorial Doctrine*. Berkeley: University of California, 1974.

Deeks, D. "The Structure of the Gospel." *NTS* 15 (1968): 107–29.

de Jonge, M. *Jesus: Stranger from Heaven and Son of God*. Missoula, Mont.: Scholars Press, 1977.

de Jonge, M., ed. *L'Evangile de Jean*. Leuven: University Press, 1977.

Dodd, C. H. *Historical Tradition in the Fourth Gospel*. Cambridge: University Press, 1963.

———. *The Interpretation of the Fourth Gospel*. Cambridge: University Press, 1958.

Duke, P. *Irony in the Fourth Gospel*. Atlanta: John Knox, 1985.

Eller, V. *The Beloved Disciple: His Name, His Story, His Thought*. Grand Rapids: Eerdmans, 1987.

Fortna, R. *The Fourth Gospel and Its Predecessor*. Philadelphia: Fortress, 1988.

Freed, E. *Old Testament Quotations in the Gospel of John*. Leiden: Brill, 1965.

Fuller, R. *The Formation of the Resurrection Narratives*. Philadelphia: Fortress, 1980.

Funk, R., R. W. Hoover and the Jesus Seminar. *The Five Gospels: The Search for the Authentic Words of Jesus*. New York: Macmillan, 1993.

Glasson, T. F. *Moses in the Fourth Gospel*. Naperville, Ill.: A. Allenson, 1963.

Gruenler, R. *The Trinity in the Gospel of John*. Grand Rapids: Baker, 1986.

Guelich, R. "The Gospel Genre." In *Das Evangelium und die Evangelien*. Tübingen: Mohr-Siebeck, 1983, 181–219.

———. *The Sermon on the Mount*. Waco: Word, 1982.

Guilding, A. *The Fourth Gospel and Jewish Worship*. Oxford: Clarendon, 1960.

Harner, P. *The "I Am" of the Fourth Gospel*. Philadelphia: Fortress, 1970.
Haenchen, E. *John 1* and *John 2*. Philadelphia: Fortress, 1984.
Hanson, A. T. *The New Testament Interpretation of Scripture*. London: S.P.C.K., 1980.
Heil, J. P. *Blood and Water*. Washington: Catholic Biblical Quarterly Monograph Series, 1995.
Hengel, M. *Crucifixion in the Ancient World and the Folly of the Message of the Cross*. Philadelphia: Fortress, 1977.
————. *Die literarische Einheit des Johannesevangeliums*. Freiburg: Universitätsverlag, 1987.
————. *The Johannine Question*. London: SCM, 1989.
————. *The Son of God*. Philadelphia: Fortress, 1976.
Hirsch, E. *Das vierte Evangelium in seiner ursprünglishen Gesalt*. Tübingen: Mohr-Siebeck, 1936.
Hoskyns, E. *The Fourth Gospel*. Edited by N. Davey. London: Faber & Faber, 1956.
Ibuki, Y. *Die Wahrheit im Johannesevangelium*. Bonn: P. Hanstein, 1972.
Jeremias, J. *Eucharistic Words of Jesus*. London: SCM, 1966.
————. *Jerusalem in the Time of Jesus*. London: SCM, 1969.
————. *The Prayers of Jesus*. 6 SBT. Naperville, Ill.: Allenson, 1967.
Johnston, G. *The Spirit-Paraclete in the Gospel of John*. SNTSMS 12. Cambridge: University Press, 1970.
Jonas, H. *The Gnostic Religion*. Boston: Beacon, 1958.
Käsemann, E. *The Testament of Jesus According to John 17*. Philadelphia: Fortress, 1968.
Koester, C. *Symbolism in the Fourth Gospel*. Minneapolis: Fortress, 1995.
Kysar, R. "The Fourth Evangelist and His Gospel" and "The Gospel of John in Current Research." *RelSRev* 9 (1983): 314–23.
Lagrange, M. J. *Evangile selon Saint Jean*. Paris: Gabalda, 1948.
Lapide, P. *The Resurrection of Jesus: A Jewish Perspective*. Minneapolis: Augsburg, 1983.
Lee, E. *The Religious Thought of St. John*. London: S.P.C.K., 1962.
Leroy, H. *Rätsel und Misverständnis: Ein Beitrag zur Formgeschichte des Johannesevangeliums*. Bonn: Peter Hanstein, 1968.
Lightfoot, R. H. *St. John's Gospel*. Oxford: University Press, 1956.
Lindars, B. *The Gospel of John*. Grand Rapids: Eerdmans, 1972.
Loisy, A. *Le quartrième évangile*. Paris: Emile Nourrey, 1921.
Lohmeyer, E. *"Our Father": An Introduction to the Lord's Prayer*. New York: Harper & Row, 1965.
MacGregor, C. *The Gospel of John*. London: Hodder & Stoughton, 1928.
MacGregor, C. and H. Morton. *The Structure of the Fourth Gospel*. Edinburgh: Oliver & Boyd, 1961.
Mackowski, R. *Jerusalem: City of Jesus*. Grand Rapids: Eerdmans, 1980.
Malina, B. *The New Testament World: Insights from Cultural Anthropology*. Louisville: Westminster/John Knox, 1993.
Malina, B. and R. Rohrbaugh. *Social Science Commentary on the Gospel of John*. Minneapolis: Fortress, 1998.
Martyn, J. L. *History and Theology*. Rev. ed. Nashville: Abingdon, 1979.
Meeks, W. *The Prophet-King: Mosaic Traditions and Johannine Christology*. Leiden: Brill, 1967.
Metzger, B. *A Textual Commentary on the Greek New Testament*. London: United Bible Societies, 1971.
Miranda, J. P. *Die Sendung Jesu im Vierten Evangelium*. Stuttgart: Katholisches Bibelwerk, 1977.
Moloney, F. *The Johannine Son of Man*. 2nd ed. Rome: LAS, 1978.
Morris, L. *The Gospel According to John*. NICNT. Grand Rapids: Eerdmans, 1995.
Newbigin, L. *The Light Has Come: An Exposition of the Fourth Gospel*. Grand Rapids: Eerdmans, 1982.

Newman, B. and E. Nida. *A Translator's Handbook of the Gospel of John.* London: United Bible Societies, 1980.

Neyrey, J. H. *An Ideology of Revolt: John's Christology in Social Science Perspective.* Philadelphia: Fortress, 1988.

Nunn, H. *The Authorship of the Fourth Gospel.* Oxford: Alden & Blackwell, 1952.

Pancaro, S. *The Law in the Fourth Gospel.* Leiden: Brill, 1975.

Porsch, F. *Pneuma und Wort: Ein exegetischer Beitrag zur Pneumatologie des Johannes-evangeliums.* Frankfurt: Knect, 1974.

Rensberger, D. *Johannine Faith and Liberating Community.* Philadelphia: Westminster, 1988.

Ridderbos, H. *The Gospel of John: A Theological Commentary.* Grand Rapids: Eerdmans, 1997.

Robinson, J. M. *A New Quest of the Historical Jesus.* London: SCM, 1959.

Robinson, J. A. T. *The Priority of John.* Edited by. J. Coakley. London: SCM, 1985.

———. *Twelve New Testament Studies.* Naperville, Ill.: Alec R. Allenson, 1962.

Ruckstuhl, E. *Die literarische Einheit des Johannesevangeliums.* Freiburg: Paulus, 1951.

Sanders, J. N. *A Commentary on the Gospel According to St. John.* Edited by B. Masten. London: Adam & Charles Black, 1968.

Sandmel, S. *We Jews and Jesus.* Oxford: Clarendon, 1965.

Schlatter, A. *Der Evangelist Johannes.* Stuttgart: Calwer, 1948.

Schnackenburg, R. *The Gospel According to St. John.* New York: Crossroad, 1987.

Schneiders, S. *Written That You May Believe.* New York: Herder & Herder/Crossroad, 1999.

Schweitzer, A. *The Psychiatric Study of Jesus.* Boston: Beacon, 1948.

———. *The Quest for the Historical Jesus.* New York: Macmillan, 1954.

Schweizer, E. *Ego Eimi.* Göttingen: Vandenhoeck & Ruprecht, 1939.

Schultz, S. *Untersuchungen zur Menschensohn-Christologie im Johannesevangelium.* Göttingen: Vandenhoeck & Ruprecht, 1957.

Segovia, F. *The Farewell of the Word.* Minneapolis: Fortress, 1991.

Sherwin-White, A. *Roman Society and Roman Law in the New Testament.* Oxford: Clarendon, 1963.

Smith, D. M. *The Composition and Order of the Fourth Gospel.* New Haven: Yale University, 1965.

———. *John Among the Synoptics: The Relationship in Twentieth-Century Research.* Minneapolis: Augsburg/Fortress, 1992.

———. *The Theology of the Gospel of John.* Cambridge: University Press, 1995.

Smith, R. H. *Easter Gospels.* Minneapolis: Augsburg, 1983.

Thompson, M. *The Humanity of Jesus in the Fourth Gospel.* Philadelphia: Fortress, 1988.

Turner, G. and J. Mantey. *The Gospel of John.* The Evangelical Commentary. Grand Rapids: Eerdmans, n.d.

Venema, J. R. "An Apologetic Role for Agency in John Five." Ph.D. diss., Golden Gate Baptist Theological Seminary, 1995.

von Rad, G. *The Message of the Prophets.* New York: Harper & Row, 1965.

vonWahlde, U. "The Johannine 'Jews': A Critical Survey." *NTS* 281 (1982): 41–54.

———. "The Witnesses to Jesus in John 5:31–40 and Belief in the Fourth Gospel." *CBQ* 43 (1981): 385–404.

Wall, D. *Johannine Christianity in Conflict.* Chico, Cal.: Society of Biblical Literature, 1981.

Wellhausen, J. *Das Evangelium Johannis.* Berlin: G. Reimer, 1908.

Westcott, John. *The Gospel According to St. John.* Grand Rapids: Eerdmans, 1954.

Winter, P. *On the Trial of Jesus.* Berlin: deGruyter, 1974.

Witherington, B., III. *The Jesus Quest: The Third Search for the Jew of Nazareth.* Downers Grove: IVP, 1995.

———. *John's Wisdom.* Louisville: Westminster/John Knox, 1995.

Selected Subject Index

abiding   142–43, 145–46, 148–149
Annas   218, 227–28, 232, 234
anointing   31

believing   66–67, 347, 353–355
beloved disciple   91, 93
Bema (See judgment seat)
branches   144

Caiaphas   218, 227–28, 232, 234, 254–55
commandment, new   99
community, new   100
covenant   98–99
cross, the   261, 264
crown of thorns   248

discipleship   44, 52, 89, 113, 171–72, 188, 196–97

election   150, 154–55
eternal life   127

falling away   160, 161
Farewell Discourses   72, 74, 96, 186
Father's house, the   103
foot washing   75–77, 79, 81, 82–83, 86–87
forgiveness of sins   309–10
friendship   149–51
fulfillment of Scripture   88, 198, 278

glorification   55–56, 59, 97
Gnosticism   153–54
Golgotha   262
Greeks, the   47–49

heaven   360–63, 366
hell   367

holiness   201, 202, 203
Holy Spirit   132, 159, 160, 165, 168, 169, 170, 171, 307, 308, 309, 358, 359
Hosanna   42, 44
hour   49, 53, 55, 78, 112, 161, 162, 181, 219, 359

incarnation   179, 191–92, 194, 351
Israel, nation of   224

Jesus
    anointing of   31, 34–35, 37
    arrest of   216, 218–22
    burial of   36–37, 279–80, 282
    crucifixion of   250, 257, 259, 261–62, 265, 267–71, 273–74
    death of   276–78, 365
    departure of   103, 105, 116, 130, 133, 196
    divinity of   79
    entry into Jerusalem   39, 41–42, 44–47
    exclusivism of   110
    glory of   208
    hearings and trials of   226, 232–35, 237–38, 240–45, 248, 250, 252–53
    "in the Father"   114
    nonabandonment of   181
    prayer for disciples   187–88, 190, 195, 197, 200–204, 206–8, 210
    resurrection of   287–95, 297–305, 364–66
    suffering of   182
    works of   114–16
Jews, unbelief of   63–65
John the apostle   229–30
    as beloved disciple   92, 268, 278, 292–95, 321, 324, 328,

339–40, 342, 372

John the Baptist   372

John, Gospel of
  epilogue in   320, 322, 326, 341, 343
  eschatological subjects in   69, 130, 144, 173–75, 199, 303
  prologue in   21, 29–30
  redaction studies of   75, 331, 332

Judas Iscariot   36, 78, 82, 88, 94, 198, 217, 219, 220, 373

judgment seat *(Bema)*   256–57

kingdom of Christ   42, 242

Lamb of God   84, 257–58, 273, 274, 278, 285

Lazarus   38

Lord's Supper   77–78, 330

love   146, 148–49, 152, 154, 178, 335–36, 355–56

Mary Magdalene   290–92, 296–302

Mary, mother of Jesus   268–69

mashal   137–40

Messiah   60

Nicodemus   374

obedience   130

papacy, the   336

Paraclete   120–24, 132, 159–60, 162, 164, 166, 170, 358

Passover   22–23, 25, 32, 34, 84, 95, 238, 258, 273, 285

peace   133, 184

persecution   155–56, 161–62, 181

Peter the apostle   75, 80–81, 92, 100–101, 193, 221–22, 229–30, 235–36, 292–94, 321, 325, 328–30, 333–35, 337–39, 374–76

Pharisees   45–46, 366, 378

Pilate   237–45, 249–56, 258, 265

prayer
  in Jesus' name   117, 119, 145, 176–78, 357
  to the Father   188, 196

rejoicing   174–75

righteousness   166

Satan   58, 134–35, 167, 200, 350

scourging   246

seed   51

servanthood   52, 84, 86–87

signs   318

sin   165–66

Son of Man   49–50, 61

sorrow   174

"the way, the truth, and the life"   108–9, 243

theophany   304

Thomas the apostle   311–13, 315–16, 377–78

tomb, the   282–83, 285

Trinity, the   117–18, 205

Twelve, the   311

unity   197, 201, 205

Vine/branches   137, 139, 140–41, 143

sashing   82

world, the   46, 152–57, 172, 184, 196–97, 199, 356

Yahweh   130, 198, 315, 351

Person Index

Abrahams, I. 232, 254
Ackroyd, P. 330
Agourides, S. 185, 189
Aland, K. 32, 111
Albright, W. F. 301
Appold, M. 206
Arav, R. 283, 284
Ashton, J. 50
Athanasius 277
Augustine 131, 330
Augustus 280

Bailey, J. A. 77
Bajsic, A. 249
Bammel, E. 159, 170, 255
Bannwart, C. 315
Barbet, P. 275
Barclay, W. 310
Barr, J. 119, 335
Barrett, C. K. 37, 44, 55, 58, 83, 88,
    122, 123, 126, 128, 134, 149, 159,
    162, 167, 169, 173, 185, 186, 197,
    207, 223, 232, 239, 292, 293, 308,
    319, 325, 328
Barth, C. 146
Barth, M. 77
Bauer, W. 265, 338
Beare, F. 307, 333
Beasley-Murray, G. 33, 47, 55, 64, 65,
    73, 83, 94, 96, 101, 102, 103, 112,

115, 124, 126, 128, 132, 137, 144,
163, 167, 173, 178, 185, 186, 192,
196, 198, 199, 202, 206, 209, 220,
230, 235, 238, 240, 242, 248, 254,
258, 268, 269, 271, 272, 278, 281,
291, 293, 300, 307, 308, 310, 316,
318, 320, 321, 322, 325, 327, 336,
338, 339, 343, 346
Becker, H. 159
Becker, J. 75, 77, 94, 168, 169
Behler, G. 165
Behm, J. 123
Bender, A. 282
Benoit, P. 238
Berger, P. 46
Bernard, J. 67, 74, 163, 169, 218, 219,
    253, 254, 255, 280, 312, 313, 327,
    337, 338
Bettenson, H. 110, 277, 310
Beutler, J. 91
Bietenhard, H. 117, 119
Bishko, H. 247
Bishop, E. 89, 268
Black, D. A. 186
Blank, J. 167, 239
Blinzer, J. 182, 224, 245, 246, 47, 255,
    264, 280, 282
Blomberg, C. L. 32, 34, 138
Bode, E. 323
Boer, H. 88

Böhling, A.   150
Boismard, M.   75, 76, 83, 206, 318, 320
Bonsirven, J.   258
Boomersheim, T.   183
Borchert, G.   21, 23, 105, 108, 115, 118, 120, 127, 130, 132, 134, 138, 141, 153, 148, 156, 161, 163, 185, 187, 194, 195, 202, 205, 207, 215, 223, 224, 226, 263, 275, 276, 277, 287, 288, 297, 299, 304, 315, 318, 319, 323, 324, 330, 336, 338, 341, 342, 348, 352, 355, 364
Borg, M.   113
Borgen, P.   113
Boring, R.   142
Brown, R. E.   32, 33, 37, 55, 57, 58, 62, 63, 64, 67, 69, 74, 80, 81, 83, 88, 90, 92, 95, 96, 99, 101, 106, 108, 116, 122, 128, 129, 130, 132, 134, 136, 137, 139, 145, 148, 155, 156, 159, 163, 165, 173, 176, 181, 183, 185, 186, 188, 194, 197, 198, 201, 203, 205, 216, 224, 227, 228, 229, 230, 231, 233, 236, 238, 245, 247, 248, 250, 254, 255, 256, 257, 258, 259, 260, 261, 263, 268, 269, 273, 274, 275, 278, 280, 281, 282, 291, 292, 293, 294, 300, 304, 307, 309, 312, 314, 315, 316, 318, 320, 321, 326, 327, 329, 332, 333, 337, 340, 343, 346
Brownlee, W.   174, 203
Bruce, F. F.   42, 197, 224, 228, 232, 242, 247, 307, 325
Bruns, J. E.   35
Buetler, J.   53
Bühner, J. A.   50, 188
Bulst, W.   281
Bultmann, R.   30, 44, 53, 59, 67, 69, 73, 74, 94, 105, 109, 110, 124, 126, 136, 137, 139, 142, 153, 163, 185, 197, 207, 209, 220, 233, 235, 236, 249, 254, 272, 274, 277, 288, 290, 293, 294, 295, 300, 325, 306, 308, 314, 318, 320, 331, 332, 333, 338, 340, 342, 378
Bundy, W. E.   288
Burge, G.   308

Cadbury, H.   222, 310
Cadier, J.   189, 205
Caird, G. B.   97
Calvin, J.   307
Campenhausen, H. von   83
Carrez, M.   119, 130, 160
Carson, D. A.   37, 45, 47, 55, 59, 64, 67, 88, 94, 96, 101, 105, 110, 111, 115, 117, 122, 123, 126, 130, 134, 137, 140, 144, 149, 151, 156, 165, 171, 173, 175, 176, 185, 186, 193, 197, 198, 203, 209, 223, 230, 238, 252, 254, 258, 267, 268, 271, 275, 278, 281, 291, 293, 294, 302, 307, 308, 316, 318, 320, 328, 331, 335, 338, 339
Cassian, B.   58
Cave, S.   184
Charlesworth, J.   113
Chatman, S.   370
Chavel, C.   244
Cheney, J.   236
Chilton, B.   61
Collins, J.   263
Collins, R.   98, 298
Corell, A.   77, 272, 346
Craddock, F.   132, 133, 141
Craig, W.   292
Crehan, J.   204, 346
Cressey, M.   189
Crosson, J. D.   113
Cullmann, O.   83, 84, 360
Culpepper, R. A.   30, 223, 230, 320, 370
Danby, H.   232, 254
Daube, D.   37, 222, 274
Dauer, A.   271

Davies, W. D.   162
de la Potterie, I.   108, 119, 253, 256
de Vaux, R.   269
Deeks, D.   30, 73
Denzinger, H.   315
Derrett, J.   80, 94
Dietzfelbinger, C.   172, 175
Dockery, D. S.   100
Dodd, C. H.   33, 41, 50, 51, 67, 83, 87,
    90, 105, 106, 107, 139, 153, 156,
    164, 180, 186, 218, 242, 247,
    261, 271, 306, 329, 341
Donfried, K.   293
Duke, P.   101, 179, 238
Dunn, J. D. G.   84, 223

Edwards, W.   275
Eisler, R.   84
Eller, V.   84
Elliott, J.   338
Ellis, E.   63
Emerton, J.   330
Enyoiha, B. U.   300
Ernst, K.   223
Eusebius   264, 284
Evans, C.   56

Farmer, W. R.   41
Feuillet, A.   33
Finkelstein, L.   366
Foerster, W.   135, 316
Ford, J. M.   275
Forster, E. M.   370
Fortna, R.   47, 231, 290, 318
Fowler, D.   301
Freed, E.   40, 42, 157, 198, 278
Frye, N.   369
Frye, W. H.   370
Fuller, R.   183, 302, 323
Funk, R.   113
Furnish, V. P.   148

Gardner-Smith, P.   288
Garland, D.   100, 222, 240
Gärtner, B.   75, 217
Gaugler, E.   77

George, A.   168, 190
Gloer, W. H.   281
Grant, R.   267, 299
Grayston, K.   123
Green, J.   113
Grobel, K.   345
Groenewald, E.   319
Grossouw, W.   78
Gruenler, R.   56, 67, 131
Guelich, R. A.   55, 100
Gundry, R.   104, 106

Haenchen, E.   94, 113, 114, 124, 136,
    185, 192, 222, 235, 243, 249,
    254, 278, 305, 338
Hanson, A. T.   42, 157, 198, 278
Harrison, R. K.   35, 272, 280
Hart, H.   41, 248, 296
Harvey, W. J.   370
Hawkin, D.   142
Heil, J. P.   214, 226, 227
Hein, K.   75, 78, 94
Hengel, M.   49, 262, 263, 338
Hennecke, E.   101
Hill, D.   224
Hill, J. H.   32
Hirsch, E.   243
Hobart, W.   222
Hochman, B.   370
Hodge, C.   348
Hoover, R. W.   113
Hopper, M. E.   200
Hort, J.   296
Hoskyns, E. and N. Davey   37, 126,
    127, 133, 136, 160, 185, 197,
    268, 290, 295, 325, 328, 329,
    330, 336
Houlden, J.   250
Howard, W. F.   165

Jacobs, L.   148
James, M. R.   101
Jaubert, A.   83, 139
Jeremias, J.   41, 55, 81, 93, 95, 224,
    236, 310
Jerome   330

Johnson, L. 223
Johnston, G. 119, 124, 160, 169, 307, 308
Jonas, H. 105, 153, 276
Josephus 41, 139, 227, 228, 238, 239, 240, 245, 263
Jülicher 138
Justin 61, 260
Justinian 246, 280

Käsemann, E. 53, 139, 192, 194
Kastner, K. 314
Kelly, J. 98
Key, A. 119
Klappert, B. 77
Klausner, J. 288, 297
Klein, G. 235
Kloner, A. 284
Koebert, R. 35
Koehler, J. 308
Koester, C. 257, 275
Koester, H. 129
Korteweg, T. 113
Krieger, N. 222
Kuhn, H. 242, 264

Ladd, G. 323
Lagrange, M. J. 156, 164, 186, 281, 317, 320, 337
Lake, K. 323
Lamouille, H. 318
Lapide, C. 336
Lapide, P. 297
Latourette, K. S. 155
Laurentin, A. 186, 191
Leaney, A. 119
Lee, E. 346
Lee, G. 149, 292
Legasse, S. 102
Legault, A. 33
Levine, E. 83
Lewis, C. S. 90, 135, 361, 367
Lieu, J. 223
Lightfoot, R. H. 136, 319
Lindars, B. 166, 220, 254

Lindsell, H. 236
Linnemann, E. 235
Lloyd-Jones, D. M. 189, 205
Lohfink, N. 99
Lohmeyer, E. 55, 77, 323
Loisy, A. 317, 325, 329
Longenecker, R. 116

MacGregor, C. H. C. 107
MacGregor, G. 83
MacKay, J. A. 376
Mackowski, R. 228, 256
Mahoney, A. 227, 233, 257
Maier, P. 255
Malatesta, E. 186
Malina, B. 52, 99, 120, 124, 140, 162
Manson, T. W. 41
Mantey, J. 104, 310
Marcion 279
Marcus, R. 250
Marthaler, B. 277
Martin, R. 224, 328
Martyn, J. L. 99
Mastin, B. 314
Matsunaga, K. 315
McEleney, N. 330
McGing, B. 239
McNamara, M. 104
Merritt, R. 244
Metzger, B. M. 38, 60, 82, 97, 105, 107, 111, 117, 121, 158, 162, 173, 176, 179, 185, 194, 197, 216, 227, 233, 244, 257, 265, 292, 296, 297, 301, 310
Michl, J. 83, 84
Minear, P. 189, 205, 292
Miranda, J. P. 188
Mommsen, T. 246, 280
Moo, D. 270
Moore, W. 48
Moreland, J. P. 113
Moreton, M. 91, 293
Morgan-Wynne, J. 124
Morris, L. 73, 106, 123, 126, 129, 135, 136, 137, 143, 148, 149, 151, 156, 161, 164, 166, 170, 171,

175, 178, 185, 195, 196, 203, 207, 209, 218, 230, 240, 242, 254, 258, 268, 272, 290, 295, 298, 299, 300, 303, 309, 329, 335, 341
Morrison, C.   189
Motyer, S.   223
Moule, C.   183, 323
Mussner, F.   119

Neirynck, F.   229, 294
Newbigin, L.   94
Newman, B and E. Nida   37, 38, 43, 47, 55, 60, 104, 105, 107, 111, 117, 140, 144, 166, 177, 185, 190, 242, 268, 310, 311
Neyrey, J. H.   99
Nicholson, C.   53
Nicol, G.   85
Nygren, A.   178, 335

O'Connell, M. J.   70
Osborne, B.   294
Osborne, G.   328

Page, S. H. T.   58
Painter, J.   64, 73, 119
Palmer, E. H.   33
Pancaro, S.   60, 70, 145
Patrick, J.   119
Pauck, W.   267
Payne, J.   282
Perrin, N.   323
Philo   238, 255, 267
Plato   364
Plautus   261
Plutarch   261
Polhill, J.   116
Pollard, T. E.   189, 205
Porsch, F.   165
Prewitt, J.   283
Price, J.   174

Quell, G.   141
Quintilian   261

Quispel, G.   193

Rad, G. von   65, 119, 242, 305
Radermakers, J.   141
Randall, J. F.   189, 205
Reiser, W.   294
Rengstorf, K. H.   203, 218, 245
Reumann, J.   293
Richter, G.   277
Ridderbos, H.   32, 146, 147, 150, 185
Rieger, J.   122
Rigaux, B.   192
Rimmon-Kenan, S.   369, 370
Robertson, A. H.   32
Robertson, A. T.   33, 375
Robinson, B. P.   217
Robinson, J. A. T.   83, 340
Robinson, J. M.   113, 299, 345
Rohrbaugh, R.   52, 99, 120, 124, 140, 162
Rousseau, J.   283, 284
Ruckstuhl, E.   290, 321
Rynen, H.   217
Sanders, E.   224
Sanders, J. N.   34, 35
Sandmel, S.   223
Sava, A.   275
Schlatter, A.   78, 94, 169, 197, 249, 310, 341
Schlier, H.   139, 250
Schmidt, K.   242
Schnackenburg, R.   30, 32, 49, 55, 58, 75, 76, 105, 111, 114, 132, 137, 141, 149, 151, 160, 163, 173, 175, 183, 185, 186, 192, 196, 201, 202, 207, 218, 221, 238, 242, 254, 259, 267, 268, 269, 272, 281, 282, 295, 298, 313, 320, 322, 327, 329, 331, 338, 339
Schneiders, S.   84
Schoon, S.   223
Schüer, E.   224
Schultz, S.   49, 103
Schürmann, H.   269
Schwank, B.   175, 190

Schwartz, E.   340
Schweitzer, A.   54, 113, 182, 183, 325
Schweizer, E.   49, 138
Segal, A.   59
Segovia, F.   96, 101, 102, 119, 122, 185
Seneca   263
Sham, F.   108
Shaw, A.   329
Sherwin-White, A.   239, 224, 246, 253, 255, 260
Simpson, A.   275
Sizoo, H.   223
Smalley, S.   61, 276, 329
Smallwood, E.   239
Smith, D.   42
Smith, D. M.   87, 346
Smith, R. H.   218, 290, 293, 313, 320, 327, 330, 346
Smyth, K.   292
Snyder, G.   81, 92
Soards, M.   261
Spurrell, J.   271
Stagg, D. and F.   33, 268
Stagg, F.   73
Stählin   148, 337
Stanley, D. M.   141, 217
Stauffer, E.   269
Stein, R. H.   33
Stenger, W.   166
Story, C.   238
Strauss, D. F.   113
Strong, A. H.   348
Suetonius   264
Suggit, J.   304

Tacitus   255, 263
Tenney, M.   325
Tertullian   83, 260
Theodore of Mopsuestia   307
Thompson, M. M.   54
Thornton, E.   304
Thüsing, W.   53, 54, 57, 170, 189, 205
Thyen, H.   75, 76
Tomoi, K.   121

Trudinger, P.   334
Tupper, E. F.   64
Turner, G.   104
Turner, M.   113
Tzaferis, V.   264

Ulpian   280
Unger, D.   269
Untergassmair, F. G.   145, 117, 176, 210

Vaganay, L.   317
van Unnik, W. C.   61
Venema, J. R.   68
Vermes, G.   261
Virgil   225

Wall, D.   107
Weber, M.   45, 46
Weiser, A.   86
Weiss, H.   84
Wellhausen, J.   75, 76, 223, 338
Wenham, D.   119, 191
Westcott, B. F.   106, 122, 125, 145, 185, 186, 254, 257, 295, 296, 299, 307, 317, 320, 321, 342
Wilckens, U.   159
Wilkins, M.   113
Wilkinson, J.   275
Wilson, B.   46
Winter, D.   87
Winter, P.   217, 222, 224
Witherington, B. III   113, 139, 140, 146, 185
Woll, D.   98, 124
Wood, J.   261
Workman, H.   334
Wrede, W.   113
Wright, N. T.   113
Wulf, F.   141, 268

Yadin, Y.   41
Yamauchi, E.   153

Zugibe, F.   274

Selected Scripture Index

Genesis
1–3 362
1:1 363
1:9–13 308
1:31 276
2:7 131, 165, 182, 211, 309, 358
3 363
3:5 . . . . 143, 166
3:10 251
3:18 363
6:5–6 175
6:9 325
9:22–27 328
12:2–3 . . . . . 151, 337
17:1 325
18:22–33 250
18:30–31 311
22:6 261
24:9–11 112
49:17 311

Exodus
3:6 367
3:13–15 198
3:14 . . . . 89, 219
4:21 64
8:15,32 64
9:23 144
12:5 274
12:10 278
20 99
20:7 55
25:8–9 130
32:1–8 166
33:11 149
33:13,18 128
33:20 113

35:7–16 130
40:1–38 130
Leviticus
10:2 144
11:44 203
15:5–11 238
19:2 203
19:17–18 149
19:18 100
20:26 203
23:40 41
24:16 251
Numbers
6:26 133
9:12 278
15:35–26 262
19:11–13 238
25:1–9 166
26:10 144
34:11 323
Deuteronomy
6:4 . . . . 52, 315
6:4–5 . . . . . 100, 148
6:8 64
10:21 144
12:3 144
13:17–14:10 139
15:19 203
18:15 70
18:15–21 89
21:22–23 273
21:23 240
31–33 73
32 189
32:22 144

32:46–47 70
Joshua
6:18 113
6:22 128
6:22–23 305
6:23 367
6:24 144
6:25–26 302
8:19 144
8:23 259
1 Samuel
8:4–9 259
13:14 375
28 366
30:1–3 144
31:8–13 298
2 Samuel
5:2 336
7:13 61
1 Kings
4:33 271
2 Chronicles
15:17 325
20:7 149
Nehemiah
8:15 41
Job
1–2 90
1:1 325
9:20–21 325
Psalms
7:10 175
10:6–17 175
11:6 144
14:1 175
16:10 295
16:11 109

18:4–6 362
19:9 166
22 271
22:1 271
22:2 181
22:18 267
22:19–21 182
22:23–31 182
25:11 117
29:3 315
31:3 117
34:21 278
34:23 315
35:19 157
41:9 88
51:2 84
57:4 199
69 271
69:3 271
69:4 157
69:21 271
69:25 198
80:8–9 139
84:11 109
86:15 315
89:35–37 61
109:6 90
118:22 43
118:25 42
118:25–26 42
118:26 42
119:4,25,28 130
139:7–12 362

Isaiah
2:11 127
2:11–19 303
5:1–7 139
6 . . . . 63, 314
6:1–4 66
6:1–5 113
6:5 . . . . . 128, 305, 335
6:8–13 302
6:10 65
6:10–11 63
8:13 305
9:6–7 . . . . 61, 133
10:25 173
11:11 303
12:1,6 303
21:3 174
26:13 259

26:17–19 174
27:2–6 139
29:17–18 173
33:20 113
34:5 199
40:1–11 . . . . 44, 210
40:3–5 109
41:8 149
52:7 133
53 . . . . 63, 247
53:1 63
55:13 363
57:19 133
66:7–9 174
66:14 175

Jeremiah
2:21 139
4:4 144
6:14 133
13:21 174
31:6,27–34 303
31:33 175
51:33 173

Ezekiel
2:1 50
3:1 50
4:1 50
11:13 182
11:19 175
15:1–6 145
15:1–8 139
17:6–10 139
19:10–14 139
34:11–12 303
34:27 130
36:26 175
37:9 309
37:24–25 61
37:26 133
37:27 130
47:9–10 330

Daniel
7:13 50
7:13–14 61

Hosea
1:4 173
10:1 139
13:13 174

Joel
2:1–2,11,31 303

Amos
5:18–20 303

Jonah
1:3 362
2:2,6 362

Micah
4:9–10 174

Habakkuk
2:11 40

Zechariah
2:10 130
3:1–2 90
9:9 . . . . 42, 43
11:12–13 198
12:10 373
13:1 278
13:7 . . . . 183, 235
13:9 183

Malachi
3:1 109

Matthew
1:22 88
2:17,23 88
2:22 225
3:1–12 109
3:4–6 372
3:12 144
3:17 56
4:1–11 . . . . . . 54, 135
4:3–10 221
5 87
5–7 100
5:1 85
5:3–10 354
5:3–12 316
5:10–11 155
5:22 144
5:43–45 149
5:43–48 100
5:44–45 148
6:9 . . . . . . 55, 182, 187
6:9,14–15 348
8:23–27 332
10:3 129
10:4 129
10:24–25 87
10:39 51
10:40 . . . . 68, 90
11:2–6 372
11:2–15 109
13:1 85

13:14 63
13:40–42 144
14:22–32 332
14:27 367
14:28–33 332
15:29 85
16:13–23 375
16:16–19 337
16:18 359
16:19 310
17:4–6 56
17:7 367
18:18 . . . . . . 310, 359
19:16–30 148
20:1–16 140
20:21 80
21:1–11 . . . . . . 34, 39
21:5 43
21:33–46 140
21:42 43
22:23–33 366
24:3 85
24:22,36 303
24:45–51 81
24:51 367
25:41 367
26:2 . . . . 32, 34
26:7 . . . . 32, 35
26:8–9 36
26:10–13 36
26:11 38
26:12 36
26:13 . . . . 35, 37
26:21 91
26:21–22 78
26:22 91
26:23 . . . . 78, 93
26:26–28 95
26:29 303
26:31 183
26:36–46 . . . 185, 216
26:39 55
26:49 219
26:50 94
26:53 . . . . . . 219, 222
26:55,64 85
26:57 . . . . . . 234, 238
26:61 234
26:63 234
26:65 . . . . . . 234, 239
26:65–66 234

26:67 234
26:71 236
27:3–10 198
27:15 244
27:19 252
27:21–22 249
27:24 . . . . . 215, 259
27:26 246
27:27 248
27:28 249
27:32 . . . . . 247, 261
27:35 267
27:38 . . . . . 215, 264
27:46 . . . . . 103, 181
27:52–53 252
27:57 279
27:59 281
27:60 . . 282, 283, 284
27:61 281
27:62–66 291
27:65–66 215
28 323
28:1 290
28:2 284
28:2–3 252
28:2–4 291
28:3 298
28:5 295
28:7 298
28:8–10 297
28:9 . . . . . . 301, 304
28:9–10 323
28:10 367
28:16 323
28:18–20 151
28:19 206
Mark
1:1–8 109
1:5–7 372
1:11 56
1:12–13 54
1:19–20 229
3:17 324
3:18 129
3:28 50
4:1–30 51
4:8 36
4:33–34 177
4:35–41 332
6:45–52 332
6:50 367

6:52 44
8:21 44
8:27–33 375
8:31 183
8:35 51
9:5–7 56
9:31 183
9:37 . . . . 68, 90
9:47 144
9:48 367
10:17–22 148
10:32–45 86
10:33–34 183
10:37 80
10:42–45 52
10:45 87
11:1–11 . . . . . . 34, 39
11:15–17 47
11:25–26 182
12:10 43
12:29–31 148
13:14–18 221
13:18 129
13:32 . . . . . . 180, 340
14:1 . . . . 32, 34
14:3 . . . . 32, 35
14:4–5 36
14:5 36
14:6 37
14:6–9 36
14:9 . . . . 35, 37
14:10–11 80
14:15 78
14:18 91
14:18–19 78
14:19 91
14:20 . . . . 78, 93
14:22–24 95
14:27 . . . . . 183, 235
14:32–43 . . . 185, 216
14:36 . . . . . . 55, 182
14:42 136
14:45 . . . . . 215, 219
14:58 234
14:61 87
14:61–62 234
14:61–64 251
14:63 234
14:65 234
14:69 236
15:6 244

15:7 245
15:11–13 249
15:15 246
15:16 248
15:21 . . . . . . 247, 261
15:22 . . . . . . 215, 267
15:23 270
15:25 257
15:26 265
15:27 . . . . . . 215, 264
15:33–38 215
15:34 . . . . . . 103, 181
15:34–36 271
15:39 215
15:43 279
15:44–45 215
15:46 . . . . . . 281, 282
15:47 281
16:1 290
16:2 290
16:3–4 284
16:4 298
16:6 298
16:7 . . . . 293, 323
16:8 295
16:9–11 297
26:39 182
27:38 215
Luke
1:2 160
1:68 87
2:2 225
3:2–17 109
3:22 56
4:1–13 . . . . . . 54, 135
4:3–12 221
5:1–11 . . . . . 331, 332
6:12–16 331
6:15–16 129
6:16 129
6:20–23 316
6:40 87
7:11 32
7:18–23 372
7:36–50 33
7:37 . . . . 33, 35
7:38 32
7:38,44–48 35
7:40 32
8:1,22 32
8:22–25 332

9:24 51
9:30–31 56
9:33–35 56
9:49 90
10:16 90
10:21 182
10:27 52
10:39–42 33
10:40–41 34
11:2 . . . . 55, 182
13:6–9 140
15:12 81
15:18,21 . . . . 187, 347
16:23 91
16:24 367
18:18–30 148
19:12,14,27 225
19:29–44 39
19:37 43
19:40 40
20:17 43
21:20–24 221
22:3–4 80
22:12 78
22:17–20 95
22:21–23 78
22:39–46 . . . 185, 216
22:42 . . . . 55, 182
22:42–44 358
22:44 . . . . 53, 216
22:47 219
22:51 222
22:58 236
22:67–69 234
22:70–71 239
23:1–2 239
23:16 245
23:18–21 249
23:23 246
23:26 . . . . . . 247, 261
23:28–31 260
23:32,39–43 215
23:33 264
23:34 . . . . . . 182, 267
23:34,46 182
23:38 265
23:46 . . . . . . 103, 183
23:50 279
23:51 279
23:53 . . . . . . 281, 283
23:55 281

23:56 281
24:1 290
24:2 284
24:4 298
24:5 298
24:5–6 299
24:6 323
24:9–11 302
24:10 290
24:11,17 295
24:11,24–25 297
24:16 300
24:25–27 45
24:30–31,35 330
24:34 293
24:36 305
24:39 263, 301, 304, 305
24:41–42 330
24:41–43 304
24:50–51 302
Acts
1:1–2 116
1:9–11 302
1:12–14 307
1:13 129
1:15–26 311
1:16–20 . . . . 198, 215
2:5–11 48
2:36 260
3:15 . . . . 260, 365
4:1–2 366
4:10 365
4:11 43
4:13 229
5:17–18 366
5:30 365
5:33–39 162
7:58 . . . . 226, 262
7:60 182
8:18–19 133
9:1–5 116
9:34 116
10:16 324
10:39 . . . . . . 260, 279
12:1–16 304
12:2 311
12:13–15 314
12:15 297
13:22 375
13:30–37 365
15:20,29 161

16:37–39 246
17:32 366
18:12,17 225
19:30 226
19:38 226
20:3 162
21:28 47
22:3 162
23:6–8 366
23:12–14 162
23:12–23 248
25:6,10 256
26:9 162
28:27 63
28:31 234
Romans
1:4 203
1:18 210
1:24,26,28 175
1:24–32 201
1:25 87
2:5,16 303
3:10–18 63
3:21–5:11 309
4:11–20 114
4:24 365
5:10 149
5:12–21 250
6:10 272
8:1 108
8:5–8 276
8:11 365
8:21 . . . . 60, 363
8:34 178
9:5 87
9–11 . . . . 63, 64
10:16 63
11:33–36 118
12:3 372
14:15 108
14:23 114
1 Corinthians
1:4–9 193
1:22–25 211
2:6–8 90
2:8 135
4:6–7 87
5:3–5 359
5:6 87
6:13 355
6:14 365

9:27 161
9–10 161
10:6–10 161
10:6–12 355
10:11 161
11:23 95
11:23–26 330
11:24–25 95
13:12 209
15:3–5 59
15:5 293
15:5–9 297
15:10 325
15:12–22 248
15:14–19 288
15:15 365
15:22 250
15:26 352
15:35–36 304
15:35–44 . . . 361, 365
15:35–50 300
2 Corinthians
2:10–11 359
3:18 208
4:4 58
4:7 155
5:7 114
5:10 256
10:21–23 325
Galatians
1:13–15 325
2:11–16 293
3:22–26 114
5:16 108
6:3–4 372
Ephesians
2:2 58
2:20 43
4:30 303
5:8 62
6:11–12 90
6:12 . . . . 58, 200
6:18 200
Philippians
1:22 365
2:5 103
2:6 134
2:6–8 365
2:6–11 . . . . 192, 207
2:7 . . . . 79, 180
2:8–9 59

2:9–11 365
3:4–6 325
3:6 325
3:18 108
4:7 133
Colossians
1:18 59
1 Thessalonians
2:12 108
4:13 360
4:13–18 337
5:2–4 303
5:5 62
2 Thessalonians
2:3 199
1 Timothy
3:16 59
5:10 86
5:15 134
2 Timothy
4:10 335
Hebrews
1:3 59
6 161
6:4–6 285
6:17–18 161
6:18 355
7:25 178
7:27 272
9:12 272
9:28 285
10 161
10:10 272
10:25 303
10:31 . . . . . . 305, 367
James
2:23 149
1 Peter
1:2 118
1:8–9 317
1:15–16 203
1:19 274
1:21 365
2:4,7 43
2:21 86
3:18 285
4:12–14 337
4:16 339
5:1–11 377
5:2 . . . . 336, 355
5:3 336

5:8 . . . . 58, 200
2 Peter
2:9 303
3:10–11 303
1 John
1:1 . . . . 304, 316
1:1–2 365
1:1–3 . . . 114, 176, 302
1:1–4 . . . . . . 132, 288
1:2–3 285
1:4 176
1:9 166
1:10 124
2:1 . . . . . 123, 166, 178
2:2 . . . . 274, 285
2:4,22 124
2:15–17 200
2:18 . . . . 99, 340
2:19 . . . . 142, 181
2:22 . . . . 276, 343, 347
2:22–25 99
2:23 285
2:24–25 347
3:1–18 100
3:2 208
3:2,13 125
3:4–10 122
3:4–18 99
3:13–17 356
3:16 . . . . 101, 148
3:18 . . . . 146, 355
3:18–19 124
4:1–3 309
4:1–6 359
4:2 . . . . 132, 365
4:2–3 . . . 276, 343, 347

4:2,14–15 285
4:4,14,17 343
4:6 156
4:7–8,20–21 141
4:7–21 . . . . 100, 359
4:7–23 347
4:9 355
4:9–10 365
4:10 285
4:14 309
4:14–15 365
4:16 356
4:19–20 356
4:20–21 356
5:2–3 121
5:4–5 343
5:6 275
5:10 124
5:20 . . . . . . 288, 309

Jude
3 285

Revelation
1:3 317
1:4 364
1:4–5 118
1:5 59
1:9 313
1:10 . . . 291, 303, 352
1:16 367
1:17 305
1:17–18 305
2:9 162
2:13 134
2:14,20 161
3:9 162

4:8 . . . . 324, 364
4:9,11 380
5:6 . . . . 59, 342
6:4 184
6:16–17 303
7:4–8 311
8:1 252
8:7–8 144
8:13 324
11:5 144
12:1–4 175
12:7 58
12:12 . . . . 90, 131
14:5 124
14:10 144
16:8 144
16:14 303
16:17 272
18:8 144
19:12–13,16 59
19:20 144
20:2 . . . . 58, 134
20:6 . . . . 81, 317
20:9–10,14–15 . . . 144
20:10,14 367
20:14 352
21:1 363
21:3 131
21:3,10 363
21:6 272
21:8 . . . . 144, 367
21:8,27 124
21:12–13 311
21–22 104
22:19 81